A COMPANION
TO OVID

BLACKWELL COMPANIONS TO THE ANCIENT WORLD

This series provides sophisticated and authoritative overviews of periods of ancient history, genres of classical literature, and the most important themes in ancient culture. Each volume comprises approximately twenty-five and forty concise essays written by individual scholars within their area of specialization. The essays are written in a clear, provocative, and lively manner, designed for an international audience of scholars, students, and general readers.

A COMPANION
TO OVID

Edited by

Peter E. Knox

WILEY-BLACKWELL

A John Wiley & Sons, Ltd., Publication

This paperback edition first published 2013
© 2013 Blackwell Publishing Ltd

Edition history: (hardback, 2009)

Blackwell Publishing was acquired by John Wiley & Sons in February 2007. Blackwell's publishing program has been merged with Wiley's global Scientific, Technical, and Medical business to form Wiley-Blackwell.

Registered Office
John Wiley & Sons Ltd, The Atrium, Southern Gate, Chichester, West Sussex, PO19 8SQ, UK

Editorial Offices
350 Main Street, Malden, MA 02148–5020, USA
9600 Garsington Road, Oxford, OX4 2DQ, UK
The Atrium, Southern Gate, Chichester, West Sussex, PO19 8SQ, UK

For details of our global editorial offices, for customer services, and for information about how to apply for permission to reuse the copyright material in this book please see our website at www.wiley.com/wiley-blackwell.

The right of Peter E. Knox to be identified as the author of the editorial material in this work has been asserted in accordance with the UK Copyright, Designs and Patents Act 1988.

Library of Congress Cataloging-in-Publication Data

A companion to Ovid / edited by Peter E. Knox.
     p. cm. – (Blackwell companions to the ancient world)
   Includes bibliographical references and index.
   ISBN 978-1-4051-4183-3 (hardcover : alk. paper) 978-1-1184-5134-2 (pbk. : alk. paper)
   1. Ovid, 43 B.C.-17 or 18 A.D.–Criticism and interpretation.   2. Epistolary poetry, Latin–History and criticism.   3. Didactic poetry, Latin–History and criticism.   4. Elegiac poetry, Latin–History and criticism.   5. Mythology, Classical, in literature.   6. Rome–In literature.   7. Love in literature.
I. Knox, Peter E.
   PA6537.C57 2009
   871'.01–dc22

                                                                        2008041557

A catalogue record for this book is available from the British Library.

Cover image: Titian, Bacchus and Ariadne, 1522–23. © National Gallery Collection; by kind permission of the Trustees of the National Gallery, London / CORBIS.

Cover design by Workhaus

Set in 10/12.5 pt Galliard by Toppan Best-set Premedia Limited
Printed in Malaysia by Ho Printing (M) Sdn Bhd

1   2013

Contents

Figures

Notes on Contributors

Benjamin Acosta-Hughes is Associate Professor of Greek and Latin and Comparative Literature at the University of Michigan. He works primarily on Hellenistic poetry, its reception of Archaic lyric, and its recall in Roman literature. He is currently editing a Loeb Library edition of Hellenistic epigrams.

Joan Booth is Professor of Latin Language and Literature at Leiden University in the Netherlands. She is the author of a commentary on Ovid, *Amores* II (1991), and of *Catullus to Ovid: Reading Latin Love Elegy* (1999). She is also co-editor (with Robert Maltby) of *What's in a Name? The Significance of Proper Names in Classical Latin Literature* (2006) and editor of *Cicero on the Attack: Invective and Subversion in the Orations and Beyond* (2007).

Barbara Weiden Boyd is Henry Winkley Professor of Latin and Greek at Bowdoin College. She is the author of *Ovid's Literary Loves: Influence and Innovation in the Amores* (1997), and editor of *Brill's Companion to Ovid* (2002). She is currently writing a commentary on the *Remedia Amoris*.

Gordon Braden is Linden Kent Memorial Professor of English at the University of Virginia. He is the author of *The Classics and English Renaissance Poetry* (1978), *Renaissance Tragedy and the Senecan Tradition* (1985), *The Idea of the Renaissance* (with William Kerrigan, 1989), *Petrarchan Love and the Continental Renaissance* (1999), editor of *Sixteenth-Century Poetry: An Annotated Anthology* (2004), and co-editor of Vol. 2 of *The Oxford History of Literary Translation in English* (forthcoming).

Sergio Casali is Associate Professor of Latin at the University of Rome 'Tor Vergata'. He has published a commentary on Ovid, *Her.* 9 (1995), and articles, notes, and reviews on Roman poetry. He is currently working on a commentary on Virgil, *Aeneid* IV, for the Cambridge Greek and Latin Classics series. A commentary in Italian on *Aeneid* II is also forthcoming.

Mario Citroni teaches at the University of Florence. His numerous publications on Latin poetry include a commentary on Book 1 of Martial (1975), *Poesia e Lettori in Roma Antica* (1995), and the edited volume *Memoria e identità: la cultura romana costruisce la sua immagine* (2003).

Jo-Marie Claassen has retired from teaching Classics at the University of Stellenbosch. She has published on Ovid and Cicero, exile in the ancient world and today, women and children in antiquity, the Classical tradition in South African architecture, academic development, and the use of the computer in the teaching of Latin. She recently completed an English translation of the verse drama *Germanicus* by the Afrikaans poet N. P. Van Wyk Louw.

Elaine Fantham taught for eighteen years at the University of Toronto before moving to Princeton in 1986 as Giger Professor of Latin. She is author of a commentary on Ovid's *Fasti*, Book 4 (1998) and a number of articles on the *Fasti*. Since her retirement in 2000 she has continued teaching and publishing, most recently *The Roman World of Cicero's De Oratore* (2004), *An Introduction to Ovid's Metamorphoses* (2004), and a biography of Julia, daughter of Augustus, *Julia Augusti* (2006).

Joseph Farrell, Professor of Classical Studies at the University of Pennsylvania, is the author of *Virgil's Georgics and the Traditions of Ancient Epic* (1991) and has published widely on Augustan poetry and other aspects of Latin literature and culture.

Laurel Fulkerson is Associate Professor of Classics at the Florida State University. She has written various articles on Ovid, particularly on the *Heroides,* and is the author of *The Ovidian Heroine as Author: Reading, Writing, and Community in the Heroides* (2005). Her current work is on the portrayal of emotions in ancient literature.

John M. Fyler is Professor of English at Tufts University, Massachusetts, and is also on the faculty of the Bread Loaf School of English. He is the author of *Language and the Declining World in Chaucer, Dante, and Jean de Meun* (2007) and *Chaucer and Ovid* (1979), as well as of a number of essays on Ovid, Chaucer, and medieval literature. He also edited the *House of Fame* for the *Riverside Chaucer.*

Luigi Galasso teaches Latin language and literature in the Faculty of Musicology at the University of Pavia. He has edited the second book of Ovid's *Epistulae ex Ponto* with a commentary (1995) and is the author of a commentary on the whole of Ovid's *Metamorphoses* (2000).

Roy K. Gibson is Professor of Latin at the University of Manchester, and the author of *Ovid, Ars Amatoria 3* (2003), *Excess and Restraint: Propertius, Horace and Ovid's Ars Amatoria* (2007), and the co-editor (with Steven Green and Alison Sharrock) of *The Art of Love: Bimillennial Essays on Ovid's Ars Amatoria and Remedia Amoris* (2006).

Julia Dyson Hejduk is Associate Professor of Classics at Baylor University. Her research interests include Latin poetry, Roman religion, and women of ancient Rome. She has written one monograph, *King of the Wood: The Sacrificial Victor in Virgil's Aeneid* (2001), a sourcebook in translation with commentary, *Clodia: A Sourcebook*

(2008), and several articles on Virgil and Ovid. She is currently at work on a monograph involving religion and intertextuality in Ovid, *Ovid and His Gods: The Epic Struggles of an Elegiac Hero.*

Martin Helzle, Professor of Classics and Chair at Case Western Reserve University, has published extensively on Ovid. Most recently he published a commentary on Ovid's *Epistulae ex Ponto* 1–2 (2003).

Geraldine Herbert-Brown is an independent scholar. She is author of *Ovid and the Fasti* (1994), editor of *Ovid's Fasti: Historical Readings at its Bimillennium* (2002), and has published articles on other Roman authors, including Lucilius, Pliny the Elder, and Tacitus.

Stephen Heyworth is Bowra Fellow and Tutor in Classics at Wadham College, Oxford. He edited *Classical Quarterly* from 1993 to 1998; and in 2007 issued a new Oxford Classical Text of Propertius, as well as a companion volume, *Cynthia*, and edited a volume of papers, *Classical Constructions*, published in memory of Don Fowler. He has also published articles on Callimachus, Catullus, Horace, Virgil, and Ovid.

Heather James is Associate Professor of English and Comparative Literature at the University of Southern California. She is the author of *Shakespeare's Troy: Drama, Politics, and the Translation of Empire* (1997) as well as numerous articles on classical reception in the Renaissance, and is editor of the *Norton Anthology of Western Literature.*

Alison Keith is Professor and Chair of the Department of Classics at the University of Toronto. She has written extensively on the intersection of gender and genre in Latin literature, including *Engendering Rome* (2000), and is currently finishing a book on *Propertius, Poet of Love and Leisure.*

E. J. Kenney is Kennedy Professor Emeritus of Latin at the University of Cambridge. His publications include a critical edition of Ovid's amatory works (2nd edn, 1995); editions with commentary of Lucretius' *De Rerum Natura* III (1971), Anon. *Moretum* (1984), Apuleius' *Cupid and Psyche* (1990), and Ovid's *Her.* 16–21 (1996); a translation with introduction and notes of Apuleius' *Golden Ass* (1998); *The Classical Text* (1974; Italian translation by A. Lunelli 1995); and numerous articles and reviews. He is at present completing a commentary on Ovid's *Metamorphoses* Books 7–9.

Peter E. Knox is Professor of Classics at the University of Colorado. He is the author of *Ovid's* Metamorphoses *and the Traditions of Augustan Poetry* (1986), as well as a commentary on selected *Heroides* (1995). Most recently he edited *Oxford Readings in Ovid* and has written articles on a wide range of topics in Hellenistic poetry and Latin literature.

Jane L. Lightfoot has been Fellow and Tutor in Classics at New College, Oxford, since 2003. All her books have been published with Oxford University Press: *Parthenius of Nicaea* (1999), *Lucian: On the Syrian Goddess* (2003) and *The Sibylline*

Oracles: With Introduction, Translation, and Commentary on the First and Second Books (2008). She is working on a volume of Hellenistic poetry for the Loeb Classical Library.

Robert Maltby is Professor of Latin Philology at the University of Leeds. His research interests are in Roman comedy and elegy and the Latin language in general, especially ancient etymology. His main publications include *A Lexicon of Ancient Latin Etymologies* (1991) and *Tibullus: Elegies* (2002).

Christopher Martin is a member of the English department at Boston University, where he serves as NEH Distinguished Teaching Professor. He has published *Policy in Love: Lyric and Public in Ovid, Petrarch and Shakespeare* (1994) and the anthology *Ovid in English* (1998), as well as journal articles on literature of the Renaissance and other topics. He is currently completing a book on conceptions of old age in late-Elizabethan literature.

Charles McNelis is Associate Professor of Classics at Georgetown University. In addition to articles on ancient poetry and intellectual life, he has written *Statius' Thebaid and the Poetics of Civil War* (2007) and is currently working on a commentary on Statius' *Achilleid* for the Cambridge Greek and Latin Classics series.

Mark Possanza is Associate Professor of Classics at the University of Pittsburgh. He is the author of *Translating the Heavens: Aratus, Germanicus and the Poetics of Latin Translation* (2004) and of articles on textual problems in Latin authors.

Efrossini Spentzou is a Senior Lecturer in Classics at Royal Holloway, University of London. She is the author of *Readers and Writers in Ovid's* Heroides: *Transgressions of Gender and Genre* (2003). She co-edited with the late Don Fowler *Cultivating the Muse: Struggles for Power and Inspiration in Classical Literature* (2002). She has just finished *Reflections of Romanitas: Discourses of Subjectivity in an Imperial Age* (co-authored with Richard Alston).

Richard Thomas is Professor of Greek and Latin at Harvard University, where he writes and teaches on Roman and Hellenistic Greek poetry, reception, and Bob Dylan. Recent books include *Reading Virgil and his Texts* (1999), *Virgil and the Augustan Reception* (2001), co-edited with Charles Martindale, *Classics and the Uses of Reception* (2006), co-edited with Catharine Mason, *Bob Dylan's Performance Artistry* (2007).

Gareth Williams, Professor of Classics at Columbia University, is the author of several works on Ovid's exile poetry, including *Banished Voices: Readings in Ovid's Exile Poetry* (1994) and *The Curse of Exile: A Study of Ovid's Ibis* (1996). Recent publications include a commentary on Seneca's *De Otio* and *De Brevitate Vitae* (2004) and several studies on Seneca's *Natural Questions*.

David Wray is Associate Professor of Classics and Comparative Literature at the University of Chicago. He is the author of *Catullus and the Poetics of Roman Manhood* (2001) and articles on Roman and Hellenistic poetry.

Theodore Ziolkowski is Class of 1900 Professor Emeritus of German and Comparative Literature at Princeton University. In addition to *Virgil and the Moderns* (1993), *Ovid and the Moderns* (2005), and the forthcoming *Minos and the Moderns: Cretan Myth in Twentieth-century Literature and Art* (2008), his recent works include *Modes of Faith: Secular Surrogates for Lost Religious Belief* (2007), *Clio the Romantic Muse* (2004), and *The Sin of Knowledge* (2000).

Preface

Another companion for Ovid . . . Arriving on the bimillenary of his exile to the shores of the Black Sea, perhaps this Companion is timely. More than one of the contributors to this volume has noted that we are living in another *aetas Ovidiana*, to borrow a famous, if somewhat problematic, phrase. Two excellent volumes of essays appeared in 2002, which offer readers of Ovid a wealth of information and provocation for future study. In preparing this volume I have had in mind the newcomers to Ovid's works, be they students or scholars, and the emphasis of the chapters has been on utility. Vast as the sweep of subjects covered in this Companion is, there are inevitably omissions, many of them deeply to be regretted. In particular, it proved impossible to do justice to every aspect of the rapidly developing field of reception studies, so the papers in the volume focus on literary receptions, with a heavy bias toward literature in English. Ovid's influence on the visual arts deserves a Companion of its own, which could not be included here.

I have allowed the contributors considerable leeway in approaching their topics, including some variation in matters of presentation, such as the use of BC or BCE to indicate dates. In the first instance thanks must go to all the contributors for their diligence, their forbearance, and their talents. I hope that my labors as editor have obscured as little as possible of their learning. I am deeply grateful to Sophie Gibson for soliciting this volume, and to Ben Thatcher and Hannah Rolls for their hard work in seeing it to completion.

Peter E. Knox
University of Colorado, Boulder, November 2007

List of Abbreviations

Ovid's works are referred to throughout the volume by the following standard abbreviations: *Amores* (*Am.*), *Heroides* (*Her.*), *Ars amatoria* (*Ars*), *Remedia amoris* (*Rem.*), *Medicamina faciei* (*Med.*), *Metamorphoses* (*Met.*), *Fasti* (*Fast.*), *Tristia* (*Tr.*), *Ibis* (*Ib.*), *Epistulae ex Ponto* (*Pont.*). All translations are the authors' own, unless otherwise indicated. References to other authors follow standard conventions to be found in, for example, *The Oxford Latin Dictionary* or Liddell and Scott. The following abbreviations for journals and reference works are used here:

A&A	*Antike und Abendland*
A&R	*Atene e Roma*
AC	*L'Antiquité classique*
AJP	*American Journal of Philology*
ANRW	*Aufstieg und Niedergang der römischen Welt*
ASNP	*Annali della Scuola Normale Superiore di Pisa, Classe di Lettere e Filosofia*
AU	*Der Altsprachliche Unterricht*
BICS	*Bulletin of the Institute of Classical Studies*
BMCR	*Bryn Mawr Classical Review*
BNP	*Brill's New Pauly*
CA	*Classical Antiquity*
CB	*The Classical Bulletin*
CFC(L)	*Cuadernos de filología clásica. Estudios latinos*
CJ	*The Classical Journal*
CL	*Corolla Londiniensis*
CML	*Classical and Modern Literature*
CPh	*Classical Philology*
CQ	*Classical Quarterly*
CR	*Classical Review*
CSCA	*California Studies in Classical Antiquity*
CW	*Classical World*
DBI	*Dizionario Biografico degli Italiani*
FGrH	*Fragmente der griechischen Historiker*

G&R	*Greece and Rome*
GRBS	*Greek, Roman and Byzantine Studies*
HSCP	*Harvard Studies in Classical Philology*
ICS	*Illinois Classical Studies*
IJCT	*International Journal of the Classical Tradition*
IMU	*Italia Medioevale e Umanistica*
JHS	*Journal of Hellenic Studies*
JPh	*Journal of Philology*
JRS	*Journal of Roman Studies*
JWCI	*Journal of the Warburg and Courtauld Institute*
LCM	*Liverpool Classical Monthly*
LEC	*Les Études Classiques*
MAAR	*Memoirs of the American Academy in Rome*
MD	*Materiali e discussioni per l'analisi dei testi classici*
MH	*Museum Helveticum*
MLatJb	*Mittellateinisches Jahrbuch*
MLQ	*Modern Language Quarterly*
N&Q	*Notes and Queries*
OLD	*Oxford Latin Dictionary*, ed. P. G. W. Glare (Oxford, 1982)
PBA	*Proceedings of the British Academy*
PCPhS	*Proceedings of the Cambridge Philological Society*
PLLS	*Papers of the Leeds International Latin Seminar*
POxy	*Oxyrhynchus Papyri*
PQ	*Philological Quarterly*
R&L	*Religion and Literature*
RBPH	*Revue Belge de philologie et d'histoire*
RE	*Real-Encylopädie der Altertumswisseschaft*
RhM	*Rheinisches Museum*
RHT	*Revue d'Histoire des Textes*
RSC	*Rivista di studi classici*
SB	*Studies in Bibliography*
SEEJ	*Slavic and East European Journal*
ShS	*Shakespeare Survey*
SH	*Supplementum Hellenisticum*, ed. H. Lloyd-Jones and P. J. Parsons (Berlin, 1983)
SO	*Symbolae Osloenses*
SSH	*Supplementum Supplementi Hellenistici*, ed. H. Lloyd-Jones (Berlin, 2005).
TAPA	*Transactions of the American Philological Association*
TLL	*Thesaurus Linguae Latinae*
TRF	*Tragicorum Romanorum Fragmenta*, ed. O. Ribbeck (Leipzig, 1871)
WJA	*Würzburger Jahrbücher der Altertumswissenschaft*
WS	*Wiener Studien*
YCS	*Yale Classical Studies*
ZPE	*Zeitschrift für Papyrologie und Epigraphik*

Chronological Table of Important Events in Roman History and Literature during the Life of Ovid

Most of the dates of Ovid's works are entirely conjectural. Those given below reflect a consensus view, but can only be considered approximate.

	Ovid's life	*Key literary events*	*Key historical events*
43 BCE	Birth of Ovid	Death of Cicero	Battle of Mutina, deaths of consuls Hirtius and Pansa.
42–40		Sallust, *Bellum Iugurthinum*	Defeat of Caesar's assassins at Philippi; civil unrest in Italy
38		Virgil, *Eclogues*	Renewal of the Second Triumvirate. Marriage of Octavian and Livia
36–35		Horace, *Satires* 1 (35). Death of Sallust	Octavian defeats Sextus Pompey; Antony's failed Parthian offensive
32–30		Horace, *Epodes*; Tibullus 1	Civil War between Octavian and Antony; defeat of Antony and Cleopatra at Actium
29–25	Ovid's first recitations	Horace, *Satires* 2; Tibullus 1–2, Virgil's *Georgics*, Propertius 1. Suicide of Gallus.	Octavian celebrates a triple triumph; closing of the doors of the temple of Janus; Octavian takes the title of 'Augustus'

Chronological Table

	Ovid's life	Key literary events	Key historical events
23		Horace's *Odes* 1–3. Vitruvius, *De Architectura*.	Augustus receives *tribunicia potestas* for life; death of Marcellus
19	*Heroides* 1–15 (?).	*Aeneid*; Horace, *Epistles* 1. Deaths of Virgil and Tibullus. Death of Tibullus	
18–17		Horace, *Carmen Saeculare*	Augustus' moral legislation. Augustus adopts his grandsons, Gaius and Lucius
16–15	First edition of the *Amores* (?)	Propertius 4	Birth of Germanicus
12	*Medea* (?)	Horace, *Epistles* 2.1	Death of Agrippa. Augustus becomes Pontifex Maximus.
8–3	Second edition of the *Amores* (?)	Deaths of Maecenas and Horace (8)	Tiberius retires to Rhodes (6).
2	*Ars Amatoria* 1–2		Julia the Elder exiled. Augustus takes the title of *pater patriae*.
2 CE	*Ars Amatoria* 3, *Remedia Amoris*		Return of Tiberius from Rhodes. Death of Lucius Caesar.
3–7	Composition of the *Fasti* and the *Metamorphoses*	Death of Asinius Pollio (4).	Death of Caius Caesar (4). Augustus adopts Tiberius, who adopts Germanicus. Tiberius granted *tribunicia potestas* for ten years.
8	Relegation to Tomi. *Metamorphoses*	Exile of Cassius Severus. Suicide of Labienus.	Julia the Younger exiled.
9–12	*Tristia* 1–5, *Ibis* (?)	Pompeius Trogus, *Historiae Philippicae*	Defeat of Varus in the Teutoburg Forest (9). Tiberius' Illyrian triumph (12).
13	*Epistulae ex Ponto* 1–3		Tiberius granted *tribunicia potestas* for ten more years.
14–16	*Epistulae ex Ponto* 4	Manilius begins *Astronomica*	Death of Augustus (14). Tiberius becomes Princeps. Germanicus campaigns in Germany.
17	Death of Ovid	Death of Livy	Triumph of Germanicus

PART I

Contexts

CHAPTER ONE

A Poet's Life

Peter E. Knox

Introduction

Late in his career, Ovid defined his place in recent literary history by drawing up a list of names (*Tr.* 4.10.41–54):

temporis illius colui fouique poetas,
 quotque aderant uates, rebar adesse deos.
saepe suas uolucres legit mihi grandior aeuo,
 quaeque nocet serpens, quae iuuat herba, Macer.
saepe suos solitus recitare Propertius ignes,
 iure sodalicii, quo mihi iunctus erat.
Ponticus heroo, Bassus quoque clarus iambis
 dulcia conuictus membra fuere mei.
et tenuit nostras numerosus Horatius aures,
 dum ferit Ausonia carmina culta lyra.
Vergilium uidi tantum, nec auara Tibullo
 tempus amicitiae fata dedere meae.
successor fuit hic tibi, Galle, Propertius illi;
 quartus ab his serie temporis ipse fui.

The poets of that time I cultivated and cherished, and for me poets were so many gods. Often Macer, already advanced in years, read to me of his birds, of poisonous snakes, or healing plants. Often Propertius would recite his flaming verse, by virtue of the comradeship that joined him to me. Ponticus, noted for epic, and Bassus, noted for iambics, were sweet members of my circle. And Horace, he of the many numbers, held our ears in thrall, while he tuned his fine-crafted songs to the Ausonian lyre. Virgil I only saw; greedy fate gave Tibullus no time for friendship with me. He was your successor, Gallus, and Propertius his; after them I was fourth in order of time.

The climate for poetry in Rome during Ovid's lifetime was electric. Ovid places himself in distinguished company, including poets whose works, though lost to us now, were celebrated in their time: Aemilius Macer, the author of didactic verse

(Courtney 1993: 292–9; Hollis 2007: 93–117), Ponticus, an epic poet (Hollis 2007: 426), Bassus, writer of iambs (Hollis 2007: 421), and Gallus, celebrated by Virgil in his *Eclogues* and widely recognized as the first Roman elegist (Courtney 1993: 259–70; Hollis 2007: 219–52). The selection cannot be random, and is not likely to have been limited only to poets whom he had met or heard. These are the names that mattered to Ovid among his contemporaries, whose works influenced his own forays into epic, didactic, invective, and the verse epistle. But when it comes to classifying himself in this company he is an elegist, following in the footsteps of Gallus, Tibullus, and Propertius, the same company he cites in his apology to Augustus (*Tr.* 2.445–66) with the concluding remark (467), 'to these I succeeded' (*his ego successi*). In the process he defined the canon, for when Quintilian turns to the chief exponents of elegy in Latin, it is these same four whom he names and no others (*Inst.* 10.1.93): 'we challenge the Greeks also in elegy, in which Tibullus seems to me particularly polished and elegant, though some prefer Propertius. Ovid is more extravagant than both of them, just as Gallus is harsher.' It is telling that Ovid thus classifies himself as an elegist, even after the achievement of his *Metamorphoses*, for the background of elegy informs even his hexameter epic: it is the wellspring from which he draws inspiration in all his manifold creative endeavors.

In His Own Words

Ovid is himself the source for most of what we think we know about his life; indeed, he provides more information about himself than most ancient poets. It is always hazardous to infer too much or too confidently from such references in a poet's own work: as Ovid himself avers (*Am.* 3.12.19), *nec tamen ut testes mos est audire poetas* ('nor is it the custom to listen to poets as if they were courtroom witnesses'). It is nonetheless possible to glean some data about his background and career, not only from the long autobiographical poem composed toward the end of his life during his exile on the Black Sea (*Tr.* 4.10), but also from numerous revealing remarks scattered throughout his works. His hometown was Sulmo (*Tr.* 4.10.3 *Sulmo mihi patria est*), now called Sulmona, situated in a well-watered valley in the Abruzzi of central Italy, and in Ovid's time one of the chief towns of the tribe known as the Paeligni. He was born Publius Ovidius Naso on 20 March 43 BCE. The significance of this date was not lost on Ovid later in life, for as he notes (*Tr.* 4.10.6) it was in this year that the two consuls Hirtius and Pansa both fell in the campaign against Mark Antony at the head of the last army of the Roman Republic. Most of the poets Ovid names in his autobiography began their careers in the confused circumstances of the civil wars that followed Julius Caesar's assassination. Virgil, who released his *Georgics* in 29 BCE in the immediate aftermath of Octavian's victory at Actium, had earlier composed his book of *Eclogues*, in which the tenor of the times is refracted through the lens of Theocritean bucolic. Horace's book of *Epodes*, probably published near the end of the Triumviral period, also meditates on the fears and apprehensions of that era. At about the same time, Ovid's two surviving predecessors in elegy, Tibullus and

Propertius, were producing books in which the harsh realities of the time impinge on their idealized visions of the life of love. Ovid, so far as we can tell, was touched by none of this. His career belongs entirely to the early Empire, a time of peace at least on the domestic front, and the great matters treated in his works are affairs of the heart and of character, rather than of state.

His first literary performances probably took place several years after the battle of Actium and the fall of Alexandria, perhaps around 25 BCE. The date can only be approximate, deriving as it does from information given by Ovid himself (*Tr.* 4.10.57–8):

> carmina cum primum populo iuuenalia legi,
>   barba resecta mihi bisue semelue fuit.

> When I first read my youthful songs to the public, my beard had been cut but once or twice.

We may suppose that Ovid was no more than about eighteen years old when this took place (Wheeler 1925: 11–17), but precision on this score is unimportant: the point that Ovid makes is about the precociousness of his venture into a life of poetry.

His family presumably preferred a different career path. As the second son of an old, equestrian family of considerable standing in the community, Ovid might have been expected to pursue a career in public life, where opportunities beckoned under the new regime in Rome. As recently as during the Social War of 91–89 BCE, Sulmo had aligned itself with the rest of the Paeligni against Rome, but there was a long tradition of alliance. In his move to consolidate power Augustus sought to draw on such communities throughout Italy to recruit new magistrates and senators. From Ovid we learn that he embarked on just such a course: he studied rhetoric in Rome and Athens, the traditional route to a political career (Wheeler 1925: 4–11). He held two positions on boards of magistrates, as one of the *tresuiri capitales* (*Tr.* 4.10.33–4; Kenney 1969b: 244), who exercised police functions in the city. And later he informs us (*Fast.* 4.383–4) that he held a seat among the *decemuiri stlitibus iudicandis* ('Board of Ten for Judging Lawsuits'), an important judicial post that was commonly a precursor to seeking the quaestorship and a senatorial career. On Ovid's testimony his earliest recitations of poetry took place at the very time when he was ostensibly embarking on a life in law and politics. He ironically remarks that his father had hoped for a more lucrative livelihood:

> saepe pater dixit 'studium quid inutile temptas?
>   Maeonides nullas ipse relinquit opes.'

> Often my father said, 'Why do you attempt a useless pursuit? Homer himself left no wealth.'

Perhaps his father might have gotten the joke, but if Augustus ever noticed this poem, he would not have been amused. Ovid abandoned public office for the life of letters, but his choices in that field were not bound to win him favor.

During the first twenty-five years of his career, a period extending roughly from the mid-twenties BCE to 2 CE, Ovid was occupied exclusively with elegy, issuing a stunning series of works: *Amores, Heroides, Ars amatoria*, and *Remedia amoris*. To this period too belong most of the lost works (Chapter 15), among which the tragedy *Medea* may be reckoned the greatest loss. The exact sequence of the release of these works is unclear and much disputed. The matter is complicated in the first instance by the fact that his earliest collection, the *Amores*, survives only in a three-book edition, which, Ovid asserts, has been reduced from an original five-book collection. There is no consensus about the date of either edition, or about the nature of the revision effected upon the earlier work, but opinions generally divide between those who argue that Ovid's final edition collects the best poems from the first edition without the addition of new poems or extensive revision (Cameron 1968) and those who contend that the three-book edition was essentially a new work (McKeown 1987: 86–9). Ovid himself seems to suggest the former, when he describes his earliest work in the autobiography from Tomi (*Tr.* 4.10.61–2):

> multa quidem scripsi, sed, quae uitiosa putaui,
>   emendaturis ignibus ipse dedi.

> I wrote a great deal indeed, but what I considered defective I myself gave to the flames for correction.

Even if this inference is correct, it is not entirely clear where in the chronological sequence to date the release of the *Heroides*, a collection that itself raises intractable questions about composition and publication. The dates given above in the Chronological Table are thus tentative at best.

By the time Ovid completed the *Remedia amoris*, the last of his amatory elegiacs, in roughly 2 CE he was probably already deeply involved in the composition of his two large-scale narrative poems, the *Fasti* and the *Metamorphoses*. It is clear that he had not completed the *Fasti* by the year 8 CE, when his life changed drastically with the issuance of a decree of relegation by the emperor. Ovid himself refers to twelve books (*Tr.* 2.549–50), but only six survive and there are clear signs of revision to the existing poem during the period of exile. There is no reason to believe that the remaining six ever left the poet's hand, and the poet's words here carry no more weight than his assertion that the *Metamorphoses* was unfinished (*Tr.* 2.555–6):

> dictaque sunt nobis, quamuis manus ultima coeptis
>   defuit, in facies corpora uersa nouas.

> And though this work lacked final revision, I also told of bodies that changed into new shapes.

The composition of this masterpiece was surely the preoccupation of the years immediately preceding his exile.

We will never know what led Augustus to send Ovid into exile, or what sense of irony or private joke led him to choose the venue for Ovid's relegation, remote and inhospitable Tomi on the shores of the Black Sea. The reason famously given by Ovid

(*Tr.* 2.207), 'a poem and a mistake' (*carmen et error*), may invert the sequence, a *hysteron proteron* of sorts, if, as many scholars believe, the poem, which Ovid identifies as the *Ars amatoria*, was brought into the indictment later to provide cover for some other offense, the *error* that Ovid never explains. Many scholars cannot escape the suspicion that Ovid's relegation was somehow related to the disgrace of Augustus' granddaughter Julia, exiled on a charge of adultery in the same year (e.g. Syme 1978: 215–29). Others incline to a scandal of a more personal nature (e.g. Goold 1983), or attempt to relate the exile to changes in the climate for literature during Augustus' dotage (Knox 2004). The consequences for Ovid were tragic, but did not sap his creative powers. A stream of innovative new works flowed from his stylus while he lamented life on the Roman frontier: the *Tristia* in five books composed during the journey to Tomi and in his first years there; that bizarre display of erudite invective known as the *Ibis*; and four books of epistles to friends and acquaintances, his *Epistu-lae ex Ponto*, the last book of which probably contains his final works. A common thread uniting all the works of exile is Ovid's return to the elegiac mode, the measure in which he began his career and by which he defined himself. Ovid began writing just a few years after Octavian assumed the title by which he is best known to history, and his death came only a few years after the emperor's. Ovid, perhaps the most Augustan poet and certainly the last, died at Tomi sometime during the winter of 17–18 CE.

FURTHER READING

Still fundamental for basic information and collection of the evidence about Ovid's career are surveys such as Wheeler (1925), Martini (1933), or Kraus (1968). In the absence of new evidence, there is always a place for re-evaluation and recontextualization. For instance, Kenney (1969b) investigates Ovid's use of legal language against the background of his public career, while Syme (1978) attempts to review Ovid's network of friends and associates within the changing political landscape of Augustus' later years. The subject of Ovid's exile continually attracts new speculation: in addition to the works surveyed by Thibault (1964), papers by Goold (1983) and Knox (2004) may be consulted for recent attempts to set the relegation within the context of the times.

CHAPTER TWO

Poetry in Augustan Rome

Mario Citroni

Introduction

The substantially unchanging judgment of the centuries has considered Virgil, Horace and Ovid, already highly admired during their own lifetimes, to be the prime examples of the greatness and the full maturity of Roman poetry. The fact that the works of these three foremost poets were all composed during the reign of Augustus, and that this same period witnessed the production of other important poets, such as Tibullus and Propertius, and of some whose works are no longer extant but who enjoyed widespread renown in antiquity (the founder of the Latin elegy, Cornelius Gallus, the epic and tragic poet Varius Rufus, the epigrammatist Domitius Marsus, the didactic poet Aemilius Macer), caused the Augustan age to be viewed, both in ancient and in modern times, as a thoroughly exceptional period of poetic splendor, and encourages reflection on the elements which determined, or favored, its development.

It has always been difficult to avoid the idea that there must have been a connection between the exceptional level of the poetic production of those years and the extraordinary success of Augustus' policies, especially in the light of the fact that the relationship between literature and political power, always very close in Rome, appears to be particularly striking in the case of Augustan poetry. Augustus maintained a personal contact with Virgil, with Horace, and with other poets, and his close collaborator Maecenas was a generous friend and patron of many of the leading poets of the period. It is clear that there was an intention to stimulate poetic production, and to orientate it appropriately, in order to create and consolidate the image of Augustus as the founder of a new period of even greater splendor for Rome, after the disasters of the civil wars. In actual fact the poetry of this period frequently includes expressions of praise and thanks for Augustus and his policies, as well as some truly encomiastic passages. Above all, a considerable part of the conceptual content of Augustan poetry can be traced back to the moral, civil, and religious themes that characterized the ideology of his regime.

Furthermore, Augustus succeeded in exploiting the prestige of his poets in order to enhance his own prestige as a political leader, publicly rewarding and honoring them, and including their compositions on occasions that were of great symbolic significance for the regime. Suffice it to recall the commission assigned to Varius to provide the text of a tragedy to be performed on the occasion of the triple triumph for the victories in Illyria, at Actium, and in Egypt, which celebrated the end of the civil wars and the starting-point of Octavian's unrivalled power in 29 BC, and the lavish recompense that Varius received. Or again, the commission given to Horace to compose the text of the hymn that was sung during the course of the solemn Ludi Saeculares, in 17 BC, which were held to acclaim the Augustan age as a new age of the world. The glory of the poets of this period was perceived even in antiquity as one of the basic components of the image of fullness and splendor that the regime of Augustus succeeded in communicating to contemporaries, and has transmitted to succeeding generations. However, Ovid's banishment at the height of his success demonstrated that the relationship between the regime and poets could also have complicated and sinister repercussions.

Actually, external conditions of a political or social nature are never able to account for the qualitative level of artistic production. Even Martial, who affirmed (8.55.5–20) that one Maecenas was sufficient to create a Virgil, was undoubtedly well aware that he was launching this paradox as a provocation against what appeared to him to be the insufficient patronage of literature in his period. On the contrary, it is clear that any patronage of the arts which is connected with the motivations and the interests of political power tends to encourage a production that is mainly conformist and celebratory, and as a result, it may even act as an obstacle to the creation of works of high quality; and modern readers have often been rather severe in their judgment of that part of the poetic production of the Augustan age which is most closely linked to the ideology of the regime. Until the Second World War, above all in Germany, but also in Italy, the dominant, albeit obviously not exclusive, interpretation of Augustan poetry was that it was deeply sympathetic to the regime of Augustus and its ideology: the greatness of Virgil and Horace was considered to stem largely from their ability to express the new imperial Rome desired by Augustus, and its values, or even to be the prophets and inspirers of the political and ideological program adopted and implemented by Augustus. In the new climate determined by the defeat of the European dictatorships, interpretations changed, and the Augustan poets have been appreciated mainly for their ability to resist pressure from the regime, seeing that none of them ever wrote an epic to celebrate Augustus, and to continue to compose poetry that was different from what their patrons would have preferred. Whenever they celebrated the regime, they were suspected of agreeing to act as mouthpieces of political propaganda, out of either weakness or convenience.

The identification of the ways in which the political, institutional and social conditions of an age may influence its literary production is always an extremely delicate question. Writers and artists follow vocations and tendencies which can only partly be attributed to the experience of contemporary society: to a certain extent, these orientations can be traced back to intellectual and aesthetic experience acquired with literary texts of the past and of the present. And writers and artists, also in the Rome of Augustus, do not respond only to their patrons and those who commission their works; they also respond to a wider reading public, whose varying expectations and criteria of judgment, can, in turn, be traced back not only to the experience of contemporary life but also to their reading of texts of the past, which inspire dreams and ideals that are projected into the future. Thus, even the temporal relationship between literary production and the political and social situation is problematic: while it is true that on the level of themes and contents the literature of this period appears to react, continually and immediately, to current events and circumstances, the motivations on the more strictly literary level of choices of genre, style and form, and the general poetic stance adopted, though linked with current experience, are rooted in, or react against, long-standing tendencies and traditions.

Nowadays, scholars are debating whether many of the social, cultural, and even the political and institutional aspects which appear to us to be typical of the Augustan age, and have usually been connected directly with the 'revolution' brought about by Augustus—that is to say, the passage to a new form of monarchy whose power was based on social forces that to some extent were different from those that had supported the *res publica*—should not rather be traced back to longer-standing processes, among which the activity of Augustus was only a conditioning factor, albeit an extremely significant one. In the case of high-quality literature, where the relationship with contemporary experience is almost always indirect and mediated, this aspect is particularly important.

An initial problem is what exactly we mean by 'Augustan age'. Discussions still aim to establish, also from the political and institutional point of view, from what date Rome may truly be defined as 'Augustan': but in the case of literature, as a result of its indirect relationship with current political affairs, the definition of the concept of 'Augustan' and the division into stages of the period called 'Augustan' raise particularly delicate problems.

The Roman Political Revolution

When Caesar was killed, on the Ides of March in 44 BC, he was governing Rome with a power that in reality was absolute, and had recently been formalized as a lifelong dictatorship; this institutional form was incompatible with the principles of the *res publica*, which only contemplated dictatorship as a short-lasting appointment, for emergencies. Caesar had shortly before concluded the complex military operations that were necessary to give stability to his decisive victory over Pompey in 48 BC: the long period of civil wars that had devastated Italy, overrun the provinces, and swept away the institutions of the *res publica* seemed to be over. The assassination of the dictator led to a new phase of wars and dramatic instability. Powerful figures, competing for supremacy, again clashed at the head of their armies.

The framework within which these conflicts found space and reason to develop was a society that was undergoing a profound transformation and did not possess adequate political institutions for its new complexity. In little more than a century, a city-state which continued to identify itself with the ethical traditions and the civic institutions typical of an ancient rural community, even if it had assumed a dominant role in the Italian peninsula, had become an enormous imperial reality. New territories, vast and distant, had entered into the political and social systems of Rome. There were new lands to be colonized and new movements of wealth had been created, together with new frontiers for trading, new tasks of administration, a new role for the armies, new opportunities for action, and new responsibilities for Roman citizens of the various classes in different areas of the world. New subjects, from faraway regions, or from previously excluded social areas, entered into the citizenship system, or increasingly pressed to become a part of it. The contacts that had long before been set up with different cultures rapidly multiplied, above all with Greece and the Hellenized regions of the East, with their customs, religious beliefs and intellectual advances. As we shall see, this spectacular renewal is particularly important for the development of a new literary public.

There was little renewal in the body of those who sat in the Senate at Rome and occupied the position of magistrates: an oligarchy of land-owning families still prevailed, who were unwilling to admit *homines novi* into the power system, and had little regard for interests that were different from those of their own class. The political system of the old city-state was totally insufficient to provide adequate representation for the forces that had now come into play. The inhabitants of Italy had only won the concession of the rights of citizenship after 90 BC, at the end of a fierce war. This tardy recognition had made it clear that it was impossible for the whole civic body to take part in assemblies and elections (which were held in Rome), which was the basic presupposition of the republican institutions (Brunt 1988: 23–6; Mouritsen 2001).

Caesar had been the most authoritative of those representatives of the Roman nobility who had tried to open up the political system to different requirements, and call into question many of the privileges of the traditional aristocracy. All the struggles of this period—the political, and subsequently military, conflict that had opposed Caesar to Pompey, the champion of the senatorial tradition, and, after Caesar's death, the series of battles in which Caesar's brilliant general, Antony, and the young Octavian, Caesar's nephew and adoptive son, fought each other for Caesar's political inheritance, and subsequently united against Caesar's assassins, Brutus and Cassius (defeated at Philippi in 42 BC), and Pompey's son (defeated in 36 BC), and in the end clashed again in a final struggle—were fought to establish the personal supremacy of men who knew that they were destined either to rule or to be ruined. Victory or defeat was decided in battle; but in order to have any chance of obtaining consensus, and a lasting power, it was necessary to find a political synthesis between the tradition of the *res publica* and the different interests and powers to which the traditional system did not assign an adequate institutional representation.

For the twelve years from the setting up of the triumvirate of Octavian, Antony and Lepidus (who were assigned special powers for a period of five years, prolonged in 37 BC for another five) by the law of 43 BC to the defeat of Antony at the battle of Actium in 31 BC, constitutional legality had been flouted, if not totally suspended. Lepidus was soon limited to a marginal role, while Octavian controlled Italy and the Western provinces, and Antony those of the East. Octavian succeeded in exploiting his position, by forming a positive relationship with the Senate, and creating for himself the image of the defender of Roman and Italic moral and religious tradition, in contrast with Antony, who behaved like an Oriental despot, accepting divine honors, and leading people to suspect that his policies were contrary to the interests of Italy. Even though Octavian also exploited his position as the son of the deified Caesar, he was aware that in order to gain lasting success it was necessary to present himself as the guarantor of the republican civic institutions and the ethical and religious tradition on which, according to the Roman and Italic collective conscience, these were based. If the revolution under way was to be accepted and consolidated, it had to be presented as a recovery of tradition, which possessed a superior prestige in Rome. Even the triumvirate had formally been instituted *rei publicae constituendae*, that is to say, for the purpose of re-establishing the *res publica* (an ambiguous expression, which could mean 'the state' or 'the state in its traditional principles', as opposed to the alterations to which it had been subjected during the civil wars: cf. e.g. Millar 1973: 63–4).

The consolidation of a regime which was in reality monarchic (and hereditary), which Octavian carried out with great skill, still required a long time after Actium, with continual adjustments and modifications to adapt to various pressures and requirements. The dominant feature was the gradual, visible, relinquishment of all special powers, and the restoration of the traditional offices. But Octavian himself held, for several years consecutively, offices which in the republican tradition were annual, he held offices at the same time, which were only to be held separately, and he maintained lifelong high civil and military powers which were typical of republican offices, without ever formally occupying them, thus setting himself above all other magistrates. A crucial stage in this process of institutional 'normalization' was the cancellation of the triumvirate laws, at the end of 28 BC, and the restoration of the traditional offices with the assumption of the title of *Augustus* in January of 27 BC. Strictly speaking, this is the beginning of the 'Augustan' age. The subsequent stages (that of 23 BC is important) continued to enhance the personal role of Augustus, as the supreme governor of the state, both in view of the powers effectively attributed to him and as a result of his superior authority (*auctoritas*), which was universally recognized. This condition was confirmed by titles which were devoid of any juridical-institutional value, but contained a strong emotional quality, like that of *Augustus*, which, in its etymological connection with *augurium* and *augere* ('to increase'), gave his figure a sacred, well-wishing aura (confirmed in 12 BC by the assumption of the highest religious office, that of Pontifex Maximus), alluding to his role as the re-founder of the city, with its reference to the *augurium* which had inspired Romulus at the original foundation. And like the title of *pater patriae*, assumed in 2 BC, these qualifications expressed his role as the guarantor not only of political life but also of every aspect of social life, customs, religion, and culture: in all these fields, his influence was considerable, in promoting laws, decreeing acts and fixing regulations.

Augustus died in AD 14, at the age of 76, after holding power by himself, unopposed, for the forty-four years that had passed since the battle of Actium, and fifty-six years after assuming power in the triumvirate, which had placed the government of Italy in his hands. For forty years, he had been Augustus. This extraordinary monarchy, clothed in the robes of the *res publica*, might seem to be an original invention of Octavian, and of the wholly exceptional situation in which he was forced to operate; however, it remained—with some adaptations—the stable form of the Roman state for centuries, which continued to have a single leader, possessing superior powers, who was supported in his government by the Senate, whose members continued to occupy the traditional magistracies of the *res publica*, and were assigned important duties, albeit essentially of an administrative nature. Already, before Octavian, Julius Caesar, and before him Marius, Sulla and Pompey, on the basis of the prestige that they had conquered in battle, had temporarily held power substantially by themselves, accumulating consulships, special powers and extraordinary honors. Under Augustus, for the first time, this recurring tendency of the republican institutions, failing a substantial legitimization, to create space for the figure of a governor—who, from a position of superior strength, could impose a different balance of forces, thus avoiding stormy conflicts within the apparatus of the state—was transformed into a permanent political system.

Poetry from Revolution to Empire

One of the first acts of the triumvirate, in 43 BC, had been the compilation of lists of adversaries to be eliminated. Antony desired the death of Cicero, who had attacked him violently, as an enemy of the Senate and of the State. Octavian, who had maintained an ambiguous relationship with Cicero, and in reality had used him, endorsed the decision. Thus, the greatest Roman intellectual died at the age of 63. By that time, almost all the poets who had acquired prestige during the age of Caesar had already died, at a more or less young age: Lucretius and Catullus about ten years earlier, and Calvus at least six years before; others had fallen in the recent civil wars. Chance and wars had caused a break in the continuity of generations between the poets who were active during the period of Caesar and those whom we usually call 'Augustan'. One exception is represented by Varius, who outlived his friend Virgil, and had become famous already before the death of Caesar.

The different age groups of the poets of the period indicate different conditions of their belonging to the 'Augustan' age. Virgil, who was born in 70 BC, seven years before Augustus, had already completed his formation before the death of Caesar. He worked on the *Eclogues* in the period of the triumvirate, from 42 to 38 BC approximately. In this work, there is only one, impersonal, reference to Octavian as a young man, who is able to right the injustices that are perpetrated at the expense of Italic farmers whose lands had been expropriated on behalf of the army veterans. Maecenas is not mentioned, and there is a reference to another patron: the intellectual and commander in Antony's army, Asinius Pollio. The *Georgics* are dedicated to Maecenas, who is addressed as their commission client, and they celebrate the new Caesar: but this work, too, which was completed in 29 BC, was largely written before the battle of Actium. Horace, who was born in 65 BC, published his first book of *Satires* in 35 BC, and Book II of the *Satires* and the *Epodes* in the year 30 BC, shortly after Actium; but many compositions in these two collections, and also some of the

Odes (the first three books of which were published in 23 BC), were written in the years of the triumvirate. Horace had been an officer in the army of Brutus at Philippi, and had fought against Antony and Octavian, but in 38 BC, he had become a friend of Maecenas, to whom he had been introduced by Varius and Virgil, who were already connected with Octavian's collaborator. Probably, of all the epodes and the satires, not more than four or five compositions date back to before his friendship with Maecenas.

Virgil and Horace, therefore, had lived through the period of the civil wars in their youth, experiencing all the risks and hardships of those years, and they developed and refined their talent as poets during the dark years of the triumvirate, before Rome became 'Augustan'. But while Virgil completed one important work before coming into contact with Maecenas, Horace became a friend of Maecenas while he was still a developing poet.

It is difficult to say to what extent, in the years of the triumvirate, being a poet connected with Maecenas already meant being involved in a project of cultural politics which could be defined as 'Augustan'. Maecenas had a sincere love for poetry, indeed, for an uncommitted, refined, sensual poetry. But at the same time, he was deeply involved in his political support of Octavian, who, as one of the leaders in a civil war, obviously did not know that he was to become 'Augustus', but realized how important it was to create an image for himself as the defender of the Italic moral and civic traditions, and to organize around himself, on this basis, a consensus of public opinion. The oath of *tota Italia* in his name, on the eve of Actium, was an important reason for his political prestige, and even for his military success. The *Georgics*, which the ancients quoted also as the 'poem of Italy' (Mart. 8.55.19), can be read against this background of cultural politics, as can also the civil and moral themes of Horace's poetry of the years of the triumvirate. As we shall see, other reasons, which were independent of political circumstances, might have led these poets to choose such themes. But it may also be admitted that Octavian may soon have developed the idea of exploiting poets, too, in order to consolidate the consensus of opinion around him. We still have some verses (*Epigr. Bob.* 39 and 40) composed by the epigrammatist Domitius Marsus in 43 BC, in support of Octavian (Mariotti 1962: 62–3; Courtney 1993: 304 suggests a later date). Also Antony had some poets on his side (Cic. *Phil.* 13.11 and Serv. on Virg. *Ecl.* 9.36), and Varius already wrote against Antony in about 43 BC (fr. 1 and 2 Blänsdorf). Today we know that some public monuments, which we are used to considering as linked to the 'Augustan' idea of a solemn imperial Rome, date back to the initiative of Octavian the triumvir and his collaborators (Millar 2000: 9–12). And it has also been observed that in the course of his years in the triumvirate Octavian was already concerned to present some of his political actions as examples of republican legality (Eder 2005: 20–2). The creation of the regime, its symbols and its ideology had thus already started before Actium. But it was a process *in fieri*, open to a variety of solutions, in which the poets could play different roles, depending on their vocations and tendencies.

Tibullus and Propertius, who were born around the year 50 BC, had only had some experience of the civil wars in their early youth. Propertius retained memories of the devastation of his region, Umbria, in 41 and 40 BC, and of a death that had occurred in his family. Tibullus may have taken part in the battle of Actium, and definitely served in the campaigns of those years, at the side of his patron, Messalla, who had passed over to Octavian's side, at least from 36 BC on, after previously fighting against him. But both Tibullus and Propertius wrote their elegies after Actium. Propertius became a friend of Maecenas in 28 BC, after publishing his first book. No relationship between Tibullus and Maecenas is known to us, but Tibullus was a friend of Horace, who was also a friend of Messalla.

Ovid is the only one among the great Augustan poets who grew up in a Rome that had been securely pacified by Augustus. In an autobiographic elegy written from exile, he says that he was born in the year in which two consuls fell victims of the same destiny (*Tr.* 4.10.6): this is 43 BC, when Antony fought against the army of the Senate, which at that time was supported by Octavian and was commanded by the two unfortunate consuls, who died in the battle. The result, in that same year, was the triumvirate, which was immediately to trigger renewed civil strife. Thus, Ovid places his birth under the inauspicious sign of one of the darkest years of the republic. But he was only 12 years old when Octavian remained alone in command, and he made his first attempts at writing poetry perhaps around the year 25 BC, when the 'Augustan' regime, strictly speaking, had already existed for two years. All his poetry before going into exile expresses a serene satisfaction with Augustan Rome, which he describes as rich in all kinds of opportunity, modern, elegant, and fully developed, in an atmosphere of peace, safety, and availability of resources. The perception of the enormous tragedy which lies at the origins of this happy condition, which we feel so acutely in Virgil, and which pervades, in different forms, the work of Horace, Tibullus, and Propertius, seems to have been put aside. Indeed, Ovid seems to believe that all the emphasis with which poets and intellectuals had celebrated the values and virtues of the ancient Roman rural community, as if they were the only reliable guarantees of the survival of the nation, is by now outdated. He evidently thinks that there is a new public that intends to turn over a page with respect to the dark memories of the past, and in literature seeks pleasant entertainment. The success that he enjoyed seemed to show that he was right. But not everybody could share this attitude, and, on the contrary, the political and cultural scene of Augustan Rome was still evolving, and was to lead to different results.

The first edition of the *Amores* can be dated around 15 BC: Ovid therefore elaborated this new poetics of lightness in the same decade which witnessed the production of the Augustan poetry with the highest ethical ideals: the *Aeneid*, the *Odes*, and the *Epistles* by Horace, the second book of Tibullus, and the last two books by Propertius. Ovid, however, did not feel that his position was polemical, or one of contrast. On the contrary, from his exile he recalls with poignant nostalgia those years when he had the privilege of being a part of that extraordinary season of Latin poetry, in a spirit of friendship and cooperation with the most prestigious poets (*Tr.* 4.10.41–52): Macer, Ponticus, Bassus, Propertius (who also mentions Ponticus and Bassus as friends), Horace, Virgil, and Tibullus. Thus, in those years there was the opportunity for free and varied literary research, in which different poetics were elaborated in an intellectual climate of friendly solidarity. But this season did not last long. Virgil and

Tibullus died four years before the probable date of publication of Ovid's first work. We have no information about Propertius after the year 16 BC, which was the date of his last book. Horace's final compositions were written no later than 10 BC, and he died in 8 BC, the same year as the death of Maecenas.

At the date of Horace's death, Augustus still had 21 years of government in front of him. And Ovid died three years after Augustus. The difference in age, which spared Ovid the sad experience of the civil wars, also meant that he was the only one, among the great poets, who lived through the years of the definitive consolidation of the regime, until the succession. And as this succession took place inside the family of Augustus, without arousing any controversy, it rendered explicit, for the first time, what had been clear for some time to everybody, and had been accepted by everybody, but had always been formally denied: a dynastic monarchy had effectively been installed in Rome. These are the years of the maturity of the regime, the years when Rome, under the strong leadership of Augustus, increasingly assumed the role of the splendid capital of an immense empire, pacified internally, proud of its superior power, and successfully involved in the consolidation of its wide-ranging boundaries. But with his exile, Ovid was the witness, and the victim, of the new relationship between power and literature, which neither he, nor the poets older than him, could have imagined in the years when he was composing the *Amores* in that happy cultural company.

Since he grew up when Rome was already governed by Augustus, and he continued to write poetry all through the subsequent course of his reign, Ovid is the most truly 'Augustan' of all poets, from a chronological point of view. Until about the year AD 2, he continued to develop the same poetics, playful and sentimental at once, which seemed to interpret so well the sensation of the new generations that they were living in an age of peace and prosperity, in which it seemed right to dedicate space also to pleasure and leisure. And the *Metamorphoses*—with its vast plot of tales in which human suffering again finds expression, through the mediation of myth and fantasy, and is recomposed, under the overarching gaze of the author, with the joys, the passions, the virtues and vices of human life in a polymorphous combination of situations and points of view—appears as an emblem of this mature Augustan civilization, absorbing into an open system, without the lacerations of the past, a great variety of intellectual and ethical attitudes. But just as Ovid was completing this composition, and was working on the *Fasti*, in which, again in the form of a pleasant tale, he was seeking a harmonious composition of Rome's present with its religious, ethical and historical past, his sudden exile, decreed by Augustus, alienated him and made him incompatible with that regime of which he had seemed to be, and felt that he was, the most genuine poetic expression.

The alleged reason for the exile of the writer who was recognized as the greatest living poet was the licentious nature of a work of his which had been circulating for some years, meeting with great success. Even if this motivation was only a pretext, which is unlikely, the very fact that such a pretext could be used, and that a work of success could be banned from libraries by decree, brutally exemplifies the change that had taken place in the relationship between literature and power since the period when Maecenas acted as a skillful mediator, making many concessions to the freedom of single authors, and thus obtaining their gratitude and their participation in the cultural programs of the emperor. The last book by Propertius (16 BC) and the last book of Horace's *Odes* (13 BC) already contained more rigid and formal panegyric passages, and more marked tones of traditional moralism, which may reflect the control that the *pater patriae* increasingly tried to exercise over the customs of Rome's citizens. It is striking that after 19 BC neither Propertius nor Horace dedicate their books to Maecenas any more (Horace, who had addressed to Maecenas all his previous books, remained a friend of Maecenas until his death, but after 19 BC dedicated only ode 4.11 to him; cf. La Penna 1963: 115–16): his role seems to have come to an end. Horace's letter to Augustus (ca. 13 BC) leads us to think that the Princeps himself intended to act as a reference point for the intellectual, as well as the moral, life of the community. However, the condemnation of Ovid in AD 8 was not an isolated fact: in the same year, or perhaps shortly afterward (cf. Syme 1978: 213–14), the writings of the orator and historian Titus Labienus were condemned to be burned, and the orator Cassius Severus was exiled: this was the beginning of the real activity of censure against writers who did not conform to the political and cultural line of the regime, which was to become so important under subsequent emperors. And the elegies written in exile—whose *raison d'être* lies in the emperor's condemnation of an author for his literary activity, and whose whole conception reflects, with the somber tone that the poet is forced to adopt, that new relationship of diffidence between cultural production and power which characterizes the literature of the first century of the Empire—can be considered to be the first works of 'imperial' Latin literature, in the waning years of Augustus' reign.

In exile Ovid thinks back to his youth, and to the happy company of those poets who seemed to him to be gods walking on this earth, as if that was an enchanted world, in which, at a certain point, the sacred figure of the supreme god, Virgil, appeared, only as a vision (*Tr.* 4.10.40–52); a world which he may be proud to have been a part of, but which now appears to him to be irremediably lost. Already during the years in which Augustus was still governing, the elegies written from exile reveal that sense of coming afterward, and a necessary decadence with respect to the 'Augustan' literary past, which is another characteristic of the literature of the early imperial age.

Professing Poetry in Rome

When Ovid decided to abandon his public career, in order to dedicate himself wholly to his poetic vocation (*Tr.* 4.10.33–40), he made a courageous choice, which is undoubtedly to be connected with the exceptional prestige that poetic activity had acquired in that period. And yet a choice like this was not a novelty. Virgil, Propertius, and Tibullus also descended from well-to-do families, and almost certainly were members of the equestrian order, who, like Ovid, could have aspired to a good career, and yet they decided to dedicate all, or most, of their energies to poetry. Gallus combined serious poetic activity with an intense, high-profile military and administrative equestrian career.

This widespread participation of the equestrian order in the production, and, as we shall see, in the fruition of poetry, was a relatively recent phenomenon, which was a part of the evolution of Roman society between the second and first centuries BC. Until about the end of the second century, the senators, that is to say, the class of landowners who traditionally held power, reserved for themselves certain areas of cultural production intrinsically connected with political and civic practices, which were reserved to them: rhetoric, historiography (understood as the registration and interpretation of political activity), jurisprudence, and agronomy. When Rome (starting from the second half of the third century BC) created a literature of its own, modeled on that of Greece, poetry was destined mainly for the production of texts for the theater. Performances were organized by the State, which, in the person of appointed magistrates, commissioned the texts from 'professional' poets: these were often slaves who came from Greece, or from regions of Italy which had long been Hellenized, but always people of a low social level. Anybody who worked to earn a living in this society of landowners was considered a marginal figure. These people were also entrusted with the task of teaching children in the houses of noble families and in the earliest form of scholastic organization, which was likewise reserved to a restricted elite. By means of these 'artisans' of the world of learning, Rome created a Greek kind of *paideia*. For this purpose, these same authors of theatrical texts, who were partly responsible for teaching duties, also produced some epic-historical texts, which had the same function in educating and creating a national identity that the Homeric poems had had for the Greeks. The theatrical performances, whose texts were modeled on the canonical authors of the tradition of Greek drama, were watched by large numbers of spectators, who included men and women, senators and slaves. This audience was largely illiterate, and followed the texts thanks to the effectiveness of the theatrical performances. The circulation of epic texts, not destined for oral presentation, must have been far more limited: through scholastic education, however, they became a part of the basic cultural patrimony of the increasing members of the elite who had access to schooling.

Even though the great theatrical texts of the past continued to be appreciated, the public turned, starting from the second half of the second century BC, to forms of entertainment that were less elevated, and original production declined. A separation developed between high-quality literary production and popular public entertainment. At the same time, however, there was a gradual growth of interest in poetry, as well as in other intellectual activities, in the upper classes, who were increasingly in the habit of giving hospitality in their homes to intellectuals, especially Greeks, who were invited to offer training in rhetoric, linguistics and literature, and cultured entertainment, including poetry. Already at the beginning of the second century BC, Ennius composed not only theatrical texts and the great national epic poem (the *Annales*) but also celebratory poems and occasional verse for the authoritative figures of public life who gave him their support, and hospitality. And a great theatrical poet like Terence was suspected of desiring to please his rich patrons more than the popular public (*Ad.* 15–21).

Around the beginning of the first century BC, we know of some Greek poets who wrote occasional verse and panegyric poems for rich Roman gentlemen, to whose houses they were invited; we also begin to hear about senators and rich knights who compose poetry themselves. This is frivolous poetry, or sentimental verse, practiced by a Roman citizen in his spare time, and clearly very different from the time-consuming production which had traditionally been reserved to professional poets. But already in those years the rich knight Lucilius made poetry his main interest in life—it is no coincidence that the genre was an ostentatiously 'amateurish' one like satire—and the senator Julius Caesar Strabo wrote tragedies. Though a serious involvement in poetry was still rare on the part of senators in the Augustan age (exceptionally, Asinius Pollio was appreciated as a tragic poet), it became common practice, starting from the age of Caesar, for an aristocrat to dedicate a part of his time to the minor genres, and it even happened that well-to-do people who had no political ambitions chose to dedicate themselves to poetry as their main activity. These were usually members of the equestrian order, which had grown considerably as a result of the new opportunities for gain offered by the imperial development of Rome; it now included a variety of very different economic conditions, and various social and professional functions. This class was undergoing a profound change, with the lively introduction of Italic and provincial elements, and was more open to innovation, seeing that they were less linked to the system of ideological values and tastes that the traditional aristocracy represented, and had transferred also to its intellectual clients and to the 'professional' poets who received the commissions for theatrical texts and epic celebrations. From this class, and from various regions of Italy, came some of the poets of the age of Caesar, and several Augustan poets. The 'professional' figure of the person who performed intellectual activities in order to make a living remained connected with teaching, with private intellectual training for representatives of the educated classes, and with various specialized scientific and cultural activities (including some that had previously been reserved to the senatorial class: cf. Wallace-Hadrill 2005), but this figure tended to disappear from the panorama of high-quality poetic production. Now, however, not only the wealthier knights but also members of the lower classes had access to this field, who had the opportunity, thanks to the new social mobility, to become rich and to emerge. Horace's father had formerly been a slave in a small mountain community in Campania, and he had made some money by means of the small-scale commercial and financial activities that were typical of freedmen, and used what he earned to give his son an education of the best quality. And Horace soon obtained access to the system of literary patronage, founded on the social prestige of literary culture, which made it convenient for an influential public figure to grant economic support to skillful writers. Thanks to this system, the great Augustan poets obtained comforts and social credit: but none of them, not even Horace, depended on this in order to survive. Horace himself became an *eques* in the year 42 BC, when he received a military rank from Brutus, which implied membership of the equestrian order: the civil wars were, in reality, an important cause of social mobility, and determined both sudden falls and sudden rises, depending on the personal faithfulness demonstrated toward losers or winners.

Naturally, it is an exaggeration when Horace says that poetry writing was a mass mania in his period, that most of the population were poets, and that everybody, learned or otherwise, given a motive, composed poetry (*Serm.* 1.4.142; *Epist.* 2.1.108–117; *Ars* 416–18). He is caricaturing a superficial kind of production, slipshod and of bad taste, from which he scornfully wishes to distinguish himself. And yet, in his last elegy written in exile (*Pont.* 4.16), Ovid mentions about 30 contemporary poets, about most of whom we know practically nothing from other sources: and these are poets that he considers to be fully accomplished. If we bear in mind that there were bound to be some amateur poets, Horace's caricature assumes a certain credibility: the practice of poetry writing was an extremely important reality in the daily customs of Augustan Rome, it stemmed from developing and changing social conditions, and it undoubtedly included more aspects, tendencies, and currents than can be documented by extant texts.

These same considerations should be extended, with further amplifications, to the composition of the public. The problem of the size of the ancient literary public has long been ignored, considering it tacitly, and uncritically, to be coextensive with the whole of society. Recently, however, the tendency has been to emphasize the limits of the public: it has been realized that the majority of the population must have been illiterate, or scarcely able to read and write, and that such refined literature could be appreciated by, and must have been destined for, restricted circles. The reality is more complex.

Since the end of the second century BC, the theater-going public had not been offered any new good-quality plays. This crisis was not solved during the Augustan age, or after: never again was a serious form of theater created that could capture the interest of a large popular public. Already in antiquity, the plays by Fundanius, a friend of Horace and Maecenas, were no longer remembered. The tragedies by Asinius Pollio still enjoyed a reputation in the first century AD, but only two plays written during the Augustan age met with success, and remained in the memories of later generations (though they are no longer extant): *Thyestes* by Varius and *Medea* by Ovid. These attempts, and Horace's discussion of the possibilities of a revival of theatrical production, in his *Letter to Augustus* and *Ars Poetica*, help us to understand that there was an awareness of the crisis, and that Augustus himself was worried about it. But while the theater only partly fulfilled its function of cultural mediation for a popular public, and while Horace considered the popular public of theaters too ignorant, and incapable of appreciating high-quality literary communication (*Epist.* 2.1.182–207), the public of readers with a certain cultural preparation had grown considerably. The prestige and the spread of culture among the upper classes, and the extension of many activities that were previously the privilege of the upper classes to the emerging local and provincial classes, who aspired, as a result of the renewal of society since the age of Caesar, to have a part in the rights, and also in the style of life, of the classes that traditionally held power, had created a varied, widespread public, genuinely interested in literature, with wider, differentiated tastes and interests. Horace, who was so diffident toward the larger public, often stated that the equestrian class was the soundest part of the public: not the senators, who were typically linked to outdated tastes and traditions, but this class, which was more dynamic and more open (*Ars* 248–50; and cf. *Serm.* 1.10.76–7 and *Epist.* 2.1.185–7). But also at lower social levels, a knowledge of how to read and write was necessary for a growing series of activities, in a society that was increasingly specialized in its func-tions and its trading, and the growing opportunities led people to seek a cultural preparation, and to demonstrate their ability to behave in the same way as the upper class, including the capacity to read (and write) literary texts.

As long as the practice of reading literary texts was limited to the upper classes, the only ones taught to read and write, books were largely produced, thanks to the labors of educated slaves assigned to this task, in the houses of their authors or their readers, and they circulated as a result of private lending and subsequent copies and domestic transcriptions. Books produced by artisans were also sold, but Cicero and his friends preferred not to purchase these, as the best-quality transcriptions were those produced at home. In the same years, however, Catullus (14.17–20) stated that it was normal to go into a bookshop in Rome and find a wide selection of books of contemporary poetry, in order to buy some presents for the Saturnalia. Horace, like the poets of the first century AD after him, spoke of the book market as a common reality of life in Rome (*Serm.* 1.4.71–2; *Epist.* 1.20.1–13; *Ars* 345, 372–3), and the book market presupposes a numerous public, not limited to a single caste, or to a circle of learned scholars. Specialized works, and particularly weighty treatises, may have maintained a circulation within private channels, but Ovid (*Tr.* 2.471–92; cf. Citroni 1989) confirms a flourishing of light works written for the Saturnalia, evi-dently to be sold to a numerous public who used books as pastimes and gave them to friends for the same reason.

Different types of texts enjoy a different circulation among different readers, and they are read to a different extent by different readers. The anecdotes about Virgil's popularity and fame while he was still alive (cf. Tac. *Dial.* 13.2), and the fact that Horace was pointed out by passers-by in the street (*Carm.* 4.3.22–3), are not incom-patible with the fact that only a restricted minority of the population could read such complex works from beginning to end, and appreciate every aspect of them. In reality, thanks to their school education, or to a knowledge of how to read and write acquired for 'professional' reasons, many members of the middle and lower classes were capable at least of reading some parts of these texts, and were stimulated to do so by the social prestige connected with the practice of reading, and by a desire to have a part, in this way, in the customs of the classes that they were trying to emulate. Even if women were in a marginal position with respect to the activities that required a knowledge of how to read and write, they, too, were an important part of the poets' public: when Ovid wrote to Augustus from exile, he judged it clearly impossible to exclude women, on the grounds of morality, from having access to poets, seeing that this was evidently a habit for them (*Tr.* 2.255).

Augustan poetry refers to a public of readers whose numerical consistency it is impossible to calculate, though they must have been sufficiently varied and wide-spread to form a representative part of society. This is the background against which we must set, and explain, the exploitation of literary production in the creation of a consensus of opinion regarding the ideological and political themes proposed and promoted by the Princeps. And Ovid, from the desolation of his exile, addressed his apologetic discourse not only to his most authoritative friends and personal protec-tors, and to Augustus himself, but also to this public, which he knew to be numerous, varied, widely representative of Roman society, and also attached to him, as he counted on having them as important allies to back up his claim to be innocent (Citroni 1995: 431–64).

Public and Private in Augustan Poetry

It was common opinion at the time of Cicero that Rome possessed a canon of great poets, thanks to whom it had achieved a dignity equal to the more illustrious Greek production in the genres that really counted: in Ennius, Rome had its Homer; in Ennius, Pacuvius and Accius, its triad of tragedians; in Plautus, Caecilius, Terence and Afranius, its comic playwrights worthy of Menander; in Lucilius, its perfect representative of a wholly Roman genre. These poets all lived before 100 BC, and Horace still complained, as late as at the time of his *Letter to Augustus* (*Epist.* 2.1.50–89), that is to say, in years when the great masterpieces of Augustan poetry, with the exception of the *Metamorphoses*, had all been published, that critics in Rome, in their blind devotion to those old sacred texts, did not recognize anything of value in any more recent writer.

In reality, a part of Roman educated society already during the age of Caesar had perceived the need for a poetry that would be different in its forms and its themes. The old canonical epic texts dealt with faraway, impersonal subjects from myth and history, and they were dominated by the traditional ideology, which assigned value only to the interests of the community and the State: questions of individual subjectivity, therefore, did not find any space, apart from in the satire of Lucilius, where, however, they assumed the restricted dimensions of the comic, and could not express the tragic element which permeates everyday experience. Furthermore, epic and tragic texts used a solemn, rigid, artificial language, which abounded in bold, incisive effects, but was distant from common language. Also the language of comedy was artificial, a clownish caricature, and it usually presented rather conventional Greek settings. The need to bring poetry closer to the concrete experience of daily life was expressed with revolutionary energy by Catullus and his young poet friends (the 'neoterics'), who operated in Rome, but almost all of whom came from well-to-do families of Cisalpine Gaul, that is to say, from those classes that were renewing the panorama of Roman society and culture. These poets had rejected the great canonical genres, the ideology on which they were based, and their high-sounding language, and had dedicated their intense artistic efforts to the minor genres (epigrams, brief elegies, lyrics, short mythological poems) which, up to that moment, had only been the occasional pastime of the literary *otium* of aristocratic salons. Catullus made these minor genres his instrument in order to propose an explicit refusal of current literary and moral values, and to express, in a new style that was both natural and elegantly refined, his own highly personal way of describing the human condition and the torments of *eros*. In their proposal for a poetics of subjectivity, Catullus and the neoterics took their inspiration from Callimachus and those Greek poets who, in the third century BC, had likewise privileged the minor poetic genres as the ideal way of focusing attention on the world of the individual and sentiments, and of dedicating a refined care to the literary form, as a reaction against the overwhelming prestige of the Homeric epic and its archaic, solemn, monumental characteristics.

The development of Augustan poetry is often seen as a process which, in the different forms and ways of expression of different poets, started from the experience of the neoterics, and tended toward an increasing participation in civic themes, and toward a corresponding assumption of more elevated literary ways of expression and more elevated genres. Thus Horace started with his iambics and satires, and arrived at the solemn Pindaric forms of his last book of odes; thus Propertius moved from his first book of love elegies and gradually opened up to wider moral and civil themes, and to a more complex type of elegy in his last book; thus, above all, Virgil, who moved from the *Eclogues*, inspired by Theocritus, a great representative of Hellenistic 'minor' poetry, to the more complex task of the *Georgics*, finally giving Rome its new national epic poem, and thus meeting with success in the very genre, and in that aim of building up a sense of national identity through poetry, which the neoteric movement had attacked. On various occasions, Propertius and Horace expressed explicit refusals (*recusationes*) to compose epic-historical poems celebrating Augustus or other eminent figures of the regime (cf. Hor. *Carm.* 1.6, 2.12, 4.2, 4.15; *Serm.* 2.1.10–20; Prop. 2.1, 2.10, 3.9; cf. also Virg. *Ecl.* 6.6–12); evidently, they knew that they were expected to write works of this kind. However, in spite of their resistance based on their faithfulness to the neoteric model, and though they never went so far as to write a panegyric epic, they nevertheless felt increasingly involved in the task of creating a poetry of far-reaching human and civil significance, which, without renouncing the neoteric lesson in terms of penetration into the depths of subjectivity and the adoption of a style that combined elegance and natural simplicity, would maintain contact with the great problems of the community, and face up to the more challenging kinds of poetry.

Unending discussions have been held to try to determine how far this process was due to the pressure of a regime that desired to make use of poets as propaganda writers, and how far these poets shared the sincere conviction of the merits of the Augustan regime as the bringer of peace, civil order, prosperity, and the recovery of ethical values. Today, many scholars have reached the conclusion that the consensus surrounding the Augustan regime was a widespread phenomenon, consisting of a combination of intricately connected economic, political, religious, and ethical aspects, which took different forms, and were differently rooted, in the different classes and areas of the population. It would be reductive and misleading to speak of propaganda, because the ways in which this consensus was created and consolidated with the passing of time appear to have been too varied and complicated. In this process, the poets' texts played an important part, but as a matter of principle it would be impossible to try to distinguish between spontaneous acceptance and adaptation to external pressure, or between an active role in the promotion of the ideology of consensus and the role of a spokesman presenting concepts elaborated by the political leaders of the regime.

On the other hand, the enhancement of the individual and private sphere, of feelings and *eros*, the penetration into the distress of the human condition, and questions about the role of the divine and of providence, destiny, and the meaning of history, raised by the ubiquitous presence of evil and suffering in the life of men and communities, are present in varying degrees in the works of all the Augustan poets, and also run through the *Aeneid*, the work which, above all others, affirms the greatness of Augustan Rome. This fact has led to the idea that an important element of the vocation of these poets, and of Virgil in particular, lies in their ability to perceive the shadowy implications of the conditions of men in their period, and thus in a sort of underground countermelody to Augustan propaganda.

These are controversial subjects, which can only be discussed on the basis of a detailed interpretation of the single authors. What I would like to point out here is that the movement of Augustan poets toward an involvement in general themes, and more challenging literary forms, also stems from reasons that are specifically literary, which already existed before the creation of the new regime. Catullus' proposal of a model of intimate, refined poetry, inwardly oriented to the individual character of the poet, had had, thanks to its 'revolutionary' nature, a widespread general significance, and had met with great success among a new, young public (while, significantly, it had been regarded with diffidence, or even hostility, by Cicero). But there was a risk that if poetry were to be maintained for a long period within exclusively private limits it might run out of motivations, and its capacity to grasp the problems of the present might dwindle. The need for an amplification of the thematic panorama had soon arisen. Already, some of the poets who were close to, or maybe members of, the neoteric movement (Furius Bibaculus and Varro Atacinus) had been induced by political pressure, or by motivations of their own, to widen the horizon of their poetry, and to write epic poems about Caesar's accomplishments. Subsequently, the great Augustan poets were also subjected to these two opposing motivations, but instead of responding to them separately in different works, they tried, in each of their works, to achieve a difficult new synthesis.

Both in the case of Horace and of Virgil, the tendency to give their poetry a more openly general character, and the tendency to take on themselves, as poets, the moral and social problems regarding the community, can be seen from the early years of the triumvirate (in some of the early epodes and early satires by Horace, and also in the *Eclogues*, even if this is, in some ways, a 'neoteric' work). Already in Book 1 of the *Satires*, published four years before the battle of Actium (*Serm.* 1.10.40–9; cf. Labate 1990: 952), Horace revealed that the poets who were friends of Maecenas felt that they were involved in the common task of giving Roman literature a new canon of works, to substitute, in the various genres, the current one, which appeared outdated and 'archaic' after the neoteric revolution. At that time, the new canon was still being formed, but the project was already clear: and it included both the minor genres, which had not been included in the old canon, but had received a new dignity from the neoteric movement, and the major genres: comedy, tragedy, and, at this early date, epic poetry, too. In the field of tragedy, where Varius and Ovid were to distinguish themselves, the most prestigious author at that time was Asinius Pollio, who was hailed as the new Latin Sophocles (cf. also Virg. *Ecl.* 8.10); in the field of comedy, it was Fundanius, the new Menander; in bucolic poetry, Virgil; in epic poetry, Varius (though his work cannot be identified with certainty), who was saluted as the new Homer (cf. also Hor. *Carm.* 1.6). From the age of the triumvirate, therefore, epic poetry was a part of the program of the poets of Maecenas' circle. Most of them preferred to limit themselves to less demanding genres, but the need for Rome to have a modern epic poem was felt before Augustus started to govern Rome. Only a few years later, Rome had, thanks to that group of poets, its Roman Hesiod with the *Georgics*, its Roman Alcaeus with the *Odes* by Horace, and its Roman Callimachus with Propertius. And in his posthumous edition of the *Aeneid*, Varius consecrated his fraternal friend as the true new Roman Homer.

In his gesture of breaking with the canon of great national literature, Catullus had opened the way to the ambition of future poets to provide Rome with a new canon of works, which would combine the new requirements of neoterism on the levels of research into subjectivity, and stylistic elegance, with the breadth and the depth of a literature that intended to represent the cultural patrimony of a nation (Citroni 2006: 211–34). This ambition, which led to the creation of a set of works soon considered as emblematic of artistic maturity, and as such called 'classic' by the moderns, found support and motivation in the policies of Augustus, but some of its reasons were already present in the literary history of Caesar's Rome. The task had largely been fulfilled, and in spite of the critics' resistance reported by Horace it had already been appreciated by a large part of the contemporary public when Ovid published his early collections of elegies, and set out, in his turn, on a journey toward a brave new world of experimentation, and growing literary ambitions. It ended in his personal ruin, which coincided with a substantial turning point in the conditions for free, creative elaboration in Roman poetry.

FURTHER READING

Important collections of essays by various authors on different aspects of the Augustan age (politics, society, religion, culture, etc.) are Millar and Segal (1984), Raaflaub and Toher (1990), Giovannini (2000), and Galinsky (2005). On politics and society, Syme (1939) and (1986) are essential reading. Wiseman (1971) and Alföldi (1985) deal with the conditions of social mobility. On the broader conditions of culture in Augustan Rome, Galinsky (1996) is an excellent introduction, while Bowersock (1965) can be recommended on the relationship with the Greek world, Zanker (1988) on the arts, and Quinn (1982), Harris (1989), and Citroni (1995) on literacy and the literary audience. Literary patronage is treated by Gold (1982) and White (1993). On poetry and Augustan ideology, La Penna (1963), Powell (1992), and Habinek and Schiesaro (1997) offer important discussions, as does Porter (2006) on Augustan 'classicism'.

CHAPTER THREE

Rhetoric and Ovid's Poetry

Elaine Fantham

Rhetoric: Its Conventional Usage and Its Wider Application

If rhetoric is an art, and needs artistry, does it have to be artful or artificial? In the generations before Ovid's birth, Romans with ambitions for public life studied not Greek *Rhetorike*, but the simpler Roman concept of *ars dicendi*, the art of public speaking. They would learn through their teacher from systematic manuals designed to help the speaker compose a law court brief or a senatorial proposal according to rules focused on content. Of the three recognized categories and contexts of speaking, judicial briefs claimed far more attention than either deliberative political speeches or display and ceremonial orations. Manuals either discussed material section by section, from proem to narration to statement of the issue to arguments and final summing up, or like the *Rhetoric for Herennius*, Cicero's early *On Invention*, or Cicero's mature and detailed *On the Orator* (Fantham 2004b), they moved through the five Aristotelian functions: finding the right arguments (heuristics, or *inventio*), arranging them in strategic order (*dispositio*), putting them into effective language (*elocutio*), memorizing the composition, and then delivering it. Oratory was determined by situation: whom the speaker needed to persuade about what issue, whether to reach a judgment on a past case or a decision on a future course of action.

But after 48 BCE, when Caesar's military victory had won him control over public life at Rome, the focus of training in oratory began to change in two ways: it shifted from the heavily monitored public sphere to private forms, and from concern for content to a growing interest in style. The circumstances of Cicero's three 'Caesarian' speeches show why: first his thanksgiving to Caesar in the senate for pardoning Marcellus, next his defense of Ligarius for his services on the Pompeian side in Africa, and finally a speech delivered before Caesar in his home in defense of Caesar's client Deiotarus against an accusation of conspiracy. Better to stay at home and practice declaiming with his young friends the future consuls of 43 BCE, Hirtius and Pansa—or to write works of literary history and theory. In 46 BCE Cicero wrote *Brutus*, a life-history of Roman oratory which was less an obituary for its honorand Hortensius than for public speaking itself; then as a rider, he composed *Orator*, also addressed to Brutus, arguing that the best and most versatile orator would be the one who commanded a rich full style and the resources of rhythmic prose.

No doubt basic training in argumentation continued, as well as the elementary exercises of paraphrasing, composing short narratives and fables, or set pieces in character (*prosopopoeiae*). But an interest in diction and rhythmic prose, together with declamation, the new practice of improvising speeches around some private or histori- cal issue, had become the dominant trend when Ovid was growing up. It is worth setting Cicero's views on the affinities and differences between poet and orator along- side our earliest report on Ovid's talent as a student.

After distinguishing the prose styles needed by an orator from the prose of phi- losophers, sophists, and historians, Cicero turns to consider poets (*Orator* 66–8):

> Even poets have raised the question in what respect did they differ from orators? In the past it was mostly in their use of rhythm and meter, but now rhythm itself has grown more frequent among orators too. For whatever is subject to measurement by the ears, even if it is not verse—for that would be a fault in prose—is called number, or as the Greeks say, *rhythm* . . . And yet this is not the poet's most important achievement, even if he is all the more praiseworthy for aiming at the virtues of an orator when he is more limited by verse. For myself, even if the style of some poets is both noble and rich, I hold that they have more freedom than us in coining and compounding words, and yet some of them still pay more heed to sound effects than sense. Indeed if they have one element in common—that is their taste and choice of words—it does not mean that we cannot recognize their difference in all other respects.

The fact that Cicero finds historians, philosophers, and poets relevant to his recom- mendations confirms the argument of Joseph Farrell that rhetoric 'is not confined to speeches' (1997: 142; see also 143–4). While Roman students had learned their techniques of narrative and description in the earlier stages of *Grammatike* before training with the rhetoricians, so that the manuals we have inherited deal only with elements of recognized oratorical genres, any systematic principles for the organiza- tion and presentation of a text are the proper material of rhetoric: we may choose instead to call it 'the art of composition'; the only advantage of this renaming is to protect the art from the suspicion which politics and publicity have cast upon rhetoric in the modern world.

Young Ovid in the Classroom

We must acknowledge that the sheer range of poetry—epic, dramatic, didactic, and epigrammatic or lyric—prevents Cicero or any other critic of the day from making aesthetic judgments on poetry. But what does it mean when the elder Seneca, looking back at young Ovid's technique in declamation, says (*Contr.* 2.2.8):

> He had a well-groomed [*comptum*] and becoming [*decens*] and charming [*amabile*] talent. Already at that time his speech could be seen as nothing but poetry free from meter.

Are the adjectives (*comptum, decens, amabile*) ones we would apply to praise an orator? Or indeed a poet? Wit, taste, elegance are all features we associate with the predominant mode of Ovid's early love poetry. As to 'freedom from meter', Ovid himself in retrospect claimed that when he was still aiming to become a legal advocate he tried to write prose (*uerba soluta modis*) but whatever he wrote turned into verse (*Tr.* 4.10.24–6). What we notice first and foremost in his elegiac distichs is his command of epigrammatic brevity and paradox. But Seneca has also preserved a sample of Ovid's prose, from a declamation on the following theme: 'A husband and wife took an oath that if anything happened to either of them the other would die. The husband went abroad on a trip and sent a message to his wife saying that he had died. The wife threw herself from a height. When she recovers she is told by her father to leave her husband. She refuses and is disinherited.' Seneca's only criticism is that Ovid neglected order in touching on each of the commonplaces (*loci*)—there must have been a list which pupils had to work into their text. The ideas reported here are sentimental (2.9): 'the only problem is for you to allow husband and wife to care for each other: if you permitted them to love each other, you must also permit them to swear. But what do you think we swore by? You were our sacred name; if we proved false she called down her father's anger upon herself, and I my father-in-law.' He goes on to complain that the father expected them to set a limit on their love (2.10): 'that is how old men love.' And ends with a melodramatic and self-pitying threat (2.11): 'I shall leave our country, flee and live in exile, enduring the deprivation as best I can with wretched and cruel patience. I would die, if I could be the only one to die.'

Did Ovid choose to declaim on this theme because it did not deal with the usual father–son conflicts but with defending a daughter, and that on the grounds of conjugal love? Or is Ovid's skillful handling of this subject the reason why Seneca remembered the poet's arguments? Seneca is particularly concerned in these two books with the techniques of his own teacher Latro, and Latro's more ornate rival Arellius Fuscus, and notes that while Ovid was a pupil of Arellius he also imitated Latro's epigrams. The example he offers may help us see how prose and verse can handle the same idea in the same vocabulary. The adjudication of the dead Achilles' arms between Ajax and Ulysses was the theme of Sophocles' *Ajax* and many lost Greek and Latin plays; it also provided a theme for a *suasoria*, deliberative declamations by either contender (cf. Juv. 7.115). Latro coined the epigram 'let us hurl the arms into the enemy and then fetch them'. Ovid adapted this in *Met.* 13.121–2 as 'let the brave hero's arms be hurled into the midst of the enemy, then order them to be fetched from there!' What makes the impact in his version is one word *inde* ('from there') and its emphatic placing at the beginning of the second line.

The adjudication of the arms is not a court case, but an impersonation of a historical figure (here of Ajax), so it is not a conventional *suasoria* advising on a deliberative issue so much as self-advocacy, a man making his own case, and we will return to this favorite theme later in connection with the mature Ovid of the *Metamorphoses*. But first let me review Seneca's other comments. He claims Ovid was averse to all argumentation, and so preferred *suasoriae* to *controversiae*, which he seldom declaimed, and then only ethical ones. What does this mean? Fortunatianus (1.11) distinguished between ethical *controversiae* (concerned with characterization) and 'pathetic', that is, emotion-rousing (he compares tragic material): his three other categories are based on the status of the evidence.

Ovid's use of vocabulary was restrained in prose, according to Seneca, but in his poems he did not so much overlook his own faults as cherish them. So when his friends asked him to prune three lines he asked for the right to excuse any three, and lo! both parties wrote down the same verses. Seneca is quoting Ovid's friend the poet Albinovanus Pedo, who gives two of the lines playing on symmetry of epithets and nouns (*Ars* 2.24), calling the Minotaur 'halfbull man and halfman bull' and (*Am.* 2.11.10) 'freezing north wind and de-freezing south.' This is one of those anecdotes improved by time, but it is worth noticing that in this one discussion Seneca has introduced four Ovidian quotations (add *Am.* 1.2.11–12) from three works spread across at least a decade from *Amores*, reissued before 2 BCE, to *Metamorphoses*, allegedly, unfinished in 8 CE.

Seneca's other discussions are supplementary rather than definitive. In *Contr.* 3.7 he reports a criticism of the tasteless Alfius Flavius' 'he was his own nurture and loss', borrowed from Ovid's final epigrammatic verdict on Erysichthon (*Met.* 8.877–8 'he began to dismember his own limbs with tearing bites and fed his body, poor fool, by stripping it'). The critic, Cestius, noted that the thought came from 'the fellow who filled our generation not only with lover's manuals but lover's sentiments'. Later in *Contr.* 7.1.27–8, Seneca quotes a criticism by Ovid of no less a poet than Virgil: Virgil had written, 'all things were resting in the calm repose of night' (*Aen.* 8.27), but as the declaimer and would-be poet Montanus reported, Ovid said the verse would be improved if the second half were cut out to read, 'all things were of night'. He was looking for a different, more elliptical, meaning; we should look out for such ellipses as sources of many of Ovid's distinctive effects. But so much depends on context. In *Contr.* 9.5.17 Seneca supports the famous comment that Ovid could not leave well alone (*nescit quod bene cessit relinquere*) with three continuous quotations from Hecuba's bitter harangue on the sacrifice of Polyxena in *Met.* 13. 503–5: *cinis ipse sepulti / in genus hoc saeuit* ('even the dead man's ashes fight against our clan'), *tumulo quoque sensimus hostem* ('we felt the enemy even from his grave'), and *Aeaci-dae fecunda fui* ('I was fertile for the benefit of Aeacus' son').

But each of these three lapidary sentences contributes some color or modification to the claim: the theme and variation would not be out of place in Virgil, and they certainly are not excessive in the context of Hecuba's powerful outcry. In *Contr.* 10.4 when Seneca is discussing *epiphonemata*—the typical closing verdict that wraps up an episode—he again recalls a contemporary, Vinicius, quoting Ovid *Met.* 12.606–7, this time on Achilles' death: *quod Priamus gaudere senex post Hectora posset / hoc fuit!* ('this was the one event that could bring Priam happiness after Hector's death'). Was the Trojan sequence of *Metamorphoses* the most read and best known in the schools?

The Early Love Elegies

Seneca's reminiscences are inevitably a diet of morsels: better to look for rhetoric directly in Ovid's own context. I would suggest that if we think of rhetoric in terms of the official genres we will find it hard to detect the rhetoric of his first work

Amores. But as Cicero recognized (*De Oratore* 2.38) every speech act has its own rhetorical form: consolations, exhortations, rebukes, protests, warnings. In the quasi-autobiographical *Amores* there is a common rhetoric based on the axiom of the primacy and irresistibility of love. Once the love-god has provided 'Ovid' with a love-object, the structure of his poems is articulated around the persuasion of direct courtship, and indirect attempts to reach her through intermediaries and obstacles that must be persuaded to desist. Consider 1.3.5–26 and 2.17.11–34, and then compare the courtship of Daphne by Apollo in a speech of about the same length (*Met.* 1.504–24).

Am. 1.3 starts with the poet speaking to the audience and claiming his right to expect, if not reciprocal love, at least that the woman will acquiesce in being loved, and Venus will heed his prayers. To the beloved he presents first his personal merits: loyalty and good faith; to compensate for lack of high birth or wealth he enjoys the favor of Apollo, Bacchus, the Muses, and Love, 'who presents me as a gift to you'. And he reprises his good credit and spotless moral record, his bare simplicity, and blushing modesty (14; this is Ovid!). The symmetry is part of the art, as is the careful introduction of good negatives (13–16) to balance the drawbacks of 7–10, and the growing prominence of the second person: 'you will be my eternal care' (16), 'with you … may I be lucky to live, and with you as mourner to die' (17–18); but the beneficiary of these protestations is inverted with 19–20: 'offer yourself to me as fertile material for poetry, and the poems will emerge worthy of their source'. With splendid effrontery Ovid offers as precedents Jupiter's reluctant beloveds, Io, Leda, and Europa. We too, he declares, will be sung together equally worldwide; or is this what he is saying? In the last line *nos* ('we') and *nostra nomina* are distinct from *tuis* (sc. *nominibus*). If 'my name will always be yoked with yours', was it not, after all, 'I' who will be sung equally (with Jupiter's women) over the wide world?

In 2.17, nearing the end of Book 2, Ovid begins by presenting himself as victim of Corinna, a woman made proud by her beauty; but—and here he turns to her—however beautiful, she should not despise him in comparison: it is legitimate to be yoked with an inferior. As in 1.3 he reaches for precedents; Calypso and Thetis and Egeria loved mortals, and Venus—here he could have cited Adonis, but instead quotes her lame but divine husband Vulcan. After all, the meter of this poem is uneven, but it is fitting for the heroic foot to march with a shorter foot. He is ready to submit to whatever laws she imposes; may she dispense the law in the heart of Rome's Forum. Now he returns to his claims of respectability; his 'record free of guilty charges' (1.3) becomes 'I will not be a guilty charge to you, nor someone you will be glad to lose, a love to be denied'. His poems are equivalent to great wealth, and many women would want to win their name from him (28 = 1.3.26). And he duly gives an anonymous example (29–32), before reaching his goal in the last couplet, echoing 1.3.23–4 in 33–34: 'no other girl but you will be sung [*cantabitur*; cf. 1.3.25 *cantabimur*] in our booklets, and you will provide the only sources [cf. 1.3.20] of my talent.'

Some of Seneca's criticisms seem to hold good for this second courtship; there are perhaps three lurches in the later part of the argument. What about Apollo's speech in courtship of Daphne? (We know it is doomed to failure because she has been struck with the leaden arrow of aversion.) First he must persuade her to stop, and he pleads that he is not a predatory animal but motivated by love—as if that would sound any less dangerous to a committed virgin. He has a good argument for persuading her to at least slow down—the risk of brambles scarring her legs (Ovid's characterization is superb as the enamored youth declares her pretty legs don't deserve to be hurt). Only at 513 does Apollo advance his own claims to her love in social terms comparable to the poet-lover of *Amores*. He is not a shepherd, some shaggy fellow watching flocks; if she only knew who he is! Delphi and other oracles do him obedience, and his father is Jupiter; he has talents too, revealing future, past, and present, tuning the lyre strings, and a sure shot with the bow—though the arrow of love has proved surer still. His archery (just demonstrated on the Python) is another talent that can be linked to his present lovesick condition, and Ovid has reserved to last the god's special art: he has invented medicine, is called Aid-bringer worldwide (fame is important, as in *Am.* 1.3) and controls the power of herbs. But it was a cliché of love epigram (e.g. Propertius 2.1.62–3, 2.12) that love's arrow wound could not be cured, and Apollo now faces failure, not in winning her but in assuaging his own lovesickness. This rhetoric is not designed for persuasive success but for effective characterization, and character drawing is the great achievement of Ovid's deployment of language in rhetorical contexts.

Bearing this literary purpose in mind, and the training Ovid and his peers received in arguing both sides of any controversy, it will be helpful to see how Ovid's pairings within the *Amores* complement each other. *Am.* 1.11–12 are paired only in the assumed reversal of genres from an honorific address to the messenger Nape, happily anticipating that Corinna will welcome his request for a rendezvous, to the virtual curse poem which damns the tablets (7–30, opening 'begone, you awkward lumps of wood') for their disappointing reply. *Am.* 2.2 and 3 are paired in sharing the same addressee, the eunuch Bagoas who guards Ovid's beloved, treated courteously in the longer first poem, then taking a different approach to make the same request for access, combining sexual condescension with thinly veiled threats if he should displease his mistress. Rhetorically the third pair of elegies, 2.7 and 2.8, makes far better use of the same kinds of argument.

In fact, 2.7 is actually a speech of self-defense, using legal language, in which his experience as one of the minor judges in civil cases had made Ovid expert (*Tr.* 2.95–6), to plead not guilty (the rhetorical *status coniecturalis*) and it draws its arguments, as the manuals recommended, from the act itself (*a negotio*) and the person or persons (*a persona*). Suppose that we are reading it for the first time and do not know what 2.8 has in store. As McKeown (1998) notes, 2.7 plausibly rejects Cynthia's accusations, though the opening, 'Am I always to be subjected to new charges', followed by 'I am weary of arguing the case so often', raises suspicion that Corinna has more cause for jealousy than lines 3–10 admit. The next section obliquely protests his innocence—if only I were guilty!—and applies first an argument from his own social pretensions: 'would I choose a low class girlfriend, or would any free man indulge in a love-union [*Veneris conubia*] with a slave scarred by lashings'; next an argument from Cypassis' loyalty to her mistress: if I had propositioned her she would have informed on me to you (*indicio*). He ends his defense with an oath by Venus and Cupid that he has been charged with a crime he did not commit—though some scholars have allowed for a double meaning: 'a crime he has not confessed'.

In 2.8, as McKeown (1998) notes, the truth is unexpectedly revealed, as Ovid switches from insulting Cypassis to flattery (1–4, what rhetoricians called the 'hunt for goodwill', *captatio beneuolentiae*) and from moral indignation to aggressive intimidation of his slave partner. Now he is addressing Cypassis, whom he has found a sophisticated partner suited to his taste. Now he demands 'who told on us?' (*index*, 5, echoes *indicio* in 7.26).

Now he calls up Homeric precedents, in Achilles and Agamemnon, who loved captive women, and reproaches her for blushing when he had not. It becomes apparent that Cypassis had been there, as audience when Ovid uttered 2.7 to Corinna. He boasts of the oath we heard him utter (17–20 = 2.7.27–8) and Venus' tolerance of perjury, before actually treating his own lies as a service he had performed for Cypassis, for which she now owes him more sexual favors. The last six lines present the situation in dramatic development; Cypassis has jibbed out of fear, but if she does not oblige, he will turn informer (*index*, 25) himself and report to her mistress where, how often, and in how many different positions the two of them had coupled (23–8). Perhaps here we should recall that participants in *furta* ('theft') could inform on their accomplices, giving details of the time, place, and nature of offenses committed.

If we had thought 2.7 aimed to persuade, the companion poem clearly overthrows the pretense; its appeal is the sheer impudence of this retooling and dismantling of any pretext of *fides*, whether 'truthfulness' or 'fidelity'.

Speech in (Female) Character

Ovid followed his quasi-narrative *Amores* with four books of practical instruction in erotics, two advising young men on seduction, one addressed to their targets on retaining their suitors while extracting gifts, and one final book on curing a love that has become inconvenient; but their didactic form offers relatively little scope for either speeches or argumentation. In contrast, his two collections of letters from heroines are rhetorical speeches in character, *prosopopoeiae*, but in many cases not *suasoriae*, since they are often more vehicles of reproach than of persuasion. Each epistolary monologue draws for its material on what is known of the writer and her addressee from earlier texts, and Ovid clearly was as concerned to exploit the events in the literary tradition as to reflect the writer's immediate mood or long-term personality. These are much longer poems, but let me illustrate his techniques selectively from two letters to Paris; the first comes from the nymph Oenone, based on a relationship not known to us from epic or drama (*Her.* 5); the second, one of the later paired letters (*Her.* 16–21), is the reply of the still chaste if weakening Helen (*Her.* 17) to Paris' solicitation (*Her.* 16).

As a nymph in love with Paris when he was still a simple shepherd, Oenone offers scope for unusual local color, and a distinctive set of values. This includes the paradox that she was renowned (*celeberrima*) when he was humble, and benefited him through her expertise in country living which he lacked. Here we can see Ovid drawing on one of the ground rules of deliberative rhetoric: to argue that the course recommended (here that Paris return to Oenone) was honorable, safe, and advantageous. Having established the success of their past relationship, she turns to his fatal Judgment of the goddesses, the *nefas* which lured him away with the promise of Helen. And from Oenone's standpoint the ultimately beautiful Helen is the opposite of morally honorable, she is a 'shameful' (*turpis*, the standard word for 'ugly') girl-friend and Paris' seduction is a shameful enterprise (cf. 97–8 *turpe rudimentum . . . causa pudenda*). In contrast, Oenone can claim that she was worthy to be Priam's and Hecuba's daughter-in-law, though she did not aspire to it. Again, her love was safe, bringing no wars and bloodshed to Troy (79–88, 89–97). Now she turns to the rich field for rhetoric of arguing from Helen's persona, and here the language comes very close to Ovid's prose declamation; Helen will not be faithful to Paris, because chastity once damaged cannot be restored. 'She is burning with love for you; that is how she loved Menelaus' (*sic et Menelaon amauit*). Later, when Oenone has reported on Helen's earlier kidnapping by Theseus, she adds, 'a woman so often ravished must have offered herself for the ravishing' (132). In the *Metamorphoses* Apollo had first boasted of his medical skill then lamented its powerlessness to cure love; this is how Ovid brings Oenone to end her letter. She has been faithful although she was courted by satyrs and even Apollo, who taught her herbal skills, but only Paris can bring her healing, and she has earned it by her loyalty to him in his youth and hopes to share the future with him.

Helen's reply to Paris is twice the length of Oenone's letter, and I need mention only one or two rhetorical features. Ovid depicts her as still proud of her chastity, even treating his overtures as hostile, though he may think her virtue unsophisticated (*rustica*, 12), but the long missive offers plenty of scope to show her mind in process, and how his protestations of love are making her waver. Initially, however, like Oenone, she claims her superior birth; if both descend from Jupiter, she is his direct child by Leda (51–63), a chaste woman deceived by his avian disguise: her culture too is superior to Paris' barbarian homeland (64); in fact, she is indifferent to his lavish gifts, but his person is a better motive for sinning (*culpa*, 68). She is on her way to surrender. If her reminiscences of their flirtation over Menelaus' dinner table reuse material from his early *Amores*, the details prepare the way for her surrender, and the poet takes her from the hypothetical, 'if I had been going to sin' (91), to signs of yielding, 'I would be made of iron if I did not love the heart that preferred me to Juno's royal power and Athena's valor; but believe me I am not made of iron' (133–6). She moves from past to future, and begins to speak more of the risks attending fleeing with him, and the decision imminent on Menelaus' return and Paris' need to depart. Resorting to paradox and the reversal of moral conventions, she reproaches him for not forcing her instead of using unsuccessful persuasion: he should have taken her simple unsophistication (*rusticitas*, 185–6; cf. 12) by storm. What is this allusion to unsuccessful persuasion? It is to his letter, which the reader has barely finished. Literary allusion has become self-allusion. She has also been reading Ovid's earlier *Heroides*, Hypsipyle (*Her.* 6) too yielded to a foreign guest, and was betrayed in her unsanctioned union, as was Ariadne (*Her.* 10), and even Oenone was abandoned by Paris himself (193–6). Worst of all, Medea (227–34; *Her.* 12) was abandoned by

Jason away from her homeland and family. Ovid cannot bear to leave any material unexploited, whether taken from tragedy or from his own work, and these lovers provide the fullest scope for the same dubious morality we met in his *Amores*.

Rhetoric in Epic Context: *Metamorphoses* XIII

You may object that Ovid's invention uses rhetorical techniques of argumentation, but the products are not rhetoric. Certainly, these arguments are not applied in the conventional contexts, but if we accept the declamatory models on which he was trained as exercises in rhetoric, we must acknowledge the similar procedure in these displays of both conscious and purposive argument and unconscious characterization. But Ovid knew well how to compose speeches for more orthodox contexts and speeches on an epic scale. We noticed above that the men who frequented the schools of declamation were particularly interested in Book XIII of *Metamorphoses*: this may well be because more than half of the book consists of extended speech (*oratio perpetua*). We have considered enough courtships, and so will pass over the eighty lines in which Polyphemus grossly mishandles the *topoi* of courtship and Glaucus ingenuously woos Scylla: instead let us return to speeches which Seneca and his peers remembered and quoted: the contest between Ajax (13.5–102) and Ulysses (128–381), and Hecuba's great speech (494–532)—the most highly developed example of a woman's lament. Both have dramatic and rhetorical precedents. Now that we have the rich and detailed study by Hopkinson (2000) of these speeches and their antecedents in the post-Homeric epic cycle and Greek tragedy, it would be a waste of time for me to repeat, or worse, to compress his analysis: readers should seek it out for themselves. The contest between Ajax and Ulysses seems to have featured in Ennius' *Ajax*, as well as the tragedies of Pacuvius and Accius called *Armorum Iudicium*. And it is Ajax's situation which seems to have been most appealing to composers: Cicero offers what may be his own translation from Ajax's speech in *De Officiis* 3.26 (*TRF* incerta fr. 31), but long before this the anonymous *Rhetoric for Herennius* touched on the situation in Book 2 (19, 28 and 30) and quoted Ajax from an unidentified tragedy at 2.26.42 (*TRF* incerta fr. 30):

> The wording speaks clearly, if you understand it; it orders the arms to be given to a man equal to the hero who bore them, if we are eager to take possession of Pergamum. This man I claim to be; it is fair for me to have use of my cousin's arms, and for them to be adjudged to me, either because I am kin or because I am his peer in valor.

Centuries later, Charisius (4.252) singles out these lines of Ajax as an example of the figure *Mukterismos* or sarcasm (*TRF* incerta fr. 32):

> I saw you, Ulysses, laying Hector low with a rock,
> I saw you protecting the Doric fleet with your shield,
> Then I was trembling, urging on a shameful flight . . .

Given the antithesis between the brawn of Ajax and brain of Ulysses, Ovid had to decide whether to fall short of his own eloquence by depicting Ajax as simple or inarticulate or, better, to give Ajax a good speech, but Ulysses a better one. As Hopkinson shows (2000: 17), Ajax loses in part because he aims his speech not like Ulysses at the princes, who will decide the contest, but at the common people. When Ajax finishes there is a murmur of assent from the *vulgus*, then Ulysses pauses for effect (as he did in *Iliad* 3.216–23, an act praised by Quint. 11.3.158), lifts his gaze to the princes, and opens his mouth for the speech they are awaiting (*exspecta-to . . . sono*). The situation is particularly promising for Ulysses (and for Ovid), because eloquence is itself the issue between the man of deeds and the man of words. We can expect certain features in both speeches, notably the claim of superior birth (Ajax, 21–9; Ulysses, 140–52) and kinship (Ajax, 29–34; Ulysses' *proximitas*, 152–6), and certain narrative elements: Ulysses' feigned madness, detected by Palamedes, and his vengeful prosecution of Palamedes for treason, and Ulysses' betrayal of Philoctetes (Ajax, 34–62, and answered by Ulysses, 306–338). Ovid also equips the two contend-ers with gesture; Ajax, more simply, stretches out his hand to the shore and the fleet he has saved; Ulysses outdoes him, first with a pathetic pretense of wiping his eyes in grief for the death of Achilles, later with a more dramatic gesture, which I will hold in reserve. But rather than discuss the material of their speeches, let us focus on two things: the theme of eloquence mocked by Ajax and exalted by his rival and their formal *elocutio*, figures of speech and thought (7–12):

> at non Hectoreis dubitauit cedere flammis,
> *quas* ego sustinui, *quas* hac a classe fugaui.
> tutius est igitur *fictis* contendere *uerbis*
> quam pugnare *manu*. sed nec mihi *dicere* promptum
> nec *facere* est isti, quantumque ego Marte feroci
> inque *acie valeo*, tantum *valet iste loquendo*.

> But Ulysses did not hesitate to give way before Hector's fires, which I withstood, which I drove off from this fleet. So it is safer to compete in false words than fight by hand. But neither does speech come readily to me nor action to him, and just as I am strong in fierce war and battle line, so he is strong in talking.

Repeatedly, Ajax mentions with scorn Ulysses' fluency (cf. 63, *licet* eloquio . . . *uincat*, 'though he may surpass Nestor in *eloquence*'; 92, *ubi nunc* facundus *Vlixes*, 'where now is the *fluent* Ulysses?'). Anaphora and antithesis, arrayed where the verse will reinforce emphasis, are Ajax's weapons. So also for example 40, *optima nunc* sumat, *quia* sumere *noluit ulla* ('Let him *take* the best because he was unwilling to *take up* any arms'); 15, quae *sine teste gerit*, quorum *nox conscia sola est* ('*the deeds* he did unwitnessed, *the deeds* which only night observed')—with variation at 100, *luce* nil *gestum*, nil *est Diomede remoto* ('he did *nothing* in daylight, *nothing* without Diomedes'). More conspicuous are the repeated verb forms: 48–9, *saxa moues gemitu Laertiadaeque* precaris / quae *meruit*, quae *si di sunt, non uana* precaris (anaphora and epiphora) ('you move the rocks with your groaning and *curse* the son of Laertes with fates, *which* he deserved, *which* if the gods exist, you do not *curse* in vain'), or

71–2, *en eget auxilio qui non tulit, utque* reliquit *sic* linquendus erat ('see, the man who did not bring aid now needs it, and as *he deserted* so *he should have been deserted*'). Is it a comment on Ajax's limited imagination that Ovid reuses striking Virgilian language for two of his insults against Ulysses? First as instigator of crimes (45, *hortator scelerum = Aen.* 6.529) and 'trembling and pale with fear, panicked at the onset of death' (74–5, *trementem pallentemque metu et trepidantem morte futura*, echoing Dido *Aen.* 4.644 *pallidaque morte futura*).

Despite his lack of sophistication, Ajax also employs paradox, sarcasm, and word play; cf. *atque utinam aut uerus furor aut creditus esset, nec* comes hic . . . umquam uenisset, 43–4 ('if only his madness had either been real or believed, and *he had never come as our comrade*'), replayed, in 55, with sarcasm, *ille tamen uiuit, quia non* comitauit *Vlixem* ('he at least lives on because he was not Ulysses' *comrade*'). Ajax can command pathos in evoking the abandoned Philoctetes (52–4), but he is best at scorn. With the declaimer's ploy, he sums up Ulysses' feats of war: he has weakened the Greeks by the exile of Philoctetes and the murder of Palamedes, 'this is how Ulysses fights, this is how he is formidable' (62, *sic pugnat, sic est metuendus Vlixes*). Ovid is truer to his own artistry than to Ajax's character in his depiction of Achilles' great armor, his *clipeus vasti caelatus imagine mundi* ('the shield engraved with the likeness of the huge universe'). Moving to the imagined future, he mocks Ulysses if he should win the award which will only lay him low, with the magnificent hexasyllabic *debilitaturum . . . te improbe, munus,* and renewed sarcasm, combined with plosive assonance. If he receives the arms, he will simply be an incentive to plunder (114–16):

> *cur spolieris* erit, non *cur metueris* ab hoste;
> et fuga, qua sola cunctos, timidissime, uincis,
> *tar*da fu*tura ti*bi est gestamina *tanta* tra*hen*ti.

> This will just be a reason for you to be stripped, not feared, by the enemy, and your flight, the only feat in which you excel all men, will be tardy as you trail such tremendous trappings.

Seneca recalled Latro's figure, 'throw the arms into the midst of the enemy and have them fetched from there', and the way Ovid transformed it. But Ajax actually uses this figure twice, and the earlier variant is perhaps more powerful than the closing lines of his speech recalled by Seneca (77–9):

> si perstas certare, locum redeamus in illum;
> redde hostem, uulnusque tuum, solitumque timorem
> post clipeumque late et mecum contende sub illo.

> If you persist in competing, let us go back to that situation; bring back the enemy and your wound and habitual cowardice, then hide behind my shield and compete with me beneath it.

This is no mean speech, and Ovid gives Ulysses twice as many lines to rebut it, but we will be more selective.

As I noted, Ulysses begins by grieving for the loss of Achilles—whom he apostrophizes with rhetorical epanalepsis ('you would have your arms and we have you', Achilles), as he wipes away an imaginary tear; he will end with a similar flourish and feigned reluctance to receive the arms—rather they should go to Minerva (whose Palladium he proudly boasts to have won for the Greeks in 337). Between these passages Ulysses makes the most of the theme of eloquence, and turns around the various charges of his rival. His first claim for his eloquence begins with mock modesty in 136–7, and shrewdly converts it to cleverness:

> quod uobis semper, Achiui,
> profuit ingenium, meaque haec *facundia*, si qua est . . .

That my cleverness always benefited you, Greeks, and my fluency, such as it is . . .

Here *facundia* neatly picks up Ajax's derisive *facundus* from 97. So too his preamble to recording his services—160, *plura quidem feci quam quae comprendere dictis / in promptu mihi sit* ('I did more than I can readily sum up in words')—recalls Ajax's rejection of ready speech (*dicere promptum*, 10). He is proud of his bravery—something Ajax has denied—in going as envoy (*audax orator*) to Troy, and of all he did, with advice and action (*consilioque manuque*), during the long siege, consoling the Greeks and instructing them in obtaining supplies (*consolor . . . doceo*, 213–14). It was his finest hour when Agamemnon acted upon Jupiter's misleading dream and even Ajax, who never talked except to talk big (*numquam nisi magna loquenti*) was ready to turn tail. It was then that Ulysses rebuked the Greeks (and he quotes his rebuke, 225–7); when the lordly son of Telamon did not dare to utter a word (*nec Telamoniades etiam nunc hiscere quidquam / audet*, 231), Ulysses saved the day by exhorting his fearful citizens against the enemy, restoring their lost valor by his voice (235): *amissamque mea uirtutem uoce repono*.

Three other moments in this long performance (for Ovid leaves no doubt that it is staged) deserve comment. At 262, after a catalogue of enemies he slaughtered, Ulysses declares, 'I too have my wounds, fellow citizens, nobly received, look and behold!' and bares his breast with frontal wounds, as the orator Antonius had bared the scarred breast of his client Aquilius (*de Orat.* 2.124, 195) and Cicero that of Sestius. But Ulysses improves on the gesture with an ingenious wordplay: *Haec sunt pectora semper . . . uestris exercita rebus* ('This breast [both physical body and brain power] has always been active on your behalf'). From here it is an easy leap to recalling how he carried Achilles' body on his own shoulders: *his umeris, his, inquam umeris ego corpus Achillis / et simul arma tuli* ('On these shoulders, these shoulders, I say, I bore Achilles' body, and all his arms').

It is difficult not to smile at the figured repetition, the display of favorite tricks. But he has brought his listeners back to the coveted prize, Achilles' arms. Ajax claimed these arms would weigh down his adversary; Ulysses offers two different retorts; first he asks how such a dolt could appreciate these heaven-sent arms (288, *caelestia dona*) such an exquisite work of art; he did not recognize the shield's engravings (*clipei caelamina*) with earth and Ocean and the constellations (*Pleiadas Hyadasque immunemque aequoris Arcton*; here the quotation from *Il.* 18.486–7 echoes the metrical form of Virgil's imitation at *G.* 1.138); later he jeers with vehement alliteration that 'if I had not obtained the statue of Minerva, the offspring of Telamon would have wielded his sevenfold oxhide shield in vain' (346–7):

> quae nisi fecissem, frustra Telamone creatus
> *gestasset* laeva *taurorum tergora septem.*

The length of Ulysses' speech also permits one extravagant figure shared by the grand style of oratory with poetry; the adynaton. Returning to the motif of 265, Ulysses elaborates the claim that his intellect has always served the Greeks: 'sooner shall Simois flow in reverse and Ida stand stripped of trees, or Greece promise aid to Troy, than my intellect will idle on their behalf, or'—here is the sting—'dumb Ajax's cleverness bring them good' (324–7):

> ante retro Simois fluet et sine frondibus Ide
> stabit, et auxilium promittet Achaia Troiae,
> quam cessante meo pro uestris pectore rebus
> Aiacis stolidi Danais sollertia prosit.

And yet—Ida was stripped for the funeral pyres of Patroclus and Hector, and Simois was choked with bodies, as readers of Homer and Virgil (*Aen.* 1.101–2) knew. Did Greece also offer aid to Troy, perhaps in Rome's eastern wars?

Ovid's final comment (382–3) reveals where his sympathies lie: 'the outcome showed the power of fluency, and the eloquent man won the arms of the brave hero' (*quid facundia posset / re patuit, fortisque viri tulit arma disertus*). He had always identified with the *facundia* of Ulysses: cf. *Ars* 2.123 *non erat formosus sed erat facundus Vlixes* ('Ulysses was not handsome, but he was fluent'). But I would like to make one point passed over by Hopkinson's analysis, perhaps because it is too obvious to mention: we do not doubt that Ajax speaks the truth, nor do we doubt Ulysses' mendacity. How did the Roman public read these speeches? Perhaps as they had read the Latin debate of *Aeneid* 11, less as partisans, or expecting to be convinced, than as connoisseurs of rhetorical grandstanding. They knew Ulysses' trickery and insincerity, they knew the tragic outcome for Ajax, but they could still enjoy the fireworks.

I turn now to Hecuba's lament, embedded by Ovid between the tragedy of Polyxena's sacrifice and Polydorus' murder. Ovid had read Euripides' *Hecuba*, and follows closely the messenger narrative of the sacrifice. But from Hecuba's two speeches he makes one lament spoken over her daughter's body, full of artful repetition and assonance (13.494–500):

> *Nata,* tuae (quid enim superest?) do*lor ultime matris*
> *nata,* iaces, uideoque t*uum, mea uulnera, uulnus,*
> en, ne *perdiderim* quemquam sine caede meorum
> tu quoque *uulnus habes.* at te *quia femina,* rebar
> *a ferro* tutam; cecidisti *et femina ferro*
> *totque tuos* idem fratres, *te perdidit idem*
> *exitium . . .*

Daughter, last grief of your mother, daughter, you lie dead and I look on your wound, my wounds. See so that I may not lose any of my dear ones without murder, you too have a wound, but I though that you as a woman were safe from steel; even you, a woman, fell by the steel, and the same destructive power that caused the loss of so many brothers. caused your loss too.

She moves through other incantatory repetitions: of *metuendus* ('to be feared', 503–4) and *finita* ('ended', 506–7) through the theme and variation of 503–5 criticized by Montanus, back to her continuing *dolor* (*in cursu meus dolor est*) and a longer syntactical period, contrasting her former glory as royal wife and mother of a growing family with her coming role as exile and slave, when Penelope will boast that her new slave is Priam's wife and Hector's mother (women in antiquity always show jealousy or fear of other women). Her daughter, comforter of her mother's mourning, has now provided atonement for enemy tombs (*hostilia busta piasti*, 516, recalls 503–5 and is in turn reworked as *inferias hosti peperi*: 'I gave birth to funeral offerings for the enemy').

Here too Ovid seems to echo Virgil, yet it is more for the ingenuity of literary allusion than from its centrality to Hecuba's grief: *at puto, funeribus dotabere regia uirgo* (523) plays on Juno's threat against Lavinia: *sanguine Troiano et Rutulo dotabere uirgo* (*Aen.* 7.318), transferring the notion of warriors as wedding offerings from the living Lavinia to Polyxena sacrificed in marriage to the dead. When Hecuba returns to the motif of loss (*omnia perdidimus*) it is to renew the opening dramatic irony of *dolor ultime matris*. She has treated Polyxena as the last living child, but now she recalls the little boy Polydorus, whom we know to be already murdered (his ghost opened Euripides' play long before his mother found his body). As she now returns to Polyxena's wounds intending to bathe them (*crudelia uulnera lymphis / abluere*) we know she is going to find Polydorus' body. So is this rhetoric or poetry? The question is misconceived. As Ovid passes from speech to narrative he maintains the same high level of musicality and pathos we have experienced in Hecuba's lament.

Ovid's Most Difficult Audience: Addressing Augustus

As it happens, not only Ovid's epic but his later elegies could not escape treating Rome's most important citizen, Augustus (we might call him the elephant in the room). He had even worked a skillful encomium of the emperor into his *Art of Love*, in the form of a poetic send-off (*propemptikon*) for the emperor's heir Gaius setting out for the East in 1 BCE, and his *Metamorphoses* both began and ended with allusions to Rome's first citizen. But both the opening portrayal of Jupiter's senate of yes-gods and execution of Lycaon without trial and the closing segue from the deification of Caesar thinly conceal cynical judgments, which can hardly have escaped the Princeps and his counselors. When Ovid hails Julius Caesar's paternity of Augustus as greater than any of his triumphs, and his deification as necessary so that his son would not be the child of a mortal (15.757–9), how could this not provoke imperial suspicion? There is some justification for the scholars who consider the *Metamorphoses* as the fatal *carmen* which brought on the poet's exile. But one should not underrate the challenge of the panegyric mode: it may have been as difficult for Ovid to compose the imperial encomia of his *Fasti* as the humble appeals (corresponding to the genre of *deprecatio*) spread across his nine books of exile poetry.

Consider the encomia with which Ovid celebrates the anniversary of the Princeps' two honorific titles, both occasions now recorded in Rome's calendar. He had obtained (and no doubt suggested) the title *Augustus* on restoring control of the demilitarized provinces to the senate in 27 BCE, but postponed for twenty-five years accepting the title of *pater patriae*, which may have brought odium upon his father, Julius. I will take the latter first, because it is the earlier of the encomia in the partially reworked edition of the *Fasti*. As Ovid approaches the Nones of February, eight lines (2.119–26) are devoted to stressing his inadequacy, and that of his meter, to deal with the epic greatness of this greatest of honors in the calendar. This preparatory fanfare enables the poet to address the emperor in simpler, more direct, language (*sancte pater patriae*) increasing the scale of public homage by dividing Rome's people between plebs, senate, and knights, adopting the first person plural for his own group: *hoc dedimus tibi nomen* ('we have bestowed this name upon you'). But public action is subordinated to Augustus' own achievements: *res tamen ante dedit* ('reality had long since bestowed it. You have on earth the name Jupiter holds in high heaven: you are father of men as he is of gods'). Another twelve lines reinforce this praise by a series of favorable comparisons (133–44) with Rome's first founder, Romulus, whom the poet addresses in order to stress Augustus' promotion of the laws, his democratic role of Princeps, his clemency, and his generosity in making his father a god, where Romulus had been deified by his own father Mars. Certainly, there is room in Ovid's allusion to Augustus' adultery laws for the cynical reader to dissent, but the poet's language is impeccable.

To complicate Ovid's rhetorical task in celebrating the name *Augustus*, the first book which contains this anniversary had to be remodeled after the Princeps' death, when Ovid changed his dedication not to the new emperor Tiberius, who was irrevocably hostile, but to Tiberius' heir, Augustus' grandson Germanicus; Ovid has begun with the Princeps' restoration of the republic, in return for which he was called *Augusto nomine*. Without our practice of capitalization, this phrase conveys two senses: the name Augustus or an august name. From the bare name the poet switches to compare all the honorifics won by Rome's past leaders and recorded in the *Fasti*; from the geographical titles of an Africanus, he moves to the title Germanicus of the Princeps' stepson, the name handed down to the new addressee, before turning back to honor the hereditary title Maximus of his patron Fabius. But the name Augustus is on a higher level, shared with great Jupiter.

Two couplets play variations on the derivation of the ancient word from *augere*, to increase or bless, and two more (613–16) transform the fact of Jupiter's blessing into good wishes to be showered on the Princeps with the gods themselves as *Au*-spicious promoters. Good wishes were perhaps the least hazardous form of imperial address; Ovid will end this first book celebrating the dedication of the Altar of Peace (709–720) with wishes for national success and the enduring prosperity of

the imperial dynasty which has guaranteed it. Given the predictability of such encomiastic material, the poet must exploit every kind of decorative figure, here alliteration
and a rare verb conspicuously placed (*Fast.* 1.719–20):

> utque domus, quae *praestat* eam, cum *pace perennet*
>   ad *pia propensos* vota rogate deos.

that the dynasty which provides peace be perpetually at peace, beseech the gods propitious
to pious vows.

Appeasing an angry ruler was an altogether tougher assignment, but once sent
into mandatory *relegatio* Ovid had no other recourse for the remaining eight years
of life except to devise forms of direct or indirect appeal to the Princeps. We know
about his relegation to Tomis (a resort in modern Romania, but then a frontier
outpost among the Dacians) only from Ovid's poems, and it remains a mystery how
and when he secured their dissemination and survival. For the first few years, indeed,
he did not dare name any addressee except his wife, and the emperor who had condemned him. So who were the intended audience of these *Tristia* ('sad epistles')?
The first poem is addressed to the book of which it is a part, the second to the gods
of sea and storm who are tossing his ship, 1.3 and 1.4 are descriptive without
addressee, and 1.5 to a nameless but loyal friend. Ovid will not dare to address the
emperor himself until he creates a petition that will fill a complete second book. If
he sent the poems to Rome, he can hardly have expected them not to be reported
to the emperor, and must have composed with the emperor's reaction in mind. I can
envisage three main possibilities: least likely, that he expected the emperor to be
persuaded that Ovid had done and would do no harm, and so change his verdict; a
little more likely, that Augustus would see his self-interest in winning popularity for
clemency to a popular figure. Failing this, Ovid might hope to create a movement
among influential readers that would make it advantageous for Augustus to display
grace in transferring him to a more urban community—as he had, for example,
brought his daughter Julia back from Pandateria to Rhegium on the mainland. But
this is not a real analogy, since the Princeps almost certainly kept his daughter under
guard as well as out of the public eye.

Rhetorically, the poet needed to call on that clemency, whether it existed or
not. As Quintilian says (5.13.6), 'if we ever must speak before a Princeps or anyone
free to make his own decision, we [advocates] must acknowledge that our client
deserves death, but that even so he should be saved by a clement ruler . . . we will
use a deliberative form rather than a judicial approach and urge him to seek glory
for his humanity rather than the pleasure of revenge.' This most probably concerns
participants in a conspiracy, and Ovid may indeed have been an accessory to conspiracy. It is contrary to his interest to hint at the *error* he had committed or offense
he had witnessed; if he stresses instead the offense create by his *carmen* it is surely
because he feels able to defend this without causing further offense or embarrassment.
Perhaps it will give a fair sample of his techniques to survey the opening section of
his first poem, and the much longer first part of his direct petition which attempts
to palliate the *error*.

The first letter bids the book dress shabbily (almost in mourning) as mark of his sorrow, and answer enquiries only by declaring that Ovid is alive, thanks to the ruler-god, avoiding the risk of any unwanted comment. 'If reminded, the reader will ask what was my offense and I will be put on trial in common gossip as an offender against the state' (24, *populi publicus ore reus*). His case is bad, and beyond advocacy. Sympathizers may hope that Caesar will be mollified, and the poet allowed to die in his home. As it is, the book may be criticized as inferior to Ovid's poetic record, but a judge should inquire not only about the facts but their circumstances (37–8, *ut res, ita tempora rerum / quaerere*). Indeed, 'a fair judge will be amazed that I can achieve even this, and read my writings such as they are with indulgence' (45–6). This talk of judging surely aims to divert the reader away from the moral issue to the literary-critical process. In the rest of the poem Ovid stays concerned with his poetry, trans-ferring to his talent responsibility for his present exile (1.1.56): *ingenio sic fuga parta meo*. Does he believe this, or is it not more likely that he believes it is safer to keep the blame on his poetry and away from his disastrous involvement in unmentionable disloyalty? Several later letters in this book contain brief claims of innocence (1.2.93–100, 1.3.37–40, 1.5.41–2, 1.9.57–64) and protestations of loyalty (1.9.43–5).

Ovid also introduces the first of many allusions to his unforeseen punishment by 'Caesar's anger' as a thunderbolt sent by Jupiter. Here it is well developed, starting from a warning to the book to stay away from the Palatine (1.1.63): *uenit in hoc illa fulmen ab arce caput* ('the blow to my person came from that citadel') and invoking the mythical precedent of Phaethon (1.1.79–82):

> uitaret caelum Phaethon, si uiueret, et quos
>   optarat stulte, tangere nollet equos.
> me quoque, quae sensi, fateor Iouis arma timere:
>   me reor infesto, cum tonat, igne peti.

> Phaethon would shun the sky if he lived now, and refuse to touch the horses which he foolishly longed for. I too admit I fear the weapons of Jupiter which I have experienced, and believe when it thunders that I am the target of hostile fire.

The motif of Augustus as Jupiter, and his anger as the thunderer's weapons, recurs with variations at 1.2.3, 1.4.25–6, 1.5.77–8, and in later books also. Thus, writing to his wife (*Tr.* 4.3.63–70), Ovid claims an offender's family should not feel shame for his offense, any more than Evadne felt shame for Capaneus, or Phaethon's kin should have repudiated him, or Cadmus disowned Semele (69–70):

> nec tibi quod saeuis ego sum Iouis ignibus ictus
>   purpureus molli fiat in ore pudor.

> Nor should shame bring a blush to your gentle face because I have been struck by Jupiter's fires.

When Ovid resolved to attempt a full-length petition to the emperor, he used many of these motifs, starting with the same comment as at 1.1.56: 'my talent caused my ruin' (2.2, *ingenio perii qui miser ipse meo*). The same (love) poems which made men and women want to know me made Caesar damn me and my way of life, ordering the removal of my *Artes*. Then Ovid tries to argue from the contrast between his mistaken writings and more recent serious works: just as Achilles' spear healed Telephus, perhaps new writings will mitigate the anger (*leniet iram*) caused by his previous writings (19–22). Here, and again later, Ovid seems to be toying with the idea of offering proper and dutiful poetry: when he cites the hymns that Caesar had commissioned for the inauguration of the temple of Ops and for the Ludi Saeculares, he may be hinting that he could write official texts, and again in 68–76 he raises the possibility of contributing to Caesar's glory; if others are more capable of celebrating him with the mighty style that is appropriate (*quanto decet ore*, 73), yet Ovid's smaller offering—mere incense to other men's hecatombs—can conciliate a god. Instead, some enemy read his frivolous *deliciae* to Augustus and prejudiced the emperor against reading his respectful poems with an open mind.

However, Ovid has to leap a gap between the official hymns of 23–8 and the central issue of his own misuse of talent. In 31 he goes as far as to suggest that if he had not offended then Augustus would have had no scope for showing mercy, a theme which he elaborates with variations and the typical parallels with Jupiter. This may have been Ovid's private strategy, but to make it so explicit is almost cheeky, more likely to enrage the emperor than lead him to relent. Can he expect the emperor to judge Ovid's offense by the same yardstick as the opposition of foreign enemies whom he had defeated and pardoned?

What makes it hard to follow Ovid's pleading is his constant oscillation between defending his life (e.g. swearing his loyal support and prayers for the emperor's long life) and defending his poetry (contrasting his weighty and serious books with the frivolous *Artes* which provoked the anger of the Princeps and his people, 78–9). Like any defendant he stands by the respectability of his former life, which was found acceptable (89) until the last fatal *error*. Although he has ruined his family, it can still be restored if Caesar uses his clemency: even his initial relegation was an act of clemency, granting him life and property and avoiding a senatorial decree of condemnation (123–42). The to and fro of Ovid's argument is supported by analogies from the natural recovery of crops or vines (143–4) or weather (149–52) as he works his way to a more elaborate structure of 52 lines: a mighty invocation (twenty-four lines, 155–78), his address and appeal to the Princeps (four lines, 179–82), and the substance of his petition (again twenty-four lines, 183–206). First then he appeals to Augustus by all the gods and every member of his dear family, reserving the language of panegyric; cf. 39, *cum patriae rector dicere paterque* ('since you are called father and guide/steersman of our country') and the echo of Jove's thunderbolt to bolster this plea for mercy:

> parce precor, fulmenque tuum, fera tela, reconde,
>   heu nimium misero cognita tela mihi.
> parce, pater patriae, nec nominis immemor huius
>   olim placandi spem mihi tolle tui.

Spare me, I beg, and sheath your thunderbolt, that savage weapon, a weapon too familiar to me in my misery. Spare me, father of our country, and do not forget this name by removing all hope of ever appeasing you.

After so intense an invocation, the modesty of Ovid's actual request may indeed be good rhetoric. What he is seeking is only a gentler place of exile, so that he is not deprived of peace as well as his country (185–206). But now he has stated his petition he can only return to the charges against him, the poem and the blunder: *carmen et error*. Skating rapidly past the *error* (207–210), he devotes the rest of the poem to a fascinating but disingenuous justification of his disgraceful poem (*turpe carmen*) by Greek and Roman precedent in all the arts, including recent Roman love elegy. At 547 this leads into a short resumptive epilogue affirming the seriousness of his life and other work. Returning in 568 to his opening ploy (2, quoted above) he again focuses on his offending Muse—I will be the only poet whom my Calliope has ruined—before repeating his plea (573, *precor . . . / non . . . ut redeam* = 183) and its modest nature (575, *tutius exilium* = 185).

Undoubtedly rhetoric, and pleaded with a greater urgency than Ovid's many earlier impersonations, this poem suffers from the sheer excess of Ovid's concerns. It is important to read as a social document, but the very arbitrariness of Augustus' power, the motives of national security (as we would call them now), which hide the real origin of Ovid's situation, prevent the poem from doing justice either to his poetic artistry or his rhetorical versatility. This versatility could handle any fictitious situation Ovid chose to invent; but the poet's situation was real and could not be disguised or argued away. For those of us who admire Ovid's command of rhetoric and creative ingenuity it is better by far to enjoy the sheer bravado of his skill in so many other genres and contexts.

FURTHER READING

A good introduction to the context of Ovid in the schools of declamation can be found in Bonner (1949; cf. especially pp. 143–4). For a shrewd and compact study of rhetoric in Ovid's many works and genres, see Higham (1958). The principal function of rhetorical education was to ready young Roman men for public careers, an aspect of Ovid's intellectual formation explored in Kenney (1969b). We neglect high-quality commentaries at our peril: Hopkinson (2000) offers a chapter-length discussion of the contest between Ajax and Ulysses and its antecedent literary and rhetorical traditions (9–22), as of Hecuba's lament (22–26); both discussions are fully accessible to readers without Latin.

CHAPTER FOUR

Ovid and Religion

Julia Dyson Hejduk

Introduction

The age of Augustus gave rise to two poets who continually confronted the problem of evil, the nature of *pietas*, and the relationship of humans to the divine. Only one of them was Virgil. Why is it, then, that Ovid is frequently characterized by modern writers as devoid of theological concerns? That, although his *Fasti* is by far the most extensive surviving poetic treatment of Roman religion, and gratefully mined for arcana of Roman rituals (see Beard et al. 1998: 6–7), he is never characterized as a 'religious poet'? And that, although nearly every one of his exile poems contains a prayer or some religious gesture, the most important modern English monograph on the exile poetry (Williams 1994) does not even contain an index entry for 'Jupiter' or 'gods'? An essay on 'Ovid and Religion' should begin by posing the question that underlies all of these: Is Ovid's indefatigable flippancy compatible with any 'real' religious impulse?

The modern answer is generally 'No'. An unspoken syllogism runs as follows: Ovid is fun; religion is not fun; therefore Ovid is not religious. Those few scholars who would take Ovid's religion seriously—focusing, invariably, on the *Fasti* alone—tend to do so at the expense of his wit, which means that scholars of Roman religion and literary critics have even less to say to one another here than usual. C. Robert Phillips, for instance, laments the lack of contact between these camps, but places the blame squarely on the literary types: 'In conclusion, then, by taking Roman religion *seriously* we take the Roman calendar *seriously*. And by taking it *seriously*, we begin to discern organizational principles and *serious* theorizing [in the *Fasti*]' (1992: 71; italics mine). Most literary scholars who study the *Fasti* are content to concentrate on politics and leave 'serious' religious considerations aside.

Those who focus on the *Metamorphoses*, on the other hand, tend to see it as a literary construction, not a religious manifesto. This poem was for the Middle Ages and Renaissance perhaps the primary source for mythology, juicy stories about the gods and heroes, but it seems refreshingly distant from myth, the menacing consort of ritual (see Graf 2002: 108 and Scheid 2003: 178–81). As Joseph Solodow puts it, 'The injection of humor [in the *Metamorphoses*] *inoculates* mythology against *excessive* solemnity; it shuts out interpretations which tend to *reduce* man to a figure within some *abstract* scheme, whether moral or historical, political or theological ... No gods preside over the course of events or represent a principle like justice' (1988: 108; italics mine). The choice of words here is revealing: Solodow appears to start from the assumption that religion is a pathology constricting human freedom and individuality, and he holds up Ovid as the hero whose humor helps to break out of religion's Procrustean 'abstract scheme'. Denis Feeney offers a similar observation, though his rhetoric implies that Ovid's absence of religious underpinning represents a lack rather than a liberation: the *Metamorphoses* 'is unique amongst ancient writings in the ruthlessness of its refusal to provide an environment which shapes the meaning of human existence' (1991: 204). Whether Ovid's anti-religious stance is seen as a strength or a weakness, both writers are reading Ovid, I believe, in the way his poem urges us to read him.

Or almost. For the question of tone, so crucial in understanding the difference between the narrative persona and the man who held the pen, is of paramount importance for a writer whose lifeblood is irony. If 'irony' means saying the opposite of what one means, and if we admit that Ovid is a thoroughly ironic writer, then why should we accept his depictions of religion at face value any more than we accept his depictions of love or politics or anything else? Ovid's approach to the Roman gods and the labyrinth of Roman ritual is humorous and satirical, like everything else Ovid does. Yet the development of his persona throughout his work, framed by the bowshot of Cupid that caused him to write love elegy and the thunderbolt of Jupiter that sent him into exile, is intimately bound up with religious issues. Though it would be impossible in an essay of this length to provide a full assessment of Ovid and religion (despite the promising title), I hope to give at least some idea of how Ovid's complex and shifting relationship with the divine is integral to the poetic autobiography that unfolds throughout his works, which in itself says something about the role of religion in Roman life.

The Amatory Poems: Ovid as Priest

If Ovid's religion and his poetry are intimately bound, humor is often the glue that binds them. The Augustan age saw the term *uates*, properly 'a prophet, seer (regarded as the mouthpiece of the deity possessing him)' (*OLD* 1.a), increasingly used to mean 'a poet (regarded as divinely inspired), bard' (*OLD* 2.a). Horace and Virgil employ the term as a synonym for 'poet' with the religious metaphor largely undeveloped, as in Horace's prayer to Maecenas to 'insert me among the lyric *uates*' (*Carm.* 1.1.35), or Virgil's 'the shepherds call me a *uates* too' (*Ecl.* 9.34). Ovid, on the other hand, plays up the 'prophet' idea by calling himself the *uates* of a particular god, following up with prayers, and repeatedly referring to himself and his poetry as 'sacred'. *Which* god, however, is subject to change, and indeed Ovid's career is characterized by various wrestling matches over whose *uates* he is to be. Again, the comparison with other Augustan poets is revealing. Virgil's Tityrus (a figure for the poet), like Ovid, was starting to sing an epic, when Apollo plucked his ear and directed him to sing the lighter genre of pastoral instead (*Ecl.* 6.3–5). But there is no further mention of the relationship between the god and the poet. For Ovid, on the other hand, the switch from epic to elegy at a god's prompting is expressed as becoming the *uates* of that god, a metaphor sustained throughout.

A glance at some programmatic passages in the *Amores* will illustrate these comic negotiations with divine beings. The poet who set out to sing an epic was, he claims, already a *uates*, but one belonging to the Muses. Cupid's fatal theft of one foot from the hexameter prompts Ovid's outraged cry that the 'savage boy' is trespassing on other gods' territory (*Am.* 1.1.5–6):

> quis tibi, saeue puer, dedit hoc in carmina iuris?
>   Pieridum uates, non tua, turba sumus.

> Savage boy, who gave you this right over poetry?
>   We *uates* are the Muses' crowd, not yours.

Cupid retaliates, sending the shaft that will—as becomes clear in subsequent decades—determine the course of the poet's entire life (*Am.* 1.1.23–4). At the beginning of *Am.* 3, Ovid's decision about what sort of poetry to write next takes the form of the epiphany of two goddess-like figures, Elegy and Tragedy, in a numinous sacred grove, the location of choice for epiphanies (*Am.* 3.1.1–14). But though he sings one more book of elegies, at the end, he lays down his charge as *uates* of the 'mother of the tender Loves' (*Am.* 3.15.1). His progression from elegy to tragedy (Ovid next wrote a *Medea*, now lost) is depicted as a sort of religious conversion from being a priest of Cupid/Venus to being a devotee of Bacchus, the god of tragedy (*Am.* 3.15.15–18):

> culte puer puerique parens Amathusia culti,
>   aurea de campo uellite signa meo;
> corniger increpuit thyrso grauiore Lyaeus:
>   pulsanda est magnis area maior equis.

> Cultivated boy, and cultivated boy's Amathusian mother,
>   pluck up your golden standards from my field;
> horned Bacchus has rattled with a heavier thyrsus:
>   by great steeds must his greater field be struck.

Note the ambiguity of *cultus* here: Cupid and his mother are 'cultivated' in the sense of both 'refined, elegant' and 'objects of cult, worshipped'. In all these instances, Ovid addresses the gods with humorous familiarity, depicting his 'conversion' from one genre to another in terms of a personal relationship with the appropriate deity.

In the *Ars amatoria*, the poet changes his tune. The persona of a humble neophgte rendered helpless by Cupid's arrow has been exchanged for the cynical arrogance of one who intends not merely to subdue the gods but to punish them (*Ars* 1.21–4):

et mihi cedet Amor, quamuis mea uulneret arcu
    pectora, iactatas excutiatque faces;
quo me fixit Amor, quo me uiolentius ussit,
    hoc melior facti uulneris ultor ero.

Love will yield to me too, though with his bow he wound
    my heart, and shake about and hurl his torches;
the more violently he pierced, the more violently he burned me,
    the better avenger I'll be of the wound he's made.

The *Ars amatoria* purports to be a didactic, defamiliarizing re-examination of this whole Love business—in spirit not unlike Lucretius 4.1030–1287, which takes a relentlessly and revoltingly physical approach to the idea of 'love as disease'. But Ovid's pose smacks so obviously of sour grapes, the bitterness of one who has been 'pierced' and 'burned' by Love and seeks revenge against his tormentor, that we are encouraged not to take his stance of scientific objectivity seriously. He is determined to tame and train Love because Love has already inflicted a violent wound on him. Having mocked other poets' claims of divine inspiration (1.25–8), he styles himself a *uates peritus* (1.29, 'prophet through practiced experience'), a willful oxymoron (Newlands 1995: 53) that might cause us to accuse him of atheism—but then adds a prayer to Venus to favor his enterprise (1.30).

Is there any meaningful sense in which these religious gestures should be taken seriously? Though the obvious answer appears to be 'No', the question is more complex than it might seem. The *Ars amatoria* is surely meant to be a send-up, even a *reductio ad absurdum*, of both didactic and elegy. Its narrator encourages his readers to engage in rape, because in fact 'that violence of yours is pleasing to girls' (1.673); to aid seduction by befriending the girl's husband, because 'he will be more useful to you when made a friend' (1.580); and to fear most one's friends, brothers, and companions, as they are most likely to be the true enemies (1.751–4). He states as simple fact the destruction of human morality by the all-consuming passion for sexual pleasure, which is increased through another's pain (1.749–51). In short, the *praeceptor Amoris* presents, in the coolly academic tone of one versifying a treatise on astronomy or agriculture, an elegiac world that—were it not merely a poetic fiction—would be one of moral bankruptcy, degradation, and horror.

It is in this context that we should read his statements about Roman religion. The quip *expedit esse deos*, 'it's convenient for the gods to exist' (*Ars* 1.637), is often quoted as representing Ovid's real view (see Miller 1991: 45, who cautions against this equation). But let us look more closely. The *praeceptor* exhorts his pupils to promise anything and call upon the gods as witnesses (*Ars* 1.631–8):

nec timide promitte: trahunt promissa puellas;
    pollicito testes quoslibet adde deos.
Iuppiter ex alto periuria ridet amantum
    et iubet Aeolios inrita ferre Notos.
per Styga Iunoni falsum iurare solebat
    Iuppiter: exemplo nunc fauet ipse suo.
expedit esse deos et, ut expedit, esse putemus;
    dentur in antiquos tura merumque focos.

Don't be timid in your promises: promises lure girls;
    add to your pledge whatever gods you like.
Jupiter from on high smiles down on lovers' perjuries,
    and bids the South Wind to carry them off unfulfilled.
Jupiter used to swear false oaths to Juno by the Styx,
    and now looks favorably on his own example.
It's convenient for gods to exist, and since it's convenient, let's think they exist:
    let incense and wine be given to the ancient altars.

The premise of the poem is that sexual conquest is the reader's ultimate concern; to that goal everything else is subordinate, including things like friendship and morality. The gods are reduced to a convenient fiction that will give weight to the lover's false promises. Yet the *praeceptor* then realizes that he has gone a bit too far in dismantling the religious underpinning of the cosmos, so he back-pedals, asserting—if rather anemically—that the divine (*numen*) is in fact the traditional guardian of human morality, on the lookout for punishable breaches of *pietas* (1.639–42). The punchline is that deceiving *girls* is perfectly acceptable, because they were the original deceivers and deserve to fall into their own trap (1.643–6). Ovid is not discarding either morality or religion, but reconfiguring them, shuffling traditional moral precepts while retaining traditional language: as the priest of Sex, he counsels us that this great cause justifies any means, religious or otherwise.

Several observations should be made about this passage. First, the *praeceptor* makes at least one statement about religion that is manifestly incorrect, even on its own terms, showing his unreliability as a reader and a teacher: no god, including Jupiter, swears an oath by the Styx that is actually *false*, even if it is (like the Delphic oracle) misleading or incomplete. Second, and more importantly, *the whole poem is a joke*. The *author himself* is not counseling seduction, rape, or betrayal: he has created a *narrative persona* who counsels these things, thus showing that they are the logical outcome of the amatory game. When an ironic writer embraces as positive goods the consequences of immorality, is it not prima facie probable that he (the man who held the pen) means the opposite of what he (the narrative persona) says? I am not suggesting that we must see Ovid's primary motivation as that of a moralist; nevertheless, an awareness of the moral pitfalls of the effete world of elegiac seduction is at least a side effect of his satiric wit.

This, then, is part of the answer to the question I posed at the beginning about Ovid's flippancy. As a sexually amoral persona *can* be created by a moral person, so an anti-religious persona *can* be created by a religious person. Philip Hardie remarks, 'For a poet who notoriously said "it is expedient that the gods should exist, and, since it is expedient, let us believe they exist" (*Ars* 1.637), Ovid has a surprising fascination for the possibility of the irruption of the divine into the quotidian, the manifestation of a *praesens deus*' (2002c: 8). This apparent contradiction ceases to be so surprising if we keep in mind, as I think we must, that the speaker of that line is an amoral know-it-all who is the poet's fiction, not the poet himself.

The *Metamorphoses*: Ovid's Anti-Theodicy

If the gods in the amatory poems appear mainly to supply generic imperatives ('write elegy!' 'write tragedy!') and perverse exempla ('Jupiter used force: you use it too!'), the gods in the *Metamorphoses* provide a full-blown model of how not to live. Their moral chaos mirrors the haphazard way the world comes into being—not without divine involvement, to be sure, but with little evidence of divine beneficence or rationality. The first appearance of 'god' (*deus*) could scarcely be more anticlimactic. In the beginning, there was a jumbled mass of 'discordant seeds of things' (*Met.* 1.9), characterized by conflicts between the elements (1.19–20). We await a divine architect to set things right, and here is what we get (*Met.* 1.21): *hanc deus et melior litem natura diremit* ('god and better nature settled this dispute'). The 'god' ('a god'? 'the god'? 'God'? the lack of articles and of a lowercase/uppercase distinction in Latin is acutely felt here) who suddenly emerges, sharing the credit with 'better nature' ('Nature'? better than what?), settles not a war but a dispute, *lis* ('litigation'). The creation of the earth seems similarly arbitrary: 'whoever of the gods that was' (*quisquis fuit ille deorum*, 1.32) gathered it into a sphere 'so that it might not not be equal on every side' (*ne non aequalis ab omni / parte foret*, 1.34–5). This is hardly a motivation calculated to inspire a sense of divine purpose, let alone divine love. After the earth's geography is sorted out, the creation of living things—including gods—merits another unmotivated negative purpose clause, 'so that no region might be bereft of its animate beings [*animalia*]' (1.72). *Why* this should be so is given no more justification than why the earth should be spherical. If Ovid has an interest in metaphysics or theology, no trace of it appears in the emergence of his cosmos.

The creation of Man is no better. It too is a variation on the theme of 'so that what wasn't there might not not be there' (*Met.* 1.76–8):

> Sanctius his animal mentisque capacius altae
> deerat adhuc et quod dominari in cetera posset.
> natus homo est . . .

> An animal holier than these and more capable of lofty thought
> was still missing, and something to lord it over the rest.
> Man arose . . .

The description of the vacancy that Man would fill is a sort of *tricolon descendens*, an anticlimax of sublimity: neither Man's participation in divinity ('holier') nor his intellectual faculty ('more capable of lofty thought') is given pride of place, but rather his capacity for domination ('something to lord it over the rest'). And while Man is in some sense made in the image of the gods, the two possibilities for how he 'arose', made either from 'divine seed' (*diuino semine*) by that anonymous 'craftsman' (*opifex*) or from some leftover 'seeds of sky' (*semina caeli*) by the Titan Prometheus (1.78–83), do not clarify the nature of the soul or of human purpose. As William Anderson notes, 'That leaves the relationship between human and divine beings ambiguous, and ambiguous it remains throughout the poem' (1997: 160).

When we see the gods in action, we can be glad that our relationship with them is not closer. The Olympians in the *Metamorphoses* are an unsavory lot, lustful, duplicitous, vengeful, petty, and, in short, having no redeeming features whatsoever. Ovid could no more be encouraging his readers to imitate these lowlifes than he could seriously be endorsing rape and betrayal in the *Ars amatoria*. As is often noted, they are thoroughly human—or worse than human—and transparent stand-ins for the Roman senate and Princeps. Ovid's description of their abode makes the analogy clear (*Met.* 1.175–6):

> hic locus est quem, si uerbis audacia detur,
> haud timeam magni dixisse Palatia caeli.

> This is the place that, if my words should be given audacity,
> I wouldn't fear to call the Palatine of the great sky.

Jupiter's behavior points up the audacity of the comparison. Whereas Virgil's Neptune calming the stormy sea is famously likened to a statesman calming the passions of the ignoble crowd with his *pietas* (*Aen.* 1.148–53), Ovid's Jupiter, incensed at the impiety of one human (Lycaon), conceives 'wrath huge and worthy of Jupiter' (*Met.* 1.166) and stirs up the passions of the sycophantic assembly himself. Ovid compares the gods' reaction to the attempted assassination of Jupiter with that of the human race to a similar attempt on Augustus (1.200–6); the *pietas* of the crowd results in a vengeful uproar that Augustus, like Jupiter, finds gratifying (1.204–5). The despotism of this Jupiter, who next whips up a cataclysmic storm—a role that Virgil, by contrast, assigns to Juno—is hardly a flattering reflection on the *clementia* of the Princeps. Jupiter then rapes a human girl, Io (1.588–600). Juno, for some reason, is not fooled by the shroud of preternatural darkness at midday with which he attempts to conceal his adultery, since she knows the tricks of a husband 'so many times caught in the act' (*deprensi totiens*, 1.606). She pulls off the covers, and the scene of marital negotiation that follows, in which Jupiter turns his lover into a cow that he gets wheedled into giving to his wife (1.607–24), is straight out of comedy.

That the most prominent interactions of Jupiter and Juno should resemble an adultery-mime is but one symptom of a pervasive Ovidian phenomenon. The running joke is that *everything* is played out in terms of sex—from generic conflict (Hinds 1992a) to the pining from exile of the locked-out lover of Rome (Holzberg 2002: 176–98). In the *Metamorphoses*, Juno's epic wrath is reduced entirely to sexual jealousy. This eroticization of religion is evident also at the linguistic level in Ovid's arch activation of the literal meaning of religious formulae. For instance, whereas *sub Ioue* ('under Jupiter') normally means simply 'under the sky', Juno's wrath is ignited when she finds nymphs lying *sub Ioue . . . suo*, (1.363, 'under *her own* Jupiter')—a choice example of what Solodow felicitously dubs 'split divinity', in which the god as metonymy (e.g. Jupiter = sky) humorously collides with the god as anthropomorphic being (1988: 94–6). Compare Juno's use of the phrase *quantus et qualis* ('how great and how fine'), a formula for the supernatural beauty of divine epiphany (e.g. *Aen.* 2.589–92, of Venus). Ovid had eroticized this formula before in his 'epiphany' of Corinna in the *Amores*, *quantum et quale latus*! ('how great, how fine her flank!',

Am. 1.5.22; see Hinds 1987b: 7–11). When Juno plays evil procuress for Semele, she cunningly suggests that the hapless mortal ask Jupiter to prove his identity by such a manifestation, making love to her 'how great and how fine he's taken in by high Juno' (*quantusque et qualis ab alta / Iunone excipitur*, 3.284–5). Juno's dirty mind has turned the august formula into what sounds like an advertisement for male enlargement.

Most of the mortals who interact with gods in the *Metamorphoses* end up like Semele, annihilated or metamorphosed into a non-human form. For the few who achieve apotheosis—like Hercules, Aeneas, Romulus, and Julius Caesar—we must wonder whether admission to the celestial club, given the obvious defects of its membership, is really desirable. Yet there is one mortal whose triumph over the wrath of Jupiter, and over death itself, rises above the pettiness of Olympian squabbles (*Met.* 15.871–9):

> Iamque opus exegi, quod nec Iouis ira nec ignis
> nec poterit ferrum nec edax abolere uetustas.
> cum uolet, illa dies, quae nil nisi corporis huius
> ius habet, incerti spatium mihi finiat aeui;
> parte tamen meliore mei super alta perennis
> astra ferar, nomenque erit indelebile nostrum;
> quaque patet domitis Romana potentia terris
> ore legar populi, perque omnia saecula fama
> (si quid habent ueri uatum praesagia) uiuam.

> Now I've completed the work, which neither Jupiter's wrath
> nor fire nor iron nor devouring age will have power to destroy.
> When it wants, that day whose jurisdiction is only over
> this body will round off the course of my uncertain life;
> yet with the better part of myself I'll be carried forever
> above the high stars, and my name will never be blotted out;
> and wherever Roman power lies over the lands it's conquered
> I'll be on the people's lips, and throughout all ages, by fame
> (if the prophecies of *uates* have any truth) I shall live.

However humorous Ovid's status as *uates* may be, this prophecy, at least, did come true.

The *Fasti*: Ovid as Victim

Readers hoping that this essay would comprehensively address Ovid's use of religion in the *Fasti* will, I fear, be disappointed. I shall offer instead a few remarks as a prelude to future study. First, Ovid's accuracy as a source for Roman religion is something of an open question, as he often provides the only information we have for particular rituals. It has recently been shown that his astronomical observations, at least, are for the most part less inaccurate than previously assumed (Fox 2004)—

though he does include some howlers, such as the Dog Star rising in May rather than in the 'Dog Days' of August (*Fast.* 5.723). Second, his inclusion of multiple explanations for various phenomena, which has rightly been seen as reflecting insecurity on the part of the narrator (Newlands 1992), is nevertheless consistent with the Roman religious system (see Beard 1987: 6–7; Feeney 1998: 127–8; Schiesaro 2002: 66). The Roman emphasis was on 'orthopraxy', getting the rituals right, rather than on 'orthodoxy', having the correct beliefs (Scheid 1992: 122–3). This is not to say that the Romans did not believe in the gods they went to such lengths to worship, but rather that a multiplicity of beliefs among various worshippers was normal; whether one thought of the Lares, for instance, as sons of the nymph Lara or as the Dioscuri or as the spirits of dead ancestors, what mattered was giving them the proper offerings (King 2003).

Sacrifice—the ritual slaughter of animals to secure the goodwill of the gods—was at the heart of Roman religious practice. I would suggest that Ovid, who may have written much of the *Fasti* in exile, implicitly figures himself as a sort of sacrificial victim, linking overt scenes and explanations of sacrifice with his own autobiography. In the victimization experienced by both his own persona and the characters in his narratives, we see, perhaps, a strand of seriousness in Ovid's religion—a strand that a sensitive reader such as Dante could weave into his own Christian fabric (see Pucci 1998: 199–222). However irreverent his depictions of the gods may be, it is evident especially in his later works how deeply engrained the sacrificial paradigm was. Not coincidentally, the *Ibis*, Ovid's fantasy of vengeance, reverses the roles, casting the poet as a priest sacrificing his nameless victim (106).

The *Fasti* poet's sympathy with sacrificial victims is apparent in his multiple aetiologies of the Agonalia in Book 1. As John Miller has pointed out, nearly all of Ovid's possible explanations focus on the fear and suffering of the animal (1992: 14–22). Yet this suffering is precisely what Roman cult practice went to great lengths to suppress: it was essential that the victim appear to go willingly, and an animal's manifest unwillingness not only rendered the sacrifice ineffective but was a dire omen requiring expiation. To focus on the animal's agony is to throw into question the central act in man's relationship to the gods. Ovid's panegyric of 'Caesar's altars' (*Fast.* 1.13) would appear to be subversive of the use to which those altars—all altars—are put.

Another feature that encourages us to see the poet as victim is his extraordinary aetiology of ritual slaughter as punishment. Sacrifice, he tells us, arose from animals' misdeeds (*Fast.* 1.343–456), an interpretation that appears to be unique among Roman writers. Ovid describes the sundry transgressions of animals against the gods, ending with birds (*Fast.* 1.441–50):

intactae fueratis aues, solacia ruris,
    adsuetum siluis innocuumque genus,
quae facitis nidos et plumis oua fovetis,
    et facili dulcis editis ore modos;
sed nihil ista iuuant, quia linguae crimen habetis,
    dique putant mentes uos aperire suas.

(nec tamen hoc falsum: nam, dis ut proxima quaeque,
      nunc pinna ueras, nunc datis ore notas.)
tuta diu uolucrum proles tum denique caesa est,
      iuueruntque deos indicis exta sui.

You birds had remained untouched, the solace of the fields,
      a harmless race and accustomed to the woods;
you who make your nests and warm your eggs with your feathers
      and bring forth sweet measures with poetic mouth;
but these don't help at all, since your tongue stands accused of a crime,
      and the gods think that you have revealed their minds.
(And yet, that's not false: for the nearer each one is to the gods,
      now with wing you give true signs, now with mouth.)
The race of birds, long safe, was slaughtered then at last,
      and the entrails of their informer pleased the gods.

To translate *facili ore* as 'poetic mouth', if loading the dice a bit (*facilis* is usually translated 'easy'), is justified by other poets' use of *facilis* to mean 'creative, makerly' (from Latin *facio*, 'to make'), a parallel to Greek *poetikos* (Wray 2003). But even with a less tendentious translation, the poet's personal bitterness in this passage is apparent. Harmless, peace-loving singers get a bit too near the gods and are punished for their big mouths: it is hard not to see an analogy with the avowedly harmless poet whose *carmen et error* (*Tr.* 2.207) aroused a god's wrath.

In the story of the expiation of Jupiter's thunderbolts by Numa, the king who traditionally introduced ritual practices to the Romans, Ovid manipulates the theme of sacrifice into an autobiographical fantasy with an exquisitely happy ending. While it has been noted that Numa's learning and poetic ability make him 'a sort of forerunner of Ovid himself' (Barchiesi 1997a: 111), the parallel with Ovid's own situation in exile is even closer. The episode takes place in the grove of Diana Nemorensis at Aricia (see Dyson 2001), a cult characterized by reciprocal human sacrifice and with mythical origins in Scythia, the place of Ovid's exile (see *Pont.* 3.2.45–98). Ovid, interestingly, inserts himself into the Roman landscape, claiming that he has drunk at the spring there supplied by Numa's wife Egeria (one of the Camenae, or Muses), whom he asks for inspiration (*Fast.* 3.261–76). Numa's task is to figure out how to expiate Jupiter's thunderbolts—just like Ovid's in the exile poetry, where Augustus' decree is constantly likened to the thunderbolt of Jupiter. Egeria tells her husband that he must capture the sylvan divinities Picus and Faunus to draw Jupiter down— just as Ovid attempts to enlist numerous intermediaries to soften the emperor. Numa then prays to them in words that could as easily have been spoken by Ovid in the *Tristia* (*Fast.* 3.309–11):

> 'factis ignoscite nostris,
>   si scelus ingenio scitis abesse meo,
> quoque modo possit fulmen monstrate piari.'

> 'Forgive my deeds,
>   if you know that wickedness is absent from my character [*ingenium*],
> and show the way the thunderbolt can be expiated.'

After Picus and Faunus employ their art and their *carmina* (3.323–4)—a word whose various meanings of 'songs', 'poems', and 'magical incantations' Ovid loves to exploit—the king engages Jupiter in a contest of wits and the outcome is a poet's dream come true. Jupiter aims for human sacrifice, demanding a head, then a man's head, then a life; Numa buys him off with puns, offering instead the head of an onion, the hair of a man's head, and the life of a fish (3.333–46): the ultimate triumph of words. It is no coincidence, then, that the nymph Egeria, whom Ovid invokes to tell this tale, is also the Muse who offers spring water for the poet himself to drink, a ubiquitous metaphor for poetic inspiration (see Hinds 1992b: 120). He all but asks her to show him, as she showed Numa, how to mitigate the human sacrifice and avert the thunderbolts of an all-powerful god.

The Exile Poetry: Ovid as Victim and Priest

In the *Tristia* and *Epistulae ex Ponto*, any covertness in the 'Augustus/Jupiter' analogy has vanished. The majority of the poems contain some sort of prayer for clemency, either directly or through the intervention of friends and relatives, from the terrible god whose punishment is the poet's obsession (Hardie 2002c: 34). Ovid figures himself as an epic hero plagued by a wrathful god, an equation he signals with such subtly allusive clues as 'my last night in Rome was just like the Fall of Troy' (*Tr.* 1.3; Huskey 2002) and 'my sufferings are just like—no, greater than—those of Odysseus' (*Pont.* 4.10.9–34; cf. *Tr.* 1.5.57–8, 3.11.61–2, 4.8.15–6, 4.10.107–8; Williams G. D. 2002: 236). His references to Augustus, almost invariably, are couched in terms of prayer to a god whose *numen laesum* ('wounded divinity') has driven our hero into exile. A typical example (*Tr.* 3.6.21–6):

> sis memor, et siquas fecit tibi gratia vires,
>   illas pro nobis experiare, rogo,
> numinis ut laesi fiat mansuetior ira,
>   mutatoque minor sit mea poena loco,
> idque ita, si nullum scelus est in pectore nostro,
>   principiumque mei criminis error habet.

> I beg you to remember me, and if your sway has given you
>   any strength, to use it on my behalf,
> that the wrath of the wounded divinity may be made more gentle,
>   and my penalty lightened through a change of location,
> and this, only if there's no wickedness in my heart,
>   and an error contains the source of my reproach.

This conflation of Jupiter and Juno—the *Aeneid*'s *numen laesum*, famously so designated in the proem (1.8)—is an acute comment on the *Aeneid*, in which the wills of Jupiter and Juno become not segregated but aligned by the poem's end. Ovid wavers between despair and hope that his own *pietas* (e.g. *Pont.* 4.6.19–20, 4.9.105–18) and that of the friends supplicating on his behalf (e.g. *Pont.* 4.8.3–4, 4.12.39–42, 4.15.23–4) will, like that of Aeneas, ultimately win over the wrathful gods.

Yet it is in the power of his own *ingenium* that we find, I think, the truest expression of Ovid's religious feeling. In the *Amores* and *Ars amatoria*, the idea of Ovid as *uates* was something of a joke, a sustained conceit to express the generic dueling of his early career. But the consolation he finds in his poetry near the end of his life, while still wittily expressed, contains more than flippant insouciance. With his Muses he has the sort of *odi et amo* ('I hate and I love') relationship that animates most of the erotic poets (see Williams G. D. 2002: 241–2): Ovid was exiled because of his art (e.g. *Tr.* 2.1–4)—or *Art*, the title of the offending *Ars amatoria* that allegedly caused his exile—yet that very art is what gives him solace from pain and a reason to live. He repeatedly refers to the holiness of that poetic process, as when he compares his poetic vocation of *caelestia sacra* ('heavenly sacred rites', *Tr.* 4.10.19) with that of his brother the orator, or confesses his unwilling love for those *sacra* (*Tr.* 4.1.27–30):

> non equidem uellem, quoniam nocitura fuerunt,
>   Pieridum sacris imposuisse manum.
> sed quid nunc faciam? uis me tenet ipsa sacrorum,
>   et carmen demens carmine laesus amo.

> I could wish, I suppose, since they were what was to bring me harm,
>   that I'd never laid hand on the Muses' sacred rites.
> But what should I do now? The very power of those rites holds me fast,
>   and wounded by song, in my madness, it's song that I love.

Though everything else may be taken away from him, his *ingenium* is the one thing that is truly immortal, that Caesar's wrath cannot touch (*Tr.* 3.7.43–8).

At the end of the *Amores*, Ovid said farewell to his amatory Muse because Bacchus, the god of tragedy, was beckoning him toward that higher genre. Ever his own best reader, Ovid, now steeped in the tragedy of his own exile, endows his youthful trope of Bacchic ecstasy with deeper meaning (*Tr.* 4.1.41–54):

> utque suum Bacche non sentit saucia uulnus,
>   dum stupet Idaeis exululata iugis,
> sic ubi mota calent uiridi mea pectora thyrso,
>   altior humano spiritus ille malo est.
> ille nec exilium, Scythici nec litora ponti,
>   ille nec iratos sentit habere deos.
> utque soporiferae biberem si pocula Lethes,
>   temporis aduersi sic mihi sensus abest.
> iure deas igitur ueneror mala nostra leuantes,
>   sollicitae comites ex Helicone fugae,
> et partim pelago, partim uestigia terra
>   uel rate dignatas uel pede nostra sequi.
> sint, precor, hae saltem faciles mihi! namque deorum
>   cetera cum magno Caesare turba facit . . .

And as the Bacchant, though wounded, doesn't feel her wound
    while in her trance she howls on the hills of Ida,
so when my heart is warmed and moved by the green thyrsus,
    that spirit rises above human evil.
Neither exile, nor the shores of the Scythian sea,
    nor does it feel that it has gods full of wrath.
And as if I were drinking goblets of sleep-bringing Lethe,
    so far away is my sense of the hostile times.
Rightly, then, do I worship the goddesses lightening my evils,
    solicitous comrades from Helicon in my flight,
and deigning sometimes on the sea, sometimes on the land,
    to follow my footsteps either by ship or by foot.
Let these, at least, look kindly on me! for the rest of the crowd
    of gods is taking sides with mighty Caesar . . .

However humorous the idea of Ovid as *uates*, what he says here about the exaltation of poetic inspiration, of losing and finding himself in his writing—his only defense against the evils of the world and the gods—has the ring of sincerity and truth. The deprivation of exile has broken his faith in the 'rest of the crowd' of conventional gods, who have all gone over to Caesar's side. But at the same time the poet's suffering, paradoxically, has tested and strengthened his faith in the holy, healing power of Art.

Ovid's Religion

This essay began by pointing to the unarticulated assumption that humor is not an acceptable or authentic response to the divine. Though I cannot prove this assumption false, I hope that this brief survey of Ovid's use of religion has at least served to reopen the question. The scholarly instinct to privilege seriousness over playfulness should not be allowed to obscure our appreciation of what must have been a key element of Roman religion in practice: fun. Religious festivals were, after all, the non-aristocratic Roman's chief opportunity for recreation. Even aristocratic social activities were often steeped in religion: one thinks of Julius Caesar offered the crown by a Mark Antony 'naked, anointed, and drunk' (*nudus, unctus, ebrius*) from the Lupercalia (Cic. *Phil.* 3.12), or of Augustus' infamous dinner party where the guests dressed up as the twelve Olympians (Suet. *Aug.* 70). Would it be going too far to say that flippancy and fun are not necessarily a contrast to 'real' Roman religious expression but at times an integral part of it?

There is another important way in which Ovid's wit is inseparable from his 'real' religion. In the *Fasti*, Ovid's Muses, discordant, brusque, and credulous (Barchiesi 1991; Newlands 1995: 65–85), are depicted as no more trustworthy or sublime than any of the other all-too-human deities in his works. Nevertheless, in his lifelong love/hate relationship with his own Muse, we see the closest thing in Ovid to a life-altering, personal relationship with divinity. The disparity between his caricature of the anthropomorphized deity and the ardor with which Ovid worships her should, I think, give us pause in making generalizations about the emotional emptiness of Roman religion—and of Ovid's playfulness. It is the Muse who gives his life meaning, whom he loves beyond all others, for whom he has given up his fatherland, and who will ultimately bring him immortality. His determination to make poetry under all circumstances reflects an unwavering sense of purpose, a quest for transcendence and beauty in a dark world, that resembles religious fervor. His declaration to Cupid at the beginning of his works, 'We *uates* are the Muses' crowd, not yours', turns out to be a vatic utterance indeed. He stands as a martyr, not to a conventional religion, but to poetry.

FURTHER READING

On Roman religion, Beard (1987), Beard et al. (1998), Feeney (1998), King (2003), and Scheid (2003) are a good starting place. Solodow (1988) and Feeney (1991) have insightful remarks about the gods in the *Metamorphoses*, as does Hardie (2002c) about the exile poetry. On the *Fasti*, all the essays in *Arethusa* 25 (1992), 'Reconsidering Ovid's *Fasti*', are useful, along with Miller (1991), Scheid (1992), Herbert-Brown (1994), Newlands (1995), and Barchiesi (1997a).

PART II

Texts

CHAPTER FIVE

The *Amores*: Ovid Making Love

In memoriam Guy Lee

Joan Booth

Introduction

Fifty or so poems in three books that the Victorian age found morally and artistically wanting (Sellar 1892: 324–30), the mid-twentieth century found frankly funny (seminally, Reitzenstein 1935; Wilkinson 1955: 44–82; contra Fränkel 1945: 11–35) and the present day finds highly sophisticated and endlessly polysemous (Hardie 2002c: 30–61; Miller 2004a: 160–83). What is it about Ovid's *Amores* ('Loves')— and their interpreters—that makes for such diverse and changing reactions? I have allowed the question to shape this chapter.

Components: Surprise, Sex, and Scherzando

I begin, traditionally, at the beginning (*Am.* 1.1.1–2):

> Arma graui numero uiolentaque bella parabam
> edere, materia conueniente modis.

> Arms in solemn meter and violent wars I was set
> to produce, with subject matching measures.

A surprise, to say the least, to find a book of poems entitled *Amores*—a title already used for a (now lost) collection of love-elegies by Cornelius Gallus (Cairns 2006: 30–2)—opening with the self-same word (*arma*) as Virgil's *Aeneid*. What immediately follows is equally unexpected (*Am.* 1.1.3–4):

> par erat inferior uersus; risisse Cupido
> dicitur atque unum surripuisse pedem.

> The lower line was equal*: Cupid laughed,
> they say, and filched a foot.

*i.e. equal in length to the one above, and thus supposedly a second hexameter

So starts the playful story of how the poet came to write about love in elegiac couplets (alternating lines of six and five feet) rather than about war in epic hexameters. Already there is a sample of Ovid's trademark verbal wit: the near-oxymoron of calling 'equal' something that is *inferior* (potentially = 'of lesser quality' as well as 'lower in position'). The aspiring composer of high-flown verse then tells how he remonstrated with Cupid for meddling and protested that he did not have the right material for love elegy: 'either a boy or a girl with coiffed long hair' (20). Thereupon Cupid settled the matter instantaneously by shooting him with one of his love-inducing arrows: '"Here's something for you to sing about, bard (*uates*)", he said' (24). End of story.

Except, of course, that it isn't: it is only the beginning. Or is it? A *different* story seems to begin in the following poem, which opens with the narrator wondering why he cannot sleep (*Am.* 1.2.5–8):

> nam, puto, sentirem, si quo temptarer amore—
> an subit et tecta callidus arte nocet?
> sic erit: haeserunt tenues in corde sagittae,
> et possessa ferus pectora uersat Amor.

> For I would know, I think, if I were under attack from love—
> or does it sneak up craftily and do damage under cover?
> Yes! That must be it: slim arrows have lodged in my heart,
> and savage Love is harassing the breast he's made his own.

'Well, of course that's it! Haven't you just told us precisely how it happened?' So may the reader well retort. The narrator, though, could equally well counter: 'Yes, but, as a poet, I'm doing only what I've been compelled to do: to start afresh.' Yet what he does next is still astonishing to anyone with a conventional view of erotic passion: he weighs up the pros and cons of resistance *versus* submission before finally deciding in favor of submission. He pictures his subjugation by way of an imaginary Roman triumph with Cupid as the *triumphator* in a golden chariot, accompanied by 'Flattery, Delusion and Madness' (*Blanditiae . . . Errorque Furorque*, 35) as his lieutenants, and himself as a chained and wounded prisoner in the procession alongside 'Common Sense . . . and Shame [*Mens Bona . . . et Pudor*] and all Love's adversaries' (31–2). He ends with an appeal to Cupid to spare his life, citing a forceful precedent (*Am.* 1.2.51–2):

> aspice cognati felicia Caesaris arma:
> qua uicit, uictos protegit ille manu.

> Look at the happy outcome of your kinsman Caesar's warring:
> *his* conquering hand protects the folk he's conquered.

The Julian family liked to derive its descent from Jupiter via Venus and Aeneas. Cupid, as the son of Venus by an unknown father, was thus related to Caesar Augustus.

'My prayer is just [*iusta precor*],' he continues. But the prayer is a different one. These words open the third poem, where the speaker begs a girl who has recently hooked (*praedata*) him to return his love or, at least, accept it. Riches and high pedigree he cannot offer, but lifelong devotion, divine backing, and good character he can (*Am.* 1.3.11–14):

> at Phoebus comitesque nouem uitisque repertor
> > hac faciunt et me qui tibi donat Amor
> et nulli cessura fides, sine crimine mores,
> > nudaque simplicitas purpureusque pudor.

> But Phoebus and his nine companions and the vine's discoverer
> > are with me and Love, who gives me to you,
> and inalienable faith, unblemished morals,
> > naked sincerity and crimson shame.

'Shame', one of 'Love's adversaries' (*Am.* 1.2.31–2), has now become one of the lover's assets: it all depends on your viewpoint, apparently. The lover's most valuable asset, however, is his poetic ability (*Am.* 1.3.19–20):

> te mihi materiem felicem in carmina praebe
> > prouenient causa carmina digna sua.

> Hand yourself to me as promising matter for poems,
> > and poems will result that do their subject proud.

Just as the heroines Io, Leda, and Europa owed their fame to verse, he tells his addressee (*Am.* 1.3.25–6),

> nos quoque per totum pariter cantabimur orbem
> > iunctaque semper erunt nomina nostra tuis.

> we too shall be sung together the whole world over,
> > and forever linked my name will be with yours.

Romantic at last? But we do not know what *her* name is!

Nor do we know the name of girl addressed at the start of the next poem (*Am.* 1.4.1–2; trans. Lee 1968):

> Vir tuus est epulas nobis aditurus easdem:
> > ultima cena tuo sit precor illa uiro.

> Your husband? Going to the same dinner as us?
> > I hope it chokes him!

Whether the *uir* is supposed to be 'husband' rather than 'partner' in the modern sense is debatable (Armstrong 2005: 66–70; a symbolic reading of the ambiguity is supplied by Miller 2004a: 184), but the relationship clearly prevents open sexual contact between the girl and the speaker. He therefore instructs her in a code of secret signs by means of which he and she can still communicate at the dinner table in the presence of the *uir*. Eventually, however, he acknowledges the inevitable (*Am.* 1.4.59–64):

> me miserum! monui, paucas quod prosit in horas;
> > separor a domina nocte iubente mea.
> nocte uir includet; lacrimis ego maestus obortis,
> > qua licet, ad saeuas prosequar usque fores.
> oscula iam sumet, iam non tantum oscula sumet:
> > quod mihi das furtim, iure coacta dabis.

> Alas, my advice is good for but a few short hours:
> > Night bids separation from my mistress.
> At night your man will lock you in; with welling tears, I sadly
> > will escort you where I can: as far as the cruel door.
> Now he will take kisses, now at kisses will not stop:
> > what you give me in secret you'll give him because you must.

How *can* the poor fellow bear it? Quite easily: 'Whatever happens tonight, just keep telling me tomorrow that you didn't oblige' (69–70).

Still, the satisfaction that night denies to the lover-narrator day apparently brings (reference to the addressee as 'my mistress' already at *Am.* 1.4.60 is perhaps not mere wishful thinking after all). Here is poem 5 complete (in Lee's 1968 translation; critical analysis of Lee's version and several others is given by Rudd 1976: 199–210):

> Siesta time in sultry summer.
> I lay relaxed on the divan.

> One shutter closed, the other ajar,
> made sylvan semi-darkness,

> a glimmering dusk, as after sunset,
> or between night's end and day's beginning—

> the half light shy girls need
> to hide their hesitation.

> At last, Corinna. On the loose in a short dress,
> long hair parted and tumbling past the pale neck—

> lovely as Lais of the many lovers,
> Queen Semiramis gliding in.

> I grabbed the dress; it didn't hide much,
> but she fought to keep it,

> only half-heartedly though.
> Victory was easy, a self-betrayal.

> There she stood, faultless beauty
> in front of me, naked.

Shoulders and arms challenging eyes and fingers.
Nipples firmly demanding attention.

Breasts in high relief above the smooth belly.
Long and slender waist. Thighs of a girl.

Why list perfection?
I hugged her tight.

The rest can be imagined—we fell asleep.
Such afternoons are rare.

This is 'making love' literally—almost. A near-cinematic sex scene, at any rate. First, a slow-paced panning around the location: the narrator lies alone in a room darkened against the heat of noon (the time of day, *mediam . . . horam*, is explicit in the Latin). A sudden change of focus: enter 'Corinna', stunningly beautiful, flimsily dressed. Next, a fast action-sequence: he tears off her frock (though she puts up a token resistance), surveys the perfection of her naked body from shoulder to thigh, hungrily presses her to himself. Then . . . cut! Use your imagination (25, *cetera quis nescit?*, lit. 'Who does not know the rest?')! Finally, forward to a quick shot of the aftermath: sleep following their exertions. In a forthcoming paper I compare the scene of Katharine's afternoon visit to Almásy in Antony Minghella's film version (1996) of Michael Ondaatje's novel *The English Patient* (1992). Despite this visual technique, however, the poem's format is still first-person narrative, with all the action in the past tense (or historic present) except for the narrator's closing wish for more of the same (26, *proveniant medii sic mihi saepe dies!*, 'May such noontimes often come my way!').

As it happens, the first five poems of the collection outlined above well exemplify the basic ingredients of the *Amores*: a lover and his lass, a rival lover, sexual passion, contemporary setting in Augustan Rome, mythological illustration, poetry itself. And these ingredients are no different from those of most (earlier) Tibullan and Propertian Latin love elegy. So what did Victorian scholars miss in Ovid that they thought they could see in the others, especially Propertius? Decency? Ovid is never verbally vulgar, but his open salaciousness in *Am.* 1.5 predictably incurred disapproval (Sellar 1892: 328), and his occasional physicality elsewhere was largely passed over in silence. So, for example, claim to unlimited sexual stamina at *Am.* 2.10.23ff., meditation on impotence in *Am.* 3.7, and the speaker's fantasized erection when, after envisaging metamorphosis into his girl's signet ring, he imagines the effect of being worn by her as she bathes in the nude (*Am.* 2.15.25–6; quite the opposite of Victorian reticence in Rivero Garcia's study (2004) of *Am.* 2.15):

sed, puto, te nuda mea membra libidine surgent,
    et peragam partes anulus ille uiri.

But, when you're naked, I think, my member will rise in lust
    And I, that ring, will act out the role of a man.

It was, however, in conveying the feeling supposed to be engendered by a unique beloved that Ovid was most found wanting. Readers of the five poems sketched above will quickly see why—especially if they come to them straight from Propertius' first book, where the opening elegies are devoted to introducing Cynthia, the beautiful, accomplished, and imperious woman with whom the Propertian lover is obsessed.

In Ovid's first two poems there is not a beloved in sight, only the warring Cupid. The third poem introduces a desired girl, but as an entirely featureless figure. The fourth adds the detail of her unavailability, but nothing more. The fifth gives her at last a name and a body, but no face (contrast the very first line of Propertius' first book: 'Cynthia first captured wretched me with her eyes'). Nowhere in the *Amores* is Corinna appreciated for anything but her sex appeal, and, despite occasional focusing on her hair (1.14; see below) and complexion (2.5.33–42), she remains an empty outline. In the last poem of Book 2 she has been displaced by another (2.19.9–10), and in Book 3 she is eclipsed altogether: the sexy legs (3.2.27–32), long hair, peaches-and-cream complexion, dainty feet, tall, slim figure, and sparkling eyes (3.3.3–10) that we glimpse there (divine face and ravishing eyes again at 3.11.47–8) are not hers.

Was Corinna even Ovid's girl at all? Over a century ago it was already suspected not. She is apparently named after a sixth-century BC (or later) female Greek lyrist, though the name is alternatively explained as cognate with *korē*, the Greek for 'girl' (McKeown 1987: 21; Armstrong 2005: 53–7). The lack of personality and inconsistently portrayed situation of the principal beloved (as good as married to another man in *Am.* 1.4 and to the narrator himself in *Am.* 2.5, 'run' by a brothel-mistress (*lena*) in *Am.* 1.8, apparently living independently in *Am.* 2.7 and 2.8) underscore the text's own hint that she is fictitious (*Am.* 3.12.43–4): *et mea debuerat falso laudata uideri / femina* 'My praising of the woman should have been seen as a lie' (Hardie 2002c: 6–7; *Am.* 2.17.29–30 is often read similarly, but wrongly so: Booth 1991:8–9). Significantly, the list of elegiac aliases supposedly unmasked by Apuleius (*Apol.* 10) does not include the Ovidian Corinna.

The lover-narrator himself in the *Amores* remains cheerfully amoral. He is prepared both to profess lifelong fidelity (1.3) and to confess to incorrigible promiscuity (2.4); quick to berate a compliant rival for spoiling his sport (2.19) and an obstructive one for being a prig (3.4). He is content to be lied to when confronted with his girl's unchastity (e.g. 1.4, 2.5, 2.11.53–4, 3.14) and to lie shamelessly when taxed with his own: *Am.* 2.7 is an outburst of righteous indignation at being accused of bedding Corinna's slave-hairdresser, Cypassis, but is followed by immediate blackmail of Cypassis in private when she refuses to oblige him again (*Am.* 2.8.27–8):

> quoque loco tecum fuerim quotiensque, Cypassi,
>   narrabo dominae quotque quibusque modis.

> And, Cypassis, I shall tell your mistress where I had you,
>   and how often, and in how many and what kinds of ways.

He dares to trivialize both his own violence in the course of a lover's row (1.7.67–8) and his girl's distress after a hairdressing accident that left her (temporarily) bald (1.14.55, 'Fix your face, and chin up: the damage is reparable'). For a generation more romantic as well as more prudish than our own, this was the work of an outrageous cad or else the pointless invention of an emotionally shallow mind. In either case, it was not the expected stuff of proper love poetry.

But need the *un*expected be inferior? So asked the post-Victorian rehabilitators of the *Amores*. All Roman love elegy contains much thematic material that is standard (e.g. separation of lovers by a locked house door, control of the beloved by a madam (*lena*), illness of the beloved). Tibullus and Propertius were nonetheless enduringly believed to have invested their stock situations and images (many inherited from Hellenistic Greek epigram and/or New Comedy) with at least emotional verisimilitude when transferring them to the social setting of first-century BC Rome; even a degree of authentic self-portrayal was not ruled out. The text of the *Amores*, however, itself strongly hints at the narrator's lack of interest in depicting unique and personal experience and emotion (*Am.* 2.1.7–10):

> atque aliquis iuuenum, quo nunc ego, saucius arcu
> agnoscat flammae conscia signa suae
> miratusque diu 'quo' dicat 'ab indice doctus
> composuit casus iste poeta meos?'

> And let some youth, wounded by the same bow as I am now,
> recognize the telltale signs of his own flame
> and in enduring astonishment say 'From what source has
> that poet learned to write about *my* troubles?'

Hence the contention that Ovid applied his virtuoso talent to turning love elegy into comedy in the *Amores*, inventing for himself as lover an absurdly unbelievable *persona* (literally 'mask'; Clay 1998), by means of which *he* could clown it where his amatory poetic predecessors had played it straight (Wilkinson 1955: 44–82; Du Quesnay 1973).

Demonstrably true, too—up to a point. Take, for example, the motif of love's slavery (*seruitium amoris*). The masochistic note sounded when this is deployed by the other elegists to convey the lover-narrator's degradation (e.g. Tib. 2.4.1–6) or obsession (e.g. Prop. 2.13.39–40) is conspicuously absent from the *Amores*. In its place comes the same humorously insouciant pragmatism as is shown in *Am.* 1.2.19–20 in the face of Cupid's attack (*Am.* 2.17.1–4):

> Si quis erit, qui turpe putet seruire puellae,
> illo conuincar iudice turpis ego.
> sim licet infamis, dum me moderatius urat
> quae Paphon et fluctu pulsa Cythera tenet.

> If anyone thinks it disgraceful to be enslaved to a girl,
> I'll go down in his judgment as a disgrace.
> I wouldn't mind the notoriety, if only she'd burn me less fiercely—
> she who holds sway in Paphos and wave-lashed Cythera.

The topic of (attempted) renunciation of love is similarly repackaged. From Ovid we get nothing that can be mistaken for genuine pathos, self-loathing, or bitterness on

the lover's part (cf. Tib. 1.5.1–8, 2.6.9–14; Prop. 3.24, 3.25), still less any psychologically convincing vacillation or mental conflict (cf. Cat. 8, a poem in lyric, not
elegiac, meter, but nevertheless comparable in sentiment; also Cat. 76). His first
tackling of the topic begins with an entertaining petition to Commanding Officer
Cupid ('commissioned' already in *Am.* 1.9; see below) for final and honorable dis-
charge from his service (*Am.* 2.9.1–24). An unheralded volte-face follows in *Am.*
2.9.25–54 (probably a separate poem, '9B'), with the observation that 'women are
such sweet hell' (26, trans. Lee). Verbal reminiscence of Tibullus 1.5.3–4 *agor
ut … turben* ('I am driven like a spinning top') at *Am.* 2.9.28 *turbine mentis agor*
('I am driven by a mental whirlwind') encourages reading as mild mockery of the
Tibullan lover's pain. A second handling of the renunciation topic in *Am.* 3.11 metes
out similar treatment to Catullus, agonizing over Lesbia. Announcing his decision
to break with an unnamed woman (*Am.* 3.11.1–32), the Ovidian lover tells himself,
'Go through with it, and stand firm' (7, *perfer et obdura*), clearly echoing Catullus
8.11: 'with mind made up, stand firm' (*obstinata mente perfer, obdura*). But the
context of facetious self-review in which Ovid's near-quotation is embedded arguably
undermines its original Catullan earnestness (a more intricately multivalent interpretation is given by Barchiesi 2001a: 155–9). Here too an immediate sequel, at *Am.*
3.11.33–52, probably also a separate poem, '11B' (the disputed unity of both 2.9
and 3.11 is largely academic, since the two parts of each pair gain much from being
read consecutively), presents sudden second thoughts. These take the form of a pretended conflict in the lover's mind between love and hate, but actually the final
decision in favor of love is from the start (33–4) never in doubt, and the passage's
bravura display of scintillating wit is at odds with any real pain (contrast Cat. 85).
Lee's translation of *Am.* 3.11B is worth quoting in full for its brilliant representation
of the flavor of the original Latin:

> Love and hate, here in my heart, at tug of war—
> and love I suppose will find a way to win.

> I'd sooner hate. If I can't, I'll be the reluctant lover—
> the dumb ox bearing the yoke he loathes.

> Your behavior drives me away, your beauty draws me back.
> I adore your face and abhor your failings.

> With or without you, life's impossible
> and I can't decide what I want.

> Why can't you be less lovely or more true?
> Why must your faults and your figure clash?

> I love what you are and hate what you do—
> but your self, alas, outweighs your selfishness.

> By the bed we shared, by all the gods
> who let you take their names in vain,

> by your face my holy icon, by your eyes that ravished mine,
> take pity on me.

Be what you will, you'll still be mine—but you must choose—
do you want me to love you or be forced to?

Make life plain sailing for me please
by helping me love what I can't help loving.

Why, then, is the mid-twentieth-century reading of the *Amores* as a highly amusing send-up of love and earlier poetry about love less than completely satisfying?
Boyd rightly addresses the question (1997: *passim*, especially 9–18), but still seeks
a somewhat reductive answer in Ovid's alleged 'intentions'. Consider a few specific
features.

First, the presentation of love as a form of soldiering (*militia amoris*). Ovid devotes
a whole poem (*Am.* 1.9) to this, supposedly to demonstrate the validity of the lover-
narrator's opening proposition (1–2):

Militat omnis amans, et habet sua castra Cupido;
    Attice, crede mihi, militat omnis amans.

Every lover is a soldier, and Cupid has his own camp;
    Atticus, take my word for it: every lover is a soldier.

Every conceivable aspect of the lover's existence is then likened to the soldier's; for
example both occupations are for the young and fit, not the old or lazy, both involve
guard duty and assault—in a military camp and against enemy positions, or on a
beloved's cold, hard doorstep and against a disobligingly locked front door. With an
exhaustiveness and ingenuity of argument that owes much to declamatory technique,
the basic ludicrousness of the idea is entertainingly pointed (not, apparently, for
Armstrong (2005: 136–7), who comes close to taking the argument seriously). Yet
this is hardly a debunking of earlier deployments of the motif: no one would judge
the spirit of its much briefer appearances in Tibullus (1.1.75–6) and Propertius
(1.6.29–30) to be anything but humorous.

Next, there is the predicament of the locked-out lover (*exclusus amator*), already
a figure of fun in Hellenistic Greek epigram. This also is accorded a whole poem in
the *Amores* (1.6), in which the comic Ovidian protagonist addresses not the beloved
within, or even the door itself, but rather the doorkeeper, at great length and with
sparkling wit and inventiveness. But arguably the Ovidian version is not as funny as
Propertius' (1.16), in which the speaker is the door itself, complaining of what it has
to put up with from locked-out lovers and quoting an extended example of their
tedious whining.

Then there is the so-called *recusatio* ('refusal'; Lyne 1995: 31–9) exemplified in
Am. 1.1, discussed above. The famous Callimachean prototype of the scenario in
which the poet starting out to write is deflected from the grandiose by intervention
of a god is already mildly amusing (Call. *Aet.* fr. 1. 23–4):

When I first took a writing tablet upon my knees, Lycian Apollo said to me, 'Poet, make
your sacrifice as fat as possible, but your Muse, my good friend, keep slender.'

Propertius' version at 3.3.1–24—the most significant of the Augustan adaptations for Ovid's own treatment—has Apollo deem the aspiring epic poet's talent inadequate for that genre. This is still amusing, but at the same time gracefully disarming in the face of any pressure, real or imaginary, that Propertius may have felt to attempt a contemporary epic. Ovid not only heightens the humor by downgrading the interferer from Apollo to a pilfering Cupid (and in his subsequent variations still further to a disgruntled girlfriend; *Am.* 2.1.11–22, 2.18.5–12), but, by beginning with the misleading *arma* and declaring his poetic *persona* well equal to the challenge of martial epic, he also adopts in the Augustan context a more confrontational artistic position. Parody of a sort, then, perhaps, but more than just parody of a motif for its own sake.

Lastly, there is *Am.* 1.5 again. This has its own comic moment: the likening of Corinna to Semiramis (a semi-legendary Assyrian queen, noted for murdering her lovers and for her own sexual forwardness) and to Lais (the name of 'at least two famous courtesans'; McKeown 1989: 11–12.) slyly retrojects irony on to the narrator's claim of the light being suitable for 'shy' girls (7–8). And it has clear points of contact with two other elegiac poems. One is a first-century BC Greek epigram by Philodemus (*AP.* 5.132 = 12 Sider), which consists entirely of a coarser, feet-upwards (rather than Ovidian neck-downwards) appraisal of a sexy woman:

> O foot, O leg, O truly to-die-for
>   thighs, O buttocks, O pussy, O flanks,
> O shoulders, O breasts, O slender neck,
>   O hands, O eyes that I am mad about,
> O wickedly skillful movement, O fantastic
>   tongue-kisses, O—finish me off!—the darling chatter!
> Even if she *is* Oscan, and called Flora, and sings no Sappho–
>   Perseus too fell for Indian Andromeda.

The other is Propertius 2.15, in which the lover-narrator opens (1–10) by celebrating a successful night of sex with a girl who 'wrestled' (5) with him bare-breasted, now and then teasingly covering up with her chemise, kissing his eyes open when he fell asleep and taunting him with 'lying there like a laggard' (8, *sicine, lente, iaces?*). *Am.* 1.5, however, does not make fun *at the expense of* either of these poems. The same is true of its treatment of the 'epiphany' motif, common in Virgilian epic, which involves formulaic specification of hour and setting preliminary to a spectacular materialization, often of a deity and often within a dream (Nicoll 1977; Papanghelis 1989). Ovid clearly adapts the motif in *Am.* 1.5 to introduce Corinna, but not in a way that mocks its Virgilian form. There *is*, then, humor in *Am.* 1.5, and the poem does apparently have a relationship with other texts. But the two features are not connected.

Suppose, then, that none of the Augustan elegists wrote poetry to express love, but that they all confected love to write poetry—in other words, that not just Ovid in his *Amores*, but all of them, invented everything? That hypothesis rests on the premise that Roman love elegy is not mimetic but semiotic. That is, although its characters and situations may resemble those of the real world, its texts do not represent anything in that world: rather, their meaning is what the reader, as much as the author, constructs from their relation to one another and from the relation of the elegiac system as a whole to other poetic systems (seminally, Veyne 1988). Such an approach can be useful not least in liberating the *Amores* from certain long-running debates. The tired, author-centered question, for instance, of whether Ovid adopts an anti-Augustan or un-Augustan political stance (Armstrong 2005: 192 n. 81) can give way to a text-centered one: what kind of Augustus does the elegiac (as opposed to, say, the epic) perspective produce? In the case of the *Amores* (helpfully dubbed a 'para-Augustan' text: Miller 2004a: 162), it is an Augustus whose real-world political significance is edited out of the love-fixated world of the poems. At *Am.* 1.2.51–2 (quoted above), for example, his much-vaunted divine lineage and foreign conquests are seen only in terms of their potential usefulness to a lover.

More of the possibilities offered by semiotic reading are also demonstrable from *Am.* 1.5. Instead of debating whether the speaker's tone there is any more or less emotionally ingenuous than in the Propertian elegy or the epigram on the same theme, the reader may ask how the Ovidian text is informed by, interacts with, or affects the earlier ones (the 'intertextual' approach). The relative passiveness of Corinna, for instance, is underlined by the proactiveness of the Propertian girl (with her sustained fighting, teasing, and eye-kissing). The Ovidian speaker's sleeping at Corinna's side only *after* sex, compared with the Propertian lover's dropping off in mid-session, with the girl still raring to go, highlights his virility (competing, perhaps, with Catullus 32.7–8, where nine repeats in one afternoon are anticipated). The sexual innuendo in the Ovidian *et nudam pressi corpus ad usque meum* (24) arguably brings out the latent sexuality in Prop. 2.15.8 *sicine, lente, iaces?*—just as easily addressed to a flaccid *penis* as to a snoozing partner (for *iacere* in the context of impotence cf. *Am.* 3.7.4, 15, 65). The last couplet of Philodemus' epigram may betray the speaker's embarrassment by his taste for a low-class woman: the Ovidian speaker's contrasting silence is readable as a rebuke. And the 're-making', elegiac-style, of the epiphany scenario familiar from a different poetic system, with the materializing deity of Virgilian epic replaced by the object of erotic desire, subtly points something quintessentially elegiac: the quasi-divine status of the beloved in the lover's eyes. This is further hinted at in Ovid's poem by the *candida diu-* of line 10, which playfully encourages expectation (in the event, frustrated) of an echo of the designation of Catullus' Lesbia as *candida diua* ('fair goddess') at 68.70 (Hinds 1987b: 7–9).

Yet even this strategy does not end the options for a positive reading of the *Amores*. All meaning can, as the post-modern position has it, be deconstructed (I use the term loosely) by the adoption of a standpoint in some way radically opposed to a previously existing one. *Am.* 1.5 will once more provide a couple of examples. (i) The narrator's man's-eye-view can be rejected and the whole episode read from the female—indeed, the modern feminist—perspective. Denied face, voice, and personality, reduced to a mere assemblage of sexualized body parts and having her thinking done for her by the lecherous speaker, the silent Corinna can mark the poem as a shameless display of male domination (Greene 1997: 77–84, with similar interpretation of *Am.* 1.7 at 84–92; 2.11 at 95–9; 2.19, 3.4, 3.8 at 99–108; and 3.12 at 108–13). Such reading is stimulating in its challenging of Roman elegy's alleged empowering of the female (Hallett 1973; cf. Wyke 1995), but I see no reason to suppose that Ovid's conscious purpose was to expose the exploitation of women in Roman culture (Greene 1997: 113). (ii) The final couplet is less closed than it may appear. Spontaneous inclination is to read the *cetera quis nescit?* ('Who does not know the rest?') as decorous confirmation that the expected sexual intercourse took place. Yet, in the light of Propertius' attempt to *describe* the ecstasy of intercourse at 2.15.2–10, this reading of the aposiopesis (= 'speech broken off') is not inevitable. Alternatively: 'Everybody knows—what the experience itself is like; so no point in wasting words on it.' Is the whole thing even a 'delusion of desire' (Hardie 2002c: 11–13)? Most literary epiphanies are dreamed: why not this one and its outcome too, including the blissful sleep in the aftermath? Anyone who would object that such a reading is precluded by the final wish for more of the same should consider the anonymous Greek epigram at *AP* 5.2: there a man tells how he dreamed that an expensive prostitute spent the night with him for nothing—which turned out to be just as good as the real thing, and a lot cheaper.

Now, it seems to me unprovable—and inherently unlikely—that the Romans themselves read all love elegy semiotically or deconstructively. Nevertheless, theory-based approaches, in asking what a text makes possible, rather than encouraging a quest for the author's definitive 'message(s)', have done much to prevent the ossification of critical opinion on the *Amores*. At times I underrated their potential (I now think) in my own commentary on Book 2 (Booth 1991), and I therefore take in this chapter a less conservative line.

Cohesion: Erotic Story and (Meta)poetic Statement?

After pulling the *Amores* apart in the attempt to explore and account for some of the collection's ever-changing faces and fortunes, it is now time to put it together again. Does the *arrangement* of poems itself make sense? Indirectly, I have already raised this question by intimating that *Am.* 1.1–5, though all apparently self-contained, are not unsusceptible to serial connection. But how about the collection as a whole? Some juxtaposed poems clearly deal with two successive phases of the same action: *Am.* 1.11 and 1.12 (sending of written message via a maid pressing Corinna to come, followed by abuse of courier and writing tablets when she has refused); 2.2 and 2.3 (polite request to a eunuch guard for access to the girl he chaperones, followed by rude riposte when he has refused); 2.7 and 2.8 (the Cypassis affair); 2.13 and 2.14 (fear for Corinna's life after she has aborted a child he thinks was his, followed by a sermon on her wickedness when she has recovered). Yet poems that depict the same situation from opposing viewpoints are placed far apart in different books: *Am.* 1.4. and 2.5; 1.3 and 2.4. Controversy surrounds the number of both poems and books. Fifteen elegies in Book 1, twenty in Book 2 and fifteen in Book 3? Perhaps. But the round and balanced figures emerge only from division of both *Am.* 2.9 and 3.11 into two and excision of *Am.* 3.5—long regarded as spurious because of its separate transmission and some stylistic oddities (Kenney 1969a), but also periodically defended (Bretzigheimer 2001: 263–72). An alternative construction retains 3.5 and accepts 3.11 as a single poem (Holzberg 2002: 61–3). A four-line prefatory epigram to the *Amores* makes the claim that the author has reduced an original five-book edition to the present three-book one—to give 'more pleasure or, at least, less pain', as he puts it. All these factors have led to endless debate. Did Ovid use the opportunity offered by a second edition to rearrange his selected poems over three books in an elaborate architectural pattern or on the principle of artful disorder (*variatio*)? Did reduction of the collection to his 'best' poems leave perhaps him with a surplus of openers—which would account for the double—if not triple—start in *Am.* 1.1–2 and 3 (so Cameron 1968; contra Moles 1991)? Did he write any new poems for the second edition? In *Am.* 2.18 the narrator tells how his attempt to compose tragedy was frustrated by his disgruntled girlfriend sitting on his knee; he therefore decided to content himself for the time being with 'the arts of love' (19, *artes . . . amoris*) and writing letters from mythological heroines to the men who have deserted them (apparently the 'single' *Heroides*). On grounds that the 'arts' point to the contemporaneous existence of the *Ars amatoria*, this poem has been canvassed as 'second-edition only' composition (McKeown 1998: 385–6). But did the second edition ever actually exist, or was the claim that it did just a witty fiction designed to act out an unexpectedly literal form of adherence to the Callimachean poetic principle of 'less is more' (so Barchiesi 2001a: 159–6; Holzberg 2002: 33)? The last, iconoclastic, question is no more definitively answerable than the others, but it is useful. For in steering attention away from preoccupation with the patterning (or lack of it) that supposedly results from *re*arrangement of the *Amores*, it makes sustained linear reading of the existing arrangement attractive; we should at least consider what the text as we have it can deliver (Boyd 1997: 136).

Holzberg (2002: 46–70) sees two intertwined linear threads holding the collection together, one essentially mimetic (though fictive) and the other essentially semiotic. His mimetic thread is a love-*story* ('erotic novel'): a comic narrative of the amatory experiences of a central fictional character, who progresses from suspecting his girl of infidelity (Book 1), through aspiring to being a Don Juan himself (Book 2), to accepting the loss of his original beloved (Book 3; in *Am.* 3.2, a racy episode at the races, he is already shamelessly chatting up a new pretty girl in the next seat). The semiotic thread posited is 'metapoetic' (that is, it says something about poetry itself). It depends not only on the text's direct references to poetry but also on its identification of the beloved and/or (parts of) her body with poetic subject-matter or poetic *oeuvre*—an elegiac phenomenon explored in relation to Propertius' Cynthia in a landmark paper by Wyke (1987) and to the *Amores* by Keith (1994/5). The metapoetic element is claimed to be both integrated with the story of frustrated amatory ambition and in tension with it. Integrated, in that the love poet travels a course in poetry comparable to that traveled by the lover in love, first committing to love elegy (Book 1), then toying with the idea of defection to other genres (Book 2), and finally bidding love elegy farewell (Book 3). In tension (especially in Book 1), in that the poet's retention of control over his elegiac brief pulls against the lover's threatened loss of control over the beloved—a tension resolved only at the end of Book 3 with the ultimate relinquishing of both. Boyd (1997: 132–64) takes a similar view, but she calls both the 'lover' and the 'poet' character 'Ovid' and declares the metapoetic narrative the 'dominant plot' of the *Amores* (165).

I sketch Holzberg's reading (2002: 46–53) of *Am.* 1 in a little more detail pre-liminary to further discussion (the purpose of the embedded quotation of his words will emerge shortly). First, the 'erotic novel'. Phase 1 (first steps): the fictional lover is reluctantly created (poem 1), accepts his role (poem 2), finds himself something to love (poem 3), overcomes a snag ['when we read the instructions . . . on how to hoodwink her current lover, we cannot help but think that they will later backfire on her new one'] (poem 4; with a forward glance at *Am.* 2.5), and finally gets what he wants (poem 5). Phase 2 (setback and suspicion): the lover is locked out of the girl's house (poem 6), they have quarreled ['why?'], and he has hit her (poem 7), he overhears a disreputable old madam (*lena*) urging the girl to favor a rich admirer above her poverty-stricken poet [this 'confirms the reasonable suspicion that he has a rival'] (poem 8), he boasts of his prowess as a soldier of love ['nothing but an . . . attempt to flee reality'] (poem 9), before warning the girl that her grasping ways ['learned . . . only from consorting with a rich man'] have changed his attitude toward her (poem 10). Phase 3 (renewed effort, setback, and success): the lover writes begging the girl to come (poem 11) and receives a refusal (poem 12), [but] he is next seen lying in bed with her, cursing the arrival of dawn (poem 13), he delivers an insensitive sermon on her folly when her hair has fallen out through her using ['so much'] dye [which 'revives our suspicions that his beloved is interested in another man'] (poem 14), before ending with a ['crowing'] prediction of his immortal fame as a love poet (poem 15).

Second, the metapoetic narrative in *Am.* 1. Holzberg finds it partly in *hair*. In poem 1 the 'coiffed long hair' (20) of the still non-existent beloved symbolizes for him the stylistically refined manner of small-scale elegy that the aspiring epic poet resists. In poem 3 the unnamed girl is read as elegiac subject-matter and the speaker's bold approach to her as acceptance of the love-elegist's task. Poem 5, with the con-quest of a named girl's body, sees him truly on his poetic way. (Corinna here, I observe, has no feet. Is this because those of a woman who doubles as 'elegy' could *not*, unlike the rest of her, be perfect? Cf. *Am.* 3.1.8–10.) Back to the girl's hair in poem 7. The lover's disarranging of it during the quarrel (11) and his ultimate plea that it be put straight again (67–8) Holzberg (2002: 53) reads as follows: 'Now that I have shown that I can write like a *poeta furens* ('raging' [*sc.* 'undisciplined'] poet') when I want to, I will again impose the ordered forms of Alexandrian poetics on my work.' Lastly, praise of the fine qualities of the girl's hair in its unadulterated state (poem 14; a different interpretation by Zetzel 1996) is taken as reaffirmation of the elegist's adherence to Callimachean principles of slender poetic composition. Meta-poetic interpretations of *Am.* 1.1–5 are pursued by Hardie (2002c: 32–45) and Buchan (1995: 56–62); of *Am.* 1.8 by Gross (1996: 205); of *Am.* 1.11 and 1.12 by Fitzgerald (2000: 69–62).

My purpose here is not to debate the plausibility of Holzberg's (or any other) individual reading. It is rather to use it as an extended example of what an interactive reader can find in the way of cohesion in the *Amores*. All remarks quoted within square brackets above are crucial to the linear thread that Holzberg traces, but none is based on anything explicit *in* the text. Yet nothing *in* the text precludes such a reader-constructed story either. If it is regarded as open to creative reading, further possibilities for 'making' sense of the order and nature of Ovid's 'making' of love in the *Amores* suggest themselves. For example, contrast between the events of (generally unhappy) night and (generally fulfilling) day is particularly strong in the sequence of poems at *Am.* 1.4–6, and in fact the two times roughly alternate (like the emotional ups-and-downs of a love affair?) through the entire first book. Day is the declared setting for poem 5, and the assumed one for poems 3, 7, 8, 10, and 14, while night is similarly the declared setting for poems 2 and 6 and the point of reference for poems 9 (l. 45), 11 (l. 14) and 12; poem 13 is interestingly liminal, dealing with the ending of a (for once, happy) night and the approach of (unwelcome) day. As for the whole collection, it seems to me that Book 1 is centered on the bedroom (his or hers), with the central poem, 8, quite literally liminal: the lover skulking by the bedroom door overhears the diatribe of the *lena* inside. Book 2 extends the perspective to the world outside the bedroom, mostly still within the city, but with occasional glimpses of non-urban horizons beyond: in poem 11 Corinna is planning a voyage overseas, and in poem 16 the lover himself has already withdrawn to his native Paelignian Sulmo. Book 3 inverts the spatial focus of Book 1. It opens with another epiphany (recalling *Am.* 1.5, the bedroom-poem *par excellence*), but *two* female figures now materialize: the personified Elegy and Tragedy, competing for the poet's allegiance (Wyke 1989; Hunter 2006b: 28–40). The setting is numinous rustic space: ancient wood, sacred stream, water-sculpted grotto, and sweetly singing birds (*Am.* 3.1.1–4). Such locations are conventionally associated with poetic inspiration, but the immediate shift to the rustic outdoors at the start of this book arguably foreshadows the elegiac poet's farewell to the poetry of the bedroom at the end (*Am.* 3.15). Only one poem in Book 3 is clearly set *in* the bedroom: the lover-narrator's experience of impotence—and with a girl who is not Corinna (*Am.* 3.7). This poem has been interpreted metapoetically as a pointer to failing elegiac commitment (Sharrock 1995; Armstrong 2005: 41–3), and it is attractive to read similarly others that puzzle by their presence in *Am.* 3, especially those which also have a rustic, outdoor setting. Can the swelling stream (made the pretext for recounting amatory river-myths) that the lover-narrator repeatedly attempts to cross in 3.6 to reach his girl stand for the grander poetic genres destined to obstruct further love elegy (Barchiesi 2001a: 54–5; Boyd 1997: 213–19)? Will 3.10, an account of the rural festival of Ceres, and 3.13, the narrator's outing with his wife (yes, wife!) to the festival of Juno at Falerii, act as trailers for the *Fasti* (Armstrong 2005: 147)? And what of *Am.* 3.12.31–40? 'We poets', says the speaker there (trans. Lee),

> made a flint of Niobe, a she-bear of Callisto,
> a mournful nightingale of Philomela,

> turned Jupiter to feathers and showers of gold
> and bulls in the ocean with virgins on their backs.

Add Proteus, and the Theban dragon's teeth,
fire-breathing oxen,

Phaethon's amber-weeping sisters,
ships transformed to nymphs.

Though part of an amatory (and non-rustic) poem, could this offer just a hint of the future *Metamorphoses*? Perhaps (cf. Boyd 1997: 203–23). But for all that metapoetic reading of the *Amores* usefully offers—or challenges—interpretation of particularly enigmatic poems (the funeral laments for Corinna's pet parrot (2.6) and for the elegist Tibullus (3.9), though not discussed here, come high on the list; see Boyd 1987, updated in 2006), not every difficulty is explained away by it. One, indeed, is created by it, and by modern theoretical approaches in general. If their logic be pressed, the poet in the *Amores* will not be Ovid-the-author any more than the lover is Ovid-the-man, such resemblance as there is between the two being coincidental and insignificant. In practice, of course, critics of all persuasions tend to be willing to identify the narrator of the *Amores* with the historical Ovid whenever he wears the poet's hat (explicitly or implicitly), but not when he wears the lover's—even though he sometimes wears both simultaneously, as, for example, in *Am.* 2.1 (Armstrong recognizes the problem (2005: 46–8)—but (136) still calls both poet and lover 'Ovid'!).

This, then, is the collection in which Ovidius Naso (sometimes) plays himself as he makes and fakes love. Literary making and faking can amount to much the same thing. 'Play' in the *Amores* is both acting and fun. And what Ovid's text makes possible is more than what it says. A teasing, shifting element of doubleness in my remarks? Such is the essence of the poems themselves (Hardie 2002c).

FURTHER READING

The *Oxford Classical Text* by E. J. Kenney (revised ed. 1994, with corrections 1995) is the standard Latin text of the *Amores*. McKie (1986) will fascinate those interested in the history of the text. McKeown's large-scale commentary (with general introduction: 1987) already covers Book 1 (1989) and Book 2 (1998); his commentary on Book 3 is still awaited (in the meantime Brandt's German commentary of 1911 remains of some use for this book). Barsby (1973) offers a running commentary (a passing fashion of its time) on Book 1, and Booth (1991) a compact but multi-purpose one on Book 2. The best English translation is Lee's inspired poetic version of 1968 (reissued in 2000 as *Ovid in Love*, with the added attraction of superbly sensual illustrations by John Ward). Melville's version of 1990 is also acceptable. Monographs on the *Amores* alone are relatively few: in the last decade, Boyd (1997), Bretzigheimer (2001) and De Caro (2003). Holzberg (2002: especially 46–70) and Armstrong (2005) offer the most lively and universally readable treatments of the *Amores* within recent general books on Ovid. Less immediately approachable, but highly original and stimulating, is Hardie's (2002c) integration of the *Amores* into his reading of the whole Ovidian *oeuvre* as a meditation on absence and presence. Among essays and articles, the overview of Lee (1962) is an outstanding 'period piece' of its kind; most newer studies address specific aspects of the *Amores* (sometimes in combination with the *Ars*): Sharrock (2002a) deals with gender and sexuality (gendered readings also by Greene 1997: 67–113; James, S. L. 2003: 155–211), Davis (1999) with politics, and Volk (2005) with the Ovidian persona. Time was when Ovid's *Amores*, rather like the first two symphonies of Beethoven, was treated discretely from the works that followed. This has been replaced by a growing awareness of its role in Ovid's overall generic development: Albrecht (2000), Gildenhard and Zissos (2000), and Harrison (2002). Marlowe's version of the *Amores* (ca. 1582) whets the appetite for its reception, and Stapleton (1996) provides an excellent introduction to this topic. Myers (1999) surveys work on the *Amores* in the 1980s and 1990s; Coletti (1981) and Martyn (1981) survey work up to 1978.

CHAPTER SIX

The *Heroides*: Female Elegy?

Laurel Fulkerson

Introduction

The *Heroides* are two series of mythological letters written in elegiac couplets, the first a group of fifteen written by women to men they have been or would like to be romantically involved with (the 'single' letters), and the second comprising three pairs of courtship letters between a couple engaged or about to be engaged in a relationship (the 'double' letters; in these the man's letter is placed first). The differences between the two sets are regularly regarded as of greater importance than their similarities, but in what follows I shall mostly treat them together. For the novice reader, the poems are likely to seem a bit daunting, as they are replete with recondite mythological references, but there is much to be gained from reading them, even for those not as enthralled as Ovid by the process of myth-making.

The twenty-one poems that comprise the collection are drawn from a multiplicity of sources, some known, others not, as indicated in the list below:

1	Penelope to Odysseus	Homer's *Odyssey*
2	Phyllis to Demophoon	Callimachus' *Aetia*?
3	Briseis to Achilles	Homer's *Iliad*
4	Phaedra to Hippolytus	Euripides' *Hippolytus* (I)
5	Oenone to Paris	*Cypria*?
6	Hypsipyle to Jason	Apollonius' *Argonautica*
7	Dido to Aeneas	Virgil's *Aeneid*
8	Hermione to Orestes	Sophocles' *Hermione*?
9	Deianira to Hercules	Sophocles' *Trachiniae*
10	Ariadne to Theseus	Catullus 64, a Hellenistic poem?
11	Canace to Macareus	Euripides' *Aeolus*?
12	Medea to Jason	Euripides' *Medea*, Apollonius' *Argonautica*
13	Laodamia to Protesilaus	Euripides' *Protesilaus*? Laevius' *Protesilaudamia*?
14	Hypermestra to Lynceus	Aeschylus' *Danaid* trilogy? The epic *Danaid*?
15	Sappho to Phaon	Sappho's poetry? Athenian comedies?
16–17	Paris and Helen	*Cypria*?
18–19	Leander and Hero	A lost Hellenistic poem?
20–21	Acontius and Cydippe	Callimachus' *Aetia*

For the convenience of the reader, throughout this chapter I refer to the writer of the letter rather than its number.

The Collection

The relative place of the *Heroides* in Ovid's *oeuvre* is not entirely clear; the order in which his poems are treated here reflects the generally held chronology. Most think that the single *Heroides* were written between the first and the second editions of the *Amores*, that is, between roughly 20 and 13 BCE (see below, for the mention of the *Heroides* in the *Amores* on which this assumption is based). The double letters, however, are often dated to about the time of Ovid's exile (8 CE) because stylistically and metrically they are more similar to his later poetry than his earlier. Another thing that remains obscure is how or whether the *Heroides* were divided into books. As the two collections stand, they are far too long for a single papyrus roll, and so the single letters are sometimes divided into three groups of five, with the six double letters as Book 4. There is, however, no manuscript evidence for this, so, although it is quite a plausible division, certainty is impossible.

The authenticity of many of the letters has been called into question; the double *Heroides* have a different manuscript tradition from the single, and the Sappho letter does not appear in its current place in any of the manuscripts. Beyond this, Ovid himself has caused no little debate by mentioning in *Am.* 2.18 some, but not all, of the letters (specifically, the single letters of Penelope, Phyllis, Oenone, Canace, Hypsipyle (and possibly Medea), Phaedra, Ariadne, Dido, and perhaps Sappho). This scholarly controversy about the letters is ignored by much contemporary scholarship, which tends either to assume without arguing it that all of the letters are written by Ovid, or to claim that it doesn't matter very much because the letters can plausibly be read as a collection, and whoever wrote them fit the forgeries in well. The reader should be aware that Ovidian authorship of all of the letters is by no means established, although for simplicity's sake I will refer to Ovid as the author of the entire corpus; the most generally suspected of the letters are the double letters and that of Sappho.

Related to the question of authenticity is the issue of monotony: frankly, a first-time reader of the *Heroides* could not be blamed for finding them repetitive. The poems can be grouped into two basic patterns: the double letters and the letters from Phaedra, Hermione, Canace, and Hypermestra are more or less letters from people interested in starting or furthering a relationship, while the letters from Penelope, Phyllis, Briseis, Oenone, Hypsipyle, Dido, Deianira, Ariadne, Medea, Laodamia, and Sappho have as their primary subject the discussion of a relationship that is seemingly over, so their overall tone is more plaintive than the first set. There are of course significant differences among them; the second set, for instance, encompasses the situations of Penelope, whose husband is about to return to her, Dido, who is genuinely abandoned by Aeneas, and Laodamia, whose husband is dead or about to die as she writes. But, given that Ovid has put the characters in similar situations, they tend to say similar things. Scholarship has exercised itself greatly over this issue; previous generations thought of it as the *Heroides'* besetting sin, but for now the general consensus seems to be that the monotony is precisely the point of the corpus (see Lindheim 2003 for an extended argument of this idea). As with Ovid's elegiac persona in the *Amores*, we are encouraged to revel in the sameness of it all and also to pay particular attention to variations on the basic themes; here, as throughout the poet's work, careful reading is amply rewarded. The primary effect of the similarities is to encourage the reader to consider what kinds of patterns emerge throughout a reading of the corpus, and some (but not enough) interesting work has been done on the significance of the order of the poems, which seems to defy a simple pattern.

Myth and Character

In a very important sense, knowledge of the mythological background of the individual stories adds to the understanding of the *Heroides*, but they are also character studies with a surprising degree of psychological plausibility and subtlety. If you happened to be the Briseis of Homer's *Iliad*, and you had just been transferred from Achilles' tent to Agamemnon's for reasons not clear to you, and if you remembered that you had once been a princess, and reflected that, while none of the Greeks was your friend, you had become accustomed to Achilles and his cortege, with some of them even showing you kindness, you might write a letter very much like *Her.* 3. For this reason, in addition to the dazzling sophistication of their revision of canonical texts, the *Heroides* have been appreciated by many different kinds of readers throughout their history, including those who read the poems as case studies of erotic psychopathology.

This kind of writing, in which the author writes in the persona of a character (sometimes historical and sometimes fictional), was a part of the rhetorical training of upper-class Romans of Ovid's time, and Seneca's *Suasoriae* and *Controversiae* provide not only examples but also mentions of Ovid's own rhetorical exercises and excesses (Chapter 3). The primary differences in Ovid's treatment of these originally rhetorical themes are, first, that he writes poetry rather than prose and, second, that the poems focus on such a small portion of human experience rather than encompassing the broader themes of the school exercises. Rhetoric, however, is not lost by these changes; the characters of the *Heroides* themselves structure their arguments with careful attention to persuading their audiences.

The *Heroides*, then, are not quite like anything that has come before them. There are probably examples of fictional letter collections before Ovid, but they are mostly the forged correspondence of historical figures who are likely to have written to one another (that is, they seek to pass themselves off as genuine, rather than counting on the reader to see through their apparent sincerity; see especially Rosenmeyer 2001). This difference between myth and reality is an important one, as it adds to the characters of the *Heroides* a significant textual history, as we have already seen: you can read any one of the *Heroides* without knowing its author's mythic tale, but you will miss many of the jokes. There is also the nearly contemporary poem of Propertius (4.3, a letter written from a fictionalized, but not mythological, woman to her husband away at war); it is not at all clear which precedes the other (Jacobson 1974 offers the most complete discussion), but Ovid himself claims to have invented this genre, whatever we understand it to be (*Ars* 3.346): *ignotum hoc aliis ille novavit opus* ('this work, unknown to others, he (re)invented'). The verb *novo* means both 'invent' and 'renew'; with this statement Ovid seems to be claiming originality, but he may merely claim, as do so many Latin authors, to be inventing a Roman form of literature known only to the Greeks. There is, however, no extant model of the *Heroides* in Greek literature. And yet the *Heroides*, while they are in some ways anomalous, are very much a part of Ovid's work as a whole. Like the *Metamorphoses* and parts of the *Ars amatoria*, they are interested in mythology, both in its canonical versions and in its contemporary, 'Romanized' permutations. Like the *Ibis* and the *Fasti*, they presume a detailed and technical knowledge of variant versions of that mythology. Like the exile poetry, they minutely examine similar themes, relentlessly pacing over the same small space. Their world is essentially the world of Roman love elegy, as seen in the *Amores* (see below). Like the *Ars amatoria* and certain books of the *Metamorphoses*, they are interested in the unhappier parts of erotic experience, particularly women's. And like all of Ovid's poetry, they are immensely playful and immensely satisfying; the more you read them, the more they draw you in to their world. Among Ovidian scholars, they have recently begun to receive a great deal of attention; several monographs and commentaries, dozens of article, and a goodly number of dissertations in the past decade have made the *Heroides* a key part of the Ovidian renaissance.

Contemporary Approaches

Some of the major trends of *Heroides* scholarship have already been alluded to, and here as well they mirror the most important and recurrent questions of Ovidian poetics. The study of intertextuality (how the poems interact with and refashion previous literature; see especially Jolivet 2001 and Hinds 1993) has provided much data about how Ovid conceived of his poetic project, as well as illustrating the poet's sophisticated incorporation of previous literature. In the few *Heroides* for which we have clear evidence, Ovid seems to have relied on one or two of his most important poetic predecessors for the basis of his story, sprinkling in allusions to other versions of the same or similar stories. That is, unlike much of Roman literature, the *Heroides* are very specifically intertextual, as they yield the best crop to the reader who has not only heard of, for example Hypermestra, but who is intimately familiar with the differing renditions of her myth as told by previous writers. This point cannot be overstressed: we tend to think of (and teach) mythology as stories 'out there', focusing on the most common versions without much attention to authorial source, but it is clear that, in the *Heroides* at least, Ovid means for us to have done our homework and read up not only the individual myth being treated but also other stories that are similar in pattern. This, too, helps to explain why the corpus is repetitive—all of mythology serves as a storehouse for Ovid's fertile mind. Much of the time, however, Ovid's primary model is no longer extant or exists only in fragments (see the table above), so hunting for these sources is speculative work; quite possibly, he uses as a framework the version of a myth we do not even know about, let alone have access to. It is clear, however, that the breadth of Ovid's sources is breathtakingly large; the poems (seem to) refer back most often to Greek tragedy, but also to Greek lyric and Greek and Latin epic, and Ovid thereby sets himself in competition with Homer, Sappho, Sophocles, Euripides, Callimachus, and even the near-contemporary but already canonical Virgil, that is, with nearly every one of the poetic heavy-hitters preceding him in the classical tradition. Given that the single *Heroides* are generally agreed to be the work of a young Ovid, this self-confidence is dazzling, to say the least.

The use of a previous poetic source does not, however, mean slavish imitation; Ovid's regular practice is to blend several contradictory or different versions of a story into his primary model, often thereby changing the story in a significant way. And, to return to the notion of repetitiveness, the poems also seem to react to one another in a sophisticated relationship of pattern- and meaning-making; depending how you read the letters and whose version of the story you believe, you get a different sense of what the outcome of each individual story is likely to be. For example, I have elsewhere argued that we are to understand the suicidal Phyllis *not* as a doomed heroine who commits suicide because her lover has abandoned her (as if she were a twin of Dido) but rather as a woman who kills herself tragically too soon: if she had only waited a bit longer, she might have lived happily ever after (Fulkerson 2002). In this way, she is much more like Penelope, the heroine immediately preceding her in the corpus, than like Dido or other women to whom she is usually compared.

Another area in which studies of the *Heroides* have been immensely fruitful is that of gender, which in this case is nearly inextricable from the genre of the poems, as we shall see. It is a peculiarity of the *Heroides* that they not only purport to be written by fictional characters but that most of the time this ventriloquism is transsexual: Ovid's voice lurks under the words of the women (and men) he personifies so vividly. One of the several things that this sex change does is render unclear where Ovid's sympathies lie; like Euripides before him, Ovid is sometimes accused of misogyny, sometimes of deep sympathy with women, and sometimes (but, here, unlike Euripides) of ironical detachment from his characters. The fact that the majority of the *Heroides* claim that they are written by women in an age when very few women attained even basic literacy is surely significant (see Hemelrijk 1999 on women's learning in Rome), and raises complicated questions about what function is served by equating women with erotic unhappiness and with letter-writing.

The poems are written in elegiac meter, as are most of the rest of Ovid's works (with the sole exception of the *Metamorphoses*). It is therefore worth comparing these women to other women of elegy, like Propertius' harsh mistress Cynthia, featured in Book 1 of his poetry. Conventional elegy features an elegiac poet, male with one exception, very much in love with a woman who is alternately generous and cruel, and who is rapaciously greedy for both presents and other lovers. Alas for the lover/poet, who cannot live without her, poetry is not a reliable source of income, and so he is forced to beg for her favors, sometimes demeaning himself by spending the night outside her door for all to see, and always proclaiming that his heart belongs to her (at least, until he tires of the game and moves on to another woman; James S. L. 2003 is fundamental to understanding what this equation means for the women portrayed in elegy). This world, in which desire is always unsatisfied, is the world of the *Amores* and the *Ars amatoria* but also of Propertius and Tibullus, elegists and contemporaries of Ovid. There is much more to be said about the *Heroides'* connections to the world of Roman elegy, as much of the recent scholarship on the corpus, even that interested in 'elegiac elements' of the poems, treats it in isolation from the rest of elegy.

For the Romans, elegy was a distinct kind of poetry from epic, tragedy, and lyric (the original generic homes of most of the heroines, as elegy does not have its own set of mythological characters). Much of the best recent work on the *Heroides* explores how these now-elegiac heroes and heroines have to change to fit into their new surroundings. For some, like Paris and Helen, or Acontius and Cydippe, the change is merely one of emphasis, but an elegiac letter of lament from such a tragic icon as Medea requires more work, and part of the delight of reading her letter is watching as she tries (often unsuccessfully) to seem elegiac (and so pitiable) and not tragic (and so melodramatic, when taken out of her context). So, for instance, Medea's letter starts off not so differently from many of the other letters, but by the time she has told the story of meeting Jason and saving his life she has worked herself up into a near-tragic frenzy of revenge (12.173–80):

> Quos ego seruaui, paelex amplectitur artus,
>   et nostri fructus illa laboris habet.
> forsitan et, stultae dum te iactare maritae
>   quaeris et iniustis auribus apta loqui,
> in faciem moresque meos noua crimina fingas.
>   rideat et uitiis laeta sit illa meis!
> rideat et Tyrio iaceat sublimis in ostro—
>   flebit et ardores uincet adusta meos!

Those arms which I saved, now your whore [*paelex*, not a polite word and rarely used in poetry] embraces, and she has the fruit of my labor. And perhaps, while you seek to puff yourself up to your stupid wife, and speak words suitable for her unjust ears, you can make up new reproaches against my appearance and behavior. Let her laugh, and let her be happy with my flaws; let her laugh as she sits, lofty on her Tyrian purple. She *will* weep, and she, enflamed, will then surpass my ardor.

Medea's words are of course meant to remind the reader that she will in fact literally set Creusa on fire, but even without reference to Euripides' *Medea* they are not without humor and irony, for Medea can only intermittently adopt the elegiac pose of helpless misery; mostly she is focused on how to punish her enemies. As scholarship on Latin poetry has made clear, the 'rules' of a genre are overlapping sets of fluid assumptions rather than solid entities, but very many of the *Heroides* are interested in pushing at these boundaries (see Hinds 1987a, a ground-breaking study on the shifting generic relationship between epic and elegy in Ovid's *Metamorphoses* and *Fasti*).

Some have seen Ovid's treatment of the figures of mythology as players in an elegiac game as part of his larger habit of conflating fact and fiction; throughout his poetry, the ('real' or 'realistic') figures of love elegy and the famous characters of mythology behave in nearly identical ways. The tales of mythology thus serve as a model for life at the same time as they are themselves subtly refashioned by reference to contemporary practices. Among the net effects of this conflation is a universalizing of Ovid's poetry; despite writing the *Heroides* within a narrow compass, the poet manages to suggest that art is not so different from life after all, and that his poetry is in fact about the sum total of possible human experience. But the world of elegy is not, or not really, the world of the *Heroides*. The predominant pattern of the single *Heroides* at least is an exact reversal of that of Latin (love) elegy. For, in the *Heroides*, it is regularly the woman who grovels and humiliates herself, not the man. Even in the double *Heroides*, the normal pattern of elegy is disrupted, for while the man does pursue, the woman hardly resists—Cydippe puts up something of a fight against her appropriation by Acontius, but by the time she writes her letter, the final letter of the *Heroides*, she has all but given up.

Further insight about this surprising reversal of the elegiac norm may be found in the figure of Sulpicia, the sole exception to the male gender of the elegiac poet and herself the subject of much debate. The third book attributed to the elegist Tibullus contains poems not written by him; of those, 3.8–12 constitute the 'Sulpicia-cycle'. Some of them claim to be written by a 'friend of Sulpicia' about her relationship with a man named Cerinthus, and some are written in the first person by Sulpicia herself, mostly to and about Cerinthus. As is the case for the *Heroides*, here too questions of authenticity are significant, but in a more fundamental sense. It is unclear—and it will likely never become clear—whether Sulpicia is a biological woman writing a male kind of poetry in the only way she can, that is, with a few necessary changes, or a biological man writing poetry as if he were a woman making those changes.

But either way, Sulpicia's poetry is a 'drag' performance: the positioning of a woman as elegiac poet is a reversal of elegiac norms, but Sulpicia's poetry (and probably the *Heroides* as well) provokes the recognition that these norms are themselves an inverted version of real life. That is, in the patriarchal society that was Augustan Rome, the notion of powerlessness portrayed so poignantly by the elegists probably has much to do with feelings of increasing political disempowerment and displacement as empire settles into Empire, but it has little or nothing to do with the poet's lived experiences in erotic relationships with women. (The thorny scholarly problem of whether we ought to read elegy autobiographically, as if it in some way reflects real men and their real love lives, or whether it is poetry about something entirely different, like the writing of poetry itself, is luckily one that the reader of the *Heroides* can ignore; on this issue see particularly Kennedy 1993.) Both the Sulpicia poems and the women of the single *Heroides*, then, redress the gender (im)balance, reminding their readers that elegy has got it wrong: it is not normal for men to have to beg women to love them, since men hold all of the cards. Part of the reason the women of the single letters (and so Ovid) are so often read as naive and sincere despite the sophistication of their textual pedigrees is simply that the abandonment of women by men is a much more regular poetic occurrence than the other way around (see Lipking 1988 on women and abandonment). In this way, too, and despite their essential literariness, the *Heroides* stake a claim to 'realism' that other elegiac poetry (before, that is, Ovid's exilic work) cannot.

The gender of the women writing the single *Heroides*, then, is key. In the later *Ars amatoria*, Ovid will suggest that it is dangerous for women to write, because they do not possess the requisite skills; he does not mean technical skills, but rather that they will be unable to hide their true feelings and so will be helpless before the superior rhetorical prowess of their male correspondents. But in the *Heroides* the mythical women write with considerable skill, and, if their writing is sometimes problematic and brings about conclusions they do not foresee, it is also an act of empowerment, despite their claims of incompetence. The men of the *Heroides*, on the other hand, present themselves as highly successful manipulators of words. Paris and Acontius, in particular, beat the elegiac poet at his own game, for one of the standard complaints of elegy is that poetry has no real effect (a claim counterbalanced by the occasional grandiose assurance that elegiac poetry is all-powerful and can open any door, literally). Yet Paris and Acontius utilize poetry in the service of their *amours*, and do so successfully. Farrell (1998) has discussed how men's writing is portrayed in the single and double *Heroides*. In the former, writing is seen as a truthful medium, and so it is reserved for women; the few cases of male writing in the single *Heroides* are duplicitous. The double *Heroides*, however, pit male writing against female, and it is not entirely clear whether we are to understand Helen, Hero, and Cydippe as winning (or losing), or if they have learned anything from the men who write to them.

The *Heroides* as Epistles

Given that some of the characters of the *Heroides*, both male and female, describe themselves as authors, we are entitled to return to the question of the question of the role of writing in the corpus, and there has been much scholarly interest in this question as well. Are we to understand these letters as fruitless cries in the night, an ancient equivalent to scribbling in one's journal after a trying day, or are they to be considered genuinely communicative? Even if we view them as poetry rather than as letters, we must face the question of how and why the mythical writers of each poem conceive of themselves within the literary tradition. As many have noted in recent years, the writers of the *Heroides* issue a challenge that is specifically literary—by attempting to (re)write any part of their story, they join Ovid in competing with their literary predecessors. And because they are characters on whom the more canonical versions of their stories have not often focused, Ovid presents them as finally having their say: if, as a reader of the *Iliad*, you have wondered what Helen or Briseis, or

Helen's abandoned daughter Hermione, thought of this Trojan War business, the *Heroides* will give you an answer. In a manner similar to Ovid's own challenging of the previous poetic tradition, then, the men and women of the *Heroides* suggest that theirs is the voice that most needs to be heard. This is all the more so given Ovid's care in choosing the moment of letter-writing. When we look at the canonical sources of the letters, we discover that some of them come at a crucial moment in the story—Medea's, for instance, which seems to be written immediately before she goes onstage to star in Euripides' *Medea*, or Penelope's, which is about to be given to the beggar who is really Odysseus in disguise (Kennedy 1984), or even Cydippe's, which makes plain that she is more or less ready to give in to Acontius. Since we rarely have information from ancient poets about how or why they write poetry, there is much to be gained from looking at the authors of the *Heroides* as themselves poets and examining their mechanics and stylistic principles (see Fulkerson 2005 on how the heroines use one another's stories to fashion their own).

In addition to their status as poetry, however, the *Heroides* also specifically identify themselves as letters; nearly every one of them has a standard epistolary opening and/or closing. If the poems are read as letters in addition to poems, they gain a further layer of meaning. As letters, they are likely to have a more specifically directed internal function than as poems: that is, whatever their value as poetry, they at least pretend that they are conveying meaning to some audience within the story rather than merely to us. But what meaning, and to whom? Previous scholarship on the *Heroides* has been greatly interested in whether the letters 'succeed' in their goal (as noted above, primarily seduction and re-seduction), but this is probably less important than noting the multiple levels of meaning thereby created. Each letter has two authors, Ovid and its nominal writer, and two purposes: revisiting a famous story with a twist, and, within the story, having some effect. Significantly, the purposes are not as clearly divided between the two authors as it might at first seem. We can view Ovid as competing with his predecessors, but we may also want to see the characters as struggling to change their stories from within (see particularly Spentzou 2003 and Fulkerson 2005, who have different views about how successful the attempt is). Finally, there are (at least) two potential readers: the character to whom the letter is addressed and anybody else who happens to come along (that is, us). From this duality, a number of effects are possible. One that is common to many works of fiction, but which is seen most clearly in epistolary works, is the creation of reader as eavesdropper; by reading something that is not addressed to us, we have made ourselves a part of the story. In addition to this, many see Ovid as creating a triangle of dramatic irony, in which he and the reader know more than (and so can feel superior to) the person in the story; for example, Hero's letter to Leander begs him to visit if he still loves her, but *we* know that when he next does so he will drown in the Hellespont and his dead body will wash upon the shore to be discovered by her—so the joke is on her. I am not, however, entirely confident that smugness is the right response to the corpus. The claim that Ovid is an anti-feminist looking to portray women in their weakest moments and making the reader complicit with his domination of them is always available, and some generations of his readership resort to it more than others. But this simplistic view occludes much of what is interesting about his poetry, and Ovid, like other elegists and Catullus before them, regularly has recourse to women as a way of talking about questions of power and powerlessness.

The efficacy of the letters as letters is always a question in the *Heroides*, sometimes explicitly, as when Penelope and Sappho respectively demand that the recipients of their letters come back rather than writing and write if they're not coming back, or when Oenone doubts whether Paris' new wife Helen will allow him to read her letter all the way through. For others, the situation is murkier, but we generally get more out of the *Heroides* when we pay attention to the internal reader of the letter and see the writers of individual poems as structuring their arguments toward a particular end. Here, too, things are more complex than they seem, as scholars have suggested that, in certain letters, there is a chance of physical interception, so the person likeliest to read the letter within the myth may or may not be its addressee, and even that the letter-writer herself may 'psychologically' address herself to someone else in the story (Williams 1997; Fulkerson 2005). For some of the *Heroides*, it is clear that the letter *does* something: for instance, Paris and Helen essentially conclude their court-ship in *Her.* 16 and 17; below are brief passages from each side of this elaborate dance (16.317–26, 17.153–4, 185–8):

> sola iaces uiduo tam longa nocte cubili;
>   in uiduo iaceo solus et ipse toro.
> te mihi meque tibi communia gaudia iungant;
>   candidior medio nox erit illa die.
> tunc ego iurabo quaeuis tibi numina meque
>   adstringam uerbis in sacra uestra meis;
> tunc ego, si non fallax fiducia nostri,
>   efficiam prasens, ut mea regna petas.
> si pudet et metuis ne me uideare secuta,
>   ipse reus sine te criminis huius ero.

You lie by yourself, on a lonely bed, throughout the long night; I too lie by myself, on a lonely couch. Let our mutual pleasure join you to me and me to you; that night will be brighter than broad daylight. Then I will swear by whatever gods you like, and I will bind myself with your choice of rites by my words; then I, once present (unless my confidence betrays me), will make you want what I have to offer. If you are ashamed, and fear lest you seem to have chased after me, I myself will assume the responsibility for the deed.

> lude, sed occulte! maior, non maxima, nobis
>   est data libertas, quod Menelaus abest . . .
> quod male persuades, utinam bene cogere posses!
>   ui me rusticitas excutienda fuit.
> utilis interdum est ipsis iniuria passis.
>   sic certe felix esse coacta forem.

Keep flirting, but be more discreet! Menelaus' absence gives us more, but not unlimited, freedom . . . What you ineffectively try to persuade me of, I wish you could more effectively compel! My naïveté should probably have been expelled by force. Injustice is sometimes useful even for its victims. In such a way, I could have been forced to be happy, surely.

Helen's response to Paris sets the stage for her 'kidnapping', but it also coyly refuses to answer the question countless generations have had about who bears most responsibility for the Trojan War, as she explains to Paris that women prefer to be taken rather than asked (a notion prevalent elsewhere in Ovid's elegies). In other cases, often because of the limitations of our sources, it is not clear whether the letter changes the story, sets it more firmly on its original track, or has no visible effect, although even here several have studied the likely therapeutic effects of the letters on their writers.

The question of authorship has particular point in the case of one of the letters, that of Sappho, who is herself a Greek lyric poet of great repute. This letter has probably received the most scholarly attention, because to the notion of Ovid pulling the puppet-strings of famous mythical heroes and heroines is added here the fact that Sappho, uniquely in the corpus, is not only a real person but also a person who has already had the opportunity to tell her story. Moderns mostly understand Sappho to have been erotically interested in women, but her letter, while aware of this fact, insists that the ferryman Phaon is her one true love; more, she claims that he is her poetic inspiration, again reversing the woman-as-Muse paradigm so prevalent in poetry! Space precludes a detailed discussion of Sappho's letter, but it is likely both that Ovid has deliberately confused Sappho with a character in one of Sappho's own poems (the goddess Aphrodite, who is linked with Phaon in mythology), and that his insistence on her heterosexuality (and so participation in the 'normal' world of elegy) is part of his larger attempt to establish himself as *the* love poet of antiquity. Many, too, have seen the Sappho-letter as Ovid's attempt to say something about his own role as poet, given that much of her poem discusses her reputation and poetic skill, but what precisely Ovid thereby communicates is a matter of no little controversy.

Conclusion

It is easy to trace the development of Ovid's increasing interest in the world of mythology; in the *Heroides* he begins a lifelong process of conflating myth with 'real life'. But the influence of the heroines appears not only in the work of Ovid; despite their relative inaccessibility to the novice reader, the *Heroides* have been enormously influential, second only to the *Metamorphoses* as a source of inspiration. Figures from the *Heroides* reappear in works by poets as diverse as Pope, Marlowe, Chaucer, Donne, and Tennyson. Further, many have traced echoes of the *Heroides* in the letters of Heloise and Abelard, in Petrarch, and in the *Lettres Portugaises;* indeed, many of the generic constraints and narrative patterns of the epistolary novel form most popular in eighteenth-century England and France derive ultimately from the *Heroides*.

FURTHER READING

Much important work on the *Heroides* appears in article form; of this, Kennedy (1984), Smith (1994), Barchiesi (1993), Desmond (1993), Hinds (1993), and Farrell (1998), are only the very most important. Jacobson (1974) and Verducci (1985) offer very different approaches; the former is probably more useful as a starting point for further research. On theoretical approaches to the *Heroides*, Lindheim (2003), Spentzou (2003), and Fulkerson (2005) offer different feminist viewpoints, while Spoth (1992), Landolfi (2000), and Jolivet (2001) concentrate on generic and intertextual elements; Edmunds (2001) is useful for intertextuality in Roman literature. On ancient letters, the epistolary form in general, women's traditional role as abandoned lovers, and their connection to letters see respectively Rosenmeyer (2001), Altman (1983), Lipking (1988), and Kauffman (1986). Works on elegy with particular interest for this chapter include Sharrock (1994a), Kennedy (1993), and James S. L. (2003); Ottone (2003) discusses specific epic influences on individual *Heroides*, and Hinds (1987a) is useful for understanding the differences between the genres of epic and elegy. Numerous recent commentaries make research into individual letters easier; just about every letter now has at least one, and often two, commentaries available (Palmer 1898; Barchiesi 1992; Casali 1995a; Knox 1995; Kenney 1996; Rosati 1996a; Bessone 1997; Heinze 1997; Reeson 2001; Michalopoulos 2006).

CHAPTER SEVEN

The *Ars Amatoria*

Roy K. Gibson

Preliminaries

The *Ars amatoria* is a witty, colorful, and often glamorous poem in three books. It employs the romantic subject matter and elegiac meter of the earlier Roman love poetry of Propertius, Tibullus, and Ovid's own *Amores*, but discards the egocentric focus of that genre on the personal erotic experiences of the poet-lover. The *Ars* adopts instead the characteristic techniques of the (largely hexameter 'genre' of didactic poetry)—exemplified in Ovid's time above all by Lucretius' *de Rerum Natura* and Virgil's *Georgics*—to produce a manual of instruction for all on the art of love. During the Middle Ages, the text could be used as a means for teaching basic Latin in the classroom (Hexter 2006), but increasingly acquired a reputation as a taboo or even pornographic text (Liveley 2006: 320 n. 2; Gibson 2007: 1–3). Today that reputation lingers on in the popular imagination, but, following the publication in 1977 of A. S. Hollis' commentary on *Ars* 1, the poem has begun to return to the mainstream of criticism on Augustan poetry and now has an established place on university curricula.

The first two books of the *Ars* offer men humorous and cynical instruction in the art of seducing the opposite sex, while the third teaches women how to play their (often) reciprocal and complementary part in the seduction. Ovid implies that *Ars* 1–2 were written together as a unit (1.35–40, 1.771–2, 2.733–44), while the third book for women is merely an afterthought written in response to female pleas for equality (2.745–6, 3.1–2). Some critics see here evidence of characteristic Ovidian playfulness and argue that the *Ars* was in fact planned from the start as a three-book work (Sharrock 1994a: 18–20; Holzberg 2002: 103; Wildberger 1998: 343–7; Henderson 2006). More certainly, this hybrid elegiac-didactic work stands at the midpoint of Ovid's (pre-exilic) literary career—as the *Georgics* had also done for Virgil—between his 'lighter' productions (*Amores*, *Heroides*) and the 'weightier' works of the *Metamorphoses* and the *Fasti* (on which he had perhaps already begun work by the time of the publication of the *Ars*). Ovid appears obsessed with the idea of ascent through the various poetic genres (Harrison 2002), and the notion of a standard literary career which progresses through the genres from low to high—

inspired by Virgil—may have already begun to make an impression on Ovid and his contemporaries (Farrell 2002, 2004).

Book 1 is divided into sections on 'where to find a girl' (1.41–262) and 'how to capture her' (1.269–770), while Book 2 is dedicated in its entirety to 'how to keep her' (for as long as the lover's interest lasts). The third book is loosely divided into 'elementary' instruction, on personal appearance, accomplishments, and making contact with men (3.101–498), and 'advanced' instruction, on controlling one's emotions and one's lover (3.501–808). The range of subject matter included under these headings is astonishingly varied, and comes laden with quasi-technical detail (as will shortly be seen). The tendency to pack in large amounts of material into a short space is increased by Ovid's fondness, particularly in *Ars* 3, for catalogues of subject matter, a traditional feature of didactic (e.g. 3.135–58, 3.169–92, 3.769–88; Gibson 2003: 6–7). The result is the creation of a text whose density and diversity serve to differentiate it from the more uniform character and leisurely style of treatment associated with the *Amores* and *Heroides*, which are dominated by various kinds of speech (rather than 'technical' exposition). In both the 'male' and 'female' sections of the *Ars*, the addressee ends the book in bed with the opposite sex, where the man learns the arts of mutual sexual pleasure (2.703–32), while the female is taught to choose her sexual position carefully and the art of faking orgasm (3.769–808). But the two journeys to these finishing posts display significant differences in emphasis. As Myerowitz (1985: 127) observes, the *Ars* involves 'for the male . . . the taming and handling of the female, for the female . . . , to a great degree, the taming and handling of herself'. Ovid's treatment of gender and the gendered implications of his advice remain important issues in modern scholarship on the *Ars* (Leach 1964; Myerowitz 1985, 1992; Downing 1990; Sharrock 2002a, 2002b).

A passage early in the first book on how to chat up a girl at the chariot races offers a good introduction to the character of the *Ars* (1.139–56):

> proximus a domina nullo prohibente sedeto,
>   iunge tuum lateri qua potes usque latus.
> et bene, quod cogit, si nolis, linea iungi,
>   quod tibi tangenda est lege puella loci.
> hic tibi quaeratur socii sermonis origo,
>   et moueant primos publica uerba sonos:
> cuius equi ueniant facito studiose requiras,
>   nec mora, quisquis erit cui fauet illa, faue.
> at cum pompa frequens caelestibus ibit eburnis,
>   tu Veneri dominae plaude fauente manu.
> utque fit, in gremium puluis si forte puellae
>   deciderit, digitis excutiendus erit;
> etsi nullus erit puluis, tamen excute nullum:
>   quaelibet officio causa sit apta tuo.
> pallia si terra nimium demissa iacebunt,
>   collige et inmunda sedulus effer humo:
> protinus, officii pretium, patiente puella
>   contingent oculis crura uidenda tuis.

Sit next to your lady, none will prevent you; sit side by side as close as you can; and it is good that the rows compel closeness, like it or not, and that by the conditions of space your girl must be touched. Here seek an opening for friendly talk, and begin with words that all may hear. Mind you are zealous in asking whose horses are entering, and quick! whomsoever she favors be sure to favor too. But when the long procession of ivory statues of the gods passes by applaud Queen Venus with favoring hand. And if perchance, as will happen, a speck of dust falls on your lady's lap, flick it off with your fingers; even if none fall, then flick off—none; let any pretext serve to show your attentiveness. If her cloak hangs low and trails upon the ground, gather it up and lift it carefully from the defiling earth; straightaway a reward for your service, with the girl's permission your eyes will catch a glimpse of her ankles. (trans. Mozley Goold)

First, the local setting for the attempted seduction is Rome's Circus Maximus, and readers—even potential readers in the provincial capitals of the Empire—are given no special explanations of specific events or conventions of behavior in the Circus, but rather are assumed to be thoroughly familiar already with the City (Volk 2006). (This is one reason why modern readers, despite the poem's reputation for hilarity, often find the *Ars* unexpectedly demanding reading.) There is a deliberate contrast here with the conventions of earlier Roman love elegy, which showed relatively little interest in the local urban setting of the poet-lover's affair (see below). Second, the context for the seduction is a public one set outdoors during daylight hours. There is another contrast here with the conventions of earlier Roman love poetry, which typically favored indoor, private or night-time occasions (Gibson 2007: 105 with n. 130). Third, the poet's style of treatment is detailed and systematic to a degree which is incongruous with the apparently trivial subject matter, and his mode is emphatically instructional, as underlined by the heavy predominance of imperatival expressions. The *Ars* in fact contains many more such expressions than either the *De Rerum Natura* or the *Georgics*, and so contrives to be more didactic than its predecessors in this sense (Gibson 1998). Furthermore, the basic assumptions behind Ovid's instruction are cynical in an uncomplicated way: he assumes that the reader wants to get physically close to his quarry (and eventually get her into bed), and—balancing wit against sleaze—supplies unromantic advice on how to achieve this. No consideration is given to the feelings of the girl, or indeed to deeper romantic longings that any male addressee might harbor. Finally (if far from exhaustively), readers familiar with Roman love elegy will instantly spot that this passage is an adaptation of the second elegy of the third book of *Amores*, where Ovid himself attempts to chat up the girl sitting beside him at the races. Readers of the *Ars* are implicitly invited to reread *Am.* 3.2 and judge for themselves the difference between elegy and didactic. Readers may also remember Ovid's striking promise earlier in *Ars* 1 that his teaching would be based on personal experience, and not, as more usually, on divine command or inspiration (*Ars* 1.25–30; La Penna 1979; Miller 1986; Ahern 1990). Yet the close adaptation here of *Am.* 3.2 teases the reader with the thought that 'personal' experience is in fact largely 'literary' experience.

After this introduction to some key facets of *Ars*, it is a good moment to introduce some critical questions which have dominated criticism on the *Ars*. In a detailed survey of the last five decades of scholarly debate on the *Ars,* Green (2006) discusses six key areas of critical activity (cf. Watson 2002). These include the date and structure of the poems; the generic status of *Ars* as a cross-breed between elegy and didactic, and the range of literary influences to which the poem is subject; a search for a 'serious message' in the *Ars,* for example implicit Ovidian commentary on the nature of love or Roman culture or contemporary politics; gender issues and the social 'status' of the women of the *Ars;* the notorious series of lengthy mythological digressions which punctuate the text of the poem; and the role of the reader. This chapter will treat a selection of these issues (and has or will simply allude to others), but will also seek to focus on some less familiar aspects of the *Ars.*

The *Ars* and Roman Love Elegy

Roman love elegy had flourished under Propertius and Tibullus in the 20s BC, with Propertius publishing his fourth and final book ca. 16 BC and Tibullus' second book appearing posthumously ca. 19 BC. Ovid had begun work on his own *Amores* ca. 26–5 BC, and may have continued revising them until 7 BC, when he published a second and definitive edition of three books. The Roman reading public would have been thoroughly familiar with elegiac love poetry as a genre when the three books of the *Ars amatoria,* at least in the form we now have them, began to appear between 2 BC and 2 AD, at a time when Ovid was now Rome's greatest living poet. (Some critics assume a 'first edition' of *Ars* 1–2 around 7 BC, and others, less plausibly, place the publication of *Ars* 3 in the year of Ovid's exile to Romania, AD 8; see Gibson 2003: 37–43, with reference to Syme 1978: 13–20; Murgia 1986a, 1986b). The common elements between elegy and the *Ars* take their most obvious form in shared conventional situations and characters. Earlier elegy had featured repeated scenarios or favored characters (Gibson 2005: 161), such as the door locked against the lover's entry (Prop. 1.16; Tib. 2.6.11–14; Ov. *Am.* 1.6, 3.11.9–16), the triangle of lover, beloved, and rival (Prop. 1.5, 1.8; Tib. 1.5, 1.6; Ov. *Am.* 2.5, 2.19), the infidelity of the poet's lover (Prop. 1.15; Tib. 1.5; Ov. *Am.* 3.8, 3.14), or the giving and receiving of advice on love (Prop. 1.10.21–30; Tib. 1.4; Ov. *Am.* 1.4). In the *Ars,* the giving of advice on love—often known as 'erotodidaxis'—becomes the dominant mode, resulting in a fundamental alteration of the other conventional elements. The locked door is no longer an occasion which allows a lover-poet to reflect on his romantic sufferings (of which the locked door is simply one more instance) but rather a practical obstacle which is to be overcome by lovers or strategically deployed against them (*Ars* 2.233–50, 2.523–32, 3.579–88). Infidelity remains a strong theme, but with a significantly different emphasis: instead of a woman's infidelity as a moment of supreme crisis, Ovid advises that lovers temper their own reactions to infidelity and accept the existence of rivals (2.535–600, 3.683–746). He also gives advice—shockingly by the standards of the exclusively male (and largely faithful) perspective of earlier love elegy—on how men may themselves be successfully unfaithful to their partners (2.373–466), and comes close to doing the same for women (3.589–610). The commitment to practical stratagems and to the achievement of particular objectives is conditioned by the mode of advice-giving, and results in an emphasis on a systematic self-restraint and long-term strategic thinking, which is new to the genre of Roman love elegy, although significant elements are anticipated in Ovid's *Amores*. (For moderation and restraint as unexpected, but sustained, themes of the *Ars*, especially *Ars* 3, see Gibson 2007.) Another characteristic feature of love elegy transformed by the didactic mode of the *Ars* is that of myth. Propertius and Ovid in his *Amores* show a particular fondness for appealing to the world of Greek myth—occasionally at some length—whether to illustrate their plights, argue a point, or even to underline a lesson (e.g. Prop. 1.1.9–16, 1.3.1–10, 1.20, 2.9, 3.15; Tib. 2.3.11–32; Ov. *Am.* 1.1.7–16, 1.10.1–8, 3.6.25–44; Lyne 1980: 82–102, 252–7). In the *Ars* Ovid continues this tradition, but characteristically develops long mythological narratives, particularly in the first two books of the *Ars*, to illustrate key points of instruction, for example 1.101–34 (Sabine women), 1.283–342 (Pasiphae), 1.525–68 (Ariadne and Bacchus), 1.681–706 (Deidamia and Achilles), 2.21–98 (Daedalus and Icarus), 2.123–44 (Calypso and Ulysses), 2.561–94 (Mars and Venus), 3.683–746 (Procris). These myths, despite the increasingly tenuous connection of some to the initial point under illustration, usually have an ingenious or deeper didactic function intimately connected to the text's core message, and continue to be the object of intense critical focus (Watson 1983; Sharrock 1994a: 87–195; Bowditch 2005; Sharrock 2006; Labate 2006).

One of the keynotes of earlier elegy is not the exaltation often associated with romantic poetry but rather personal alienation from both the loved one and from society (Gibson 2005: 161). This alienation is reflected in the metaphors which the earlier elegists use to describe their experience of love, such as slavery, mania and disease (Prop. 1.1, 1.5.21–30; Kennedy 1993: 53–63), and also in their striking obsession with death (Prop. 1.19, 2.13b, 2.26, 4.7, 4.11; Tib. 1.1.59–68, 1.3, 1.10; Ov. *Am.* 2.10.29–38; Griffin 1985: 142–62). Mania, disease, and death are prominent features of the world of the mythological characters of the *Ars* (where they play an important role in negative didactic lessons). But they are not offered as metaphors through which the addressees of the *Ars* are invited to articulate their own experiences. If the earlier elegists like to think of love as an invasive external force of overwhelming power (Prop. 1.1; Ov. *Am.* 1.1), in the *Ars*, as Ovid makes clear in the preface to Book 1 (1.1–24), love is a force that will now be subject to the control and direction of the lover. Some critics see here a potentially serious comment on love and its expression in the cultures of civilized societies (Fyler 1971; Myerowitz 1985; Sharrock 2002b: 152–3). The amatory environment constructed for the lover in the *Ars* is, then, relentlessly positivist, where—to paraphrase Epicurus' famous dictum on pain—emotional suffering is either short lived or (for strategic purposes) easily borne. Those who do end up experiencing love as a mania or disease are unsuccessful readers of the *Ars*—and the natural audience of the *Remedia*.

Propertius and Tibullus had described themselves as slaves of their mistress or of love in order to express their alienation from the values of contemporary society (Gibson 2005: 162–3). Such alienation, again, has little role to play in an instructional poem dedicated to the goal of erotic success, and the 'slave' role figure of earlier elegy is discarded in favor of the rather more positive (if hardly respectable) model of the *kolax* ('flatterer'). Rather than assuming the degraded role of slave in order to express their willing self-degradation outside society's structures, Ovid's lovers are to model themselves on a figure who possesses a familiar (if contested) role inside the normal operation of society (1.503–4, 1.611–16, 2.199–232, 2.281–6, 2.295–314, 2.641–62, 3.513–14, 3.673–86, 3.793–808; Labate 1984: 175–226; also Solodow 1977: 117–20). Where the slave performs services for his mistress because his condition of subjection offers no other choice, the flattering lover of the *Ars* may demean himself by holding his mistress's parasol or taking off her shoes (2.209–16), but always does so as a means of securing her affection (and eventually getting her into bed).

Ovid avoids identifying the male addressee of the *Ars* with the hero 'ego' of love elegy. This is appropriate to a non-exclusive didactic work addressed to *si quis in hoc . . . populo* (*Ars* 1.1 'If anyone among this people . . .'), but leads to the virtual disappearance from *Ars* 1–2 of the elegist's overwhelming obsession with the value and standing of his love poetry (e.g. Prop. 1.7, 2.1, 2.34, 3.1, 3.3, 4.1; Tib. 1.4.57–72, 2.4.13–20; Ov. *Am.* 1.3, 1.15, 2.1, 2.18, 3.1, 3.8, 3.15)—albeit not to the disappearance of Ovid's concern with the poetics of his own text (Sharrock 1994a; Gibson 2007: 82–99). It also produces as an apparently necessary correlative some sharp humor at the expense of the male addressee; note, for example, Ovid's acid comment on the likely quality of the love poetry written by his readers, at 2.283–6. If the male addressees of the *Ars* are not thought to be poetic geniuses like Ovid or Propertius, then the female addressees of *Ars* 3 are likewise carefully differentiated from such goddess-like creatures as Corinna and Cynthia. Ovid, for example, emphasizes the dearth of natural beauty among his readers (3.101–4, 3.251–6), in a manner that both justifies the need for controversial beauty aids and sets the tone for physical humor against his female addressees (Gibson 2003: 24–5, 35–6). Yet, for all that, Ovid cannot resist playing the lover to his pupils, and makes one last attempt to secure a privileged place for love poets in their affections (3.525–54). The character of Ovid's persona as *praeceptor* here and elsewhere in the *Ars*—self-interested, over-confident, prone to pedagogical errors—continues to attract the attention of scholars (Durling 1958: 163–4; Fyler 1971: 200–3; Wright 1984; Watson 2002: 149–51).

The Women of the *Ars* and the *Lex Iulia*

The dissociation of the women of the *Ars* from the goddess-like creatures of earlier elegy inevitably raises the hoary issue of the status of the women of the *Ars*. There has been something of a critical consensus in recent years that Cynthia and Corinna are largely fictional creatures, frequently symbols for the poetics of the elegists (Gibson 2005: 165–6). (For the women of *Ars* 3 also as expressions of the poetics of the work, see Sharrock 2000: 23–5; Gibson 2007: 143–7.) One of the factors fueling an unwillingness to believe that these are 'real' women concealed behind a pseudonym is the observation that the status markers provided for Cynthia and her ilk shift (confusingly) between those of, for example, low-status courtesans and

libertines of 'respectable' birth (Wyke 2002: 29–31). Readers of the *Ars* find something similar: the *puellae* appear now to have the stereotypical attributes and attitudes
of sexually available non-elite women (1.399–436, 3.417–24, 3.461–66, 3.479–82,
3.749–68, 3.805–8), now to possess the luxuries of upper-class women (1.351–74,
1.487–90, 2.251–60, 2.295–302), and now to appear like respectably married women
in search of tips for adultery (2.355–72, 2.535–600, 3.483–98, 3.601–10). Yet there
had been one crucial change in society between the heyday of love elegy and the
publication of the *Ars*. The majority of earlier elegy was written—not insignifi-
cantly—before 18 BC. In or around that year, Augustus promulgated his revolutionary *lex Iulia de adulteriis coercendis*, whereby illicit sexual relations with married
women (including widows and divorcees)—whether freeborn or of freed status—
became subject to serious punishment. In such an environment, the question of the
status of the women in the *Ars* necessarily became urgent. Ovid responds with assur-
ances that respectable married women are excluded from his poem, whether as targets
for men or as readers of *Ars* 3 (1.31–4, 2.599–600, 3.57–8, 3.483–4, 3.613–6). It
is clear, however, that these disclaimers raise as many questions as they answer, since
their phrasing is often ambiguous, or they appear in contexts where it is hard to take
them seriously (Rudd 1976: 3–4; Little 1982: 330–1; Sharrock 1994b: 109–22;
Holzberg 2002: 111–13). This is obvious already from Ovid's assurance at 1.34 *inque
meo nullum carmine crimen erit* ('and in my verse there will be no wrong-doing'),
where the alert reader will spot subversive intent in the fact that the letters of *crimen*
fit literally inside *carmine* (Sharrock 1994b: 110–12). Furthermore, the *lex Iulia*
appears to have offered some notable difficulties of interpretation and application to
jurists. The latter, for example, found it hard to offer a positive definition of the category of women actually liable to prosecution. Thus, when Ovid declares that his
legitimate female readership is made up of those whom 'shame and the laws and their
own rights permit' (*Ars* 3.57 *quas pudor et leges et sua iura sinunt*), his intent is
clearly disingenuous, since few of his readers can have had a clear idea of the exact
extent of this group when even legal experts were at something of a loss (Gibson
2003: 25–32). One result of these (unreassuring) disclaimers is that readers are
invited to watch for passages where Ovid appears to break the law. In this context,
the continuation of earlier elegy's habit of providing inconsistent clues to female
status appears provocative. Furthermore, as in the 'Circus' passage quoted above,
Ovid often takes no great care to make clear how the seduction of his female prey
might differ from attempted adultery. In *Ars* 3, however, Ovid changes his approach,
and, as I shall argue below, tackles the polarity between *meretrix* and *matrona* implicit
in the *lex Iulia* to produce a female addressee who is more consistently a hybrid of
these two stereotypical figures.

The *Ars*, Society, and Augustus

If the *Ars* seems dedicated to a subversion of Augustus' *lex Iulia*, it would be easy
to infer from that a general program of subversion of society's values. At first sight,

the *Ars* offers plenty of material for such a reading, being filled with recommendations for behavior which is variously unscrupulous, manipulative, unethical, or
simply lacking in magnanimity (frequently all four together). In the first book alone,
lovers are encouraged to bribe and corrupt slaves (1.351–6), to avoid birthday
gifts (1.417–8), make empty promises (1.443–4, 1.631–6), make overtures of
friendship to men with the intent to deceive (1.579–88), take advantage of others'
high opinions of themselves (1.611–14), act with the conscious aim of duping
the opposite sex (1.645–6), simulate tears of love (1.661–2), and hide erotic intent
behind a deliberate facade of innocuous friendship (1.719–22). Is this then a text
dedicated to the destruction of Rome's social fabric? It was suggested earlier that
the *Ars* does not in fact share earlier elegy's general stance of alienation from
society. That argument can be extended here if the peculiar ethical character of
the *Ars* is observed closely. It had been long asserted that love is a special arena
where the normal rules of society do not apply (Plato *Symp.*182e–83c). At several
places in the *Ars amatoria*, Ovid appears to make a related point (often as a coda
to some piece of shocking instruction just offered): the advice which he gives
on gift-giving or deception is not to be applied outside the erotic arena to normal
social intercourse (e.g. 1.641–44, 2.271–2; Labate 1984: 97–120). An illuminating
parallel is suggested by Labate (1984: 225–6), who notes a connection with the
special status awarded the sphere of electoral competition. Love and electioneering
are separated from the rules of normal society, and constitute arenas where behavior
that would elsewhere provoke outrage—such as simulation, ingratiation and flattery—are condoned (as explicitly for electioneering at [Q. Cic.] *Comm. Pet.* 42). But,
crucially, both are arenas contained within the broader ambit of society, rather than
being set up in opposition to it, and are not meant to threaten society's operation.
Contrast the rhetoric of the earlier elegists, who drew a sharp line between 'their'
society and 'normal' society, and affected that the former was in fact a threat to the
latter (e.g. Prop. 2.15; Gibson 2007: 44–6). Ovid's 'moralizing' codas, nevertheless,
have been ignored, or dismissed as window-dressing, sometimes even excised from
the text on the assumption they are the interpolations of later readers. At 1.583–8,
for example, Ovid sets down the following circumscription, after advising his readers
to make a pretense of friendship with the *uir* of their female prey:

> siue erit inferior seu par, prior omnia sumat,
>   nec dubites illi uerba secunda loqui.
> [tuta frequensque uia est, per amici fallere nomen;
>   tuta frequensque licet sit uia, crimen habet.
> inde procurator nimium quoque multa procurat,
>   et sibi mandatis plura uidenda putat.]

Be he below you or hold an equal place, let him take of all before you; nor hesitate to
yield him place in talk. ['Tis a safe and oft-trodden path to deceive under the name of
friend; safe and oft-trodden though it be, it is the path of guilt. Thus too an agent
pursues his agency too far and looks after more than was committed to his charge.]
(trans. Mozley Goold)

Lines 585–8, as Labate (1984: 108–9) points out, are routinely bracketed off from the text as interpolations, but on the grounds of incongruity with the context rather than on strong doubts about the language or style of the couplets (cf. Labate 1984: 98–9 on the 'interpolated' lines at *Ars* 2.669–74). Yet it is obvious that the sentiments here cohere with other moralizing passages in the *Ars*, which attempt to draw a line between the ethics to be practiced in the erotic world and those to be practiced outside it (cf. 1.739–40). Nevertheless, even if all critics agreed on the authenticity of the excluded lines, it would be easy to interpret them, along with the other moralizing codas, in a subversive manner. Like Ovid's disclaimers of teaching adultery, these codas may be read as drawing attention to the possibility of transgression as much as to denying intent to encourage it. But Ovid's moralizing codas, I suggest, lack the playfulness and charged ambiguity of the adultery disclaimers: critics are more often worried by the earnestness of the former. The difference in tone between these codas and the disclaimers of adultery may be polemical. Many of the old urban elite in Rome can only have found Augustus' revolutionary sexual laws unforgivably intrusive on their traditional freedoms (Gibson 2003: 31–2, 334–5). As such, the *lex Iulia* appears in the *Ars* as a legitimate target for subversion, while elsewhere Ovid pointedly makes clear that 'established' ethics remain unaffected by his teaching.

There is a wider context for this reading of Ovid's moralizing codas. It is evident that in the *Ars* Ovid is trying to move love elegy in a new direction—away, in fact, from the characteristic binary oppositions of earlier love elegy (Gibson 2007: 72–86). In earlier elegy, for example, the life of love and civil life were strongly opposed: lawyers and government officials were excluded from the fun (e.g. Prop. 1.6; Ov. *Am.* 1.15). But the *Ars* seeks rather to include such figures within its ambit (1.79–88, 3.525–54), even if they are ultimately made to appear a second best to love poets. Connected with this is Ovid's determination to move love elegy out onto the streets of Augustus' Rome. Earlier love elegy had either ignored Augustus' new Rome, applauded lukewarmly from the sidelines, or ultimately seen there a potential for corruption of the poet's beloved girl (Gibson 2005: 163–4). In Book 4 of his elegies Propertius had even contrived largely to turn his back on Augustus' Rome in preference for the city's grottoes and waters (Fantham 1997). But in the *Ars*, Ovid conspicuously mingles his pupils with the other citizens on Augustus' streets (1.67–176, 1.213–62, 1.487–504, 3.387–96, 3.631–44).

Yet, for all that, there are limits to Ovid's willingness to cooperate with new Augustan realities, and, as with the *lex Iulia*, the Emperor's city is regarded as a target for subversion. Many of the buildings associated with Augustus and the imperial family—picked out by name in the *Ars* (cf. Barchiesi 2006 on the prominence of the imperial family in the *Ars*)—incorporated within their decorations the values of the Emperor's new morality (Zanker 1988: 101–66). It is hard to resist the conclusion that Ovid's use of these buildings as places for his lovers to meet is an act of mockery (Holleman 1971: 463–6; Wallace-Hadrill 1989: 162–3; Davis 1995: 186ff.). Furthermore, Ovid works hard to expose the tension between the modern splendor of Augustus' transformed Rome and the Emperor's claim to adhere to traditional Roman values—a tension which previous Roman poets had tried to

diffuse (Gibson 2003: 134–5, 140–1 on *Ars* 3.113–28). Ovid offers instead a celebration of the modern and a rejection of the archaic and rustic. (Ovid's thorough-
going preference for the modern in his society is a significant feature of the *Ars*, and
is the driving force behind his rejection of the 'anti-cosmetic' tradition for women—
which even the earlier elegists had embraced—and of a consistent targeting of Horace
in order to expose the contradiction between the latter's modernist poetics and
'archaic' moral standards; see, for the former, Gibson 2006; for the latter, Gibson
2007: 93–9).

This subversion of Augustus' Rome involves, nevertheless, the acceptance of its
existence. In a sense, this is a less radical move than the tendency of earlier elegy to
ignore Rome's new cityscape. Yet the *Ars* does contain—in Book 3—one subtle yet
strong refusal to acknowledge Augustan 'realities'. Here I have in mind Ovid's refusal
to accept the binary polarity of 'matron' and 'whore'. According to a persuasive
reconstruction of the *lex Iulia*, Augustus' law, whatever its other obscurities, attempted
to introduce a moral clarity into Roman society by dividing all citizen women, for
legal purposes, into two highly symbolic categories: prostitutes (and procuresses) on
the one hand, and, on the other, all remaining women, who either were or should
aspire to be *matronae* (McGinn 1998: 147–56, 194–203, 209). The categories of
matrona and *meretrix* carried great resonance in ancient culture, even if they bore
little relation to the complex realities of the spectrum of women's social and legal
statuses. It is this new clarity, precisely, which is resisted in *Ars* 3, where Ovid instead
drives an unexpected middle path between the stereotypical attributes of matron and
whore, and invites addressees to turn themselves into a hybrid which mediates the
'extremities' of the matron–whore polarity (Gibson 2006; 2007: 86–92). Implicit in
all this is Ovid's refusal to accept the binary polarity offered by Augustus as a moral
reality in his new Rome.

The *Ars* and Erotodidaxis

It was stressed earlier that the giving of advice in love had been a significant
element in love elegy, and became the dominant mode of the *Ars*. However, the
'erotodidactic' tradition in elegy (Wheeler 1910, 1911) is itself only one part of
a much larger tradition of giving advice in love relevant to understanding the *Ars*.
In this informal tradition (covered more fully in Gibson 2003: 13–19), it is usual to
find an experienced person passing on (sometimes systematic) advice about a particular loved one or love affairs to an addressee (who may not always be strongly characterized). This tradition, partly philosophical in inspiration (Kleve 1983; Dillon 1994),
may take the glamorous form of Aspasia as instructor of Socrates (Athen. 5.219d;
Halperin 1990: 119–24; Henry 1995: 40–56) or the scandalous form of prose treatises allegedly written by famous prostitutes on sex and sexual positions (Baldwin
1990; Parker 1992: 92–4). The most notorious of the latter was the treatise attributed
to Philaenis (Tsantsanoglou 1973; Vessey 1976; Parker 1992). When a few scraps
from Philaenis were published as *POxy* 2891 in 1972, the treatise turned out instead
to be a more general work on the subject of seduction, and may thus be an important

forerunner of the *Ars* itself. Rather clearer is the influence of New Comedy, where (often older) women offer instruction in their trade to fellow prostitutes (Plaut. *Cist.* 78–119, *Poen.* 210–32; Ter. *Eun.* 434–53). Of particular importance is a scene in Plautus (*Most.* 159–290), where a *lena*-procuress passes on lengthy advice to a younger female prostitute while a lover of the latter listens in the wings. This is scenario repeated by both Propertius in his fourth book (4.5) and Ovid in his *Amores* (1.8); cf. also Tibullus 1.4 (where the god Priapus assumes the role of formal instructor in love to men).

Women dominate this informal tradition, both as pupils and (more often) as teachers of love. This tradition is of particular importance for understanding the third book of the *Ars*, since the rather more respectable tradition of didactic verse represented by Virgil and Lucretius set no precedent for the instruction of an exclusively female audience. Much of *Ars* 3 makes sense when understood against a background of cynical instruction of prostitutes by older women. For Ovid contrives not only to usurp the role of *lena*-procuress (3.57–82, 3.83–98) but also to change the *lena*'s traditional emphasis on manipulation of lovers for the extraction of money and presents into the kind of manipulative behavior likely to flatter men's egos and sustain their erotic interest (3.525–54, 3.577–610, 3.673–86; Gibson 2003: 19–20). Furthermore, the scenario of a male audience eavesdropping in the wings is one explicitly maintained by Ovid in *Ars* 3 (3.1–8), and also serves to make sense of much of the humor directed by the figure of the *praeceptor* at his female pupils (Gibson 2003: 20–21, 35–6).

The *Ars* and Didactic Poetry

Nevertheless, for all the importance of the erotodidactic tradition, didactic poetry remains important to understanding all three books of the *Ars*. As a didactic poem in elegiacs, the *Ars* is an extreme rarity in the ancient literary landscape: few other writers appear to have attempted formalized instruction in this meter (Obbink 1999: 64; Gibson 2003: 8–9). But what exactly is a didactic poem? As a 'genre', didactic poetry shares with the novel the difficulty that both, while apparently familiar forms, display little or no corresponding ancient critical categories. One recent attempt to specify necessary and sufficient conditions for membership of the 'genre'—for example explicit didactic intent, the 'teacher–student constellation' (Volk 2002: 36–41)—is useful and suggestive, but may be open to criticism (Farrell 2003: 384–5, 394–5, 400–1; Sharrock 2003). Another approach is to list an open-ended set of characteristics drawn from a wide range of poems normally thought of as didactic. The danger of circularity of argument here is obvious, but the set produced by Toohey (1996: 4) is undoubtedly good to think with, including instructional subject matter, technical treatment, illustrative (often mythological) inset panels, and a single authorial voice directed explicitly to an addressee. The *Ars*, it will now be clear, possesses all of these characteristics, but it nevertheless lacks two others listed by Toohey: seriousness of form and the hexameter meter.

Whatever the difficulties of defining didactic, and the imperfect fit of the *Ars* with any phenomenological description of the genre, it is obvious that the poem belongs to a tradition of 'frivolous' instructional verse, and is influenced both by the general character of the didactic tradition and some of its classic texts. The playful tradition of didactic verse is illustrated by *Tr.* 2.471–96, where the poet, as part of his defense of the *Ars*, catalogues works on dice and board games (cf. *Ars* 3.353–80), on ball games, swimming, cosmetics (cf. Ovid's own *Medicamina*), and dining (cf. *Ars* 3.747–68) etc. The ancestry of this tradition is often traced back ultimately to the Hellenistic poets Aratus and Nicander, who produced sophisticated versifications of prose treatises on (respectively) the constellations, and poisonous creatures and antidotes. Aratus and Nicander in their turn looked back to Hesiod's *Works and Days* (Hollis 1973: 89–90)—the text traditionally seen as the foundation stone of the didactic tradition—and Ovid certainly alludes to all three authors or their characteristic style in the *Ars* (see Hollis 1977: 107–8 on *Ars* 1.411–12 (Aratus), *idem* 47 on 1.75 (Nicander); Gibson 2003: 140 on 3.121–2 (Hesiod)). However, a rather more useful example of the 'frivolous' didactic tradition for thinking about the *Ars* is perhaps the fourth-century BC *Hedupatheia* ('*Life of Pleasure*') by Archestratus of Gela, which combines notoriety of reputation with a similar emphasis on personal restraint; see Gibson (2007: 64–6, 110–12).

The *Ars* is also clearly influenced by the general character of the didactic tradition (Küppers 1981). It employs, for example, a range of traditional imperatival expressions (Gibson 1998); affects abrupt changes of subject in a style associated particularly with Hesiod and Lucretius (e.g. 2.467–8, 3.99–100, 3.499–500); sets out its instructional program in advance, and marks its own progress through that program in a manner established already in Hellenistic didactic (Hollis 1977: 39 on *Ars* 1.35–40; Gibson 2003: 4, and *idem* 130 on 3.101), often with nautical and chariot imagery also found in earlier didactic poetry (Kenney 1958: 205–6); and uses conventional formulae of introduction, transition, and closure (Kenney 1958: 201–4). For more examples, see Gibson (2003: 430, General Index s.v. 'didactic poetry').

On top of this one can highlight the intertextual relations of the *Ars* with the *De Rerum Natura* and the *Georgics*. The *Ars* is hardly alone in Latin poetry in making frequent reference to these two monumental works, but it is fair to say Ovid privileges reference to his two didactic predecessors, often by alluding to them at key moments, such as the reference to the halfway point of Virgil's *Georgics* (2.541–2) at the corresponding point of Ovid's own project of instructing men (*Ars* 1.771–2). In this way Ovid invites the reader to read the *Ars* alongside, and potentially in the same manner as, the two great didactic works of his time. Ovid's engagement with Lucretius and the *Georgics*—often comic or subversive in effect—is now well documented in the literature on the *Ars*: for uses of the arguments and imagery of Lucretius, see Sommariva (1980), Shulman (1980–81), Steudel (1992), and Miller (1996–97); for the use of Virgil, see Leach (1964: 149–52), Hollis (1973: 91–92, 97–100), and Steudel (1992).

The *Ars* and the *de Officiis*

The privileging of reference to Lucretius and Virgil (and indeed earlier love elegy) has served to obscure another author to whom Ovid makes especially frequent reference in the *Ars*. That author, perhaps surprisingly for a poetic text such as the *Ars*, is Cicero, and the particular text to which Ovid refers is his *de Officiis*. Parallels between the two texts had long been noted, but it fell to Mario Labate to demonstrate why the parallels were important for understanding the *Ars* (Labate 1984: 121–74). The *de Officiis*, addressed to Cicero's son Marcus, offers practical and systematic ethical advice to the young elite of Rome, nothing less than 'a set of guiding principles for life' (Dyck 1996: 16). The target of much of Cicero's reflection and advice in this treatise is the smooth operation of society, and he emphasizes that individuals should aim to earn the esteem of their fellows and foster consensus. Paramount, in Cicero's view, are personal flexibility, the practice of the social virtues and considerate manners, and the observation of the principle of *decorum* (appropriate or becoming behavior). In earlier love elegy, relations between male and female were often characterized by violence, drunkenness, and dysfunction (e.g. Prop. 3.8; Ov. *Am.* 1.7). But in the *Ars*, Ovid regularly emphasizes that the lovers must play their part in the smooth running of a love affair, conduct themselves in an obliging manner, and practice personal *decorum* (cf. e.g. 1.709–12, 2.107, 2.145–6, 2.177–8, 2.497–500). The allusions of the *Ars* to, or consonances with, the *de Officiis* are symptomatic of this new drive toward cooperative behavior between lovers; in *Ars* 3 alone, cf., for example, 89–100 (*Off.* 1.51–2), 299–310 (*Off.* 1.128–9, 131), 305 (*Off.* 1.130), 433–66 (*Off.* 1.130), 501–8 (*Off.* 1.88), 517–24 (*Off.* 1.108), 535–48 (*Off.* 1.45), and 555–76 (*Off.* 1.47) (with Gibson 2003: ad loc.). Central to this new ethic is the concept of *decorum* (and its near relation 'moderation', mentioned earlier as a feature of the *Ars*), which Cicero helpfully insisted could 'be seen in every deed and word, and, indeed, in every bodily movement or state' (*Off.* 1.126). Although intended by Cicero as a serious guide to moral behavior among the Roman elite, *decorum* proved an easy target for transplantation to the arena of merely 'appropriate' (and not necessarily ethical) behavior for lovers (Gibson 2007: 122–26). The concept of *decorum* had been conspicuous by its near absence in earlier elegy (Gibson 2007: 118–19), but Ovid makes it central to a range of behavior in the *Ars*, from appropriate complexion and proper gift-giving for men (1.729–30, 2.262) to becoming hairstyles, clothing, and sexual positions for women (3.135–6, 3.188–91, 3.771–2); see Gibson (2007: 126–29) for a fuller analysis.

Coda

All codas to the *Ars* are obliged to tell some version of the tragic sequel. I suggested earlier that throughout the *Ars* Ovid appears to invite readers to watch out for passages where he may break the spirit or letter of the *lex Iulia*. A dangerous game—and one which Ovid lost, if, as many critics believe, the *Ars* was the main reason for the exile of the poet in AD 8 to a small provincial town in Romania on the outermost reaches of the Empire (see most recently Knox 2004; for powerful dissenting voices, which place emphasis instead on Ovid's mysterious 'mistake', see Green 1982a; Goold 1983).

FURTHER READING

This short chapter inevitably presents only a partial view of the range and complexity of the three books of the *Ars*, and should be read alongside the general contributions also of, for example, Hollis (1973), Watson (2002), Sharrock (2002b), and Holzberg (2002: 92–113). The standard text for the poem is E. J. Kenney's superb revised *Oxford Classical Text* of 1994 (corrected 1995). The *Ars* has attracted numerous detailed commentaries: Hollis (1977) and Dimundo (2003) on Book 1, Janka (1997) on Book 2, and Gibson (2003) on Book 3, plus useful single-volume commentaries on all three books by Brandt (1902) and Pianezzola et al. (1991). The collection of essays edited by Gibson et al. (2006) brings together many of the critics who have worked on the *Ars* in both Europe and the United States since the 1980s, and introduces the reader to a representative range of issues and styles of criticism connected with the *Ars*. The first essay in that volume—Green (2006)—offers a detailed survey of the most important criticism on the *Ars* from the late 1950s onwards. As Green's survey shows, criticism on the *Ars*—for reasons that are unclear—has often proceeded in article form rather than in monographs. Nevertheless, two rather dissimilar monographs published in the 1980s have remained influential: Labate (1984) and Myerowitz (1985), where the first works within the traditions of German and Italian philological criticism and the second adheres to an American tradition of sociological and cultural approaches to the text. More recent monographs include Steudel (1992), Sharrock (1994a), Wildberger (1998), and Gibson (2007). On the reception of the *Ars*, Janka (2006), Hexter (2006), and Liveley (2006) provide a useful starting-point.

CHAPTER EIGHT

Remedia Amoris

Barbara Weiden Boyd

Introduction

Ovid's interest in testing the boundaries of didactic elegy is evident from both his extended exploration of the confrontation of *ratio* and *furor* in the three books of *Ars amatoria* and his juxtaposition of time and (the absence of) consequentiality in *Fasti*. The basic function of a boundary is to define, to establish a division between yours and mine, history and myth, love and war. Ovid's consistent commitment to the transgression of such boundaries is evident, beginning with the opening lines of his first published work (or at least the first surviving published work: cf. Cameron 1968; Boyd 1997: 142–7; Holzberg 1997: 41–3; Barchiesi 1988: 101–3), *Amores*: *arma graui numero uiolentaque bella parabam / edere* (*Am.* 1.1.1–2). That commitment finds what is perhaps its most mature and challenging expression in the poet's one non-elegiac work, *Metamorphoses*: the unceasing cycle of change, expressed repeatedly on the levels of language, style, subject matter, and organization all interacting with and responding to each other, constantly blurs the boundaries between animate and inanimate, reward and punishment, male and female, life and death, and even between human and divine. As a result, Ovid's readers are challenged repeatedly to revise, reconsider, and rethink their own understanding of the natural order of things, and to contemplate the implications of a literary universe in which the boundaries that separate us from the chaos in which Ovid's poem opened are as contingent and variable as the temperaments of the gods who inhabit so many metamorphic myths.

Much of the energy that animates contemporary discussion of Ovid and his poetry is driven by a desire to capture and get a grip on this definitively Protean poet. The poet's slipperiness, his ability to switch back and forth between themes, genres, and perspectives, ensures the engagement of readers drawn to (and by) his intellectual brinksmanship. In this context, *Remedia amoris* has had little opportunity to seize the limelight: as at once both explicit sequel and apparent conclusion to Ovid's career as erotodidact, its thin veneer of novelty is repeatedly breached by its overly determined character. Thus, scholarship on *Remedia* has until very recently looked at the poem as nothing more than an appendage to *Ars*, and has found little to add to what has already been said about the earlier work (e.g. Hollis 1973: 110–12; Küppers 1981; Holzberg 2002: 107–11; Gale 2005: 109–11). The same tendency informed my decision, made about a decade ago, to give *Remedia* subordinate status in *Brill's Companion to Ovid* (Watson 2002; cf. also Sharrock 2002b). The opportunity to correct this oversight by taking the poem on its own terms here is therefore both welcome and timely: several scholars have only recently begun to do the same, and I gladly join their ranks (e.g. Brunelle 1997, 2000–1, 2002; Fulkerson 2004; Rosati 2006; Hardie 2006). In the following discussion, therefore, I shall aim to open up our usual perspectives on *Remedia*, and to follow Ovid's example in transgressing the usual boundaries that characterize discussions of this poem. This essay is meant to serve as both an introduction to work on the poem and an attempt to take this work a step or two further by suggesting alternatives for framing the discussion in the future.

Remedia has typically invited analysis and discussion on a number of different topics: its date and, by implication, its relationship to the three books of *Ars* (Geisler 1969: 47–54; Syme 1978: 8–15; Murgia 1986a, 1986b; Brunelle 1997: 10–19; Woytek 2000: 182; Gibson 2003: 37–43); its central panel (357–96), in which Ovid as *praeceptor amoris* interrupts his amatory advice, directed at an audience of *decepti iuuenes* and *puellae* (41 and 49), to speak *in poetae persona* on behalf of his Muse and to mount a defense of his poetic choices (Woytek 2000; Hinds 2000: 223–5; Holzberg 2002: 110; Holzberg 2006: 45–50; Casali 2006: 219–22); its deployment of the conceit of *medicina amoris* in the context of a didactic tradition going back to Nicander, who with *Theriaca* and *Alexipharmaca* offers a model, in his catalogues of poisons and their cures, for the didactic investigation of both illness and its cure (Hollis 1973: 110; Henderson 1979: xiv; Pinotti 1988: 15 and n. 4; Toohey 1996: 62–77); and its *exempla*, particularly the agricultural analogies (Leach 1964) and the extended mythological scenes involving Circe (263–90) and Phyllis (591–608) (Davisson 1996; Michalopoulos 2000–2; Brunelle 2002). In part because these topics have received ample, if not conclusive, treatment elsewhere, and in part because my goal is to look at *Remedia* with fresh eyes, each of these topics may appear at least superficially underdeveloped, more or less, in what follows; in fact, I hope at least by implication to contribute to our ability to engage each of these topics by bringing some underappreciated features of *Remedia* to readers' attention here.

The Metapoetic Frame

The poem's structure is noteworthy. An essentially linear sequence of therapeutic precepts is framed by an extended proem and a brief *envoi*, each of which draws attention to the poet's control of (and interference in) his subject matter. The poet does not otherwise withdraw from *Remedia*, however—rather, his omnipresence makes itself felt throughout the poem's sections of instruction, in repeated appeals to autopsy and allusions to fictive 'experiences' that exist in the worlds of myth and of Ovid's other poems. Ovid also inserts himself quite literally into the poem, playing a, or the, central role in a metanarrative about the interplay of genre and authority.

This metanarrative consists of three episodes, or scenes: the first is depicted in the opening forty lines, as Ovid describes the conversation in which he explained and justified to Cupid the title of the current work; the second draws attention to itself by breaking quite literally into the climactic center of the poem, where Ovid interrupts his own instructions on how to avoid being overpowered by desire in the midst of sexual intercourse with an *apologia* for his choice of elegy and a comparison of his elegiac accomplishment to Virgil's achievement in epic; and the third recalls a dream which the poet (thinks he may have) had, in which *Lethaeus Amor* appeared to offer him instruction *in paruo* mirroring the more extensive instruction Ovid himself gives in *Remedia*.

The last of these in particular has inspired puzzlement in readers—what exactly is the function of Cupid's intrusion into *Remedia* at this point? It has been suggested that we may wish to read the last several hundred lines of *Remedia* as evidence of Ovid's waning interest in the poem's ostensible goals. Kenney (1990: 253) summarizes this view with his comment, 'Many readers have felt that as the end of the *Remedia* comes in sight Ovid's treatment becomes increasingly more perfunctory.' Such a reading, while perhaps too reductive to be taken literally, does have some value, in that it highlights the odd lack of closure that characterizes the poem as a whole. Conte (1994) demonstrates that the burden of *Remedia* is to resist the closure that defines the elegiac genre, and that it is this resistance, rather than the autobiographical fiction Ovid constructs to convey it, that explains how *Remedia* can be the end of erotic elegy. Before proceeding forward from Conte's premise, however, I want to look at this last scene in the context of the other two metapoetic episodes I have mentioned. I suggest that the affinity between and among the three episodes helps Ovid's readers to make sense of each of them, and that together they reflect on the place of *Remedia* in Ovid's elegiac *corpus*.

The *Remedia* proem invokes a dramatic scenario, the realism of which is undercut by its very allusiveness: that is, even as Ovid describes a challenge from Cupid and his own lively self-defense, his readers cannot help but recall the formally similar scene with which *Amores* opened. Ovid thus both exposes the current fiction and draws his readers back into the poetic world created in *Amores*—but with a twist (cf. also Rosati 2006: 143–6; Hardie 2006: 171–3). In the earlier scene, Cupid was in control: Ovid's ostensible determination to write *Aeneid*-style epic could not resist the all-powerful god of love. By the end of *Am.* 1.1, therefore, the poet's course has been dramatically altered, and epic aspirations are but a distant memory; through the remainder of *Amores*, Ovid uses first-person dramatic narrative to explore the subject matter selected for him by Cupid (Boyd 1997: 132–42; Holzberg 2002: 46–70). The *Remedia* proem, on the other hand, entails no such capitulation: now Cupid is the one caught up short, as the poet rebukes him for misconstruing the title of this new work (1–4):

Legerat huius Amor titulum nomenque libelli:
  'bella mihi, uideo, bella parantur' ait.
'parce tuum uatem sceleris damnare, Cupido,
  tradita qui toties te duce signa tuli.'

Amor had read this book's label and name: 'Wars, I see, wars against me are afoot,' says he. 'Cupid, cease and desist from accusing your poet of crime—I who, under your leadership, have so often borne the standards entrusted to me.'

This time, furthermore, Cupid cannot divert Ovid from his chosen course: in fact, most of the remainder of the proem is given over to Ovid's logical argument that Cupid should not be rebuking him, for Cupid is, after all, not a fighter but the god of love—a perfect instance of what Galinsky (1975: 30) describes as Ovid's tendency to *reductio ad amorem*. The mirror image of *Am.* 1.1 thus effected in the *Remedia* proem concludes with Cupid's inevitable capitulation; whereas the triumphant god of *Am.* 1.1 had nullified Ovid's attempt to stay on course with the crisp command: '*quod . . . canas, uates, accipe . . . opus*' (*Am.* 1.1.24), he now yields, however begrudgingly: '*propositum perfice . . . opus*' (40).

At the close of this scene, *Remedia* proceeds to a second proem; the little drama with Cupid is over, and the god has exited the stage. Ovid now addresses his audience, and offers an impressive résumé (41–70). After asserting his continuing identity as *praeceptor* and, indeed, as liberator of those enslaved by love (71–4), Ovid welcomes the inspirational presence of Apollo, who as *medicus* is an apt patron for the current work (75–8). The double-proem construction establishes a model for the kind of reading Ovid asks his audience to undertake in this poem: that is, he invites a reading on two levels: one that considers the instruction offered by the *praeceptor* within the closed framework of erotodidactic poetry and the other that invites, even demands, readers' attentiveness to the paradoxical nature of Ovid's inspiration.

This model for reading reasserts itself at *Rem.* 357–96, just as the *praeceptor* launches into a discussion of how best to control one's desires even when engaged in intercourse (357–60):

> nunc tibi, quae medio Veneris praestemus in usu,
> > eloquar: ex omni est parte fugandus Amor.
> multa quidem ex illis pudor est mihi dicere, sed tu
> > ingenio uerbis concipe plura meis.

> And now, what we advise in the middle of the sex act itself, I shall tell you: love must be routed on every side. It is indeed embarrassing for me to say many of these things, but you should imagine in your mind more than my words say.

Readers pursuing the wisdom to be gleaned from Ovid's wide-ranging advice on all things erotic can hardly be blamed for thinking that the poet has chosen a decidedly inappropriate moment to interrupt his instructions—made even more off-putting by his sudden introduction of a lengthy reflection upon his literary reputation (361–4):

> nuper enim nostros quidam carpsere libellos,
> > quorum censura Musa proterua mea est.
> dummodo sic placeam, dum toto canter in orbe,
> > qui uolet, impugnent unus et alter opus.

> In fact, recently some people have found fault with my books, and in their judgment
> my Muse is naughty. So long as this makes me pleasing, so long as my poetry is sung
> throughout the world, one or two people are welcome to impugn my verse.

In place of the expected consummation of desire in sexual intercourse—the single
end-point and goal of almost all the instruction dispensed until now—Ovid intrudes
with a defense of his Muse and his elegiac calling. He shifts, in other words, from
one level of reading to the other, and so draws attention to the fictiveness of his
didactic world.

Ovid's self-defense is articulated in terms that are explicitly literary, and perhaps
implicitly political as well (Casali 2006; Holzberg 2006): unnamed critics (*quidam*;
unus et alter, cf. *quicumque es*, 371) are assimilated to the notorious opponents of
the great epic poets, from Homer's fault-finder Zoilus (365–6) to Ovid's own contemporaries, critics of the *Aeneid* (367–8). Framing Ovid's central defense, furthermore, is a series of allusions to *Liuor* (369, 389; cf. *inuidia*, 397), the personified
Envy with roots in Pindaric epinician that became a focus of Callimachean polemic
(Call. *H.* 2.105–13). Ovid's *Liuor*, unlike Callimachus', however, has targeted the
poet's alleged epic pretensions (*summa petit Liuor*, 369); Ovid's defense asserts that
such criticisms are misplaced, since the license and playfulness of his verse are entirely
in keeping with the character of his elegiac Muse (387–8):

> si mea materiae respondet Musa iocosae,
>   uicimus, et falsi criminis acta rea est.

> If my Muse complements my playful subject, we have won, and she is found to have
> been falsely charged with crime.

Ovid thus makes explicit the division between art and life that, at least since Catullus
(16.5–6; cf. Holzberg 2006), had been a feature of self-conscious poetic discourse;
at the same time, he not only exposes but also invites critical scrutiny of the choices
he makes in style and subject. The fact that the erotodidaxis of the poem experiences
virtual *coitus interruptus* with this *apologia* is, therefore, not simply a clever mimicking
of sexual frustration—though it is certainly that—but also a way for Ovid to call
attention to his own seductive abilities as poet (Sharrock 1994a). The poetic metanarrative both insulates the integrity of the Ovidian *praeceptor*'s instructions and
arouses the paradoxical desire of his reader to bypass them in his (the reader imagined
here is surely male) pursuit of erotic *and* narrative satisfaction.

A third metapoetic moment interrupts Ovid's erotic instruction at 549–78, even
as it adds to the authority of his advice: this is the dream sequence to which I have
already referred (Hardie 2006: 178–86). The *praeceptor* has just recommended
overindulgence as a sure means of abating one's desire, and has suggested that
fears of infidelity be banished, too (531–48). Suddenly the scene and tone of
the poem shift, as Ovid embarks upon an ecphrasis describing one of the two temples
of Venus Erycina in Rome (549–50). In this temple, Ovid claims, Cupid in the
character of *Lethaeus Amor* spoke to him, and offered him further instruction on

how to dampen one's desire. The nature of Cupid's appearance is described by Ovid as something of a puzzle: was it really Cupid, or a dream of Cupid, that he saw (555–6, 575–6)?

> is mihi sic dixit (dubito uerusne Cupido
>   an somnus fuerit; sed, puto, somnus erat) . . .
> plura loquebatur; placidum puerilis imago
>   destituit somnum, si modo somnus erat.

> So he spoke to me (though whether he was really Cupid or a dream, I'm not sure; but I think he was a dream) . . . He had more to say; the boyish apparition departed my deep sleep—if in fact it was sleep.

The emphasis thus placed on the ambiguous nature of Cupid's epiphany locates this scene in a long tradition of poetic *Dichterweihen*, beginning with the appearance of the Muses to Hesiod and wending its way, through the Hesiodic dream with which Callimachus opened *Aetia* (Pfeiffer 1949 on Callim. *Aet.* 1 fr. 2.1–5 and on the scholia to *Aet.* fr. 2; Cameron 1995: 127–32; Fantuzzi and Hunter 2004: 6–7), and the Homeric dream that appears to have begun Ennius' *Annales* (Skutsch 1985 on *Ann.* 1.ii–x) all the way down to Ovid himself, who has in fact repeatedly described the experience of divine epiphany as part of his own experience, even as he uses the cliché to assert his independence from it. Each book of *Amores* opens with an epiphany (1.1, Cupid; 2.1, Cupid; 3.1, *Elegia* and *Tragoedia*); the first book of *Ars amatoria*, on the other hand, opens with an explicit disavowal of Apollo and the Muses, making *usus* the vehicle of poetic inspiration instead (25–30). And of course *Remedia* opens with a scene that gestures to all these familiar models even as the poet punctures Cupid's sense of injury by asserting that Cupid remains as central to Ovid's poetic purpose as ever. In the present scene, that centrality is implicitly reaffirmed, as Cupid assumes the role of *fons et origo* for the *praeceptor*'s instructions; yet Ovid simultaneously exposes the logical problem at the heart of this sequence of events by putting into Cupid's mouth the very advice that will make Cupid's power obsolete. As the epithet *Lethaeus* indicates, the one sure release from desire is forgetfulness; in the context of the elegiac tradition, in which memory and desire are united as a single source of inspiration, *Lethaeus Amor* is a conundrum whose role in the metanarrative of *Remedia* effectively writes him out of a career. It is hardly illogical, then, albeit surprising, that Ovid closes this episode with an allusion to the loss of the helmsman Palinurus by Aeneas (577–8):

> quid faciam? media nauem Palinurus in unda
>   deserit: ignotas cogor inire uias.

> What am I to do? In mid-sea Palinurus abandons ship, and I am compelled to enter upon unfamiliar paths.

This allusion casts Ovid in the role of Aeneas, a reference to epic models to which I shall return below (**Genres**). Less clear, however, is the role played by Cupid here:

are we to see him in the role of Palinurus, fallen overboard and no longer able to guide Ovid's ship-poem, or should we be reminded instead of the god Somnus, who effected Palinurus' demise? As Virgil describes him, Somnus bears a striking resemblance to *Lethaeus Amor* (*Aen.* 5.854–6):

> ecce deus ramum Lethaeo rore madentem
> uique soporatum Stygia super utraque quassat
> tempora, cunctantique natantia lumina soluit . . .

> Lo! the god shakes a branch, soaked with Lethe's water and drowsy with Stygian force, above both temples; although Palinurus resists, the god closes his swimming eyes . . .

Ovid appears to have conflated Somnus and Palinurus, aggressor and victim, in describing the disappearance of Cupid from his poem and so characterizing his own state of abandonment as comparable to that of Aeneas at the loss of Palinurus. With Ovid's final experience of erotodidactic inspiration, therefore, we are left to wonder whether Cupid's misreading of *Remedia*'s title, as imagined in the opening scene of the poem, was indeed a misreading after all. The erasure of Cupid and of the situations in which Cupid determines desire spells the conclusion of *Remedia*, and leaves Ovid to guide his poem single-handedly to shore. The lack of closure I have already noted can be understood as a distinguishing feature of love elegy in which Love himself has abandoned ship.

Praecepta

The instruction Ovid offers in *Remedia* is abundant, even excessive; every sort of temptation or allurement is imagined only to be dispelled. If we wish to locate the sense of order that operates behind this apparent jumble of recommendations—at times self-contradictory—it is most helpful to consider them not as 40 discrete *praecepta* but as belonging to five general categories of advice, in each of which Ovid gathers together a series of permutations on the theme. These categories in turn all draw at least to some extent on the medical metaphor that gives the poem its title. They also gradually but definitively deconstruct the world created by elegy—its pastimes, preoccupations, and landscapes, its way of viewing the world.

Time provides Ovid with his first organizing principle. The importance of time in the management of a love affair is a theme derived from medical discourse, in which the importance of 'the opportune moment' (ὁ καιρός) is central (see e.g. Hippoc. *Praec.* 1; and cf. Pinotti 1988 on *Rem.* 107–34). Ovid begins with delay, which should be avoided at all costs (*mora dat uires*, 83). The longer one delays, the less efficacious any medicine is likely to be (91–2): *sero medicina paratur, / cum mala per longas conualuere moras.* A survey of natural phenomena provides evidence to support this thesis: as time allows trees to grow and flourish so does it nurture love. The external evidence of a tree's growth (*umbras*, 85) is matched only by the tenacity of its roots, the insidiousness of which Ovid parallels to the flame of passion working silently within someone whose love has been allowed to last (105–6).

In this desperate situation, hope would appear to be lost; yet it is at this crucial juncture that the Ovidian *praeceptor* promises not to abandon his patient. In fact, Ovid suggests, he is up to the task, however heroic may be the measures required: with the words *maius opus* (a Virgilian tag: *Aen* 7.45) describing his own assistance and an apt reference to Philoctetes, whose cure, albeit long overdue, brought the Trojan War to a close, Ovid claims an ability to dispel even the longest-lasting disease of love (107–18).

The application of a timely cure is not simply a matter of swift defensive action, however; Ovid proceeds to provide complementary advice and urges that a cure not be attempted too soon. *Furor*, he observes, can be dangerous to face head-on (119–20):

> dum furor in cursu est, currenti cede furori:
>   difficiles aditus impetus omnis habet.

> While passion is in midcourse, yield to coursing passion; all headstrong force is difficult to confront.

Moderation in all things is the instructor's watchword: for *medicina* to be most effective, it must be neither delayed nor hurried (131–4).

Ovid's second organizing principle is activity, a concept that by its very nature is frequently linked to place. Thus, *otium* is to be avoided: *fac monitis fugias otia prima meis* (136). Action is the opposite of *otium*: *res age, tutus eris* (144). Ovid here inverts all the truisms about love as like a form of military service so spectacularly developed in *Am.* 1.9; there, Ovid constructs an opposition between *amor* and *desidia* (*qui nolet fieri desidiosus, amet*, 46), that is here rejected by the *amator*-turned-*praeceptor*. As Ovid develops a list of specific *res agendae*, he links them closely with particular locations: thus, there is the law, and its intrinsic connection to the Forum (151); there is war, in this post-Actium era exemplified here as elsewhere by reference to a distant campaign in Parthia (153–8; cf. *Ars* 1.177–228 and Hollis 1977: ad loc.; Fulkerson 2004: 213–16). Then again, there is agriculture; one need not go to Parthia when the Roman *rura* themselves can keep one very busy (169–98). Ovid's advice throughout this section is a reprise of scenes familiar from not only *Georgics* but also *Eclogues*; Ovid offers a revisionist reading of the bucolic world, however, filled as it is here with goats, calves, and shepherds playing reed-pipes, but with nary a lover to be found. Yet another locus for escape is that provided by hunting and fishing (199–212); sheer physical exhaustion will provide respite. Again, Ovid evokes an erotic landscape only to revise it: the pursuit of hunting—so central to the Milanion *exemplum* with which Propertius inaugurates his elegiac *opus* and most likely a central feature of Gallan erotic elegy (Prop. 1.1.9–16; Ross 1975: 61–5; Rosen and Farrell 1986)—is now explicitly stripped of its amatory associations (205–6):

> nocte fatigatum somnus, non cura puellae,
>   excipit et pingui membra quiete leuat.

> At night, sleep rather than love of a girl gets hold of a weary man, and relaxes his limbs in easy calm.

Ovid thus constructs a sequence of venues for escape that moves outward as he proceeds, from the Forum at the center of Rome, to the *rura* outside of the city, to the forests and mountain ridges where wild animals hide. Finally, he evokes the entire world—travel is the best medicine, and the farther from one's beloved, the better (*i procul, et longas carpere perge uias*, 214). Ovid thus revises his *Amores* again, now transforming the heartfelt desire to be reunited with his *puella* (e.g. *Am.* 2.16; Boyd 1997: 55–66) into its exact opposite. In so doing, Ovid mounts an assault on the entire elegiac tradition of love, as encapsulated in Virgil's tribute to Gallan amatory excess. In *Eclogue* 10, Virgil depicts a Gallus who resorts to virtually all the same escapes—escapes that link activity and place—in his attempt to cure his love for Lycoris. Gallus considers a military career as diversion (44–5), and then the life of a shepherd (50–1); then he imagines the career of a hunter (52–60)—only to reject them all in the end, acknowledging that, however far he may travel in pursuit of the points of the compass, he cannot escape Love (64–9):

non illum nostri possunt mutare labores,
nec si frigoribus mediis Hebrumque bibamus
Sithoniasque niues hiemis subeamus aquosae,
nec si, cum moriens alta liber aret in ulmo,
Aethiopum uersemus ouis sub sidere Cancri.
omnia uincit Amor: et nos cedamus Amori.

Our efforts cannot change him, neither if we should sip from the Hebrus in midwinter or endure the watery winter's Sithonian snows, nor if, when the dying bark dries on the lofty elm, we should tend the Ethiopians' flocks under the sign of Cancer. Love conquers all: let us too yield to Love.

The movement away from Rome that Ovid recommends through this series of remedies parallels a movement away from Rome within the narrative of *Remedia*, as the *praeceptor* recognizes the extreme nature of his prescriptions (225–48). Severe though his remedies are, they are practical, unlike the other-worldly cures embodied by magic. Allusions to Medea and Circe illustrate the difference between his own effective cures, sanctioned by Apollo, and the desperate (and, in Circe's case, ultimately ineffective) measures taken by the witches of myth (249–90).

Ovid's rejection of magic complements the narrative's return to Rome (291–2), where we can locate the third category of advice. The *praeceptor* acknowledges the power a *puella* can have, even (or especially) when her venality and faithlessness are evident—indeed, he admits his own vulnerability (311–14), and so confirms the relevance of *Amores* to his assertion of experience. Working from this experience, Ovid advises his pupil to accentuate the negative, and provides a detailed catalogue of the many ways in which a girl's physical defects can be emphasized (315–40; cf. Lucr. *DRN* 4.1160–70 and *Ars* 2.657–62; Sommariva 1980: 135–42). In fact, once begun this manner of thinking allows a lover both to find fault with a girl bereft of *cultus* and to be nauseated by the cosmetics she resorts to (341–56). Again, then, every illusion of love is to be dissected by the reluctant lover; simultaneously, the conceits that make the wheels of the elegiac machine run are stripped of their power.

This advisory section is interrupted pointedly by the address to detractors discussed above (see **Introduction**); when the *praeceptor* redirects his attention to his audience, both the poem and its precepts reach a climax in instructions for the conduct of intercourse itself. Ovid's advice here is fundamentally problematic—he at first endorses an encounter in which sexual arousal is delayed and then compromised by distaste and even disgust (399–418); the paradox inherent in this advice is reflected in his ambivalence about the relative desirability of various positions for intercourse (425–40). Ovid thus neatly reaches (in the company of his readers) a climax that is no climax, as he raises the curtain on elegiac illusion.

The fourth category of *praecepta* set forth in *Remedia* is characterized by excess. Ovid begins by recommending a more appealing alternative to the anticlimax of the preceding series: have two girlfriends (or even more, if you're able), not one (441–2). This option lends itself to a wide variety of *exempla* drawn from nature and, *in extenso*, heroic myth (445–86). Here Ovid turns aside for a moment to acknowledge that feigned love may sometimes become real in spite of one's intent; the only solution is to resort to the very deception that is a *puella*'s stock in trade, and to deceive oneself (489–522). After this deconstruction of elegiac deception, Ovid returns to the theme of excess, and recommends that his pupil overindulge to the point of tedium (523–48); novelty itself loses its appeal in a world not controlled by the rules of elegiac love.

After the dream excursus, a complementary extension of Ovid's eulogy of excess returns us to the *praecepta* proper: just as many partners can provide ample distraction, so the lack of companionship can drive one to suicidal thoughts, even behavior: look at Phyllis, whose obsessive longing for Demophoon, played out in her repeated—and repeatedly frustrated—journeys to the shore in search of him, led her to hang herself (579–608). Thus, Ovid again exposes the difficulty of self-control, as he demonstrates that only physical excess can hope to trump emotional excess.

A fifth category of advice proceeds logically from the fourth category's preoccupation with excessive contact with others: that is, Ovid now turns to discuss the company one keeps in general, and develops a series of *praecepta* around the sorts of situations in which contact with others can work to one's advantage or disadvantage. The medical conceit around which this category of precepts is organized is *contagium*: *facito contagia uites*, 613 (Pinotti 1988: ad loc.). Thus, avoidance of places and situations in which one is likely to run into an old love is recommended, and Ovid's recovering patients are advised to inhabit a universe (*alter orbis*, 630) different from that previously frequented. In effect, the world of amatory elegy is to be avoided (627–8):

> nec, quae ferre solet spatiantem porticus illam,
> te ferat, officium neue colatur idem.

> Neither should the portico that typically hosts her when she goes for a stroll welcome you, nor should the same activity she engages in be cultivated by you.

In one quick couplet, Ovid thus advises his pupils to keep away from the very places he had previously described as such fertile ground for the seeds of love, the porticoes of Pompey, Octavia, Livia, and Palatine Apollo (*Ars* 1.67–74; Hollis 1977: ad loc.). All once characterized by their erotic associations, these places become in *Remedia* generic locales for the spread of *contagium*, and thus are summarily excluded from the new world of the recovering lover.

Again, this *praeceptum* lends itself to extension: not just places but particular people and topics of conversation should be avoided (635–54). Thus, contact with her relatives and other members of her household is not welcome, especially since the woman in question is likely to come up in conversation; and even if mention of her is unavoidable, denials of love should be restrained: the lover who too vehemently or frequently declares himself out of love (*qui nimium multis 'non amo' dicit*, 648) betrays his continuing vulnerability to contagion. The dangers of excess culminate in Ovid's recommendation that a lover not hate his former *puella*, for the very extremity of such emotions brings love and hate too close. He neatly reminds his reader of the truth to be found in the Catullan declaration *odi et amo* (85.1), and in recommending moderation in its stead puts paid to the premise on which erotic elegy is founded.

Moderation remains the watchword for the succeeding *praecepta*: thus, concealment of emotions is to be preferred over confrontation (673–98). Comparisons, too, are effective—after all, there are many more desirable women than the *puella* in question (707–14). This point allows Ovid to return yet again to the topic of contagion and its avoidance: his pupils are to get rid of reminders and tokens of the beloved, and to avoid the places associated with the affair (715–34).

Like his pupils, Ovid is now approaching the end of the lesson; the remainder of *Remedia* therefore offers a miscellany of last thoughts, most of which add to one of the categories of advice already set forth. Thus, the suggestion that a sexual liaison with a poor girl is ideal extends the idea of avoiding contagion—so long as you do not become poor yourself, the class barrier is a perfect solution for controlling desire (741–50). And then there are forms of entertainment: the theater is a dangerous place, since performers can arouse unanticipated emotions in their viewers; the verses of *teneri poetae*, too, should be shunned—and Ovid stunningly undercuts the *praecepta* heretofore offered his readers by including his own poetry in this category: *summoueo dotes impius ipse meas* (758). The avoidance of rivalry, on the other hand, complements Ovid's earlier advice regarding excess—rivalry has been the cause of any number of famous poetic struggles, from the rape of Helen to the competition between Achilles and Agamemnon over Briseis (767–84). Epic *exempla* yield a last time to medical concerns as Ovid turns to considerations of diet (cf. Celsus *proem.* 9; Pinotti 1988: ad loc.), again offering a middle course between extremes (795–810). His task completed along with his cure, Ovid declares both *Remedia* and his pupils safely to have reached port after the end of their poetic voyage (811–14).

The *praecepta* of *Remedia* offer solutions for the management, treatment, or avoidance of a wide variety of symptoms associated with the disease of love; in the process, they also demonstrate what Fulkerson (2004) calls the 'failure' of *Remedia*, that is, its failure to disassemble the elegiac system which it presumes to undermine. The irony of this failure is itself engineered by Ovid, who expands elegy even as he claims to make it obsolete.

Genre(s)

In the central excursus in defense of his elegy (361–96), Ovid draws an explicit paral-lel between his own work and Virgil's (395–6):

> tantum se nobis elegi debere fatentur,
>   quantum Vergilio nobile debet epos.

> Elegy acknowledges that it owes as much to me as distinguished epic owes to Virgil.

Like the two distinct lines on the page that constitute this Latin couplet, the trope of 'parallelism' embodies a safe separation: that is, even as Ovid claims a sort of equality with Virgil, he establishes a boundary between the two genres the two poets represent. At the same time, however, Ovid's couplet instantiates a challenge to its contents: the hexameter is used to characterize Ovid and elegy; the pentameter, to characterize Virgil and *epos*. This subversive gesture, so typical of Ovid, characterizes the generic play that runs throughout *Remedia*. I shall devote the remainder of this survey, therefore, to a brief examination of the importance of generic transgression in the poem.

The tension between elegy and *epos* is fundamental to Ovid's deployment of the elegiac couplet for didactic poetry. The tradition of didactic poetry is closely identi-fied with epic hexameter, from Hesiod's *Works and Days* to the *Phaenomena* of Aratus, from Nicander's *Alexipharmaca* and *Theriaca* to Lucretius' *De Rerum Natura* and Virgil's *Georgics* (Toohey 1996; Dalzell 1996; Volk 2002). Ovid, however, follows an alternative tradition, offering a brand of didactic which formally aligns itself with both Callimachus' *Aetia* and the erotic subject matter of Hellenistic and Roman elegy.

The Callimachean inspiration behind Ovid's elegy is evident and familiar: meta-poetic scenes and language regularly illustrate the links between and among Ovid's various elegiac works, and establish a decidedly subversive tone when the poet turns to patriotic themes. I have already mentioned some of these formative scenes, and refer readers to some of the many studies of Ovid's poetry that examine the intersec-tion of elegiac values and epic technique in *Metamorphoses* (e.g. Knox 1986; Hinds 1987a; Hinds 2000). I want to conclude this discussion by looking at the mirror-image of this intersection in *Remedia*—that is, at the intersection of epic values and elegiac technique in Ovid's last amatory work.

I have already noted in passing a number of occasions in which Ovid deploys epic imagery and metaphors as he dispenses *praecepta*. Taken together, these figures can be seen to create a sort of 'epic within elegy' narrative—that is, they both assimilate epic to elegy through the *reductio ad amorem* effect, and reveal the tensions that pull Ovid's didacticism in two directions at once. The formal qualities of the poem—its meter and, generally speaking, its diction (Kenney 2002)—are typical of erotic elegy; yet its didactic pose assimilates it to epic, an assimilation that finds repeated expres-sion in the allusions to epic themes and characters that fill the poem (Davisson 1996). In the course of offering *praecepta*, Ovid casts himself at least momentarily in the roles of a variety of epic figures; a healthy recovery from the disease of love is thus given the status of an epic achievement.

The ship metaphor that appears repeatedly through the poem provides an ideal example of the generic complexity of *Remedia*. The conceit that a didactic poem progresses like a journey through time and space is, as many scholars have shown, an essential organizing principle of didactic narrative (Volk 2002: 20–1 offers a summary). Traveling along a path, riding in a chariot, or sailing in a ship is a way of expressing the idea that a didactic poem has a beginning and an end, and that skill and attention are required for the successful completion of the journey. This complex of imagery is pointedly appropriated by Callimachus for non- or only superficially didactic purposes, as when he uses the metaphors of wagon and untrodden paths (*Aet.* 1 fr. 1.25–8 Pf.; Asper 1997) to characterize his own poetic techniques and values. But these same metaphors and others like them are also associated with epic, in particular with the journeys that epic heroes themselves undertake as part of their destinies, especially the wandering heroes Ulysses and Aeneas.

In comparing his progress and that of his readers (and pupils) through *Remedia* to an epic voyage, Ovid offers a reading of epic that brings out its inherently didactic features. Thus, his first application of the metaphor constructs an analogy to the speech given by Aeneas to his men in *Aeneid* 1. Aeneas' men have just survived a ruinous storm at sea; their captain suppresses his own concerns (*Aen.* 1.208–9 *curisque ingentibus aeger / spem uultu simulat, premit altum corde dolorem*) and speaks soothing words (*dictis maerentia pectora mulcet*, 197). His very first words to them are '*O socii*' (198)—an effective acknowledgment of their shared travail and a token of his empathy, as well as a reminder of the Homeric Odysseus' similar, and similarly problematic, role (Hardie 2006: 177). Ovid both retroactively characterizes Aeneas as a *praeceptor* and demonstrates the structural similarity of *Remedia* to its epic models as he takes on Aeneas' role (69–70):

> me duce damnosas, homines, compescite curas,
>   rectaque cum sociis me duce nauis eat.

> With me as your leader, men, calm your ruinous cares, and with me as your leader may our ship sail with our comrades straight ahead.

Ovid evokes a purely metaphorical voyage, but the (ironic) message is the same: those who follow his directions faithfully should reach homeport safe and sound (albeit without the very *curae* that launched this ship of love).

The nautical imagery of *Remedia* reappears in a variety of contexts: thus, when Ovid wants to establish a contrast between the efficacy of his *praecepta* and the ineffective magic of witches, he offers an extended description of Circe's failure to hold on to Ulysses (263–90; Brunelle 2002). In this *exemplum*, the fundamental distinction is that drawn between the down-to-earth advice of Ovid *praeceptor* and the incantations and love magic of Circe; but a parallel distinction is developed from the choice offered to Ulysses, namely, to stay in Circe's thrall or to sail off into his epic identity (*illa loquebatur, nauem soluebat Vlixes*, 285). Ulysses' sea voyage represents both an escape from amatory tedium and an opportunity to continue his journey home, and so to be restored to the narrative of the *Odyssey*. Simultaneously, he provides a model for Ovid's pupils of successful disentanglement from a love affair, and so of successful progress through *Remedia*.

Other nautical images are less obviously epic in their associations, but continue to promote the analogy between success in learning (and applying) the lessons of *Remedia* and a successful voyage. Thus, after an extended discussion of the advantages of having multiple *amicae*, which culminates in an *exemplum* featuring the central events of *Iliad* 1 (Agamemnon's loss of Chryseis and appropriation of Briseis from Achilles, 465–86), Ovid uses the image of a well-stocked ship to underline his advice (487–8):

> quaeris ubi inuenias? artes tu perlege nostras:
>   plena puellarum iam tibi nauis erit.

> Where should you find them, you ask? Read these instructions carefully; your ship will soon enough be full of girls.

Again, after describing the gentleness of his *medicina* (523–8), Ovid imagines a delicate pupil whose resistance cannot stand up to a persistent lover; he uses a nautical image (here as elsewhere in a double entendre: Adams 1982: 167; Janka 1997 on *Ars* 2.9–10) to endorse the course of least resistance as a means to escape for even the most passive:

> desine luctari; referant tua carbasa uenti,
>   quaque uocant fluctus, hac tibi remus eat.

> Stop struggling; let the winds take your sails, and where the waves call, there let your oar carry you.

When Ovid next employs this metaphor, he reminds us of its metapoetic connotation, in the allusion to Palinurus I have already discussed (577–8). There, the poem itself is conceived of as a ship, the poet its helmsman; as Ovid assumes the role previously held by Palinurus, he blurs the distinction between epic and his own didactic *Remedia*, and assimilates the problematic directionless of Aeneas to his own poetic self-consciousness. His indecision quickly fades, however: the next occurrence of the image reasserts the authority of Ovid's *praecepta* as he warns his pupils to avoid their favorite places (737–40):

> praeterita cautus Niseide nauita gaudet:
>   tu loca, quae nimium grata fuere, caue.
> haec tibi sint Syrtes, haec Acroceraunia uita;
>   hic uomit epotas dira Charybdis aquas.

> The cautious sailor rejoices once past Nisus' daughter Scylla: take care to avoid places once too pleasing. Consider these your Syrtes, avoid these as if they were Acroceraunia; here dread Charybdis spews forth the waters she has drunk.

These locales are virtually synonymous with the dangers weathered by Aeneas and his men at various points in their journey (cf. the frustrated catalogue of Juno, *Aen.* 7.302–3). A similarly evocative pair of natural threats, reminders of Ulysses' voyage (Lotus-eaters: *Od.* 9.82–104; Sirens: *Od.* 12.154–200), illustrates the dangers of allowing oneself to be provoked by the thought of a rival (789–90):

> illo Lotophagos, illo Sirenas in antro
>   esse puta; remis adice uela tuis.

> Imagine in that cave the Lotus-eaters, the Sirens; add sails to your oars.

Both Ovid's ship-poem and the lessons it contains equip his pupils to weather the most dangerous seas, just as his epic models have done. These dangers successfully passed and the poetic journey over, Ovid announces the end of the voyage at the end of *Remedia* (811–12):

> hoc opus exegi: fessae date serta carinae;
>   contigimus portus, quo mihi cursus erat.

> I have completed this work; adorn my weary ship with wreaths; we have reached port, where my journey led.

As the epic voyage that is contained within the elegiac *Remedia* comes to a close, Ovid provides a script for both life and poetry that succeeds by deconstructing the boundaries between the two (and so asserts his authority over both). This play with boundaries is both the signature his readers expect and the challenge they confront repeatedly in Ovid's poetry; in *Remedia*, Ovid exposes the points of convergence between elegy and epic even as he exploits their parallelism.

FURTHER READING

Conte (1994) has renovated interest in *Remedia* on its own terms; since his essay first appeared (1986b), the poem has attracted the interest of a new generation of scholars: for general treatments see, for example, Brunelle (1997), Woytek (2000), and Fulkerson (2004); recent studies of individual episodes or features include Davisson (1996) and Brunelle (2000–1) and (2002); finally, the volume edited by Gibson et al. (2006) heralds a new engagement with *Remedia*, treated prominently in several essays contained therein: *Remedia* is the central focus of Hardie (2006) and Rosati (2006), while Casali (2006) and Holzberg (2006) offer opposing approaches to Ovid's engagement with the political landscape of Augustan Rome by considering the role of the reader in both *Ars amatoria* and *Remedia*. For literary treatments of *Remedia* in relation to *Ars amatoria*, Hollis (1973) remains *primus inter pares*; other introductions to Ovid's amatory didactic barely graze *Remedia* but have much general value, for example Watson (2002), Sharrock (2002b), and Volk (2002). Of older studies, Prinz (1914) and (1917) deserve particular mention; though his argument is no longer of particular urgency, the catalogues of parallels and motifs that he provides remain useful and offer evidence of an unusual early appreciation of *Remedia* as an independent work. Although his perspective on the constraints of genre differs significantly from that taken in the present essay, Fyler (1971) signals a new and important appreciation for Ovid's divergence from generic decorum in *Remedia* and elsewhere. Küppers (1981) and Myerowitz (1985) assemble and discuss thematic elements that unite the three books of *Ars amatoria* and one book of *Remedia*.

Remedia has attracted more than its share of commentators in recent decades: Geisler (1969) on *Rem.* 1–396 and its complement, Lucke (1982) on 397–814, both dissertations directed by Franco Munari and packed with detail; Henderson (1979), in most university libraries but no longer in print; and Pinotti (1988), not easy to locate but very much worthwhile. Lazzarini (1986) is not a comprehensive edition but offers a handy text (with Italian translation), broadly annotated, and is available in bookstores throughout Italy. This edition also contains Conte (1986b) as an introductory essay, the original version of Conte (1994).

The relative priority of *Ars amatoria* 3 and *Remedia* remains a topic of debate: see Geisler (1969: 47–54), Syme (1978: 8–15), Murgia (1986a, 1986b), and Woytek (2000: 182). Brunelle (1997: 10–19) offers a judicious evaluation of Murgia's scheme, more fully analyzed and ultimately refuted by Gibson (2003: 37–43). I agree with Gibson that it seems most likely that *Remedia* can be dated to shortly before the conclusion of Gaius Caesar's Parthian campaign in AD 2; I would suggest further that there is no reason not to imagine Ovid working on *Ars amatoria* 3 and *Remedia* simultaneously, much as he appears to have done with *Fasti* and at least parts of *Metamorphoses*: the artistic appeal of creating two 'alternative' conclusions for *Ars amatoria* seems to me at least a typically Ovidian motive.

CHAPTER NINE

Fasti: the Poet, the Prince, and the Plebs

Geraldine Herbert-Brown

Introduction

Why would the famous love elegist versify the Roman calendar? Ovid anticipates the question and answers it himself: the *Fasti* is his *militia*, or military service, to the Prince (2.9). He does not need to explain to his contemporaries what the Roman calendar was, of course, because they lived it everyday. The same cannot be said for *Fasti* readers of two thousand years later. To comprehend what the Roman calendar meant as a cultural institution to Ovid's first audience requires some effort if we want to understand the significance of his *militia* to Augustus.

The welcome surge of interest in the *Fasti* over the last two decades has been focused primarily on the poem's engagement with its literary tradition and its status as a sophisticated literary artifact. Its engagement with the extra-textual calendar has not received equivalent scrutiny. The way one interprets the *Fasti* and its wealth of literary intertexts hinges largely upon one's notions of what the Roman calendar was. Sometimes modern preconceptions can be unwittingly superimposed upon ancient ideas of morality and Augustus' restoration of the traditional religion. For this reason I will begin by considering the Roman calendar in its most alien aspects to highlight the chasm which exists between ancient Roman religion and modern notions of what a religion should be, encumbered as they are with a Judeo-Christian frame of reference. I will then discuss Ovid's calendar in the light of that religious 'otherness' and try to show how important it is as an intertext for appreciating the *Fasti*.

The Calendar

In 46 BC Julius Caesar, Dictator and Pontifex Maximus (head of the priestly college in charge of regulating the calendar), employed mathematicians to align the solar and civil year to create what became the Julian calendar, in essence the same as the modern, Western calendar of 365¼ days divided into twelve months. Before Caesar's reform, the Roman year was lagging behind the solar by ninety days. In 46 BC the day celebrated as New Year should have been 14 October of the old year, and the harvest thanksgiving was celebrated long before the harvest had begun. Ovid (*Fast.* 3.155–165) is just one of seven authors who testify to the chaos generated by the old Roman calendar in comparison with the new (Herbert-Brown 1994: 20). The year 46 BC was described by Macrobius as 'the final year of confusion' (1.16.3).

It was not his power as Pontifex Maximus, however, which enabled Caesar to carry out the reform. In Republican times religious authority was not invested in one office but was fragmented across four priestly colleges. The Pontifex Maximus was head of just one, all of whose members were also magistrates drawn from, and controlled by, the senate. It was the senate which decided whether or not to act on priestly advice (Beard et al. 1998: 29). When Caesar reformed the calendar as Pontifex Maximus, it was his authority as Dictator which enabled him to carry it out, whether or not the senate agreed with it.

Caesar's reform was as much a political maneuver as it was a mathematical adjustment. From 1 January 45 BC the Julian calendar began to provide unprecedented stability, not just in diurnal time-reckoning but also in every aspect of Roman daily life. It liberated the populace from the tyranny of unscrupulous *pontifices*, who had the power to manipulate the old calendar with arbitrary intercalations for partisan political purposes, such as altering the dates of election days or extending a magistrate's term of office (Scullard 1981: 42). At the same time it preserved continuity with the traditional religious calendar in form and emphasis: it retained the names of the months, their division by Kalends, Nones, and Ides, the character of the days, and the names of all the state-funded festivals (*feriae statiuae*) throughout the year. The custom of oral announcements by the priests was maintained (and necessary for the illiterate), but now, except for moveable feasts such as the Sementivae (*Fast.* 1.659–60), the importance of their major calendrical role was minimized. For the first time in living memory the Roman people could know in advance when to sacrifice to the gods, when to celebrate their festivals, when to begin sowing and harvesting, when the sailing and fighting seasons began, when there were no religious impediments to initiating lawsuits, transacting business, or voting in the Comitia. The only social class that did not benefit from Caesar's reform was the governing class, who could no longer manipulate it to its own advantage. Caesar effectively transferred control of time from the senate to the people of Rome.

Nevertheless, it was a partisan-stacked senate which introduced the most innovative religious aspect of the Julian calendar. It decreed *feriae* (holidays) on the anniversaries of Caesar's victories and on his birthday, and renamed the seventh month *Iulius* in his honor. These new holidays were marked 'NP', the same designation as the major state festivals. The insertion of Caesar into the calendar appears to have been an attempt to rationalize his superhuman, god-like power in relation to the whole community (Gradel 2002: ch. 3). The result was that the reformer's personal cult was included in the yearly round of religious, cultural, and civic life, and the collective consciousness of the entire social order. His anniversaries also increased the number of annual holidays (there were no weekends) that working people, including slaves, could enjoy. The Roman calendar became an annual replaying of the relationship between Caesar and the Roman people at every social level, both rural and urban.

But what sort of company was Caesar keeping in the Roman calendar? Many of the state *feriae* were not only agricultural festivals but also celebrations of events in Roman legend or history. The ritual performed at such festivals evoked aspects of those distant events and linked them to the present in what Mary Beard (1987: 11) calls a series of tableaux, which offered to participants a conceptual pageant of Rome and what it meant to be Roman.

That picture of Romanness, however, was not always one of dignity and decorum by modern standards. Some festal evocations of the past presented an occasion for getting drunk, having sex, or watching obscene mimes. At the Saturnalia, the people celebrated with drunken revelry and gambling, a custom which dated back to a senatorial decree of 217 BC (Liv. 22.1.19–20). At the Consualia, games were held in the Circus Maximus at which priests (*sacerdotes*) enacted the rape of the Sabine virgins (Var. *L.* 6.20). The Nonae Caprotinae festival, which recalled the demand by the Latins for the wives and daughters of the defeated Romans, and the latter's response of surrendering servant girls (*ancillae*) dressed as free women in their place, presented similar sport in a comedy on an historical theme (*togata praetexta*) at the games of Apollo (Var. *L.* 6.18 with Wiseman 1998: 8–11, 68, 'explicitly erotic'). At the Floralia, mimes were featured at which *mimae/meretrices* (showgirl/prostitutes) stripped on stage at the behest of the audience. In 55 BC a puritanical Cato left the show, but knew better than to try and curtail the 'ancient custom' of the games (Val. Max. 2.10.8; Sen. *Ep.* 97.8). At the Lupercalia, naked men (Luperci) glistening with oil, ran around whipping women with goatskins (Var. *L.* 6.34). Livy wrote that the god being honored was Inuus (from *ineo*, 'to penetrate sexually'). The Luperci ran through the streets playfully and licentiously (*per lusum atque lasciuiam*: 1.5.1–2). The presence of the Vestal Virgins signaled the importance of this licentious festival, as, indeed, it did of the Consualia on 21 August.

The idea that sex shows were a feature of some festal celebrations is a challenging one to modern sensibilities; however, in a slave-owning culture where humans as well as animals were killed to entertain the crowds (*RG* 22: 1, 3), it was a relatively tame one. Quite incidentally, Cicero reveals that gang rape of showgirls was a traditional prerogative at *ludi scaenici* (scenic games). In his defense of Plancius, accused (among other things) of joining in the gang rape of a *mima*, he says: 'What a tribute to the propriety of my client's youthful days. He is reproached with an act which he was permitted to commit, yet even that reproach is found to be baseless' (*Planc.* 30–1). Cicero's retort implies that Plancius was just doing what it meant to be Roman.

Caesar knew better than to interfere with the cultic traditions associated with the public festivals, just as Cato did. He was also careful not to move the festivals about in the process of reform. When the Julian calendar required an extra day to the month of April, he inserted it before rather than during the Floralia, which extended into May, to avoid upsetting the dates of the festival claimed by prostitutes as their own (Macr. 1.14.6–9; Scullard 1981: 110; Degrassi 1963: 449). He demonstrated support for the Lupercalia by founding the college of the *luperci Iulii* to add to the two others already in existence, the *Quinctiales* and the *Fabiani*. It was in the role of a *lupercus* that the Consul, Mark Antony, *nudus, unctus, ebrius* (Cic. *Phil.* 3.12), offered Caesar the diadem in 44 BC (Plut. *Caes.* 61.3–4). Caesar's choice of the Lupercalia is indicative of the importance he saw in the festival as an expression of Roman identity. It was an ideal opportunity to test public opinion about any political innovations he had in mind. It is there that the Roman people let him know by their lack of applause that they did not want a king. It was not the people who murdered him exactly one month later, but members of the senate. On the Ides of March, 44 BC, the Julian calendar was less than fifteen months old.

Caesar's heir recognized the value of the legacy he inherited in the Julian Calendar. From the victory of Actium onwards, he allowed his anniversaries (birthday, victories, honorific titles, the naming of a month 'Augustus') to be gradually incorporated into the calendar and spread more or less evenly throughout the year without interfering with the ancient festivals (we can compare the latter in the Julian calendars with those in the pre-Julian *Fasti Antiates Maiores*: Michels 1967). The calendar was more than just an advertisement of his status as *diui filius*; the honors system in Roman society was a reciprocal arrangement. To accept honors entailed a moral obligation to reciprocate with benefactions (Gradel 2002: 59). Augustus did not accept all honors offered to him (*RG* 5: 1, 3), which highlights the significance of those he did. His acceptance of calendrical honors meant that in return for recognition of his superior status he accepted the moral obligation of safeguarding the Julian calendar. He fulfilled that obligation in two ways: he corrected an error of the *pontifices* who had intercalated an extra day every three instead of every four years, so that it was brought into full alignment with the solar year again by AD 8; he preserved the ancient festivals and their cultic traditions alongside the emerging Julian cult as a part of his policy of restoring the old religion.

This included the old religion's less than dignified aspects. He revived the Lupercalia and the only change he made was to forbid beardless youths from participating in the running (Suet. *Aug.* 31.4). The traditional male nakedness was maintained, as Ovid's words attest (*Fast.* 2.301–2, 379–80; cf. D. H. 1.80.1). Ovid's mention of the *flamen Dialis* (*Fast.* 2.282), a priesthood which had been vacant since 87 BC but restored by Augustus in 11 BC, signals that it was the Augustan Lupercalia he was describing, not one from the Republican past. Augustus boasted of having restored the position of Lupercal as a public service in his *Res Gestae* (19.1).

Augustus did not spoil the fun of the people by censoring the erotic stage acts on festal days. Propertius (2.22.3–10) alludes to the impact naked female flesh in such shows had on him. Horace, idealizing the past, sniffed that satyr plays on festal days had evolved to include nudity and obscene dialogue and aimed to please the uneducated, rustic workers in the audience, not the sophisticated, urbane classes (*Ars* 208–50); Vitruvius (5.6.9; 7.5.2) describes the set of such plays.

The lascivious content of stage plays is confirmed by Ovid, both before and after exile. In the *Remedia amoris* (751–6) he counseled the man anxious to end a love affair to abstain from theaters, where the actor's art taught forbidden pleasure. At *Tr.* 2.497–506 he describes comic mimes, obscene both to ear and eye. Some of the scripts of these lewd shows were from the pen of poets, much to Horace's disgust (*Ars* 220–4). Ovid said such scripts could be very lucrative for a poet (*Tr.* 2.507). His verse had been, and still was, danced on stage as pantomime (*Tr.* 2.519–20, 5.7.25–8). Pantomime, based upon mythological, tragic, and erotic themes including adultery, and danced by masked soloists to musical and vocal accompaniment, was introduced to Rome in 22 BC by Pylades and Bathyllus, freedmen of Augustus and Maecenas. Augustus not only indulged such entertainment but also enjoyed it, according to Tacitus, and thought it civil to mingle in the pleasures of the populace (*Ann.* 1.54.2).

Augustus' active interest in the theater, games, and in the performers themselves is confirmed by Suetonius (*Aug.* 43–5). The biographer also says that he segregated the theater audience by social, political, and sexual stratification. Women were banished to the back rows (cf. Prop. 4.8). This sexual segregation indicates that Augustus did nothing to curtail the traditional content of the performances; it merely demonstrates women's place at the bottom of the social hierarchy. The Vestal virgins, Suetonius says (and we assume, the imperial women: Dio 60.22.2), had front seats. Ovid, in his defense to Augustus (and Rome at large) from exile, was saying what everybody knew: that the Prince, wives, husbands, boys, and nubile girls—and senators too—watched sex(y) acts on stage, all funded by the *praetor* and Augustus himself (*Tr.* 2.497–518; Dio 54.2.4). Augustus' patronage of the theatrical spectacles enabled him to interact in a controlled way with the entire social hierarchy, and offered him the ancient equivalent of the photo-opportunity: to be seen fulfilling his obligation to preserve and to share in the religio-social traditions of the Roman festival calendar—and what it meant to be Roman.

What, then, of the *lex Julia de adulteriis coercendis* of 18–17 BC, which made sexual laxity a public crime? How could erotic shows, particularly those flaunting adultery, receive the patronage of Augustus after that date? The first clue presents itself in the extant fragments of the once majestically proportioned calendar of Praeneste, dated AD 6–9 (Degrassi 1963: 141). This was a calendar created by Verrius Flaccus, scholar-freeman of Augustus who had lived under his roof and been entrusted with the education of his sons (Suet. *Gram.* 17). Like the many epigraphical calendars which had been proliferating in Italian towns since the introduction of the Julian reform, it organizes in tabular and abbreviated form diverse information, such as letters marking the character of the days, the Kalends, Nones, and Ides, notices of festivals and games, foundation dates of temples, Julian anniversaries, etc., divided across the year in twelve months without any apparent connection. Because of its size, however, the

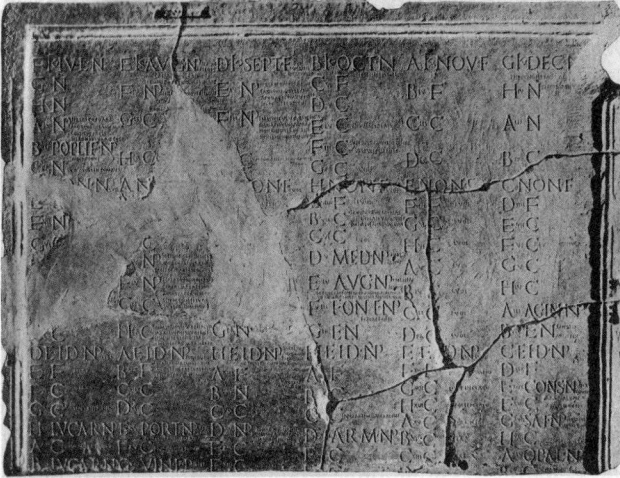

Figure 1: Inscribed calendar from the city of Amiternum in central Italy, of the first century CE, with notations of Augustan festivals (reproduced from Degrassi 1963). Courtesy of the Istituto Poligrafico e Zecco dello Stato, Rome.

author of the Praenestine calendar was able to offer more information in the form of exegeses on certain festivals, giving alternative etymologies, names, origins, and *aetia* for rituals without offering a definitive version. Unfortunately, he does not say what people did on *feriae*, or mention the dramatic shows which featured as part of festivals, but he does provide information as to who might have performed in them.

Under 1 April it reads (Degrassi 1963: 126–7, 434):

> frequenter mulieres supplicant Fortunae Virili, humiliores etiam in balineis, quod in iis ea parte corpor[is] utique uiri nudantur qua feminarum gratia desideratur.

> women in great numbers supplicate Virile Fortune, the humbler ones also in the baths, because in them men expose in particular that part of the body by which the favor of women is desired.

These words offer a glimpse into how a socially distinct group of women within a larger generic group participated in a public religious festival. *Mulieres* tells us nothing about the marital, social, or moral status of the group, but *humiliores* has a distinct moral flavor. The word cannot simply mean 'lower-class women', as women of that status could also belong to the first group. That they supplicate the goddess in the baths also distinguishes them from the general group. The sexual overtones of this *aetion*, furthermore, cannot be ignored. The *humiliores* are clearly in the men's section of the baths, not the women's (Var. *L.* 9.68). Could the word be a euphemism for *meretrices*? Is Verrius telling us that prostitutes offered their services as part of the ritual of Virile Fortune? The idea becomes more plausible when we read that on 25 April (Degrassi 1963: 131, 448):

Festus est pu[e]rorum l[e]noniorum, quia proximus superior mer[e]tricum est

Holiday for pimps because the preceding day is a holiday for prostitutes.

These words from Verrius Flaccus must be the closest we have to an official acknowledgment that pimps and prostitutes were a recognized social category in the Julian
calendar and Augustan religious discourse. Augustus' law against adultery prohibited
women, not men, from having extramarital sex. Infidelity was an issue pertaining only
to them. Men were free to indulge with prostitutes and slaves (Bauman 1992: 105–6;
Treggiari 2005: 145). The law—which forbade *adulterium* with married women,
and *stuprum* (fornication) with a single free woman, widowed or unmarried—would
have increased the profile and social need of the sexually available class as never
before.

The lacunose and incomplete state of this calendar unfortunately deprives us of
any further elaboration of that role. For this we must turn to Ovid's *Fasti*. But first,
let us look at the reaction of the populace to Augustus' fulfillment of his calendrical
obligation. On 6 March 12 BC there flocked to Rome from the whole of Italy such
a multitude as had never before been seen, to elect him Pontifex Maximus (*RG* 10).
That election made him the official head of the college in charge of the calendar,
although he had been acting head for decades. Syme observes (1939: 469): 'This
unique and spontaneous manifestation bore the character of a plebiscite expressing
loyalty to the Princeps and confidence in the government.' He might have added,
'and gratitude for the Julian calendar'. There can be no doubt that the Julian calendar
was a means by which the Prince bound the Roman people to himself in gratitude,
for giving them a stability in their daily life unknown to their forebears, for reviving
their ancient religion, and for joining in their fun at their religious festivals. They, in
their turn, were able to embrace the Julian cult alongside their traditional gods in
the same way tribal communities later adopted Christianity while still clinging to their
old idols and myths of identity. Augustus gave enormous importance to his new title.
Pontifex Maximus is the only one of all his religious offices which he advertised in
his coinage and inscriptions, and it preceded every other title.

Ovid's Calendar

Now we can look at the relationship between the Julian calendar and Ovid's *militia*
to the Prince. Verrius Flaccus and Ovid were creating their works in the years leading
up to AD 8, the year in which Caesar's reform, thanks to Augustus' intervention,
began to function without error. The date of inception of either cannot be known,
but we can make a conjecture about the *Fasti*. Ovid refers to Augustus' restoration
of the temple of Cybele in AD 3 (4.352). At the time of his exile in AD 8, he claimed
all twelve books existed (*Tr.* 2.549–52). Evidence for this can be seen in anniversaries
from the second half of the year, such as Hercules' Ara Maxima, transferred from 12
August to 11 January (1.543–86), the Fabii from 18 July to 13 February (2.195–
242), and (possibly) Mars Ultor from 1 August (Dio 60.5.3) to 12 May (5.545–98).

However, only the first six books, partially revised and rededicated to Germanicus, have come down to us (with Herbert-Brown 2002b: 126–8). Scholars speculate that the *Fasti* could have been in progress from 2 BC onwards, but we will see that the real impetus for Ovid's *militia* becomes apparent with the adoption, in AD 4, of Tiberius Nero into the house of Caesar.

Ovid might have witnessed the *Fasti Praenestini* in progress, although he does not distinguish this calendar from others he mentions (*Fast.* 1.11, 289; 3.87–96; 6.59–63). His poem can be read in many respects as a filled-out version, however, in pattern and in detail (Wallace-Hadrill 1987: 227). Its opening couplet is followed by the dedication to Germanicus (1.3–62), which develops the calendrical theme announced in the first hexameter, promising sacred rites (1.7; cf. 2.7, 6.8), imperial anniversaries, and research into their origins (1.7; cf. 4.11). It provides a potted history of the calendar (cf. 3.99–166) and includes an explanation of the names of the months and the notation of the days (cf. 1.328, 3.429, 5.727, 6.649).

Beginning on the Kalends of January, Ovid's poem proceeds through the annual cycle. Throughout he brings to bear the resources and techniques bequeathed to him by his literary forebears, particularly Callimachus and Propertius. Adopting a Callimachean-style scholarly pose in elegiac couplets, he dates, makes enquiries about, and offers multiple explanations for festivals and many other religious, cultural, and historical categories, both antiquarian and Julian, which are listed in abbreviated form in the epigraphical calendars. He draws regular attention to his new poetic identity of *uates* of the Roman year (*Fast.* 1.101, 2.3–8, 3.177, 4.1–18, 6.21–4). The Roman year as both subject and framework is the most important and pervasive motif of the poem, which fulfills its programmatic statement: *tempora cum causis Latium digesta per annum /... canam* ('of times and their causes distributed through the Latin year ... I shall sing').

Where the *Fasti* bears no resemblance to Verrius' calendar is in Ovid's accounts of popular festivals, which highlight their most vulgar aspects, such as drunkenness, sex, dirty songs, and obscene mimes. It is these bawdy tales, recounted with an elegiac relish redolent of his earlier, erotic love poetry, that cause discomfort among some modern commentators, who feel that a focus on such aspects creates tension between the popular cults and the 'serious' Julian anniversaries. Some go so far as to assert that Ovid's enthusiastic attention to such details was a deliberate attempt to undermine Augustus.

But was it? Scholarship over the last thirty years has made significant advances in tracing features of popular drama in many of Ovid's narratives. Ovid himself refers to the theater in the *Fasti* (e.g. 3.535; 4.326, 946; 5.189, 347), which encourages the idea that he drew inspiration from it. Littlewood (1975: 1063–7) detects the characteristics of a satyr play in the story of Faunus, Hercules, and Omphale, which Ovid associates with the Lupercalia (2.303–56), while Fantham (1983: 200–1) sees in it the characteristics of pantomime, and suggests it would have been understood as such by an audience.

We have seen that both types of popular drama were current entertainment at festival time. Other stories of sexual desire and rape, frustrated or otherwise, and dressed up in mythological burlesque or transvestite farce—such as Priapus and Lotis

(1.391–440), Jupiter, Lara, and Mercury (2.583–616), or Anna Perenna and Mars (3.675–96)—also have affinities with these types of popular drama (Wiseman 2002: 283–4). Many foundation stories entailed the rape of a Vestal virgin or nymph whose offspring became the founder of Rome or Arcadia. Divine rape was viewed as an acceptable basis for popular entertainment as well as a mythical explanation for a community's divine heritage. Laughing at the gods was not blasphemous in a religion that easily accommodated humor (Liebeschuetz 1979: 21–2). If Ovid's bawdy tales were drawn from the entertainment presented at festival celebrations, then their place in his calendar would have been seen as logical. They could have been understood as the genre of Augustan calendrical entertainment.

It is in the genre of Augustan entertainment that we discover the religio-social role played by the sexually available class mentioned in the Praenestine calendar. On 1 April, the same day that Verrius' *humiliores* were in the men's baths, Ovid describes two cults of Venus (4.133–62). He accordingly addresses her worshippers as two distinct social groups: 'mothers and brides' (*matres nurusque)* in the hexameter on the one hand and 'you who do not wear the headband and long gown' (*et uos, quis uittae longaque uestis abest*, 4.133–4) in the pentameter on the other. The poet maintains the distinction between the two groups and describes the different rituals performed by each (contra Wiseman 2008: ch. 6; Boyle 2003: 241; Barchiesi 1997a: 224; Herbert-Brown 1994: 93).

He instructs the first group to bathe the statue of Venus (we are not told where: 135–8). His apostrophe then shifts to the second group, at 139, signaled by the repetition of the pronoun *uos (quo) que*, which harks back to *et uos* in the pentameter at 134 and which he now places in the hexameter to give it priority. This second group is privileged with the poet's paraphrase of Venus's own instructions (*ipsa iubet*): she herself bids them bathe under the green myrtle, he says, then commands them to learn (*discite*) the cause. She was naked on the shore drying her dripping hair when a lecherous lot of satyrs caught sight of her. She covered her nakedness with myrtle in the nick of time, which saved her (from being ravished). 'And she tells you to re-enact it' instructs the poet: *uosque referre iubet* (144).

Ovid's words sound like instructions to *mimae* of a satyr play with a wet, naked Venus in the starring role. Having told them why they should bathe in emulation of the goddess, he proceeds to tell them where (the reiteration and expansion of the imperative *discite* at 140 into *discite nunc quare* at 145 indicates that he is addressing the same group). Learn now why you give Fortuna Virilis incense in the place 'moist with warm water' (*calida qui locus umet aqua*, 146; the variant *calida* is more sexy than *gelida*, preferred by Alton et al. 1997). That place (i.e. the baths) accepts all women stripped of clothes (and so excludes the mothers and brides), and sees all blemishes of the naked body, but Fortuna Virilis undertakes to hide them from the men in exchange for a little incense. It is clear from these words that Fortuna Virilis is a kind of assistant deity to Venus, and that the second category of worshippers also offer their services as prostitutes on this day. Ovid concludes his address to them by giving them permission to take a little poppy seed crushed with milk and honey (*nec pigeat . . . / sumere*, 151–2). The modern working girl would interpret this as permission to inject herself with a little heroin to see her through the ordeal ahead.

This was the sort of ordeal experienced by Venus, says Ovid (53–4), for she, too, needed the poppy mind-bender when being escorted to her lustful (but hideous) husband (Vulcan). This couplet is crucial as it serves as a linchpin to converge then separate again Venus' two cults with two interlocking ideas: it conveys a close conceptual link between prostitution and marriage, and it morphs the sexy stage star into a submissive wife. Venus' dual nature is succinctly encapsulated. It tells us that the poppy seed she takes as a reluctant bride is a ritual shared by her two sets of worshippers, who, in so doing, are united with the goddess but separated from each other according to which of her two aspects—the chaste or the erotic— they desire for themselves. Venus the bride now (*ex illo tempore nupta fuit*) signals the transition from the cult of those who do not wear the headband and the long gown back to the cult of the respectable mothers and brides of the first line, which continues through to the last word, *nurus* (162). The imperative (*supplicibus uerbis illam placate*) is addressed to them now to propitiate Venus in her wifely role to secure for them her favor in acquiring all that a husband could desire: *forma et mores et bona fama.* Ovid proceeds to lecture them on the lapse of (female) morality in Rome's past, and concludes the passage with an exhortation to Venus Verticordia, or Changer of Hearts (of their morally lax predecessors?), to look benignly on her descendants, the Aeneadae, and to guard all their young brides (155–62; cf. Val Max 8.15.12 *quo facilius uirginum mulierumque mens a libidine ad pudicitiam conuerteretur*).

Ovid's second social group is clearly equivalent to Verrius' *humiliores*, but the poet's allusion to the satyr play and the *aetion* for their ritual tells us more about them. They are *mimae/meretrices* who worship Venus as goddess of erotic power. The satyr play may well have been staged on this her festal day, with men in the audience achieving with the *mimae* in the baths after the show what the satyrs had failed to achieve with Venus—the *Thermae Agrippae*, willed by Agrippa to the Roman people in 12 BC (Dio 54.29.4), were convenient to the theater of Pompey. Venus' first group, the mothers and brides (no wonder the sexes was segregated!), worship her as goddess of marital chastity. They do not strip, nor do they enter the water. The chastity required of them is not required of the second. They worship Venus Verticordia. Ovid's Augustan Venus, worshipped on the Kalends of April, is indeed *geminorum mater amorum* (4.1), mother of both chaste and erotic love. In the *Ars amatoria* she was *mater amoris*, mother of erotic love only (*Ars* 1.30–4).

The role of prostitute/showgirl in Roman religious discourse is evident elsewhere. Verrius had told us about the holidays for pimps and prostitutes on 24 and 25 April. On 23 April Ovid exhorts *uolgares puellae* to celebrate the divinity of Venus because a lot of sex appeal (*multa . . . uenus*: the meaning is better represented by lower case: Fantham 1998: ad loc.) is advantageous for the profits of sex-workers (*professarum quaestibus*). Ovid instructs them to pray for beauty and popular favor, coaxing ways and words suitable for a dirty joke: *formam populique fauorem . . . blanditias dignaque uerba ioco* (4.865–8).

The word *iocus*, along with it adjectival form, is used by Ovid almost exclusively in the sense of seduction stories or risqué drama. In the *Fasti* the tales of Priapus and Lotis (1.396), Faunus, Hercules, and Omphale (2.304), Anna Perenna and Mars

(3.695), Silenus, Bacchus, and the bees (3.738), the plays at Flora's games (4.946, 5.332), and the tale of Vesta and Priapus (6.320) are all characterized as *ioci* (Newlands 1995: 141; Barchiesi 1997a: 240). These are the sorts of plays, starring naked satyrs from scripts written by poets, that a conservative Horace found so shocking (*Ars* 220–32).

Ovid's *uolgares puellae/professae*, who pray to Venus for popular favor and words suitable for *ioci*, are the most likely candidates to play naked goddesses in bawdy tales. They are also the likely candidates to star as respectable women made victims of rape in foundation stories such as Lucretia at the Regifugium, the Sabine women at the Consualia, or slave girls dressed as *matronae* at the Nonae Caprotinae in *fabulae togatae* or *ludi scaenici* evoking Rome's past on festal days. Their presence in the calendar makes sense of Ovid's words when he says that *matronae* and Vestals saw *corpora meretricia* poised for sex of every kind, with no reproach for their pimps (*Tr.* 2.309–12). It also makes sense of the fact that Ovid could castigate Romulus for the rape of the Sabine women and still praise Augustus for ordering wives to be chaste (*Fast.* 2.133–44), even as Augustus allowed the Consualia to be re-enacted every year for the merriment of all (D. H. 2.31.2; Ovid *Ars* 1.101–34, *Fast.* 3.199).

This dual role of *meretrix/mima* can be seen as fulfilling an important function in the Augustan religious revival. It offered a low social category the vital role of enabling the traditional festivals—and what it meant to be Roman—to be celebrated without violation of the Julian law against adultery. It is possible that the Venereal festivals celebrated by prostitutes according to Verrius and Ovid were an Augustan calendrical innovation, as Varro and Cincius knew nothing about them (Macr. 1.12.12–13). Their role will be explored further when we come to look at some of the popular festivals described in the *Fasti*.

Reading the *Fasti*

How are we supposed to read the *Fasti*? As fragmented pieces of information without coherent connection linked only by a shared date, like a calendar? Or as a continuous text as reproduced in the manuscripts before nineteenth-century editors began what is now the convention of dividing it up into days by following the poet's regular signals of the passing of time? Ovid himself provides cues. The first word, *tempora*, both signals a link with and a separation from the *Metamorphoses*, which also announces *tempora* as a theme. Ovid's instructions are to read the latter's *tempora* as an unbroken transition with no divisions or breaks (1.1–4; cf. *Tr.* 2.559–60). The structure of time is teleological. The temporal structure of the *Fasti* is the opposite: *tempora . . . digesta per annum* (times divided through the year). *Digesta* is from *digero*, meaning 'to force apart', 'separate', 'divide', or 'distribute'. It is a word used by later writers such as Macrobius in the sense of the division of time into a calendar (*anni . . . ordinationem a C. Caesare digestam*, 1.11.50). Before Ovid, Varro (*L.* 6.3) had put it differently—*Id (tempus) diuisum in partes aliquot maxime ab solis et lunae cursu*—but the concept is the same. Romulus divided the year into ten months (*Fast.* 1.27). Each month was subdivided by the Kalends, Nones, and Ides, and even days were subdivided into different categories (*Fast.*1.45–63). Ovid creates further division in the *Fasti* than one would expect even from a calendar. His poem was not to be a day-to-day calendar and he wanted to avoid repetition (1.61–2; cf. e.g. 2.475). One could not consult it, for example, to find out when *Nundinae* (market days) fell in May. It was a festival calendar, a series of events (*series rerum*) rather than a continuum, which means many days between them were left blank. Roman time is doubly divided by the non-Roman stellar calendar which weaves in and out of it. Proleptic and retrospective temporal references (e.g. 4.947–8, 5.721–8) tell us that *tempora* in the *Fasti* are segmented and cyclical, not linear and continuous.

The elegiac medium conveying these festivals further discourages the idea of textual continuity. Elegy was the meter of episodes and a short concentration span, not epic narrative. It was also a declared affiliation with Ovid's elegiac predecessors, Callimachus and Propertius, who had written collections of disconnected poems, and with his own amatory elegies written on a small scale. His claim that the *Fasti* is an application of elegy to grander themes familiar to epic (2.3–8, 119–26; 4.3, 9–12, 948, 6.23) is a pointed reminder of its inherent nature as a little work (*exiguum opus*). The closed elegiac couplet, a hexameter line followed by a pentameter (six feet and five feet respectively), drags the progression of stories and checks the forward narrative movement afforded by hexameters. This enabled Ovid to separate calendrical entries with stellar interjections, or insert a great variety of *aitia* without bias or resolution. It also enabled him to add and subtract or cut and paste material as necessary as he revised from exile.

However, the *Fasti* is not just an elegiac calendar but also, in part, a didactic poem. In the poem's segmented Julian anniversaries, Ovid explains Augustus' relationship with the gods to his contemporaries, and in the process allows his modern reader to witness the emergence of the Ruler cult from the State cult in Roman religion (Herbert-Brown 1994). Ovid employs continuous as well as fragmented elegiacs to a similar didactic purpose: to explain Augustus as a semi-divine champion of the lower orders against the senatorial, governing class of Rome.

One might assume that Augustus was careful in selecting particular dates for his key anniversaries. The Ides of March, however, was one anniversary he did not choose. Did Caesar's assassins choose it to be the date of his murder? Suetonius (*Div. Iul.* 80.4) gives the impression that it was the selection of the Campus Martius, traditionally associated with the Roman plebs, that was more meaningful in their deliberations than the date itself. It was the plebs who, initially stupefied by the murder and unresponsive to the conspirators' explanations and blandishments, unleashed their rage the following day when Caesar was defamed as a tyrant by Cinna, a former Caesarian protégé (Yavetz 1969: 63, 65–6).

Yet the character of the day might have had a bearing on their decision. All the Ides were sacred to Jupiter, but many had a double character. Caesar was killed on the day also sacred to Anna Perenna. Her name tells us she was a goddess of the yearly cycle, or the continual succession of years. March was the first month of the old ten-month year, and the 15th was the original, first full moon. Anna Perenna's day was an old New Year festival, celebrated by the urban plebs on the Campus Martius.

There is little to connect Anna Perenna's holiday and Caesar's death in the sources apart from the date itself. Its significance as a New Year festival could perhaps be read into the fact that Dolabella, a man once popular with the plebs who then betrayed Caesar, allegedly proposed that the birthday of Rome should be transferred to the Ides of March (Appian *BC* 2.122, 511; 3.35, 141). It was the year before, in 45 BC, that Caesar had exploited the Parilia, an ancient festival also celebrated as the birthday of Rome (21 April), to parade his honors and create a cultic basis for a relationship between himself and Romulus, founder of the city (Weinstock 1971: 175, 184, 190). Dolabella's suggestion of 15 March as the new birthday of Rome could have been intended to symbolize a return to the traditional senatorial government. But any real connection between the events is missing, until we look at Ovid. On the Ides of March, Ovid gives Anna lavish treatment, culminating in a short but powerful panegyric compressed into six couplets to a murdered Pontifex Maximus (3.523–696, with Littlewood 1980). In the proem to March Ovid had prepared us for the association between the two when he introduced her as a New Year goddess in his retelling of the history of the Roman calendar, which culminated in Caesar's reform (3.135–66).

Ovid presents Anna's day as one celebrated by the plebs with sex, drunkenness, and the singing of obscene songs from the theater. The togas he mentions at this plebeian festival (3.530) betray the presence and role of *mimae/meretrices* (Hor. *Serm.* 1.2.63; Wiseman 1998: 67–74). The *puellae* at line 675 could be further identified as Venus' *uolgares puellae/professae*, discussed above, whose talents would have been touted by Verrius' *pueri lenoni* so that they could be hired to participate in the festival *ioci* (695) in their dual role. Their presence makes sense of the erotic *aetia* Ovid devotes to Anna, including the elegiac inversion of the *Aeneid*, which bear the hallmarks of comic theater, both mimic and farcical (Littlewood 1980: 316–17; McKeown 1984). It also makes sense of the fact that the (male) revelers could celebrate Anna's day without breaking the Julian law against adultery. The succession and accumulation of verbs in the present tense describing the revelers and their rituals (3.523–42; cf. 675–6) indicate that Ovid is not referring to a defunct festival from Republican times but a contemporary festival in Augustan Rome.

Among Ovid's different versions of Anna's identity, three of them are consistent with her status as a goddess of the year: Luna, the moon goddess who fills the year with the months, Themis, mother of the seasons, and Io, the cow identified with the horned moon (3.657–8; Wiseman 1998: 66–7). Then Ovid relates the one 'not unlike the truth' (3.661–74, 77). Anna was the old woman of Bovillae who fed the plebs at a time when they were hungry and unprotected by tribunes (from the patricians, whose name was then synonymous with the aristocracy), during their secession to the Mons Sacer (in 493 BC). They erected a statue in her honor because she had aided them in their distress. She was made a goddess.

The underlying message in Anna's story is clear: the Mons Sacer gives historical antiquity and authority to her (human) identity and role as protectress of the plebs against the aristocracy; her service in their interests earned (we infer) her deification as a calendrical goddess. The plebs worshipped her annually on the Ides as a mark of their gratitude. Bovillae, the origin of the gens Iulia and a site with both Trojan and Julian cultic associations (Weinstock 1971: 5–7), insinuates her divine Julian connections. Ovid concludes the passage with an amusing story which might well be based on a mime called Anna Peranna by Laberius (Wiseman 1998: 72), who wrote mimes for Julius Caesar (Macr. 2.7.1–5).

The connections Ovid makes between Anna, the calendar, and the plebs are continued in the account of Caesar's death. Following the jollity of the story of Minerva and Mars, Ovid was not going to mention the swords that stabbed the Prince (why spoil the fun and remind the plebs of such a terrible event?). But Vesta objects. She identifies Caesar as her priest, *sacerdos Vestae*, that is, as Pontifex Maximus (3.699, 706). It was her Pontifex whom she transported to heaven, who was deified, who had a temple dedicated to him in the Forum. The pontifical identity of Caesar is important. So, too, is the focus on the assassins. The daggers of the conspirators were aimed at the incumbent in the office in charge of the calendar, and, through that, at Vesta herself. The office, the apotheosis of its incumbent, and the goddess of the Roman hearth are inextricably linked.

Why Vesta? At *Met.* 15.843–6 it was not she but Venus who transported Caesar to heaven. Venus was Caesar's divine ancestress, and he had dedicated a temple to her as Genetrix in 46 BC. The transferal of this role to Vesta in the *Fasti* is significant. Vesta was a much older goddess than Venus, who had been annexed into the Roman pantheon relatively late. Her lack of antiquity and claim on the calendar posed problems for Ovid, who had to go to great lengths to justify the naming of the fourth month after her (4.1–132). Vesta, on the other hand, was introduced to Rome by Numa Pompilius, reformer of Romulus' ten-month calendar and traditional founder of the city's religion and cult (*Fast.* 1.43–4; 3.152, 276; 6.260). She was the people's goddess, *Vesta publica populi Romani Quiritium*. Her sacred flame was the guarantor of Roman identity and continuity. It was Vesta whom Ovid's Carmentis ordered (with some chronological sorcery) to welcome the Ilian gods into Rome so that it could come to pass that a god would guard her flame and the world and perform her sacred rites (*Fast.* 1.527–30).

Ovid/Carmentis has chosen the ancient goddess of the people Vesta over Venus to provide the aetiology for the new Julian god(s) in the Roman calendar. The idea is reiterated and developed on 6 March, the day Augustus was elected Pontifex Maximus, and in which role he is honored as *cognatus* of Vesta and so incipient god himself (3.415–28). This was the day that the goddess of the hearth was annexed into his Julian/Trojan ancestral worship, the day she acquired a male priest for the first time (an idea retrojected onto Caesar: Herbert-Brown 1994: 66–73). His sacred hand guarding her flame on 6 March (3.427) is a pointed contrast to the sacrilegious hands of the assassins which struck her priest on 15 March (3.700). What Ovid does not have to say, because it was common knowledge, is that those sacrilegious hands which had defiled (*polluerant*, 3.706) the pontiff's head (cf. Vesta's guardianship of it at 3.426) belonged to senators. It was senators who dared the unspeakable act against the will of the gods (3.705–6), it was their bones and those of their supporters which whitened the ground at Philippi. Their ignominious fate at the hands of Caesar's heir was a pious act, both filial and national, and so fully justified.

The attack on Vesta's priest is a crime against the Roman people by the aristocracy. Ovid has Augustus avenging the conflated interests of the goddess of the hearth and the author of the Julian calendar. Both are benefactors of the Roman plebs. In avenging them, Augustus was also their benefactor. The interplay between Anna Perenna's festival and Caesar's murder is clear. Anna Perenna, Vesta, Caesar, and Augustus are all Julian gods, calendrical gods, and defenders of the Roman people against their senatorial oppressors. The implication is that the plebs are enjoying Anna's day because of the benefaction of the current Pontifex Maximus.

The next important Julian anniversary is 28 April, signified by the fact that it was made an NP day like 6 March. Both Ovid and Verrius Flaccus confirm that this day, the first of the five-day games of Flora, was also the date chosen *ex senatus consulto* to commemorate the new cult of Vesta in Augustus' home on the Palatine (Degrassi 1963: 133; *Fast.* 4.943–54). Yet both writers give precedence to Flora in their entries. The poet postpones his lavish exposition of Flora and her games until the next available date of 2 May, presumably because his book of April was, at nine hundred and fifty-four lines, the longest and so quite full up. Nevertheless, he injects a provocative detail about the comic and licentious nature of her rites (4.946, *scaena ioci morem liberioris habet*) before tackling the more pressing business of Vesta and her *cognatus* (*nunc me grandius urget opus*), and showing how they were united conceptually and topographically on the Palatine. The word *iocus* recalls ribald scenes described earlier, including Anna Perenna, so we know what to expect (5.332).

Why would Augustus want Palatine Vesta to have a date with the infamous Flora? Flora's festival (5.331–78) and that of Anna Perenna have much in common: whores, drinking, and bawdy songs from the theater. Flora offered the additional titillation of *ludi scaenici* performed by prostitutes. Flora's girls constituted a *chorus plebeius* (5.349–52). Her games had been founded by plebeian aediles, the Publicii (5.283–94). The senate had neglected Flora, a crime against her which it only made good in 173 BC after she had manifested her anger on the earth (5.312–30). The senatorial guilt of 15 March is repeated in Flora's festival on 2 May. Augustus must have chosen the first day of the festival for prostitutes (ironically through the *iusti patres*, 4. 950), to link Palatine Vesta ideologically with Flora and her history (see below).

Both Anna Perenna and Flora are defenders of the plebs against the senate. Their festivals are occasions of institutionalized license for the common people. Both share a date with Vesta and her new Julian gods. Flora even imbues Mars, the god of war, with an (incongruous) elegiac nature and association with the plebs where she claims responsibility for his fatherless, flower-powered conception, and his patronage of her cult in return (5.229–60). Ovid highlights his own ideological allegiance to them all by poking his *cognomen* Naso in as he bids farewell to Flora, praying to her to endow him with her gifts to ensure his own poetic eternity (5.377–8). Anna Perenna, Vesta, Caesar, Augustus, Flora, Mars—and Ovid too—are all linked conceptually in this elegiac *militia* to the Prince.

Vesta and her priest appear again on 12 May, not against the backdrop of an ancient festival this time but in connection with Mars in his Julian guise as Ultor. Their appearance here is brief but pivotal, as they are invoked in the *aetion* for his temple (5.573–5). The theme is familiar. Augustus replaces Vesta as spokesman this time (her words on 15 March had provided the authoritative precedent), but once again we are told (there's that hand motif again: *ille manus tendens*, 5.571; cf. 3.427, 700) that the crime against the *sacerdos Vestae* was an impious act against Vesta and so justified the speaker's taking up of *pia arma* to wreak revenge upon those who murdered him (5.567–78; cf. his *iusta arma* at 3.710). Again, the divide between the pious and the impious, delineated on 15 March, is evident on 12 May: *hinc stanti milite iusto, / hinc coniuratis* (571–2, 'a just military on the one side, the [senatorial] conspirators on the other').

But now the link between Mars and Vesta in an *ultio* context expands the theme considerably. She and her priest provide the catalyst for bringing the god of war into the frame. It is they who authorize Augustus to bid Mars do his worst and so earn the Julian epithet Ultor. Again, we find the people's goddess performing a duty which belonged to Venus. Ovid mentions neither the Forum Iulium with the temple of Venus Genetrix which intersected that of the Augustan Forum nor Venus' iconography which decorated the Avenger's huge temple there (Zanker 1988).

For the third time we find Vesta selected over Venus to incorporate a Julian god into the Roman calendar—and more. The god of war had never been allowed inside the *pomerium* before but Vesta provides the pretext for the construction of a temple to Caesar's avenger in the city itself (5.553). Now we learn it was by Mars' favor that Augustus had wrought that revenge upon the assassins whose guilt and fate were detailed on 15 March. Vesta's appearance at 6 March, 15 March, and 28 April had prepared us for her connection with Mars Ultor. The surprise comes in the exploitation of her name to allow Mars to unleash his revenge in another direction: on the Parthians for their capture of the Roman standards. Ovid, in effect, instructs us that it was the goddess of the Roman hearth who invited the Julian god of revenge into the heart of Rome. May 12 must have been chosen so that the games could be held in his honor without having to compete with another popular festival. One wonders how many of the old aristocracy heeded Ovid's exhortation to attend them in the Circus every year.

The next appearance of Vesta and her priest occurs on 9 June in the climactic anecdote of the ancient festival of the Vestalia (6.249–460). This is not Palatine Vesta, but Vesta of the Roman Forum. Yet the presence of Vesta's priest serves to merge the two cults ideologically. So, too, do features apparent in Ovid's Vestalia and the *feriae* Vesta had shared with Anna Perenna and Flora. Vesta gets fulsome treatment, although she is made complex by being presented in several guises. On the one hand, she is a symbol of the earth and hearth of the home, a living flame with no cult statue, served by virgin priestesses beside the Regia (6.249–304); on the other hand, she is patroness of bakers and millers, who honor her anthropomorphized form in association with a donkey (6.319–48; cf. Prop. 4.1.21). The low social status of Vesta's worshippers triggers a farcical tale about her attempted rape by Priapus, thwarted just in time by the braying of a donkey (6.319–48). The scene is populated with satyrs and nymphs, drinking, dancing, and pairing off, and is characterized as *iocus*, with all its phallic associations (6.320). It bears the features appropriate to the *leuitas* of the stage, just as Flora's had done (5.347). (Littlewood 1980: 317; Barchiesi 1997a: 238–56; Wiseman 2002: 284). In conclusion, Ovid indicates that this comic play was indeed a current holiday entertainment for the bakers' cult of Vesta (*Fast.* 6.347–8): work ceases; the mills are deserted and silent (*cessat opus; uacuae conticuere molae*).

Further familiar themes emerge in the coda of the passage (6.437–69). There we discover that it was not the terrified senate and the timid Vestals who had once saved Vesta's pious flame but her trusty pontiff, this time in the person of L. Caecilius Metellus (241 BC). He broke with tradition to save her, with her approval. He provided the historical precedent that only the Pontifex Maximus was fit to attend to Vesta's welfare (and that of Rome), as we heard before on 6 March and 15 March, Anna's day. Now her sacred flames were safe in the care of Caesar, the present incumbent, as we heard before on 28 April, Flora's day (4.943–54).

The scene it not yet complete, however. A military anniversary on the same day as the Vestalia—of one Brutus Callaicus (who built a temple to Mars with his booty)—provides a handy catalyst for Ovid as a reminder of another military victory, that of the avenger of Crassus. The transition between the two is his sentiment that 'sorrow sometimes mingles with joy, and festivals are not a source of unalloyed pleasure to the populace' (6.463–4). It is a sentiment which recalls the Ides of March, where Anna's happy day was clouded by Vesta's ominous words which led into the finale of Augustus' revenge on the assassins of her Pontifex Maximus (Littlewood 2006: 143). Now we hear Vesta's voice again, not addressing Augustus this time but the Parthians. *Parthe, quid exultas?* recalls her similar apostrophe to the vanquished foe at 5.591–93. Vesta's words, concluding the entire passage on the Vestalia, *quique necem Crassi uindicet, ultor erit* (6.468), endorse a second time since 12 May her inauguration of Mars Ultor into the Roman calendar.

In the four Julian passages considered above, we see that Ovid invokes and enhances Vesta as the authoritative agent who introduces three new Julian gods into the Roman calendar. Augustus' *cognata dea* is not a lofty remote goddess but patroness of the plebs. It is an image strategically fragmented and augmented across March, April, May, and June, and consistently reflects Vesta and her new gods as protectors of the Roman people against their aristocratic oppressors. Anna Perenna and Flora, juxtaposed with Vesta and her pontiff on 15 March and 28 April, are made in the same image to blend tradition with innovation and so imply continuity with the remote past. The *ioci* Ovid inserts on their anniversaries and the Vestalia serve two purposes: they link the three ancient goddesses with each other and with other ancient festivals such as the Lupercalia and Fors Fortuna (24 June, 6.775–80), and with the Roman plebs and the fun they have on their festal days; they serve as a literary device to provide relief—and to deflect attention—from the generically confronting seriousness of a didactic scheme which, like a theological exposition, can be traced across Ovid's contrastingly short, sometimes deceptively light-hearted or irreverent, Julian encomia. Ovid's elegiac, anti-epic calendar (*Fast.* 1.13 *Caesaris arma canant alii*), can be read as an annual replay of the relationship between the Prince and the plebs to the exclusion of the traditional governing class of Rome.

The theme could account for a curious omission in the *Fasti*. On the Nones of February 2 BC, Augustus was hailed *pater patriae* by the senate, equites, and plebs. The Praenestine calendar and the *Fasti Antiates Maiores* note that the day was also sacred to the cult of Concordia on the Capitol (Degrassi 1963: 119, 407). It was Augustus' ability to conciliate the senate *and* espouse the cause of the plebs that ensured his success where Caesar had failed, so his choice of Concord's day is not surprising. His pride in the *concordia ordinum* he had achieved is reflected in the fact that he lists all three classes who voted him the honor in their traditional hierarchical order (*RG* 35).

Ovid, by contrast, gives the plebs precedence over the senate and equites to reflect their historical role in initiating the offer of the title to Augustus (2.127; cf. Suet. *Aug.* 58.1: 'as he entered the theater'). And he ignores Concordia. This is odd, considering how often Concordia is mentioned elsewhere in the *Fasti*. Did he think it might detract from the *Fasti*'s Prince and plebs theme here? The time of writing could be relevant. These were the worst years of Augustus' career. The social cohesion celebrated on 5 February 2 BC (Suet. *Aug.* 58.2) began to disintegrate within months. His daughter Julia, darling of the plebs, was banished for adultery in the summer of that year. Following the deaths of her sons Lucius and Gaius in AD 2 and 4 respectively, the people demonstrated unsuccessfully to have her recalled (Dio 55.13.1). The deaths of the youths moved Augustus to adopt her estranged ex-husband, the conservative Tiberius, as his new heir and (provocatively), to give him the tribunician power for ten years (Dio 55.13.2). Further provocation was the passing of the *lex Valeria Cornelia* the following year, which gave precedence to the upper orders in voting at consular and praetorian elections (Levick 1999: 51). Augustus became more conservative with age and reluctant to risk causing offense to any senators (Dio 55.12.13). In the years 5–8 AD, a severe famine ensued. Dio records that the mass of people suffered grievously, which generated an atmosphere of crisis. Senators, however, were free (and wealthy enough), to leave the city and go wherever they pleased. The crisis was exacerbated by a series of natural disasters (fire, earthquake, and plague) and the imposition of a new tax and conscription as a result of demands of wars in the north. There was a threat of a popular rebellion. Dio maintains that Augustus only succeeded in levying the tax by appealing to the authority of Caesar as a precedent (Dio 55.22.3, 23.1, 25–27, 31.1–4, 33.4).

Augustus' move to a more conservative position clearly generated deep divisions between the social orders. Popular support for him had all but collapsed, as his attempts at damage limitation reveal. He began restoration of the Aventine temples of Flora, and of Ceres, Liber, and Libera, which had burned down in 31 BC (Dio 50.10.3), but which mysteriously had not been included in his restoration program of 28 BC. Was it because, as a patrician, he was ineligible to preside over these temple cults which tradition dictated be served only by plebeians? His membership of every priestly college (*RG* 7.3) would not have overcome such a problem. Ovid mentions neither temple, even as he celebrates the *ludi* of both goddesses. This omission is particularly noticeable in the case of Flora on 28 April (cf. Verrius Flaccus, Degrassi 1963: 132–3, 451–2), the same day Augustus selected to install Vesta into his house which he made partly public property and so effectively partly her 'temple'. He made it all public property following its restoration in AD 3 or 4 after a fire (Dio 54.27.3, 55.12.4–5). (The image of Metellus rescuing Vesta from the flames (6.437–69) must have had powerful contemporary resonance at this time.) The dedication in 12 BC of Palatine Vesta's 'temple' on the *dies natalis* of Flora's unrestored Aventine temple indicates that the latter, over which Vesta's pontifex could not have presided, had been subsumed into the Julian popular cult (*aufer, Vesta, diem*, 4.949), over which he could. Both goddess and her *cognatus* could then have 'presided' over Flora's games below in the Circus Maximus, which more people than ever could enjoy now because of the day's elevated status as Vesta's public holiday.

The idea of Palatine Vesta and her priest ideologically annexing Flora may have been seen as a compliment by the populace in times of fun and plenty, but not so in times of famine and social injustice. It is contemporary events which explain Augustus' late decision to restore the adjacent plebeian temples, both of which had been founded under similar conditions. He did not live to see their completion and perhaps did not expect to, for his dedication of an altar to Ceres mater and Ops Augusta on 10 August AD 7, which was created an NP day (Degrassi 1963: 493), is suggestive of an interim measure.

Haec Mea Militia Est

Before 1 BC, Ovid had reveled in the Augustan age (*Ars* 3.121–8). The dedication of his *Fasti* to Augustus (2.9) was made during an atmosphere of civil unrest unknown since his childhood in the 30s BC. This prompts the question: was his *militia* a reminder to the Prince of his calendrical obligations to the Roman people in return for their support of his claim to be *diui filius*? Was Mars Ultor's view that his huge temple was greater for bearing the Dictator's name (5.563–8) a warning to Augustus not to forsake his Caesarian legacy? If Augustus knew about Ovid's calendar, it was to no avail, for his political savvy had long deserted him (Plin. *Nat.* 7.149). His banishment of Agrippa Posthumus and Julia II tilted the balance of power irrevocably in favor of Tiberius by the summer of AD 8, although in the public eye the adopted son would defer to the Prince as usual (Knox 2004: 2–3).

The power realignment affected Ovid's personal life and the fate of his *Fasti*. His *relegatio* later that year 'ruptured' his poem, he says, even though all twelve books had been completed (*Tr.* 2.549–52). This must mean his *militia* had been in vain. The poem's 'Prince and plebs' theme would render it redundant now that Tiberius, champion of senatorial government, was in control. Tiberius was not interested in the plebs or their entertainment, and hated attending theatrical performances (Tac. *Ann.* 1.54, with Levick 1999: 122–3). But he knew literature. When the second adultery scandal rocked the imperial *domus*, it was Ovid's *Musa iocosa* (*Tr.* 2.354) which provided the public excuse to eject the popular poet who had rejected membership of the senate (*Tr.* 4.10.35). The man whom Augustus called 'warrior of the Muses' (Suet. *Tib.* 21.4), who wrote bawdy verse (Plin. *Ep.* 5.3), would have understood the conventions of erotic poetry, but had reason to fear its *popularis* ideology in these critical years. Who would defend Ovid? Not the Prince. Five decades earlier, in the year of Ovid's birth, Octavian had sacrificed Cicero to conciliate Mark Antony, even though he admired the orator's works (Plut. *Cic.* 47–9). In AD 8 his career had come full circle. The age of Augustus was over. Yet it seems Ovid experienced a brief surge of optimism after AD 14. His short-lived rededication of the *Fasti* to the populist prince Germanicus indicates that, in both a physical and ideological sense, he had reason to hope for a return to the Rome of Augustus he once knew and loved.

FURTHER READING

Degrassi (1963) provides all extant inscriptions with commentary of the Roman calendar. Michels (1967) is a study of Roman religion, history, chronology, and institutions in relation to the major festivals of the pre-Julian calendar. Scullard (1981) is a more reader-friendly guide. Miller (1991), Newlands (1995), Barchiesi (1997a), and Gee (2000) are important studies of the *Fasti*'s engagement with its literary tradition. Herbert-Brown (1994) focuses on the poem's engagement with contemporary politics and religion. Boyle (2003) locates and comments on all monuments and sites mentioned in the entire Ovidian corpus. For characteristics of popular drama evident in Roman poetry, see McKeown (1979b), Wiseman (1998), and Horsfall (2003); in the *Fasti* in particular, see Fantham (1983) and Wiseman (2002). The twelve essays in Herbert-Brown (2002a) provide a variety of recent approaches to the *Fasti*. Three Commentaries on Books 4, 1 and 6 of the *Fasti*, by Fantham (1998), Green (2004), and Littlewood (2006) respectively are an invaluable aid to readers of varied interests. Yavetz, (1969, 2nd edn 1988) is essential for the importance and power of the plebs in the first principate. For Roman religion in general and a salutary reminder of the scarce resemblance between ancient and modern ideas of religion, see Ruepke (2007).

CHAPTER TEN

The *Metamorphoses*: A Poet's Poem

E. J. Kenney

The Metamorphoses is like no poem written before it, although virtually everything in it can be found elsewhere (Mack 1988: 99)

The Metamorphoses luxuriates in its own novelty, making virtues of narrative discontinuity and ruptured expectations (Boyd 2006: 171)

Great Expectations

Virgil's debut as an epic poet had been heralded by a trumpet-blast from Propertius, proclaiming the *Aeneid* to be *nescioquid maius . . . Iliade* ('something greater than the *Iliad*', 2.34.66): an epic, that is to say, in the heroic, Homeric, mode. Ovid was his own slyly allusive harbinger. The first hint that the poet of the *Amores* nurtured higher generic expectations is dropped in the opening couplet of the first poem of the collection (1.1.1–2):

> arma graui numero uiolentaque bella parabam
>   edere, materia conueniente modis.

> It was arms and violent wars that I was preparing to write about in weighty verse, the meter matching the matter.

Arma is also the first word of the *Aeneid*, and Ovid's first hemistich is an unmistakable echo of Virgil's: *arma graui numero ~ arma uirumque cano* (McKeown 1989: 11–12). However, this intention was promptly scotched, we learn, by higher authority (1.1.3–4):

> par erat inferior uersus; risisse Cupido
>   dicitur atque unum surripuisse pedem.

> Every second verse was equal to its predecessor; but it is said that Cupid laughed and stole one foot from it.

So at a stroke the weighty epic hexameters were transformed into light elegiac couplets, and the great plan aborted. But that Ovid was confident that he could have brought it off is made wittily explicit in the opening poem of the next book. The aborted epic turns out to have been about the wars between the Gods and the Titans and their monstrous progeny. (These originally distinct conflicts had already become conflated by the Hellenistic period, and Ovid's scenario is correspondingly vague (McKeown 1998: 10–11).) That was an ambitious undertaking for a poet who was probably not yet out of his teens (McKeown 1987: 74), and one of which both Horace (*C.* 2.12.6–9) and Propertius (2.1.19–20, 39–40) had fought shy. Ovid proclaims that he is equal to it in an untranslatable pun, 'and the words were there' (*et satis oris erat*, 2.1.12). *Os* can mean not only the necessary poetic equipment but also 'assurance' (*OLD* 2b, 4b, 8b; McKeown 1998: 12–13), that sense here, bearing in mind the writer's age, bordering on 'nerve', 'cheek'.

The hints become even more plain in the first and last poems of Book 3. In the encounter with Tragedy and Elegy in the sacred grove, Ovid is adjured by Tragedy to abandon love poetry and to 'embark on a greater work' (*incipe maius opus*, 3.1.24), another Virgilian echo, here of his styling the second, Iliadic, half of the *Aeneid* as *maius opus* (*Aen.* 7.44); these are also the words with which Ovid was to describe the *Metamorphoses* (*Tr.* 2.63). He is, says Tragedy, to 'sing the deeds of heroes' (*cane facta uirorum*, 3.1.25). Though this is Tragedy speaking, it seems rather to be epic which she is pressing him to turn to, and his own reference in the last line of the poem to the 'loftier work' (*grandius . . . opus*, 3.1.70) that awaits him carries the same implication. All this is finally brought to a head in the last poem of the collection, a formal farewell to love elegy. It is now Bacchus who appears, in an epiphany corresponding to and, since he is par excellence the source of poetic inspiration, overruling Cupid's decree and tacitly endorsing Ovid's protest that Cupid had no business to interfere in the first place in matters which did not concern him (1.1.5–16). Picking up Tragedy's use of the same phrase (3.1.23), he summons Ovid 'with a weightier rod' (*thyrso grauiore*) to 'a greater field' (*area maior*, 3.15.18). That phrase also recalls Tragedy and her description of the deeds of heroes as 'a worthy field' (*area digna*, 3.1.26), for the display of Ovid's poetic powers.

The cumulative effect of all these hints is clear: the young Ovid is seemingly bent on challenging Virgil on his own ground and believes himself equal to the challenge. The reader alert to such allusive techniques, the *doctus lector* whom scholars postulate as the necessary complement to the *doctus poeta*, is being led to expect a heroic epic aspiring to rival, if not outdo, the *Aeneid*.

Prospectus

We do not know whether Ovid read parts of the *Metamorphoses* to friends in advance of publication, as Virgil had done with the *Aeneid*. Even those so privileged, if any such there were, could hardly have been prepared for what they found when the poem appeared. The first hint that this might be a rather different kind of epic from what they had been led to expect would have confronted them in its physical shape:

fifteen papyrus rolls, a poem in fifteen books, signaling 'its proper distance from the traditional epic which is instead characterized by a number corresponding to a multiple of six' (Merli 2004: 36), and an affinity with elegy, which favored multiples of five. That the *Metamorphoses* was indeed not going to be like any poem, epic or otherwise, written before it would have become further apparent to our hypothesized *doctus lector* on unrolling the first of the fifteen *uolumina* and reading the astonishingly brief proem, ushering in a poem of some twelve thousand verses in four lines (1.1–4):

> In noua fert animus mutatas dicere formas
> corpora: di, coeptis (nam uos mutastis et illa)
> aspirate meis primaque ab origine mundi
> ad mea perpetuum deducite tempora carmen.

> My spirit carries me to tell of shapes changed into
> new bodies. You gods—for you have changed that too—
> further my enterprise and conduct a continuous song
> from the first origin of the world to my own times.

No translation, however literal, can capture all the nuances of the original, in which every word and phrase is loaded with programmatic implications. These can only achieve full recognition from a reader already primed by the hints dropped in the *Amores*: for what is now promised is not heroic epic, let alone a Gigantomachy as foreshadowed there. The first four words form a complete sentence which can be read autonomously: *in noua fert animus* ('my mind carries me on to new things'). We are quickly undeceived as to the syntax by *corpora* picking up *noua* in the next verse, the enjambment slyly nudging the reader to appreciate the little joke that has been played on him. The appreciation is further sharpened if it is remembered that the first hemistich of the *Aeneid*, 'arms and the man I sing' (*arma uirumque cano*), does stand on its own as announcing the subject of the poem. At the outset Ovid can be seen signaling that he is taking his own, unVirgilian, way. The sense of that opening phrase is sustained by the following parenthesis: this poem is indeed new, because the gods have set the poet on this new course. The metamorphosis protestingly suffered in the first poem of the *Amores* is now reversed: the gods—all of them this time—have again intervened to change the poet from elegist to epicist. The first metamorphosis in the poem is that of its creator; and as the transformations to be described in what follows often do, it includes an *aition*, the explanation of an origin (on aetiology as a leitmotiv of the poem, see Myers 1994): *here* is to be found the poem's *prima origo*. The intervention of a deity to guide a poet in his choice of genre or theme had become something of a cliché since its first attested appearance in Hesiod's meeting with the Muses on Mount Helicon (*Theog.* 22–34) and its subsequent exploitation by Greek and Latin poets, including Callimachus, Ennius, Virgil, and Propertius. Ovid, as we are now coming to expect, has given it a new lease of life.

Paradox now supervenes. The poem which Ovid asks the gods to 'conduct' (*deducere*) to its planned conclusion will, if that prayer be literally granted, be a *deductum carmen*, a 'fine-spun song' (*OLD deduco* 4b), something *à la* Callimachus, such as that to which Apollo had directed Virgil on finding him beginning to sing of 'kings and battles' (*reges et proelia*), the material of heroic epic; he admonishes him that a herdsman/poet 'should fatten his flock but sing a "thin" song' (*Ecl.* 6.4–5) in 'Virgil's pastoral rendering of Callimachus' rejection of epic' (cf. Clausen 1994: 174–8):

> pinguis
> pascere oportet oues, deductum dicere carmen.

Ovid then, it would seem, is setting out to write that contradiction in terms, a Callimachean epic. It is certainly consistent with this intention that when 'kings and battles' are allowed to figure in the *Metamorphoses* they are apt to be handled satirically. A well-read student might also note that in electing to begin his narrative from the creation Ovid is flouting the authority of Horace, who in the *Ars Poetica* (as acutely remarked by Fantham 2004a: 5) had expressly warned aspiring epic poets against the fault of beginning their stories too far back (*AP* 146–7).

Clearly for Ovid innovation was the name of the game. The scale on which the game was to be played is further signaled by a hint in these closely packed lines (see Myers 1994: 1–7; Wheeler 1999: 8–30; Barchiesi 2005: 133–45 for further discussion of the Proem), which could not have been apparent to even the most switched-on reader if they were all he had to go on. The phrase *ad mea tempora* ('to my own times') can also be read as 'down to where my *Fasti* take over', for the first word of that poem and its alternative title is *Tempora* (Barchiesi 1991: 6–7, 19 n. 13)—in antiquity books could be identified by their opening words and the *Aeneid*, for example, was often referred to as the *Arma uirumque* (Kenney 1970a). The *Fasti*, composed simultaneously with the *Metamorphoses*, is likewise a generic hybrid, an aetiological poem in elegiacs, planned on an epic scale in twelve books, as anomalous a number for elegy as was fifteen for epic. The two poems were clearly designed as a literary diptych, a combined *chef d'oeuvre*. '[T]aken together the *Fasti* and the *Metamorphoses* represent Ovid's typically indirect answer to the challenge of Virgil's epic, on the one hand a Callimachean elegy on the central subjects of the *Aeneid* and on the other a hexameter epic on themes for the most part not Roman' (Hardie 1991: 47; cf. Merli 2004 and Kenney 2005). This was a unique example on a monumental scale of what Wilhelm Kroll famously christened 'Kreuzung der Gattungen', generic miscegenation (Kroll 1924: 202–24). Ovid had previously claimed that in the *Heroides* he had 'created a work unknown to others' (*ignotum hoc aliis ille nouauit opus, Ars* 3.346). It can be argued that the word *nouauit* there is ambiguous, for the word can mean both 'invent' and 'reinvent' or 'renew' (*OLD* 1, 4; cf. Gibson 2005: 239), hinting at a debt to Propertius' 'Arethusa' elegy (4.3). Applied to the *Metamorphoses*, the claim would call for no such qualification: the achievement here is Ovid's and his alone.

From all this one conventional element is missing: invocation of a Muse or Muses. Ovid, indeed, has invoked the whole pantheon, but all he asks of them is a favorable wind and an escort to speed the undertaking on its course and to its conclusion. The word *aspirate* evokes the familiar image of the progress of a poem as a sea voyage, frequently exploited by Ovid (Kenney 1958: 205–6), and among the various senses of *deduco* is also that of providing a ceremonial escort (*OLD* 8b). There is nothing here about *in*spiration; that is to come from within the poet himself, from his *animus*. The *Ars amatoria* had begun with a similar assertion of independence: Ovid welcomes—indeed, rather seems to take for granted—Venus' support, but insists that he draws his inspiration not from Apollo or the Muses but from *usus*, his own experience (*Ars* 1.25–30). In the coda to the *Metamorphoses*, as we shall see, he expressly denies the power even of Jupiter, the supreme overlord of Olympus, over the fate of the poem and of its creator (15.871–2). The gods have their uses—*expedit esse deos*, they are useful to have around, as he had cynically observed in the *Ars* (1.637)—but when it came to writing poetry Ovid was his own man.

Materials

In the *Georgics* Virgil had claimed to be embarking on a new and unfrequented path to Helicon, dismissing Callimachean mythological themes (*G.* 3.3–8). The complaint may be an old one, dating back to Choerilus of Samos in the fifth century BC (Courtney 1980: 85; *SH* no. 317), but in later poets the rejection of myth as played out becomes a familiar cliché (e.g. Manil. 2.49–52; *Aetna* 17–23; Stat. *Silv.* 5.3.80–8; Nemes. *Cyn.* 15–47; Juv. 1.7–13). Their lists of ostensibly hackneyed myths contain many which Ovid was to demonstrate were far from being played out when he went on to turn them to brilliant effect in the *Metamorphoses*. Indeed, his whole poetic career, until it was abruptly and brutally derailed by Augustus' sentence of exile, is an implicit refutation of that idea. Hints of what myth meant to him as a poet begin to emerge in the third book of the *Amores*, in the series of hints of his coming emancipation from the role of love poet imposed on him by Cupid. The thematic character of the catalogue of rivers which prefaces the story of Ilia and Anio (3.6.23–44) perhaps suggests resort to a mythological handbook (see below). (In passing, it is worth noting that that story from Roman prehistory is the first foretaste in the *Amores*, followed by the overtly aetiological 3.10 and 3.13, of the *Fasti*. There Ilia was to appear in her more familiar guise as Rhea Silvia (*Fast.* 3.1–54, 2.381–422).) The list of myths at 3.12.29–40 is something different. Ostensibly in that poem Ovid is lamenting the part played by his poetry in the loss of his mistress to rivals: his praises of her beauty proved all too credible. What poets write, he insists, is not to be taken literally. There follows a catalogue of stories to illustrate the power of poetry to invest the miraculous or incredible with plausibility. This is articulated on an emphatic sequence of pronouns and verbs which drive the point home: it is *we*, the poets, who have *made* these things happen. In apparently deprecating the power of his poetry Ovid is in reality celebrating it, even though in his capacity of elegiac lover it has done him no favors (McKeown 1979a; Bretzigheimer 2001: 169; Kenney 2001b: 1). The stories in that list, unlike those of the rivers of 3.6, were all familiar, a point emphasized by the stock rhetorical formula which introduces the last six, *quid referam . . .?* ('need I go on to mention . . .?'). The ambiguity informing the poem is maintained in its last four lines. Poets enjoy unbounded license to exploit their material, but they also have a right to expect not to be identified with their characters or persona (3.12.41–4)—a grievance of writers from Euripides to Kingsley Amis. The art of the poet is 'to lie so as to persuade the ear of the listener'—the ear, be it noted, not the intelligence (Call. *Hymn* 1.65). Those who have filched Ovid's girl from him may be good judges of beauty, but they are poor literary critics. Aristotle had remarked that in storytelling 'plausible improbabilities are preferable to unconvincing possibilities' (*Poetics* 1460a.26–7). Ovid's achievement in the *Metamorphoses* was to transform the world of myth, by imparting plausibility to the fantastic or incredible, into a parable of the human condition.

Making

The *Metamorphoses* is about metamorphosis in the obvious sense spelled out in the Proem: all the stories in the poem incorporate or can be linked in some way to a story of transformation. It is also an exercise on a vast scale of literary metamorphosis, a demonstration of the poet's power to shape an amorphous mass of material into a work of literary art. The word 'poet' (*poeta*, ποιητής) means literally 'maker'; poets saw themselves as craftsmen. The immense corpus of myth and legend handed down by tradition and put on record by mythographers had been selectively exploited by poets over the centuries. Ovid's program was nothing less than to lay it all under contribution on a chronological plan so as to fashion from it an artistic whole. The first episode in the poem, the creation of order from chaos, the transformation of a shapeless, unordered mass of elements, *rudis indigestaque moles* (1.7), into the world about us, is a paradigm of the act of creation that has brought into being what now awaits the reader. The catalogue of myths at *Am.* 3.12.21–40 exemplifies a figure common in Latin poetry in which the poet is said to do what he describes (Nisbet and Hubbard 1978: 21 on Hor. *C.* 2.1.18; Clausen 1994: 194 on Virg. *Ecl.* 6.46). This is more than a *façon de parler*: the poet does indeed make these things happen by reenacting them. In the *Metamorphoses* Ovid set out to do that on an unexampled, indeed a universal, scale by an act of literary creativity implicitly equated with that which brought the universe itself into existence.

The undertaking faced him with a number of technical problems. First, that of selection: to choose from the vast stores of mythological and legendary material at his disposal what best suited his purpose. Second, and perhaps more taxingly, to accommodate what he selected to his grand chronological scheme. These stories had been transmitted in differing and not infrequently contradictory versions, and mythical chronology was not an exact science. There was no accepted overall coherent chronological structure into which a 'continuous song' could be fitted: such stories or groups of stories as did have some sort of chronological shape had to serve as a series of frameworks into which could be fitted other stories linked in various ways—thematic, geographical, genealogical, by contrast, and sometimes by pure invention and 'outrageously contrived synchronization' (Cameron 2004: 289). It seems probable, though the idea has more often than not been pooh-poohed, that

Ovid drew on mythographical handbooks as well as literary sources for some of his material (Cameron 2004: 261–303, esp. 286–303). What he made of it was all his own.

The architecture of this great literary edifice is complex: '[t]here is no simple key to the structure of the *Metamorphoses*' (Cameron 2004: 286). The body of the narrative falls naturally into three main divisions, centering respectively on the activities of the gods (1.452–6.412), heroes (6.413–11.193), and what can be described, if history be taken as having begun with the Trojan War, as historical characters (11.194–15.870). Attempts to detect more formal and symmetrical structures, apart from proving contradictory, rest on an unlikely assumption. Such elaborations, which most readers then and now could hardly be expected to notice or appreciate, add nothing to the enjoyment and understanding of the poem, and Ovid was not one to waste time and effort on buried virtuosity. There were other and more effective ways for him to display his art (cf. Crabbe 1981: 2327).

The overriding imperative was to hold the reader's attention through a poem of some twelve thousand verses. The secret was to keep the narrative moving and the reader guessing. The *Metamorphoses* differs from most epics in one important respect: it has nothing that can be described as a 'plot'. In this it resembles Ennius' *Annales* rather than the Homeric epics or the *Argonautica* or the *Aeneid*. It is true that there is an overarching theme, but the episodes, though thematically or otherwise linked, are as regards their individual plots autonomous. In this it resembles Callimachus' *Aetia*, and the resemblance, as has been noted, is not coincidental. The reader is not obliged to bear in mind an earlier episode in order to make sense of some later development. That is not to say that on a second or third reading interesting or piquant echoes, correspondences, and subtleties of construction may not suggest themselves; but there is no immediate temptation to listen to them. What makes this one of the most enjoyable books ever written is the feeling that it communicates of constantly beckoning the reader on to see what comes next: it is what reviewers are apt to call a 'page-turner'. In the conduct of his narrative it is above all variety and surprise that Ovid is seeking to achieve.

In an approximately central position in the poem (on the pivotal role of Book 8 in the poem, see Crabbe 1981), Ovid has located one of his most brilliant *tours de force*, the comparison of the Cretan Labyrinth, in which its creator, Daedalus, nearly gets lost himself, with the windings of the river, which has bequeathed a word to the English language, the Maeander (8.159–68):

> Daedalus ingenio fabrae celeberrimus artis
> ponit opus turbatque notas et lumina flexa
> ducit in errorem uariarum ambage uiarum.
> non secus ac liquidis Phrygius Maeandros in undis
> ludit et ambiguo lapsu refluitque fluitque
> occurrensque sibi uenturas aspicit undas
> et nunc ad fontes, nunc ad mare uersus apertum
> incertas exercet aquas, ita Daedalus implet
> innumeras errore uias uixque ipse reuerti
> ad limen potuit! tanta est fallacia tecti.

Daedalus, famous for his architectural genius, built this work, confusing the guide-marks and leading the eyes astray in a maze of alternative routes. Just as Phrygian Maeander amuses himself with his liquid waves and in his deceptive course flows now backwards, now forwards, meeting himself and seeing waters that have yet to arrive, as he presses on his undecided current, now back to its source, now on to the open sea, so Daedalus built error into the innumerable ways, and could scarcely find his own way out: such was the trickery of his building.

Just as Ovid's account of the Creation can be read as a metaphor for the poem that it prefaces, so in this passage we have an image of the poet's management of his narrative and of his role as creator of and guide—though now and again momentarily perplexed by his own ingenuity— through a literary labyrinth (Tsitsiou-Chelidoni 2003: 144–7; Boyd 2006: 175–84). Like one traveling down a great river, the reader is borne effortlessly along by a narrative current which now broadens out into a placid pool, now divagates into a picturesque backwater, now suddenly breaks into rapids or whirlpools, as the joys and sorrows of the characters are reflected in their predicaments and emotions. The only predictable feature of Ovid's telling of these stories is its unpredictability. A poetic Daedalus, 'he leads (the reader) wandering through the twists and turns of various paths' (*ducit in errorem uariarum ambage uiarum*); '*Variarum, viarum*—these look so alike that one seems a blurred image of the other: the very diction dramatizes the confusions of the maze' (Nims 1965: xxvii). As the Maeander repeatedly turns back on itself, *refluitque fluitque* (the '*hysteron proteron*' reversal of the 'natural' word order, imaging the paradox), so Ovid's narrative may backtrack to spring a surprise.

The humor of this ploy is brought out rather cruelly in what happens to Daedalus himself. His story seems to be about to fade out on a tragic tableau: the bereaved father mourning the death of his son Icarus, apparent closure rounded off, as often, with an *aition*, explaining why the Icarian Sea is so called (8.231–5). Pathos is, however, abruptly dispelled by what follows. There is a witness to this spectacle, who greets it with glee: Perdix, the boy genius killed by Daedalus in a fit of jealous rage and transformed into a ptarmigan (8.236–59). The loss of a child—Ovid leaves it to the reader to draw the inference—is a just retribution for child-murder.

There can be few if any poems in which the poet makes his presence so constantly and wittily felt as in this one. A particularly amusing example is that of Pirithous. He is identified on his first appearance as *Ixione natus* (8.613), the son of the man who, as the reader would know and had indeed been previously reminded (4.461) and would be reminded again (9.123–4, 12.210–11), was undergoing eternal torment in Hades for the attempted rape of Juno, and as a 'despiser of the gods' (*deorum spretor*, 8.612–13). When he asserts that the story of metamorphosis that Achelous has just finished relating is pure fiction and that the gods have no such powers, his hearers round on him in outrage and dismay (8.614–16), as well they may, for he is in effect calling into question the credibility of the poem in which he, and they, are characters, robbing them of their literary identities and denying his and their Maker. Ovid's characters, no less than his readers, are left in no doubt as to who is in charge.

Crucial to Ovid's success in continuously engaging the reader's attention is his management of the narrative medium, the hexameter. Wilkinson's description of it as 'a comfortable, well-sprung, well-oiled vehicle for his story' (Wilkinson 1963: 202) neatly hits off its function: to keep the narrative moving. Compared with Virgil's, Ovid's verse moves at a faster overall pace, achieved by a higher proportion of feet containing short syllables and a more even distribution of metrical emphasis. 'Metrically . . . Ovid is far more Greek than any previous Roman poet, far more "Homeric" than Vergil, and almost as "Homeric" as Homer himself' (Duckworth 1969: 73). This 'Greekness' is in keeping with and arises out of the general character of the *Metamorphoses* as having more in common with Greek poetry, especially that of Callimachus, than with his Roman predecessors. As with most, if not all, of the meters of classical poetry, based as they are on syllabic quantity rather than stress accent, these metrical characteristics are hardly reproducible in English translation, but they are integral to Ovid's purpose and to his poetic art (for technical discussion see Duckworth 1969: 71–80; Kenney 1971b; Kenney 1973 = 2002: 57–89 *passim*; Dee 2006).

A 'hero-free' Epic

The *Metamorphoses* is, among many other things, an anthology of genres, and it duly includes as stock features of heroic epic three battles and a legendary hunt. Of the battles, one depicts a relatively brief encounter on conventional lines between Greeks and Trojans, its function being to introduce the metamorphosis of Cycnus into a swan (12.64–145). Those of Perseus against Phineus and his followers (5.1–235), and of the Lapiths and Centaurs (12.210–531), are exaggerated to the point of burlesque, full of grotesque variations on a familiar epic theme: gory death on the battlefield. The Calydonian Hunt (8.267–444) wittily transposes battlefield motifs into hunting mode, but Ovid has transformed the whole episode into non-stop knockabout farce, a competitive display of heroic ineptitude (Due 1974: 80; Horsfall 1979). It includes as one of the star turns a vivid vignette of the young Nestor, who according to his reminiscing in the *Iliad* had been a devil of a fellow in those days (Hom. *Il.* 11.670–762), using his boar-spear, not to transfix his quarry, but to pole-vault into a tree to escape its charge (8.365–8). Since it is nowhere else recorded that he was among those present, it is tempting to wonder if Ovid included him expressly to satirize his traditional epic image. When after repeated fiascos first blood is eventually drawn, it is not by any of the heroes, poor marksmen all—Jason indeed managing to spear a hound (8.412; Kenney 2001a: 547–8)—but by the maiden huntress Atalanta; and it is the infatuation with her of Meleager, the titular hero of the Hunt, that precipitates the catastrophic denouement, his murder of his uncles and his own death at the hands of his mother (Keith 1999b: 224–30).

With this intrusion of love into the heroic arena, the tone of the narrative modulates abruptly from farce to tragedy, allowing Ovid to revert to a favorite theme. The murder of her brothers confronts Althea with the choice of condoning the crime of shedding kindred blood or committing it herself by killing the perpetrator, her own son. She literally holds his fate in her hands, in the shape of a magic brand on which his life depends. Her agonized soliloquy, as she decides whether or not to commit it to the flames (8.481–511), is one of a series of dramatic monologues by heroines that punctuate Books 7–10 of the poem. All turn on conflicts between the claims of *pietas* in its different aspects—duty to family, to country, to the gods—and those of love. It had been with Medea, who opens the sequence, that 'the famous duel of *amor* and *pudor*'—best defined as the feeling of shame evoked by conscious disregard for what is fitting (*OLD*)—'enters the *Metamorphoses*' (Otis 1970: 172–3), and it is with Medea that we meet much the most conspicuous example of the power of Ovid's heroines to subvert traditional epic values. 'Encounter with the female . . . inevitably results in the unmanning of the Ovidian epic hero' (Keith 1999b: 239). Jason's failure to distinguish himself in the hunting field is no more than we ought to expect in the light of the performance that he had put up in Ovid's version of the story of the Argonauts (7.7–424). As leader of this famous expedition to recover the Golden Fleece he was, so to say, *ex officio* a hero of the first rank; and it is he who is chosen by Ovid as the victim of his most brutal exercise in (if the word may be permitted) deheroization. The Jason of Apollonius' *Argonautica* does not dominate the action; his role is rather complementary to that of Medea. In Ovid's treatment of the story that role is further downgraded to that of a virtual automaton manipulated by an all-powerful sorceress who holds the very forces of nature, the Sun and the Moon, in thrall (7.199–209). His ordeals are a put-up job stage-managed by Medea, and it is she, from the moment she sets eyes on him, who determines the whole subsequent course of events. The three soliloquies in which Apollonius had explored his Medea's fluctuating states of mind (*Arg.* 3.464–70, 636–44, 771–801) are telescoped by Ovid into a single monologue by a woman who has evidently made up her mind and is fighting a battle already lost against the claims of family and country (7.11–71; see Kenney 2001c for a fuller discussion). Indeed, it turns out that in all these duels *pudor* is on a hiding to nothing.

Ovid had begun to explore the possibilities of the dramatic monologue in the *Heroides*, commandeering, as was his way, and promoting to sub-generic status, a feature of Euripidean and Hellenistic tragedy (Heinze 1960: 389, 395–9; Jacobson 1974: 7). There the speakers have for the most part little choice: there is not much they can do about their situations but complain. The heroines of the *Metamorphoses* are confronted with urgent moral dilemmas requiring a decision and calling forth an anguished display of warring emotions. The first and last monologues of the series, those of Medea and Atalanta (10.611–35, not the Atalanta of the Hunt, but a namesake; the two are often confused by the poets), complement each other, even more obviously than is true of the rest, in presenting an open-and-shut case. Medea, as she says in lines perhaps quoted more often than any in Ovid, sees the better course and follows the worse (*uideo meliora proboque, / deteriora sequor*, 7.20–1). Her dilemma and that of Atalanta are identical: do I rescue this man or do I condemn him to death? Between Medea and Atalanta (Althea standing somewhat apart) we have the stories of Scylla (8.6–151), Byblis (9.450–665) and Myrrha (10.298–502), their themes respectively high treason, incest frustrated, and incest consummated. The story of Byblis is a tour de force, incorporating two monologues (9.474–516,

585–629) and between them what is in effect a third in the form of a letter to her brother declaring her infatuation (9.530–63). This is a remarkable demonstration of Ovid's ability to produce fresh variations on what was by now a fairly well-worn theme. As with Althea's soliloquy, uttered while she stands holding the fatal brand before the sacrificial fire (8.479–80), the incorporation of the motif of the heroine's letter into a narrative setting adds an extra dramatic dimension.

'The sweet witty soul of Ovid'

Byblis is the only heroine in the *Metamorphoses* to take example from the heroines of the *Heroides* and declare her passion in writing. A woman whose name suggests an etymological connection with βύβλος, βίβλος, 'paper', is clearly the right person to take that plunge (Ahl 1985: 211–13; Tissol 1997: 44). This is typical of many such allusive strokes of metapoetical and inter- or intratextual wit in the poem, such as the reaction provoked by the blasphemous outburst of Pirithous, which Ovid's *docti lectores* were presumably equipped to appreciate. But he did not write only for the learned. There is much straightforward comedy, as when Juno notices the coincidence of her husband's absence and a thick cloud covering the earth, and leaps immediately to the correct conclusion—that he is up to no good. But the reader sensitive to Ovid's use of language and meter will additionally relish the way in which her instantaneous reaction is mirrored in the rapid movement of the verse, accentuated by enjambment (1.607–9):

> quem postquam caelo non repperit, 'aut ego fallor
> aut ego laedor' ait delapsaque ab aethere summo
> constitit in terra nebulasque recedere iussit.

> The moment she failed to find him in heaven, 'either I'm wrong or I'm wronged,' said she, and dropping down from the topmost *aether* she arrived on earth and ordered the mist to lift.

From the outset the gods of the *Metamorphoses*, like the heroes, are fair game for Ovid's ironical wit (for a general survey of Ovidian humor in the *Metamorphoses* see Frécaut 1972: 237–9). Their Council is portrayed as a parody of the Roman Senate (1.167–76), recalling the use of the same motif by the Republican satirist Lucilius (Coffey 1976: 42–3); when Jupiter invites their acquiescence in the deification of Hercules (9.243–58), it is in the manner of the Princeps thanking his colleagues for, while taking for granted, a favor done to a member of his family (Wilkinson 1955: 195; Due 1974: 82–3; Feeney 1991: 206–7). That speech concludes with a sideswipe at Juno, the sworn enemy of Hercules as another of her husband's by-blows: a reminder of the cat-and-dog relationship of Zeus and Hera in the *Iliad*, and a far cry from the dignified reconciliation and adjustment of aims between Virgil's Jupiter and Juno (*Aen.* 12.791–842). We seem perhaps to catch here a prefatory hint of the process of 'appropriation and reappropriation' informing Ovid's intertextual dialogue with the *Aeneid* in Books 13–14, as brilliantly and invigoratingly argued by Stephen Hinds (Hinds 1998: 99–122).

Few of the gods who figure in the *Metamorphoses* are presented in a dignified light. They more often than not behave cruelly and arbitrarily, and they, no less than the human beings whose destinies they purport to control, are subject to violent and irrational passions. Indeed, so far from being absolute rulers of the world, they frequently seem to be themselves equally subject to forces outside their control. That raises a vexed question of which Ovid's readers would have been made aware in their reading of Homer, the relationship between the gods and Fate (Guthrie 1955: 130 and n. 3; Onians 1954: index, s.v. 'fate'). As with much else in the Ovidian universe, this is left for the reader to puzzle over; but its lurking presence in the poem prompts the asking of a fundamental question: what *are* we supposed to make of this world? What, if anything, is the poem essentially about? What has it to say to us in the twenty-first century?

Why Read the *Metamorphoses*?

That Ovid is a supremely gifted storyteller and that the poem makes continuously entertaining reading does not need demonstration. But is there a case for taking the fun of the *Metamorphoses* seriously (Hinds 1989: 271)? A crucial pointer is to be found in the long speech of Pythagoras (15.75–478), a passage which has provoked widely differing critical reactions ranging from outspoken admiration to outright boredom. Technically it is another tour de force, a full-scale demonstration of generic versatility in the shape of a specifically Lucretian excursus in didactic mode. Though its text is the Pythagorean prohibition of the eating of flesh (15.75–142, 456–78), its real theme is that of the poem itself, change—not mutations but the principle of mutability. That theme is essentially Epicurean and Lucretian, and Lucretius is a pervasive presence in the text, but its real message is flatly at odds with his. There is, says Pythagoras, one thing and one alone in the physical universe that is immune from the law of universal mutability: the soul. The *Metamorphoses* describes a world in a state of perpetual flux, in which no identity is secure and nothing is certain but uncertainty, a world-picture reflected textually in the kaleidoscopic variations of genre and tone from episode to episode, and the often arbitrary character of the transitions between them. This latter feature was to call forth a magisterial rebuke from Quintilian, who called it playing the fool (*Inst. Or.* 4.1.77); it should rather be understood as a verbalization of the often inconsequent course of events in the world inhabited by Ovid's characters, and by implication in the real world. 'The haphazard chain of association is entertaining, but it also reinforces the Ovidian theme of the very contingency of connectedness' (Feeney 2004: xxi). It is the behavior of those characters in the face of such challenges that the poem is essentially 'about'.

This has been well expressed by Otto Steen Due in his admirable and too little appreciated monograph. 'The *Metamorphoses* are not really an epic poem. They are a descriptive poem. And what is described is the innumerable aspects of man, and not least of woman, and of their behaviour as individual in this fantastic world' (Due 1974: 164). Other writers before and after Ovid have exposed their characters to predicaments arising from far-fetched or ridiculous or otherwise improbable premises, whether like Aristophanes to make a serious political point or like W. S. Gilbert for purely comic effect. The tone of Ovid's exploration is ironical: he views human life as a tragicomedy. His humor is not infrequently black, sometimes, as in the famous description of the flaying of Marsyas (6.385–91), macabre. His attitude is that of the detached observer, recording with sympathy, rather than sharing with empathy, the emotions of his characters as he documents what the soul of man is capable of enduring when subjected to ultimate breaking strain.

The dominant character in the *Metamorphoses*, however, is the poet himself. It is his mind, his *animus*, the one indestructible part of him, that has brought the poem and the world it portrays into being; and it ends with his own apotheosis (15.871–9):

> Iamque opus exegi, quod nec Iouis ira nec ignis
> nec poterit ferrum nec edax abolere uetustas.
> cum uolet, illa dies, quae nil nisi corporis huius
> ius habet, incerti spatium mihi finiat aeui;
> parte tamen meliore mei super alta perennis
> astra ferar, nomenque erit indelebile nostrum;
> quaque patet domitis Romana potentia terris
> ore legar populi, perque omnia saecula fama
> (si quid habent ueri uatum praesagia) uiuam.

> And now I have accomplished a work which neither the anger of Jupiter nor iron nor devouring old age will be able to destroy. When it will, let that day, which has power only over this body of mine, put an end to my uncertain life; yet in the better part of me I shall be borne above the lofty stars and my name shall be indestructible, and wherever the power of Rome extends over the conquered lands I shall be read by the voice of men, and through all ages, if prophets prophesy truly, I shall live in fame.

Whether Virgil, had he lived to complete the *Aeneid* to his satisfaction, would have rounded it off with a coda or *sphragis* (Greek for 'seal', conventionally used to describe an epilogue in which the poet identified himself and appraised his work; see Mynors 1990: 323–4 on Virg. *G.* 4.559–66), as he had rounded off the *Georgics*, is much debated. His only explicit reference to his poetry in the *Aeneid* is in the apostrophe in which he promises immortal renown to Nisus and Euryalus while Rome endures, 'if there is any power in my songs' (*si quid mea carmina possunt*) (see Hardie 1994: 153–5 on *Aen.* 9.446–9). That modest qualification is a far cry from Ovid's triumphalism. The soul of Ovid will be borne above the stars, thus outsoaring all the catasterized heroes of myth, most particularly, in the world of the *Metamorphoses*, Hercules, established by Jupiter only *among* the constellations (9.271–2). As we have seen, Ovid's account of Hercules' promotion to the pantheon had been tinged with satire. In the coda the words 'in the finer part of me' (*parte . . . meliore mei*) picking up Hercules' survival 'in the better part of him' (*parte sui meliore*, 9.269) drive home the ironical comparison. Less overtly the words 'above the stars' (*super astra*) might recall the self-predication of Aeneas as 'known by repute above the heavens' (Virg. *Aen.* 1.379 *fama super aethera notus*). In that echo of Odysseus' introduction of himself as one 'whose fame reaches to heaven' (Hom. *Od.* 9.20) Austin is surely right to detect, though he does not develop the point, 'a Virgilian emotional contrast and significance' (Austin 1971: 137). In introducing his hero thus Virgil can be seen implicitly staking his own claim to immortality. What Virgil had been content to imply, Ovid proudly proclaims.

In the poems written in exile at Tomis Ovid frequently equates his situation with death. He was not alone among the banished in doing so (Gaertner 2005: 353 on *Ex P.* 1.5.86). In his case the theme takes on a special resonance. In thanking a friend for loyally cherishing his memory in the shape of his portrait on a ring, he insists that it is only his poetry that truly portrays him (*Tr.* 1.7.11–12):

> grata tua est pietas, sed carmina maior imago
> sunt mea.

> Your affection is dear to me, but it is my poetry that is my real portrait.

The lines play on the sense of *imago*: not only 'likeness' but 'form' (*OLD* 12). It is in the physical shape of the *Metamorphoses* that Ovid lives on. The poem is Ovid, Ovid is the poem.

FURTHER READING

Of works mentioned in this chapter, two may be especially singled out. Fantham (2004a) provides the most recent and accessible introduction to the *Metamorphoses*; and Due (1974) can be recommended for 'the sanity of [his] judgement and the number of intelligent and enlightening observations that he makes both on single passages and on wider matters' (Reeve 1977: 113). Tissol (1997) fruitfully examines how Ovid's wit contributes to shape his narrative so as continually to spring surprises and divert the reader. Ovid's relationship with the epic predecessor whom, as suggested above, he aspired to rival, Virgil, is entertainingly explored in Chapter 4, 'Repetition and change', of Hinds (1998). The volume including Keith (1999b) offers a collection of essays which strikingly illustrate the range and diversity of current scholarly response to the interpretative challenges posed by this unique poem. Detailed analysis of the language and style of the *Metamorphoses* is offered by Kenney (1973 and 2002); also in Boyd (2002a) there are chapters on various topics by Keith (2002b), Rosati (2002), and Tissol (2002). Turning to writers not cited here, essays exemplifying further similarly varied approaches to different aspects of the poem can be found in Hardie (2002a) by Graf (2002), Hinds (2002), Feldherr (2002), and Barchiesi (2002). Earlier works still meriting attention include the pioneering exploration of the symbolic part played by landscape in Ovid's narrative by Segal (1969); and the useful and timely clearing away by Galinsky (1975) of a number of current misconceptions to pave the way to a fresh appraisal. To the vast subject of the exploitation of Ovid's poetry, more particularly the *Metamorphoses*, by artists, a succinct introduction, with illustrations, is provided by Allen (2002); a briefer discussion, with illustrations, is offered by Llewellyn (1986). On his influence on garden design, see Hunt (1996: 42–58).

CHAPTER ELEVEN

The *Metamorphoses*: Politics and Narrative

Gareth D. Williams

Introduction

To write of politics in the *Metamorphoses* is to broach a topic of great range and interest, extending beyond the familiar question of Ovid's relation to Augustus—is he pro- or anti-Augustan, somewhere between the two, or non-Augustan in his political indifference?—to embrace important topics such as gender and sexuality, Roman imperialism, class difference, and Roman power (individual or collective) as a tool of social oppression and exploitation. While welcome attention has been drawn in recent years to this wider notion of 'politics in Ovid' (Habinek 1998: 13–14, 151–69; 2002, esp. 55–7), especially gender politics (Myers 1999: 200–1 with Sharrock 2002a; then Richlin 1992b; Segal 1998; Keith 2000: 81–6, 122–6; and now Salzman-Mitchell 2005), the Augustan question nevertheless remains inescapable and dominant, and in the approach taken below it is inextricably linked to important aspects of narratology in the *Metamorphoses*. Augustus himself is an explicit presence at structurally significant points in the first and last books, but in another sense he is *always* present, whether as a god-like ruler who naturally invites comparison, for better or worse, with the Ovidian gods (especially, of course, Jupiter) or as an all-pervading influence who lurks as a permanent subtext of sorts, a symbol of Roman fixity that contradicts the fluidity essential to Ovid's metamorphic world-view. In the next section, **The Idea of Augustus**, Augustus is nevertheless drawn as a fluid commodity in his own right; quite apart from Ovid's own elusiveness as both or neither pro- and/or anti-Augustan, the Augustus we shall encounter similarly resists simplistic labeling and one-dimensional characterization. In the following section **Metamorphic Narrative**, we turn to larger-scale testing of narratological instability in the poem as a prelude to our attempted conjunction of Augustan meaning and Ovidian poetic form in the final section, **Imperial Portraiture**: Ovid's always self-qualifying treatment of Augustus, as elusive as it is seemingly effusive, will be seen to be a natural tendency of a metamorphic poetic mode that necessarily resists fixed meanings and unambiguous political positionings.

The Idea of Augustus

In contrast to more traditional modes of analysis, a more nuanced approach to the Augustan question that has gained important ground in recent scholarship emphasizes Augustus' significance not as a person but as an idea (Kennedy 1992: 35), the emblem of an all-embracing system of government that leaves no Roman life untouched by its ubiquitous influence. Non-involvement in this Augustan discourse is no realistic option, while strong or wavering pro- or anti-Augustan sentiment, at least on an individual basis, amounts to a mere point on a scale of overwhelming Augustan measurement and prevalence. If in this respect Ovid is hailed as a subversive ironist who subtly undermines Augustus through doublespeak in the *Metamorphoses* and elsewhere, his 'success' arguably amounts to nothing more than a mere (even a pathetic) pinprick in the context of an unassailable Augustan omnipresence. Hence the cold fact that nothing, not even his preeminence as Rome's greatest living poet, could countermand his exile by imperial decree in 8 CE.

Whether in his rebuilding program or his moral reforms, his 'restoration' of the Republic or his intervention in Rome's religious and ritual life (not least through the many interventions that he made in the festival year, either by creating new commemorative days or revising the significance of traditional days; cf. Pasco-Pranger 2002 and 2006: 174–216; with Barchiesi 1997a: 69–73), Augustus was an all-penetrating phenomenon, Augustan ideology 'a whole way of thought, a total value system' (Wallace-Hadrill 1987: 223) which appealed to 'notions of continuity, stability, fixity—the *urbs aeterna*' (Hardie 1992: 61). Yet in certain respects flexibility and tension nevertheless underlay this solemn facade. After all, Augustanism was not a static, unilateral imposition from above but a phenomenon partly generated and sustained by external energies and needs; as Kennedy well puts it (1992: 35), Augustus' power was 'a collective invention, the symbolic embodiment of the conflicting desires, incompatible ambitions and aggressions of the Romans, the instrumental expression of a complex network of dependency, repression and fear'. The power-center that exploited this collective energy was in part an open-ended reading of Roman attitudes, 'an all-embracing discourse, which [was] able to take over and transform to its own ends the resources of the collective imagination' (Barchiesi 1997a: 8); and this (control of) discourse was also always in development, feeling its way as the Principate grew from infancy after the *nefas* of civil war—a process of adaptation and adjustment that is too easily underestimated in synchronic approaches to the Augustan age. The gradual narrowing of the limits of free speech in the later part of Augustus' reign, especially after the disgrace of his daughter, the elder Julia, in 2 BCE, offers one obvious example of climate change on this developmental basis (Feeney 1992: 6–7; Newlands 1995: 175–6; Knox 2004, esp. 1–3, 12–17), while ongoing uncertainties about the succession were at least one factor that long unsettled the dynastic self-assurance of the regime and the air of Augustan permanence, at least down to the adoption of Tiberius in 4 CE.

The tension that Hardie detects between this 'ideology of permanence' and the still fresh memory of upheaval in the late Republic (1992: 61) exemplifies the broader challenge faced by Augustan discourse as an uneasy mediator between past and present. As both the upholder of Republican tradition and a *de facto* autocrat, Augustus hovered ambiguously between republican and imperial images of authority, and as Princeps he reached for language that 'admirably suited [his] pretence that he was simply a leader among equals' (Nisbet and Hubbard 1970: 39, on Hor. *Carm.* 1.2.50). Restorer of a Golden Age but (*qua* Jupiter) by definition a post-Golden Age ruler (Feeney 1991: 221); a Roman citizen and yet a god on earth (Barchiesi 1997a: 44); architect of a lavish rebuilding program at Rome, yet committed to the moral values of *paupertas* and modest living (Feeney 1992: 2): in these and other ways Augustus represents an internal contradiction, for Feeney (1992: 2) 'an anomaly, a novelty, a challenge to Roman powers of definition, occupying novel, uncategorisable conceptual areas'; the Augustus who appeals to notions of fixity and permanence himself defies fixity. In this respect the ambivalences that notoriously complicate Ovid's treatment of him throughout his *oeuvre* need hardly amount to a game of sniggering innuendo played for its own sake, or to the irreverence of a poet indifferent to the serious politics of the age. No: through those ambivalences Augustus is strategically cast as a problem of representation, 'a shifting signifier' (Barchiesi 1997a: 255) who is always multidimensional and internally inconsistent—a complex picture sold short by reductionist efforts to define Ovid's general attitude to Augustus, be it pro-, anti-, or studiously indifferent. He writes not against or for but *about* (Feeney 1992: 6) Augustus.

On this 'open' approach, Ovid's deep engagement not so much with Augustus himself but with the foundations of his authority suggestively offers a reaction against the closural tendencies, the sheer exhaustiveness, of an all-encompassing system. Within Augustan discourse, Barchiesi asserts (1997a: 11), '[a]ll aspects of Roman life are involved: sacrifices, religious cults, horoscopes, processions, coins, pottery, funerals, games, inaugurations . . . The more closely woven our discursive fabric becomes, the greater is our need for poetry, whose signifiers are so difficult to pin down.' That fabric is tested in diverse ways in Ovid's works other than the *Metamorphoses*, but by its very preoccupation with change the latter offers a natural forum for experimentation with the protean Augustus theme. Beyond the superficial, metamorphic potential of the Augustan idea, however, the *Metamorphoses* shares a deeper affinity with the underpinnings of that idea: if Augustus and Augustanism represent a floating and flexible problem of signification, they find suitable expression and complication in a medium that is *itself* fundamentally unstable on so many levels of narratological operation.

Metamorphic Narrative

As proof of his consistent loyalty to the Emperor, the exiled Ovid invites Augustus to peruse those few (*pauca*) lines in the *Metamorphoses* 'in which, after beginning from the earliest origin of the world, Caesar, I brought the work down to your times' (*in tua tempora*, *Tr.* 2.559–60; cf. *Met.* 15.745–870). Does *pauca*, so sonorous in its repetition (*Tr.* 2.558, 559), disconcert in the attention that it draws to Augustus' relative absence (at least in terms of explicit presence) from the *Metamorphoses*, that ever so 'loyal' poem? He is not entirely candid, at least to judge by *Met.* 1.3–4, where the work is projected to extend 'from the beginning of the world down to *my own times*' (*ad mea . . . tempora*): the poem will indeed be brought down to 'my times' in the epilogue's endless vision of Ovid's post-Augustan immortality (15.871–9). Yet if we momentarily overlook the self-serving implications of *mea*, the preface to the *Metamorphoses* is suitably respectful in projecting an Augustan teleology for the work. Later in Book 1, Jupiter, angered by Lycaon's offense against him, convenes a divine assembly (1.167–76) that is indeed 'a parody of the Roman senate' (Chapter 10), but whose Roman color also anticipates Augustus' imminent entry into the text: 'And your people's loyal devotion is no less welcome to you, Augustus, than was that of his subjects to Jupiter' (1.204–5). This show of 'loyal devotion' comes after the disconcerting vision of a conspiracy against Augustus' life (cf. 1.200–3 with Galasso 2000: 765; Feeney 1991: 199–200). After another passing allusion at 1.562, Augustus disappears from view until Book 15, where Ovid's apparently effusive praises (cf. 15.750–9, 818–39, 852–70) bring to a climax the Roman section of the poem, with Augustus' projected apotheosis (15.861–70) aligning him with Aeneas (14.581–608; cf. already Hercules at 9.229–72), Romulus (14.805–28) and Julius Caesar (15.745–851) in a textual variation on the iconic symbolism of those same presences in the Forum of Augustus (Tissol 2002: 311–12).

An august frame and teleology for the *Metamorphoses*, then; but certain tonal difficulties give pause even before we explore more radical fault lines in this Augustan structure. If we press the analogy between Jupiter and Augustus in Book 1, how troubling is it that Jupiter indiscriminately punishes an entire race out of anger (cf. 1.166) at Lycaon's particular offense (cf. Habinek 2002: 51; already Ahl 1985: 79)? After all, Lycaon himself has already been punished (cf. 1.209) *before* Jupiter announces his vengeance on all of humankind at his hastily convened council of the gods. To what extent does this Jupiter fall tellingly—even programmatically, at this early point in the poem—short of the measured rule that Ovid imputes to him (and, by extension, to Augustus) at 15.858–60? Is this Jupiter so different from the serial rapist pictured by Arachne on her tapestry at 6.103–14—a picture borne out in so many other scenes in the *Metamorphoses*, with Io his first victim not so long after the Lycaon episode (cf. 1.588–600)? Beyond these localized hints of discordance, however, the chaotic operation of time within the *Metamorphoses* works against the Augustan frame by continually slowing and disrupting the poem's teleological journey toward its Augustan arrival-point in Book 15. For all its clear sense of chronological direction at the outset, progressing from chaos down to the Augustan/Ovidian present, this 'continuous poem'—a *carmen perpetuum* (cf. 1.4) presumably also in Ovid's anticipation of its immortality (cf. 15.871–9)—proves to be chronically *dis*continuous in its erratic regressions and digressions. More than a third of the poem is delivered through secondary narrators who go off on their own chronological tangents, often speaking in a 'timeless' present of events in the indeterminate mythical past (e.g. the Muse who tells Minerva of the singing contest between the Muses and the daughters of Pierus at 5.300–678; Orpheus' song, 10.148–739). In Book 15 Numa is shown, impossibly, imbibing the philosophy and teaching of Pythagoras (cf. 479–81)—just one, albeit extreme (cf. Cic. *Rep.* 2.28–9, with Zetzel 1995: 184–5;

Liv. 1.18.1–3; D. H. 2.59.1–2), example of the anachronisms and other distortions that cumulatively recast 'reality' in the *Metamorphoses* as 'an artificial construct, depending on subjective choices rather than on an objective and absolute truth' (Rosati 2002: 280).

This undermining effect has suggestive Augustan repercussions, 'introducing uncertainty and disorder . . . into the teleological structure of the "Age of Augustus" . . . it is as if the deliberate fragmentation of time that controls the "fictitious world" of the poem is aimed at unmasking the arbitrary, indeed even fictitious character of the supposed cosmic order established by the power of Augustus' (Rosati 2002: 280–1, referring to Feeney 1999, Zissos and Gildenhard 1999, and Hinds 1999). In contrast to the fate-driven teleology of the *Aeneid*, fate in the *Metamorphoses* is rather 'an historical prop' (Tissol 2002: 309) that struggles to assert itself amid the seemingly fortuitous twists and turns of a metamorphic narrative; and the anarchic functioning of time is only one cause of attrition to the Augustan sense of destiny. As with time, so with generic form: if the *Aeneid* offers a re-codification of Roman epic, setting an 'ideal' generic standard that is part of its wider Augustan meaning, the *Metamorphoses* moves from one state of chaos (cf. 1.7) into another by obliterating generic boundaries in a kaleidoscopic fusion of epic, tragic, pastoral, elegiac, and other elements. While traces of generic mixture can of course be discerned in the *Aeneid*, Ovid's juxtapositions are so much more obtrusive and jarring. Virgil may traverse epic, erotic, and tragic ground in *Aeneid* 4, but Ovid makes much more jolting progress in, for example, the story of Meleager and the hunt for the Calydonian boar (8.260–546) from grandiloquent epic (the hunt, 260–444, with elegiac stirrings when Meleager falls in love with Atalanta; cf. 324–8) to high tragedy (445–525, featuring Althaea's soliloquy as, Medea-like, she ponders killing her son) and then on to the moving picture of Meleager mourned at Calydon and Althaea committing suicide (526–32)—only for comic bathos when (at last, the metamorphic point of the whole extended Meleager episode!) his grieving sisters are transformed by Diana into guinea-fowl (533–46; cf. Hollis 1970: 95, 96; for the hunt itself as epic burlesque, Horsfall 1979).

In still other ways the Meleager episode well illustrates Ovid's rich repertoire of generic play. At 8.301–23, for example, his catalogue of the heroes who accompany Meleager on the boar hunt—so epic a feature in one way, such a triumph of Alexandrian minimalism in another—takes on a momentum and fascination of its own (cf. 305 for 'Caeneus, now a woman no longer', to whom we shall soon return) as a bravura performance that does not so much enable as divert us from the main story that it is meant to carry forward. The parallel catalogue of Actaeon's hounds (3.206–25) is similarly disruptive and indulgent, an incongruous counterfoil to the catalogue in Book 8 as high epic form goes to the dogs (Galinsky 1975: 133, 195); and this doubling of one passage or scene in another further complicates the forward (Augustan) movement of the poem as one episode gives way to a subsequent 'remaking' of it. So epic retrospectively competes against itself when, after battle is waged at the wedding banquet of Perseus and Andromeda at 5.1–249 in a parody (or perhaps rather a drastic reinterpretation; cf. Keith 2000: 245; Newlands 2005: 481–2) of heroic warfare, still greater battle rages between the Lapiths and Centaurs at the wedding feast of Pirithous and Hippodamia at 12.210–535; there, still more bizarre weaponry of an impromptu kind—goblets, a table leg, a chunk of the threshold floor, even a far-flung altar, fires and all (cf. 12.260–1)—far outstrips the mere brand from an altar (5.57), the door-bars (5.120), and the odd mixing-bowl (5.82) that are deployed along with more conventional arms in the Perseus scene. The battle between the Lapiths and Centaurs is recounted by Nestor in a sequence of episodes related to the Trojan War (12.4–13.622)—a section that is in one sense so Iliadic, yet in another so unHomeric in the tangential episodes featuring, for example, Cycnus (12.64–145), Caenis (12.189–209), and Periclymenus (12.536–76) that are loosely collected within the Trojan mainframe. This process of decentralization from a famil- iar story represents a form of generic play that immediately recurs in 'Ovid's '*Aeneid*' (13.623–14.580), that 'miracle of summarizing and miniaturization' (Hinds 1998: 104) in which Virgil's almost 10,000-line epic is reduced to some 1000 verses of retelling; or perhaps rather of studied omission and careful editing, to the effect that 'wherever Virgil is elaborate, Ovid is brief, and wherever Virgil is brief, Ovid elabo- rates' (Hinds 1998: 106). Through these manipulations, Hinds' Ovid mounts 'a kind of bid for teleological control', with Virgil emerging 'as a hesitant precursor of the *Metamorphoses*' (1998: 106). And this rewriting of Virgilian epic also exposes a pro- found relativity within the form, to the effect that Ovid's '*Aeneid*' is conspicuously an exercise in editorial choice and manipulation, not unlike the *Aeneid* itself—a consideration that has compromising implications not just for Ovid's treatment of Augustus later in the *Metamorphoses* but also for our subsequent re-engagement with the Augustan politics of the *Aeneid*.

Another factor that importantly complements the chronological and generic elas- ticity of the *Metamorphoses* is Ovid's cultivation of a multiplicity of narrative voices—a form of delegation that undercuts the controlling authority of his own master voice and strips narratival 'truth' of any absolute value (Wheeler 2000; Rosati 2002: 282– 304; Barchiesi 2002); that 'truth' is constructed partly by the teller of a given story, partly at the story's point of audience-reception. These complexities are well exempli- fied by Nestor's broader performance as a narrator in Book 12, including his account of the battle of the Lapiths and Centaurs (just sampled above). For present purposes, his performance is of special interest for three reasons, The first is Nestor's careful self-positioning as he embarks on his narrative (12.182–579). The scene is a celebra- tion for Achilles' victory over Cycnus, Neptune's son, whose divine pedigree gifts him with invulnerability on the battlefield (cf. 12.86–94). Pursued by Achilles in a chase with shades of the Homeric pursuit of Hector (hence the irony of 12.76–7: Achilles 'joined battle with Cycnus—his encounter with Hector was not to take place until the tenth year'), Cycnus finally succumbs, only to elude his victor by transfor- mation into a swan as Achilles readies to strip the corpse. At the celebration Cycnus' immunity to injury is the object of wonder (12.164–7), only for Nestor gently to assert his seniority and 'superior' knowledge as one two hundred and more years old (cf. 12.187–8) by going on to recall from the distant past the story of Caeneus (see Keith 2000: 83–6 on Nestor's/Ovid's play on gender stereotypes in Book 12). The latter was similarly invulnerable, but his exploits are all the more remarkable because of the detail that the eloquent (cf. *facunde senex*, 12.178) and, we may surmise, the thoroughly calculating Nestor adds in closing: 'He was born a woman' (12.175). Nestor's audience is rapt, captured by 'the novelty of this strange phenomenon' (*monstri nouitate*, with a neat play on *nouus*–Greek καινός–Caeneus; cf. Raeburn 2004: 660). But which *monstrum* in particular? Caeneus' miraculous invulnerability, or his change of gender? Achilles' enthusiastic call for Nestor to tell all (12.177–81) plays both sides, wanting to know who Caeneus was, and why he changed sex (12.179), but also asking for details on a military front (cf. *militia*, 12.180). Or does Achilles subtly correct himself, reverting to *militia* after *first* enthusiastically inquiring into the gender change? And could it be that, at this celebration where Achilles holds court, Nestor has carefully tailored his speech to draw the special interest of that one audience member above all? After all, who can forget that, in his different way, Achilles *too* made the transition from one gender to the other in his own formative years (cf. *Ars* 1.681–704, *Met.* 13.162–70, and Dilke 1954: 10–12)?

Second, after Nestor tells of Caenis' transformation into Caeneus (12.189–209), he proceeds to his apparently first-hand account ('I too was present', 12.213) of the battle between the Lapiths and Centaurs—including Caeneus' heroism against the Centaurs before he is finally killed and transformed into a bird (12.459–535). But this emphasis on Caeneus' heroics merely draws attention to a conspicuous absence in Nestor's whole account, as Tlepolemus, Hercules' son, is quick to observe (12.539–41):

> atque ait: 'Herculeae mirum est obliuia laudis
> acta tibi, senior. certe mihi saepe referre
> nubigenas domitos a se pater esse solebat.'

> 'I marvel, old Nestor,' he cried, 'at your forgetfulness of Hercules'
> glorious deeds. I'm sure that my father often used to tell me
> the Centaurs were conquered by him.'

'Old age has slowed my memory,' Nestor remarks at 12.182–3, 'and I've forgotten much that I saw when I first took up arms.' But this frailty is also self-serving, giving him license to edit his storytelling under the pretense that studied omission is an accident of memory. In Hercules' case, however, Nestor makes no apology for the conscious omission, which is due to the hatred (*odium*, 12.544) that he has long harbored because Hercules killed all eleven of Nestor's brothers. Hence his self-justification at 12.573–6:

> nunc uideor debere tui praeconia rebus
> Herculis, o Rhodiae rector pulcherrime classis?
> nec tamen ulterius quam fortia facta silendo
> ulciscor fratres; solida est mihi gratia tecum.

> Does it now seem, Tlepolemus, most handsome leader of the Rhodian fleet,
> that I owe your father any public praises of his exploits?
> Nevertheless, my silence about *his* deeds is the limit of my vengeance
> for my brothers; my friendship with *you* is unaffected.

Here is a relatively straightforward example of truth constructed and manipulated by an internal narrator in the *Metamorphoses*; but there is a sting in the tail. In mythological tradition Hercules more conventionally battles against the Centaurs in Arcadia (cf. 9.191–2), not in Thessaly, the Ovidian setting in Book 12 (Galasso 2000: 1426–7). Could it be that we are to imagine that Hercules was indeed involved in the incident Nestor describes, but not to the glorious extent that Tlepolemus believes? Tlepolemus cites his father as a reliable source (12.540–1), but Musgrove (1998: 228) fans the doubts already raised by the slender evidence for Hercules' *Thessalian* action against the Centaurs: 'either Tlepolemus interpreted his father's story incorrectly, conflating the various Centaur incidents, or Hercules misled Tlepolemus about his exploits. Are stories heard at the feet of one's elders to be believed? Are such stories always interpreted correctly by their audiences, or can they be colored by the audience's personal biases?' The truth of Nestor's story is made yet harder to pin down because of the difficulty of judging the truth (or otherwise) of what Tlepolemus has been led to believe by (Ovid's shadow construction of) yet another intermediary narrator: Hercules himself.

Third, another perspective on Nestor's seemingly unreliable memory: so beautiful was Caenis, he recalls before Achilles and the rest of his audience at 12.193–5, that 'even your father, Peleus, might perhaps have tried to win her, but he had already married Thetis, your mother, or was firmly engaged to her'. How can there be such vagueness about the chronology of the famous marriage, that 'landmark event in the mythological history of Greece' (Musgrove 1998: 226)? Perhaps Nestor does indeed show the effects of age; but his uncertainty is also beguiling, at least in the sense that it conceals—or does this enlightened Ovidian Nestor in fact share?—Ovid's (and the learned reader's) recognition that the 'true' chronology of the marriage of Peleus and Thetis is a matter contested in the mythographical/literary tradition (Musgrove 1998: 226 and n.11). And yet if Nestor shows an indirect awareness at 12.193–5 of the tensions between competing versions of narrative truth, he also reveals a more innocent side when, after recounting Caeneus' fate in the battle against the Centaurs, he asserts that 'No one is sure about what finally happened' (12.522). One body of opinion held that Caeneus was dispatched to Hades by the mass of trees that crushed him, but the seer Mopsus asserted that he was transformed into a bird (12.524–31). Nestor himself offers a somewhat diffident endorsement of Mopsus' claim (12.526: 'on that day I sighted the bird for the first time, and also for the last time')—a claim whose plausibility is strained further by the fact that 'Ovid seems to have made up this particular metamorphosis' (Galinsky 1975: 178). Yet 'because the prophet said it we believed it' (12.532): in taking the reverend Mopsus at his word, Nestor ends his account of the battle of the Lapiths and Centaurs by inadvertently highlighting the dangers latent in accepting at face value any subjective viewpoint or version of events. At this late point in his narration he may want obliquely to claim for himself the reverend authority of a Mopsus, thus enhancing the credibility of his version of the battle; but the unintended effect of his 'naive' appeal to Mopsus is to put us squarely on our guard about taking *any* given speaker, even one of hallowed reputation, at his every word.

The need for guardedness is already signaled by Ovid's treatment of *Fama* early in Book 12 (Feeney 1991: 247–9; Barchiesi 2002: 195–6; Hardie 2002c: 236–8; Rosati 2002: 297–9; Tissol 2002: 307–9). In contrast to his fantastic and dream-like description of the god of Sleep and his cave at 11.592–649, his picturing of the house of Fama at 12.39–63 is studded with evocations of Rome: as Zumwalt observes (1977: 211), '[a]*tria turba tenet* [12.53] suggests perhaps a *turba clientum* . . .; these are *clientes* who serve *Fama* as their *patrona*. But *turba, leue uulgus* [12.53], and *Seditio recens* [12.61] also suggest the familiar characterization of the Roman mob, as a fickle and irresponsible force in Roman political life'. These echoes, and also Ovid's focus not on the fantastic monstrosity of Fama herself (as in his Virgilian model at *Aen.* 4.173–97) but on place (Due 1974: 148), create the illusion of contact with a more 'real' world as the poem takes a quasi-historical turn in Books 12–15. For Otis, the *Fama* ecphrasis 'is, of course, absurdly out of any proper context: Ovid's *Fama* only spreads the news of the approaching Trojan War' (1970: 282). On the basis of this incongruity, Otis finds 'the first hint to the reader that Ovid's attitude to the Roman world of Virgil is not without its share of paradox and subtle parody' (1970: 282); yet in detecting this parodic whisper, Otis inadvertently activates a key symbolic point of 12.39–63 that fully vindicates the 'incongruous' dimensions of Ovid's description. Located 'at the middle of the world, between the earth, the sea and the celestial region, on the boundary of all three parts of the universe' (12.39–40), the house of *Fama* is also centrally positioned in the *Metamorphoses*, at least in the senses that (i) the Trojan War that opens in Book 12 'occupies a place on the borderline, so to speak, between legend and history' (Zumwalt 1977: 212), so marking a loose division between the 'legendary' and more 'historical' portions of the poem; and (ii) as a repository of rumor and report, whether true or false (cf. 12.54–5), this chamber, 'open night and day' and busy with the comings and goings of the fickle throng that crowds it (12.46, 53), offers a central emblem for the *Metamorphoses* too as 'a place in which a polyphony of autonomous, biased, and distorted voices resounds, and in which the external narrator—in his omniscience—refuses to make distinctions and impose order. *Fama* herself does this, too: she too repeats what she hears, gathering and diffusing a proliferation of stories that mix truth and invention, voices that assert constructed, manipulated, and self-interested truths' (Rosati 2002: 299).

After her appearance early in Book 12, *Fama* supplies a boundary of sorts for Books 12–15 as a whole through her striking recurrence at the poem's close, albeit there with 'privatized' reference to Ovid's projected renown: 'Through every age, if the prophesies of poets have any truth, I shall live in my fame' (*fama*, 15.878–9). *Fama* is at last fixed and made firm in Ovid's confident prediction, in ironic contrast to the flux that she embodies earlier in the poem, and especially in her resistance in Books 12–15 to 'the tendency toward interpretive simplicity and transparency that the introduction of historical and political topics might lead us to expect' (Tissol 2002: 309). On this approach, our visit to the house of *Fama* formalizes an essential feature of Ovid's poetics in the *Metamorphoses*, but with particularly challenging consequences as we read on toward Ovid's Augustan climax. If *Fama* symbolizes the polyphony of Ovid's competing narrative voices more generally, and if Nestor's performance in Book 12 conveniently exemplifies the shifts of tone and irony that potentially complicate any of Ovid's secondary narrative voices, our accumulated experience of the *Metamorphoses* conditions us always to tread warily, to suspect complication, to resist the plain reading—all of which preconditions us to approach the Roman/Augustan books with an eye for more of the same, and to take nothing, not even imperial praise, for granted.

Here, after all, is a poem that surprises to the last, and comes close to collapsing upon itself as a consequence of Pythagoras' enormous pseudo-scientific discourse in Book 15 on reincarnation and the fundamental mutability of the world (15.75–478). This speech may seem at first to offer an attractive paradigm for the 'philosophy' of transformation underlying the *Metamorphoses* as a whole (Wheeler 2000: 116–17). But how then to account for the fact that Pythagoras' doctrine of the divine soul's reincarnation contradicts the entire apparatus of metamorphosis in the prior fourteen books (Graf 2002: 120–1; Barchiesi 2002: 184–5)? Whereas reincarnation presupposes an ongoing state of metamorphosis from life to life, body to body, Ovidian metamorphosis brings about a single, irrevocable transformation. A devastating irony at this terminal point in the poem, it would seem—only for the master-narrator, Ovid, to have applied a prescient touch before Pythagoras speaks: his words 'were learned, to be sure, but not given credit' (15.74). The *Metamorphoses* is vindicated, it would appear, by Pythagoras' failure to persuade. Yet the slipperiness of the Ovidian flux is still felt in the further consideration that, within the fictive world of the *Metamorphoses*, Pythagoras' words may not be believed, but they are not for that reason necessarily untrue . . .

Imperial Portraiture

The elusive idea of Augustus and Augustanism that we traced in the **Introduction** above now merges with, and into, the narratological flux sampled in the next section, **The Idea of Augustus**. The ambivalent and multisided Augustan significance of the *Metamorphoses* is no detachable layer of meaning that is superimposed on the poem, but rather an *intrinsic* function of Ovidian narrative: beyond the 'official' Roman/Augustan allusions and movements of the poem, a continuous subtext resonates (not unlike the house of *Fama*) with Augustan whisperings and suggestions, some obtrusive, others fainter, but all persistently audible as an underlying sound—a sound that is especially disturbing in the many passages where divine justice proves to be high-handed and partial, the gods so often humanized in their passions, wiles, and obsessions but ever immune to human consequence and suffering (Feeney 1991: 202). We have already touched on the disconcerting implications of Jupiter's punishment in Book 1 of *all* mankind for Lycaon's shocking transgression. For all the exiled Ovid's tactful emphasis on Augustus' anger as merciful (*mitissima, Tr.* 1.2.61), moderate (*Tr.* 5.2.55, *Pont.* 2.9.77), and just (*Pont.* 1.8.69), a more complicated version of the Augustan reality comes into view if we press the inviting Augustus/Jupiter analogy in the Lycaon episode: which dimension of Augustus— 'natural' identification with Jupiter, that identification strategically played down in inconvenient circumstances, or an uneasy tension between the two extremes?—are we to invoke (or suppress) in this first extended display in the poem of Jovian (in)justice in action, and of wrath that may at first seem righteous (cf. 1.166) but which soon overflows into anger that is apparently as indiscriminate as the flood that Jupiter unleashes with Neptune's help (cf. 1.260–1, 274–5)? Or, to cast his actions in a different light, should we rather commend Jupiter for his firmness of mind and decisive action, killing the many to root out the corruption epitomized by Lycaon's crime, and so to clear the way for a new moral start? Tempting as it may be to opt for a dark Augustan reading, especially from the perspective of Tomitan hindsight, a more balanced approach is to accept Augustus as a multivalent signifier who is simultaneously open to *all* of the available possibilities.

Ovid's direct allusion to Augustus (1.204) and the distinctly Roman feel of Jupiter's council of the gods (1.167–76) provide a helpful entrée-point into the Augustan subtext underlying the Lycaon episode. Other episodes may offer no such direct guidance; but after the Augustan dimension has explicitly asserted itself so early in the first book, it is hard not to invoke the shadow of that presence in so many later scenes, especially those that focus on the harshness of divine justice. 'Anger too can move the gods' (*tangit et ira deos*, 8.279): this much in the way of theological rumination before Ovid's Diana, offended at the Calydonian king Oeneus' failure to pay her due honor, unleashes the dreaded boar, her 'servant and avenger' (*infestae famulus uindexque Dianae*, 8.272, where *infestae* itself suggests animal-like ferocity on Diana's part; cf. *Ars* 3.670, *Fast.* 2.800, and *Pont.* 2.2.38). The word order at 8.279 itself disconcerts, with *et* placed not to the effect that the gods *too* feel anger but that *ira* is but one of the 'nobler emotions' (Hollis 1970: 70)—or should that be raw and fickle passions?—that touch them; given this faint hint of flippancy, we are indeed 'a long way from Virgil's probing question *tantaene animis caelestibus irae?* at *Aen.* 1.11 (Hollis 1970: 71). The justification or otherwise of Diana's *ira* here is complicated by her characterization elsewhere in the *Metamorphoses*, and notably by her punishment of Actaeon when he stumbles upon the goddess as she bathes naked with her attendant nymphs in Book 3 (138–252). Transformed into a stag who is killed by his own hounds, Actaeon is exquisitely tortured by his voicelessness: as the animals that he knows so well relentlessly track him down, he is powerless to call off the very hounds that are devoted to him. Ovid explicitly introduces Actaeon's transgression as an innocent error (3.141–2):

> at bene si quaeras, Fortunae crimen in illo,
> non scelus inuenies; quod enim scelus error habebat?

> But if you look thoroughly into the matter, you'll find that his was a chance misdemeanor, not a deliberate crime; for what crime lay in his simple mistake?

After Actaeon's death, opinion was allegedly divided (3.253–5):

> Rumor in ambiguo est: aliis uiolentior aequo
> uisa dea est, alii laudant dignamque seuera
> uirginitate uocant; pars inuenit utraque causas.

Common talk varied: to some the goddess appeared more cruel
than was just, while others praised her and called her act worthy
of her strict virginity. Both sides found good reason for their verdict.

If we incline to the view that Actaeon is a blameless victim of divine pique (so Galinsky
1975: 66), he is but one of numerous figures in the *Metamorphoses* whose treatment
at the hands of the gods hardly inspires confidence in the consistent fairness of divine
justice. What, then, of Augustan justice?

Several of Actaeon's fellow victims are consummate artists, prominent among them
the Arachne who is transformed into a spider by Minerva after brashly challenging
the goddess to a weaving-contest in Book 6 (1–145), a much discussed episode
(Salzman-Mitchell 2005: 125–39 and 227 n. 25 for bibliography, adding Oliensis
2004: 286–96). We are shown the tapestries of each: in contrast to the carefully
controlled, highly formalized ('Classical') structure within which Minerva weaves
austere images of the gods and ominous representations of divine punishment exacted
(6.70–102), Arachne applies a lighter, distinctly non-conformist ('neoteric') touch
in picturing the many seductions carried out by the gods (Harries 1990: 69–76;
Feeney 1991: 191–2); the roving Jupiter leads the way in metamorphic disguise
(6.103–28). Minerva's violent response to Arachne's masterpiece (6.129–38) ambiguously blends personal jealousy with righteous outrage at such disrespect toward
divine authority, while Arachne herself is partly the blameless victim of her sublime
talent, partly ruined by her irreverent arrogance. Beyond Arachne's fate, the transformation of the daughters of Pierus into magpies after they are beaten in their poetic
competition with the Muses (5.662–78) and Apollo's sadistic flaying of Marsyas after
the latter is defeated in their piping-contest (6.383–400) offer notable examples of
Ovid's broader preoccupation in the *Metamorphoses* with the persecution of artists—a
theme that appears all too prescient in the light of his own banishment by Augustus'
order in 8 CE. Could it be that, in the years before his exile, Ovid expressed through
the likes of Arachne a growing uneasiness at 'the real-world potential for an analogous
silencing of artists' (Johnson 1997: 243) under Augustus (cf. further Harries 1990:
76–7; Keith 1992: 135–6)? Moreover, Diana's cruel silencing of Actaeon is but one
(albeit extreme) example of voicelessness as punishment in the *Metamorphoses*: could
it be that those silences speak volumes, quietly conveying Ovid's 'increasing sensitivity
to the precarious position of any creative artist under a totalitarian regime' (Forbis
1997: 248)? Given his own fate at Augustus' hands, the controversial nature of divine
justice in the *Metamorphoses* offers good reason why the exiled Ovid should continue
to find in the work a 'reminder of me' (cf. *admoneant . . . mei*, *Tr.* 1.7.26, adduced
by Harries 1990: 77); and still better reason why, in revisiting the two causes of his
exile in his entreaty to Augustus in *Tristia* 2 (cf. *carmen et error*, 207), he should
picture himself as a second Actaeon (105–8), one who inadvertently incurred (vastly
excessive?) divine wrath—an Actaeon in his *error* (Williams 1994: 174–7), even if the
provocations of his *Ars amatoria* might cast him more in the mold of an overconfi-
dent Arachne or Marsyas in his incriminating *carmen*.

If divine justice is an evolving problem in the *Metamorphoses*, gathering ever com-
plicating nuances and (Augustan) shades as the poem progresses, a different textual

sequence similarly generates accumulated complexity in Books 14–15. We have already glimpsed (p. 157) the interrelation between the apotheoses of Aeneas (14.581–608), Romulus and his wife Hersilie (14.805–51), and then Julius Caesar (15.745–851)—a sequence that culminates in Augustus' projected apotheosis at 15.861–70. But while on one level we make unruffled progress through Roman time and genealogy toward the Augustan climax, on another level Ovid's multivalent tone in the three preceding apotheoses disrupts and resists that comfortable Augustan line, as if gently testing the underpinnings of an intimidating and seemingly official facade that the poet simultaneously appears to endorse. Again, the task before us is not to try to fix Ovid's position on Augustus, whether pro-, anti-, or somewhere in between, but rather to monitor how the text wrestles with the multivalent phenomenon that *was* Augustus. Already in Book 9 Hercules' apotheosis (229–72) prefigures the later sequence in its own Augustan overtones, especially when, in losing his mortal form, Hercules 'begins to seem greater and to grow in the awesomeness of his august majesty' (*augusta . . . grauitate*, 270; cf. *augusta grauitate sedent* at 6.73, of the gods on Minerva's tapestry; Feeney 1991: 207); but the Augustan gravity of the scene is at once alleviated by Ovid's light play on the literal connotation of *grauitas* (cf. 'Atlas felt the added weight', 9.273), and by his subsequent allusion at 9.287 to Alcmene's weight (*grauitas*) of pregnancy with Hercules. If such plays threaten gently to compromise the (Augustan) grandeur of this Herculean moment, Aeneas' apotheosis in Book 14 blends 'the trappings of epic' (Feeney 1991: 207) and religious solemnity (cf. 14.607–8 for Aeneas entering state cult) with potentially comic traces that begin with Venus canvassing the gods on Aeneas' behalf in decidedly Roman political fashion (Tissol 2002: 325, after Feeney 1991: 207); and the gravity of the scene is also compromised in part by its context, set as it is in breathless juxtaposition to the bizarre vision of Turnus' town of origin, Ardea, transformed into the first heron after it is destroyed by Aeneas' Trojans (14.573–80; cf. Tissol 2002: 326–7).

When we reach Romulus' apotheosis (14.805–51), it is further disconcerting to find that the landmark achievement that qualifies him for divinity, his foundation of Rome, receives only the briefest coverage in a phrase cast in the passive (*festis . . . Palilibus urbis / moenia conduntur*, 14.774–5), his role virtually effaced from the proceedings (at 14.773 he is introduced merely as Numitor's 'grandson'). It is Mars who secures his son's elevation by calling on Jupiter to meet his own promise (14.812–15):

> tu mihi concilio quondam praesente deorum
> (nam memoro memorique animo pia uerba notaui)
> 'unus erit quem tu tolles in caerula caeli';
> dixisti: rata sit uerborum summa tuorum!

> Long ago, in the presence of all the gods in council (for I heeded
> your gracious words with unforgetting mind, and now recall them to you),
> you declared: 'One man will there be whom you will raise up to the blue of heaven.'
> Let your words now find their fulfillment!

In repeating Jupiter's words here, Mars also quotes Ennius' Jove: *unus erit quem tu* (i.e. Mars; cf. Skutsch 1985: 205: 'Romulus will be carried up to heaven *Martis equis'*) *tolles in caerula caeli / templa* (*Ann.* 1 fr. xxxiii Skutsch; cf. *Fast.* 2.487 for the same Ennian line echoed in similar circumstances). The likelihood that Romulus first received deification in Ennius (Skutsch 1985: 205) is arguably bolstered by Ovid's transparent allusion as if to an *Urtext*; but in vital respects Ovid's treatment of Romulus appears to depart fundamentally from its Ennian precedent. 'Whereas in the narrative [of Ennius' *Annales*] the ascension must have appeared as the conse-quence of Romulus' divine origin,' observes Skutsch (1985: 260), 'the Euhemerist and political moralist Ennius . . . will have used the speech [in which Skutsch locates 1 fr. lxii *Romulus in caelo cum dis genitalibus aeuom / degit*] to affirm that virtue and political merit open the gates of heaven.' In the *Metamorphoses*, however, Ovid's drastically reduced coverage of Romulus' founding achievement and his focus instead on Mars' intervention provocatively cancel the euhemerist emphasis in Ennius (Tissol 2002: 328–31): while the latter's Romulus conspicuously earns his apotheosis, Ovid's relies on divine lobbying. The unhelpful Augustan implication of this underpowered Romulus is aggravated by the 'poor allegorical fit' (Tissol 2002: 332) when Mars asserts to Jupiter that the time is ripe for his son's apotheosis because Rome is now securely established 'and does not rely on a single protector' (14.809); contrast Augustan Rome, all too dependent on *praeside uno* amid the problems of the imperial succession. We may yet view the apotheosis of Hersilie (14.829–51) as tactfully Augustan in the parallel that it suggests with Livia, but here too Ovidian levity gently challenges the apparent gravity of the occasion. Iris, Juno's emissary, prepares the way for Hersilie's reunion with Romulus (14.829–39). Hersilie is not explicitly told that apotheosis awaits her, and so she responds with delightfully unwitting irony in asserting that, if fate allows her to look upon Romulus for one last time, *caelum accepisse fatebor* (14.844): 'I'll declare that I'm in seventh heaven!' (Tissol 2002: 334–5).

   Before Ovid turns to Julius Caesar's apotheosis in Book 15, the stories of how Cipus refused to become king at Rome (15.565–621) and of how the god Aescula-pius arrived there from Epidaurus, establishing his temple and cult on the Tiber island (15.622–744), constitute the only tales drawn in the *Metamorphoses* from the Repub-lican period. If Cipus stands in suggestive Republican contrast to Caesar (or is Cipus rather to be counted as a heroic paradigm for Caesar and/or Augustus? Cf. Galinsky 1967 and 1975: 258; Myers 1994: 129–31; Feeney 2004: xviii), Aesculapius plays the accepted foreigner to Caesar's native Roman divinity (15.745–6):

> Hic tamen accessit delubris aduena nostris;
> Caesar in urbe sua deus est.

> Aesculapius arrived, a stranger from abroad, to dwell in our shrines,
> but Caesar is a god in his native city.

But whereas Aesculapius is invited to Rome through collective action to save the state in a time of crisis, and whereas he enters the city amid the acclaim of all (cf. 15.729–31), the introduction of Caesar's cult is cast here as a more private affair, as if 'the sole responsibility of his son and his "mother"' (Feeney 1991: 212) rather than a communal undertaking. As we hover between the Republic and the Empire, or between different versions of Caesar as a Roman champion of traditional stamp ('outstanding in war and peace', 15.746–7) and yet as a novelty who strains Republican modes of definition, Ovid's tone is similarly indeterminate in its open-endedness (15.750–4, 757–8):

> neque enim de Caesaris actis
> ullum maius opus quam quod pater exstitit huius.
> scilicet aequoreos plus est domuisse Britannos
> perque papyriferi septemflua flumina Nili
> uictrices egisse rates . . .
> et multos meruisse, aliquos egisse triumphos,
> quam tantum genuisse uirum?

> For of Caesar's achievements
> none is greater than this, that he found glory as the father of this man [i.e. Augustus].
> It should evidently be thought a greater thing to have tamed the islander Britons
> and to have led a victorious fleet through the seven-mouthed delta
> of the papyrus-bearing Nile . . .
> and to have celebrated several triumphs, to have merited more,
> than to have fathered so great a man!

As Hinds points out (1987: 25), *scilicet* is delicately balanced here: for is it an evident truth, or evidently an absurdity (cf. *OLD scilicet* 3, 4), that Caesar's fathering of Augustus outweighs all of the formidable military achievements catalogued in lines 752–7? And how fitting is it first to touch a raw nerve by casting Caesar as Augustus' biological father (cf. *pater*, 15.751; *genuisse*, 758), and then to imply that Caesar was made a god perforce, and not necessarily through his own compelling merit? (15.760–1): 'Consequently, lest this great prince be derived from mortal seed, his father had to be made a god [*ille deus faciendus erat*].' When we finally reach Augustus' own anticipated apotheosis and Ovid's extravagant prayer (15.868–70) that

> tarda sit illa dies et nostro serior aeuo,
> qua caput Augustum, quem temperat, orbe relicto
> accedat caelo

> slow be that day in coming, and long after my time,
> when Augustus leaves the world that he controls,
> and rises up to the heavens

this Augustan climax in one sense resists the entire poem's impetus and motivation; for it delays the moment of Augustan metamorphosis into 'literal' divinity, and it projects so immutable an image of Roman tradition and permanence in its appeal to the establishment gods (15.862–6: Quirinus, Mars, Vesta, Apollo, Jupiter) and in its evocation of Aeneas' pioneering voyage (cf. 15.861).

Yet how to reconcile this solid vision—if truly solid it is, with no ironic underlay (cf. Feeney 1991: 214–19, esp. 217)—with our unsettling experience of the apotheoses of Aeneas, Romulus, and Caesar thus far in the poem? If Ovid's treatment of those earlier deifications is seen to be complicated by disconcerting shades of ambivalence, the Augustan climax is arguably compromised from the outset by association with such inviting but troubling *comparanda*. On this approach there are no exceptions to the general rule: everything, even apparent Augustan certainties at the close of the *Metamorphoses*, are made vulnerable to the great Ovidian flux that controls, or rather disorientates, the text; and the Augustan politics of the poem recede into that flux as a function or an effect of narrative, and not as something that somehow exists independently ('politics' as opposed to 'literature') of that fluid operation. And this primary emphasis on narratival flux, and secondarily on Augustan political play as a main constituent within that flux, has important implications for how we interpret Ovid's defiant tone in his celebrated epilogue. His appeal to a familiar topos at 15.871–9 (Nisbet and Rudd 2004: 367) barely disguises the provocative effect of his words, predicting the immortality of a work, which nothing can destroy, 'not Jupiter's wrath, not fire or sword, not all-devouring time' (15.871–2). Certainly, from an exilic perspective these lines take on added bite, especially if we find Augustus powerless to impede the spread of Ovid's fame 'wherever Roman power extends over lands she has conquered' (15.877), and perhaps even in remote Tomis. A still more satisfying irony, however, may lie not so much in Ovid's defiance of Jupiter/Augustus, but in his triumph over the irrepressible forces of flux and change that have prevailed in the previous fifteen books: as long as he lives on in the disembodied text, his *Metamorphoses* defies metamorphosis.

FURTHER READING

Fine starting-places on narrative technique and narratology in the *Metamorphoses* are now provided by Barchiesi (2002) and Rosati (2002), but important precursors include Hinds (1987a), Tissol (1997), Wheeler (1999, 2000), and Barchiesi (2001a), as well as several essays in Hardie et al. (1999). Recent contributions that importantly complicate the Augustan politics of the *Metamorphoses* (and other Ovidian works) include Hinds (1987b), Kennedy (1992), Feeney (1991, 1992), Hardie (1992), Barchiesi (1997a), and Tissol (2002). But for the politics of the Ovidian corpus extended significantly beyond the Augustan question, see Habinek (2002) with (on gender politics) Sharrock (2002a) and now Salzman-Mitchell (2005).

CHAPTER TWELVE

Tristia

Jo-Marie Claassen

Introduction

A prominent literary figure, when relegated to the ends of the earth, loses his audience but not his readership, for he has at his fingertips the means to maintain contact (if not to find redress). How Ovid's poems from exile were interpreted by his contemporaries can remain an object of speculation only; Ovid's tragedy as humorist has been that later generations often took these missives *literally*. The first of his exilic works, the *Tristia*, is a collection of poems of varying length, written in elegiacs. It comprises five books of poems, which are, contrary to a commonly held assumption, not all personal letters set to verse, but considerably more varied. Some are open letters to unnamed friends or to the poet's wife; others pretend to be monologues with a variety of 'speaking' personae (Evans 1983). One, the second volume, is a book-long 'speech for the defense' aimed at the exile's imperial accuser. Except for this, and the poems to his wife and stepdaughter, these missives are anonymous, and Ovid's contemporary readers could choose to read themselves into them.

Problems of Interpretation

Why Ovid was relegated is a non-question that has led to much ingenious but fruitless surmise. To ask the right questions, and to find answers through careful, consecutive reading of the five books of the *Tristia* as a literary creation without parallel, must be the aim of research. The key lies in its nature as a work of art. A valid question is: how should readers of the twenty-first century react to these quasi-autobiographical outpourings of an erstwhile humorist when racked by the pain of isolation and rejection?

We may speculate on why Ovid chose to write his appeals to Rome in poetic form. And if in verse, why not in a 'serious' medium like hexameter, at which he was also an adept? Why elegiacs? Why, if elegiacs had to be the medium of choice (Nagle 1980; Harrison 2002), did he not continue writing love poetry, of a more innocuous kind, an antidote to the 'poison' that had caused his relegation? Why, too, all the secrecy and innuendo over his addressees? The letter poems of the *Tristia* are sent anonymously, the danger his friends will be in for reading them is stressed; the reasons for his relegation (for which the poet so profusely and abjectly continues to apologize throughout five volumes) are ostensibly suppressed, yet frequently emphasized. Why did Ovid choose to continue living dangerously? These questions cannot be answered, but may be rephrased, to give them greater legitimacy.

A legitimate question is: who were Ovid's readers? At whom was he aiming these anonymous missives, whether letters or monologues? The deliberate act of publication placed ostensibly private letters and personal monologues into the public domain. Who were really in Ovid's mind as potential readers in his ostensible address to Augustus in *Tristia* 2, or to his wife in the letters naming her? Whom was he trying to reach or impress, or was he, as he sometimes claimed, merely trying to entertain himself and relieve the tedium of exile? Both modern and ancient literary theory can give us pointers. Ancient theorists focused on authorial function. The Horatian generic criterion of purpose ('aim') essentially focuses on authorial intent, more specifically, the notional audience for whom an author writes. 'Authorial purpose' as concept is considered suspect in post-modern literary criticism, and 'intentionalism' is often denigrated as a critical solecism, yet use of a particular medium must still be ascribed to an author's intentional choice.

Modern theory frequently considers how the author visualizes his potential audience. Reception theory stresses the importance of this audience. The mediating role of the reader in decoding texts as signals is paramount in modern semiotics. Eco (1994: 15–17) postulates an 'empirical reader', the person in the act of reading, and a 'model reader', the notional audience at which the 'empirical author' pitches his material. The empirical reader, in turn, by a continuous interpretative process, mentally creates the 'model author' who has made the text into what is discovered in this process. Perhaps one cannot speak of *a* or *the* reader, for a shifting series of readerly actions conceptualizes a shifting series of aims by a shifting series of model authors. Ovid as 'model author' has changed considerably in the last hundred years, each generation of readers finding new Ovids. In autobiographical or quasi-epistolary texts the area of reception envisaged by the author is important, but also the author as persona. Hence we may attempt to seek 'Ovid the empirical author as person' behind 'Ovid the poet' and 'Ovid the exile'. Sometimes these personages overlap; often they do not.

It is equally legitimate to interrogate the contents of an ostensibly self-revelatory work. Readers in the nineteenth and early twentieth century tended to accept Ovid's hyperbolic outpourings of grief and contrition for a literary life ill-spent, also his protestations of undying loyalty to, and belief in, the great god Augustus, the arbiter of his weal and woe. With this, equal sincerity was taken to underlie all Ovid's protestations of 'waning literary powers', even loss of language. In the second decade of the twentieth century an earnest German scholar could offer 'proof' of Ovid's pathetic loss of skill and inspiration, if not outright moral turpitude, with an analysis of one of his Pontic epistles, where the scholar had identified some 125 'borrowings' from other poets (Ganzenmüller 1911). Some forty years later came Allen's refreshing call (1950) for the reappraisal of the term 'sincerity' as applied to the elegists. What he said applied as well to Ovid's exilic elegies as it did to erotic elegy: that not *literal fact* but *plausibility* and *emotional impact* are the dual touchstones of interpretation. Soon after, Kenney (1965) alerted the anglophone Classical world to the beauty and originality of Ovid's exilic poetry.

The poet's style is another legitimate area of research, but style and content are almost inseparable. I started working with the poems in the early 1980s, originally because I was impressed by Ovid's functional word placement in his humorous poems, particularly his use of hyperbaton to convey graphically the sense of what he was saying. Would he still use the device when he was (as I then still thought) '*sincere*'? It came as a pleasant and growing surprise, and a source of lasting admiration, that this urbane and urban writer, when sent on a journey whence there was no return, to a place without hope, could continue as sprightly and subtly as when he was pretending to be the world's greatest lover, dispensing gratuitous advice on well-known techniques to novices in the art of love. Ovid the master lover cocked a snook at the morality of his time, where 'don't ask, don't tell' applied to relationships with females of the *demi-monde*. In exile, Ovid's snook was still cocked, no less at himself than at the august author of his banishment (Boyle 2003: 1–15; Williams 1994).

Stylistics and Intertextuality

Ovid avers (4.10.23–6) that even when he attempted prose, verse would flow from his pen. This scintillating wordsmith continued to display all the devices that contribute to the charm of his other works: sound- and wordplay (*figura etymologica*), tmesis and zeugma, punning and double entendre: every verse can be examined as evidence of its author's endless verbal ingenuity. The poet appears to delight in verbal experimentation while maintaining his metrical proficiency (Claassen 1998, 1999b, 1999c).

Characteristic stylistic and rhetorical devices such as oxymoron and paradox, exaggeration, hyperbole and bathos, sustained (and sometimes conflicting) imagery, lend interest to every line. Even here Ovidian ingenuity leads to innovation. An apparent increasing use of aphorism (expressing 'eternal truths') seems a precursor to later 'silver age' sententiousness (e.g. 2.33–4, 75–6, 141; 3.4.4, 11–12, 25; 3.7.33–44; 4.3.74, 79–80; 5.14.12). Elegiac poets tended mostly to avoid multisyllabic words, but in exile Ovid experiments with these, too. In 4.7 the exile affects to believe in all the monsters of myth rather than to think his friend has deserted him, in deliciously playful lines bristling with five- and six-syllabic portmanteau words (*quadrupedesque*, 4.7.15; *tergeminumque*, twice in 16; *serpentipedesque*, 17; *centanimumque, semibovemque*, 18). Elsewhere he claims to be losing his Latin, in poems that are as elegant as ever (3.14.43–52, 5.7.51–58), but with subtle stylistic indications of severe stress (Claassen 1988: 165; 1990b; 2003: 101). Loss of language is often symptomatic of the alienation felt by exiles, and that is what he is expressing.

Ovid's intertextual debt to predecessors is well-known, but Ovid was also an 'intratextual' adept. Myth as metaphor is a prime example of Ovidian generic cross-pollination. The influence of Ovid's epic-style *magnum opus*, the *Metamorphoses*, is discernible in his choice of illustrative material. The *Metamorphoses* and *Fasti* were probably finally revised during his exile. Myth is an important leitmotiv in the *Tristia*, with certain characters predominating. Of these, the wanderers, Odysseus, Jason, and Aeneas, and their divine antagonists, are the most important, but also the theme of friendship as evidenced by the pairs Achilles–Patroclus, Theseus–Pirithous, Orestes–Pylades, Nisus–Euryalus. The last two pairs are not mentioned in the *Metamorphoses* (Claassen 2001: 48–56).

The *Tristia* exhibits intertextual links with Ovid's other works and with his earlier essays into generic experimentation. Ovid had earlier established a precedent for non-erotic Roman elegy with the *Fasti*, representing the first six months of the Roman calendar, and with his didactic elegies. These book-length poems set a new precedent for Roman elegiacs. The longest Latin elegies are seldom longer than 100 lines: Propertius 4.11 (102 verses) and Catullus 68 (160) are exceptional. After the *Amores* and the offending *Ars amatoria* and *Remedia amoris*, Ovid had ventured into epistolary elegiacs. His *Heroides* are fairly long poetic letters purporting to come from mythical heroines to the men who had deserted them. Their central theme is desolation and loneliness. In his exilic poetry several of these heroines re-engage Ovid's interest, most frequently Medea, also the heroine of his lost tragedy, who, he claims, gave the place Tomis its name, from the Greek *temnô* ('cut'), when she here *cut up* her brother in her flight from Colchis (*Tristia* 3.9.33).

Miller posits, as answer to the question of why Roman elegy virtually disappeared as a genre after the *Tristia* and *Epistulae ex Ponto*, the theory that in the early Empire there was a fatal slippage between the 'Imaginary', a poet's self-view, and the 'Symbolic', the codes that control his projection of self. This was caused by the intrusion of the 'Real', here Augustan intervention into all aspects of public and private life. Miller argues (2004a: 158) that the gradual restructuring of the social, discursive, and power relations that had made elegy possible in the late Republic ultimately rendered elegy impossible to practice, in spite of the pretense that the Republic had been restored, with Augustus as monarchical pivot of all attention. For Miller (2004a: 266), the reason why, of all the elegists, Ovid alone felt the Emperor's wrath was precisely *because* 'he accepted the new regime for what it was', thereby reproducing its 'founding contradictions', and this ideological and generic displacement led to the physical displacement of the author. 'The exilic poetry does not abandon the subject position of amatory elegy but recasts it', so Miller (2004a: 211). The abandoned lover is recast as abject exile, the object of his desire his lost city, the space within which he could function as poet now filled by an all-powerful antagonist. Ovid is free to continue publishing precisely because he acknowledges this power: every poem acts as a warning against potential elegiac subversiveness (Miller 2004a: 229). Erotic elegy simply could not survive under such oppressive freedom.

Cicero established what may be considered a separate genre, 'laments from exile'. He penned mostly brief, not completely artless, prose outpourings of grief and despair to his wife and friends when he fled Rome in 58 BC (Claassen 1999a: 83–5, 105–10). Cicero's topics of lamentation are continued by Ovid: a feeling of hopelessness and alienation, abject misery, appeals for aid in returning, self-justification alternating with self-loathing, both a fear of and a longing for death, death and illness as metaphors for exile. These topics continue to haunt those expelled from their homeland anywhere, at any time, for they are psychological, rather than literary, manifestations. Cicero and Ovid may together be seen as the initiators of a genre that has gained in importance as the twenty-first century limps along its bloody way, with the growing dispossession and alienation of millions of mute victims of war (Claassen 2003, 2004).

Chronology

The dating of the decree of relegation and the poet's departure has been much debated: Ovid's statements about his year of birth, his age at exile, and the position of celestial bodies at his departure are difficult to reconcile. That Ovid was relegated to Tomis in AD 8 is now generally accepted (Green 1994: xviii). Internal evidence suggests that from December AD 8 to the autumn of AD 9 his time was spent composing *Tristia* 1 and 2 (totaling 1280 verses), which were sent to Rome simultaneously. The next two books (1466 verses) were composed in 10 AD and 11 AD, reaching Rome during AD 11. *Tristia* 5 (800 verses) was completed and sent to Rome on its own at some time during AD 12.

Although critics like to observe symmetry and parallels in the arrangement of individual poems within each book, and often treat as units those with similar topics (e.g. Evans 1983), it is consistently rewarding to read the poems consecutively. This is the order in which ancient readers were likely to have read the poems, given the exigencies of the ancient book-roll—only since the advent of codices has it become easy to dip at random into a book. A review of Books 1 and 2, together with some poems from the other books, will illustrate themes and topics central to the exiled poet's thought.

Contents

Tristia 1, comprising eleven poems ostensibly written on board ship, on Ovid's way to the place of exile, reads like an elegiac epic in miniature, complete with flashbacks and elaborate divine machinery (Hinds 1985). The introductory poem was probably composed after the others, but it should be read first, to gain the effect presumably intended by the author. So, poem 1 starts anonymously: an author-parent in an unspecified location sends his rather bedraggled book-child to the big city, giving it explicit instructions about where to go, what to avoid and what to answer when questioned. The reader deduces that the speaker is in disgrace, for the book must avoid the house of Caesar (whence had come the thunderbolt that struck its author down), but also the collection of books that had harmed this author (1.1.111–16). It will also find some stories about 'changed forms', and of these the new book must ask to include in their ranks their own author, as the ultimate changeling (117–22).

The second poem shows the unhappy traveler in the midst of a violent storm at sea, where the elements conspire to support the ire of the greatest god. He prays to the tempestuous deities to prove his innocence by allowing the storm to abate. When, by the end of the poem, the storm slackens, the author triumphantly proclaims that the gods have shown him innocent (1.2.107–10).

The third poem is a flashback to the night of the fugitive's departure, redolent with pathos, a memory wreathed in tears. No practical details are given, but the scene is evoked in emotional outpourings that recreate his initial dismay and distress, his night of grief watched over from on high by an impassive moon (1.3.28). Equally impassive was the seat of his divine adjudicator that unresponsively heard his protests of innocence (29–40). We learn the fugitive's destination, Scythia, but not yet his name. Poem 4 returns us with the fugitive to the teeth of a storm; the steersman is helpless, and the ship tends back toward *Italia interdicta*. The victim prays that the storm gods obey the greater god, as he does, and spare his life—that is, if someone who has died, is still capable of 'living' (1.4.28).

Tr. 1.5 is at last a letter, to a friend whose steadfastness was proven in adverse circumstances (15–30). The missive becomes an open letter to all his remaining friends. They need not fear Caesar's anger, for their unfortunate friend has merely been silly, not wicked. They must pray for the Princeps' anger to diminish (35–44). The letter ends with an elaborate comparison of the author's sufferings with those of Odysseus, where the latter emerges as by far the more fortunate (57–84; cf. Claassen 2001: 33).

Almost predictably, the next letter-poem, in an important central position in the book (1.6), is addressed to the exile's wife. The order of verses 22–35 is much debated but the sense is clear (Green 1994: 214). The poem sets the tone for future missives: praise for her steadfastness (1.6.5–16), favorable comparison with the virtuous wives of myth (17–22), a glancing reference to her virtue as stemming from the example set by the wife of the Princeps (23–28), and a promise to immortalize her in his song, weak though his powers may be (29–36).

Tr. 1.7 is an open letter to steadfast friends. At last the anonymous sufferer is named. A friend is imagined exclaiming sadly over the distance that separates his boon companion, Naso, from him (1.7.10). This friend is requested to embrace Naso's works, as his true image (11). Two consistent themes are hereby introduced: poetics and the lasting value of the poet's creations as 'absent presences' (Hardie 2002c: 322). Another Virgil, this unfortunate claims to have tried to burn his works (15–22), and that they are unfinished (23–32). The last three couplets (35–40) offer a new inscription for the initial lines of the *Metamorphoses*: 'If anyone should pick up the volumes, bereaved of their father, at least give them a place in your city. And (to make you like them more), they were not published by him, but virtually snatched from the funeral of their master. So, I would have fixed (if I could) whatever solecisms my rough-hewn song in these books may have.'

Friendship and flight are the overriding themes of Book 1. *Tr.* 1.8 and 9 form a pair: reproach of a faithless friend, praise of a true one. The tenth poem depicts the exile's journey, featuring the tutelary goddess of his ship, the *Korax*, named after Minerva's helmet. It starts and ends with prayers, and gives a brief description of the various ports of call. The last poem in this book, as befits an envoy, explains the circumstances in which the short collection was penned: shivering on board ship in the cold month of December, the traveler was driven to write by his overriding obsession (1.11.1–8). It is amazing that his talent has not flagged in the midst of such storms, but writing took his mind off his sorrows and the tempests buffeting him (9–18). A generic storm, one example of the many that he encountered, is described in hyperbolic detail (19–24). Next follows a description of the bare, savage-ridden wasteland that is to be the fugitive's future home (25–38). The storm-tossed poet has the very pages torn from his unwilling hands by the fierce wind (39–42). The coda (43–4) strikes a jaunty note: he prays that the tempest end its howling with the end of his song. Such jauntiness often undercuts the exile's apparently most abject pleadings for forgiveness and stay of sentence. Ovid the humorist has not lost his sense of fun.

The second book is, as we have noted, unusual as elegy, in that it comprises a single, 578-verse 'speech for the defense'. It is both an *apologia pro vita arteque sua* and a wide-ranging criticism of Augustus' moral double standards. Verses 1 to 212 are concerned with Ovid's relationship with Augustus: his loyalty, his inadvertent error, Augustus' greatness and clemency, Ovid's frequent celebration of the great man in his earlier works, the fact that someone had maligned him to the Emperor. He had seen something he should not have (2.103–4). Some undefined *error* (109) had led to his ruin. When in the past the Emperor had favored him, all had fawned on the poet, but since experiencing Augustus' just anger, he found all turned against him. Humbly and gratefully he praises Augustus for sparing his life (127–8). The reader is led to wonder at the despotism of a ruler who would even consider putting to death the inadvertent perpetrator of a mere peccadillo. The exile's hopes and fears ebb and flow, his praises of the imperial household grow, and he hopes only for a milder place of punishment (185–6, 201–2). Lurid details depict the terrors of his surroundings, embellished with the names of tribes that ethnology tells us lived far distant from Tomis (190–8; cf. Claassen 1990b).

The passage that most succinctly typifies the reasons for Ovid's banishment reads (2.207–10):

Perdiderunt cum me duo crimina, carmen et error,
    alterius facti culpa silenda mihi:
nam non sum tanti, renouem ut tua uulnera, Caesar,
    quem nimio plus est indoluisse semel.

Although two accusations ruined me, a song and a mistake, I have to keep mum about one of the misdemeanors, for I'm not the kind of person to rake open your wounds, Caesar, and it's more than enough to have hurt you once.

Intriguing as these verses are, to seek further illumination is fruitless: what Ovid's 'fault' was, and what he 'saw' that hurt the Emperor, cannot (and will never) be known. It is another non-question, and although frequently speculated upon (Thibault 1964; Holleman 1976; Verdiére 1992) may be set aside while we enjoy the poet's continued artistry. Much has been written about Ovid's attitude to Augustus as evinced in this poem: many of his protestations of loyalty and elaborate prayer formulae (e.g. 2.155–84) may be interpreted as gibes, protected from further imperial retribution by the poet's ability to retreat into the surface meaning of what he says (Claassen 1999a: 126, 210–11, 226–7), a frequent refuge for poets critical of a regime (Ahl 1984).

The second part of the poem (2.213–578) is a tour de force of ebullient wit: some ill-natured person had brought the poet's works to the attention of the Emperor, who had found them lacking in *grauitas*, or worse, obscene. If a poet is to be punished for writing about love and its effect upon humanity, then the whole of the Greek and Roman literary corpus is equally at fault. From Homer and the Greek dramatists, to hallowed Roman classics, all treat of love and all must be punished. Yet even Gallus (Augustus' friend, former Prefect of Egypt, who committed suicide when he lost the Emperor's favor) was not punished for his elegies (445–6). All things are pure to the pure of heart; all things may be tainted by the guilty (301–2): even the great porticoes of the Augustan building program can lead to illicit liaisons. The circus, the theater, even temples, none is exempt. Authors writing about games or pastimes are equally lacking in *grauitas*, all are iniquitous (471–94). The only poet ever punished for his poetry was Ovid, although his poetry stopped short of the obscenities of mime and was merely danced to (495–520). Finally, Augustus has, in his own house, pornographic decorations and pictures of a naked Venus (521–8). Even the *felix . . . auctor* of Augustus' revered *Aeneid* was reprehensible (533–4, with a wicked echo of that poem's opening lines: *contulit in Tyrios arma virumque toros*, 'He thrust arms and the man into a Tyrian marriage bed'). Finally: the poet published the offending poems quite long ago, and has since been approved by the Emperor in the annual knights' parade (541–2).

The poem ends with a plea that Augustus make time to read some of the poet's other, more 'serious' works and, ultimately, to commute his punishment by sending the poor victim, who harmed no one in his writings, to a pleasanter place of exile, where his punishment might more aptly fit his delict (547–78). The whole poem reads as a subtle indictment of Augustus' bigotry, hypocrisy, and apparent willingness to punish, unexamined, the author of a work that he had himself not read (Williams 1994: 154–209; Claassen 1987).

The third book chronicles the exile's first year at Tomis, and his experience of the changing seasons, interspersed with appeals to family and friends. It was probably sent to Rome together with the fourth book, which has as motif the interconnected concepts of *place* and *time*. The final poem of Book 4 is famous as Ovid's autobiography, one of the first of the 'modern' genre, with its stress on the personal and emotional life of the author, rather than on his public image, although, with Ovid, these are closely intertwined. The poem starts with a Virgilian evocation—*Ille ego qui fuerim* . . . ('That I that I was . . .')—and by verse 6 dates the poet's birth with a significant political reference, in the year of the death of two consuls. As a piece of self-promotion, 4.10 closely parallels Augustus' own autobiographical writings that culminated in the *Res Gestae*, the official documentation of the great man's deeds, that was published throughout the Empire after his death (Fairweather 1987). The poet emphasizes family life, a topic not mentioned by Augustus, but notably similar: both men were married more than once, each had a daughter, who each was married more than once, both were grandfathers, both honored their parents. A reference to the susceptibility of the poet's heart to tender emotion is followed by a description of his various marriages, first to a woman 'neither worthy nor useful', next to someone 'blameless but temporary', finally to a woman, his source of constant happiness, who bravely bore the fate of seeing her husband exiled (4.10.65–74).

A large part of the poem consists of a description of Ovid's poetic career and his relationship with other poets and with poetry (19–26, 39–63, 111–132). The young Ovid and his brother had attempted the usual career in public service and the courts, but the poet had hated this life and had turned to poetry, much to his father's dismay. He could not help it: poetry flowed from his pen (21–26). The last eight couplets (117–32) offer a paean of praise to his Muse, who relieves the exile's misery. The fame she brings will last forever, thanks to his kind readers. Predictably, parts of this poem are also devoted to exculpation of his 'fault' (89–90, 99–102), interspersed with biographical details (91–8), and an evocation of his present sorry state and the dreadful surroundings with which he must now contend (103–10).

The fifth book, now predominantly epistolary, appears as a compendium of poetic experiments, regarding both genre and content, and with more poems addressed to his wife than in any other. It starts more plaintively than any of its predecessors. The first poem typifies the book as the poet's 'swan song' (5.1.11–14). It again treats of Ovidian poetics and elaborately denies any lapse into lasciviousness, blandly quoting as a 'more suitable candidate' the earlier elegist Gallus, who also fell victim to a vindictive Augustus (17). He admits that his Muse had formerly been playfully amorous (*iocosa*, 'jocular') but that his terrible place of exile offers no hospitality to 'quiver-bearing Amor' (22). The poem goes on to explain that the contents of the new book will again reflect the endless miseries of its author, but, bad as it is, the book is better than its place of origin (72). He no longer seeks glory, but merely comfort. He sends these missives to Rome, in order still to be with his friends in some way. Again poet and works are identified. The rest of the book reflects the exile's ever-changing fluctuations of hope and despair.

Themes and Topics

Ovid's frequent references to his *carmen* and *error*, and to the wounds that he caused his 'divine' antagonist, appear as central and consistent themes in the *Tristia*. Other, equally important, themes together formed the fabric of Ovid's exilic writings, serving as the model for others after him, from Seneca and Boethius to Lawrence and Van Wyk Louw (Claassen 1999a: 241–58; 2003). Time and space loom large as important themes (cf. Hinds 1999). For example, *Tr.* 5.10 depicts the exile's third winter at Tomis. Time goes slowly (5.10.5–14). The place and the people are wild and he is treated unkindly. He is the speechless, unintelligible barbarian (35–44) that has outlived himself (45–50). Tomis is consistently depicted as 'under the Pole star', although it is demonstrably on the same latitude as Firenze or Bologna. It is a frozen waste, as wild and bare as its savage inhabitants, and infinitely removed from Rome. Here time stands still and the seasons do not perform their normal functions. At Rome life goes on and time passes normally, but no one heeds the exile's constant appeals. Rome and Italy contain all that is sweet and dear, and the exile's only comfort is his increasing ability to travel vicariously, by means of his books, but also with his mind's eye (Claassen 1999b; Hardie 2002c: 291).

The personages that populate the *Tristia*, apart from Ovid himself, his wife, and (possibly) her daughter, remain nebulous. Augustus is the most certainly named addressee. The poet lavishes love and praise on his wife for her constancy as another Penelope, Evadne, or Laodamia, without reference to the negative aspects of the latter two mythological figures. Occasionally, he sounds querulous, even petulant. His friends are offered an equal mix of praise, appeal, and blame, but address of unnamed enemies offers interesting reading (3.11, 4.9). An enemy has caused the exile unnamed ills: at *Tr.* 4.9.2–26 the exile threatens to expose him, even to posterity, by means of his verse. With the hindsight of close on two thousand years, we can say that the threat was carried out, if only partially. We know about this enemy, yet his identity has remained unrevealed, and the hyperbolically threatening tone of the poem undercuts its ostensibly serious purport.

Exile often creates a certain depersonalization of the victim. The exile appears to have lost his sense of self (3.8.38, 3.11.25; Claassen 1990a, 2003). His use of poems as virtual ventriloquist's dummies (1.1, 3.1, 5.4) indicates an eclipse of the exile's inner consciousness of self, an externality whence the creator-poet both observes himself as protagonist and manipulates the poetic strings of his *alter ego* poems. Self-hatred is another typical exilic trait, with Ovid, as with any other exile the world over (2.82). Strong identification with his poetry results in this self-hatred fluctuating between his person and his poems (2.316, 4.10.63–4, 5.7.31–34; Claassen 1989a).

The exile's physical and mental well-being, or lack of it, looms large. Ovid the poet shows Ovid the exile as suffering an all-encompassing, anxious misery (5.7.7, 5.11.4). On occasion he admits that there is a 'certain pleasure in crying' (4.3.37). His personified book depicts the poet weeping (1.3.1–4, 5.4.39–40). A central metaphor is exile as illness (3.8.27–8, 33–4; 5.2.7). With illness, *death*, including the desire for suicide, features frequently (1.5.5–6, 3.2.23–4, 3.8.39–40, 4.6.49–50, 5.10.45–52). The exile is simultaneously dead and desires death (1.4.28) but hopes for immortality through his verse (5.14.5–6), and promises to confer it upon others, including his wife (5.14.1–14; Claassen 1996).

The second poem of *Tristia* 3 reflects an attitude of extreme despair. The excitement of the journey had buoyed up the exile's spirits, but now he is totally despondent and longs for unattainable death. In the following poem, written to his wife by an amanuensis, the exile reports physical illness and extreme lassitude. He wishes that he could have died en route, imagines himself dying alone (3.3.29–36), but gives instructions for his funeral (65–72). He composes his own epitaph, claiming to have 'died though his own genius' (73–6). His 'last will and testament' ends with a confident statement of the immortality of the poet's works (77–80) and final instructions to the prospective widow to tend his ashes and accept a 'farewell' from lips that cannot say that their owner is faring (equally) well (81–88) (Miller 2004a: 224–9).

Humor

Ovid's depiction of the exile's emotional fluctuations and inconsistencies is not an indication of the poet's flagging powers, but the central characteristic of Ovidian wit. Ovid's spirit certainly owed its survival to the fact that he was still able to compose and that he had not totally lost his sense of humor. Humor lends distance, and can tone down tragedy. Its interpretation is an intensely personal thing, depending upon the reader's perception (Claassen 1999a: 233–8). Ovidian humor is displayed in irreverence, whimsy, and self-irony, also comic juxtaposition or contrast, of either concepts or words. Playful personification of the poet's book (1.1, 3.1, 5.4) is supported by its inverse: the poet becomes an exemplum of the ultimate metamorphosis (1.1.119–20). Elsewhere we find sexual innuendo. At *Tristia* 3.3.21–4 he assures his wife, that, were he at death's door, on hearing that she had arrived, he would 'rise up'. In the same poem, the picture of one helpless little Roman ghost, terrified by the overpowering Scythian and Sarmatian ghosts around it (63–4), is proof, not of Ovid's new, superstitious belief in the supernatural, but of his continued playfulness.

Sure and controlled intertextual allusion works to ironize apparently solemn statements of fact (Williams 1994: 3–49). The hyperbolic equation of his departure as another 'fall of Troy' in 1.3.25–6 seems not wholly unhumorous to a reader aware of the Virgilian pastiche: Ovid is a 'dying male Dido'. Ovid's depiction of life at Tomis and the appearance and customs of its inhabitants is tinged alternately with humor and pathos. *Tr.* 3.10.19–24 invites laughter at the Getae as trousered savages, their hairy locks tinkling with icicles, serving chunks of frozen wine to their guests, a scene borrowed from Virgil and transported several hundred miles southward from the swamps of Lake Maeotis. Well-attested geographical details about the river freezing over and allowing transport wagons to be trundled across the ice (25–34), or marauding hordes to cross from the other side (53–6), lend verisimilitude to the more outrageous aspects of his comical depiction. The genuine pathos in a cameo of innocent farmers being carried away to slavery (58–66) renders acceptable the surprising next assertion that 'no one ploughs here anyway, from fear of war' (69–76) and that there are no trees nor viticulture. Would the 'frozen wine' thus have been *imported*? The *stolidi . . . Getae* of *Tr.* 5.10.37–44, who consider Ovid a barbarian, because he does not understand them, come straight from Greek Middle Comedy, where the stock 'stupid slave' is often named Geta (Williams 1994: 18–23; Claassen 1990b).

In his attitude to Augustus we discern Ovidian humor at its most stringent (Williams 1994: 154–209; Claassen 1999a: 219–28). Throughout, the Emperor looms large as both persecutor and only haven of appeal, a powerful god that has eclipsed the divine pantheon that Augustus strove to restore. The greater part of *Tristia* 2 is an extended prayer to the man-god that holds absolute sway, his divine consort at his side, 'without whom he would have had to remain celibate' (161–4). A web of subtle and not-so-subtle imagery permeates the collection. Ovid is the composite Actaeon–Odysseus–Aeneas, long-suffering and thunderstruck victim of a vengeful (male) Diana–Poseidon-Juno–Jupiter. His victimization is frequently signaled by references to Callisto, Jupiter's innocent victim from *Met.* 8, now turned into a cold, Northern constellation that oppresses the hapless wanderer under the Pole star (1.3.48, 1.4.1, 1.11.15, 2.190, 3.4.47, 3.11.8; Nisbet 1982). Suetonius (*Aug.* 80) avers that Augustus had seven birthmarks resembling this constellation. Perhaps our poet was slyly alluding to this (Claassen 2001: 23–4 n. 26).

Ovidian *nequitia* is never more apparent than in the exile's abject protestations of devotion to Augustus. In 4.4.1–22 the poet justifies his address of (probably) M. Valerius Corvinus Messalinus (Green 1994: 261) with reference to Caesar (15) and Jupiter (17) as 'both allowing their praises to be sung'. Of these personages, *hic aspicitur, creditur ille deus* ('the latter is seen, the former believed to be a god', 20). Application of the conventional rules of translation makes of *hic . . . ille* a Jupiter who is *seen* to be a god, and a Caesar who is (merely) *believed* to be divine. The apparently bland exemplum is a subtle gibe. In *Tr.* 4.8.45–50 the central tenet of the consolatory tradition, that man's fate is uncertain and subject to the divine will, is followed by the poet's usual semi-confessional acceptance of blame for having brought divine wrath upon himself. Friends at Rome are adjured to try to deserve the approval of the 'man who is equal to the gods' (51–2). 'Man' (*uirum*) appears in the emphatic final position in both verse and poem. This apparently guileless admonishment is not without a barb. Arbitrary and powerful as he may be, Augustus is still only human, and mortal. *Tr.* 5.11.23–8 fulsomely praises Augustus, praying for his continued life on earth (the gods must keep heaven's door closed to him, allowing him to be 'a god apart from them', 25–6). Finally, the Emperor is abruptly reminded that 'even the smallest stream eventually reaches the sea'; by implication: death is inevitable (27–8).

Ovid's *culpa* is irrecoverable but appears closely tied to the Emperor as person. Sometimes he claims that it was a minor peccadillo (5.8.23–4). At *Tr.* 5.10.51–2 he admits to having deserved punishment, even death. These statements, like his gratitude in the intervening poem to Caesar for having 'spared his life' (5.9.11–12), subtly show the Emperor to be a despot who would not hesitate to wreak supreme vengeance for a minor offense. Equally irrecoverable is a final decision on whether Ovid was 'pro- or anti-Augustan'. The common consensus today is that this, too, is a nonquestion. Ovidian ambivalence invites multiple readings of every statement, of each fleetingly ironical nuance in the delicate quadrille that was the poet's relationship with the Prince (Barchiesi 1997a: 1–44; Miller 2004a: 217–35).

Poetics

Less uncertain is interpreting Ovid's attitude to his own works, drawn as his 'children' and 'ambassadors', but also the 'parricides' that caused his civic death (1.1.113–4). Throughout the *Tristia* he claims that his poems are bad because his situation is bad. The introductory poem of Book 4 spells out the concept of 'the suitable blemish': just as the poet's life is flawed, so his poetry reflects his misery. As an exile, his aim was to entertain himself, not to seek fame (4.1.1–4). An ingenious list of laborers that alleviate with song their menial tasks illustrates this thesis (5–14). Two mythical exempla lift the mundane comparison to a higher plane: Achilles and Orpheus were both comforted by their music (15–18). The poem becomes a double-edged song of praise to the exile's Muse, both the comforting witness to his innocence and the cause of his downfall (19–30). Another mythical example (at 31–36, Odysseus' companions relishing the plant that brought their doom) shows him loving the books that harmed him. The poet's love/hate relationship with poetry is explored in all its dimensions (37–52), culminating in a pathetic description of his miseries. All the gods follow Caesar's wrath, his ills mount up innumerably. A doomed lot brought him into warlike surroundings where he has donned helmet and shield to keep off the poisoned darts of barbarian hordes (53–86). Yet he continues to compose, with no audience to hear his poems, tears flowing down his cheeks, remembering what is past, often burning what he has written (87–102). What remains, he now entrusts to *Roma interdicta*, with the entreaty that she accept it, however feeble, for it matches his lot (103–6).

Writing poetry clearly sustained the exile's spirits, but poem after prolific poem claims to deny this, culminating in a supreme negation of all that his Muse ever stood for. *Tristia.* 5.12 claims that poetry needs the calmness of spirit and peace of mind, which Ovid lacks (1–6); his talent has wasted away from disuse (21–2); he is weighed down by his troubles and no longer seeks glory (37–44); his Muses caused his relegation (45–50); bookless, he is surrounded by illiterate savages jabbering in a foreign tongue (51–6); he has lost his Latin (57–60); he writes, but burns what he has written (61–6). The poem ends on the futile wish that he had burned his *Ars* before it could have destroyed him (67–8). Yet this poem is less memorable than the hymn to his Muse that closes Ovid's autobiography (4.10.117–20):

> Gratia, Musa, tibi: nam tu solacia praebes,
>   tu curae requies, tu medicina uenis.
> Tu dux et comes es, tu nos abducis ab Histro,
>   in medioque mihi das Helicone locum.

> Thank you, dear Muse, for you offer comfort,
>   you are my rest from care and come as balm.
> You are my leader and companion, you take me away from the Ister
>   and give me a place on the slopes of Helicon.

That is the lasting memory that readers of the *Tristia* take away with them (Claassen 1989a, 1989b).

FURTHER READING

Luck's German edition (1967) with commentary (1977) remains standard. André's French edition appeared in 1968, followed by an Italian translation and commentary by Della Corte in 1973. There are commentaries by De Jonge (Book 4, 1951) and Bakker (Book 5, 1946). Slavitt's verse translation (1990) of all three exilic works is rather free; so, too, is Melville's (1992). Green's verse translation of the two longer collections (1994) offers almost line-by-line equivalence, with an excellent, up to-date commentary, fully appreciative of Ovid's wit. Few authors, with the exception of Videau-Delibes (1991), concentrate on the *Tristia* alone in monographs on Ovid's exilic poetry. Of these, Nagle (1980), Helzle (1988), and Barchiesi (2001a) are particularly useful; Chwalek (1996) takes Ovid rather too seriously. An extensive bibliography appears in Claassen (1999a); for updates, see Claassen (2003, 2004 and 2007), as well as Citroni Marchetti (2000) and Martin (2004).

CHAPTER THIRTEEN

Ibis

Martin Helzle

Introduction

At the age of at least 50, so Ovid tells us in the first couplet, he wrote the invective poem entitled *Ibis*, not as one might expect in some form of iambic meter, which had become the generic convention since Archilochus, but in his favorite elegiac couplets. Since he was born in 43 BC, the earliest year in which it could have been written is AD 7. Scholars generally agree that it was composed no later than AD 12, and one of them (Leary 1990: 99–101) narrows it down to the years between AD 10 and 12. In this extraordinary poem, Ovid directly addresses an enemy whom he condemns to hell and damnation following the model of and explicitly invoking Callimachus' invective poem called *Ibis*.

This is probably Ovid's least-known poem, and so a brief overview of its contents is called for. In lines 1–66 the poet claims that nobody but himself has been hurt by his works, but now one person is trying to hurt him even in exile. Then he damns that individual as Callimachus damned his enemy Ibis. Lines 67–134 invoke all the gods for help and wish that Ibis may be bereft of everything, hated by all, and die miserably. In lines 135–62 Ovid announces that he will hate his opponent beyond death and will haunt his every waking hour. Lines 163–208 proclaim that his dead body will not be buried, but eaten by wolves and that he will dwell in the Underworld with sinners like Sisyphus and be tortured in unspeakable and countless ways. Lines 209–50 talk of his having been born on the anniversary of the lost battle of the Allia. Everything at his birth spelt disaster, the Fates even predicted that a poet would sing about his fate. 'I am that poet!' exclaims Ovid. Then he launches into a long tirade (251–634), in which he wishes that, like the heroes of myth, legend, and history, his enemy shall suffer endless forms of mutilation, torture, and death, even be killed by his own brother like Remus (635–6) or, worst of all, die among the Getae like himself (637–8). At the end (639–44) Ovid wishes that the gods may multiply his almost 400-line tirade and announces that he will name his enemy later and write iambic verse about him.

Identifying Ibis

There can be no certainty as to who is hiding behind the pseudonym Ibis. There is not even agreement on whether he is the same enemy as the one addressed in the *Tristia* and *Epistulae ex Ponto*. Even if this were certain, it would not tell us anything else about his identity. One clue can be found in line 232, where it is said about Ibis that he 'barks canine words in the entire forum'. On the basis of this he has been thought to be Titus Labienus (Herrmann 1938: 709–12) or Caninius Rebilus (Herrmann 1938: 710). I argue elsewhere (Helzle 2005) that the enemy mentioned in the *Tristia* and *Epistulae ex Ponto* may well be Sabinus, one of Ovid's earlier friends who imitated his *Heroides*, but relied on Ovid's patronage and had to find another source of support after Ovid was sent to Tomis.

More recently, scholars (e.g. Williams 1996, following Housman 1920) have dismissed the question as 'literalist' and focused instead on the only reality that exists, which is the text. Literature, however, consists not just of products of the imagination but also of fragments of reality. Otherwise, it would become an inextricable and inexplicable maze of hallucinations (Iser 1983). Ovid's poem, like all literature, obviously combines purely imaginative passages with some real details. If a poem like this were circulated in Rome and no reader had any idea who Ibis could be, the conclusion would have to be that Ovid was hallucinating. It is therefore safer to assume that a real person or a group of people is hiding behind the pseudonym Ibis. After all, the whole purpose of using a pseudonym is to have the reader ask 'who could this be?' Two thousand years after Ovid and Ibis we simply have to accept the question of his identity as one of the myriad unsolved mysteries in life.

Genre

Another unanswerable question is how much Ovid depends on Callimachus' poem of the same name. Unfortunately, no single line of this Hellenistic model survives, only references to it (fr. 381–2 Pfeiffer). Many scholars assume that Ovid's lines 67–250 are modeled on a corresponding passage in Callimachus, but, again, there is no proof. In the absence of Callimachus' poem, all we can do is take Ovid on his own terms, which may be, as Williams suggests (1996: 13), a good thing. What we can say is that Ovid's poem was significantly longer than Callimachus', especially because of its huge catalogue of curses. These in themselves depend on Hellenistic poets' curses, or *Arai*, which at times use overkill as a humorous device juxtaposing a crime with its overdone punishment.

Another major difference between Ovid and traditional invective poetry is clear: Ovid writes in elegy, while the Greek tradition of attacking personal enemies in verse, begun by Archilochus, used iambics. As in the *Fasti* and the *Ars amatoria*, Ovid crosses the literary genres by couching a subject that would ordinarily call for another meter in his favorite elegiac couplets. The same had been done by Callimachus, whose narrative poem entitled *Aitia* was not composed in the usual dactylic hexameter but in elegiac couplets. Maybe a parallel should be drawn between

Ovid's mode of operation in the *Ars amatoria* and here in the *Ibis*: in the *Ars*, the poet humorously adapts the didactic genre, customarily written in hexa- meters, in his irreverent manner. Similarly, he could here be seen as using a subject usually expressed in iambic verse in this overdone elegiac effusion of curses (Schiesaro 2001). If Ovid is poking fun at the genre of didactic in the *Ars*, the possibility that he is equally making fun of the genre of iambic invective and of *Arai* must certainly be entertained, especially in light of the grotesque catalogue of mythical punishments.

Moreover, one cannot help but notice the discrepancy between the extremely harsh words and the poetic meter known for being *mollis* ('soft'). While the poets of Latin love elegy shun *militia* ('military service') in favor of the *mollitia* ('softness'), 'gentleness', even 'effeminacy' of their own verse, Ovid in the *Ibis* is actively and explicitly engaged in a war, *bella geram tecum* ('I will wage war with you', 139), which contrasts sharply with his literary production up to this point, *omne fuit Musae carmen inerme meae* ('My Muse's every song has been unwarlike', 2). Elegy is *inermis* ('unwarlike'), but here it undergoes a metamorphosis. Ovid, the peace-loving elegist, turns into an invective elegist, *prima quidem coepto committam proelia versu* ('I shall fight the first battles in the verse in which I began', 45). Williams further argues (1996: 90–1) that the *Ibis* crosses poetic genres with epic since its mythical catalogue constitutes a new kind of *carmen perpetuum* that employs characteristically Callima- chean lack of symmetry.

Such poetic transformations are the hallmark of Ovid's poetry. At the beginning of the *Amores*, Ovid portrayed himself as setting out to write an epic, but Cupid stole a foot of hexameter from every other verse thus forcing the poet to write in elegiac couplets. In the second line of the *Metamorphoses*, the gods change Ovid's poetic undertaking from elegy to epic (Kenney 1976). In exile, the *tenerorum lusor amorum* ('the jokester of tender love affairs') becomes the author of *Tristia* ('sad songs'). In the *Epistulae ex Ponto*, the son of Sulmo in the Abruzzi ends up as *Tomitanae iam non novus incola terrae* ('already no new inhabitant of Tomis', 1.1). And now the *inermis poeta* ('the unwarlike poet') turns into a vicious attack-dog. Just as the figures in his *Metamorphoses* turn from one shape into another, so Ovid's poetry keeps on changing from love elegy to epic to the lament of the exile to invective.

Curses!

One of the most important readings of Ovid's *Ibis* takes its cue from modern psychol- ogy. Williams (1996) focuses on the futility of Ovid's curses and the author's aware- ness of this very pointlessness. Ovid does not envisage any of the maledictions, such as the following, ever to come true (551–8):

> nudaue derepta pateant tua uiscera pelle,
> > ut Phrygium cuius nomina flumen habet.
> saxificae uideas infelix ora Medusae,
> > Cephenum multos quae dedit una neci.

Potniadum morsus subeas, ut Glaucus, equarum,
   inque maris salias, Glaucus ut alter, aquas.
utque duobus idem dictis modo nomen habenti,
   praefocent animae Cnosia mella uiam.

Or may your entrails lie open, skin ripped off,
   as in the case of the one [i.e. Marsyas] whose name a Phrygian river bears.
May you unhappily see the face of petrifying Medusa,
   who alone handed many of Cepheus' men over to death.
May you suffer the bites of the Potnian steeds
   and jump into the sea like one of the Glauci.
And as for the one who has the same name as the two just mentioned,
   May Cretan honey choke the path of your breath.

According to Williams, the poem constitutes a letter in which Ovid essentially reveals his psychological state in exile. The *Ibis* is thus another manifestation of the poet's consistent need for self-revelation in the exilic corpus. Williams takes the exile-poetry to be an emotional outlet for the poet's anger and frustration, a coping mechanism for the banished, powerless, marginalized individual. Ovid's gratification comes from anticipating getting his own back on his enemy, rather than actually exacting vengeance on him. The entire catalogue is therefore couched in optative subjunctives from line 251 *neue sine exemplis aeui cruciere prioris* (You shall not be tortured without the examples of the previous age'), down to the culminating wish in lines 637–8:

denique Sarmaticas inter Geticasque sagittas
   his, precor, ut uiuas et moriare locis.

Finally I pray that you live and die in this place
   among the arrows of the Sarmatae and the Getae.

None of this will ever come true, nor is it intended to become reality. The long list of curses is so overdone because the speaker is unbelievably angry and has to let his wrath out. Ovid is 'venting'. Maybe there is a hint at this in the fact that Ibis is an anagram for *sibi* ('for himself'). He is expressing his anger for himself.

His list is also exaggerated because Ovid gives free rein to his imagination and does not control his cruel impulses, which are already evident in some passages in the *Metamorphoses*, such as the simile that compares the dying Pyramus's pulsating blood to water shooting from a burst pipe (*Met.* 4.121–4). This cruel streak goes far beyond just Ovid, and can be found in Roman culture's delight in blood sports in general (as it can in modern cultures). The poem's cruel wishes represent the dark complement to Ovid's light, frivolous, and witty earlier works.

In spite of its manifest violence, one cannot help but find some humor in these frequently exaggerated curses. The tone is set by Ibis' birth (209–50), which is described ironically after his non-burial and descent into Tartarus have been predicted: he was, of course, born unlucky (209) in accordance with the gods' wishes.

None of the lucky stars, such as Venus, Jupiter, Luna, or Mercury, shone at his birth, but the unlucky Mars and Saturn did (211–16). His birthday is the unluckiest of all days, the *dies ater* ('black day') of the anniversary of the Roman defeat at the River Allia on 18 July 387 BC. His mother is predictably *impura* ('morally impure'), that is, sexually promiscuous, which is why no father is even mentioned. This ignoble birth under malignant stars inverts commonplaces used in ancient birthday poems (Gordon 1992: 28–32). Instead of the spinning Fates appearing at his birth, as in the case of Achilles in Catullus 64.303–22, the Furies are present, of whom Klotho, who is usually one of the Fates, is one (Hinds 1999: 63 n. 31). They are the first to feed the newborn infant (229–32):

> gutturaque imbuerunt infantia lacte canino—
>   hic primus pueri uenit in ora cibus:
> perbibit inde suae rabiem nutricis alumnus,
>   latrat et in toto uerba canina foro.

> they filled the infant throat with dog's blood:
>   this food first came into the boy's mouth:
> from there the nursling imbibed his nurse's rage
>   and barks canine words in the entire Forum.

Scholars have focused on the 'canine words' as a possible hint at identifying Ibis. These rhetorically inferior words (cf. e.g. Sall. *Hist.* fr. 4.54 *canina, ut ait Appius, facundia exercebatur*, 'a dog-like eloquence, as Appius calls it, was being practiced') are, however, only the outward expression of the *rabies* (or 'rage') which the infant has imbibed from its nurse's milk. The conceit that Ibis was nursed on dog's milk by the Furies is so hyperbolical that it has to be taken humorously. After all, the basic principle of ancient literary criticism is that all aspects of literature have to be appropriate to their subject matter, what in Latin is called *decorum* (e.g. Hor. *Ars* 308) and in Greek *tò prépon* (e.g. Arist. *Rhet.* 1408a.10–36). What is funny in the burst water pipe simile in the *Metamorphoses* is exactly its inappropriateness in the tragic romance of Pyramus and Thisbe. Like the simile, the image of the Furies nursing Ibis with dogs' blood and this causing his rage is beyond the limit of decorum and therefore becomes humorous despite its gruesomeness. Humor and gruesomeness strangely coexist so as to make the reader recoil and a moment later smile at the same image.

This wavering perspective is typical of Ovid. Tissol (1997) convincingly shows that such constant shifts in the reader's point of view are characteristic of Ovid's art in the *Metamorphoses*. One minute one sees Apollo's pursuit of Daphne through the young woman's eyes as rape, the next moment it is seen through the god's eyes as just plain fun. Similarly, Ibis being nursed with dogs' blood by the Furies and therefore barking in the Forum is at once nauseating and so hyperbolical as to be funny.

An even more extreme example is the passage in which Ovid predicts that Ibis will indulge in cannibalism and be himself served as a meal to Jupiter (427–34):

nec dapis humanae tibi sint fastidia, quaque
    parte potes, Tydeus temporis huius eris.
atque aliquid facies, a uespere Solis ad ortus
    cur externati rursus agantur equi.
foeda Lycaoniae repetes conuiuia mensae
    temptabisque cibi fallere fraude Iovem.
teque aliquis posito temptet uim numinis opto:
    Tantalides tu sis, tu Tereidesque (Teleique *La Penna*) puer.

Nor may you feel disgust at eating human flesh, and as far as
    you can you will be the Tydeus of our time.
You will also provide some cause why the terrified horses
    of the Sun are driven back from evening to morning.
You will repeat Lycaon's dinner
    and try to trick Jupiter with deceptive food.
I hope that someone may test the power of a god by serving you, too,
    may you be Tantalus' son, you Tereus' boy.

The first three couplets cast Ibis as engaging in some really outrageous acts of cannibalism. Ibis will be a latter-day Tydeus, who was one of the seven heroes who laid siege to the city of Thebes. He and his opponent Melanippus dealt a deadly blow to each other; before he died, Tydeus ate Melanippus' brains. Ibis can parallel Tydeus' cannibalism, but not his heroism. The Sun ran backwards when king Atreus served his brother Thyestes his own sons as a meal. Ibis will commit *aliquid* ('something') which will have the same effect. He will also repeat Lycaon's attempt at testing Jupiter by serving him the flesh of his own guest, a particularly appalling deed for the ancients, to whom hospitality was so sacred that it was the domain of Jupiter (Zeus xenios). All three mythical examples are extremely nauseating. A hint of humor may be contained in the qualifying *quaque parte potes* ('as far as you can', 427–8) since this suggests that Ibis isn't really up to Tydeus' standard. However, better still than Ibis eating human flesh and incurring a punishment of mythical proportions, why not just have him eaten and served up as a meal himself? The fourth couplet then provides the climax to the series. It is the most gruesome of all and takes the idea of cannibalism to its logical extreme: why have Ibis punished for serving or eating human flesh if he can be eaten himself? Not only that, *aliquis* ('somebody') without a name will serve him up to a divinity. The harshness of this idea is brought out by the alliteration in both lines, the climactic effect by the emphatic *teque* ('you, too') at the beginning of verse 433. Everything about these examples is overdone, and yet Ibis is not really up to mythical standards. This contrast generates a somewhat macabre element of humor.

    On a larger scale, the sheer length of Ovid's curses already strikes one as humorous. While there are plenty of gruesome predictions and descriptions in the sections on his death and birth, the curses proper take up 388 lines (251–638). By way of comparison, there is a passage in Plautus' comedy *Pseudolus*, in which Calidorus, the master, and Pseudolus, the trickster slave, pile terms of abuse on the pimp Ballio. This is called a *flagitatio*, which was a form of popular Italian justice. It takes up just ten lines (359–68) with nineteen terms of abuse consisting mostly of single words. Ovid usually takes a whole couplet for a single mythical example. There has to be some point to the length of Ovid's tirade other than the ancient critic Quintilian's remark that Ovid would have been better 'if he had rather controlled his genius than indulge in it' (*si ingenio suo imperare quam indulgere maluisset*, Quint. 10.1.98). It seems that most readers would reach a point in the poem where they would say to themselves: 'This can't be serious!' While one cannot deny that Ovid might have a just reason to be angry at Ibis, at some point, which will vary from reader to reader, his endless tirade becomes humorous.

Myth and Erudition

Since Ovid's mythical examples never become dull, but constantly pose challenges to the reader as to who is meant, the lengthy catalogue also never becomes dull. If we take the whole poem, with Williams (1996), as a letter to Ibis, then the contents and the style are very likely to have something to do with the addressee. The length of the curses could therefore be an indirect comment on Ibis' manner of writing. Maybe he had an even greater propensity than Ovid to indulge his *ingenium* and go on? While that has to remain a matter of speculation, it is fair to say that Ovid's mythical learning, which at times leaves modern commentators stunned, is designed to stun Ibis, too. Ovid's 388 verses provide a vast display of Callimachean learning (*doctrina*) and ingenuity (*ingenium*), qualities of which Ovid was known to have been proud. In short, he simply buries Ibis under an avalanche of myth with all the powers at his disposal.

Lines 601–20 illustrate Ovid's *doctrina*, or learning:

> natus ut Althaeae flammis absentibus arsit,
>   sic tuus ardescat stipitis igne rogus.
> ut noua Phasiaca comprensa est nupta corona,
>   utque pater nuptae, cumque parente domus;
> ut cruor Herculeos abiit diffusus in artus;
>   corpora pestiferum sic tua uirus edat.
> qua sua Pentheliden proles est ulta Lycurgum,
>   haec maneat teli te quoque plaga noui.
> utque Milo robur diducere fissile temptes,
>   nec possis captas inde referre manus.
> muneribusque tuis laedaris, ut Icarus, in quem
>   intulit armatas ebria turba manus.
> quodque dolore necis patriae pia filia fecit,
>   uincula per laquei fac tibi guttur eat.
> obstructoque famem patiaris limine tecti,
>   ut legem poenae cui dedit ipsa parens.
> illius exemplo uioles simulacra Mineruae,
>   Aulidis a portu qui leue uertit iter.
> Naupliadaeue modo poenas pro crimine falso
>   morte luas, nec te non meruisse iuuet.

As Althaea's son burns in far-off flames
  may your pyre start burning on the flame of a tree trunk.
As the new bride was ignited by the crown from Phasis,
  as the bride's father caught fire and the house with her parent,
as the blood was shed and spread over Hercules' limbs
  may a destructive poison eat your body.
May the blow of a novel weapon with which his own offspring
  took vengeance on Lycurgus, son of Penthelius, await you.
May you try to separate the split oak like Milo
  and not be able to remove your caught hands from there.
May you be hurt by your own gift like Icarus on whom
  a gang of drunks lay their armed hands.
And what the dutiful daughter did out of grief for her parent's death,
  see to it that your throat is tied by a noose.
And may you go hungry with the front door locked
  like the one for whom his own mother set the legal punishment.
May you violate Minerva's statue like the man
  who easily changed course from the port of Aulis.
Or like Nauplius' son may you suffer the punishment of death
  for a crime you did not commit and may it not help you not to have deserved it.

In these ten couplets, which contain one myth per distich, four of the ten mythical people are explicitly named: Hercules (605), Lykurgos (608), Milon (609), and Ikaros (611). All others are paraphrased in the characteristic manner of Hellenistic and Roman poetry.

Althaea's son (601–2) is Meleager (Ov. *Met.* 8.446–532; cf. Gordon 1992 on *Ib.* 599–601), who killed his two uncles in a quarrel following the Calydonian boar hunt. Out of anger, his mother threw into a fire the log on whose existence Meleager's life depended. Hence the paradox of the far-off flames, which Ovid also uses at *Met.* 8.515–16, *Fast.* 5.305–6, and *Rem.* 721 of Meleager's brand. Plays on absence and presence are a favorite of Ovid's; for example, cf. *Met.* 3.247 *uellet abesse quidem, sed adest* ('he wished he were absent, but he is present'), *Pont.* 2.10.48 *et ades celeberrimus absens* ('and you, most famous one, are here and gone'). The new bride of 603–4 is Creusa, daughter of the Corinthian king Creon, whom Jason married after divesting himself of Medea, who had saved him from certain death at Colchis and helped him win the Golden Fleece. Out of revenge, Medea sent Creusa a crown or wreath as a bridal gift which set her on fire, then Creusa's father and finally his palace (cf. Eur. *Medea* 982–8, Ov. *Met.* 7.394–5, and Sen. *Medea* 817–842). Note that this couplet does not name anybody and even refers to Colchis poetically only by its river Phasis (Gordon 1992 on 601–2). Hercules' death through a poisoned robe sent to him by Deianira is another example of being burned by a poisoned piece of clothing (cf. Soph. *Trach.* 1053–5 and Ov. *Met.* 9.166–174; Gordon 1992 on 603–4). The connection with Creusa is immediately apparent, while Deianira is also linked with Meleager since she is his sister (cf. Ov. *Met.* 9.149–150).

The reference in 607–8 is open to speculation. The most likely solution seems to be La Penna's (1957) suggestion that Ovid is referring to a descendant of Penthilos, son of Orestes, who is on record as having ruled Lesbos with an iron fist (Strabo 9.2.3, Pausanias 3.2.1; cf. Gordon 1992: ad loc.). This solution, however, does not explain the name Lykurgos, which is not attested anywhere for a descendant of Penthilos.

A much better attested figure is Milon (609–10), the most famous athlete of antiquity (Strabo 6.1.12), although of all the Augustans only Ovid mentions him. He was so sure of his bodily strength that he tried to separate a partly split tree trunk whose halves were kept apart by wedges. In the process, he got himself caught and was eaten by wolves (Val. Max. 9.12. ext. 9; Gordon 1992 on 607–8). Ikaros in 611–612 is more commonly known as Ikarios to whom Dionysos is said to have given the art of wine-making (Eratosth. fr. 22–27 Powell; Hygin. *Fab.* 130; Gordon 1992 on 609–10). He passed the wine on to his neighbors, who thought they were being poisoned and consequently killed him. His daughter, Erigone, found her father's unburied body and hung herself. Dionysos is said to have taken his revenge by causing young Athenian women to commit suicide en masse, whereupon the festival of Aiora in Erigone's honor was instituted (Call. fr. 178 Pf.; Servius on Virg. *G.* 2.238; Gordon 1992 on 611–12).

A historical figure follows in Pausanias, the nephew of the Spartan Leonidas who put up the famous last stand against the Persians at Thermopylae. Pausanias was suspected of plotting with Persia and convicted on mere suspicion, whereupon he took asylum in a temple of Athena. The Spartan leaders and his own mother therefore immured him there until the point of starvation when they removed him in order not to pollute the sanctuary (Nep. *Paus.* 5; Gordon 1992 on 613–14).

The following couplet contains a mythical Greek figure who violated a statue of Athena and then set sail from Aulis. This could be Odysseus (Ellis 1881: ad loc.), who stole the Palladium together with Diomedes and persuaded Agamemnon at Aulis to sacrifice Iphigenia in order to set sail for Troy. Since, however, Athena was Odysseus' patron goddess, Housman (1920) favored Oilean Ajax, who angered Athena when he tore Cassandra from her altar. The drawback with this solution is that at 341–2 Ajax has already been mentioned as having been drowned for this very outrage. Further suggestions include Theseus' son Akamas (Ellis 1881: ad loc.) and, if one changes *Mineruae* to *Dianae*, Agamemnon (La Penna 1957: ad loc.). There is no satisfactory solution to the problem and we are left to conclude that Ovid alludes to a myth or a version of a myth that we do not know.

Nauplios' son in the final couplet of this section is Palamedes, who was falsely charged with treason by Odysseus at Troy and stoned to death (cf. Virg. *Aen.* 2.81–85 and Ov. *Met.* 13.56–62; Gordon 1992: ad loc.). Other versions have him being drowned by Diomedes and Odysseus (Paus. 10.31.2) or lured to a well and then stoned by Diomedes and Odysseus (Dictys 2.15). In any case Odysseus was taking revenge for Palamedes' exposing his pretended madness as a ploy in order not to join the expedition to Troy.

These twenty lines alone are only comprehensible if one has a handbook of Greek myth and history or a compendium of rhetorical exempla at one's disposal. Ovid must have had one to write them (Cameron 2004), and his use of recherché examples must have a special point: simply outdoing Callimachus at his own game and topping the tradition of literary curses could easily have been accomplished in half the length. Since the catalogue of examples is hard to take seriously both because of its length and because of its sustained violence, Ovid's catalogue of punishments may be directly related to his addressee and may be making fun of some of his stylistic hallmarks, among which could have been a tendency to go on endlessly, the use of abstruse myths, or a fondness for gruesome details, a tendency which reaches new heights in Seneca and Lucan (Fuhrmann 1968) and for which Ovid gives the blueprint in this extraordinary poem.

Conclusion

Like many of his other works, the *Ibis* straddles the lines of literary genre between iambic invective and elegy with an epic-style catalogue thrown in for good measure. This 'crossing of genres', as Kroll (1924) calls it, is accompanied by a tone that starts with vicious hatred but at some point slips into an irony generated by the sheer excess of heinous maledictions. Clearly Ovid is venting his anger and frustration generated by his banishment and abandonment. At some point the venting becomes so much that it becomes humorous both for the reader and, I think, for the poet. In the end, then, the poem's true use lies in the poet's self-therapy by means of it. It shares this purpose with the *Tristia* and *Epistulae ex Ponto*, which ultimately allowed the poet to cope with his lot.

FURTHER READING

An up-to-date commentary on the *Ibis* is a desideratum, but recourse may be had to La Penna (1957) and Gordon (1992). Housman's paper (1920) remains fundamental not only for textual matters but also for interpretation; and Leary (1990) helps to establish the date of composition. Hinds (1999) and Williams (1996) illustrate contemporary critical approaches to the poem.

CHAPTER FOURTEEN

Epistulae ex Ponto

Luigi Galasso

Introduction

Traditionally, an author starts his work by highlighting its innovative character. The case of Ovid and his *Metamorphoses* is a signal example: *in noua fert animus mutatas dicere formas / corpora* ('my soul leads me to recount the forms turned into bodies never seen before'). The *Epistulae ex Ponto* opens instead with a rather strikingly different claim, in fact the opposite claim (1.1.1–2):

> Naso Tomitanae iam non nouus incola terrae
> hoc tibi de Getico litore mittit opus.

> Naso, who is by now no stranger to the land of Tomi,
> Is sending you this work from the Getic shores.

Ovid is by now a *non nouus* inhabitant of the land of Tomis. This poetry, as the *Tristia* explains, is the direct reflection of the author's existential situation (a complex concept; Claassen 1999a: 110–14). Furthermore, set as it is in the context of his still ongoing exile, it is also an expression of continuity. The following couplet, however, with its apostrophe to Brutus, introduces a significant novelty, for in the collection about to start the recipient is overtly revealed, as is made clear in lines 17–18:

> rebus idem, titulo differt, et epistula cui sit
> non occultato nomine missa docet.

> The topic is the same, the title is different, and the epistle reveals
> its recipient, without concealing the name.

Here the elements of continuity and discontinuity are expressed clearly and concisely. The facts upon which Ovid's poetry focuses remain the same, but by unveiling the recipient's name a means is provided to endow elegy with a new structure. This process was set in motion in the fourth and fifth books of the *Tristia*, where, as the collection unfolds, the elegies increasingly presuppose a well-defined recipient who is a basic component in the structure of the poems. The *Epistulae ex Ponto* constitutes the final stage in this process, vividly ushering in the concrete figure of each individual recipient, who is linked to a complex discourse—not shying from hints of veritable blackmail—on the concept of proposing behavioral models. The momentous impact of this novel element is fully exploited dramatically when Ovid imagines that Brutus, faced with an unexpected event (*nouitate . . . sub ipsa*), wonders what he has received (1.1.13) and has to be persuaded to accept the writings coming from afar. Ovid's friends in Rome cannot prevent such letters from being delivered to them, but—so the poet reassures them—they have nothing to fear: not only because the works by Mark Antony and Brutus are still widely read but also because the new work abounds in praise of Caesar (19–20). From the start, then, the very difficult balance Ovid has to keep between the requirements of self-accusation and his proclamation that he is fundamentally devoid of guilt is clearly delineated. These contradictory impulses were to be mirrored in the tension between *ira* and *clementia* experienced by the figure of Augustus, and would pervade and profoundly affect the entire work.

Chronology

The *Epistulae ex Ponto* comprise four books of epistles in elegiac couplets, giving a total of forty-six compositions. The first three books (thirty elegies) form a well-defined collection that make up a clearly structured organic whole. They were written between AD 12 and 13: more precisely, none of these elegies contains references to events falling outside that time span. The pivotal event that shapes the chronology of the collection is Tiberius' triumph in the Pannonian War (23 October AD 12), which acts as a landmark allowing conclusions to be drawn on the chronology of several poems.

The poems of Book 4, on the other hand, cover a broader time span, from the second half of AD 13 (4) up to the summer of AD 16 (9). The dating of the other poems can be approximately determined accordingly. Thus, poem 5 dates back to early AD 14, poem 10 to the summer of AD 14, 6 and 8 to the autumn of AD 14, poem 13 to the winter of AD 14/15, while 7 probably dates back to AD 14. Poem 12 was written before Augustus' death. None of the poems in Book 4 can be said definitely to precede those in the other three books. The first poem, dedicated to Sextus Pompeius, makes no reference to his consulate of AD 14, to which elegies 4 and 5 are dedicated. Since the poet states he had felt remorseful because the name of his powerful dedicatee was never read in his work, the epistle must certainly have been written after *Pont.* 1–3. The Severus mentioned in *Pont.* 4.2 is the poet Cornelius Severus, who for the first time was also the dedicatee of a poetic epistle. If he were also to be identified with the Severus of *Pont.* 1.8, we would be compelled to hypothesize the potential chronological overlapping of the two collections. But the absence of any allusion to the poetic activity of the friend described in 1.8 (it is merely said that he spends little time in the Forum, 1.8.65–6), whereas this activity is prominently highlighted in *Pont.* 4.2, constitutes a serious difficulty. The elegy against the friend who has rejected him (4.3) has been placed in the early years of exile on the basis of purely subjective motives; in Book 4, on the other hand, it represents the negative model which Books 1–3 set in 3.6 and 3.7.

Structures and Themes: *Pont.* 1–3

The position in which the elegies are placed in *Pont.* 1–3 offers an excellent example of the organization of the *liber* typical of Hellenistic and Augustan authors. A complex network of symmetries has been discovered (Froesch 1968: 127–44), which revolves around an axis set between 2.5 and 2.6. Without considering, naturally, the prologue and the epilogue, there is a correspondence between the second (1.2) and the penultimate (3.8) poem, which feature the same dedicatee: Fabius Maximus (Froesch 1968: 209 n. 328). A further correspondence exists between the two poems in Book 2 dedicated to Atticus (2.4 and 2.7), placed in the fourth position from the beginning and the end respectively. A similar patterning holds true for the six poems dedicated to Cotta Maximus: the fifth poems in Books 1 and 3 (1.5 and 3.5), the penultimate of Book 1 (1.9), and the second of Book 3 (3.2); and within the second book two poems occupying the third position from the beginning and end (2.3 and 2.8).

Furthermore, the four elegies immediately following the prologue of Book 1 (dedicated to Fabius Maximus, Rufinus, his wife, and Cotta Maximus) and the first four of Book 3 have the same dedicatees, albeit with a slight *variatio* in their order (his wife, Cotta Maximus, Fabius Maximus, and Rufinus). This impulse for symmetry has prompted editors to transfer 2.11 into Book 3, after 3.4, so that the elegies appear to be distributed in a uniform manner and divided into groups of ten in all three books (Froesch 1968: 139–44). The mistake probably originated from an erroneous interpretation of the term *opus* (2.11.2), which was held to refer to the whole of Book 2, and not to a single elegy. This proposal, however, does not seem convincing. In the first place, it is not clear why, if 2.11 was placed after 3.4, *opus* was necessarily to be associated with Book 2 instead of Book 1. The epistle itself, though short, was certainly appropriate for the end of the *liber*, all the more so if compared to 1.10, which is longer but by no means more significant. Also, 2.11 adequately introduces the topic of the next epistle, 3.1, that is, the duties of Ovid's wife toward her exiled husband, and it is the only one (with the exception of the brief mention in 2.10.10) where this topic is addressed in Book 2. The peculiar status of 2.1 may explain why there are 11 poems. Poem 2.1 basically addresses Germanicus, but it represents a more general celebration on the occasion of the triumph and has no explicit dedicatee. In this manner, it fully becomes a part of the complex system of symmetries, while still retaining its independence. Book 3, which contains no more than nine elegies, is held to absorb the excess number, precisely by virtue of the well-structured organic arrangement of the collection (Galasso 1995: 36–7). Therefore, with regard to the overall number of poems, the rule of ten is respected as a whole, especially if one considers that Latin poets did not seek absolute regularity (Helzle 2003: 41–2). For instance, Book 1 of the *Tristia* has eleven elegies, where the first one likewise functions as a proem and the second closely corresponds with the last one. The hypothesis is thus only weakly supported, although it currently seems to be predominant (Gaertner 2005: 4). In *Pont.* 1–3, the majority of the dedicatees are linked to Augustus and Tiberius, but the presence of Germanicus begins to be more strongly felt, and becomes predominant in Book 4.

Further patterns in the arrangement of the elegies can also be perceived, and Book 3 is particularly significant from this point of view. It opens with three long elegies, the first of which is dedicated to Ovid's wife and tackles the duties of the poet's *bona coniunx* by utilizing a didactic perspective which recodifies the teachings of the *Ars.* Within the context of the celebration of true friendship, the second elegy recounts the events already narrated in *Iphigenia among the Taurians* by Euripides. In the third elegy, Love himself takes center stage, appearing to his ill-fated *magister* to exculpate him and invite him to have trust and confidence, as the triumph of the Emperor has ushered in a period of joyfulness. This leads into the subject of the fourth elegy, which provides a fresh description of the triumph, but this time accompanied by some thoughts on the limits that the condition of an exile imposes on the celebratory poetry the writer wishes to compose. The next epistle, 3.5, is dedicated to Cotta Maximus, the friend whose presence is felt most keenly throughout the letters from exile. This epistle focuses once again on the theme of absence: Cotta has sent him the text of an oration he delivered in the Forum, and Ovid regrets having been unable to attend so that he could listen to the very words in his friend's own voice. The subject of *nouitas* ('novelty') in literary production is therefore at the heart of both this poem and 3.4.

The final sequence is extremely interesting. The sixth elegy is dedicated to a friend who does not wish to be explicitly mentioned. Therefore, it explores the problems posed by the choice which lies at the very basis of the composition of the *Epistulae ex Ponto*. In the seventh poem, the exile announces he will no longer send his friends entreaties and prayers: rather, he is determined to die courageously in the lands of the Getae. Scholars, who are always in search of demonstrations of heroism, appreciated this epistle even when Ovid's critical reception was at its lowest ebb. The poem is fraught with tragic overtones, which add to the expressive potential of the elegy. Placed before the epilogue, which is addressed to Brutus and tackles the themes of poetics, which pervade the collection, there is a short note to Paullus Fabius Maximus which is intended to accompany, in an overtly metaliterary gesture, a present that is emblematic of the situation in Tomis: bow and arrows.

The collection *Pont.*1–3 is extremely homogeneous and features a situation which undergoes no evolution. As it focuses on its dedicatees, it represents the various ways in which Ovid seeks to relate his current situation to the different personalities of the individuals to whom he addresses his letters. The most salient public event mentioned is Tiberius' triumph (achieved with the participation of Germanicus), which is awarded the most prominent position and upon which many of the instructions given by Ovid are centered.

The one and only diachronic element can be found in 3.7, the *renuntiatio querelae*, which may suggest an interesting parallel with Propertius. At the end of Book 3 (24–5), Propertius pronounces a *renuntiatio amoris*: he declares he no longer loves Cynthia. The end of their love obviously means the end of the work. Something similar was presented in Book 3 of the *Amores* (11), although the effect was more muted and the development of the poem showed a different manner of elaboration.

Hypothetically, two further parallels may be found, albeit very tentatively, between the structure of the *Epistulae ex Ponto* and Propertius' work. Thus, in *Pont.* 3.3, the poet experiences a nocturnal vision of Love, though the conjecture that this apparition may be a dream is not fully dispelled. In Prop. 3.3, Apollo gives the poet apposite instructions on poetics in a dream. *Pont.* 3.4, another epistle that focuses on Tiberius' triumph—seen from the point of view of its poetic rendition and of the problems this creates for the exile—forms a parallel with Prop. 3.4, which is the representation of an 'elegiac triumph', where the poet is content to simply cheer the parade as he stands beside his ladylove. The two elegies share the prophetic vision of the forthcoming triumph heralded by the poet. Propertius, who will be present, is to be its dispassionate bard. Ovid, against his will, is destined to be far from the scene and unable to take part in it.

Structure and Themes: *Pont.* 4

It is a commonly held view that Book 4 was published posthumously. This opinion is based on the length of the book and its lack of the carefully woven system of symmetries which can be found in *Pont.* 1–3. As a matter of fact, however, these elements merely highlight the differences between this collection and the preceding one (Holzberg 2002: 193) and no sign of incompleteness is to be found.

The structure of the book is rather clear. The first epistle is addressed to Sextus Pompeius, as is epistle 15, and both are so closely linked by shared themes and images that they can be considered complementary. The last epistle (16), the only one dedicated to Cotta Maximus, features the apostrophe to Envy (*Livor*) as well as the list of famed Roman poets who were Ovid's contemporaries, with regard to whom he highlights the great renown he enjoyed. This epistle clearly has a special status; furthermore, it seems to evince a sense of closure which is too evident to be constrained within Book 4 only, as is also the case for *Tr.* 4.10. In addition, this elegy also possesses considerable documentary value since on numerous occasions its references to various authors mentioned in the poem constitute the only remaining testimony of their works. It is also worth noting that 4.8, in the honorary central position, addresses some basic poetical issues, besides extolling the value of poetry. The preceding elegy (7) and the following one (9) provide an eloquent account of the perils of living in the Pontus, but they are mainly centered on the celebration of Vestalis' virtues as a warrior and of the consulates of Graecinus and Flaccus. The consulate is a central topic of the fourth composition, where Fame foretells the consulate of Sextus Pompeius, as well as of the fifth, which describes him entrusted with the full powers of the Consul. *Elegy* 4.7, with its *arma* that were foreshadowed by references to the confrontation in the Forum in which Brutus is involved (4.6.29–36), constitutes a significant exploration of the boundaries of this genre, as is also the case, within didactic, for 4.10.

Among the recipients of these epistles there figure persons not encountered previously. A significant shift of Ovid's attention is perceived, which is now centered on Germanicus, to whom the new dedication of the *Fasti* is addressed. The young prince, a poet himself, becomes the member of the imperial family on whom the exile sets his hopes. *Pont.* 1–3 partly anticipates this change: in 2.1, Ovid directly addresses him (49), while in 2.5 Ovid describes the young prince's skills as an eloquent speaker. In Book 4, Germanicus plays a crucial role: he is the real protagonist of 4.8 (which is dedicated to Suillius, the pedagogue of his children), and the majority of the other recipients are in fact part of Germanicus' circle. Significantly, there is no further mention of Messallinus, a *nobilis* who was closely linked to Tiberius. However, Graecinus is still present with one epistle which, as already mentioned, testifies to his long-lasting influence and that of his brother Pomponius Flaccus, a member of Tiberius' inner circle. Ovid had chosen which side to support, and was determinedly coherent with his choice. He did not live long enough to realize that his plans were not well thought out.

Interesting considerations are raised by the manner of presentation of the death and apotheosis of Augustus, although it should be borne in mind that Ovid had written a specific work on this issue (*Pont.* 4.6.18). The death of the Princeps, which is set alongside that of Paullus Fabius Maximus, is said to have been caused, in a completely 'egocentric' perspective, by Fate's relentless assault against the poet: the old Emperor was about to have mercy on the exile, and therefore he passed away. In 4.8.63–4, the apotheosis itself is presented as a product of poetry, and is included in a line of events beginning with the origin of the cosmos: in a sense, this is the further development of the final part of *Metamorphoses*. In 4.13, where Ovid sets forth the content of the *Geticus libellus*, he maintains he made clear to his audience the divine nature of Augustus' soul (25–6). (The brief mention of 4.12.39–40, where it is apparently assumed that he is still alive, does not seem to be significant.) When the presence of Augustus can no longer be of assistance, it effectively dissolves: instead, it is the poet who has the last word on him, even though it is motivated by opportunism.

This collection actualizes what was already observed in the first three books of the *Epistulae ex Ponto*: one notes a considerable expansion of the scope of celebratory compositions, as well as the final and strongly emphasized reintroduction of the greatness and importance of the art of poetry. All this stands side by side with a strikingly innovative tone with which the now elderly Ovid can still amaze us.

The Recipients

Ovid is endeavoring to set in motion a strategy of persuasion designed to ensure him a milder place of exile—he seems to have abandoned all hope of returning to Rome. The existence of this practical objective is of crucial importance for the poetic production of his late years, and it cannot be ignored. Of course, these compositions give voice to complex feelings—how else could it be? Augustus' attitude toward him could not but be called into question, and there is undeniably an appeal for a more positive reappraisal of the poetic production the Princeps had judged so sternly.

Yet there seems to be little room for an attack on power. In the end, this consideration shades into something more in the nature of an act of faith or a prejudice: however, it is better to state it overtly. It is not a question of being either in favor of or against Augustus: the necessity the poet finds himself confronted with has to be acknowledged.

Ovid sent his correspondents prose letters (*Pont.* 4.2.5–6) which were clearly reserved for private correspondence. The decision to compose and publish elegiac epistles was determined by his status as a formerly successful author who could still count on a number of affectionate readers (Citroni 1995: 431–59). His recipients, who thus are well-known figures on the public scene—from his wife to the powerful persons with whom he was probably less well acquainted such as Fabius Maximus or Messallinus—ought, in Ovid's perspective, to conform to certain well-defined ethical models. The models he offers—the good wife, the good friend, and the good patron—display before our eyes a panoply of characters embodying the fundamental moral values of the Augustan age, on which more is said below. Ovid's recipients are presented as if they were the repositories of morally unquestionable gifts who cannot refrain from acting accordingly. The underlying rationale of this approach betrays something akin to a blackmail, making a new use of poetry's immortalizing power and thus producing a new kind of courtship poetry, *werbende Dichtung* (Stroh 1971: 250–3). Among the elements underlying elegiac poetry there was the promise of eternal fame made by the poet to his beloved: rich suitors could be defeated by the poor poet purely through the might of this weapon. Now he is promising the persons he is addressing that their behavior will be eternalized through his lines—and this means good, but conceivably also bad, behavior. A further variation presupposing and, indeed, confirming this basic principle is to be found in Book 4, in an epistle to an ungrateful friend who has deserted him (3): Ovid is not willing to reveal the friend's name in order to ensure that the addressee does not benefit by obtaining any kind of celebrity (3–4): 'I won't utter the name lest my grievances should recommend you and you derive fame from my poem.' The exile produces a poetry of *mores* where he himself is the touchstone: he is in difficulty, and his friends must prove to have moral virtues and fulfill their duties toward him.

Of course, Ovid must present his request as absolutely legitimate and therefore he insists on the non-compromising character of his guilt, which can bring ruin to no one save to himself who bears the stain of guilt. Anyone who provides him with assistance has nothing to fear and may therefore fulfill his duties toward the ill-fated poet without concern. Furthermore, as is overtly stated from the start in Book 1 of the *Tristia* (9.23–36), Augustus approves of the feeling of devotion and the sense of duty toward a friend, even in his enemies (Citroni Marchetti 2000: 325–9).

The pattern of events presented to us is further enriched by the fact that the recipients of the *Epistulae ex Ponto* are often active members of literary society and are duty-bound to demonstrate their loyalty to the exile, all the more so because in the past the latter involved them in the production of writings, which are therefore flawless thanks to their very testimony, even though it may be implicit. This gives a vivid portrayal of literary composition in Rome, depicting the lively and close relationship among the poets. The commitment involved in the elaboration of a friend's poetic work is very concretely and effectively conveyed. Retrospectively, this attitude takes on a strong moral component: if a work of art was the cause of the exile, then the fact of having contributed to it entails a degree of joint responsibility. That is precisely the reason why Ovid shows on numerous occasions that his lines gained him appreciation as well as criticism, and that he responded to critical assessments by making changes to his poems, thus putting into practice what his friends had told him. That is to say, his friends had acted as well-wishers but with appropriate severity. In this manner, Ovid partly reproposes the complex issue of the distinction between friend and flatterer, one of the most significant illustrations of which is to be found in the character of Quintilius by Horace in *Ars Poetica* 438–52. Those who previously read his compositions did not restrict themselves to unreserved praise, or an attitude of compliant patronizing, as a flatterer would do. Rather, they also admonished and corrected him, thus taking their task seriously and behaving as true friends: and this was all the more reason for them to feel duty-bound to come to the aid of an exiled friend.

A confirmation of this manner of pleading his case is found in the topic of the poets' *communia sacra* (2.10.17), which sets forth the image of the *collegium scribarum histrionumque* at a symbolic and metaphorical level. Harking back to ideas that once again can be traced to Horace, poets are represented as a group of people characterized by strong ties and ideally supposed to be committed to solidarity and sympathy (White 1993: 47–8), though this is rather obviously a significant embroidery on reality. It is the same principle which, suitably adapted, is put into action with regard to his powerful friends: Ovid strongly emphasizes the institutional side of his relation with the figures he is addressing, perhaps endowing them with a more upstanding character than their true colors. To some extent, his desire to create a network of sound relationships and strong ties that would allow him to put forward his requests with some hope of receiving an answer is quite natural. This seems to suggest—and herein lies perhaps the most interesting feature—the existence of a veritable hierarchy of feelings pointing in two directions: Ovid's attitude and state of mind toward his *nobiles amici* are typical of those of friends toward the imperial *domus*, and forms of interpersonal relations typical of court society are already prefigured. By this stage, the aristocracy was clearly subordinate to the Emperor, who in turn constituted the yardstick against which to measure one's ambitions and goals. What is more, the pair of friends (i.e. Ovid and his recipient), whose relationship could be simply a superficial social contact or an extremely deep companionship, were inevitably affected by the disrupting necessity of having to take Augustus into account as a point of reference. The pair of friends, whose models are to be found in myth, had to reckon with what has been called the 'third character', who is a source of problems and alters the dynamics in the relationship between the two (Citroni Marchetti 2000: 345–68). Loyalty must be shown first and foremost to Augustus, and Ovid is a master in dramatically representing this through Cotta Maximus' reaction to the news of his exile: Cotta Maximus' first reaction was a righteous ire no less indignant than that felt by Augustus himself (2.3.61–2); but when he learned about the reasons behind his friend's disgrace, he wept at the mistakes his friend had made (65–6). Therefore, Ovid can seek Cotta Maximus' help because he presented the latter not only as a model of loyalty but also as the very hypostasis of the Emperor's spirit.

The Poetry of *Mores* and the Role of Augustus

In seeking to analyze Ovid's late poetic production, the very fact of its tendency to communicate behavioral models allows us to gain insight into the realities of the late Augustan age, while at the same time becoming aware of some of its innovative aspects. Significantly, this late poetic production anticipates several of the themes that would recur in the poetry of the following imperial period.

Ovid, who is experiencing an extreme situation, projects onto his past the rules he needs now. His former environment is reshaped on the basis of a configuration where mutual obligations and duties are of crucial importance. Therefore, what we find is a redefinition, albeit partial, of Roman high society, to which the traditional values that are supposed to be the foundation of its morality apply. Just as is the case with Horace's *Epistles*, here too one could speak of the poetry of *mores*, though it is not characterized by a personal and problematic approach but tends instead to adapt the individual to a previously defined paradigm. In a sense, it might even be said that one could hardly imagine a 'more Augustan' form of poetic composition than this poetry from exile, which portrays individuals endowed with the virtues the Emperor would wish them to have.

Augustus himself acts as the guarantor of this morality but, at the same time, he himself is likewise reminded of the duties proceeding from his role, the public image he has built up for his own figure and his own virtues. In a sense, he too is required to act according to the needs imposed by the construction of his persona. Here one may perceive a sort of challenge by the exile: since in any manifestation of his power, Augustus has insisted on declaring himself *clemens*, he must therefore apply the *clementia* he claims to embody (Mader 1991: 147–9). Of course, Ovid has to approach the Princeps in an extremely cautious manner, and in so doing he displays an almost frantic endeavor to shield himself from harm. A significant example can be seen in the concept used by Ovid to explain Augustus' attitude toward him, depicted as poised between opposing forces, yet reluctant to punish, analogous to Jupiter, who often thunders without striking with his flash of lightning (e.g. *Tr.* 2.33–4, *Pont.* 2.2.116). This has been interpreted as the probable development of an Apollonian element in the ideology of princedom (Lechi 1988). Naturally, there is an obvious opposition between the overt avowal of such clemency and the wrath exhibited in punishing the poet's *error*, and this opposition underlies all the problems of exile, be it poetic exile or otherwise. Ovid was punished—this is indisputable—by a *numen iratum*—and this might seem a univocally negative characterization. But the god was rightly angry with him (*merito*). Further oppositions of this kind can be found in the *Epistulae ex Ponto*: the entire world enjoys the *pax Augusta* save for that corner of land where the exile is now spending his life. Indeed, the necessity springing from the request for a different place of exile effectively highlights the limits of the Empire. Ovid has experienced the true state of affairs and begs the Prince to conform to the representation, to the 'propaganda'. The reality/fiction dialectic that extends throughout Ovid's *oeuvre* is thus brought to a paradoxical conclusion precisely in the poems from exile: the poet of forms is working to endow them with the substance of reality.

Present Poetry and Future Poetry

Ovid presents his call from the exile not only as a necessity Augustus must bow to by virtue of the coherent behavior the Emperor should display but also as a demonstration that he intends to offer something positive in exchange: upon his return, Ovid will be the bard of Augustus' regime and will purge his own poetry of the ambiguities that appeared to underlie such works as the *Ars*. He provides significant examples of this production, the signal example being 2.1, the poem dedicated to Tiberius' triumph, where Ovid repeats the narration of the events as Fame had recounted them to him. Examples from Book 4 of *Epistulae ex Ponto* include the fourth and ninth elegies, the inaugural celebrations for the consulates of Sextus Pompeius (to whose public activity 4.5 is also dedicated) and Graecinus. It is therefore occasional poetry, a new poetry of the city with marked characteristics of panegyric, although it can be seen as basically developing characteristics already present in erotic elegy (Labate 1987: 104).

The exile is therefore now facing a specific problem: how can he write an occasional poem if he is not present? Epistle 3.4 of *Epistulae ex Ponto*, to Rufinus, is in fact devoted to some considerations on this task in the framework of Ovid's role as a poet. One can rely on the intermediation of Fame, as in *Pont.* 2.1, or, to some extent, in 4.4, but an important aspect is the emphasis placed on the inspired mental vision, a theme that is pervasively present in many of the elegies from exile. Ovid feels he is possessed by an *enthousiasmos* which in some sense compensates for his inability to be present in person and for the lack of visual contact with the monarch. He is a *uates* who foreshadows the events so that he may experience them in the first person despite being far away (*Pont.* 3.4.87–114). Celebrations, which call for this high degree of inspiration, exploit the very same general principle that lies at the basis of epistle writing itself. Unknowingly, friends pay visits to the exiled poet, and, just as he goes to Rome, so they come to the Pontus and are made present by means of a mental force which might well be compared to the force of Lucretius' Epicurus and of Pythagoras in the *Metamorphoses*. Thus, in the elegies from exile there is a further and suggestive development of the theme of illusion/reality/disillusionment, which is one of the cardinal issues in the whole of Ovid's poetry (Hardie 2002c: 307–15). This opens up a pathway toward a fuller appreciation of this poetry, which seems forever in need of deliverance.

The acclaim this poetry has today finally achieved exempts us from the need to add to it in order to transform Ovid into an indomitable opponent of the regime, one who launched a whispered assault on imperial power through a system of sarcastic allusions. That he justifies his poetic creation by pointing to its potential usefulness for him is in stark contrast with the damage which, the poet accusingly adds, was inflicted on him by his *Ars amatoria*. But now, the three books of the *Epistulae ex Ponto* are fully capable of filling the gap left by the removal of the *Ars* from the

libraries (1.1.11–12). It is as though Ovid sought to offer us a completely irreproach-
able *Ars amicitiae* in place of an *Ars amatoria* that had given rise to such misunder-
standings (Claassen 1999a: 120). However, his relationship with the work on which
the blame had been laid is rather complex. Suffice it to say that the indications Ovid
gives his recipients, and his wife in particular, concerning the manner of approaching
Augustus are in effect a recodification of the *Ars*. Furthermore, the poetry from exile
is anything but monolithic, as it was developed over many years (Claassen 1988: 163)
and there is a noticeable difference between the way Ovid discusses the imperial guilty
verdict in Book 2 of the *Tristia* versus the way he celebrates the delivery of the object
(most probably a relief or a group of three small statues, but it might also have been
a coin) with the busts of the three main members of the imperial family (Augustus,
Tiberius, and Livia) in *Pont.* 2.8.

Ovid's Character and the World of the Exile

Ovid further pursues the construction of his persona, which was already a feature of
the *Tristia*: he himself makes his entry as an author and a character in the fictional
world, which thus takes on special traits. Ovid remains an elegiac poet whose poetry
is the direct and immediate expression of life, according to a model still drawn from
Tibullus and Propertius, which had been the object of the clever literary game of the
Amores. All the defects exposed in his production are a reflection of his wretchedness.
Life is monotonous, and so is poetry. Life is generally horrible, and poetry can hardly
be different. The quality of the lines composed is a metaphor of existence, and must
be acknowledged as such. Even today, one is amazed at how readily the least sympathetic critics have opted for a literal interpretation of the poet's statements, to the
point that a detailed defense has been called for even in relatively recent times
(Williams 1994: 50–91). In order to give voice to a new state of affairs, the poetry
from exile must therefore offer us a new configuration of the literary universe. The
landscape surrounding him is the wintry Scythic environment of the *Georgics* (3.349–
83: Williams 1994: 10–25), which is depicted through very effective stylistic features—such as the sequence of negations—which were to prove a highly successful
choice. But it is the very essence of Ovid's experience that is structured according to
the scheme of his previous works, and of elegy in particular, from the *Amores* to the
Heroides. The mechanisms governing the events in the lives of literary characters are
unveiled (Lechi 1993: 15–31), and Ovid assumes a position of superiority vis-à-vis
these figures: for none of them has suffered what he has gone through. Indeed, as
early as the *Amores* it can be noted that the poet already contemplated the idea of
playing with the rules of the elegiac world and the intention of revealing their functioning. In the exile poetry the poet acquires the status of a mythical character, the
protagonist of both *epos* and tragedy. In this regard, the experience of the *Heroides*
cannot be overestimated. Besides all else, the *Heroides* successfully feature a poetics
of repetitiveness—or, if we consider it from a positive perspective, of variation on a
theme. Compared to the *Heroides*, the *Epistulae ex Ponto* also exhibit a practical
motive, the need to bombard the recipients with his calls for help and impress the

question on their minds (*Pont.* 3.9.39–42). The rhetoric of repetitiveness therefore can be seen as an outcome of the rhetoric of sincerity: literature reflects reality without mediation, that is to say, by means of its own mechanisms and not through the mere recording of anecdotes (Cucchiarelli 1997). It is in this sense that life in exile, in its concrete and objective manifestations, actualizes the momentous flow of events and, indeed, goes beyond the heightened reality of literary forms. Of course, a certain degree of evolution during his exile can also be perceived. Thus, at the opening of the *Tristia* (1.1), Ovid presents the sudden change in the aspect of his lot as a possible addition to the poem of the *Metamorphoses* (119–20). On the other hand, in the *Epistulae ex Ponto*, Niobe and the Heliades are the object of a paradoxical *makarismos* (1.2.29–32): by turning into stone and poplars, they lost their ability to suffer. Ovid, by contrast, can undergo no metamorphosis: even Medusa would lose her powers (33–6). In this case, we can see the elucidation of one of the fundamental mechanisms of the structure of the *Metamorphoses*, where transformation excludes tragedy. But Ovid cannot experience this solution, the sole aim of his life being the perpetuation of suffering, which can be compared only to the pains of the great damned of the Afterworld: Tityus' liver is never consumed, so that he may continue to suffer (37–40).

Even in his exile, then, the world in which Ovid is living is modeled on and by poetry, and it is no coincidence that in the very last book of the *Epistulae ex Ponto*, in a composition vicariously addressing Germanicus (4.8), we find a passage extolling poetic creation that is one of his most passionate pieces of writing. It starts (51, *scriptis Agamemnona nosti*) with a reference to Hor. *Carm.* 4.9.25–8: many lived before Agamemnon, but they remained unknown because there was no poet to celebrate them. This leads in to a momentous concept: it is poetry that endows individuals with existence, shapes the universe, and to some extent even creates the gods, among whom stands Augustus himself (55–64). In short, a veritable new role is created for what had been one of the central themes of Ovid's poetry ever since he composed the *Amores*.

In the context of the rereading *sub specie litterarum* of life in exile, it is of interest also to address the problem of Getic poetry. For Ovid, being a Getic poet is one of the traits that becomes most prominent in his new poetry, suffusing it with a decadent tone. Learning the language of the barbarians implies being overwhelmed by the new situation and despairing of ever returning home or being transferred to a different place. Yet here, too, one may identify certain features that suggest an evolution. In 4.13, Ovid writes to his friend Carus stating he has composed a poem in the Getic language, which he recited before an audience of barbarians: it was a poem where he praised the late lamented Augustus and the imperial family. The Getae showed their approval and maintained that, by virtue of such works, he should be reintegrated into his homeland. There has been much debate over the existence of this poem, composed by a figure who would thus have been the 'first Romanian poet'. It seems unlikely that Ovid would have had to learn the language of the Getae in a town where the most educated inhabitants were Greek. Rather, here Ovid aims to present himself as the member of a loyalist elite who, in the most distant provinces, acts as the spokesperson upholding the values and interests of the imperial family. At one point, he even mentions the shrine he consecrated to Augustus, Livia, and Tiberius, along with Drusus and Germanicus (4.9.105–12). The Getae are an audience who, paradoxically, represent the final judgment against which there is no appeal: if even the barbarian living far from Roman civilization realizes that the poet should be allowed to return to his homeland by virtue of his writings on Augustus (4.13.37–8), how can such an aspiration be denied him in Rome?

The *Epistulae ex Ponto* concludes with the elegy where Ovid celebrates his victory over envy and offers us, evidently with self-congratulatory intent, a list of the poets of his generation. This is a powerful statement of self-awareness and confidence in himself and in his art: by virtue of its position, it molds the whole collection.

This collection not only has the aim of positively reappraising the values of poetic creation but also comprises some compositions where poetry is approached with a tone of disenchantment, but a tone that is distinct from the rejection he had mentioned in the past. Apart from a number of elegies influenced by their specific function, such as 3.7, there are some moments that are quite striking in the disillusionment to which they bear witness. Lonely and isolated, tormented by boredom, Ovid wonders (4.2.45–6):

> quid, nisi Pierides, solacia frigida, restant,
> non bene de nobis quae meruere deae?

> what is left for me if not the Pierides, cold comfort,
> goddesses who have not deserved well of me?

Not only were the Muses one reason behind the sentence pronounced against the poet, they also have little more than cold ineffective comfort to offer as consolation. His dejection seems total in this daily life, where Ovid is imagined as simply in search of a way to while away the time. Of course, the scholar cannot judge the sincerity of a statement, but only the manner in which the poet builds his own character. One is not obliged, however, to stifle feelings and be insensible to the force stemming from this total disenchantment.

FURTHER READING

Today, the standard editions of the *Epistulae ex Ponto* are Richmond (1990) and Pérez Vega (2000). Other editions that are authoritative or significant for the history of the text in the twentieth century are: Owen (1915), Lenz (1938), and André (1977). There are commentaries by Helzle on Books 1–2 (2003) and 4.1–7, 16 (1989), Scholte on Book 1 (1933), Gaertner on Book 1 (2005), Galasso on Book 2 (1995), and Staffhorst on Book 3.1–3 (1965). The translations and studies cited for the *Tristia* (Chapter 13) include the *Epistulae ex Ponto* as well. Froesch (1968) and Syme (1978) are still extremely useful, while Labate (1987) offers an innovative approach. The eight articles in *Ramus* 26 (1997), a volume on the poetry from exile, are also worth consulting.

CHAPTER FIFTEEN

Lost and Spurious Works

Peter E. Knox

Lost Works

When did it become impossible to read the elegies of Gallus? Who was the last owner of a copy of Ennius' *Annales*? In the fluid and informal circumstances of the book trade in antiquity, it was distressingly common for the work of even a very prominent author to go out of circulation and eventually disappear, as we know from the number of important titles that were no longer available to readers even in late antiquity. Ovid's works were not immune from the vagaries of book production in the ancient world, and we hear of several works from his stylus that are no longer accessible to us. How much, or how little, we might have to learn about him as a writer from any of these works is a matter of pure conjecture. Ovid is himself the source for most of what we know, or think we know, about his works that have not survived. As was often the case, the most vulnerable to loss were works of the poet's youth. In Ovid's case we learn, from an epigram prefixed to the *Amores* in the manuscript tradition, of an earlier five-book edition, no trace of which otherwise survives:

> Qui modo Nasonis fueramus quinque libelli,
>   tres sumus; hoc illi praetulit auctor opus.
> ut iam nulla tibi nos sit legisse uoluptas,
>   at leuior demptis poena duobus erit.

> We who just before had been five books of Naso now are three; the author preferred this version to the former. Though even now there may be no pleasure in reading us, at least with two books subtracted your pain will be lighter.

Such is the state of the evidence that some scholars even doubt whether this original edition existed (Holzberg 1997: 33). If indeed Ovid's earliest elegies were released in five books, there might be much to learn from the decisions he made in reducing them to three, which he evidently did in fairly short order, since he later refers only to the three-book edition (*Ars* 3.343–4). Was this a process of amalgamation and rearrangement only, as some scholars believe (e.g. Cameron 1968)? Or were new poems included, as the consensus of scholarly opinion would have it (e.g. Hollis 1977: 150–1)? It is perhaps a mark of the slight interest shown in Ovid by ancient scholars that none of them seized the opportunity to display his erudition by citing from the first edition, that is if the first edition even outlived Ovid.

Ovid also refers several times to his one effort in dramatic composition (*Am.* 2.18.13–18 3.1.23–30, 67–70, 3.15.17–20; *Tr.* 2.553–4), the tragedy *Medea*, and for this work we have the corroborating testimony of Quintilian, who admired the play very much, considering it an illustration of his squandered potential (*Inst.* 10.1.98): 'It seems to me that Ovid's *Medea* shows just how much that man could have offered if he had preferred to govern his talent rather than indulge it' (*si ingenio suo imperare quam indulgere maluisset*). By reputation Ovid's *Medea* was coupled with the only other memorable tragedy of the Augustan period, the *Thyestes* of L. Varius Rufus, also lost (Tac. *Dial.* 12.6). Only two fragments of Ovid's play were quoted in ancient sources, one by the Elder Seneca (*Suas.* 3.7 *feror huc illuc, ut plena deo*, 'I wander here and there, as if full of the god') and the other by Quintilian (*Inst.* 8.5.6 *seruare potui: perdere an possim rogas?*, 'I was able to rescue you: do you ask if I can destroy you?'). Ovid did not stake his reputation on his dramatic prowess, but surely he is engaging in characteristic self-deprecating irony when he refers to his earlier theatrical work from exile (*Tr.* 5.7.27–8):

> nil equidem feci—tu scis hoc ipse—theatris,
>   Musa nec in plausus ambitiosa mea est.

> I have done nothing for the theater, as you yourself know, nor is my Muse ambitious for applause.

A complete tragedy would be an attractive addition to the Ovidian corpus, not least for the sake of comparison with other treatments of Medea in *Her.* 12, *Met.* 7, and Seneca's later tragedy on the same theme (Leo 1878: 166–70).

One of the most popular works of Greek Hellenistic poetry, the *Phaenomena* of Aratus (ca. 315–240 BCE), was translated several times by Roman writers, with versions by Cicero and Germanicus Caesar known from the late Republic and early Empire, and it was a work that Ovid knew well and exploited in his *Fasti* (Gee 2000). But there is some evidence to suggest that Ovid's interest in Aratus was also manifested in a translation or adaptation. Two late antique sources, pseudo-Probus on Virg. *G.* 1.138 and Lactantius (*Inst.* 2.5.24), quote from an otherwise unknown translation (fr. 3–4 Lenz = 1–2 Blänsdorf = 1–2 Courtney), which they attribute to Ovid. No contemporary evidence from Ovid supports this attribution, but none refutes it either, although one may harbor some doubts about the legitimacy of such an ascription in the fourth century CE. It would indeed be surprising if this work by Ovid had survived so long only to otherwise entirely vanish then from the record.

The attack of the Giants on the Gods was also an extremely popular theme in Greek literature and art (Vian 1952), which may have been handled by Ovid in another lost work. The only *testimonium* is Ovid's own declaration in the *Amores* (2.1.11–16):

ausus eram, memini, caelestia dicere bella
   centimanumque Gygen (et satis oris erat),
cum male se Tellus ulta est ingestaque Olympo
   ardua deuexum Pelion Ossa tulit.
in manibus nimbos et cum Ioue fulmen habebam,
   quod bene pro caelo mitteret ille suo.

I had dared, I remember, to tell of the wars of heaven—and I had the voice for it—and
Gyas of the hundred hands, when Earth botched her attempt at revenge and steep Ossa
bore sloping Pelion and was piled on Olympus. I had the thunder clouds in my hands,
and Jupiter with his lightning bolt, which he would fire on target in defense of his own
heaven.

Among the Augustans the topic recurs as typical of the kind of theme rejected by
Roman poets following the example of Callimachus (Nisbet and Hubbard 1978:
189–91), and one likely explanation for the reference in these lines is that Ovid's
Gigantomachy was no more a reality than Virgil's epic on the Alban kings, conjured
up by ancient critics to account for his claim to have written on 'kings and battles'
(*Ecl.* 6.3 *reges et proelia*). Most modern scholars remain extremely skeptical about the
existence of this poem (McKeown 1998: 10–11), and it seems quite unlikely that
such a poem, had it ever been released to the public, would have escaped notice as
the only Latin example of the species.

   In his exile poetry, Ovid refers to several examples of occasional verse, none of
which survives: a wedding song for Paullus Fabius Maximus (*Pont.* 1.2.131); an *epicedion* for the death of his one-time patron, Messalla Corvinus (*Pont.* 1.7.30); a
panegyric on the Pannonian triumph celebrated by Tiberius late in 12 CE (*Pont.* 3.4);
and an *epicedion* for the death of the emperor Augustus (*Pont.* 4.6.17, 9.131). In
addition, Ovid refers to another poem on the death of Augustus in praise of the
imperial family composed in Getic, the local language of his place of exile in Tomi
(*Pont.* 4.13.19–36). How much credence one is to invest in such professions by Ovid
varies according to one's critical orientation toward the exile poetry. That Ovid did
produce occasional verse is certainly credible; that much of it long survived the
occasion for which it was composed, perhaps less so. Ovid's frequent references to
such poetry could only serve as an incentive to a host of other attributions to him
by ancient sources quoting without the benefit of a secure bibliography (fr. 3–18
Blänsdorf; fr. 3–16 Courtney).

   Two other losses from the corpus of Ovid's works may be attributed to different
circumstances, the one to the vagaries of the medieval manuscript tradition, the other
perhaps to imperial ire. Only a fragment survives of the didactic poem that Ovid
recommends to women readers of the third book of the *Ars* (3.205–6). The *Medicamina faciei femineae* is transmitted separately from the other didactic elegies, its
text being chiefly represented by one eleventh-century codex. The poem breaks off
after a hundred lines, and it is not clear how much has been lost, but it is likely that
the text extended a few hundred lines beyond the surviving fifty couplets (Rosati
1995: 43–5). The truncated condition of the *Fasti*, which ends with the sixth of a

projected twelve books, has been variously explained. Ovid himself asserts that he completed all twelve books—*sex ego Fastorum scripsi totidemque libellos* ('six books of *Fasti* and as many more have I written', *Tr.* 2.549)—but most modern scholars doubt that *Fast.* 7–12 ever passed out of Ovid's hands, and surmise that in any event the revision of the work that he began in exile was abandoned when he lost faith in the prospects for recall (Herbert-Brown 1994: 204–12).

Doubtful Works from Antiquity

The same circumstances of the Roman book trade that sometimes made the survival of a writer's works a precarious proposition also made it rather easy for a text to be falsely attributed to someone other than its real author. In fact, Cicero relied on these circumstances when he asked his friend Atticus (*Att.* 3.12.2) to help him claim that a pamphlet that he had in fact written was actually a forgery (Starr 1987: 219). More commonly a work that bore a generic resemblance to a well-known author's might be ascribed to him, not out of any intent to foist an imposture on the unsuspecting reading public but out of a simple error of attribution. This might occur, for example, with rhetorical exercises in which the writer is assuming the persona of a famous author, as with the pseudo-Ciceronian speech against Sallust. Poems written by some unknown practitioner in the manner of a great poet might also be taken for the real thing, as with some of the works transmitted in the *Appendix Vergiliana*. Outright forgery, though hardly unknown in antiquity (Speyer 1971), is not usually at issue in such cases. Ovid's influence on the style of later poets was immense, and it is certainly the case that some surviving poems that were ascribed to him in antiquity are now generally acknowledged as spurious, while still others are, with varying degrees of probability, suspected of being so.

Included in this group are some poems transmitted together with Ovid's works that have been suspected as spurious for a variety of reasons, including some combination of stylistic anomalies, irregular appearance in the manuscript tradition, or other external circumstances, such as Ovid's own statements. One example is the so-called *Somnium*, transmitted in some, not all, manuscripts as the fifth poem in the third book of the *Amores*, but also circulated independently of the rest of the collection (Kenney 1962: 11–13). This poem represents the poet relating a strange dream he has had to an interpreter: while seeking refuge from the midday heat, the poet spots a white heifer and beside it a bull. A crow glides down through the air and pecks at the heifer's breast, leaving a mark, whereupon the heifer leaves its mate for greener pastures frequented by other bulls. The interpreter explains (3.5.35–44):

> quem tu mobilibus foliis uitare uolebas,
>   sed male uitabas, aestus amoris erat.
> uacca puella tua est: aptus color ille puellae;
>   tu uir et in uacca compare taurus eras.
> pectora quod rostro cornix fodiebat acuto,
>   ingenium dominae lena mouebit anus;

quod cunctata diu taurum sua uacca reliquit,
    frigidus in uiduo destituere toro.
liuor et aduerso maculae sub pectore nigrae
    pectus adulterii labe carere negat.

The heat you wished to avoid beneath the fluttering leaves, but failed to avoid, was the heat of love. The heifer was your girl: that color is fit for a girl. You were her man and bull with a heifer for a mate. The pecking of her breast by the crow's sharp beak meant that a pandering old woman was meddling with your mistress's heart. The fact that the heifer lingered for a long time before leaving her bull was a sign that you will be left cold in a deserted bed. The dark color and the black spots on her breast in front were signs that her heart is not free of the stain of adultery.

The poem's focus on the interpretation of dreams is consonant with widespread interest in the subject in antiquity, and its symbolic interpretation has resonances with other ancient literature on the subject. Although the poem is a relatively polished piece, with many stylistic features consistent with Ovidian authorship, it has nevertheless been argued with considerable persuasiveness that some anomalies simply cannot withstand scrutiny (Kenney 1969a). Other critics have also noted that unlike all the other elegies in the *Amores*, this poem departs from the tradition of Tibullan and Propertian elegy, with which it has little intertextual relationship (McKeown 2002). Of course, not every reader is convinced (e.g. Holzberg 2002: 61) and it is unlikely that any definitive solution can be obtained, given the subjective nature of the evidence. But the circumstances match what we know of literary life in the early empire, when we know of many anonymous poets—and there must have been many more of whom we do not know—who imitated the masters of the Augustan age. Indeed, the *Somnium*, like many other pseudonymous works, may hold more interest for us as 'the independent production of an anonymous elegist rather than as a constituent poem of the *Amores* or the work of Ovid' (Kenney 1968: 7).

Ovid's authorship of some of the poems transmitted in the *Heroides* has also often been questioned. The diverse content of the collection may be divided into three groups: (1) epistles (1–14) from women of myth to their absent lovers or husbands; (2) the *Epistula Sapphus*, a letter from the seventh-century poet Sappho to Phaon; and (3) the so-called 'Double Epistles', three pairs of letters between star-crossed mythical lovers. The Double Epistles are distinguished from the other *Heroides* by their different design from the first part of the collection, as well as by significant stylistic and metrical variations that are largely inconsistent with Ovid's practices as attested in other elegies from the first phase of his career (Kenney 1979). Although skeptics remain, the consensus of scholarly opinion now inclines toward accepting the ascription to Ovid and dating their composition to a later phase of his career, perhaps in the period immediately preceding his exile in 8 CE (Kenney 1996: 20–6).

No such consensus has yet been reached on the *Epistula Sapphus*, which was transmitted in a medieval manuscript tradition separate from the rest of the *Heroides*. When the poem first came to the attention of scholars in the fifteenth century, its authorship was hotly contested, but the early consensus settled on Ovidian authorship, and in the edition of Daniel Heinsius (1629) the poem was set in the position it now occupies in the collection. Apart from the circumstances of its transmission the principal bar to Ovidian authorship in the view of some critics is the dense concentration of non-Ovidian features of language, style, and meter (Tarrant 1981). The situation is complicated by the fact that in a disputed passage in the *Amores* (2.18.26 and 34), Ovid mentions an epistle by Sappho. So, the counterargument runs, the alleged anomalies can be explained on other grounds and, despite the objections of a vocal minority (e.g. Knox 1995: 12–14), many scholars continue to consider the poem as Ovid's.

The authorship of some of the single epistles (*Her.* 1–14) also continues to be disputed, although the consensus in favor of Ovid as author of the entire section is far more solid than in the other parts of the collection. In *Am.* 2.18.21–6 Ovid explicitly refers to at least eight of the *Heroides* (1–2, 4–7, 10–11), and the authenticity of each of the remaining poems has been challenged (Knox 1995: 5–12). Ovidian authorship has been vigorously defended (e.g. Hinds 1993), and very few recent critics now doubt that all of these poems are rightly attributed. The genesis of the collection remains a mystery, since, taken as a whole, it is too long to be accommodated in a single ancient book. If any of the epistles are spurious, they probably did not infiltrate the collection until late antiquity, during the time when parchment codices became the standard format for literature, supplanting the papyrus roll.

Some other works ascribed to Ovid in antiquity reach us through medieval manuscript traditions, in which they have not been integrated with Ovid's authentic works, as happened with *Am.* 3.5 and later with the *Epistula Sapphus*. When writing of the marvels of the sea and marine life, the Elder Pliny (*Nat.* 32.11) referred to a poem called the *Halieutica* ('On Fishing'), which he attributed to Ovid. Pliny believed that Ovid began this poem in Tomi in the last days of his life (*Nat.* 32.152), and a fragment of this work, containing 130 poorly preserved hexameters, survives in one Carolingian manuscript (Reeve 1983). Although some scholars accept this as a genuine work of Ovid's, the more general consensus is that Pliny's attribution is in error (Richmond 1976).

It is highly unlikely that Ovid was the author of another poem of ancient, but suspect, pedigree, the *Nux* (or 'The Walnut Tree'), in ninety-one elegiac couplets. It is transmitted in many medieval manuscripts from the eleventh century onward (Tarrant 1983b), and in language, style, and meter there is little that would be hopelessly inconsistent with an ascription to Ovid. The poem's conceit is an entreaty by a nut tree to passers-by not to pelt it with stones to get its fruit. The elegy elaborates themes found in Greek epigram, such as the address to passers-by typical of sepulchral epigram, and indeed this very theme is found in one epigram (*AP* 9.3) that may be contemporary with Ovid. In this short poem, generally attributed to Antipater of Thessalonica (Gow and Page 1968: 103), an approximate contemporary of Ovid, a nut tree complains that boys throw stones at it to bring down the nuts. A similar lament by a nut tree is found in Aesop (188 Halm). The *Nux* is probably intended as a rhetorical elaboration of this minor theme, and the poem has its wry moments, as when the tree essays a criticism of contemporary *mores*. Once, it laments, trees vied in fruitfulness, but now all honor goes to the barren plane tree, and so (19–24):

nos quoque frugiferae (si nux modo ponor in illis)
    coepimus in patulas luxuriare comas.
nunc neque continuos nascuntur poma per annos,
    uuaque laesa domum laesaque baca uenit;
nunc uterum uitiat quae uult formosa uideri,
    raraque in hoc aeuo est quae uelit esse parens.

We fruit-bearers also (if as a nut-tree I am ranked among them) have begun to luxuriate in spreading foliage. Now fruits do not grow year after year, and grapes and berries come home injured; now the woman who wants to look beautiful harms her womb, and rare in this time is the woman who is willing to be a parent.

Proof of the poem's antiquity, however, is not proof of authorship by Ovid, and the arguments advanced by A. G. Lee (1958) have convinced most scholars that it incorporates imitations of Ovid that would be inconsistent with his authorship, although some few scholars still maintain the attribution to Ovid (Pulbrook 1985). If the poem is not by Ovid, then it is another document in the dossier on the reception of Ovid in antiquity by contemporary, or near-contemporary, poets who were heavily influenced by, and thoroughly absorbed, his manner.

The *Consolatio ad Liuiam* is less securely anchored in antiquity, but there is no reason to suspect, as Moritz Haupt once did (1875: 371–4), that the poem is a Renaissance forgery. This previously unknown poem came to light in the mid-fifteenth century in a manuscript now lost. All the surviving witnesses to the text derive from this source, which was already badly corrupt (Reeve 1976b). The author identifies himself as a Roman knight who was present at the funeral (202) of Drusus, and the manuscripts ascribe the poem to Ovid. The view that it is a Renaissance imposture has been generally rejected, since language, style, and meter all point to composition in antiquity, even though they cannot confirm the Ovidian authorship claimed in the manuscripts. The poem consists of 474 lines addressed to the empress Livia in consolation for the loss of her son.

Early scholars assumed that the *Consolatio* was the poem referred to in the opening lines of the *Elegiae in Maecenatem*, a work set in the immediate aftermath of the death of Maecenas in 8 BCE (Scaliger 1572: 528). It is no longer considered certain that there is a connection between the two poems (Schoonhoven 1980: 57), and there is thus even less reason to date the composition of the *Consolatio* close to the death of Drusus. Most critics agree that a much later date suits the style and treatment of the subject matter. And a considerable amount of internal evidence points in this direction, for example references to the temple of Castor and Pollux (283–4, 287–8) dedicated in 6 CE and imitations of Ovid's *Epistulae ex Ponto*. Indeed, it is difficult to imagine how Livia might have responded to the description of her imagined welcome of Drusus in the opening of the poem (31–6):

iam ueniet, iam me gratantem turba uidebit
    iam mihi pro Druso dona ferenda meo.
obuia progrediar felixque per oppida dicar
    collaque et hoc oculos illius ore premam.
talis erit, sic occurret, sic oscula iunget,
    hoc mihi narrabit, sic prior ipsa loquar.

Soon he will come; soon the crowd will see me giving thanks; soon I must bear gifts for my Drusus' safety. I shall go forth to meet him, and throughout the towns I shall be called fortunate. And with my mouth I shall press his neck and eyes. So shall he be, so shall he rush to meet me, so shall he kiss me. He will tell me this story, so I shall speak to him first.

Emendation of the troubled text of line 34 hardly dampens the erotic overtones of this scene, built as it is upon imitations of amatory elegy. If Ovid (or any other author) truly had presented the empress with this poem in the aftermath of her son's death, it is likely that he would have found himself in Tomi long before 8 CE. If Richmond's surmise (1981: 2780) of a date before the death of Tiberius in 37 CE is correct, then the poem's interest for us is somewhat enhanced as a reflection of the literary climate under his repressive regime.

Medieval and Renaissance Pseudepigrapha

Ovid's emerging status as a model for style in the medieval schoolroom is reflected in an extraordinary number of new poems taking their cue from his works. Medieval collections of Ovid's works frequently include contemporary poems falsely ascribed to him, reflecting not the activity of forgers but the obsession with Ovidian style and expression that increasingly characterized the classrooms of the high Middle Ages. As the number of manuscripts of Ovid's works testify to his increasing popularity among readers, so too do the number of individual poems that were extracted from collections like the *Amores* or *Epistulae ex Ponto* and circulated separately. And so elegies from the *Amores* circulated under titles like *Ovidius de psittaco* ('Ovid on the Parrot') (*Am.* 2.6). Particularly popular was the poem known to us as *Am.* 3.5, which had a life of its own as *Ovidius de Somno*. Whatever doubts one might harbor now about the ascription to Ovid, in the Middle Ages it was regarded as genuine and it inspired imitation in a poem, *De Sompnio*, depicting a struggle among allegorized figures of Death, Anger, Fear, and Misery (Lenz 1968). Inspired perhaps by the pseudo-Virgilian *Culex*, one medieval Ovidian penned a poem on the 'The Flea' (*De Pulice*); another took his inspiration from Ovid's *Medicamina faciei femineae* to write on 'The Treatment of Ears' (*De Medicamine Aurium*). Ovid's status as a source of wisdom in the *Metamorphoses* is reflected in a poem 'On the Wonders of the World' (*De Mirabilibus Mundi*). The number of such poems circulating under Ovid's name is large and many additions can be made to published lists (Lehmann 1927: 89–91).

The relative dearth of information about the details of Ovid's life has been an invitation to the imagination of readers over the centuries, and fictional biographies figure large in the Ovidian reception of the Middle Ages (Trapp 1973) and after. The most ambitious pseudo-Ovidian poem of the Middle Ages comes under this heading, *De Vetula* ('About the Old Woman'), composed in the thirteenth century and presenting itself as the poet's own autobiography, written after he had become convinced that he would not be pardoned. In the prose life prefaced to the poem, doubtless by the same author as the poem, the circumstances of its discovery are described (Klopsch 1967: 193):

> Recently there was discovered in a suburb of the city of Dioscori, capital of the kingdom of Colchis, when certain ancient pagan tombs were being removed from the public cemetery which is beside Tomis, one tomb among the rest, with an epitaph engraved on it in Armenian characters, of which the interpretation goes like this: *Hic iacet Ovidius ingeniosissimus poetarum*. At the head of this tomb an ivory casket was found. In it, unconsumed by the ages, was a book. The local inhabitants, unable to read what was in it, sent it to Constantinople, where there were many 'Latins'. This happened in the time of Prince Vathasius, by whose command the book was handed over to Leo, Protonotary of the Sacred Palace and he, when he had read it over, published and distributed it in many countries.

In the poem that follows, in three books comprising approximately 3000 hexameters (hardly any of which could be recognized as genuine), 'Ovid' gives an account of his life, beginning in the first book with his youth, which was devoted, of course, to his love affairs, but varied with other pursuits, such as hunting, fishing, and games, especially chess. In the second book 'Ovid' relates the story of a love affair gone awry when an old woman, who was to act as a go-between, substituted herself for Ovid's lady at a night-time assignation. The final book is his account of how, disillusioned with love and banished to Tomi, he turned to philosophical studies (3.12–18):

> Sed scio, quid faciam: Studio complectar anelo
> lucem, quam mecum dixi prius esse reclusam,
> lucem doctrine, que rerum sedula causas
> rimatur, sublimis apex in philosophia,
> lucem doctrine, que cum sit celica, terras
> non dedignatur, sed in exilio peregrinat
> isto nobiscum solacia vera ministrans.

> But I know what to do: with breathless enthusiasm I shall embrace the light that I have said was shut within me before—the light of learning, which tirelessly roots out the causes of things, the sublime peak in philosophy; the light of learning, which does not disdain the earth, though it is of heaven, but wanders in this exile with me, administering true consolation.

The poem merits serious study not only as an instance of the medieval reception of Ovid, but as a work in its own right, employing the Ovidian persona to challenge the conventions of thirteenth-century scholasticism (Godman 1995), a stance that the classical poet would have appreciated.

The adoption of an Ovidian persona as a conceit in Latin composition did not end with the Middle Ages. In the edition of Ovid's *Heroides* published by Stefano Corallo in Parma in 1477, three epistles addressed to Penelope, Phyllis, and Oenone are included, described as the work of 'Aulus Sabinus, a celebrated Roman knight and poet'. Although some harbored doubts, until the nineteenth century these poems were often treated as the work of Ovid's friend, whom he describes as writing the earliest responses to the *Heroides* (*Am.* 2.18.27–34):

quam cito de toto rediit meus orbe Sabinus
   scriptaque diuersis rettulit ipse locis!
candida Penelope signum cognouit Vlixis,
   legit ab Hippolyto scripta nouerca suo.
iam pius Aeneas miserae rescripsit Elissae,
   quodque legat Phyllis, si modo uiuit, adest.
tristis ad Hypsipylen ab Iasone littera uenit,
   dat uotam Phoebo Lesbis amata lyram.

How quickly has my Sabinus returned from the ends of the earth and brought back writings from far places. Blameless Penelope has recognized the seal of Ulysses; his stepmother reads what was written by Hippolytus. Now devout Aeneas has written back to wretched Elissa, and a letter is here for Phyllis to read, if only she lives. A sad letter has come from Jason for Hypsipyle, and the woman of Lesbos, now loved, offers to Phoebus the lyre she vowed.

The author of these epistles was in fact the humanist Angelo Sani Di Cure, also known as Angelus Sabinus (Canali 1961), a poet and editor of classical texts. A different epistle from Ulysses to Penelope, also attributed to 'Sabinus', turned up in a humanist manuscript (Meckelnborg and Schneider 2002), perhaps representing the efforts of another precocious scholar, or an earlier work by the same Angelo Sani Di Cure. By observing classical norms in meter and diction and drawing on literary and mythographic resources, scholars such as Sabinus employed imitation as a means of working toward interpretation. Imposture was almost certainly not Sabinus' goal: he refers to his responses to Ovid's *Heroides* in the dedicatory letter of his *Paradoxa* dated 1467. Rather like similarly inspired efforts to flesh out and make sense of the narratives of classical literature—Maffeo Vegio's thirteenth book of the *Aeneid* (Putnam and Hankins 2004) comes to mind—Sabinus takes up the implicit challenge of re-imagining Ovid. Like the imagined Ovid of the medieval *De Vetula*, Sabinus sought to interpret Ovid by reconfiguring his work, a form of reception that Ovid's works still inspire in contemporary artists and writers.

FURTHER READING

A good introduction to the production and circulation of books in the Roman world can be found in Kenney (1982), to be followed up with Reynolds and Wilson (1991). Speyer (1971) is the standard reference work on literary forgery in the ancient world, while Grafton (1990) is a very accessible study of the engagement of scholars with the problems posed by forgeries since the Renaissance. Fragments attributed to Ovid, not including the *Medea*, are collected in Blänsdorf (1995: 283–90) and, with some discussion, in Courtney (1993: 308–14). The complete (sic) fragments are to be found in Lenz (1956), with notes in Latin. This remains the standard edition as well of the *Halieutica, Nux,* and *Consolatio.* Richmond (1962) should also be consulted for the *Halieutica.* For medieval pseudo-Ovidiana, the discussion by Lehmann (1927) is still basic. There is no comprehensive collection of Ovidian pseudepigrapha from the Middle Ages, many of which can only be found in scholarly journals, but there are two editions of the *De Vetula* (Klopsch 1967; Robathan 1968): the field is ripe for further study. Sabinus' epistles were edited most recently in Häuptli (1996).

PART III

Intertexts

CHAPTER SIXTEEN

Ovid and Hellenistic Poetry

Jane L. Lightfoot

Recent finds show Hellenistic poetry as ever more important for Latin poetry; they also reveal how little we know about it. (Hutchinson 2006: 84)

Introduction

My task in this chapter is not easy. The period (as my epigraph attests) is extremely important for Ovid, but neither it nor its influence on him is something that can be captured by a snapshot. Hellenistic poetry is a conduit through which earlier poetry reaches Ovid, and in turn a staging post, only a point on a journey all of whose later stages we also have to follow in order to understand him. Hellenistic literature is not a static category. We can trace developments between the high Hellenistic period and the later centuries, for example the way bucolic develops between Theocritus and Bion in the late second century BC, or elegy between Callimachus and Parthenius in the first. Ovid is heir to all of this.

Another difficulty is that we are comparing something extant in enormous dimensions with works that, for the most part, are extant, if at all, in scrappy, fragmentary form. Apollonius' *Argonautica*, Callimachus' *Hymns*, Theocritus' *Idylls*, and a huge corpus of epigrams with a Hellenistic bedrock (the Palatine Anthology) are precious legacies of the manuscript tradition, where more typical patterns of survival are disjointed excerpts in later authors or papyrus fragments in a greater or lesser state of disrepair. On any account the *Metamorphoses* are a bigger, more polymorphous affair than anything that preceded them, but trying to delineate this background is certainly not aided by the scrappiness of the remains. Another problem is the sheer lack of evidence for Hellenistic prose. Where the relationship between poetry and prose may be crucial—as with the reciprocal relations between didactic poetry and prose treatises, or in mythography; as with the versification of prose treatises and prose paraphrasis of verse, and the borrowing of conventions from the one into the other—progress is hampered by the wreck (although not quite total wreck) of

Hellenistic prose. All these problems have tended to divert critical attention from Ovid's Hellenistic background.

However, it is also an area from which enlightenment may reasonably be expected from new papyrological finds and publications. No discovery yet has had quite the revelatory impact on the study of Ovid as the publication in 2001 of the papyrus roll containing over a hundred epigrams by Posidippus (Bastianini et al. 2001). But we have seen the recent publication of fragments of an elegiac poem on metamorphosis, containing three stories which overlap with the *Metamorphoses* (see below). Even without lucky windfalls, there remain areas of Ovid's Hellenistic background that have simply not received the attention they deserve. Emma Gee's book (2000) on the astronomical content of the *Fasti* attempted to redress one, but there are many more.

Alexandria

I begin with some characteristics of Hellenistic literary culture that provide a useful background to Ovid; but I have to acknowledge the partiality of my account. Our evidence for literature in the Hellenistic period is dominated by Alexandria, where the Ptolemies established their capital and endowed a museum and library, which they filled with literary men from across the Greek world. The qualities of the literature I am about to describe are above all associated with this tone-setting culture, but it is neither the case that all new developments originated there, nor the case that the outside world could only react passively to its influence. Conditions in Alexandria were exceptional. When the first Ptolemy founded its library, he had, according to Eusebius, the ambition to 'equip it with the writings of all men as far as they were worth serious attention' (*Hist. Eccl.* 5.8.11). To the *philologoi* who worked there, earlier literature must have been available in unprecedented abundance, and an astounding legion of talent was attracted there. Yet they were also working with the legacy of earlier scholar-poets who had prepared editions of texts; critics and theorists who had developed literary taxonomies and critical terminology; and compilers of miscellanea, who gathered biographical traditions and anecdotes. Other royal courts, at Pella, Pergamum, and Antioch, had their own constellations of literati. They were, moreover, living in a culture in which important developments in meter, music, dialect, and performance scenarios had long been underway.

First, critical reflection seems to have produced a more formal understanding of genre. While, in the archaic and classical periods, there seems to have been a strong association between types of poem or song and the occasion for which they were intended, in the Hellenistic period genre was increasingly marked by formal means and markers, whether the literary works in question were supported by a given performance scenario or not (Rutherford 2001: 4–5, 72, 128–9; Fantuzzi and Hunter 2004: 22–6). With the tightening of expectations that a certain type of poem would contain a certain kind of meter, dialect, and perhaps other features (tone, ethos, a certain kind of narrator), it was also possible to undercut them by making new and unexpected combinations of these elements. This is the so-called 'Crossing of Genres' for which Hellenistic poetry is so well known (Hutchinson 1988: 15–16), with the important qualification that it was not impelled simply by 'a ludic spirit of contamination' (Fantuzzi and Hunter 2004: 17–41, 457–61). This kind of recombination is hardly new then, though: for one thing, there was an established tendency for the hexameter and elegiac couplet (which always had a wide compass) to conquer ever more territory as the Doric and Aeolic lyric traditions went into decline, and elegy, in particular, was an increasingly popular choice for many different kinds of poem. It was used for narratives sometimes of several books' extent; for catalogue-poetry in the tradition of the Hesiodic catalogues, which of course were in hexameters; for various types of song where lyric was no longer used; and for occasional poetry: hymns, laments, epinician, and epithalamium all now fell within its compass (Cameron 1995: 46, and, from a different perspective, Hunter 1996: 3–5). It is worth noting, however, that as yet there is no certain example from the Hellenistic period of the use of elegiac meter for didactic verse (Obbink 1999: 64), although elegiacs on medical themes seem to appear at the beginning of the imperial period.

The scholar-poet Callimachus illustrates many of these tendencies, but in a heightened, whimsical, idiosyncratic form. In producing his catalogue or taxonomy of literature in the Alexandrian Library—the famous *Pinakes*—he had given much theoretical attention to genres and species in Greek literature (Pfeiffer 1968: 127–34; Fraser 1972: I.452–5; Fantuzzi and Hunter 2004: 43; Call. frr. 429–53 Pf.). As a result he was supremely well placed to produce literature of his own with a sophisticated understanding of genre. He flaunts his versatility (fr. 203 Pf.), which was even more diverse than his extant output shows (the *Suda* also credits him with satyr-plays, tragedies, and comedies). He revives archaic genres, but in reviving, transforms them: the Ionic iambus, now purged of its crudity and (mostly) of its vitriol; the victory-ode, now running more smoothly in elegiacs (or iambics), and with an eye for local detail rather than grand, pan-Hellenic settings; and hymns, which combine the conventions of different hymnic traditions, meters, and settings. In this chapter I aim only to highlight a number of issues that arise from Callimachus' *oeuvre* that seem to me most important for understanding Ovid's background.

First, he favors a poetic persona which is highly articulate about itself and about poetics, and is the most outspoken spokesman in the Hellenistic period for the aesthetic of small, exquisite, finely crafted poetry. His embattled but unspecific pronouncements were read and mis- or over-interpreted by all subsequent poets. The Romans produced one reading of him, and modern scholarship another, which was perhaps no less of a distortion than the ancient one. Callimachus never banned the imitation of Homer, or elevated Hesiod in Homer's place (Cameron 1995: 362–86), any more than he was a poet of softness, love, and love's delights. Yet in spite of the untenability of the idea of a 'ban' on Homeric epic, it remains the case that the Hellenistic period in general (not only under Callimachus' influence) saw the emergence of forms that offer alternatives to martial epic: narrative poetry in both hexameters and elegiacs whose subject matter is often erotic, sometimes rustic, and in any case non-martial. These poems have a cozy, storytelling feel (many have a once-upon-a-time *incipit*); they seem to enjoy the evocation of character; the *Iliad* is clearly not the model, though (aspects of) the *Odyssey* sometimes may be. The so-called 'epyllion' (*BNP* s.v.) will go through more stages of development before it reaches Ovid, but it is obviously of enormous importance for Ovid's narrative style.

Second, although it cannot be true that Callimachus elevated Hesiod above Homer in some notional hierarchy of poets, it remains the case that Hesiod enjoyed a particularly high reputation in the Hellenistic period (see Asquith 2005; Hunter 2005b). The elegist Hermesianax, in a work which was itself an imitation of Hesiod, called him 'keeper of all knowledge' (fr. 7.22 P. πάσης ἧρανον ἱστορίης). But it was not only as a repository of lore that Hesiod attracted interest. The scene at the beginning of the *Theogony*, where Hesiod was invested as a poet by the Muses, was reworked by Callimachus at the beginning of his *Aitia* and in Theocritus' seventh *Idyll*, and is progressively elaborated and loaded with significance, until, by the time it is inherited by Roman poets, it has taken on priestly as well as poetological overtones (Cameron 1995: 364–8; Fantuzzi and Hunter 2004: 6–7; Hunter 2005b: 240). The *Works and Days* is transformed in Aratus' *Phaenomena*: the rambling, moralistic archaic poem is hybridized with a modern astronomical prose treatise by Eudoxus in accordance with the Hellenistic taste for technical, recalcitrant subject matter. Just enough myth and Zeus-based theodicy is left in to gesture in Hesiod's direction. In his erotic didactic poetry, Ovid will take quite a different path; but we will shortly consider what he makes of the *Phaenomena* in his own didactic poem on the Roman calendar.

The other poem or poems ascribed to Hesiod in antiquity were genealogical catalogues, a *Catalogue of Women* and a *Megalai Ehoiai*, which traced family stemmata from their origins in the union of a god with a mortal woman. The importance of these works for the Hellenistic poets is becoming clearer as more and more papyrus fragments are published. So too is the extraordinary range of responses. In the first place, the form itself exerted a fascination. We have several substantial excerpts of catalogue elegies which reduce the Hesiodic original to the essential form of a list, and adapt its connective formulae to *catenae* of stories, anecdotes, or otherwise bite-sized pieces of information. Ovid is heir to this material. He refers to it occasionally. In *Tr.* 1.6.1–2 he refers to the *Lyde* of Antimachus (end of the classical period) and the *Bittis* of Philetas (early Hellenistic), both of them supposedly elegies which amassed self-consolatory stories, and in *Pont.* 3.1.58 he refers again to Philetas' beloved Bittis. He hits off the catalogue manner, which he takes to its most virtuoso extremes in his own curse poem *Ibis*, modeled on Callimachus' poem of the same name (Call. frr. 381–2 Pf.; cf. Watson 1991). No fragment survives of Callimachus' work, though we do have substantial fragments of a Hellenistic curse poem in which the narrator threatens to tattoo his enemy on various parts of the body (Huys 1991; cf. Watson 1991: 260–3). The relatedness to the catalogue genre appears in that successive sections are introduced with the formula στίξω ('I shall tattoo'), in each case introducing a new myth. Each myth seems to have been told fairly concisely, but not with the opaque brevity characteristic of some of the later Hellenistic curse poems. Most of column i (24 lines) is devoted to the story of Heracles and Eurytion; in column ii (= *SSH* 970), lines 4–13 are devoted to Tantalus, and 14–24 (where the fragment breaks off) to the story of Oeneus and the Calydonian boar.

But the Hellenistic poets also develop different, and less formal, approaches toward Hesiodic catalogue poetry. Callimachus' *Aitia* is the apotheosis of poetry built out of connected narrative segments, yet with a method of connection that is anything other than formulaic. Analogies have also been discerned between the *Catalogue*'s narratives about (the erotic adventures of) women and the Hellenistic epyllion, a concrete example of which is Moschus' light and highly pictorial *Europa*, a story we know figured in the Hesiodic *Catalogue* and in Bacchylides (Hunter 2005b: 254–6). Ovid is heir to this anti-formalist approach no less than to the formalist one, and clearly it is the inventive, narrative experiments whose method he adopts and makes his own. In antiquity it appears that Hesiod's *Theogony* and *Catalogue* circulated together with a transition directly from the one poem to the other, so that cosmogony and theogony was followed by the unions of gods with mortal women (West 1966: 48–9, 437; 1985: 126–7). The *Metamorphoses* have been seen as a version of this kind of progress from primordial chaos through to the recognizable world, a *carmen perpetuum* (1.4) that conveys at least an impression of catalogic comprehensiveness—but a version run riot, with orderly sequence swept aside by unlimited, fantastical ingenuity (Hunter 2005b: 265; Hardie 2005: 296–88). Some of that ingenuity must be due to what Ovid learned from the Hellenistic poets: the eroticization of what was originally genealogical myth, and the literary manner of the epyllion, certainly is. But it is true that no mythographical poem survives from that (or any other) period which combines such comprehensiveness with such virtuosity in binding its material together.

The importance of the theme of aetiology will recur throughout this chapter. Archaic and classical poetry had of course been deeply concerned with the origins of the present order of things, but in Hellenistic literature this interest takes the form of the just-so story: a discrete narrative whose punchline is the establishment of something familiar in the present day (Kirk 1970: 256–8; 1972; 1974: 53–63). The motif of 'even now', 'to this very day', is characteristic of Hellenistic aetiology. Human institutions, especially cults, festivals, divine statues, and temples, attracted particular attention; so too the foundation-traditions of the communities of which they formed part. But the natural world was no less fascinating: aetiological stories gathered around about species of animals, birds, and plants, features of the landscape (springs, rivers, rarely hills), and natural curiosities (curiously colored stones). Starmyths which told how a person or thing was translated to the heavens, although by no means new in this period, achieve a far higher profile than ever before (Condos 1997). Why this shift of emphasis? The preference for the local over the pan-Hellenic in the Hellenistic period, certainly; perhaps also the intellectual interests of the Peripatetics, who loved to describe and catalogue things in all their individuality, their quiddity. Aetiology now occurs in epic (Apollonius Rhodius' *Argonautica*; Callimachus' abbreviated epic, the *Odyssey*-like *Hecale*); it implies the adoption of a perspective that no longer, as in the Homeric poems, wishes to create a gulf between past and present but rather is interested in portraying their continuity one with another. By evoking the opening of the *Theogony*, a poem that explained the genesis of the gods, Callimachus' *Aitia* presented itself as its sequel, an explanation of present-day

cults, rituals, and local traditions (Fantuzzi and Hunter 2004: 49–51). The Hellenistic catalogue poems drop genealogy as the connecting link between items, but
several of them put aetiology in its place (Asquith 2005: 278; for the *Aitia* itself,
Fantuzzi and Hunter 2004: 56). A new type of poetry appears on the theme of
foundation-myths, or *ktiseis*. It is of obvious importance for the metamorphosis
theme, for what else is metamorphosis myth but a special way of explaining how
something took on its present form?

Ovidian Aetiologies

Among Ovid's works the Hellenistic interest in aetiology is most obvious in the
Fasti (Porte 1985). Its subject, cults and ritual practices, is the very choicest theme
of Hellenistic aetiology, and although it has been transmitted to Ovid across generations of Roman antiquarians, it is Callimachus' *Aitia* that Ovid chooses as his principal literary model. The elegiac meter itself in an aetiological poem is an inheritance
from Callimachus' *Aitia*, transmitted across the fourth book of Propertius. At the
same time, the *Fasti* is also a didactic poem. Unlike Callimachus' gaily eclectic *Aitia*,
the *Fasti* is an attempt, albeit an unfinished one, to compass a single field of knowledge. The *Aitia* already had certain affiliations to didactic poetry, of course: in
depicting his encounter with the Muses as a dream encounter, Callimachus is alluding
to the 'teaching dream' (ὄνειρον διδάσκαλον, 3 B 1 D-K.) of Epimenides. But
the *Fasti* draws the two skeins closer together, and also engages closely with the most
influential didactic poem of the Hellenistic period, Aratus' astronomical epic, the
Phaenomena (Kidd 1997; Fantuzzi and Hunter 2004: 224–45). Like several Republican literary figures before him, Ovid himself may have translated the *Phaenomena*
(Chapter Fifteen), although he seems only to have covered the first section, dealing
with the fixed stars. Announcing that its theme will be the Roman calendar, the
first couplet of the *Fasti* promises 'times and causes' and the risings and settings of
constellations (*tempora cum causis . . . lapsaque . . . ortaque signa*). That is, we are to
expect a combination of the 'causes' of Callimachus, the rising and setting constellations of Aratus—and Ovid's own calendrical, chronological format, which is not
found in either.

   The hybrid of Callimachus, Aratus, and Roman antiquarian writing on the calendar
results in a work that is quite unlike anything that came before it. The voice of the
persona loquens now elicits information, like Callimachus conversing with the Muses
in the first and second books of the *Aitia* (Fantham 1998: 16–17), and now expounds
it like a didactic narrator. The question-and-answer format was also employed in the
second and third books of Timon's *Silloi* (Diog. Laert. 9.111), which depicted the
narrator in dialogue with Xenophanes. The cast of characters from whom Ovid elicits
information is far richer than Callimachus' closed circle of Muses: he conjures up
whoever is likeliest to know the answer, whether human or divine, and sometimes
that person is himself, replying to someone else's questions. The obsession with
causae (the word occurs over eighty times) is hyper-aetiological, unmatched by Callimachus, in whom, as far as we know, the word αἴτιον does not occur. His obsessive

question 'why' (*cur, quare*) has an analogue in Callimachus' 'how' (πῶς; Pf. on Call. fr. 3.1), but again far exceeds anything in the earlier poem (it could be a legacy of Varro). While Callimachus had carried his antiquarian learning to the point of self-parody (frr. 75, 178 Pf.; Hutchinson 1988: 26–32), Ovid takes his to the point of self-defeat when he lays side by side several alternative explanations or etymologies without attempting to judge between them, resulting in a state of complete *aporia* as to the 'true' cause (Miller 1992). The *Aitia* already offered some alternative aetiologies, as at Schol. Flor. on frr. 3–7, ll. 32–5, where, however, Klio proposes a definitive solution (cf. also fr. 79; Fantuzzi and Hunter 2004: 56–8).

As for the *Phaenomena*, this was yet another Hellenistic reinterpretation of Hesiod. The main body of the poem describes the position of the constellations, the tropics, equator, and ecliptic, and the Paranatellonta, or constellations that rise and set at the same time as those of the zodiac. It supplements and modernizes the very rudimentary astronomy in the *Works and Days* by versifying a prose treatise by Eudoxus. The last section turns the 'Days' to account by presenting Aratus' own version of rustic lore—a list of weather signs from celestial phenomena, animal behavior, and other signals. Hesiod's pious traditionalism is recast in terms of a providential Stoic Zeus, but the distance between the archaic and Hellenistic poems is marked by the characteristic preference of the latter for a 'hard', technical subject (in the main body of the poem at least). Aratus wrote other poems on astronomical themes that have not survived (*SH* 86–91), as well as a poem on medicine (*SH* 92–8): both subjects were favorites of later didactic writers, to judge from fragments of other *Phaenomena* by Alexander of Ephesus (*SH* 20–2), Artemidorus (*SH* 213), Hegesianax (*SH* 465–70), Hermippus (*SH* 485–90), and fragments of medical poems (*SH* 18, 471–2, 595, 690). We also hear of poems on hunting and fishing and are still in possession of poems on snakes, poisons, and their antidotes attributed to Nicander of Colophon (Gow and Scholfield 1953; Jacques 2002). The elegant versification of abstruse, (semi-)technical or scientific subject matter was essential to the poet's purpose (*BNP* s.v. 'Didactic Poetry'). When Ovid adopts the didactic mode in the *Fasti*, then, it produces a tension between 'hard' astronomy and the calendrical material, a human institution that is only semi-scientific at the best of times, a cheerful amalgam of colorful and bizarre practices. The technical, astronomical arcana interspersed throughout the whole are not treated systematically, but as isolated curiosities. Moreover, Aratus' framework is spatial, not chronological like Ovid's. Stars and meteorological phenomena become 'signs' of calendar dates, as they were not in Aratus. Ovid distributes his astronomical aperçus around his calendar, principally as and where they pleased him—with blithe disregard for scientific accuracy (Fantham 1998: 35–6; Gee 2000).

Ovid's poem is thus the product of two quite different traditions and approaches: the didactic one that treats of a subject of forbidding technicality and abstraction, and the aetiological one that deals with a muddled human one; the didactic one that describes a calm, perfect, ordered whole, and the aetiological one that describes teeming, superabundant, local variation, sometimes with alternative explanations available for the same phenomenon, which in Aratus' Stoic system could never be. Just as the sources of the subject matter are multiple, so too is the form highly eclectic.

It is a witty combination of the information-dispensing narrator of traditional didactic, transmitted across the Roman didactic of Lucretius and Virgil, with the information-seeking narrator of Callimachus' *Aitia*, further combined with the narrative personae of epic and epyllion, who delight in narrative for its own sake. At times we seem to be hearing Aratus' withered little voice (1.313: 'at such-and-such a time you will look in vain for a certain constellation'), but more often Ovid lays on color, humor, and narrative *joie de vivre*. The setting of a constellation is focalized through the eyes of a viewer; that same individual is perplexed by the setting of Lyra, as if there were a dramatic difference in the position of the stars from day to day, and the constellation had suddenly fallen out of the sky (2.75–8). Indications of time are an opportunity for florid, hyper-epic descriptions of natural processes and human activities (4.165–9). Aratus is not wholly devoid of mythical narrative, but out of deference to his literary model he confines it to a very restricted number of passages. Ovid, on the other hand, loves to take the opportunity of the rising of a constellation, or the sun's movement into another sign of the zodiac, to tell elegant, miniature stories of *katasterismos*.

Sufferings in Love

I move on now from aetiology to another dominant theme in Hellenistic poetry: love. Its newfound prominence in Hellenistic literature appears to mark a change of taste, but it was prefigured, as in so many other respects, by Euripides' dramas about good and bad women. Partly, it is a case of a particular kind of subject matter moving upwards and across genres which, in archaic and classical literature, had been less associated with it (a common enough Hellenistic phenomenon); it is also a case of re-reading old genres in new ways, and of the emergence of new genres (such as bucolic, which is steeped in *erōtika pathēmata*).

In epic, it is represented above all by the third book of Apollonius' *Argonautica*, with its famous treatment of the story of Jason and Medea, although traces survive of other Argonautic poems (*SH* 339, cf. 339A). The eroticization of its tone is achieved especially by blending epic narrative with the subjective tone of the archaic lyricists and with tragedy. Imagery from Sappho and Ibycus, emotional monologues by characters, and an emotive, interventionist narrator commenting on the action in the style of a tragic chorus all contribute to a far more affective tone than anything found in earlier epic. The Hesiodic *Catalogue of Women* had already laid significant emphasis on the sexual attractiveness of its women, the 'plot of sexual attraction' (Osborne 2005), and much of the literature inspired by it—whether it adopted the 'formal' or 'anti-formalist' approaches that I described above—took the erotic element even further. An extreme example of the former is an erotic catalogue (fr. 7 P.) attributed to the third book of Hermesianax' *Leontion*, three books of elegies bearing the name of his beloved (Asquith 2005: 279–81, a skeptical reading). Phanocles' Ἔρωτες ἢ Καλοί dealt with the loves of gods and heroes for beautiful boys: an extract attributes Orpheus' death at the hands of the Thracian women to Orpheus' passion for a boy (fr. 1 P.); and Alexander of Aetolia's *Apollo* ingeniously presented love stories in the form of Apolline prophecy (fr. 3 P.). Callimachus' *Aitia*—not in itself a terribly erotic poem, despite Callimachus' later reputation—contained the celebrated story of Acontius and Cydippe (frr. 67–75 Pf.), and that of Phrygius and Pieria, a variation on the love of an enemy commander for a native maiden (frr. 80–3 Pf.). And the short, detached narratives of epyllion were the domain par excellence of Eros: Hellenistic examples are Theocritus' *Hylas* poem (*Id.* 13) and Moschus' *Europa*, discussed above.

In this perspective, Ovid's *Metamorphoses* could be seen as a hugely eroticized revision of his manifold sources—epic, catalogue, mythography—blown up with all the narrative sophistications and virtuosity that the Hellenistic poets and their neoteric heirs devised. But before I turn to the *Metamorphoses*, which will occupy the remainder of this chapter, I will deal very briefly with that other, all-important aspect of Ovid's erotic *oeuvre*, his subjective love elegy and the didactic poetry associated with it. Whether there is any background in Hellenistic poetry for subjective Latin love elegy, where a first-person narrator dramatizes and analyses his emotional experiences, is still very controversial. While one can argue for the emergence of an ideology of love, especially over the second and first centuries BC, which approximates to that of the Latin elegists (Fantuzzi and Hunter 2004: 186, 190), the formal criterion—the first-person speaker and formal coincidence between the *persona loquens* and the author—is harder to meet, except in Hellenistic epigram (Gutzwiller 1998: 118, 120). It relies on testimonia which are difficult and dangerous to interpret because the works themselves are extant only in fragments at best, and on papyri of the imperial period which may or may not contain Hellenistic poetry, or poetry with Hellenistic antecedents (Asquith 2005: 279–86; *POxy* 2884 fr. 2 (*SH* 962); 2885 fr. 1 (*SH* 964); 3723 (*SSH* 1186)).

This is an area where it is impossible to measure Ovid directly against a corpus of earlier literature without taking account of all that intervened between them. Treating 'Ovid as a love poet' adequately within the scope of this paper is out of the question, since it would also entail a study of his Roman precursors—themselves, of course, the heirs of Hellenistic literature as well, in a constant process of reinterpretation (e.g. Hutchinson 1988: 277–329; Fantuzzi and Hunter 2004: 444–85). Ovid's love elegy shares some of the attitudes of earlier Latin love elegy toward its Hellenistic legacy. At the end of his *Hymn to Apollo* the god commends the small, pure spring over the great, filthy river Euphrates (105–12), and on this basis Callimachus is read as having rejected epic in favor of elegy, which now becomes a choice of lifestyle and ethical character rather than merely one of literary genre. Following Propertius, Callimachus is interpreted, highly tendentiously, as a love poet (*Ars* 3.329–30, *Rem.* 759–60, *Tr.* 2.367–8): this despite the fact that his 'love poetry' in subjective mode is in fact confined to some highly quizzical homosexual epigrams. No matter: it is Acontius and Cydippe which was supposed to seal his status as erotic master (*Rem.* 381–2). The language of *mollitia* is applied to him (*Pont.* 4.16.32; Hutchinson 1988: 282–3). Roman poets love to restage the end of the *Hymn to Apollo* as an encounter in which the god pulls the poet back from epic to a less pretentious genre (Virg. *Ecl.* 6.3–5; Hor. *Od.* 4.15.1–4; Prop. 3.3); in Ovid's version of this trope, Amor pulled him back from writing tragedy and reclaims him for his own (*Am.* 2.18.13–18).

The *Metamorphoses*

The *Metamorphoses* combine interests in all the subjects of this chapter so far: Eros and aetiology; experimentation with 'catalogue' poetry, epyllion, and brilliantly unorthodox narrative technique. My aim here must be modest. It is to consider whether and what sorts of precedent Ovid's most famous poem had in the metamorphosis literature of the Hellenistic period, and to compare it with them as far as possible in terms of its use of the metamorphosis theme, and in the literary texture of the resulting work of art. It may be true that 'Ovid's most primary Hellenistic models had not aroused great enthusiasm in critics' (Hutchinson 2006: 84), but if we are to appreciate Ovid's achievement then it is obvious that we must pay careful attention to his predecessors not only as inert collections of data but also as literary works in their own right. Two of these texts have been known about for a long time; a questionable third has only just come to light.

Like love and aetiology, metamorphosis is a theme that emerges into greater prominence in the Hellenistic period (Lightfoot 1999: 241–2). There are, of course, antecedents, especially in Hesiod and in tragedy, but it is in the Hellenistic period that metamorphosis comes to be applied aetiologically to the natural world, and that mythographical collections specifically on that theme start to come to light. In addition to the collections about to be discussed, note those by Antigonus (*SH* 50), Didymarchus (*SH* 378), and Theodorus (*SH* 749–50). A 'dictionary' of metamorphoses preserved on a second or third century BC papyrus, possibly with a Hellenistic source, is particularly interesting (Renner 1978). It contains summaries of five stories whose protagonist's name begins with the letter 'a'. Three come from Hesiod, two expressly from the *Catalogue of Women*. Metamorphosis is a theme in Hesiod and in tragedy (Forbes Irving 1990: 12–19), and in its 'terminal', aetiological, form also spreads into later epic, contrasting with its very restricted presence in Homer (Forbes Irving 1990: 8–12): consider, for example, the stories of Cleite (1.1067–9) and the Heliades (4.604–26) in Apollonius' *Argonautica*.

The first work that can be linked directly with Ovid is an *Ornithogonia*, attributed pseudonymously to a mythical Delphic priest(ess) 'Boio(s)' (Powell 1925: 24–5; Forbes Irving 1990: 33–7). It probably dated from the early Hellenistic period, because it is referred to by Philochorus (*FGrH* 328 F 214), and Ovid seems to be referring to it at *Tr.* 4.10.43 when he describes how his friend Aemilius Macer read to him from a work on birds (Courtney 1993: 292–4). The *Ornithogonia* explained how every species of bird had its origins in a human being, so it was aetiological and apparently ambitious in scope; the author seems to have been particularly interested in the birds' mantic significance. The work seems to have been in hexameters, but no citation preserves the original wording. Our evidence depends mainly on a prose collection of metamorphoses by a second- or third-century AD mythographer, Antoninus Liberalis, ten of which are expressly attributed by source citations in the manuscript to Boios and a further two can be assigned to the work with a high degree of probability (Papathomopoulos 1968; the stories from Boios are: 3, 5, 6 (probably), 7, 11, 14 (probably), 15, 16, 18, 19, 20, 21). Ovid knew the work, then, but it seems to have had little in common with the *Metamorphoses*. The biggest overlap is in the story of Tereus, but Boios' strongly exhibits his own personal style in storytelling—the setting is urban, the characters bourgeois and given untraditional names—and clearly did not serve as a source for Ovid. Ovid refers to a further four stories unique to Boios, but none is more than three lines long: *Met.* 6.90–2 ~ Ant. Lib. 16; 7.390 ~ Ant. Lib. 18; 7.399–400 ~ Ant. Lib. 6; 13.717–18 ~ Ant. Lib. 14 (Knaack 1880: 4–12; Lafaye 1904: 51–3). It is impossible to say much about the literary texture of Boios' poem, but while Antoninus' plot summaries imply that the stories were told at some length and with attention to detail, their translation to a middle-class setting, in a novelistic but not-quite-rationalizing spirit, does not suggest much similarity with Ovid.

Rather more illuminating is the comparison between Ovid and Nicander. Nicander wrote a hexameter *Heteroioumena*, in four or five books, which dealt with the origins of stones, birds, plants, and animals (Gow and Scholfield 1953: frr. 38–67): our main evidence again consists of the stories ascribed to him in Antoninus Liberalis, although there is also an intriguing four-line excerpt on the transformation of Hecuba quoted by a scholiast on Euripides (fr. 62; cf. Schneider 1856: 42–6; Forbes-Irving 1990: 24–32). The interest of the collection was intensely aetiological: some eight stories explain the origins of festivals, cults, or temples (1, 4, 13, 17, 25, 26, 29, 32), while others concern species of animal, bird, or plant, or natural curiosities such as rocks and stones. The 'to this very day' motif seems to have been extremely prominent. Indeed, the end often seems more important than the means by which it was reached. Although metamorphosis certainly occurs, Nicander is often content with disappearance (1.5, 8.7, 13.6, 25.4, 26.4, 27.2–3, 37.5; cf. also 5.4, 12.8, 25.1, 32.5) or substitution. After all, the title means 'alterations', 'becomings-other', rather than specifically 'changes of shape', and while the verb 'to transform' (μεταμορφόω) is found in 2.6, 15.4, commoner are verbs meaning 'to change' (μεταβάλλειν or μεταποιεῖν). In either case, the emphasis is on *x* making *y* into *z*, rather than (as so often in Ovid) on the process of *y*'s becoming *z*. What goes for Boios, goes for Nicander too: Antoninus presents each as a self-standing little narrative, each one with a sense of independence and completeness in itself (suitable, Otto Schneider thought, for treatment as an epyllion). The paraphrases seem to indicate quite complex narratives, not brief anecdotes that could be got out of the way by a poet in half a dozen lines. There are, moreover, signs of the typically Hellenistic interest in digression or outward extension of narrative: the story of Leucippus, a maiden who changed sex, contains a catalogue of other instances of sex-change (17.4–5), while the story of Cerambus contains an inset narrative about Poseidon's rape of one of the nymphs (22.4). There is no indication how, if at all, the stories were connected together, nor much sign of any principle of linkage: no more than tendencies and loose groupings can be observed—stone stories all come in Book 1; springs occur in both 2 and 4; birds in both 3 and 4; in all cases, the books also contain other types of story—nor any principles of geographical ordering.

Some twenty-one of Nicander's stories overlap with Ovid, and of these eleven are unique to the two authors (Knaack 1880: 54–6; Lafaye 1904: 53–6). But Ovid is nothing if not inventive in his use of earlier literature; in no case should we expect him soberly to follow a 'source', nor has he here. The stories where it seems most plausible that Ovid was at least familiar with Nicander's version, which he then turned to his own ends, include those of the boy who was changed into a lizard for mocking Demeter when she drank (*Met.* 5.438–61 ~ Ant. Lib. 24; Nicander called the boy Ascalabos, but Ovid uses the name Ascalaphus for the boy who was turned into an owl because he revealed that Persephone had eaten a pomegranate, *Met.* 5.538–50); Iphis, turned from a girl into a man at adolescence (*Met.* 9.666–797 ~ Ant. Lib. 17, where the 'boy' is called Leucippus); and Galanthis turned into a weasel by Juno because she helped Alcmena to give birth to Heracles (*Met.* 9.281–323 ~ Ant. Lib. 29, Galinthias). The two authors also tell similar stories about the Minyades, transformed into creatures of the night for refusing to worship Dionysus (*Met.* 4.1–415 ~ Ant. Lib. 10); the Emathides (*Met.* 5.294–678 ~ Ant. Lib. 9); Cycnus (*Met.* 7.371–81 ~ Ant. Lib. 12); the daughters of Orion (*Met.* 13.692–9 ~ Ant. Lib. 25); and Lycian peasants (*Met.* 6.317–81 ~ Ant. Lib. 35) (*RE* xvii.1 (1936), s.v. Nikandros, 264–5).

    If anything can be said to characterize Ovid's adaptations, it is their sheer versatility. What Antoninus presents as one of a series of discrete narratives may in Ovid be blown up to epyllion proportions, with inset narratives of its own (Minyades), become a narrative within another narrative (Galanthis), an item in an ecphrasis (the daughters of Orion), travelogue (Cycnus), or merely a passing reference (*Met.* 13.713–15 ~ Ant. Lib. 4, Cragaleus). Very often, names are altered, but this seems to have been common storytelling practice, to judge from the heading to Parthenius, *Narr. Am.* 8: 'the story is told by Aristodemus of Nysa . . . except that he changes the names' (cf. Papathomopoulos 1968: on Ant. Lib. 16, n. 2). While the *Metamorphoses* are dotted about with aetiology, sometimes even reproducing the *adhuc/nunc quoque* motif, Ovid cannot be relied on to reproduce Antoninus' aetiological punchlines. A revealing instance is the story of Iphis. In Nicander, the story explained a Cretan cult, festival, and prenuptial rite. Ovid has dropped all this. He has, indeed, picked up the themes of adolescence, nubility, and changes of status, but has rewritten these in the form of a wedding story, lavishing all his rhetorical embellishments on a titillating *scena* in which a girl expresses frustrated desire for another girl, and wraps it all up with a happily-ever-after ending. In cases like this, it is unfortunate that we cannot get any closer to the literary texture of the original. Take one of Ovid's purplest masterpieces, the story of the heroine Myrrha who seduced her father through the intermediary of her nurse and bore a son to him (*Met.* 10.311–502 ~ Ant. Lib. 34). Ovid has loaded this with hyper-Euripidean coloring. We can tell that there was already Euripidean coloring in Antoninus' source (probably Nicander) as well—the nurse is called 'Hippolyte', and promises the girl an ambiguous 'cure' (cf. Eur. *Hipp.* 509–12)—but not how far it went. The prose paraphrast ventures one or two prudish little comments; but we cannot tell how much (if at all) earlier treatments anticipated Ovid's lurid sensationalism and tabloid moralizing.

    Our total yield of verbatim quotations from Nicander amounts only to six hexameters and a couple of half-lines. In Boios' case, unless one is prepared to play the game of extracting hexameters from Antoninus' prose, there is nothing at all. Another lost work of unknowable importance for Ovid is a work on metamorphoses—not assuredly, but very probably a poem—by the late Hellenistic elegist Parthenius of

Nicaea, who was brought to Rome in the late Republic and supposedly became Virgil's tutor in Greek. It is mentioned by the *Suda* (v 261, π 664); the scholiast on the geographical poet Dionysius Periegetes ascribes to it the story of Scylla, who betrayed her city and father for her love of the enemy commander Minos and was transformed into a seabird (*SH* 637*a–b*); and it may also be the home of five lines of elegiacs which describe how a Cilician maiden fell in love with the river Cydnus and was transformed into a spring by Aphrodite in order to be united with him (*SH* 640). Interest has been aroused by the recent publication of some new elegiac fragments of metamorphosis stories whose first editor cautiously put forward Parthenius' *Metamorphoses* as a possible source (*POxy* 4711, ed. W. B. Henry; Hutchinson 2006; Bernsdorff 2007). In the longest fragment, the story of Adonis (fr. 1↓ ll. 1–6) ends with his transformation into a flower, and the aetiology of the name of the river Adonis. (So too, the story of Scylla ended with her transformation into a bird, and the aetiology of the name of another body of water, in this case the Saronic Gulf.) The beginning of the story of the nymph Asteria (fr. 1↓ ll. 7 ff.) follows immediately, and the next most substantial fragment contains part of the story of Narcissus (fr. 1).

It is too early to say what consensus will emerge about these fragments, but it is already clear that the attribution to Parthenius will not go unchallenged. Indeed, we may not be dealing with the remains of a Hellenistic poem at all (Bernsdorff 2007 argues that in fact this is a late-antique specimen of διήγημα as a rhetorical exercise, and that the writer knows and imitates Nonnus). If it is not—indeed, if it is not even pre-Ovidian—then its interest for Ovid is reduced to that of a specimen of another verse treatment of the metamorphosis theme. The genuine fragment of Parthenius (*SH* 640) makes some nice use of alliteration and rhetorical conceit (the play on metaphorical fire and literal water; the transition from metaphor to metamorphosis, a technique whose similarity to the *Metamorphoses* is noted by Bernsdorff); but—while it cannot be complete in itself—the bulk of the story is already over within five lines. As for the new fragments, these stories, too, were short: at most a page (45 lines), and possibly appreciably less (for the calculation, see Hutchinson 2006: 73–4). They were too short to be called epyllia; shorter, too, than the poetic treatments implied by Antoninus Liberalis' summaries. Compression and density are the consequences of brevity; this is married to genealogical learning and some straightforward rhetorical figures (a pair of antithetical, and a second pair of synonymous, verbs in fr. 1→ 10–11, 12–13). Diction is epic, but there are also a few inept or infelicitous expressions (see Bernsdorff 2007 on fr. 1↓ 10, 12, and fr. 1→ 12). All told, the yield for Ovid is small.

Two negative results emerge from this. First, there is no sign of any Hellenistic metamorphosis literature even remotely approaching the length of Ovid's poem. Fifteen books belong in the league of the Homeric poems and the *Aeneid*: they contrast with Nicander's four or five, Didymarchus' work in at least three books (*SH* 378A) and Boios' in at least two (Ant. Lib. 16, 18–21). Second, we simply cannot tell whether any Hellenistic predecessor span out his stories to the same length as Ovid's longest, or exploited the full range of Ovid's repertoire, from blink-and-you've-missed-it brevity through to full-scale epyllia. Antoninus' summaries imply units considerably longer than either the old fragments of Nicander or the new poem(s) in *POxy* 4711. Neither exhibits anything like the versatility of Ovid—nor his endless inventiveness in connecting stories together.

Yet it is precisely here, where Ovid's invention is at its most fertile, that Hellenistic poetry, with its fascination for lists, catalogues, and accumulations of information, might have been most helpful. In asking about connectivity, we are really talking about two different things: 'internal' or formal connections (whether the stories are held together by particles, by a connecting frame, or whatever) and 'external' or thematic (whether they are held in place by juxtaposition, contrast, or other felicities of placement). Ovid's stories are both formally and thematically connected. The poem is very broadly chronological, but the sense of temporal progression is really only strongly marked at the beginning and end; after the opening creation and flood sequence, we soon lose much sense of orderly, forward momentum and are free to impose patterns limited only by the ingenuity of the critic. As our knowledge of both Hesiod and Hellenistic poetry increases, so we can better grasp what precedents Ovid had (Cameron 1995: 382–4; Hutchinson 2006: 74–6). Our long fragment of Hermesianax' *Leontion* shows formal connection but extremely sclerotic arrangement, with its long list of paired poets and philosophers (fr. 3 P.). The new fragments in *POxy* 4711 seem to consist of separate segments (cf. fr. 1↓ 6–7), but possibly exploited thematic connections between proximate stories (flowers, water, Eros). But it seems once again to be the *Aitia* that offers the most complex techniques of formal (in Books 1–2 through dialogue with the Muses) and thematic conjuncture. It is also the *Aitia* that seems to offer the best parallels, in its treatment of aetiology, for Ovid's use of metamorphosis (Hutchinson 1988: 330, 338)—not only to supply the final punchline, but also interwoven, integrally or incidentally, throughout the whole. Callimachus' 'Acontius and Cydippe', for example, is notable for having no main aition, but several incidental ones (Fantuzzi and Hunter 2004: 60–6).

While a case can be made out for the 'Hellenistic' quality of much of the tone and register of the *Metamorphoses* (Hutchinson 1988: 329–52), it is striking how little sign there is in the Hellenistic metamorphosis poems—which admittedly are very fragmentary—of Ovid's fascination with the moment of change itself. The bizarre sensibility that delights in the similarities between hair and leaves, or 'puns' on the similarities between veins in flesh and veins in stone, is not to be found in Nicander, Boios, or Parthenius—though it is perhaps closer, for example, to Apollonius' depiction of the Heliades as semi-personified, soughing, wailing trees (4.624–6).

One can hardly identify story types and themes per se as 'Hellenistic', though some do seem to attain especial popularity in this period. For example, consider the 'hospitality theme' (Hollis 1970: 106–8). Callimachus popularized a particular form of it: a hero's entertainment by a virtuous cottager, with emphasis on the poverty of his/her surroundings. Ovid has many examples of the story pattern, though he invests his most celebrated example, that of Baucis and Philemon in *Met.* 8, with a specifically Roman ethos (Hutchinson 1988: 346–7). Consider also the incest theme (Lightfoot 1999: 243–4), to which Ovid devotes two of his most famous epyllia, those of Byblis (*Met.* 9.454–665) and Myrrha (10.298–502). The story of Byblis' incestuous passion for her brother (or vice versa) seems to have been particularly popular among Hellenistic poets: we learn from Parthenius' review of the story in *Narr. Am.* 11 of treatments by Apollonius Rhodius (fr. 5 P.), Nicaenetus (fr. 1 P.), as well as by Parthenius himself (*SH* 646). It may have been from one of these poets that Ovid derived the tradition of Byblis' wanderings (Lightfoot 1999: 434–5), though not from Parthenius himself. His own version is exquisite, but short: six lines take us from the girl's repulse to her death. In Myrrha's case, we have what we are lacking in Byblis', that is, evidence for an earlier extended treatment in epyllion. For in addition to the version by (?) Nicander, discussed above, the story has also reached Ovid via Cinna's famous epyllion, *Zmyrna* (frr. 6–8 Courtney) and a putative earlier treatment by Parthenius (Lightfoot 1999: 183). It is in cases like these where we most regret our inability to trace the development of style and ethos from the early to the later Hellenistic masters, thence to the Roman neoteric poets and beyond.

It is with the treatment of love and the erotic sensibility of Hellenistic poetry that I wish to end this chapter. Hellenistic literature famously loves to explore the psychology of women in love. Often it does so through 'interior' means such as soliloquies, dramatic monologues, and accounts of dreams, all of which are in evidence in Apollonius' Medea. A newly published, probably Hellenistic, hexameter fragment describes how Medea utters a monologue, falls asleep, has a nightmare, and awakes (*POxy* 4712, frr. 1–2): this recalls Apollonius' Medea, though the order of monologue and nightmare are reversed (3.616–44; cf. also fr. 1.4 and 3.794–7). The subject is at home in mime. Among several erotic monologues in Theocritus' *Idylls*, the second is spoken by a woman who is performing love magic in order to conjure back an errant lover. A famous piece of declamatory rhetoric, the so-called Alexandrian Erotic fragment, or Fragmentum Grenfellianum, preserved on a papyrus of the second century BC, uses imagery of fire and madness and a free, dochmiac-based meter to portray the hysteria of an excluded lover: it might indicate the development of *verismo* and heightened emotionalization in certain strands of second-century poetics (Powell 1925: 177–80; Hunter 1996: 8–10; Fantuzzi and Hunter 2004: 485). Clearly, soliloquies by Ovidian heroines stand in a long tradition of dramatic *ethopoeia* (e.g. Medea (7.11–71); Byblis (9.474–516, 585–629); Iphis (9.726–63); Myrrha (10.320–55); also Narcissus (3.442–73)), and Ovid was obviously aware of developments between the high Hellenistic period and his own day. Yet it is Apollonius' Medea on whom I wish to concentrate. She is a particularly influential model on account of her psychological complexity and the literary techniques involved in depicting her split state of mind. It is worth pursuing the comparison with Ovid's heroines a little in order to expose the mechanics of both (compare Gill 1987, whose study of Medea's monologues in Euripides and Seneca reaches important conclusions which can be extended, *mutatis mutandis*, to Ovid).

Consider Apollonius' depiction of Medea's vacillation. She makes three attempts to pull herself together, each consisting of movement in contrary directions, then stasis (3.464–70, 636–44, 772–801). Her indecision is expressed through a similar triple movement or set of choices in the first and third monologues: she will give

Jason the drugs to overcome the serpent; she will die; she will carry on just as she is. Each speech begins with an expression of woe which evokes, to some extent, scenes of irresolution in epic; but in epic the person making the speech always comes down on one side or another (e.g. *Il.* 11.404–10, 17.91–105, 21.553–70, 22.99–130). Apollonius' heroine's portrayal is more in the style of the monologues of self-division in Euripides' *Medea*, especially 1040–55, where Medea debates whether to kill her children. Here, too, we have swerves in contrary directions. Apollonius builds on and develops this technique, making Medea change her mind mid-sentence, even mid-line, with abrupt asyndeton. Euripides' speech has the character of a dialogue insofar as it contains several shifts of addressee (children, chorus, Medea's own self), but Apollonius' heroine is self-addressed and correspondingly more self-absorbed. Apollonius makes third-person imperatives and optatives, wishes, and potentials, possibly taken from *Med.* 1044, 1048, the keynote of Medea's three monologues (first: 3.466, 467, 468, 469; second: 3.639, 640, which, however, concludes with a future indicative and a definite resolve, 3.642; third: 3.773–4, 778, 785–6, 787, 789). But they do not serve the same function as in Euripides. Apollonius' Medea reckons with public opinion, but does not engage with anyone other than herself. This is all in Medea's imagination. It is Medea playing with possibilities, fantasizing, self-engrossed.

When it is Ovid's turn to render Medea's soliloquy, he bundles away the earlier stages of the narrative in order to reach it; once there, he makes it last as long as possible (*Met.* 7.11–71). This is Medea's big aria. The debt to Euripides remains, and, indeed, is made obvious by Medea's famous formula: 'I see and approve the better, but follow the worse' (20–1, cf. Eur. *Med.* 1078–9 and *Hipp.* 380–1). Apollonius is there, too: the *ethopoeia*, the rapid vacillations, repeated many times over, the questions and exclamations that spill across line-divisions and mimic spontaneity and agitated thought—all these are techniques he learned from the earlier poet. But Ovid's Medea is a different creature from her earlier incarnations. Where Apollonius' Medea had looked to die, Ovid's looks to live, and the most decisive way in which her mastery and self-mastery expresses itself is in her command of rhetoric. She apostrophizes herself throughout, and displays a remarkable detachment and analytical ability. She is not simply vacillating between two static positions but reviewing in turn all the obstacles that will face her if she decides to help Jason; the speech ends with a euphoric fantasy of elopement, and there is humor in the prim sentiments with which she forecloses this line of thought in the last three lines. Other Ovidian soliloquies heighten the color still further. First, there is more playfulness and irony. Slippage between two states of mind is now an amusing spoof (Byblis would rather die than yield, but wants her brother to kiss her lips as she lies dead: *Met.* 9.503–4). Second, and crucially, beside the *ethopoeia* now is deliberative rhetoric and displays of ingenuity in front of an imaginary audience. When Myrrha puts the arguments for and against incest, she is indulging in a full-scale *controversia* (*Met.* 10.320–55); when Byblis tries to persuade herself that it is acceptable for her to court her brother, it is a miniature *suasoria* that we are hearing (*Met.* 9.497–9, 507, 511–14). The Hellenistic poets had created psychological complexity through the heightened subjectivization of the epic voice. It was left to the Romans to add formal rhetoric.

Conclusion

Ovid's debt to Hellenistic poetry is a complicated but very important question. It is complicated because of the sheer state of the preserved material, by the fact that Ovid's inheritance has reached him across many earlier generations of re-interpretation, and, of course, because of his own transformative genius. Yet it was the Hellenistic period that saw the development of many of the sophistications of which Ovid avails himself. Curiously, it is some of the most central aspects of Ovid's *oeuvre* that are most in need of further work: the narrative technique of both the *Metamorphoses* and the *Fasti*; their organization, structure, and transitions, and the bearing on this of catalogue literature and mythography. Hellenistic poetry has a fundamental contribution to make here; for example Ovid's stories would benefit from sustained comparison with the techniques that Hellenistic poets use in expanding narratives outward, or deviating from a main narrative trajectory. His indebtedness to such Hellenistic narrative experiments shows in his famous imitation of the talking crow in Callimachus' *Hecale* (*Met.* 2.534–632); other experiments in mythology-as-prophecy, such as Lycophron's *Alexandra* or Alexander of Aetolia's *Apollo* (West 2000: 160; cf. already *POxy* 2509; Hunter 2005b: 257–8), could underlie passages such as the prophecy by Cheiron's daughter, Ocyrrhoe, in *Met.* 2.642–54. Just as fundamental is the contribution of Hellenistic poetry to the tone, ethos, and sensibility of Ovid's work. One hopes for an end to its undue neglect in Ovidian studies.

FURTHER READING

Secondary literature can be followed through references in the chapter, but the only way to make real progress with this topic is to return to the primary sources. The standard edition of Callimachus has long been Pfeiffer's (1949–53); but, as new finds have come to light, it has been supplemented by the editions (both with Italian translation and commentary) of Massimilla (1996; Books 1 and 2) and d'Alessio (2001). For a translation, see Nisetich (2001). There are editions of Apollonius Rhodius' *Argonautica* by Fränkel (1961) and Vian (1974–81), and separate commentaries on Book 3 (Hunter 1989) and, in Italian, Book 4 (Livrea 1973). For a translation, with introduction and notes, see Hunter (1993). The standard text, translation, and commentary of Theocritus is by Gow (1952), and there are also selections by Dover (1971 on *Idylls* 1–11, 13–16, 18, 22, 24, 26, 28) and, with excellent commentary, by Hunter (1999 on *Idylls* 1, 3, 4, 6, 7, 10, 11, 13). There are two indispensable collections of fragments of poetry written in the Hellenistic period, the first by Powell (1925), and the second (with more generous limits of 300 BC–AD 1) by Lloyd-Jones and Parsons (1983). This latter contains recent papyrological discoveries, both of anonymous authors and, crucially, of Callimachus; a further supplement has been edited by Lloyd-Jones (2005).

CHAPTER SEVENTEEN

Ovid and Callimachus: Rewriting the Master

Benjamin Acosta-Hughes

Introduction

Ovid's rapport with the poetry we broadly term 'Hellenistic' (the term is a better historical than literary one, cf. Dover 1971: lxx–lxxi; Hollis 2006: 102), is, as has been acutely shown in the previous chapter, a complex mosaic of recall, appropriation, and enhancement. This is particularly true of Ovid and Callimachus, and in some ways, differently true; for this reason alone a separate treatment of these two figures is justified. While all three of the major surviving third-century BCE Alexandrians, Theocritus, Callimachus, and Apollonius, find extensive artistic reiteration in Roman poetry, Callimachus is the only one to become himself a cultural monument in Roman poetry to the extent that he does; each generation's evocation of Callimachus implicates earlier evocations of Callimachus—the Cyrenean Greek poet becomes, paradoxically, a cornerstone of Roman poetics. And Ovid's use of Callimachus is emphatically multigeneric; Callimachus is a presence throughout Ovid's artistic career and, in one way or another, in all of his *oeuvre* (Tarrant 2002b: 21). Callimachus' appeal for Ovid is multifaceted, hence Ovid's 'Callimacheanism' is the composite of more than one artistic impulse. No one of the following aspects of this complex translation completely predominates in Callimachus' significance for Ovid; the whole, however, is a compelling confluence of factors in this rapport.

From Catullus onward Callimachus is periodically invoked by name in Roman poetry. By the time Ovid at *Pont.* 4.16.32 recalls the *Callimachi . . . molle iter* he follows in a long line of invoking this figure in Roman poetry—Callimachus is now not only the third-century Alexandrian poet alone, but also the many faces, or personae, of Callimachus that have appeared in the verse of Ovid's Roman predecessors.

Already with, for example, Ennius and Lutatius Catulus, Callimachus finds extensive imitation in Roman poetry; in other words, imitation of Callimachus becomes itself something of a *trope* of Latin poetics, and Ovid has a long imitative tradition before him (well noted by Tarrant 2002b: 22). The degree to which the elite Roman was effectively bilingual (or perhaps better bi-cultural) is often easy for us, who come to these languages (and literatures) as largely separate entities, to misapprehend. It's worth noting too that Hellenistic poetry and early Latin literature are more or less contemporary. *Aetia* 4 includes the episode of the Roman Gaius (frr. 106–7 Pf.); albeit there is much about this episode that is uncertain (D'Alessio 1996: 520 n. 28; Cic. *de Orat.* gives a parallel to the story), the appearance here of Rome, and, indeed, the attention overall to the Greek west in the *Aetia*, is revealing. This is, after all, an area where the Roman republic and the Alexandrians likewise interacted with local figures and events (e.g. the Sicilian dynasts, the Pyrrhic Wars).

Unlike Theocritus and Apollonius, even given what we know of their lost poetry, Callimachus was, in generic terms, truly multifaceted. An author of works in both prose and verse, and in verse of a wide variety of metrical genres, he prefigures Ovid (indeed, outdoes him, metrically if not thematically) in the varied scope of his poetry. Even if we cannot judge the accuracy of the *Suda* entry on Callimachus, which attributes inter alia comedy and tragedy to him (although there is no reason prima facie for doubting this, and the case of Ovid's *Medea* might suggest caution here—had we not the knowledge we do, we might hesitate to ascribe tragedy to Ovid), we know from his surviving poetry that he composed in hexameter, elegiac couplet, and a variety of meters that can be termed iambic (the issue of whether or not Callimachus composed lyric poetry is a somewhat complex one; see Cameron 1995: 163–66; Acosta-Hughes 2003: 478–82; Lelli 2005: 17–19). His poetry includes hymns, epigrams, the four-book elegiac *Aetia* (now fragmentary), occasional court pieces, invective, and the fragmentary hexameter *Hecale*. And in terms of quantity there was clearly a lot of Callimachus, as there was a lot of Ovid. The role of the *Aetia* in the development of elegy as a predominant metrical form in the Alexandrian period (where increasingly elegy and hexameter came to subsume much of the realm earlier occupied by e.g. lyric meters, Callimachus' own elegiac *Victory of Sosibius*, frr. 384–84a is a telling example) may also be a factor in Callimachus' later significance particularly (though not only) among Roman elegiac poets.

Callimachus composed a number of fairly celebrated occasional court pieces. One, the *Lock of Berenice*, which came to be included at the end of the fourth book of his elegiac *Aetia*, was a poem that captured the imagination of Catullus, Virgil, and later Ovid; poetic narrative of *apotheosis* came to serve as an important model for the poets of the early Roman Empire. One of Callimachus' poems, now largely lost, that may have been especially important in this regard was his poem celebrating the apotheosis of Arsinoe II (fr. 228 Pf., the term *ektheosis Arsinoes* preserved in a later prose summary may be a definition rather than a title); one scholar has suggested (Barchiesi *per litteras*) that this poem in particular may hold a key for understanding Callimachus' later popularity in Latin verse. Ovid's *Metamorphoses*, like Callimachus' *Aetia*, concludes with (a series of) apotheoses, culminating in that of the poem itself (*Met.* 15.871–79). Callimachus *Ep.* 15 GP (51 Pf.) is now read by some scholars as a poem on the apotheosis of the *Aetia*; Ovid appears, at the end of his long hexameter poem, to be doing something very similar.

A scholar of Hellenistic poetry raised the question 'How important *was* "Acontius and Cydippe?" '(Hunter 2006a: 129). The question is apt. This episode of the *Aetia*, whether known to its Roman admirers as a separate poem or not (Cameron: 1995: 255–61), clearly enjoyed a long life in Roman imitation; Catullus 65, Virgil *Ecl.* 10, Propertius 1.18 all recast portions of this erotic narrative. Ovid devotes two of his *Heroides* to this episode, and I'll touch below briefly on the figure of Acontius as poet that may have caught the attention of Ovid and others before him. The point I would stress here, however, is Callimachus' importance as an erotic poet. While it is true, as Lightfoot (Chapter 16) observes, that this is an aspect of Callimachus the loss of so much of his work has made somewhat obscure for us, nevertheless the degree to which he becomes an erotic model for later poetic (and in the case of Aristaenetus prose) tradition *does* suggest that here the Romans were 'reading' differently (Catullus' parallel treatment of Sappho and Callimachus is very telling in this instance).

A part of Callimachus' appeal for Ovid is clearly the way in which he wears a great deal of learning lightly, indeed, elegantly. Scholarly sources are alluded to, and even appear *in propria persona* in some of Callimachus' extant verse (Hipponax in the first *Iambus* and Pythagoras at the end of the *Metamorphoses* make an intriguing parallel). Callimachus' elegiac *Aetia* covers a large geographical and temporal canvas (the earthquake on Ceos (fr. 75) is a particularly early event in Greek cultural memory; the *Lock of Berenice* at the poem's end is more or less contemporary). It is less the facile management of didactic poetry per se, though, that prefigures Ovid, than the marriage of didactic and narrative. The structure of the *Aetia*, inasmuch as we can perceive the whole given the poem's fragmentary state (Harder 1993 and forthcoming) is especially important here not only for Ovid's composition of the *Fasti*, which is clearly in part modeled on the *Aetia*, but also his long hexameter *Metamorphoses*.

Surely the single most important aspect of Callimachus for his Roman emulators is his confrontation with the 'poetic' past. Not alone of Hellenistic poets, but perhaps most idiosyncratically and with the most variation, Callimachus appropriates (or subsumes) a matrix of earlier voices into his verse. The first fragment of the *Aetia* alone (Acosta-Hughes and Stephens 2002: 246–53) includes those of Homer, Hesiod, the *Homeric Hymn to Aphrodite*, Mimnermus, Aesop, Pindar, Plato, possibly Antimachus, Aristophanes, Euripides, perhaps Choerilus, and quite likely alludes to the New Sappho (Janko 2005). Earlier Greek poetry had always responded to other poetry (as Anacreon evokes Sappho, or Sappho reconfigures Homer, or Solon recasts Mimnermus etc.), but the manner of the response in poetry that engages at once with its heritage as physical texts and poetic models is more textured. Roman poets, in engaging with the Greek poetic past, had a model for doing this in Callimachus (see Hardie 2002c: 38)—in a sense his dream of poetic metempsychosis becomes theirs in turn.

A complete treatment of Ovid's use of Callimachus would need a book-length study of its own; indeed, though a number of works of secondary literature undertake aspects of this relationship, the definitive work on Ovid and the Callimachean tradition remains to be written. My purpose in the pages that follow is far less ambitious, though I hope it may suggest to this chapter's readers something of the wealth of this intertextual association and serve as an incentive to further appreciation of these two figures together. I highlight several of the different ways in which Ovid recalls Callimachus, beginning with the Roman poet's subtle, yet startling, assessment of Callimachus in the *Remedia amoris*. The study then turns to a paired general consideration of the legacy of Callimachus' *Aetia* in two different Ovidian works, in narrative structure (the *Metamorphoses*) and in poetic structure (the *Fasti*). The following sections focus on Ovid's enhancement of a Callimachean subject (Acontius and Cydippe in *Her.* 21–22), and here I then briefly outline some of the problematic issues involved in assessing Callimachus' influence as an erotic poet on Ovid, a tricky topic that is nonetheless worth rethinking. In conclusion this discussion turns to two texts on stylistic debate, *Am.* 3.1 and Callimachus *Iambus* 4, whose surprisingly parallel nature well deserves further study.

Callimachus in the Canon

Callimachi numeris non est dicendus Achilles,
    Cydippe non est oris, Homere, tui.

Achilles ought not to be sung in Callimachean meter, nor is Cyddipe a subject, Homer, for your voice. (*Rem.* 381–82)

Ovid's stylistic comparison of elegiac and epic subject material in the couplet above is typically light, elegant (with Achilles appropriately at the end of the hexameter, Cydippe at the beginning of the elegiac pentameter) and tongue in cheek—since, for Ovid, Achilles, too, may appear in the light of elegiac love poetry (*Her.* 3), and Achilles is indeed, throughout the *Remedia amoris*, sung in the Callimachean meter of elegiac couplet. Continuing this juxtaposition, the *Remedia* utilizes both Homeric and Callimachean material. Line 597: *perfide Demophoon* is a quotation *both* of the mythological Phyllis and of the poet Callimachus (fr. 556 Pf.: νυμφίε Δημοφόων, ἄδικε ξένε). Lines 747–8 (*cur nemo est, Hecalen, nulla est, quae ceperit Iron? / nempe quod alter egens, altera pauper erat*) recall one of the most celebrated of Callimachus' descriptive narratives, and one Ovid reconfigures elsewhere (in the Philemon and Baucis episode at *Met.* 624–724), and further again juxtaposes Callimachus and Homer. At *Rem.* 761–2 Callimachus appears again, this time in company with the lyric poets Sappho and Anacreon, and the Roman elegiac poets Tibullus, Propertius, and Gallus. The whole passage (*Rem.* 757–66) is important as an assessment of Callimachus, as well as of the evolution of love elegy:

eloquar inuitus: teneros ne tange poetas;
    summoueo dotes ipsius ipse meas.
Callimachus fugito, non est inimicus amori;
    et cum Callimacho tu quoque, Coe, noces.
me certe Sappho meliorem fecit amicae,
    nec rigidos mores Teia Musa dedit.

carmina quis potuit tuto legisse Tibulli
    uel tua, cuius opus Cynthia sola fuit?
quis poterit lecto durus discedere Gallo?
    et mea nescioquid carmina tale sonant.

Let me speak out, though against my will: touch not the gentle poets; I my gifts I myself
subtract [from their number]. Avoid Callimachus, for he is no enemy to love; and with
Callimachus you too, Coan, do harm. Sappho truly made me better for my girlfriend,
nor did the Teian Muse grant puritanical habits. Who could have read your poems,
Tibullus, safely, or yours, of whose work Cynthia was sole care? What man can be
impermeable to Gallus on reading him? And even my poems, for what they're worth,
have some such voice.

Lines 759–60 are a variation on Propertius 3.1: *Callimachi Manes et Coi sacra Philitae*
(see Hunter 2006b: 7–16). Puelma (1982: 224–25 = 1995: 363–64) suggests that
it was unlikely that the Romans in fact read Philetas (see also Lightfoot: 1999: 88;
Knox 1993). The association with Callimachus, which had become itself traditional,
was probably derived from later readers' familiarity with the opening of Callimachus'
Aetia. The same may well be true of Mimnermus in *Rem.* 381–2, where Ovid is
clearly recalling Propertius 1.9.11–12: *plus in amore ualet Mimnermi uersus Homero:
/ carmina mansuetus lenia quaerit Amor*. This may be an even closer model than
at first appears, since for Ovid Mimnermus may well be not so much the seventh-
century BCE elegiac poet as the Mimnermus Propertius knew from the opening of
Callimachus' *Aetia*.

Philetas here is not only, as usual, associated with Callimachus (cf. Quint. 10.1.58,
Puelma 1982, and Lightfoot 1999: 88), and characterized, as often, by his epithet
'Coan' (see Hollis 2006: 104 and n. 34), but subordinate to him to the extent of
being 'Callimacheanized'; Callimachus' name appears twice, and as subject he occupies three-quarters of the distich. The juxtaposition of Callimachus and Sappho is
one that is particularly Catullan, and one that suggests, in this light-hearted history
of erotic poetry, that the association itself had become conventional. At the same
time Callimachus appears at the head of a short history of elegy, with Callimachus,
Sappho, and Anacreon as artistic models for Augustan elegy, and Gallus, Propertius,
and Tibullus its primary pre-Ovidian practitioners. This is almost the mirror image
of the catalogue of erotic poets Ovid gives at *Ars* 3.329–334; again Callimachus and
'the Coan poet' head the list (*Ars* 329 *sit tibi Callimachi, sit Coi nota poetae*, 'be
familiar with Callimachus, and the poet of Cos').

Rem. 381–2, the distich that opens this discussion, contrasts Callimachus and
Homer *in elegy*, with Homer appearing, again in a slightly tongue-in-cheek moment,
in the elegiac pentameter, the metrical unit of which he is indeed *not* the composer.
The couplet also highlights something else: the cultural value of Callimachus for a
later audience of poets and readers of poetry, and particularly for Ovid. The juxtaposition of the two is no accident. As Ennius can define himself in terms of a reincarnation of Homer (*Annales* 1 frr. 2–10; see Skutsch 1985: 147–53), Propertius
can claim to be the 'Roman Callimachus' (4.1.64). Ennius' dream itself has a Callimachean precedent in that poet's dream of transfer to a youthful form on Mount

Helicon. Callimachus' stamp on Roman poetry begins early, and remains constant in the evolution of this later literature. It is in Ovid that we find, to cite Propertius' apt phrase—and Hunter's (2006b) recent title—the 'shadow of Callimachus' at perhaps its most pervasive.

The Panel and the Frame

With these terms K. Galinsky, in an early-modern study of Ovidian poetic structure (1975: 82–4), characterized the structure of the *Metamorphoses* in a compelling comparison with contemporary Roman wall painting. Yet in terms of the structure of a long poem, the same designation might be said to work equally well for Callimachus' *Aetia*. An elegiac poem in four books that is estimated to have consisted of some four to five thousand lines (Cameron 1995: 357 n. 76), the *Aetia* was not a continuous poetic narrative but a series of episodes artfully linked together, as the poet himself characterizes his work at fr. 1.4–5: οὐχ ἓν ἄεισμα διηνεκές . . . ἤνυσα ('I did not complete one continuous poem'). Our appreciation of the structure of the whole poem is in part obscured by the fragmentary state of what has survived; but of some facts we are fairly sure. The first two books, which many scholars believe were composed earlier (Parsons 1977: 49–50; Cameron 1995: 103–9) were framed as a dialogue of the Cyrenean poet, now transfigured as a youth on Mount Helicon, and the Muses Calliope and Clio and perhaps others, for example Erato. The first book was largely concerned with heroic legend, particularly the return of the Argonauts from Colchis and Heracles. The second book, of which we know perhaps the least, included an extensive account of Sicilian city foundations preceded, it now appears (Zetzel 1981: 31–33; Massimilla 1996: 399–401), by a symposiastic scene in Alexandria—there seems to have been a contrast of East and West, with Alexandria perhaps at the center, which is of some interest when thinking of the structure of the *Metamorphoses*. The latter two books lacked the dialogue format, rather the transition from one episode to another seems to have been differently configured. The third book comprised a greater number of erotic episodes, the fourth those that might be frankly termed 'bizarre'. But this is not to over-schematize; there is marked variation throughout the poem. One particular feature that sets off the last two books, at least in the work's final form, is the inclusion of occasional poems celebrating Berenice II Euergetes at the beginning and end of this part of the poem (the *Victory of Berenice* and the *Lock of Berenice* respectively).

In some aspects the narrative structure of Ovid's *Metamorphoses* is clearly very different. Ovid specifically characterizes his poem as a continuous work (*Met.* 1.2–4 *coeptis adspirate meis primaque ab origine mundi / ad mea perpetuum deducite tempora carmen*, 'breathe favorably upon my beginnings, and from the world's first origin, lead on a continuous song to my times'), and the choice of hexameter, the meter associated particularly with heroic epic, supports the expectation of continuity in the reader's mind. The poem proceeds from the origin of the world to the reign of Augustus, so presenting in some sense a (more or less) linear history. While there are a variety of temporal settings in the *Aetia*, there does not appear to be an overarching temporal linearity (though it is clear from both the *Epilogue* (fr. 112 Pf.), thought by some scholars to be the conclusion of an earlier two-book edition (Knox 1985, 1993), and the *Lock of Berenice* (fr. 110), that the poet has returned to his contemporary setting, and so to the point of departure from which the original dream (fr. 2 Pf.) began. Nor is there anything like the division of gods/heroes/ historical figures that marks the *Metamorphoses*. The first *aition* of *Aetia* 1 (frr. 3– 17.14 Pf. *The Parian Graces*) tells of Minos learning of the death of his son Androgeos; among the final episodes of *Aetia* 4 are one that figures the same Androgeos (fr. 103 Pf., though here possibly a statue) and the *Argo*'s anchor left at Cyzicus (frr. 108–9 Pf.), which returns us to the Argonauts, whose return journey is one of the themes of *Aetia* 1.

Yet there are also some striking features that the two long poems share. One is the 'Chinese box' character of embedded narrative of individual episodes: smaller narratives arise in the context of larger ones (e.g. those of the nymphs Cyane and Arethusa in the larger narrative of Cere's search for Proserpina in *Met.* 5, and the destruction of the Telchines in the context of the Acontius and Cydippe episode in *Aetia* 3). Another is the subsumption of multiple poetic genres and generic features into a larger poem, a compositional strategy that is typically Hellenistic (e.g. Theocritus *Id.* 7, which incorporates multiple lyric moments into bucolic hexameter) and of which the *Aetia* is the most outstanding example on a large scale and in the multiplicity of generic features involved (Harrison 2002: 89). Both poets use the ordering technique of related or similar episodes. Both poems have a marked interest in local lore and certain kinds of recondite detail, which reflect their common character as 'Hellenistic' poems if not a more specific rapport with each other. And we should not overlook two other commonalities. The relationship, as Lightfoot observes (Chapter 16) of *aition* and metamorphosis is a peculiarly close one (and see Graf 2002: 115). Narrative of a metamorphosis explains the *aition* of a subject's present state: the *Lock of Berenice* narrates the change from lock of hair to star. While not a model in exactly the same sense as Nicander's *Heteroioumena*, a long poem that details the *aitia*, the 'coming into being' of rituals and behavior, would clearly be of great compositional interest to Ovid in his *Metamorphoses*. And, indeed, Ovid's disinclination to follow Callimachus' path in his choice of composing a *perpetuum carmen* ('continuous song') does not demonstrate inattention to his predecessor but rather close reading. For Ovid's poem will be at once a *perpetuum carmen* and one that is *deductum*; continuous, yet finely wrought in the Callimachean tradition of stylistic refinement (on the Callimachean overtones of the opening of the *Metamorphoses* see Wheeler 1999: 8–30). Although we now know that the text of *Aet.* 1.11 *cannot* have been αἱ κατὰ λεπτόν (Bastianini 1996; Lehnus 2006: 133– 147), the equivalence of *deductum* and λεπτότης elsewhere in Callimachus remains a valid one.

And in both cases there is the appropriation of traditional mythology from a new topographical perspective. Callimachus dreams that he is transported as a youth from North Africa to Helicon (an image Ovid will recall, also in retrospect, at *Tr.* 4.10.58: *carmina cum primum populo iuuenalia legi, / barba resecta mihi bisue semelue fuit,* 'when first I read my youthful poems to the people, my beard had been only cut twice or for the first time', where Ovid is also clearly recalling the image of Callimachus as child-poet at *Aet.* fr. 1.21–2; see also McKeown 1987: 74), where he engages in dialogue with the Muses; in fr. 178 (*The Ician Guest*), now thought to have come early in *Aetia* 2, he is the guest of an Athenian resident in Alexandria. The *Victory of Berenice* narrates the arrival of the queen's success from Nemea to Pharos (the same episode tells of the common origin of the Egyptians and the Colchians). In fr. 110 (*The Lock of Berenice*) Zephyr bears the Egyptian queen's hair from Zephyrium (Alexandria) to Heaven. The episodes of the *Aetia* occur over a wide geographical canvas; the perspective, though, is a North African one; Ovid's *Metamorphoses* culminates in the arrival of a Greek god (Aesculapius) in Rome, but more largely in the transition/continuation of his Greek mythological journey on Italian soil. Both poems can be seen as mapping the Greek cultural heritage from a new vantage point, and claiming it as their own.

The individual episodes of Ovid's poem that have the most striking Callimachean counterparts do not find these in the extant fragments of the *Aetia* but in other of Callimachus' poetic works (particularly the *Hecale*, in the case of the crow and the raven in *Met.* 2, on which see esp. Keith 1992: 9–61, and Baucis and Philemon in *Met.* 8, and the *Hymn to Demeter* in the case of *Erysichthon* at *Met.* 8). In part this is unsurprising. *Aetia* and metamorphosis, while related, are not identical: Ovid's poem is of the transformation of individuals; Callimachus' of the instantiation of cult and ritual practice. Hence it is only to be expected that a poem like Nicander's *Heteroioumena*, though we know it only in a partial and epitomized form, would have a greater proportion of one-to-one correspondences in terms of individual figures with Ovid's *Metamorphoses*.

It's worth noting that Nicander's poem may itself in some ways have imitated the structure of Callimachus' *Aetia*, and this is significant indeed when appraising Ovid's use of both poets. The opening summary of Antoninus' *Metamorphoseon Synagoge*, the tale of Ctesilla, includes the startling comparison (1.11): ὥσπερ ὅτε Κυδίππην Ἀκόντιος ἐξηπάτησεν ('as when Acontius deceived Cydippe'), a tale famously related in the third book of Callimachus' *Aetia* (frr. 67–75 Pf.). The hand that inscribed the tag above the summary notes that Nicander recounted the tale of Ctesilla in the third book of his *Heteroioumena*. So the text reads its model, and leaves a tantalizing trace of intertextual associations: Callimachus as read through Nicander as read by Antoninus as read, possibly, by yet another figure, the author of the inscription. A careful reading of the summaries contained in Antoninus Liberalis whose themes the inscriptional hand assigns to Nicander (22 of the 41 episodes) reveals a complex relationship between the fragments of the *Heteroioumena*, as we discern them in Antoninus, and Callimachus' long elegiac poem. Nicander composed, in four books, a poem that recounted metamorphoses, many of these markedly aetiological in character. There appear to be marked structural similarities as well: Nicander in his first book recounted a meeting of singer and muses (Ant. Lib. 22 Cerambus), in his second a tale (the Messapiens, Ant. Lib. 31) set in the Greek west: the third book of the *Heteroioumena* included the tale of Ctesilla; the fourth the metamorphoses of the gods into the animal figures of Egyptian cult, one of the stranger episodes in the collection. The immediate structural parallels with Callimachus' *Aetia* are striking;

and, indeed, a close reading of the shards of the *Heteroioumena* suggests more than structural similarity—Nicander's poem must have been much indebted to the *Aetia*. Ovid's long hexameter *Metamorphoses* implicates both models. The actual surviving fragments of the *Heteroioumena* are few (frr. 43–62 Gow and Scholfield), but what we can establish with these and the summaries in Antoninus is that this was a hexameter poem in four books that comprised stories of metamorphosis possibly ordered in a way that reflected, as the number of the books, Callimachus' *Aetia*. This would in turn suggest that Ovid had already in Nicander a model for adapting features of Callimachus' elegiac poem to hexameter. The fragmentary state of both the *Aetia*, and more so in this case of the *Heteroiouma*, impede closer comparative reading. It is nonetheless quite likely that Ovid's poem is in some senses a (very) large-scale example of what Wills has terms 'double-reference' in Latin allusion: 'B refers to C by single reference, then A refers to both B and C . . . Example: Catullus refers to Callimachus; then Virgil simultaneously refers to Callimachus and the Catullan imitation' (Wills 1998: 284; McKeown 1987: 37–45).

Further, Ovid's recall of Callimachus *tout court* might be termed a very large-scale (and very multifaceted) example of what Wills (1998: 285) terms 'divided reference': 'Two cross-references, A and B, each refer to C in different ways. Example: Virgil takes a single passage in Catullus and divides it into two passages in the *Aeneid*.' A striking case in point would be the opening of the *Aetia*; this Ovid evokes at the opening of the *Metamorphoses*, the *Fasti*, and the *Amores*. The structure of the *Aetia*, particularly the first two books, must in turn have been an important model for the *Ars* (Harrison 2002: 83) and clearly individual episodes (especially it would seem Acontius and Cydippe) play a role not only in Ovid's choice of thematic material (as in *Her.* 20 and 21) but also in Ovid's characterization of Callimachus as an erotic poet in the *Tristia* and the *Remedia*. Ovid's recall of Callimachus not only implicates earlier Roman renditions of Callimachus (Catullus c. 66 would be one example; Virgil's recall of the *Aetia* in the *Georgics* another) but also involves his own use of Callimachus in the many Callimachean appearances in his own work—Ovid's Callimachus is a complex *intratextual* rapport as well. The opening lines of the *Fasti*, *tempora cum causis Latium digesta per annum / lapsaque sub terras ortaque signa canam* ('times arranged with their causes throughout the Latin year, and the constellations set below the earth and risen again, these I'll sing'), a clear echo of the theme of Callimachus' poem (*causae* = *aitia*), read differently against the opening of the *Metamorphoses* (where Ovid will compose a poem both Callimachean and not) and the opening lines of *Am.* 1.1, which recall a long tradition of Roman readings of the *Aetia*'s opening lines. All are Ovidian representations of Callimachus, and all are different from one another.

The *Fasti* is, in some senses, the most exact Ovidian reflection of Callimachus, with the possible exception of the *Ibis*, though here ordering, structure, and theme are distinctly Ovid's. In the fourth book of his elegies Propertius, who, like Ovid, is a poet whose rapport with Callimachus is multilayered (Harrison 2002: 85; Hollis 2006: 115–23; Hunter 2006b: 7–21), had in some sense prefigured Ovid's adaptation of Callimachus' *Aetia* to an assembling of Roman monuments. Ovid's twelve-book poem (of which only the first six survive; see Newlands 2002a: 201, 215) of connected *aitia*, historical, religious, and astronomical, narrated in the 'frame' of the Roman calendar, is clearly modeled, in many ways, on Callimachus' long elegiac poem. This is true both of the poem's larger goal (the explication of cultural monuments) and in many details of its narrative structure (the presentation of material framed as question and answer) and narrative style (the occasional longer, self-contained episode set amidst smaller ones). The extended relationship of these two works is the subject of a number of studies (e.g. Miller 1982, 1992) and ongoing scholarship. In the necessarily limited context here, I would like just to highlight a couple of features of the engagement of the two texts.

Ovid's poem opens with a dedication to Germanicus Caesar; here the gesture to the Roman *recusatio* tradition, found both at the beginning of the *Am.* and in a more nuanced way at the opening of the *Metamorphoses*, is differently configured at lines 13–14:

> Caesaris arma canant alii: nos Caesaris aras,
> et quoscumque sacras addidit ille dies.

> Let others sing of Caesar's arms; I shall sing of Caesar's altars and the holy days he added to the calendar.

The *causis*, third word in the poem's first line and immediately at the poem's first *caesura*, clearly evokes Callimachus' poem and at the same time the Roman tradition that this poem informs (Schiesaro 2002: 64); the address to a royal family member *may* do so. While we know that *Aetia* 3–4 were framed by poems in honor of Berenice II Euergetes (the *Victory of Berenice* and the *Lock of Berenice* respectively), we know somewhat less about the framing of *Aetia* 1–2. A scholion to line 41 of *Aetia* 1 suggests that Arsinoe figured in the opening of the poem, perhaps numbered as tenth among the Muses (Harder forthcoming: ad loc.); the reference to a queen in fr. 112.2 (the 'Epilogue' to the *Aetia*), possibly to an original version consisting of *Aetia* 1 and 2, may further suggest that Arsinoe also figured in the poem's first conclusion (Cameron 1995: 160–62, 371; Harder forthcoming). The suggestion that the *Fasti*'s initial dedication to a member of the imperial house reflects a similar gesture (now obscured in part by the loss of so much of the poem) at the opening of Callimachus' *Aetia* seems on the surface very likely—Ovid has recast much of Callimachus' poem in his own. And the parallel case of Propertius 4 and its rapport to *Aetia* 3–4 is very revealing (Hollis 2006: 115–16).

One feature from the opening lines of his Alexandrian predecessor is the poet's first interaction with one of his informants, the god Janus (1.89–94):

> quem tamen esse deum te dicam, Iane biformis?
> nam tibi par nullum Graecia numen habet.
> ede simul causam, cur de caelestibus unus,
> sitque quod a tergo, sitque quod ante, uides?
> haec ego cum sumptis agitarem mente tabellis,
> lucidior uisa est, quam fuit ante domus.

> Yet what god am I to say you are, double-shaped Janus? For Greece has no divinity like you. Tell at the same time the reason, why alone of the heavenly ones, you see both from the back and the front. While I was musing thus, on taking up my writing tablets, the house seemed brighter than it was before.

The observation that Greece has no god like Janus playfully misdirects the reader from the Callimachean model for this scene, the child poet, on taking up his writing tablet, whom Apollo addresses at *Aetia* fr. 1.21–2: καὶ γὰρ ὅτ‚ε πρ‚ώ‚τιϲτον ἐμοῖϲ ἐπὶ δέλτον ἔθηκα | γουναίϲ‚ιν, ᾿Α[πο]λλων εἶπεν ὅ μοι Λύκιοϲ ('for when first I put my writing tablet on my knees, Lycian Apollo said to me'). Janus is the first divine source of 'information' to appear in the *Fasti* (Apollo is subtly and cleverly diverted on to Germanicus in the simile at 19–20: *pagina iudicium docti subitura mouetur / principis, ut Clario missa legenda deo*), as Apollo is the first divinity of the *Aetia*. The *tabellae*, a setting for either juvenile or playful writing, as in another passage of Callimachean resonance (Cat. 50.2 *multum lusimus in meis tabellis*), here recall the intentionally puerile gesture (note *sumptis*) of Callimachus' pupil-poet. The Callimachean scene of a god instructing a poet, which already had a long history in Roman poetry before Ovid's *Fasti*, has been recalled in a new way with the focus not on song interrupted, let alone on sacrificial imagery, but on the writing tablets.

Ovid seems to have disposed of another structural feature (the Muses) differently than Callimachus. For one thing, in the latter's poem, the Muses, Calliope and Clio (though *SH* fr. 238a.8: ᾿Ερατὼ δ᾿ ἀνταπάμειπτο τά[δε somewhat complicates this picture), appear as interlocutors in the first two books, in the *Fasti* in the later books that are extant. Ovid, on the other hand, has a distinct plurality of individual Muses (including Erato at 4.195–6, whose name the poet etymologizes). Both poems have a variety of speakers and interlocutors, both offer multiple explanations (Schiesaro 2002: 65), and in both the dialogue form allows for the exposition, often humorous, of the *doctus poeta*.

There are, however, many aspects in which Ovid's poem is distinctly Roman. The *causae* of its opening line align it with a tradition of Roman didactic poetry (Schiesaro 2002: 64–66), just as the god that comes upon Ovid with his *sumptae tabellae* is a distinctly Roman god. Indeed, the confluence of Roman and Greek mythologies is something that Ovid himself highlights at 2.359–60: *adde peregrinis causas, mea Musa, Latinas, / inque suo noster puluere currat equus* ('add Latin origins, my Muse, to foreign ones, that my horse may run in its own dust'). Above all, there is that very Roman subject: the Roman calendar. It is perhaps this most Roman of subjects that allows for the close alignment with Callimachus in other respects—the *Fasti* is indeed a collection of *aetia*, but *aetia* of a Roman institution.

Acontius the Poet

The Acontius and Cydippe episode of *Aetia* 3 has a long reception in Roman poetry. Here we are doubly fortunate in having not only the later reworkings of this Callimachean poem but also, thanks to papyrus fragments found at Oxyrhynchus, large portions from the poem's opening and conclusion (although not, sadly, the two parts of this work that were to have the greatest afterlife, the trick of the inscribed apple and Acontius' monologue). This poem may well have enjoyed a circulation independent of its insertion in the *Aetia* (Cameron 1995: 255–61), and it is possible (though not certain) that Ovid knew this as an independent elegy; *Rem.* 381–2, while they do not prove that Ovid is referring to a title rather than simply the poem's heroine, are suggestive here (the main figure in Callimachus' poem is Acontius, so Ovid's choice of Cydippe as referent is intriguing). In Callimachus' version, Acontius, in a trope that 'Eros makes one a poet who was Museless before' (Eur. fr. 663 Kannicht; cf. also Nicias *SH* fr. 566), by composing an oath on an apple (and subsequently wishing his love inscribed on trees) is figured as an elegiac poet. For him love and loss are the motivation for elegiac composition (love and sorrow are two of the *topoi* of elegiac composition, cf. (on Antimachus' *Lyde*) Hermesianax fr. 7.41–6). The inscribed oath, whether or not it actually figured verbally in the poem, and the inscription of Cydippe's name, both play on the 'theme' of the elegiac poet; Callimachus the poet lurks behind the 'poet' Acontius. The oath as it originally appeared in Callimachus' text, if indeed it did, we can only surmise, since the text as preserved at Artistaenetus 1.10 (μὰ τὴν Ἄρτεμιν, Ἀκοντίῳ γαμοῦμαι) does not scan. It clearly did figure in the poem; hence Ovid's play on the inscription at *Her.* 20.240–2: *effigie pomi testatur Acontius huius, / quae fuerint in eo scripta fuisse rata* ('by the image of this apple let Acontius declare that the words once inscribed thereon have found fulfillment'). And it resembles a conceit we find elsewhere in Callimachus at play with dedicatory inscriptions, for example in the concluding fragmentary lines of *Iambus* 6 (Acosta-Hughes 2002). Note that Cydippe reads the apple, as she would any other inscribed object, in a sanctuary of Artemis (Aristaen. 1.10; Ov. *Her.* 20.5–6). Three lines of Acontius' monologue, of which there is a lengthy paraphrase in Aristaenetus 1.10, and Propertius' rendition at 1.18, survive in two fragments (frr. 73–4 Pf.):

> ἀλλ' ἐνὶ δὴ φλοιοῖσι κεκομμένα τόσσα φέροιτε
> γράμματα, Κυδίππην ὅσσ' ἐρέουσι καλήν.

But may you bear as many letters inscribed on your bark as will call Cydippe beautiful.

λιρὸς ἐγώ, τί δὲ σοι τόνδ' ἐπέθηκα φόβον;

wretched am I, why did I set this fear upon you?

Callimachus has taken the conceit that Acontius, admired for his beauty by older men (frr. 68–9), has changed the *graffito* he might see of himself, Ἀκόντιος καλός into an appeal itself figured as an elegiac couplet celebrating Cydippe (in, however, a remote setting, where it is not part of the public erotica of his male world). λιρὸς ἐγώ *can* be rendered into Latin by *me miserum* (e.g. *Her.* 20.133; cf., however, Magnelli on Alexander Aetolus fr. 3.30: λιρὰ νοσεῦσα γυνή); and it's worth noting that the poem, as we have it (the opening distich is widely, though not universally, thought to be missing) begins *pone metum*, which works both contextually (Cydippe's reading will not implicate her in another oath) and as an allusion (to Acontius' lament in the Callimachean version).

In Callimachus' version the central figure is Acontius. Cydippe is silent, read as an erotic object, a patient, and finally part of a genealogical history (it is widely assumed that she would read the inscribed oath, but again we don't actually know how this reading was configured in Callimachus). Acontius, from the opening to the last line (happily both preserved, frr. 67.1 and 75.76–7), is both narrative agent and primary focus of attention. Further, there is a close rapport of poet (Callimachus) and poet (Acontius), underlined by the apostrophes at fr. 75.44, 53, 75) as well as by Acontius' first-person utterances. Both Virgil, in his portrayal of the poet Gallus in love at *Ecl.* 10, and Propertius, at 1.18, have built on this. Catullus in the concluding simile of 65 appears to evoke Cydippe (see now esp. Hunter 2006b: 88, 101; Barchiesi 2001a: 127), but again as object of another's gaze. The blush elicited by the apple rolling forth is perceived by another. Ovid appears to play on this with Acontius' perceiving the course of the apple—*Her.* 20.209 *postmodo nescio qua uenisse uolubile malum* ('then, I know not whence, came this rolling apple'). Whereas further at Cat. 65.20–22 the apple falls forth from the girl's lap, it's very striking that at *Her.* 20.207–10 the apple's projection is somehow loosely (note *nescio qua* at 209) connected to Acontius' cloak slipping off his shoulder—one of several moments in Ovid's treatment that recall not only Callimachus' poem but also its Roman renditions.

Ovid gives Cydippe a voice, though, appropriately, in secret (*Her.* 21.19–28). Acontius, in Ovid's version cast in the roll of an *exclusus amator*, composes from a public, she from a private, setting. So even in the variation of moving Acontius to Naxos, Ovid intriguingly maintains the 'places' of the two figures in Callimachus' poem: where Acontius is either in an urban or sylvan exterior, Cydippe is portrayed as ill in her chamber. And Acontius thus effectively in Ovid's version takes on the role of the poet 'Callimachus' who details Cydippe's illness. Both letters are replete with Callimachean references, which can be conveniently categorized as:

A. recollections of the inscribed oath of the Callimachean original, however this figured in the Callimachus text (20.33 *iterum scribo*; 21.108 *ei mihi, iuraui nunc quoque paene tibi*; and of course the final inscription at 20.239–40).

B. recollections of individual moments of the Callimachean original: 20.25–30 *non ego natura nec sum tam callidus usu; / sollertem tu me, crede puella, facis* etc. (recalling Callim. fr. 67.1–3: Αὐτὸς Ἔρως ἐδίδαξεν Ἀκόντιον . . . τέχνην / οὐ γὰρ ὅγ᾽ ἔσκε πολύκρατος;); 20.55–56 *tu facis hoc oculique tui, quibus ignea cedunt / sidera, qui flammae causa fuere meae* (recasting Callim. fr. 67.8: καλοὶ νησάων ἀστέρες ἀμφότεροι,, with the nice touch that Acontius, the Callimachean 'narrator' of Ovid's version, takes on this observation himself); 20.97–8 *adfuit (sc. Diana) et uidit, cum tu decepta rubebas, / et uocem memori condidit aure tuam* (recalling Callim. fr. 75.26–7: Δήλῳδ᾽ἦν ἐπίδημος, Ἀκόντιον ὁππότε σὴ παῖς / ὤμοσεν, οὐκ ἄλλον, νυμφίον ἐξέμεναι—here with *adfuit* subtly translating ἐπιδήμιος). A particularly lovely rendition is the transition from actor to figure acted upon in Cydippe's (Ovid's) *Forsitan haec spectans a te spectabar, Aconti* (*Her.* 21.103) for Acontius (Callimachus) fr. 70 ἀλλ᾽ ἀπὸ τόξου /

αὐτὸς ὁ τοξευτὴς ἄρδιν ἔχων ἑτέρου. Even the legalistic image (part of the larger legal coloring of both poems, see Kenney 1970b) of *Her.* 20.30 *consultoque fui iuris Amore uafer* is prefigured in Callimachus' ψήφου δ᾿ ἂν ἐμῆς ἐπιμάρτυρες εἶεν / οἵτινες οὐ χαλεποῦ νήιδές εἰσι θεοῦ.

C. recollections of other Callimachean poems. Here the most immediately striking are the recall of the *Hymn to Delos* at *Her.* 21.83–4 (Cydippe envisions Delos in flight) and 21.100 (recalling the image of the olive at line 322 of the *Hymn to Delos*, repeated at *Iambus* 4.84, and again at *Iambus* 13.62), and the *Hymn to Apollo* with the altar of bone at 21.99. I wonder too whether *Her.* 20.21–3 (*Deceptam dicas nostra te fraude licebit, / dum fraudis nostrae causa feratur amor. / fraus mea quid petit, nisi uti tibi iungerer, unum?*) is not in part modeled on Callim. *Ep.* 62 Pf. with its play on the definition of love as 'wrong' (line 6: εἰτοῦτ᾿ ἔστ᾿ ἀδίκημ᾿, ἀδικέω, where the poet-speaker is, among other things, an *exclusus amator*).

Her. 20–21, the letters of Acontius and Cydippe, are the third of three pairs of letters (on these poems as *Gedichtbuch* see Kenney 1996: 18–20). It's worth noting that the Callimachean original was one of several erotic episodes of *Aetia* 3; the following episodes are those of the Elean marriage rites (frr. 76–7), and shortly after those of Phrygius and Pieria (frr. 80–3). Further, it is possible that the episode of Phyllis and Demophoon, of which only fr. 556 Pf. remains, also occurred in *Aetia* 3 (cf. D'Alessio 1996: 725 n. 63); this episode is also the artistic impetus for Ovid *Her.* 2 and in part for Dido's farewell to Aeneas in *Aen.* 4 (Heinze 1915: 134 n. 1). It's worth noting that the arrangement of the first three *Heroides* also juxtaposes Homer and Callimachus: Callimachus' erotic *aitia* read love in a variety of contexts, particularly in both peace and war—the points of tangent with Ovid's *Gedichtbuch* are obviously many, and this is a rapport of these two poets that merits further study.

Epigraph and Poet

Before *Am.* 1 Ovid prefixes an epigram that serves as the epigraph to the collection (in other words attests its completion or reconfiguration in the present form):

> Qui modo Nasonis fueramus quinque libelli,
>   tres sumus; hoc illi praetulit auctor opus.
> ut iam nulla tibi nos sit legisse uoluptas,
>   at leuior demptis poena duobus erit.

> Who once were five little books, we are now three; this form the poet preferred to that. That though even so you may have no pleasure in reading us, yet with two books gone your pain will be lighter.

The scholarship on this epigram has been concerned primarily with its value as historical witness to a second edition of the *Amores* (McKeown 1987: 76–7; Cameron 1968). One immediate model is obviously Catullus 1, which Ovid recalls verbally in *qui modo . . . libelli* (Catullus' poem opens: *Cui dono lepidum nouum libellum, arida modo pumice expolitum?*) and thematically in the juxtaposition of the pleasure and labor of reading (or lack thereof). Catullus is certainly the proximate model, but the original is very likely a Callimachus epigram (*Ep.* 15 GP = 51 Pf.) that I have argued elsewhere (Acosta-Hughes and Stephens 2009; see also Petrovic and Petrovic 2004) is the epigraph for the completed *Aetia*.

τέσσαρες αἱ Χάριτες, ποτὶ γὰρ μία ταῖς τρισὶ κείναις
    ἄρτι ποτεπλάσθη, κῆτι μύροισι νοτεῖ
εὐαίων ἐν πᾶσιν ἀρίζηλος Βερενίκα,
    ἇς ἄτερ οὐδ' αὐταὶ ταὶ Χάριτες Χάριτες

Four are the Graces. For amidst the other three just now a new one has been fashioned, still moist with perfume, Berenice, splendid, blessed among all, without whom the Graces themselves would not be Graces.

Especially pertinent to Ovid's epigraph are the revision of the number of books, the reference to authorial 'fashioning', and a slight but nonetheless noticeable repetition of ἄρτι in *modo*. Ovid here, as elsewhere, is heir to a tradition of Roman imitation of Callimachus; in this case the Catullus poem provides the 'window' on to the Callimachean original.

One of the *Amores* that has a striking Callimachean precursor, one little studied, is *Am.* 3.1, Ovid's *agon* of Tragedy and Elegy (both, we remember, genres in which he composed). The precursor is *Iambus* 4, a poem that contains a lengthy fable of an *agon* of a laurel and an olive tree, a fable that serves as an allegory for poetic styles in which, notably, Callimachus composed (see further Acosta-Hughes 2002: 191–2). In part *Am.* 3.1 is a rendition of another Augustan theme evolved from Callimachean poetics, the *recusatio*. Aside from the parallel structure, the order of the speeches, and the manner of speaking, Tragedy wroth, Elegy slightly sardonic, there are some rather more specific possible allusions to *Iambus* 4. Whereas Tragedy points out that the poet's elegiac composition is making him an object of ridicule, Elegy takes some pride in her more popular role. The initial response of Elegy to Tragedy (lines 37–8) is very like that of the olive to the laurel: the adversary has provided the best argument for her own defeat. Elegy's denomination of Tragedy as *grauis* and *sublimis* reflects that of the olives' denomination of the laurel as καλή—all are adjectives that can be understood, in terms of literary criticism, to refer to certain kinds and perceptions of elevated literature. Many other parallels, among them the physical descriptions of the speakers, particularly the haughty manner of Tragedy and the mock self-deprecation of *Elegy*, encourage a closer comparison of the two poems. Finally, *Lydius* at line 14, while appropriate, seems at first somewhat unnecessary and stands out as the only such adjective of place aside from the name *Romana tragoedia*. Might not the point be a subtle allusion to *Iambus* 4, where οἱ πάλαι Λυδοί (line 7) are designated the origin of fable? Callimachus' poetic rendition of a popular fable in choliambic trimeter (he may be drawing here on a number of folk traditions, most likely in prose) reappears in Ovid's elegiac debate on poet and genre—a perfect example of one *poeta doctus* reworking the craft of another.

FURTHER READING

The standard Greek edition of Callimachus is still Pfeiffer's (1949–53); a new edition of the fragmentary poetry, edited by Lehnus, is shortly forthcoming with Teubner. Nisetich (2001) offers a comprehensive translation in English with substantial notes; some readers may prefer the 1987 translations of Lombardo and Rayor. An excellent introduction to Callimachus' *Aetia* is now provided by Fantuzzi and Hunter (2004) in their second chapter on 'The aetiology of Callimachus' *Aitia*'. On Callimachean poetics see Bing (1988: 1–90), and for a different assessment Cameron (1995), especially Chapters 1–3. Both volumes of the *Hellenistica Groningana* series on Callimachus contain important pieces on Callimachus' influence on roman poetry; see Thomas (1993). On the same topic a new wide-ranging study is Hunter (2006b). Keith (1992) gives a close reading of an extant Callimachean text and its Ovidian re-creation; for readers of the *Fasti* interested in Ovid's use of the *Aetia* in this poem, Miller's monograph (1991) has much of value, as do several of his other works on Callimachus and Ovid.

CHAPTER EIGHTEEN

Ovid's Catullus and the Neoteric Moment in Roman Poetry

David Wray

Predecessors in Roman Poetry

Ovid's relation to Catullus, like that of any Roman poet to an important predecessor, needs to be understood in the broader context of the culture they shared by inheritance and changed and reshaped, in some measure, by their poetry. In nearly every aspect of life, Romans were deeply traditional social agents, looking back to illustrious forebears as standards for measuring their own achievements, models to imitate, and rivals to outdo. Roman literature was no exception in this regard, and from the earliest history of the literary language we hear of a number of poetic 'fathers' being held up as exemplary predecessors in a recognizably Roman way. So, for example, in the late third century BC, Livius Andronicus made a Latin translation of the *Odyssey* in Saturnian meter, a native Roman verse form. Renowned as the first long poem written in Latin, Livius' *Odisia* was still being used two centuries later as a beginning textbook when Horace was a schoolboy. But early in the second century BC, well within living memory of Livius' achievement, a younger poet named Quintus Ennius had made his own bid for poetic firstness, a considerably more impressive one, by writing the first Latin epic that was an original poem rather than a translation. If Ennius' *Annales* successfully staked a claim to be acknowledged as the first authentically Roman epic (by its Roman mythological and historical themes and its powerful statements of Roman values) and therefore could be said in some sense to have fathered Latin poetry, it is also the case that, from the viewpoint of poetic form, Ennius had scored a different kind of victory over his immediate predecessor, namely he had achieved a more deeply engaged response to Greek poetic tradition. Ennius' was the first Latin verse to be composed in dactylic hexameter, the metrical structure that all Greek epic had taken from Homer, and that all subsequent Roman epic would now take from Homer by way of Ennius.

Livius Andronicus and Ennius, whose works survive only in fragments, are just two of the more historically prominent early examples of Roman poets establishing strong claims to precedence and being remembered for it. Getting there first was a claim that poets writing in Latin, even in the classical period and beyond, continued to stake with pride whenever they could. And, just as in Ennius' case, acknowledged originality continued to reside, for Roman poets and their knowledgeable readers, in the achievement of a new kind of response to Greekness. Belonging to the imagined community of Roman poetic tradition always entailed thinking in at least two languages, living in at least two cultures, and negotiating a complex set of reverential and aggressive relations with competing and overlapping lines of predecessors.

This way of conceiving a poetic tradition and poets within it, while not totally unrecognizable from a modern viewpoint, looks and feels importantly different from the model of the 'strong poet' as a towering original genius that has featured prominently in much modern talk about poetry by poets and critics. Saying this is not to deny that ancient Roman poets did sometimes talk about individual poets as possessing inimitable greatness. Horace, for example, says this about Pindar. And original genius, as a broad critical notion, does go a long way toward adequately describing the ambitions and highest achievements of ancient Roman poets as well as modern European and American ones. From the standpoint of our own place in history, the first unfragmented poetry in Latin that merits being described in terms of genius can be found in a smallish corpus of mostly short poems, a little over a hundred in number, probably published together and purchasable for centuries thereafter as a set of three bookrolls in a single case. The young man who wrote these poems was called Gaius Valerius Catullus. He was born in the Eighties of the first century BC in Verona, spent much of his adult life in Rome, and was probably dead by the end of the Fifties.

Catullus and the Neoterics as Predecessors to Ovid

For modern readers, Catullus has long stood at the head of Roman poetic history, and this is true even though we know something about some of his predecessors. Catullus is the first artist of the Latin language we can still read today whose claim to authentic, authoritative status as a poet has been acknowledged by nearly every reader who has cared about poetry, both in later antiquity and through every modern century since the rediscovery of his poems at the beginning of the fourteenth century. The Renaissance prized him as a poet of wit and verve, a nobler and stronger predecessor to Martial. The Romantics thrilled to his searingly intimate voice in the poems of love and disillusionment focused on the woman he calls Lesbia. Twentieth-century poets and critics found a kindred modernist spirit in his concision, directness, and psychological realism.

And twentieth-century classical scholars, for their part, have enabled us to see the deep truth beneath Cicero's apparently dismissive characterization of the younger poets of his day when he called them *novi poetae* in Latin and *neoteroi* in Greek: the 'new poets'. As the only surviving representative of a fiercely erudite and subtly allusive mode of literary production now generally described as 'neoteric', Catullus has come into critical focus over the past few generations of scholarship as a chief ringleader in a set of innovations in Roman poetry, innovations that were strong and bold enough to merit being called a revolution. It is true, nonetheless, that our focus will be more skewed than it has to be if we fail to acknowledge that terms like 'revolution' and 'movement', when applied figuratively to the context of art and criticism, have certain historically specific resonances for us, simply because our formation as readers includes the effects of cultural and social processes that are historically specific to the avant-garde modernism of the twentieth century.

Even 'neoteric', it is important to emphasize, is not a historically attested ancient term for an ancient poetic movement or aesthetic school to which Catullus could plausibly be said to have belonged in the straightforward way that Paul Éluard and André Breton, for example, belonged to the artistic movement called Surrealism. A modern scholarly usage (not exactly a coinage) and too convenient not to keep using, the term's currency is based partly on the fact that Roman grammarians used the word *neotericus* as a general descriptor referring (sometimes, but not always, in a tone of condemnation) to writers of a later and so 'newer' time than the one under discussion. Its principal origin, however, resides in a remark of Cicero's, made probably a few years after the death of Catullus, delivered in a curmudgeonly tone somewhere between playfulness and outright hostile indignation, and bearing some relation or other (hard to say just what) to the actual literary critical judgment of its author, a man who was one of the most accomplished artists of the language's entire history, who had written and translated poetry himself and held passionate critical opinions about it. Writing to his friend Atticus in 50 BC about a recent sea voyage, Cicero offers up a Latin dactylic hexameter of a kind we might call mock epic—'came wafting us on from Epirus that gentle gale, Onchesmites' and then adds, 'you can pawn off that *spondeiazon* [line with a fifth foot spondee] as your own to any of the *neoteroi* you please' (*Att.* 7.2.1).

For all its malicious high spirits, this offhand remark by Cicero already gives us a conjectural basis for imaginative reconstruction of a contentiously polarized literary scene in the last decades of the Roman Republic. We picture, on the one side, a set of talented young poets finding new resources in Hellenistic Greek poetic models and drawing on those resources to produce new effects in Latin. On the other side, we envision a set of older or more conservative Romans finding themselves by turns amused, rebuffed, or outright scandalized at the sight of their inherited tongue made into a vehicle for the mannerist excesses of a new and unaccustomed experimental art. Cicero gives us two further pieces of evidence that have seemed to many scholars to corroborate this plausible if speculative picture. Writing again to Atticus, Cicero quotes a Hellenistic-sounding Greek line of poetry, of unknown authorship: 'tossing his horns in vain, in the insubstantial breeze' (*Att.* 8.5.1). Remarkably enough, Catullus seems to have worked a translation of precisely this same verse into his longest and most elaborate surviving work, Poem 64 (111). This miniature epic, or 'epyllion' (another convenient scholarly term), on the wedding of Peleus and Thetis, is a poem in which an 'ecphrasis', or descriptive passage (often, as in this case, on the subject of a work of visual art), on the woven or embroidered design of the wedding bed's coverlet tapestry enters the narrative as a detail and then, astonishingly, balloons out into a vivid and dramatically powerful tale featuring a soliloquy by the abandoned Ariadne.

Cicero drops a third and final clue in the *Tusculan Disputations*, a major philosophical work he completed a year or two before his death in 43 BC. After quoting some lines from a tragedy of Ennius, Cicero pauses long enough to praise the poetic strength (and psychological astuteness) of that good old Roman author, while lamenting the current devaluation of his critical stock: 'What an extraordinary poet! though he is regarded with contempt by these singers of Euphorion' (*Tusc.* 3.45).

Was Cicero referring to Catullus and his friends by the term 'singers of Euphorion'? If so, what was the significance of his remark? Of Euphorion's actual writing we have only fragments, but we do know he was a scholar-poet of the third century BC who crafted poems of challenging difficulty and intricacy, often on obscure mythological themes. What is more, Euphorion's name appears several times in a remarkable document written during Cicero's lifetime, a text that seems to add yet another piece to the neoteric puzzle. A handbook of sorts for Roman poets bearing the title 'Erotic Sufferings' (*Erotika Pathemata*), this was written, in Greek, by one Parthenius of Nicaea, a scholar-poet in the tradition of Callimachus and Euphorion who arrived at Rome early in the first century BC as a slave, is said to have tutored the young Virgil in Greek, and dedicated his prose catalogue of poetically useful love themes to Virgil's friend and fellow poet Cornelius Gallus. Parthenius identifies Euphorion as the source for three of his most lurid tales of incestuous love and grisly death.

Admittedly, not every scholar agrees that these bits of evidence from the writings of Cicero all refer to a single group of poets or kind of poetry. Many others, however, have taken them as sufficient grounds for asserting the historical reality of a neoteric moment during the last decades of the Republic, even if no poet of Catullus' generation actually identified himself with that term. What we call 'neoteric poetics' does appear to have represented, if not an organized movement in the modern sense, at least a shared set of aesthetic values: an allegiance to polished dictional elegance in the Alexandrian mode of Callimachus and Euphorion, coupled with a strong interest in erotic themes and the depiction of psychological interiority, especially that of female characters, in extreme dramatic and narrative situations. To the degree these conjectures are all valid, then, the Hellenistic poetic tradition that includes creations like Euripides' Phaedra in the *Hippolytus* and Apollonius Rhodius' Medea in the *Argonautica* can be said to have found, in the poetry of the neoterics, its first fullthroated Roman response—but certainly not its last. Catullus' Ariadne in Poem 64 and (probably) the heroines of his friends' poems trace an important line through Latin poetry. That line continues in the tragic grandeur of Virgil's Dido and arguably finds its culmination in the many erotically transgressive heroines Ovid portrays in the *Heroides*, the *Metamorphoses*, and elsewhere on a smaller scale throughout his work. The sly ethical psychology, lurid eroticism, and elegantly light touch of Ovid's characterizations of female interiority add up to one of the principal set of qualities that many readers have identified as quintessentially 'Ovidian': qualities that were no less all his own, to be sure, for having been inherited from Hellenistic Greek and neoteric Roman predecessors.

In the mannered spondaic verse he tosses off in a letter, Cicero does sound as though he is parodying exactly the kind of poetry Catullus gives us in Poem 64. And it does seem more than likely that, if we had them, we would find a similar kind of poetry in the miniature epics of Catullus' friends, poems he describes with appreciative enthusiasm. His friend Gaius Helvius Cinna spent nine years, Catullus tells us, writing a short, aggressively difficult poem on the story of Myrrha, presumably focused on or at least including her sexual desire for her own father and her consummation of that desire through deceit and the cover of darkness. Even the title of Cinna's epyllion, named after its heroine, needs a commentator's gloss: he called his poem not Myrrha but *Zmyrna*. In Poem 95 Catullus compares Cinna's epyllion to the work of Volusius, a poet contemporary in time but very distant in sensibility from Catullus and his fellow neoterics. Volusius, it seems, was writing annalistic poetry in the old Roman tradition, and had even given his poem a plain Latin title taken from Ennius: *Annales*. Catullus predicts that Cinna's *Zmyrna* will outlast the centuries and continue to be read on shores as exotic as its title, which he repeats three times in seven lines, as if entranced by its exuberantly wild accent. To Volusius' poem, on the other hand, Catullus assigns an ignominious demise in his author's native Padua, where fishmongers will use it as cost-effective packaging for their merchandise.

From the vantage point of our own historical moment, we might say that Catullus' prophecy in Poem 95 came true only in part, in the sense that both poems are lost to us. But in another sense, from the long view of poetic tradition, Catullus can be said to have gotten it right on both counts. The annalistic poetry in the style of Ennius that Volusius wrote and Cicero admired belonged to an exhausted tradition never to be successfully revived in the Latin language. And if Cinna's poem itself did not outlast the centuries, his incestuous heroine did, thanks to Ovid, who incorporated the story of Myrrha into his *Metamorphoses* (10.298–502). That Ovidian episode was a favorite piece for translation among Renaissance poets, and in our own time the American poet Frank Bidart has reworked the challengingly transgressive narrative theme of Myrrha into an epyllion-length poem bearing a title after Ovid: 'In the Second Hour of the Night'.

Another neoteric poet, Caecilius, is known to us only through Catullus. In Poem 35 he is depicted hard at work on a poem about the goddess Cybele, apparently called *The Great Mother*, but Catullus also refers to it more exotically as *The Lady of Dindymus*. Caecilius' epyllion may have told the same story as Catullus' Poem 63, in which Attis castrates himself in a devotional trance and must spend the rest of his life as the goddess' eunuch and votary. And Catullus' great friend Licinius Calvus, whose named is coupled with that of Catullus in several later Roman sources (including Ovid), wrote an epyllion called *Io*, another female protagonist of an erotically charged narrative who shows up prominently in the opening book of Ovid's *Metamorphoses* (1.568–746). In view of these pieces of evidence it is tempting to surmise that composing an epyllion, and spending years of painstaking labor on it, was viewed by Catullus and his friends as a kind of requisite apprenticeship in a shared craft, and that the young poet's successful completion of an epyllion was rewarded with full acceptance into a kind of poetic circle—however loosely and informally those terms are to understood. What is fairly clear, in any case, is that Ovid studied these neoteric epyllia carefully and looked to them as important predecessors. Throughout Ovid's poetry, but especially in the *Metamorphoses*, an episodic epic that has some-times been described as a series of epyllia loosely stitched together, we are almost certainly seeing a later poet's reception, at multiple levels of diction and theme, of lost neoteric models.

The poets we call neoteric actively set themselves a goal of responding to Helle-nistic Greek poetic achievements in a new and newly adequate way, and of thereby achieving something unprecedented for the Latin language as a poetic instrument. It is true that when we speak of the particular qualities of neoteric poetry we are in some measure always extrapolating from our reading of Catullus, because the other neoterics survive only in a very few fragments and second-hand reports. What survives of Catullus, at any rate, can be said to have brought Latin poetry into its own and made it matter to all subsequent histories of the development of European literature. Whether you think poetry's true task and true dignity lies in the poet's ability to enrich the socially shared artifact of a given human language through coura-geous intellectual play grounded in painstaking erudition and craft, or whether you think good poets are good to the degree that they touch depths and intensities of particular or general human experience that ordinary language lacks the fineness to convey and the wildness to contain, or whether you think that these and similar standards and definitions of poetry can be only partially right at best and that the only valid touchstone is a given reader's response to a given poem, you will be an exceptional reader indeed if you make a serious study of Catullus, think poetry matters, and come away from your study having found nothing you think worth taking seriously as poetry.

The view just now reported is a modern one, and it belongs more to literary criticism than to philological scholarship. It may look unfamiliar to some readers for being told in a mood of praise and appreciation rather than couched in suspiciously resentful terms, looking to debunk, or as part of some scientifically objective inquiry In any case, as a modern view it is at least partially conditioned by all the accidents of Greek and Roman antiquity's survival into modernity and all the intervening events of a long modern reception history. This view of Catullus' poetic preeminence is also at the same time conditioned by the artifacts that are the poems themselves: rhythmed sequences of written words that, however variously construed and received (and however textually unstable: most of our text of Catullus comes to us through a single manuscript that must have been lamentably corrupt and is now lost), still retain enough family resemblance to be classed as referents of the phrase 'Catullus' poems'. What this means for us is that, when we study Ovid's relation to Catullus as a poetic predecessor, we are putting ourselves in the presence of a reader (Ovid) of a poet (Catullus) to whose works we have our own readerly and critical response. Doing this might teach us something new about Catullus, not only because Ovid had information we lack but also because he was as shrewd a reader of poetry as any modern literary critic. It might teach us something else. We stand to learn new things about what kind of poet Ovid was by studying what kind of reader he was when he read Catullus.

Catullus in Ovid's Poetic Program

How much did Catullus matter to Ovid? How seriously, that is, did he take Catullus' poetic achievement as a predecessor to his own? Did Catullus loom anywhere near as large in Ovid's poetic imagination as he has in the imaginations of modern poets and readers? These are questions we can never ask from a place fully outside our own historical moment and our own role as receivers of ancient and modern poetry and criticism, but that consideration does not bar or excuse us from asking them. Answers, if anywhere, are to be found in Ovid's own poetry. To get a sense of how Catullus looked to Ovid, we need to study not just what Ovid says about Catullus explicitly but also what traces and likenesses of Catullus we can find in Ovid's own poetic themes and language.

Our most explicit and direct evidence for Ovid's estimation of Catullus comes at the beginning of Ovid's own career as a poet. In his first work, the *Amores* ('Loves' or 'Cupids'), he mentions Catullus by name twice, both times in the third and final book of the collection of love elegies as we have it. *Am.* 3.9 commemorates the death of Albius Tibullus, Ovid's elder contemporary and fellow elegist, a poet whom Quintilian would later regard as the foremost exponent of the genre. Ovid's poem imagines a fictional version of Tibullus' funeral rites. The mourners in attendance include three divinities—Elegy herself, personified as a goddess (she had already appeared at the beginning of the book, in *Am.* 3.1), along with Venus, and her son Cupid—and two mortal but in some measure fictional women, Delia and Nemesis, who feature as recipients and love objects of Tibullus' two books of elegiac poetry. At the end of the poem, Ovid completes his fictional narrative with the picture of Tibullus arriving at the Elysian Fields of the Underworld. There he is greeted and welcomed with honor by the three poets whose number he will increase. These are Tibullus' chief poetic predecessors in the genre of Roman erotic elegy. They are, of course, Ovid's predecessors as well (*Am.* 3.9.59–64):

> si tamen e nobis aliquid nisi nomen et umbra
>   restat, in Elysia ualle Tibullus erit.
> obuius huic uenies hedera iuuenalia cinctus
>   tempora cum Caluo, docte Catulle, tuo;
> tu quoque, si falsum est temeratit crimen amici,
>   sanguinis atque animae prodige Galle tuae.

> But if it's really true that something of us lasts besides a name and a shade,
>   then the Elysian valley is where Tibullus will be.
> And you will come to meet him, wearing an ivy crown on your youthful temples,
>   learned Catullus and with you your friend Calvus;
> and you too (if the charge of violating a friendship is false)
>   Gallus, spendthrift of your life and your life's blood.

As captain of this elite band of three poets, Catullus is the only member whose name is qualified by a specifically literary descriptor. A word with special resonance among poets by Ovid's time, being 'learned' (*doctus*) seems to have meant possessing full mastery of an aesthetic of allusive, recondite, formally painstaking, urbanely witty, and unheroically slender modes of production associated chiefly with the third-century Alexandrian scholar-poet Callimachus, whom Catullus had translated in part. Poem 66, his version of the episode on Queen Berenice's lock of hair from the *Aetia*, is our only surviving example, but Catullus claims to have made other translations as well. During the intervening years, between Catullus' neoteric generation and Ovid's late-Augustan one, the influence Callimachus exercised over Roman poets appears to have become, if anything, even more pervasive.

Significantly, the *Amores* as we have it opens with Ovid's own programmatic pledge of allegiance to Callimachean poetics and a strong bid to be recognized as a 'learned' poet in his own right. *Am.* 1.1 references a scene from Callimachus' proem to the *Aetia* that Virgil had already rehearsed in the sixth poem of his ten bucolic *Eclogues*. Callimachus in the *Aetia* had portrayed himself with a tablet on his knees setting out to write a continuous epic narrative on heroic themes, until Apollo himself intervened with the critical advice to keep his Muse slender and avoid the well-worn tracks of poetic composition. Virgil, in turn, had fairly closely reproduced this scene of so-called *recusatio*, in which the poet 'recuses' himself from writing heroic epic (by recourse to a plea of divine intervention) and thereby gives a sideways announcement of an aesthetic that assigns the highest value to exquisite poetic craft showcased in intricate work on a thematically and formally miniature scale. Ovid in *Am.* 1.1 gives the familiar metapoetic scene a generically appropriate twist, by making the divine intervention come in the form of Cupid, *Amor* personified, who upsets the poet's epic ambitions aggressively, with an arrow to the heart and a stern command to be a love poet.

Of all the poets Ovid mentions in the *Amores*, and these are numerous, only Catullus receives the epithet *doctus*. We are probably not overreading if we take this fact as signaling Ovid's special esteem for Catullus as the first thoroughly accomplished exponent of the Callimachean aesthetic that Ovid claims as his own informing tradition at the opening of his first poetic collection. As for Callimachus, his name appears in the *Amores* only once, in a passage where Ovid clearly shows the degree to which he takes his Hellenistic predecessor as the undisputed benchmark, the standing record to meet (or preferably beat) for exquisite learning in poetry. The context of that passage, characteristically Ovidian, has the poem's speaker owning up to a playboy's unapologetically catholic taste in beautiful women, whom he addresses collectively and with more frankness than gallantry (*Am.* 2.4.17–22):

> siue es docta, places raras dotata per artes;
>   siue rudis, placita es simplicitate tua.
> est quae Callimachi prae nostris rustica dicat
>   carmina: cui placeo, protinus ipsa placet;
> est etiam quae me uatem et mea carmina culpet:
>   culpantis cupiam sustinuisse femur.

> If you are learned, you appeal through your gift of rare arts.
>   If unschooled, your appeal lies in your simplicity.
> Say there's a girl who calls Callimachus' poems rustic

compared to mine: since I appeal to her, she does to me too, instantly.
Say there's another who criticizes the poet I am and the poems I write:
   I'd like to be holding up my critic's thigh.

This throwaway joke about Callimachus' poems being called rustic compared to his
own is more telling, arguably, than the most extravagant literary praise on Ovid's
part would have been. The joke makes sense only on the assumption that its reader
will agree with Ovid in taking Callimachus as the model and summit of what Romans
called *urbanitas*: a combination of dictional elegance and sharp wit that Catullus had
prominently championed and exemplified in his often aggressive but always fiercely
learned poetry.

   Putting Catullus at the head of the chorus of dead elegiac poets welcoming Tibullus into Elysium and giving him the unique epithet *doctus* already signal a very high
valuation of Catullus' poetic achievement on Ovid's part. On the other hand, given
that Catullus is being honored specifically as a predecessor in the miniaturizing minor
genre of elegy, we might be tempted to suppose that Ovid means not just to praise
Catullus but also in some measure, for purposes of Ovid's own future poetic career,
to bury him, leaving his shade in the undergloom with the other chief exponents of
a mode of poetic creation Ovid thinks his own developing genius has now outgrown.
If *Am.* 3.9 is a farewell poem to a dead elegist, the entire third and final book of
Ovid's *Amores* (as we have them—an earlier version contained five books) announces
itself as Ovid's farewell to Roman erotic elegy. Along with the usual narrative of a
young man's fortunes and setbacks in love, the *Amores* also tells the story of a young
poet testing his own powers of language and imagination against the tight constraints
of Roman erotic elegy's inherited set of thematic and dictional conventions. That
story's end seems to show Ovid deciding, with a young man's characteristic bravado,
that he has strained the capacities of Roman elegy to exhaustion and thereby given
proof of poetic strengths and ambitions in himself that demand and deserve a wider
playing field.

   The first poem of *Am.* 3 stages an allegorical vignette strangely reminiscent of
a Greek story well known to Roman readers (Cicero, for example, is fond of it)
about the young Hercules coming to a crossroads and having to choose between
the path of pleasure and the path of excellence. Ovid's poem shows us the young
poet wandering in a sacred grove and visited by two female personifications competing for his loyalty. Tragedy, the first of these, urges him to stop wasting his time and
talent on trifles: 'begin a greater work. You constrain your genius with [elegiac)]
material. Sing the deeds of men! "*This*," you will say, "is a playing field worthy of
my spirit"' (*Am.* 3.24–6). Elegy, in turn, does plead her own case, but only weakly
and with all the passive-aggressive, masochistic pathos of an elegiac lover (a mode
that never seems to fit Ovid comfortably when he writes in the first person, at least
not until the poems of exile). Elegy is easily—almost too easily—persuaded to accept
the speaker's small concession, an offer to put off tragic poetry just long enough to
finish his present elegiac project. We might wonder, then, if Ovid at this point is also
implicitly bidding farewell to the influence of Catullus and, by joining the ranks of
tragic poets (and a long series of Roman predecessors in that noble genre, including

Livius Andronicus and Ennius), renouncing the slender aesthetic of Callimachean neotericism altogether.

Ovid as Emulator of Catullus

Putting the question that way almost surely oversimplifies. It ignores the fact that Catullus, elegy, and neotericism are three distinctly separate, if mutually overlapping, items. It probably also puts too much implicit credence in a poet's representation of his own program and his complex, developing relation to an interwoven set of generic precedents and traditions. In any event, Ovid ends the *Amores* by giving us strong reason to suppose that he is not done with Catullus. Catullus' is the last proper name (of a historical person) that Ovid mentions in the final verses of the *Amores*. What is more, he couples it with the name of Virgil, the poet whose achievement, only recently completed, had already been promoted by its community of readers to the position it would thenceforth occupy at the summit and center of the Latin language's canon (*Am.* 3.15.7–8):

> Mantua Vergilio gaudet, Verona Catullo;
>   Paelignae dicar gloria gentis ego.

> Mantua rejoices in her Virgil, Verona in her Catullus;
>   I in turn shall be called the glory of the Paelignian people.

This prophetic boast—whether from a young poet at the outset of his career or (if we suppose Ovid added these lines to his second edition of the *Amores*) a fully mature one—sounds aggressively strong, even after we make all the necessary cultural adjustments for the high degree of self-aggrandizement, in the name of personal and familial honor, that went into the self-fashioning of a high-born Roman man. And note that Ovid's closing poem in the *Amores* fulfills the function of a poet's *sprhagis* or signatory 'seal', complete with a proud assertion of his family's long-standing equestrian rank. It is worth noting that neither Catullus nor Virgil, the two poets whose work Ovid invokes here as likenesses of his own self-eternizing achievement, ever presumed to speak with such straightforward confidence of 'work that will remain and survive [its author's] death' as Ovid does in the final words of the *Amores* (3.15.20).

The overall narrative arc of *Am.* 3 as an autobiographical story of poetic program, and the ringing self-confidence of this closing signature in which the speaker of *Am.* 3.15 proudly identifies himself by rank and birth, give us strong reasons to take the couplet just now quoted as a fully serious claim that Ovid himself is making about his own poetic achievement as a whole, from an imagined temporal perspective in which he has joined the ranks of dead great poets whose names live on in their work. Ancient readers would have recognized this bold claim as an instance of *aemulatio* ('emulation'), a stance in which the piety of imitation is conjoined with the aggression of rivalry. They would have acknowledged, further, that Ovid was issuing a kind of promissory note with respect to his own poetic achievement as a whole, by claiming that it would one day win him membership, alongside Virgil and Catullus, in a constellar triumvirate of poets occupying the summit of their language's tradition. Many subsequent readers seem to have judged that Ovid went on to make good on his promise.

While the poetic concerns, values, problems, and solutions of Catullus and the other neoteric poets continued to influence Ovid throughout his career, and while individual poems in the *Amores* seem to be closely engaged with aspects of Catullan and neoteric poetics, it is harder to say for sure whether he continued to fix his sights on Catullus specifically as a chief model and rival. In any case, Ovid's later poetry does contain some remarkably specific references to specific passages in Catullus' poetry. While the precise significance of any given reference is an inexhaustibly complex question, it is worth looking here, by way of conclusion, at what is probably the most notable instance from among these.

Ovid's most extensive and specific Catullan reference in the *Metamorphoses* comes in the Narcissus episode. The narrator is describing Narcissus' sexual inaccessibility and the character trait it manifests (3.353–6):

> multi illum iuuenes, multae cupiere puellae;
> sed (fuit in tenera tam dura superbia forma)
> nulli illum iuuenes, nullae tetigere puellae.

> **Many a boy and many a girl wanted him.**
> But in that tender beauty was a pride so hard
> **no boy at all, no girl at all ever touched him.**

In the first and third lines, highlighted here, Ovid is referencing—almost quoting—a long poem of Catullus' written in the form of a poetic contest between a chorus of youths arguing on behalf of marriage and a chorus of virgins arguing against it. In this stanza, the virgins liken virginity to the blossom of a flower that, once plucked, fades and loses its desirability (Catullus 62.39–47):

> ut flos in saeptis secretus nascitur hortis,
> ignotus pecori, nullo conuolsus aratro,
> quem mulcent aurae, firmat sol, educat imber;
> multi illum pueri, multae optauere puellae:
> idem cum tenui carptus defloruit ungui,
> nulli illum pueri, nullae optauere puellae:
> sic uirgo, dum intacta manet, dum cara suis est;
> cum castum amisit polluto corpore florem,
> nec pueris iucunda manet, nec cara puellis.

> As a flower, born in an enclosed garden,
> unknown to the flock, torn by no plow,
> that breezes soothe, sunshine strengthens, showers nourish:
> *many a boy and many a girl desire it.*
> But when once it comes unflowered, plucked by a slender fingernail,
> *no boy at all, no girl at all desires it:*

so a virgin, while she remains untouched, dear to her own.
But when her body has been stained, her flower lost,
she remains neither delightful to boys nor dear to girls.

Ovid's reference to Catullus is specific, perspicuous, readable off the page. It merits the designation 'intentional allusion' to just the degree to which any human action merits being called 'intentional x' when other people regard it as (1) deliberate not accidental and (2) recognizable as an instance of the kind of action they call by the name 'x'. (Literary scholars who fret the question of intentionality, or carefully avoid using the word, sometimes seem to forget that intentionality is no less complex a philosophical problem outside literature and even outside language.) Rather more complex than the questions surrounding intentionality and allusiveness are the questions that come into play once we begin to interpret the meaning and significance of this poetic reference in the context of the Narcissus episode. While some readers have been content to find fairly simple versions of irony and wit—the chorus of girls is making an extended simile on the tenor of a flower, and a flower is what Narcissus will become at the end of the story—we are entitled, I would argue, if not obliged, to read more ethical and psychological subtlety than that into Ovid's poetic choice. Once we have done that, we are likely to decide that Ovid's reappropriation of Catullus is a reference in the strictest sense, in that it invites us to refer back to Catullus' poem, reread it carefully, and ask the deepest and broadest questions we can muster about the relation between the human condition of female virginity on the one hand and the pathological but also miraculous story of Narcissus pursued by Echo (who wastes away and loses her body), falling in love with his own reflected image, and being changed from a young man into a flower. Once we have done this, we may decide that Catullus' poem, and Ovid's implicit reading of it, are integral to the experience of reading this episode of the *Metamorphoses* in ways that are so complex as to baffle our vocabulary and our understanding of intertextuality and allusion.

Conclusion

One of the principal differences between Ovid and Catullus, we might say, is that Ovid's poetic tradition includes, and his poetry in large measure incorporates, the poetic achievements of Catullus and, almost certainly, the achievements of the other poets of the neoteric generation. By Ovid's time, the profession of poetry at Rome had become considerably better established, and that consideration, along with the existence of a canonical body of Roman poetry that could arguably rival the best poetic productions in Greek, goes a long way toward accounting not only for Ovid's lighter dictional touch but also in some measure for the remarkable self-confidence of his poetic persona in comparison to the embattled machismo and theatrical delicacy of Catullus. Still, if we take Ovid at his word in what he tells us at the end of the *Amores*, the chief way in which Catullus figured in Ovid's own poetic imagination was as an illustrious predecessor of the highest artistic order, a model and rival whose accomplishments challenged him to become the poet he was.

David Wray

FURTHER READING

Ferguson (1960) gives a concise and nearly complete catalogue of clear verbal echoes of Catullus in the poems of Ovid. A classic study of Catullus as a poetic revolutionary in the modernist mode is Quinn (1959), and for the Latinist reader Ross (1969) is a crucial study of Catullus' poetic diction. Recent book-length studies of Catullus include Miller (1994), Fitzgerald (1995), and Wray (2001). On Catullus' rediscovery and early-modern reception, see Gaisser (1993). The poem 'In the Second Hour of the Night' is published in Bidart (1997).

CHAPTER NINETEEN

Propertius and Ovid

S. J. Heyworth

Introduction

Gallus (*Tr.* 4.10.53) was the first and Tibullus (*Am.* 3.9, *Tr.* 2.447–64) was the elegist most celebrated by Ovid; but in the range of material and approach, Propertius is the predecessor to whom Ovid is closest. This closeness is asserted as a biographical truth by Ovid himself at *Tr.* 4.10.45–6:

> saepe suos solitus recitare Propertius ignes
> iure sodalicii, quo mihi iunctus erat.

> Propertius was often accustomed to recite his fires [i.e. passionate poems] according to the rules of the society through which he was joined to me.

It is not surprising therefore that the influence of the Propertian corpus is profound. In Books 1–3 Propertius developed the exclusive concentration on love of a mistress that Ovid pursues in the *Amores*, both poets combine love as theme with repeated discussion of their poetic models and aims, and from the first they use imagery most familiar to modern readers from the poetry of the Hellenistic poet Callimachus. In Book 4 Propertius broadened the elegist's field through erotodidaxis, laments for the dead, and a letter written by a wife to her absent husband, and with material on ritual and aetiology, and on transformation, and thus prepared the way for the *Ars amatoria*, the Ovidian epicedia, the *Heroides*, the *Fasti*, and the *Metamorphoses*. Like Ovid, Propertius wrote poems that on the surface at least praise Augustus, but there is always uncertainty about the level of commitment, and some sign of outright opposition, in Ovid's case manifested by his relegation in 8 CE, in Propertius' by the revelation in two epigrams at the end of Book 1 that a member of his family fought against Octavian's forces in the Perusine War of 43 BCE.

The Role of the Love Elegist as Defined by Propertius

Key elements in Propertius' love poetry from the start are the tropes of *militia amoris* ('the warfare of love') and *seruitium amoris* ('the slavery of love'). Already in the first poem (1.1.21) he talks about his beloved as *domina* ('mistress': the term is found already in the Gallus fragment; Catullus uses only the synonym *era*, at 68.136; see Lyne 2007: 89), no dead metaphor in a society supported by the labor and attention of slaves. He goes on to imagine the torture she might inflict on him (1.1.27–8), but acknowledges the imagery by claiming at least a limited freedom for himself:

> fortiter et ferrum saeuos patiemur et ignes,
>   sit modo libertas quae uelit ira loqui.

> Boldly I shall suffer iron and fierce fire, if only I have the freedom to say what my passion would wish.

domina is thereafter a default way of denoting the beloved, along with the more neutral *puella* ('girl'). In 1.16 and 3.6 she is the mistress at one and the same time of the poet and the door (1.16) or the slave (3.6) addressed. At 2.13.36 the poet's role as a 'slave of one love' encapsulates his nature for his future epitaph. It is against this background that Ovid makes the slave porter the addressee of *Am.* 1.6, offering to take on his chains (47), asserting his own readiness to undergo iron and fire (57), and finally condemning the unhelpful man to imprisonment (64): typical realism from the later poet, to address the figure who is more likely to hear, and to bring out the truth of slavery. But he does not avoid the emotive hyperbole of the trope, and the very next poem begins (1.7.1): *Adde meas in uincla manus (meruere catenas)*, 'Put my arms in fetters (they have deserved chains)'. The juxtaposition has a comic effect; but so does the anticlimax at the end of the poem, when the horror with which Ovid speaks of his act of violence against his mistress leads only to advice that she should rearrange her hair. The realistic mode reasserts itself in Book 2 of the *Amores*, where slaves play an important part, and there are pairs of poems concerned with the eunuch Bagoas (2.2–3) and the hairdresser Cypassis, more distinctive creations than the Lygdamus of Propertius 3.6 and 4.7–8.

Even more prominent in Propertius 1.1 is the imagery of warfare (1–4):

> Cynthia prima suis miserum me cepit ocellis,
>   contactum nullis ante Cupidinibus.
> tum mihi constantis deiecit lumina fastus
>   et caput impositis pressit Amor pedibus.

> Cynthia was the first; she caught me with her eyes and made me miserable—I had never been infected with desire before. Love forced me to drop my look of resolute pride, put his feet on my head, and pressed it down.

These lines are based on an epigram (*Anth. Pal.* 12.101) by the Greek epigrammatist Meleager, who wrote about 100 BCE; but in Latin, the language of the city that has conquered the Mediterranean world, the picture of the victor standing on the head of the defeated seems far more vivid: it is a picture displayed on Roman coins. More-over, Propertius chooses this image for the start of his collection. At times, the poet-lover will be the conquering hero (e.g. 1.8.28); rivals are his enemies (2.8.4, 2.9.51–2, 3.8.29–30). At others, it is Cynthia he fights with (3.5.2), and these battles may be violent and angry (and thus proof of true passion: 3.8.1–10), or sexual (3.8.32, 3.20.20, 4.8.88), or both (as in 3.8). The image is acknowledged to be a flexible one, though always valid: 'I shall always have fights either with you, or over you, with rivals: in your case no peace satisfies me' (3.8.33–4). This is real campaigning for Propertius, and persistently contrasted with the warfare of the Roman state (1.6, 2.7, 3.4–5). *Militia* is a dominant image for the Ovid of the *Amores* too. He is shot by Cupid's arrow in his first poem, and surrenders to him in the second, which develops into a long account of the triumph the god may enjoy. The culmination of the trope comes in 1.9, an exploration extended with rhetorical invention to comic length of the ways in which lover and soldier are alike; and if one of the two is tougher, it is not the soldier.

One detail in Propertius' opening couplet not drawn from Meleager's epigram is the figuring of love as an infection (in the epigram the poet is previously 'unwounded'). The imagery of medicine is resumed in lines 26–7, where Propertius talks of the need for a cure for his madness. However, when in the next poem the word *medicina* itself appears, it has a rather different sense: in context *non ulla tuae est medicina figurae* (1.2.7) means 'there is no treatment to improve your beauty'. This sense will bear fruit in an independent Ovidian poem, the *Medicamina faciei femineae* (of which only the first 100 lines survive). Ovid responds to the attack Propertius had mounted on cosmetics and dressing up in 1.2 by singing the praises of *cultus* (a theme resumed at *Ars* 3.101ff.; see Gibson 2003). Whereas Propertius had complained that Cynthia was destroying her natural beauty by adopting imported perfumes and clothing, seeing this as an attempt to attract other men when she already had him, Ovid sees personal *cultus* as a symbol of modernity, as productive as agriculture (*Med.* 1–22). Propertius had asserted *uni si qua placet, culta puella sat est* ('if a girl pleases one man, she is cultivated enough', 1.2.26); Ovid's response is *culta placent* ('cultivated things please', *Med.* 7).

However, one should not imagine that it is a simple model Ovid overturns to create his complexity. When Propertius attacks Cynthia's clothing as 'Coan' (1.2.2), thus evoking his Greek predecessor in elegy, Philetas of Cos, or when he brings out the natural beauty of mythical heroines by comparing it to the coloring in the paint-ings of Apelles (22), he draws attention to the mismatch between his claimed hatred of imported art and the Greek form in which he advertises the delights of his girl. He is an example of the *formae artifex* ('creator of beauty') he sees as hated by Love (8). For the reader who is aware of this background of playful ambiguity, it is hard to ignore the alternative sense of *non ulla tuae est medicina figurae* ('there is no cure for your beauty'), a sense repeated at 1.5.28, and a claim borne out by his repeated assertions of undying love (1.12.19–20, 1.19, 2.6.41–2). Though he is unable to cure himself of the love with which he has been infected, he can help others: 'there is no small medicine in my words' (1.10.18). This force of *medicina* also gets taken over by Ovid, not so much in the *Amores* (where he presents love as an art or a game and largely avoids the notion of sickness) as in the *Remedia amoris*, his farewell to love poetry. Here it becomes entirely apt to represent himself as a doctor, able to cure those who need assistance. Some of the possible cures he discusses replicate those Propertius has considered already in 1.1 (Henderson 1979, esp. xiii–xvi; cf. also Hardie 2006: 184–5): travel to faraway places is commended at *Rem.* 213–48; but magic, brought in by Propertius as an evocation of *psychagogia* ('transport of the soul'), is condemned by Ovid as old-fashioned, useless, and potentially harmful (249–90). This art is also rejected as a way of instilling love, at *Med.* 35–42 and *Ars* 2.99–107, and thus Ovid again becomes like his mentor.

Propertius 1.16 is another poem that expresses intense desire, in the form of a traditionally emotional *paraclausithyron* ('a song outside a closed door'), but comments in a distanced way on the lover's absurdity. The *paraclausithyron* is a type of poem that developed from the Greek *komos*, drunken wandering through the streets in search of more fun. We have an isolated fragment of the lyric poet Alcaeus (178 Page), which reads: 'Let me in, I beg you, I beg; I'm on a *komos*'; and there are ten or so epigrams in the fifth book of the Palatine Anthology that explore the situation (e.g. 5.23, 167, 191). Ovid, as we have seen, has a realistic take on the pattern: he addresses not the beloved, the door, or the weather, but the door-keeper. Propertius plays with the form in a different way: he sets his lover's lament in a monologue spoken by the door herself (thus picking up on the speaking door of Catullus 67, and more generally the voices given to inanimate objects by the Alexandrian elegist Callimachus). The mannered distress of the lover is thus humorously set off against the snobbery of the ancient door, whose threshold has previously welcomed triumphant generals, and the scurrilous lampoons others have attached to the door, attacking the immorality of the woman who lives there.

Humor

Humor is a frequent element in Propertius. We find humor at the expense of his addressees: the iambic poet Bassus, whose genre implies invective and disgust about sexual partners (as in Hor. *Epod.* 8 and 12), is presented as praising girls (1.4.1); Gallus has trusted Propertius to be a witness of his love-making, and he repays the trust by broadcasting an account of it (1.10.11–14); Tullus is sent off to govern the empire in 1.6, and then presented in 1.14 as so idle that he spends his time drinking and watching boats on the Tiber. But he invites the attentive reader to laugh at him too, hoping in 1.18 that the woods will not repeat his painful lamentation (and this in a published poem), describing in 2.19 how he will boldly go and hunt while Cynthia is on holiday in the country, and he'll tackle—not lions and boars but—hares and birds. So mighty is his prowess as a lover that he can be called both an Achilles and a Hector (2.22.34). When he receives a night-time summons to attend on Cynthia in Tibur (3.16), he's afraid to go; but he's more afraid not to go.

Amusing too is the choice of images and words: he imagines himself trying to drink from the enormous fountain where Ennius found inspiration (3.3.1–6), and having the power to 'gape' (*hiscere*) the kings of Alba, a most improbable topic, improbably articulated. When he announces, at 3.4.9, that he sings propitious omens for Caesar's money-spinning campaign against Parthia, the next words are *Crassos clademque*, 'the Crassi' (father and son killed at Carrhae in 53 BCE in an earlier attempt to overcome Rome's eastern rival) 'and disaster'. This may be more subtle than Ovid's humor (but Ovid's humor tends to be both obvious *and* subtle; Hinds 1987b), but it should not be neglected, and readers of the later poet are doing an injustice to both if they imagine Ovid parodies the seriousness of his predecessor. One can see the methods of some of Ovid's jokes anticipated. The comparisons extended at such length that they becomes laughable (e.g. the soldier and lover in *Am.* 1.9; Ovid and Ulysses as exiles in *Tr.* 1.5b) can be seen as modeled on Propertian poems like 3.11 and 3.12. In the latter Postumus is made a second Ulysses, and the events of the *Odyssey* are summarized over twelve lines; but it is only in his wife's fidelity during his absence that Postumus is like the epic hero. This point comes out in the final line. The twist in the final couplet is a famous aspect of the *Amores* too, occurring in places such as 1.13.47–8 and 1.7.67–8, where after many lines cursing his violence toward his mistress he tells her simply to put her hair back in order so no one will know. Propertius begins 2.14 with a sequence of similes describing his triumphant and immortal joy at winning Cynthia back, but in the last couplet he fears something will change—and then he will die lying outside her front door. Poem 1.15 ends with him 'perishing' once again for the changes of color and the tears that he has been attacking, along with her makeup and slowness, in the preceding lines.

On the other hand, some of Ovid's humor does derive from his undermining of Propertian patterns. Mythological similes are a major feature of Propertius' work, and three times he begins a poem with a triple (or quadruple) comparison to figures of myth or history (1.3, 2.6, 2.14). At 1.3.1–8 he expresses the loveliness of the sleeping Cynthia:

> Qualis Thesea iacuit cedente carina
> languida desertis Cnosia litoribus;
> qualis et accubuit primo Cepheïa somno
> libera iam duris cotibus Andromede;
> nec minus assiduis Edonis fessa choreis
> qualis in herboso concidit Apidano:
> talis uisa mihi mollem spirare quietem
> Cynthia non certis nixa caput manibus.

> Like the Cretan girl, lying languid on empty shores as Theseus' vessel departed; like Cepheus' daughter Andromeda too as she lay in her first sleep, now free from the harsh cliff; and also like the Maenad who tired by constant dancing collapses on grassy Apidanus: so Cynthia seemed to me, breathing soft sleep, her head supported by restless hands.

Verses 1–2 and 5–6 illustrate Propertian mythological writing at its best. While glorifying the sleeping Cynthia through romantic association, they also offer alternative senses of Propertius's place in the *exemplum*: he may fancy himself a lustful Bacchus or a satyr, but in Cynthia's eyes he may prove to be a Theseus, or the Maenad may wake and tear him limb from limb. Ovid caps this pattern in *Am.* 1.10:

Qualis ab Eurota Phrygiis auecta carinis
    coniugibus belli causa duobus erat,
qualis erat Lede, quam plumis abditus albis
    callidus in falsa lusit adulter aue,
qualis Amymone siccis errauit in agris,
    cum premeret summi uerticis urna comas,
talis eras: aquilamque in te taurumque timebam
    et quidquid magno de Ioue fecit Amor.

As was the girl carried off from the Eurotas on Trojan ships, a cause of war for two husbands, as was Lede, whom the cunning adulterer hidden in white plumage deceived in the form of an unreal bird, as Amymone wandered in the dried-up fields when an urn was pressing the hair on top of her head, such were you: I feared the eagle might come for you and the bull and whatever Love has created out of the mighty Jupiter.

After his three couplets, comparing the beloved to Helen, Leda, and Amymone (raped by Neptune), he adds implicit comparisons to Ganymede and Europe, to secure whom Jupiter was transformed into eagle and bull; but, as it turns out for the poem that follows, it is the tense that matters most here: this is how she *used* to appear; this is the fear he *used* to feel, but now . . . (*Am.* 1.10.9–10):

nunc timor omnis abest animique resanuit error,
    nec facies oculos iam capit ista meos.

Now all fear is absent and the madness of my mind has healed, nor does her beauty captivate my eyes any longer.

And so it has been since she started asking for presents (11–64). This multiple comparison wittily serves to emphasize not desire but disgust.

Cynthia and Corinna

Cynthia, Propertius' beloved, is named from a title repeatedly given by Callimachus to the god Apollo after the hill Cynthus on Delos below which he and his sister Artemis/Diana were born. She is presented as a *femme fatale*, fatally attractive, hard of heart but seductive in appearance and behavior. The paradox is summed up in the paired epithets *durus* ('hard') and *mollis* ('soft'), which are both repeatedly used of Cynthia (*dura* at 1.7.6, 1.16.30, 1.17.16, 2.1.78; *mollis* (or *molliter*) of her behavior at 1.3.7, 1.11.14, 2.12.24), but also of epic on the one hand (2.1.41, 2.34.44, 3.1.20) and elegy itself on the other (1.7.19, 2.1.2, 2.34.42, 3.1.19, 3.3.18, 3.9.57). She is seen by the poet as untrustworthy, intent on using dress and cosmetics to display her beauty for the world to see. He cannot live without her, a notion he explores in poems that describe the journeys or death of one or the other. The two lovers come to seem male and female equivalents: each considers departure and then remains in Rome (1.6; 1.8a and b); she complains about his staying out late at night (1.3) and he about her bothering to dress up when he has given her an urgent summons (1.15).

The extraordinary prominence of Cynthia's name as the opening word of the first book seems to have provoked reticence in Ovid, as in Tibullus. Tibullus talks about a number of alien things in his opening poem before he turns to Delia: the first two words *Diuitias alius* immediately dramatize the point. Ovid takes the delay much further: he twice submits to Love, asks a *puella* for the opportunity to love, and gives detailed instructions for behavior at a symposium, before he utters a name (at *Am.* 1.5.9). The high point of this play comes in the final couplet of 1.3 (25–6):

> nos quoque per totum pariter cantabimur orbem
> iunctaque semper erunt nomina nostra tuis.

> We too will be sung together throughout the whole world, and our names will ever be joined with yours.

At first it seems that *nos* means Ovid and the girl, a pair to be sung across the globe like Jupiter and his various *amours*. But the pentameter invites us to remember that we do not yet know the girl's name (whereas *Naso* has appeared in the introductory epigram; and an anagram can be found at the junction of *nomina nostra*), and then forces us to reconsider our interpretation of *nos*: for *nomina nostra*, set against *tuis*, must mean 'my name'.

Cynthia is so closely identified with Propertius that Ovid twice uses her name to evoke his predecessor (*Ars* 3.536, *Rem.* 764). Ovid also uses *Cynthia* of the goddess Diana (to whom the title is not given before Propertius). Some of the contexts (*Met.* 2.465, 7.755, 15.537; *Fast.* 2.159) do not obviously allude to the elegist, but in at least two there is manifest evocation of Propertius. Newlands (1995: 182–3) discusses *Fast.* 2.91–2; another case is *Her.* 18.71–4 (Leander recalls addressing the moon as he swims the Bosporus):

> quantum, cum fulges radiis argentea puris,
> concedunt flammis sidera cuncta tuis,
> tanto formosis formosior omnibus illa est.
> si dubitas, caecum, Cynthia, lumen habes.

> To the extent that all the stars yield to your flames when you shine silver with untarnished rays, to that extent is she more beautiful than all beauties. If you doubt it, Cynthia, you have a blind eye (*or* a dark light).

Leander has been hymning the moon that shines on his path to Hero, but the belief that his beloved is the greater beauty and thus a greater goddess keeps coming to the surface; and here at the end he uses his words to force her to agree: if she cannot see it, she must be blind, and the pun on *lumen* (light/eye) simultaneously blacks out the moon. But in addition, by calling her *Cynthia*, he evokes Propertius 2.15, where much attention has been paid to the bedside light, and has Hero outdoing Propertius's girl for beauty.

Propertius 2 distances itself from 1 at the beginning through the omission of Cynthia's name. Having been absent from 2.1, the name does not appear until poem 5 (though earlier lacunae may mislead us here). What are we to make of the opening lines, 2.1.1–4?

Quaeritis unde mihi totiens scribantur amores,
    unde meus ueniat mollis in ora liber.
non haec Calliope, non haec mihi cantat Apollo:
    ingenium nobis ipsa puella facit.

You ask how it happens that so often I write of love affairs, how my book comes in elegiac form onto people's lips. It is not Calliope who sings this for me, nor Apollo: it is my girl herself who creates my poetic talent.

Readers may see *ipsa puella* ('my girl herself') as potentially a sign of coyness about his own fickleness, or as carrying the implication that Cynthia's identity is so securely linked with the poet's that he could not possibly mean any other girl. In either case, he is playing against the preconceptions built up by the existence of his first book. In fact, he maintains his career as the lover of Cynthia, and this clearly persists, despite a variety of divagations and distractions, till the end of Book 3. Even after the apparently final farewell there she reappears, first unnamed in the programmatic claims of the astrologer Horos (4.1b.140–6), then as a ghost (4.7), and finally in 4.8 triumphantly alive once more, and, as the poem closes, we see the two of them for the last time, in bed together.

Corinna has a very different role, though she remains the shorthand for Ovid's *puella* (at *Ars* 3.538, *Tr.* 4.10.60). It is a joke when *Am.* 3.12.16 *ingenium mouit sola Corinna meum* ('Corinna alone stimulated my poetic genius') combines rewriting of Propertius 2.1.4 (above) and 2.7.19 *tu mihi sola places* ('you alone are my love'): for the collection has a number of poems in which other girls have succeeded Corinna (and not just replaced her temporarily, as when Propertius tries in vain to escape his love for Cynthia: 2.23, 4.8). At 2.19.9–26 Corinna's past success in playing hard-to-get is cited as a model for the new girl. At 3.7.23–6 active sexual trysts with Chlide, Pitho, and Libas are described as 'recent'; but the night when Corinna demanded his attentions nine times is a memory. And, whereas for Propertius a wife is a fantasy figure (2.7), already at *Am.* 3.13.1 Ovid speaks of his wife (and another wife, his third, will play a major role in the exile poetry).

Progressive Narratives

Propertius regularly develops stories through linked poems. Already 1.7, the poem contrasting the elegiac production of Propertius himself with the Thebaid of Ponticus, grand but useless for a lover, is followed by 1.9, in which the epic poet has fallen in love, his mockery turned to subservience; and 1.8a, where he pleads with Cynthia not to go off to Illyria, leads directly on to 1.8b, in which she has decided to stay with the poet in Rome, and is then picked up in 2.16a, where the praetor who has now returned from Illyria is seen as no rival but a sheep to be fleeced by her (7–10). Ovid has analogous developments: there are adjacent pairs, such as *Am.* 1.11 and 12, where the writing tablets sent with a message to Corinna are first promised a place in Venus' shrine and then (when they bring back a negative) cursed as useless, ill-omened, and fit only to lie at the crossroads. And there are pairs where the argument progresses across a book division: in a classic inversion of expectations 2.19 encourages the beloved's husband to keep a closer eye on her—the ease of access is diminishing Ovid's desire; but then 3.4 complains about the arrival of just such a guard.

Book 3 marks Propertius' movement away from single-minded concentration on Cynthia with a greater variety of subject matter: alongside occasional poems such as 3.6 (the slave Lygdamus reports on the behavior of the temporarily estranged Cynthia), 3.8 (the pair have fought the night before), and 3.10 (Cynthia's birthday), we have more general pieces, reflecting on moral questions, such as the relationship of wealth with war (3.5) and travel (3.7) and women (3.13). The book ends with a farewell to Cynthia (3.24–5), which has every sign of being final, though there is no hint of what the poet may go on to write in future. This has elements that echo 1.1, in particular the reference at lines 9–10 to friends and witches. The reader is prepared for this development by the loss of the poet's writing tablets in 3.23, and before that by a pair of poems that reprise and overturn material from Book 1: 3.21 has Propertius heading off for Athens, the trip Cynthia has prevented at 1.6.13, while 3.22 addresses Tullus for the first time since Book 1, and summons him back to Italy from Asia, where he apparently lives the life of a tourist rather than the imperial soldier depicted in 1.6.

Ovid's *Amores* does not end with so marked an evocation of a failing affair, though he plays with such a narrative throughout Book 3. Thus 3.2, a seduction piece set at the chariot races, matches Propertius' offering of consolation to a new girl abandoned by her lover (3.20). The poem that describes Ovid's impotence when with a beautiful girl also reminisces about past performance (3.7.23–6), and contains phrases like *lassus amore* ('tired of love', 3.7.80). The theme comes most obviously to the fore when 3.11a opens with an assertion that love has been conquered by *uitia*; lines 29–30 reprise the completed voyage imagery of Propertius 3.24.15–16; the final couplet begins *desine* ('cease', with echoes of Prop. 1.15.25 and 4.11.1). However, 3.11b resiles from the determination to say farewell, and offers an extended version of Catullus' *odi et amo*. Poem 3.12 then reflects on the publication of the *Amores* (cf. e.g. Prop. 2.24.1–2; *Am.* 2.17.29) and sees Corinna's attractiveness as being due to Ovid's broadcasting of her charms: his readership should have not been so credulous, but taken this poetic fiction as lightly as those that describe metamorphoses (an introduction to a theme that will become central to his work). The final poem (*Am.* 3.15) goes even further in elevating concern for poetry and fame over concern for the mistress. For Propertius it is a novelty at the start of Book 3 to write about poetry in a way that subordinates Cynthia's importance, whereas Ovid is returning to the emphasis already found in 1.1 and 1.15. But like Propertius he also broadens the range of material in Book 3, with his epicedion for Tibullus in 3.9 and the reflections on the Cerealia in 3.10 and the festival of Juno at Falerii in 3.13. However, these extensions of the boundaries of his elegy are closer to poems in Propertius 4: though Marcellus' death is the occasion for 3.18, fuller and more emotional explorations of recent death come in 4.7 (Cynthia) and 4.11 (Cornelia); and *sacra* is the topic Propertius announces for his book at 4.1.69.

An interesting case is *Am.* 3.5 (known as *Somnium*, 'the Dream'), a poem transmitted separately as well as in the older group of MSS. The poet describes how, as he slept, he watched a beautiful white cow and her mate resting in a wood on a hot day; a crow pecks at the cow's breast, leaving a black mark, before she wanders away to where some other bulls are pasturing. An interpreter of dreams then reveals that it points to the infidelity of the poet's girlfriend. The authenticity of the poem has been much debated, most recently in McKeown 2002, where it is argued that, though the arguments from transmission and style are indecisive, the small quantity of identifiable allusion to Propertius and Tibullus would make the poem unusual within the collection. This is a significant point, and McKeown may be right. However, he does not include in his count the usage of *pastus* ('pastured', *Am.* 3.5.18) with an unusual passive sense, as at Propertius 2.33a.12, with reference to Io, another loved female figured as a cow and about to stray. Nor does he note that *Nox erat* at the start inverts *Mane erat*, the opening of Propertius 2.29b, the poem that is paired with the dreamlike night-time narrative of 2.29a, where the poet is described as straying, drunk, till captured by Cupids; 2.29b is also related to the Ovidian *Somnium* when lines 27–8 describe Cynthia heading off to tell Vesta her dreams, potentially harmful to her or the poet. Another Propertian dream (3.3) begins with the poet dreaming that he is lying in the shade; but he encounters Apollo, Venus's doves, and the Muses, not cattle and crows: though there is no verbal reminiscence, *Am.* 3.5 reads like an Ovidian inversion of this. It certainly fits into the pattern of the final book with its prognostication of infidelity and separation; and the encounter with the *nocturnae . . . imaginis augur* can be linked with Propertius' introduction of Horos, the astrologer, in 4.1b.

Propertius 4 and Ovid's later works

Books 1–3 are thus a vital model for the *Amores*, constantly recalled and entertainingly inverted. But in some ways Propertius' final book can be seen as more important for Ovid's career as a poet. As we have seen, the opening poem (4.1.69) announces a new topic: *sacra deosque canam et cognomina prisca locorum* ('rites and gods I shall sing and the ancient names of places'). Religious observation and the names and shrines of particular deities are the major concerns of Poems 2 (Vertumnus), 4 (Tarpeian Jupiter), 6 (Palatine Apollo), 9 (Hercules as Sancus; Ara Maxima, Bona Dea), 10 (Feretrian Jupiter), and the start of 8 (Juno at Lanuvium); and Ovid takes over the theme of *sacra* as one of the major topics of the *Fasti*, along with *tempora* ('times') and *stellae* ('stars'). The transmitted text of Propertius 4.1.69 makes the connection broader, for it reads *sacra diesque* (though that looks like a scribal assimilation to the *Fasti*, as it scarcely works even as a partial account of Propertius 4). Then poem 4.3 is a letter from a Roman matron, Arethusa, to her husband, who is ever absent on military campaigns at the margins of the empire; as Ovid acknowledges with repeated reminiscence, this is the vital model for his *Epistulae heroidum*. Of course, there are considerable differences: Propertius brings out the mismatch between the marital and the imperialist policies of the regime (already touched on in 3.12); Ovid leaves that point implicit (Davis 2006: 49–70), but increases the literary complexity of his letters by attributing them to women with significant identities within the poetic tradition (see e.g. Kennedy 1984 and Barchiesi 1993).

Erotodidaxis ('education in matters of love') is given in the speech of the *lena* ('bawd') Acanthis in 4.5, and this leads on to *Am.* 1.8 (O'Neill 1999), and less directly to the *Ars amatoria* (Tibullus 1.4, and poems in the didactic tradition, in particular the *Georgics*, are more important influences in this case). What Propertius provides for the *Ars* is material that can be turned to educational purpose (as happens with other authors in the erotic tradition). In 2.31–2 (a sequence wrongly divided by editors) he envisages Cynthia frequenting the newly opened portico attached to the temple of Palatine Phoebus (and thus close to the Library where he is likely to be reading); in 3.4 he looks forward to a triumph to celebrate victory over the Parthians—he'll be a spectator leaning on the bosom of his girl: the portico and the triumph inevitably feature in the list in the *Ars* of places and occasions where men can pick up girls (1.73–4, 177–228), and so do Baiae and the shrine of Diana at Aricia (1.255–62), both places that Cynthia heads off to without Propertius, much to his consternation (1.11; 2.32.9–10).

Verbal similarities reinforce these reworkings; in the case of the *Metamorphoses* such echoes are the main way in which Ovid shows his continuing debt to Propertius. Erotic narratives dominate the poem from the first story of Deucalion and Pyrrha in 1 to Vertumnus and Pomona in 14. Both the start and the end of the theme are signaled by use of the concepts *mollis* and *durus*, developed by Propertius as markers of elegy and epic (*Met.* 1.400–2, 14.757–8):

> *saxa* (quis hoc credat, nisi sit pro teste uetustas?)
> ponere *duritiam* coepere suumque *rigorem*
> *molliri*que mora *mollita*que ducere formam.

> Who would believe it unless antiquity served as a witness? The *stones* [i.e. those thrown by Deucalion and Pyrrha] began to lay aside their *hardness* and natural *solidity*, and as time passed to grow soft, and as they *softened* to take on form.

> paulatimque occupat artus
> quod fuit in *duro* iam pridem pectore *saxum*.

> And little by little the limbs [of Anaxarete, whose indifference has killed Iphis] are taken over by the *stone* which has long been in her *hard* heart.

The epic tale of the flood leads to the married pair, Deucalion and Pyrrha, and on to Python, heroically killed by Apollo; but then Amor enters the poem, and historical sequence is abandoned. The god of love shoots Apollo and makes him fall in love with Daphne: the scene has much that recalls *Am.* 1.1, but, with the stress on *Amor*, *primus*, and the girl's name, the first verse, 1.453 *primus amor Phoebi Daphne Peneia* ('Apollo's first love was Daphne daughter of Peneus') recalls Propertius' opening

Cynthia prima etc. (p. 266). Throughout the poem, lovers' soliloquies and attempts at seduction have phrasing that echoes the elegiac lover. The nymph Salmacis does not hunt but pays the attention to her appearance shown by an elegiac mistress (*Met.* 4.288–388). She addresses Hermaphroditus with the kind of compliments Odysseus offers to Nausicaa (*Od.* 6.149–97), but far from showing the delicacy of the naked, salt-encrusted, lion-like epic hero, she seizes and rapes the beautiful boy as he swims: *uicimus et meus est*, she cries ('we have won and he is mine'), like Propertius celebrating Cynthia's staying in Rome (1.8.28, 34, 42, 44). As he struggles, she warns that he will not escape (4.371; *non tamen effugies* echoes Prop. 2.8.25).

At the start of Book 8 reminiscence of a Propertian passage contributes to another context where the elegiac voice competes with an epic setting. Scylla, daughter of Nisus, king of Megara, watches the war against Minos and his army from a tower on the walls: this is an imitation of the scene in *Iliad* 3 where Helen and Priam look down on the Greek warriors outside the walls of Troy, and the language is suitably epic (8.20 *rigidi certamina Martis*, 'the contests of harsh Mars'; 8.22 *armaque equosque habitusque Cydoneasque pharetras*: '[she recognized] the weapons and horses and clothing and Cretan quivers'). But, like Tarpeia in Propertius 4.4, Scylla falls in love with the enemy leader, and we find a sequence of balanced clauses, each matching an aspect of his behavior or dress with her approving response (8.25–9):

> seu caput abdiderat cristata casside pennis,
> in galea formosus erat; seu sumpserat aere
> *fulgentem* clipeum, clipeum sumpsisse decebat;
> torserat adductis hastilia lenta lacertis,
> *laudabat* uirgo iunctam cum uiribus *artem*.

> If he had covered his head with a helmet crested with feathers, he was handsome in a helmet; or if he had taken up a shield *gleaming* with bronze, it suited him to have taken up a shield; he had applied his strength and hurled pliant spears: the maiden *praised* the mixture of *skill* and might.

As is noted by Hollis (1970: 39), the structure and theme are found a number of times in Latin love poetry. But the closest is Propertius 2.1.5–16, where six consecutive couplets begin with *seu* or *siue*, and each matches an action or outfit of Cynthia with the poet's response (the generic play here has been explored by Wiggers 1977 and others). Ovid repeats three further words from his model (Prop. 2.1.5–10):

> siue illam Cois *fulgentem* incedere cerno,
>   totum de Coa ueste uolumen erit;
> seu uidi ad frontem sparsos errare capillos,
>   gaudet *laudatis* ire superba comis;
> siue lyrae carmen digitis percussit eburnis,
>   miramur faciles ut premat *arte* manus.

> If I observe her out for a walk *gleaming* in Coan silks, the whole roll will be about [*and of*] Coan cloth; or if I have seen her hair undone and wandering on her brow, she

rejoices to advance made proud by the *praise* of her locks; or if she strikes a song on the lyre with her ivory fingers, we are amazed how *artfully* she applies her skillful hands.

Propertius has a climactic pun in 13–14: when Cynthia wrestles naked with him, he both composes long Iliads and sheathes his long *ilia* ('groin'); Ovid matches this with his own double entendre, the uncontrollable excitement of Scylla as she watches Minos riding his horse, and touching his spear (8.32–6).

As has been said, it is the Propertian figure Vertumnus who brings the erotic sequence to a close in the *Metamorphoses*, telling the tale of Iphis and the hard-hearted Anaxarete (14.698–764) as a warning story to Pomona, the goddess he desires (and to whom he is allied through his interest in gardens). In Propertius, Vertumnus presents himself as a god of the people, standing within sight of the Forum and taking on the characteristics of any figure whose clothes he is dressed in. His name is derived from *uertere* ('to turn' or 'change'), and his ability to shift shape from day to day is mimicked in the poem itself, as it changes direction line by line. It is thus no surprise that Vertumnus appears in Ovid's poem of transformation. He retains many of the accoutrements that mark the Propertian Vertumnus, but sometimes changes their meaning, and makes the god's varied appearance serve a narrative purpose, as he keeps turning up in different disguises (*Met.* 14.643–56: highlighted words are repeated from Prop. 4.2.21–42):

> o quotiens habitu duri *messoris* aristas
> *corbe tulit* uerique *fuit* messoris imago!
> tempora saepe gerens *faeno* religata recenti
> desectum poterat *gramen* uersare uideri; . . .
> *falce data* frondator erat uitisque putator; . . .
> miles erat gladio, piscator *harundine sumpta*; . . .
> ille etiam picta redimitus tempora *mitra*,
> innitens *baculo* positis ad tempora canis
> adsimulauit anum cultosque intrauit in *hortos*, . . .

> O, how often in the garb of a hardy *reaper he carried* corn *in a basket*, and *was* the image of a real reaper! Often, having his head bound with fresh *hay*, he could seem to be turning cut *grass*; . . . *given a sickle* he was a gatherer of leaves and a pruner of a vine; . . . he was a soldier with a sword, a fisherman *when he took up a rod*; . . . his head bound with an embroidered *turban*, white hair placed on his head, leaning *on a stick*, he also put on the disguise of an old woman and entered the cultivated *gardens*.

The shifty, Etruscan Vertumnus may seem a strange first item for a Roman poet fulfilling his promise to sing *sacra deosque*; but there is significance in Propertius' choice of a deity who is symbolic of poetic creativity and open to revision at the hands of the crowd in the street. With his version Ovid marks a debt to the predecessor who brought into Augustan poetry this image of unpredictable change, an effective alternative to the immovable *fatum* that determines history in the *Aeneid*.

FURTHER READING

There is a dedicated discussion of the influence of Propertius on the *Amores* in Morgan (1977); also on the *Amores* see Berman (1972, 1975), Du Quesnay (1973), McKeown (1987: 11–115), and Boyd (1997); and O'Neill (1999) for discussion of one case where the direction of influence is not certain. For a more general account of Propertius and Ovid's love poetry, see Armstrong (2005: esp. 11–19). However, for detailed examination of particular Ovidian allusions to Propertius, the best sources are the commentaries, for example Henderson (1979), McKeown (1989, 1998), Barchiesi (1992), Casali (1995a), and Gibson (2003). For the Propertian background to the *Fasti*, there are excellent observations in a number of more general accounts such as Miller (1991), Barchiesi (1997a), Newlands (1995), and Gee (2000: esp. 23–34). On Propertius and the *Heroides*, the fullest account remains Jacobson (1974; see also Merklin 1968).

For examination of the many fraught questions raised by the transmitted text of Propertius, see Goold (1966, 1992), Butrica (1997), Günther (1997), and Heyworth (2007a). Helpful literary introductions are Boucher (1965), Commager (1974), Hubbard (1974), La Penna (1977), and Papanghelis (1987). Tränkle (1960) is an admirable discussion of his diction; on politics, see Stahl (1985) and Heyworth (2007b).

On *seruitium amoris*, see Copley (1947) and Lyne (1979 = 2007: 85–100); on *militia amoris* Thomas (1964), Murgatroyd (1974), Cahoon (1988); on paired poems, Jäger (1967) and Davis (1977).

CHAPTER TWENTY

Tibullus and Ovid

Robert Maltby

Introduction

Ovid would have been only sixteen or seventeen when Tibullus' first book of elegies appeared in 27 or 26 BC. It was around this time, or perhaps a couple of years later, that Ovid started reciting the poems of his own *Amores*, published first in an edition of five books and then later, not before 16 BC, in the three-book collection as we now have it. The influence of Tibullus can be seen in almost every poem of this work and reaches its climax in *Am.* 3.9, an elegy commemorating the death of Tibullus in 19 BC. Tibullan influence does not end with the publication of the *Amores* but continues to make itself evident throughout Ovid's career. Even in the poems of exile, for example in *Tr.* 2.445–68, Tibullus is singled out for detailed treatment, in this case as Ovid's predecessor in erotodidactic poetry of the kind which had been responsible in part for Ovid's banishment from Rome.

The aim of this chapter will be to bring together and analyze the evidence for Tibullan influence on Ovid with a view to explaining why Tibullus in particular of all Ovid's Latin predecessors in the elegiac genre had such a hold over his poetic imagination. Beginning with an analysis of those passages in which Ovid specifically names Tibullus, we will move on to look at the ways in which Ovid reacted intertextually with his predecessor's work, both at the level of the individual elegy and at the more detailed level of his use of specifically Tibullan themes, ideas, and phrases. In the course of the discussion it will become clear that while Ovid frequently acknowledges Tibullus as an important predecessor in the genre he is always at pains to emphasize his own originality in his treatment of Tibullan material. Only the genuinely Tibullan first two books of the Tibullan corpus will be discussed, as it is now generally agreed that the third book was composed much later, probably at the end of the first century AD.

Tibullus in Ovid's Elegiac Canon

The most frequent context in which Ovid mentions Tibullus by name is to establish his position as a leading exponent of elegy. Already in the final poem of the first book of the *Amores*, where Ovid is stressing the immortality to be achieved through literary works, Tibullus is named first among the Latin elegists, even before Gallus, against the true chronological sequence (*Am.* 1.15.27–30):

> donec erunt ignes arcusque Cupidinis arma,
>   discentur numeri, culte Tibulle, tui.
> Gallus et Hesperiis et Gallus notus Eois,
>   et sua cum Gallo nota Lycoris erit.

> For as long as flames and the bow are Cupid's arms your verses will be learned, elegant Tibullus; Gallus will be famed both in the West and in the East and with Gallus will his Lycoris be famed.

An important feature of this first mention of Tibullus is the stress laid on the elegance of his style in the epithet *culte*, also applied to Tibullus in the elegy on his death at *Am.* 3.9.66. Here Ovid's appreciation of Tibullus' polished style as an elegist coincides with that of Quintilian, who describes him at *Inst.* 10.1.93 as *tersus atque elegans maxime auctor* ('the most terse and elegant author [of elegy]'). In applying the adjective to his own *Ars amatoria* at *Ars* 3. 341–2—*culta magistri carmina* ('elegant poems of the master')—Ovid implicitly acknowledges the influence of Tibullus on his own work. The reference to Cupid's torches and bow echoes Tibullus' wish in his final elegy (2.6.15–16) that Cupid's weapons, the source of his unhappiness as a lover, should be destroyed: *acer Amor, fractas utinam, tua tela, sagittas, / si licet, extinctas aspiciamque faces* ('Cruel Love, if it be allowed, would that I could see your weapons, the arrows and the torches, broken and burned out'). This couplet of Tibullus' is also reworked, for pathetic effect, in *Am.* 3.9.7–8, as we shall see below. These echoes from Tibullus' final elegy in the two passages in which he is named in the *Amores* may indicate that Ovid wishes to be seen as Tibullus' successor in the genre. The emphasis in *discentur* (28, 'will be learned') is on Tibullus' importance as a teacher of love (*praeceptor amoris*). It is this aspect of Tibullus' work that is also stressed in *Tr.* 2.447–68, where Tibullus is presented as an important predecessor of Ovid in this field. Erotodidaxis, or the teaching of love, will be an important element in Ovid's own work, culminating in the *Ars amatoria*, but already foreshadowed in the present poem (*Am.* 1.15) at line 38: *atque a sollicito multus amante legar* ('and I shall often be read by an anxious lover'). While Gallus is mentioned as bringing fame to his mistress Lycoris, there is no mention at this stage of Tibullus' mistress. This is perhaps because, unusually for an elegist, he celebrated two different mistresses: Delia in Book 1 and Nemesis in Book 2, a point that will be emphasized for comic effect in *Am.* 3.9. Finally, it is interesting that there is no mention of Propertius among the elegists in this poem, although he was a near contemporary of Tibullus. From the time of the *Ars* it became Ovid's custom to mention Tibullus in combination with Gallus and Propertius as his three predecessors in the genre (*Ars* 3.333–4, 535–8; *Rem.* 763–6; *Tr.* 2.445–68, 4.10.51–4, 5.1.15–20).

The importance of Tibullus to Ovid is stressed by the dedication to him of a whole elegy (*Am.* 3.9) commemorating the poet's death at an early age in 19 or 18 BC. The elegy is given the emphatic middle position of the third book and, as a farewell to an admired elegiac poet, parallels Ovid's farewell to the elegiac genre at the end of the book in 3.15. It also repeats at a more serious level the theme of the central poem of the second book on the death of a parrot (2.6). More significant from our point of view is the fact that this central position in the first book (1.8) is reserved for the speech of the *lena* Dipsas, a theme which may have been influenced by the speech of the *lena* in Tibullus 1.8.47–58. The poem reveals Ovid's deep knowledge of Tibullus' writings, not only at a thematic level but also on more detailed points of technique and meter. The clearest echoes come from the beginning of Tibullus' first book, poems 1.1 and 1.3, both of which contain passages envisaging his own death (1.1.59–68, 1.3.5–10) and the last poems of his second book (2.5 and 6). Lines 37–8 (*uiue pius—moriere; pius cole sacra—colentem / mors grauis a templis in caua busta trahet*, 'Live in piety—you will die; piously observe the rituals—in your very act of observance heavy death will drag you from the temples to the hollow tomb') echo Tibullus' description of his own observance of ritual in 1.1.15–24 and 35–40, which precedes the imagining of his own death in Rome (1.1.59–68). There is a direct verbal echo in *pius cole sacra* (37) of Tibullus' description of Delia's worship of Isis in 1.3.25 (*pie dum sacra colis*, 'while you piously observe the rituals'). The reference in 53–4 to Nemesis and Delia joining their kisses to those of Tibullus' kin at the funeral (*cumque tuis sua iunxerunt Nemesisque priorque / oscula*, 'Nemesis and your former love added their kisses to those of your kin') echo Tibullus' injunction to Delia at the end of 1.1 to unite with him in love: *iungamus amores* ('let us unite in love'). Humor is never far from the surface of this funeral elegy, especially in Ovid's description of the imagined argument between Tibullus' two mistresses at his graveside (3.9.55–8):

> Delia discedens 'felicius' inquit 'amata
>   sum tibi: uixisti, dum tuus ignis eram.'
> cui Nemesis 'quid' ait 'tibi sunt mea damna dolori?
>   me tenuit moriens deficiente manu.'

> Delia departing said, 'I was more happily loved by you; you were alive while I was your flame.' To whom Nemesis replied, 'Why is my loss a source of grief to you? It was I he held in his failing grasp as he died.'

Her last line is a pointed quotation of Tibullus' words to Delia at 1.1.60: *te teneam moriens deficiente manu* ('I will hold you in my failing grasp as I die'). Similarly, Ovid addresses both mistresses in the words: *quid uos sacra iuuant? quid nunc Aegyptia prosunt / sistra? quid in uacuo secubuisse toro?* (33–4, 'What use are your rituals? What help are your Egyptian sistrums? What help your sleeping alone on an empty couch?'), in an echo of Tibullus' address to Delia alone while sick on the island of Phaeacia (1.3.23–6):

> quid tua nunc Isis mihi, Delia, quid mihi prosunt
>   illa tua totiens aera repulsa manu,
> quidue, pie dum sacra colis, pureque lauaris
>   te (memini) puro secubuisse toro?

What help is your Isis to me now, Delia; what help are the bronze rattles shaken so often in your hand; what help, while you piously observe the rituals, and are washed in purity for you, as I well recall, to sleep alone on a pure couch?

The phrase *quid prosunt* ('what use are . . . ?') is characteristic of Tibullus, occurring no fewer than nine times in his poetry, but Ovid fails to follow the purity of Tibullus' Latin to the extent of avoiding the Greek loanword *sistra*, as Tibullus does by his use of the circumlocution *aera repulsa manu*. Another feature of Tibullus 1.3 echoed in *Am.* 3.9 is the use of the funerary epigram. At 1.3.55–6 Tibullus imagines the following epitaph for himself should he die abroad:

> hic iacet immiti consumptus morte Tibullus
>   Messallam terra dum sequiturque mari.

Here lies Tibullus wasted by cruel death, while accompanying Messalla on land and sea.

The phrase *iacet . . . Tibullus* recurs in Ovid's poem at 3.9.40, suggesting that the whole of the section 3.9.37–40 could also be taken as a funerary epigram, addressed in Hellenistic fashion to a passer-by (text of Showerman/Goold):

> uiue pius—moriere; pius cole sacra—colentem
>   mors grauis a templis in caua busta trahet;
> carminibus confide bonis—iacet, ecce, Tibullus:
>   uix manet e toto, parua quod urna capit.

Live in piety—you will die. Piously observe the rituals—in your very act of observance heavy death will drag you from the temples into the hollow grave. Put your trust in good poetry—behold, Tibullus lies dead. From his whole self there scarcely remains the contents of a small urn.

Other elements of Tibullus 1.3 are reworked in the poem. The reference to death in Phaeacia—1.3.3 *me tenet ignotis aegrum Phaeacia terris* ('Phaeacia holds me sick in its unknown lands')—is echoed at *Am.* 3.9.47–8 (*sed tamen hoc melius, quam si Phaeacia tellus / ignotum uili supposuisset humo*, 'and yet this is better than if the Phaeacian land had buried you a stranger in its mean soil'), where Ovid transfers the epithet *ignotus* from the unknown foreign land in Tibullus to Tibullus' nameless corpse. Whereas in 1.3 Tibullus complains of the absence of his mother (5–6), sister (7–8), and Delia (9) at his funeral, should he die abroad, Ovid mentions the same mourners in the same order at his actual funeral in Rome: mother (49–50), sister (51–2), and Delia (55), but adds, as we have seen, as an extra piquant detail, the presence of the mistress of his second book, Nemesis (53) and the quarrel between the two mistresses discussed above. Whereas in 1.3 Tibullus imagines his spirit being led after death by Venus to an Elysium reserved for lovers (57–66), Ovid imagines Tibullus' spirit living on in an Elysium reserved for love-poets, where he will meet the shades of Calvus (62), Catullus (62), and Gallus (64). The terms in which Catullus and Calvus are described as running to greet his shade (*Am.* 3.9.61–2),

> obuius huic uenies hedera iuuenalia cinctus
> tempora cum Caluo, docte Catulle, tuo;

> You will come to meet him, learned Catullus, your youthful temples encircled with ivy and your Calvus with you.

recall those in which Tibullus bids Delia run to meet him on his safe return from Phaecia (1.3.93): *obuia nudato, Delia, curre pede* ('run to meet me, Delia, in bare feet').

Alongside these echoes from the early poems of Tibullus' first book come reminiscences of the last two poems of his second. So at *Am.* 3.9.12 Cupid is described as weeping at the funeral of his brother Aeneas. The only earlier reference to Aeneas and Cupid as brothers comes from Tibullus 2.5.39 in the opening of the Sibyl's prophecy: *impiger Aenea, uolitantis frater Amoris* ('tireless Aeneas, brother of winged Love'). The twice-repeated idea that bards are sacred in *Am.* 3.9.17 (*at sacri uates et diuum cura uocamur*, 'but we bards are called sacred and the care of the gods') and 41, referring to Tibullus, *tene, sacer uates, flammae rapuere rogales* ('have the flames of the pyre snatched you away, sacred bard?'), again has its origin in Tibullus 2.5, in this case in Tibullus' warning to Nemesis at the end of the poem (113–4): *at tu (nam diuum seruat tutela poetas) praemoneo, uati parce, puella, sacro* ('but since divine protection watches over poets, I warn you, girl, spare the sacred bard'). Finally, as discussed above, the breaking of Cupid's arrows and the extinguishing of his torches, wished for by Tibullus in his final poem (2.6.15–16) in order to bring an end to his sufferings in love—*acer Amor, fractas utinam, tua tela, sagittas, / si licet, extinctas aspiciamque faces* ('Cruel Love, if it be allowed, would that I could see your weapons, the arrows and the torches, broken and burned out')—is seen in Ovid as coming about because of Cupid's grief at Tibullus' death: *Am.* 3.9.7–8 *ecce puer Veneris fert euersamque pharetram / et fractos arcus et sine luce facem* ('Behold, the son of Venus carries his quiver upturned, his bow broken, and his torch without a flame').

This echoing of Tibullan themes marks out *Am.* 3.9 as a sincere tribute to an elegiac predecessor, but Ovid takes this appreciation further by echoing in the poem some characteristic features of Tibullan metrics. Pentameters in which the penultimate word ends in *-isse(t)* are more frequent in Tibullus than in the other elegists (Tib. 6.26%, Cat. 1.53%, Prop. 1.05%, Ov. *Am.* 3.26%). There are no fewer than five occurrences of this type of pentameter ending in *Am.* 3.9 (lines 22, 24, 34, 46, 48), giving a total for that poem of 14.7% (Luque Moreno 1995). Two other Tibullan metrical features are also prominent in this poem, namely a weak caesura in the third foot and diaeresis in the second foot of the hexameter. Examples of weak third-foot caesura are concentrated in lines 35–40 and in the two lines in which Tibullus is named in the poem (15 and 39) and one of the poem's two examples of second-foot diaeresis is also found in line 35 (McLennan 1972). In the course of the poem, then, Ovid made a serious effort to recall within the space of a few lines the metrical style of Tibullus (Maltby 1999: 382–4; 2002: 68–72).

It will suffice here to list quickly the other poems in which Tibullus is named as a poetic predecessor before going on to look in detail at *Tr.* 2.445–68, where Tibullus is given detailed treatment as a predecessor, specifically in the area of erotodidaxis. At *Ars* 3.329–46 Ovid reviews the type of literature which it would be suitable for girls to use to woo men, and the recitation of works by Propertius, Gallus, and Tibullus is recommended at 3.333–4, before Ovid passes on to his own compositions at 3.339–46, where his reference to them as *culta . . . carmina* (3.341–2) acknowledges his debt to Tibullus, as discussed above. At *Ars* 3.535–8 the fame won by Tibullus' Nemesis, Propertius' Cynthia, and Gallus' Lycoris is used to illustrate the immortality which elegiac poetry can confer upon a mistress. As in 3.333–4 Gallus is named out of chronological sequence. Only Nemesis is mentioned here, but the omission of Delia must simply be for the sake of parallelism with the single mistresses of Propertius and Gallus. In *Am.* 3.9.31 Ovid mentions the fame to be won by both Tibullus' mistresses. In *Rem.* 763–6, when listing poetry to be avoided by those wishing to be cured of love, the four elegists are mentioned, again out of chronological order, as Tibullus, Propertius, Gallus, and Ovid. No details are given here of the elegists, except for Propertius' devotion to Cynthia alone, a particularly dangerous aspect of his work in this context.

Ovid as a Tibullan Erotodidact

Next in his autobiographical elegy (*Tr.* 4.10) Ovid mentions Tibullus along with Gallus, Propertius, and himself as exemplifying the canonical four elegists (*Tr.* 4.10.51–4):

> Vergilium uidi tantum, nec auara Tibullo
>   tempus amicitiae fata dedere meae.
> successor fuit hic tibi, Galle, Propertius illi;
>   quartus ab his serie temporis ipse fui.

> Virgil I only saw, and greedy fate allowed Tibullus no time for friendship with me. Tibullus was your successor, Gallus, and Propertius was his; I came fourth after these in order of time.

It is significant here that Tibullus occurs out of chronological order before Gallus and is given a longer treatment than the other poets mentioned. Of the four, Tibullus alone is singled out as a possible object of Ovid's friendship, if only he could have lived longer. Similarly in the introduction to *Tristia* 5 Ovid mentions his own work along with that of the three canonical elegists, in this case in chronological order. The point is that now Ovid is no longer able to write wanton verse (*lasciua carmina*) such as they had all produced in the past (*Tr.* 5.1.15–19):

delicias siquis lasciuaque carmina quaerit,
    praemoneo, non est scripta quod ista legat.
aptior huic Gallus blandique Propertius oris,
    aptior, ingenium come, Tibullus erit.
atque utinam numero non nos essemus in isto!

If anyone is looking for amusement and lascivious verse, I warn him, there is no reason for him to read such writing as this. Gallus will be more suitable for such as he, and Propertius of the charming voice; more suitable Tibullus, that winning genius. And would that I were not of their number!

Again, prominence is given to Tibullus, who has a whole line to himself, as compared with the half-line each for Propertius and Gallus; in addition Tibullus is given the flattering description of *ingenium come* ('winning genius').

We come now to *Tr.* 2.445–68, lines which contain Ovid's most sustained interaction with Tibullus' verse. *Tristia* 2, written from exile in AD 9, consists of an open letter to Augustus in which he pleads against his banishment. In *Tr.* 2.207 Ovid gives the two reasons for his exile as *carmen et error* ('a poem and a mistake'). He is unwilling to give further details of the mistake for fear of paining Augustus further (208), but of the poem he says (211–12) *qua turpi carmine lecto / arguor obsceni doctor adulterii* ('the charge is that I am accused of being a teacher of foul adultery through reading a disgraceful poem'). The poem in question is in all likelihood the *Ars amatoria*, for at 471–96 he goes on to point out how other writers of *Artes* have escaped punishment. His defense in general is to show that he was not the only poet to write of love, although he has been the only one to suffer for doing so: 361–2 *denique composui teneros non solus amores: / composito poenas solus amore dedi* ('moreover I was not the only one to write of tender love: but for writing of love I was the only one to be punished'). There follows a catalogue of Greek and Latin writers on love, beginning with Greek lyric, epic, and tragedy (363–420); of the Roman writers Catullus heads the list (427–30) followed by a dozen further writers from Calvus to Sisenna (431–44). Then begins the section on Roman elegy with two lines on Gallus (445–6), no fewer than seventeen lines on Tibullus (447–64), and two on Propertius (465–6), all of whom wrote without punishment, and finally Ovid himself (467–70), the only poet to suffer for his verse on love. Tibullus, then, is discussed at far greater length than any other author in the piece, Greek or Latin. The Tibullan passage itself (447–64) consists mainly of a close rewriting and rearrangement of Tibullus 1.6. In this poem Tibullus had complained that Delia was using the tricks he had taught her against her husband to cheat Tibullus himself with other men. In a fit of jealous despair he bids her husband to keep tighter rein on her. Each couplet in Ovid's reworking corresponds closely to a Tibullan couplet from 1.6 (447–58) or in one case from the end of 1.5 (459–60): only Ovid's summary in 461–2 has no direct Tibullan model. The best way of illustrating the construction is to take Ovid's reworking couplet by couplet, showing the Tibullan origin after each one:

credere iuranti durum putat esse Tibullus,   (*Tr.* 2.447–8)
   sic etiam de se quod neget illa uiro.

Tibullus thinks it hard to believe what his mistress swears, since she makes the same denials about himself to her husband.

illa quidem iurata negat, sed credere durum est: (Cf. Tib. 1.6.7–8)
   sic etiam de me pernegat usque uiro.

She denies it on oath, but it is hard to believe her: she constantly makes the same denials about me to her husband.

fallere custodes idem docuisse fatetur,   (*Tr.* 2.449–50)
   seque sua miserum nunc ait arte premi.

The same admits to teaching her how to deceive the guards and says that he is now a wretched victim of his own device.

ipse miser docui, quo posset ludere pacto   (Cf. Tib. 1.6.9–10)
   custodes: eheu, nunc premor arte mea.

It was I in my wretchedness who taught her how to trick the guards: alas I am now a victim of my own device.

saepe, uelut gemmam dominae signumue probaret,   (*Tr.* 2.451–2)
   per causam meminit se tetigisse manum;

Often, on the pretext of trying his mistress's gem or signet ring, he remembers how he touched her hand.

saepe, uelut gemmas eius signumque probarem,   (Cf. Tib. 1.6.25–6)
   per causam memini me tetigisse manum:

Often, on the pretext of trying her gems or signet ring, I remember how I touched her hand.

utque refert, digitis saepe est nutuque locutus,   (*Tr.* 2.453–4)
   et tacitam mensae duxit in orbe notam;

As he tells, he often spoke to her with finger signs and nods and drew a silent message on the round table top.

neu te decipiat nutu, digitoque liquorem   (Cf. Tib. 1.6.19–20)
   ne trahat et mensae ducat in orbe notas.

Let her not deceive you with a nod, and let her not draw with her finger in the wine and trace a message on the round table top.

et quibus e sucis abeat de corpore liuor,   (*Tr.* 2.455–6)
   impresso fieri qui solet ore, docet:

And he teaches what lotions cause to disappear the marks made by the mouth's imprint.

tunc sucos herbasque dedi, quis liuor abiret,   (Cf. Tib. 1.6.13–14)
     quem facit impresso mutua dente Venus.

Then I gave lotions and herbs to make disappear the marks passion made with the imprint of our teeth.

denique ab incauto nimium petit ille marito,   (*Tr.* 2.457–8)
     se quoque uti seruet, peccet ut illa minus.

Finally he asks her too careless husband to watch him also, so that she should sin less.

at tu, fallacis coniunx incaute puellae,   (Cf. Tib. 1.6.15–16)
     me quoque seruato, peccet ut illa nihil.

But you, incautious husband of a deceitful girl, guard me also, so that she should not sin.

scit, cui latretur, cum solus obambulet, ipsas   (*Tr.* 2.459–60)
     cur totiens clausas excreet ante fores,

He knows who the dog barks at as someone passes by alone, and why someone coughs so often before the closed door.

instabat tota cui tua nocte canis   (Cf. Tib. 1.6.32)

(I was the man) your dog was barking at all night.

solus et ante ipsas excreat usque fores.   (Tib. 1.5.74)

(He returns) alone and coughs persistently at the very door.

Ovid has rearranged the Tibullan material to suit his special purpose. The Tibullan lines 25–6 are inserted before 19–20 and 19–26 are placed before 13–16. The resulting structure moves away from Tibullus' theme of tortured jealousy and gives the impression more of a self-confident Ovidian lover, a teacher of love who revels in his own success. The address to the husband comes not as act of desperation but as a climactic (note Ovid's emphatic *denique*, 547) demonstration of arrogance. The concluding couplet (*Tr.* 2.461–2) has no direct correspondence in Tibullus and is added by Ovid to stress Tibullus' role as a teacher of love *dat . . . praecepta docetque*, who has written an *ars* (*arte* in 462 recalling *arte* of the opening 450) to show married women (*nuptae*) how to trick their husbands. This stress on trickery in Tibullus' teaching is stressed structurally by the triple *fallere . . . docuisse . . . arte* of 449–50 being picked up in *furti . . . docetque . . . arte* of 461–2. Although Tibullus names Delia as the girl in question in 1.6.5, Ovid intentionally suppresses the name: the girl is referred to only in the participle *iuranti*. The intention here seems to be to emphasize Tibullus' role as a teacher of secret love (*furtiuus amor*) in general (cf. 461–2) rather than in the context of a specific affair. In this sense Tibullus is presented in this poem as perhaps more Ovidian than he actually was. The didactic content is stressed throughout: *docuisse* (449), *meminit* (452), *refert* (453), *docet* (456), *scit* (459), *dat . . . praecepta docetque* (461), as is the element of trickery and secrecy involved: *fallere* (449), *nutu . . . locutus* (453), *tacitam . . . notam* (454), *peccet* (458), *furti* (461).

Tibullus, then, is presented here by Ovid as a master in the teaching of love and hence an excellent precedent for Ovid's case that such teaching has not been punished in the past, even though Tibullus was at the height of his fame in Augustus' early principate (*Tr.* 4.464). Erotodidaxis had in fact played an important role in Tibullus' work in other poems apart from 1.6. It had featured in Venus' advice to lovers at 1.2.15–24, and, in particular, in Priapus' lecture on homosexual love in 1.4. But 1.6 serves Ovid's purpose here better than the two earlier examples because the teaching is given not through the mouth of a god but directly in Tibullus' own voice, as it is also in 1.8.5–16 and 1.8.55–66. It is this element of his work in particular, then, that causes Ovid to see in Tibullus an important literary predecessor both for the *Amores* and, more significantly, for the *Ars amatoria*.

Tibullus in the *Amores*

Tibullus 1.6 had influenced Ovid even in his *Amores*. The final poem of the second book (*Am.* 2.19) consists of a *suasoria* addressed to a husband who is seen as too lax in guarding his wife. The whole elegy is a development of the address to the husband in Tib. 1.6.15–38, but, whereas Tibullus wishes the husband to keep her from other men (16) and, if necessary, hand her over to himself to guard (37), Ovid's purpose is to have the husband put difficulties in his way in order to enliven his own enjoyment of the affair. A comparison of Ovid's opening couplet with the beginning of Tibullus' address makes the difference in emphasis clear:

> si tibi non opus est seruata, stulte, puella,   (*Am.* 2.19.1–2)
>   at mihi fac serues, quo magis ipse uelim.

If you have no need of guarding your girl, stupid man, then see that you guard her for me, so that I may desire her all the more.

> at tu fallacis coniunx incaute puellae,   (Tib. 1.6.15–16)
>   me quoque seruato peccet ut illa nihil

But you, incautious husband of a deceitful girl, guard me also, so that she should not sin.

Tibullus' opening line is also reworked, with different emphasis, in line 37 of Ovid's treatment: *at tu, formosae nimium secure puellae* ('o you, who are too careless of your pretty wife'). In line with Ovid's different viewpoint he makes use of detailed echoes from Tibullus to different effect. So Delia's feigned headache, used as a ruse against her husband in Tibullus (1.6.36 *et simulat subito condoluisse caput*, 'and she pretends to have a sudden headache') is cited by Ovid as an example of the way his previous girlfriend, Corinna, had understood the necessity of putting difficulties in Ovid's way in order to spice up their affair (*Am.* 2.19.11–12 *a, quotiens sani capitis mentita dolores / cunctantem tardo iussit abire pede*, 'Oh, how often, when quite well, she feigned a headache and bade me depart, though I with tardy foot delayed'). At 2.19.42 Ovid advises the husband to ask his wife *cur totiens uacuo secubet ipsa toro* ('why so often she sleeps apart in an empty bed'). In Tibullus this had been a trick that Delia had first learned from him to use against her husband (1.6.11 *fingere tunc didicit causas, ut sola cubaret*, then she learned reasons for sleeping alone'). Similarly, Tibullus' confession to the husband (31–2) *ille ego sum, (nec me iam dicere uera pudebit), / instabat tota cui tua nocte canis* ('I was the man—I am no longer ashamed to tell the truth—at whom your dog barked all night') is again turned by Ovid into a question the husband should ask his wife (40): *quaerere, quid latrent nocte silente canes* ('ask her why the dogs bark in the silence of the night'). At 34, Ovid echoes Tibullus' complaint that Delia uses his own tricks against him (Tib. 1.6.10): *eheu, nunc premor arte mea* ('alas, now I am the victim of my own teaching') in the words *ei mihi, ne monitis torquear ipse meis* ('alas, may I not be tortured by my own advice'), but here such anguish is amusingly inconsistent with Ovid's overall thesis that lovers welcome difficulties.

It is easy to see how the outrageous request that lies at the center of Tibullus 1.6—that the husband should hand over his wife for Tibullus to guard (37)—would have appealed to Ovid's sense of humor, and it is perhaps no coincidence that this, of all Tibullus' elegies, is the one most frequently quoted by Ovid. We have already seen its central importance in *Tristia* 2 and as the starting point for *Am.* 2.19. In view of Veremans's detailed discussion (Veremans 1987) other echoes of this poem can be reviewed in less detail. At 1.6.19–20 Tibullus warns the husband not to let his wife write secret messages to admirers in wine on the table top. At *Am.* 1.4.20 Ovid proposes using this device to communicate with his mistress at a party at which her husband is also present, whereas at *Ars* 1.571–2 this method of communication with a mistress is recommended to male suitors. Finally, at *Her.* 17.89–90 Helen reminds Paris how he had used this method of conveying his secret love to her. Another trick used against the husband by Tibullus in 1.6 is to get him drunk while remaining sober himself (27–8), in the context of the party mentioned above in *Am.* 1.4 Ovid advises his mistress to get her husband drunk by serving him neat wine (*Am.* 1.4.51–2). At the end of 1.6 Tibullus expresses the wish that Delia will impose strict rules upon him (69–70) *et mihi sint durae leges, laudare nec ullam / possim ego, quin oculos appetat illa meos, et siquid peccasse puter, ducarque capillis / in medias pronus proripiarque uias* ('Let her impose strict rules upon me, may I not be able to praise another girl without her attacking my eyes; and, if I am thought to have erred in any way, may I be dragged by the hair and thrown face down along the middle of the street'). This punishment is echoed by Ovid in *Am.* 2.7.7, where he describes his mistress's reaction, should he praise another woman: *si quam laudaui, miseros petis ungue capillos* ('should I praise any girl, you make for my poor hair with your nails'). Similarly, at *Her.* 20.83–6 in a similar context Acontius specifies all the punishments Cydippe can inflict upon him, provided she does not harm herself in the process. At 1.6.73–4 Tibullus expresses the wish that he should lose his hands rather than use them to harm his mistress: *non ego te pulsare uelim, sed, uenerit iste / si furor, optarim non habuisse manus* ('I would never want to strike you, but, should such madness arise, I would wish to lose my hands'). This rather exaggerated wish is taken even further by Ovid in his adoption of the same idea at *Am.* 1.7.23: *ante meos umeris uellem cecidisse lacertos* ('I would that my arms had sooner fallen from my shoulders'). Finally, Tibullus' wish at the end of the poem that Delia should remain true to him out of faithfulness rather than fear (1.6.75–6 *nec saeuo sis casta metu, sed mente fideli: / mutuus absenti te mihi seruet amor*, 'may you not be true through savage fear, but may mutual love guard you for me in my absence') is picked up by Ovid in his address to the cruel guardian at *Am.* 3.4.1–3: *Dure uir, imposito tenerae custode puellae / nil agis: ingenio est quaeque tuenda suo. si qua metu dempto casta est, ea denique casta est* ('Harsh husband, you achieve nothing by setting a guard upon your tender girl; each girl must be guarded by her own character. She who is chaste when fear is removed is chaste indeed').

In the case of 1.6 it has been shown that a single elegy of Tibullus made a lasting impression on Ovid and details from it were echoed in Ovid's work throughout his career. In some cases the influence was at the level of a single phrase or couplet influencing a phrase or couplet in Ovid, but in the case of the address to the husband at 15–38 a single section of the poem was used as the basis of a whole elegy in Ovid (*Am.* 2.19). Similarly, the whole of *Am.* 1.4 on the theme of flirting at a banquet was based on ideas found in this same passage of Tibullus (1.6.17–28). Here we see one of the main differences between Ovid's method of composition and that of Tibullus. Whereas an elegy of Tibullus consists of a number of distinct but related themes carefully organized into a single unit through the use, in particular, of Hellenistic narrative techniques involving balance, contrast, and repetition, Ovid prefers to develop a single theme in each elegy through the techniques of rhetoric. So 1.6.15–38 of Tibullus is developed into a Roman *suasoria* in *Am.* 2.19. Other examples of this type of Tibullan influence on Ovid are not difficult to identify. So in *Am.* 1.7 a whole elegy is built on the theme of how serious a matter it is to raise one's hand against a mistress, using the rules of rhetoric to amplify themes used in passing in Tibullus (specifically 1.10.53–66; cf. 1.6.73–6, 2.5.101–4). The theme of impotence, touched upon in passing in Tibullus 1.5.39–44, is turned in *Am.* 3.7 into a dramatic poem, examining in detail Ovid's state of mind and his mistress's reaction. But whereas in Tibullus an explanation is provided, namely that his passion for Delia prevents him from performing with other women, in Ovid the drama of the situation stands alone, with no explanation offered. It is not certain whether Tibullus' curse on the *lena* at 1.5.47–58 gave rise to the description of the old procuress Dipsas in *Am.* 1.8. This poem of Ovid's also contains echoes in lines 9–10 of the witch controlling the winds and weather in Tib. 1.2.51–2; and in 17–18 of the practice of necromancy described in Tib. 1.2.47–8. A closer parallel for Ovid is found in this case in Prop. 4.5, with its bitter attack on a procuress containing a central erotodidactic section and offering many verbal similarities with *Am.* 1.8. Both Propertius and Ovid create a single poem out of ideas that are used only in passing in Tibullus, but the priority between Propertius and Ovid is in this case difficult to establish (McKeown 1998: 200). Another poem which takes its starting point from a passing theme in Tibullus (1.5.9–18) but is also influenced by Propertius (in this case Prop. 2.28) is the poem on the mistress's illness (*Am.* 2.13, which forms a pair with *Am.* 2.14). The opening of *Am.* 2.13, in the second line, *in dubio uitae lassa Corinna iacet* ('when Corinna lay exhausted in peril of her life') is clearly dependent on Tibullus' description of Delia's illness at 1.5.9: *cum tristi morbo defessa iaceres* ('when you lay exhausted by a sad disease'). The repeated *ipse* at 2.1323–4 emphasizing Ovid's personal involvement in Corinna's care also recalls the repeated *ipse* in the same context in Tibullus in lines 11, 13 and 15. Both Propertius and Ovid use the theme of the mistress's illness for the subject of a whole elegy (or pair of elegies). In this case Propertius would be earlier than Ovid. Whereas neither Tibullus nor Propertius specify the nature of the mistress's illness, Ovid handles the theme in a novel manner which is clearly intended to shock. His mistress's illness is due to the mishandling of an abortion, a theme he was to treat again in *Her.* 11.39–44.

It is not our purpose here to trace all the Tibullan reminiscences in Ovid but simply to outline the main areas of influence. Other authors provide fuller lists (e.g. Zingerle 1869–71, and, particularly on Tibullan influence on the *Metamorphoses*, Albrecht 1983). However, one further point needs to be emphasized: Tibullan themes and echoes are not scattered randomly throughout the Ovidian corpus but concentrated at points of specific significance. We have already discussed the emphatic positioning of the elegy on the death of Tibullus as the central poem in the third book of the *Amores*. Tibullan influence is particularly marked also in the programmatic opening poems (1–4) of the first book of the *Amores*, perhaps in an attempt by Ovid to establish himself as Tibullus' successor in the genre. In *Amores* Cupid is depicted as interfering in Ovid's poetic composition, turning what was going to be epic into elegy (1.1.1–4). This theme has a special resonance with the end of Tibullus' final book, where at 2.5.105–112 Cupid takes up arms against Tibullus with the result that the only verse he can compose is on the subject of his mistress, Nemesis. Ovid's remonstration with Cupid—(1.1.5–6) *quis tibi, saeue puer, dedit hoc in carmina iuris? / Pieridum uates, non tua, turba sumus* ('Who gave you jurisdiction over poetry, savage boy? We bards are the company of the Pierides, not yours')—although recalling initially a warning from Apollo to Propertius at Prop. 3.3.15–16. to avoid epic, nevertheless also seems to echo Tibullus' words to Cupid at Tib. 1.6.3: *quid tibi saeue, rei* [v.l. *saeue puer*] *mecum est?* ('What have you to do with me, savage one [*v.l.* savage boy]?') Also *uates* in Ovid possibly looks back to Tibullus' reference to himself at 2.5.114 as *uati ... sacro* ('sacred bard').

In *Am.* 1.2 the witty treatment of the triumph of Cupid (lines 34–48) is based on the serious treatment of the triumph theme in Tibullus at 1.7.5–8 (triumph of Messalla) and 2.5.115–120 (projected triumph of Messalla's son, Messallinus). This debt to Tibullus becomes particularly plain at *Am.* 1.2.34 (*uolgus 'io' magna uoce 'triumphe' canet*, 'The crowd will cry "Io, triumph" in a loud voice') with its direct echo of Tib. 2.5.118 (*miles 'io' magna uoce 'triumphe' canet*, 'The soldier will cry "Io, triumph" in a loud voice'). In the same poem the picture of Cupid's mother Venus looking down in pride from Olympus on her son's triumph (39–40 *laeta triumphanti de summo mater Olympo / plaudet*, 'His mother will applaud him in his triumph from high Olympus') is an adaptation of Tibullus' picture of Venus looking down from Olympus on the faithless mistress (1.6.83–4 *hanc Venus ex alto flentem sublimis Olympo / spectat*, 'Aloof on high Olympus Venus looks down upon her tears').

The third poem of the first book of the *Amores* completes Ovid's introductory sequence by introducing the girl who is to be the subject of his love elegies. Like poems 1.1 and 1.2, it too draws on programmatic themes from the beginning of Propertius' third book, but again there are significant Tibullan reminiscences. The theme of the poet's poverty (*paupertas*) in *Am.* 1.3.7–10 echoes one of the most important themes running through Tibullus' first elegy (especially 1.1.5 *me mea paupertas uitae traducat inerti*, 'May my poverty transfer me to a life of inaction'; cf. 11–22, 33–4, 77–8). Other programmatic themes in this elegy reminiscent of Tib. 1.1 are slavery to a mistress (*Am.* 1.3.5; cf. Tib. 1.1.55–6) and the wish that the mistress should mourn at his death (*Am.* 1.3.18; cf. Tib. 1.1.59–68). After the introductory three elegies comes *Am.* 1.4, whose detailed echoes of Tib. 1.6 are discussed above. At the opening of his first collection of poetry, then, Ovid is at pains to make his debt to Tibullus clear.

Looking to Tibullus from Tomi

Finally, just as the beginning of Ovid's first work echoes Tibullan programmatic material, so in Ovid's last composition, the *Epistulae ex Ponto*, there is a detailed echo of a closural theme from Tibullus' final poem (2.6). In that poem Tibullus describes how the cruelty of love had almost driven him to suicide. The only thing to rescue him was personified Hope, with her promise that tomorrow things will be better: *fore cras semper ait melius* ('she always says that tomorrow will be better'). Tibullus then goes on to illustrate the role of Hope in bringing consolation to farmers (21–2), hunters (23–4), and slaves in fetters (25–6), before ending with the statement that in his case Hope promises him better treatment from his mistress, Nemesis. In the corresponding passage in *Pont.* 1.6.27–46 Ovid begins by stating that some hope remains of lessening his punishment (i.e. of bringing him home from banishment): 27–8 *spes igitur menti poenae, Graecine, leuandae / non est ex toto nulla relicta meae* ('Hope therefore of lessening my punishment, Graecinus, has not totally left my mind'). From the beginning of his account of the benefits of Hope Ovid is intent on outdoing his Tibullan model. He begins with a mythological reference, a feature beloved of Ovid but alien, for the most part, to Tibullus' style; the myth referred to here is the story of Hope alone remaining on Earth when all the other deities had departed to Heaven (29–30). When Ovid lists those to whom Hope brings consolation, he begins with an example from Tibullus, the chained field-worker (31–2), but then goes on to add more dramatic instances: the shipwrecked man (33–4), the sick man (35–6), the prisoner (37), the convict on the cross (38), and finally those contemplating suicide (39–40). Whereas Tibullus had begun with the role of Hope in preventing his own suicide, in Ovid this point comes as a climax at the end (41–6), a passage enlivened by a direct address from Hope to the poet (43–4). In this, then, Ovid's final tribute to his elegiac predecessor, there is a clear attempt to out-do his master.

Conclusion

The weakness of any chapter devoted to the influence of a single poet on Ovid is that this particular influence is necessarily taken in isolation and not seen in the full context of the sophisticated interplay of the numerous sources that were always at work in Ovid. Propertius, in particular, was never far from Ovid's thoughts when composing elegy, as a number of the above examples have illustrated. However, the present chapter will, I hope, have demonstrated the central importance of Tibullus to Ovid not just in the *Amores* but throughout his work. This importance is reflected in particular in the significant positioning of reminiscences of, and tributes to, his elegiac predecessor throughout his work. Ovid was perhaps the best read of the Roman elegists, but in his reading of Tibullus he displays a depth of detailed understanding and sympathy which attests to a genuine admiration.

FURTHER READING

The fullest list of parallels between Tibullus and Ovid is provided by Zingerle (1871), but this is simply a list of similar passages, with no discussion of their literary implications or of their possible status as intentional echoes. A more detailed discussion of selected parallels is to be found in (Albrecht 1983), who makes a strong case for the idea that Ovid saw himself as the elegiac successor of Tibullus. These arguments are developed further by Veremans (1987), who confines his discussion to the ubiquitous influences of a single poem, Tibullus 1.6, in the work of Ovid, and by Lenz (1997), with his detailed investigation of Tibullan echoes in the *Tristia*. Specific studies are devoted to Tibullan influence in *Am.* 3.9 (on the death of Tibullus) by Taylor (1970) and Otón Sobrino (1999). Finally, more on the metrical influence of Tibullus on Ovid, particularly in *Am.* 3.9, is to be found in McLennan (1972), Luque Moreno (1995), and Maltby (1999: 382–4).

CHAPTER TWENTY-ONE

Ovid's Reception of Virgil

Richard F. Thomas

Career and Genres

Ovid's Virgil is unlike that of the other, older Augustans. He had clearly been writing individual poems of the *Amores* in the mid-20s BCE (*Tr.* 4.10.57–60), well before the death of Virgil on September 21, 19 BCE. However, he was, as James McKeown has shown (1987: 74–89), still working on poems from the first edition after the death of Virgil, for instance 1.14, which mentions the Sygambri, and so can hardly be before 16 BCE, when the German tribe came to the attention of the Romans. He therefore was the first poet of note, his slate perhaps as yet publicly uninscribed, who either had before him or was aware of the corpus of what must have emerged with Varius and Tucca's issuing of the *Aeneid* as the most important cultural phenomenon in Roman history. 'I only saw Virgil,' he said, confirming what the chronology suggests, namely that Ovid saw himself as a newcomer in relation to the Rome's great poet. As Tarrant well puts it (1997: 61), Ovid was the first poet 'for whom the poetic career of Virgil is a given rather than a gradual discovery, and the first to see it as paradigmatic'. But he was also a neophyte who knew his own genius and had something to offer, something that would take a permanent and prominent place among the genres and genius that had flourished among the poets writing in the generation between his own birth and Virgil's death.

Ovid's career in a sense tracks that of Virgil, but in ways that suggest a disruptive nexus. The opening of the *Amores* (*arma graui numero uiolentaque bella parabam / edere*, 'I was preparing to issue arms and violent wars with a heavy rhythm'), until the purported loss of foot, is an incipient epic, a first successor to the *Aeneid*, published a couple of years before publication of the *Amores*. But Ovid's opening is also an adaptation of the opening Callimachean program of *Eclogue* 6 (*cum canerem reges et proelia* . . . , 'When I was to sing kings and battles . . .'), which likewise justifies the poem and type of poetry at hand. The choice of love elegy, a generation after the *Eclogues* placed the elegiac voices of Corydon and Gallus (*Ecl.* 2, 10) in pastoral settings, serves to reappropriate the genre of elegy to the center of Callimacheanism.

The *Amores* of Ovid are generically kindred to the genre with which those poems of Virgil contested. Similarly, the *Heroides*, *Ars amatoria*, and *Remedia* play generically with erotics and with expanded notions of the elegiac.

In the context of that expansion of the generic territory of the erotic, let us turn to the *Ars amatoria*. Formally and in many other ways it responds to Virgil's second poem, the *Georgics*. Kenney (1958) and Leach (1964) have treated some of the ways Ovid's poem responds to Virgil's. The maxim that 'every woman can be caught' (*Ars* 1.269–70 *cunctas / posse capi*) leads into an assertion that women enjoy furtive love more than men, as observation of the animal world will show. There follows a lengthy mini-epyllion on Pasiphae (289–326), whose transgressive coupling reflects the animal–human boundary-crossing of the *Georgics*. Leach (1964) notes that many of Ovid's images are quintessentially georgic: on the erotic chase (hunting nets and dogs), on becoming acclimatized to the girlfriend (a graft taking), on ignoring the age of the woman (different soils are ready for different types of crop), on the mistress becoming sick in August (recalling the plague of *G.* 3). As she also notes (1964: 150), learning *cultus* is vital for the success of farmer and lover alike. And likewise the lover, like Virgil's farmer, must confront toil, the thematic essence of Virgil's poem, and so reused by Ovid (*Ars* 2.669 *tolerate labores*, 'put up with hard work'). As Virgil assimilated his georgic style to that of Lucretius (taking phrases such as *nonne uides*, *principio*, and the like) so, as Kenney notes (1958), Ovid gives the poem a sense of didactic stylistic veracity by lifting such tags from Virgil and from Lucretius, in some cases from both, for example *ergo age*, *hactenus*, *iubeo/iubebo*, *nunc dicam* and the like. As for the point of this generic—and at times stylistic, dictional, and thematic—intertextuality, to that we shall return presently.

The *Metamorphoses* and *Fasti*, in different ways, match up to the *Aeneid*, with the first uniquely among Ovid's works in dactylic hexameter, the meter of epic. The Roman focus, the Romanizing of myth that is so fundamental a part of the *Aeneid*, and the continuing evolution of aetiological poetry all mark the *Fasti* as a poem that is post-Virgilian in similar ways to the *Metamorphoses*, with its elegiac couplets binding it to Callimachus' *Aetia*. As O'Hara puts it (1996: 257), 'explicit etymologies fit the aetiological nature of both the *Aeneid* and the *Metamorphoses* and are particularly at home in the *Fasti*'. As for the rest of the Ovidian career, Virgil died with his epic and his final work pretty much finished, but Ovid lived on after these two poems. The Virgilian Lives hold that the poet had determined at the time of his death to work on finalizing the *Aeneid*, after which he would remove himself from Rome and Italy and go to Greece and Asia Minor to pursue philosophy. The exiled Ovid in reality got close to Asia in his final years, and wrote in a mode (epistles) not distinct from the philosophical (*Tristia*, *Epistulae ex Ponto*). Those who believe the exile poems were written in the comfort of Rome might look for support to this detail of the Virgilian Lives. The same goes for *Tr.* 1.7.17–40, where Ovid perhaps helps the parallel along by claiming to have burned his copy of the *Metamorphoses*, as Virgil himself had tried to do, at least according to Suet. *Vita Verg.* 39. If the story was current when Ovid was writing, it would be hard for any reader to avoid the connection, particularly given the Dido intertext at *Tr.* 1.7.20–1 (cf. *Aen.* 4.494–7, 504–8, 642–7).

Virgil by Name

Ovid mentions Virgil by name three times, in each case in the context of literary history, and in each case along with other Greek and (mostly) Roman authors. At *Am.* 3.15.7–8 he talks of the posthumous fame he will have in his native land, equal to that currently enjoyed by Catullus and Virgil (who is clearly dead, as the tense difference demands): 'Mantua delights in Virgil, Verona, in Catullus; I shall be called the glory of the Paelignian race'. At *Rem.* 395–6 Ovid is as great in the world of elegy as Virgil is in that of epic (with other genres and authors through the poem). And at *Tr.* 4.10.51–2, Ovid's 'autobiography', again a poem full of other poets, we find 'I only saw Virgil, and the greedy fates gave no time for my friendship with Tibullus' (*Vergilium uidi tantum, nec auara Tibullo / tempus amicitiae fata dedere meae*). Here there is a sense of greater affection for Tibullus, named twelve times by Ovid, as also emerges from *Am.* 3.9—the lament for the elegist's death, which accounts for five of the instances of his name. But the difference may have more to do with generic affiliation, since Gallus is mentioned in seven different contexts, Propertius in five. And in any case such statistics are not so very useful, since at *Tr.* 2.1.533 Virgil is named by periphrasis 'that blessed author of your [Augustus'] *Aeneid*', and also at *Pont.* 3.4.83–4: 'highest bard of the sons of Aeneas'. The *Eclogues* or, more often, the *Aeneid* are named or alluded to at *Am.* 1.15.25–6, *Ars* 3.337, and *Tr.* 2.533. That is not to mention the fact that *Her.* 7, the *Fasti*, and the last books of the *Metamorphoses* are sustained engagements with Virgil's epic. As Barnes (1995: 257) puts it, 'Virgil is everywhere in Ovid.'

Virgil as Intertext

Recusatio and Dichterweihe

Like each of his Augustan predecessors, Ovid subscribes to the mandatory Callimacheanism in programmatic utterance as in practice, and he does so from the beginning by way of an engagement with Virgil's own Alexandrianism, which serves as an intertextual window onto the poetics of the Hellenistic poet. The first word of the *Amores*, presumably the first word of Ovid's the Roman reader encountered, is the same word that began the *Aeneid*, and the verbs represent an inceptive version of Virgil's *cano: parabam edere* ('I sing / I was preparing to issue'). By the third line, of course, everything changes, and as with every *recusatio* the martial theme is withdrawn. But there is a difference: no Callimachean/Virgilian epiphany here from Apollo, no Cynthia telling Propertius what he can write, no Horatian lack of *ingenium* or sense of *pudor*. Ovid was fully equipped and had the right stuff: 1.1.2 *materia conueniente modis* ('subject appropriate to meter'). As McKeown notes (1989: 8), 'he protests that his epic would have been a success'. The problem was rather an external one: Cupid stealing a foot, and leaving him with no option but to follow in the steps of Gallus, Propertius, and Tibullus, even though he as yet has no woman about whom to elegize. The lines, playful as they are, are a profound deflation of the positive, Callimachean component of the preceding examples of the trope, as the opening poem conducts itself with indignation against the preventer. Then there is the opening epigram, the reduction of the five-book collection, again well-treated by McKeown (1989: 1–4). There is no other evidence of an earlier edition, and it is legitimate to wonder whether one existed. The epigram is self-justificatory. Any Callimachean would know that nightingales are sweeter for being shorter, big books are big evils, and so on: at least if you don't enjoy reading me 'the unpleasantness will be less since I've removed two books' (*at leuior demptis poena duobus erit*).

Virgil is also to be found in the *recusatio* of *Ars* 1.25–30, through reference to Hesiod and Callimachus, the genre model and programmatic model respectively for the *Georgics*: 'Apollo, I won't lie that I got my arts [pun on the *techne* of the *Aetia* preface, but also the three books of the *Ars*] from you, nor, Ascra [home of Hesiod, cf. *G.* 2.176, where the poem is *Ascraeum . . . carmen*, 'Ascraean song'], did the Muses appear to me as I was watching my flocks in your valleys [*Theogony* and *Somnium* of Callimachus]. No, this work is set in motion by experience.' The echo is most notable in line 29 (*usus opus mouet hoc*, 'experience puts this work in motion'), which looks to *G.* 1.133–4 where *usus* is the didactic machine that will hammer out the various arts. Ovid's experience, of course, is different, archly so, namely based on his experience as a lover. His lines also look to Virgil's apparent abandonment of Callimacheanism at *Aen.* 7.45: 'I put in motion a greater/bigger work' (*maius opus moueo*). At the same time, line 30 (*uera canam: coeptis, mater Amoris, ades!*, 'I shall sing the truth; mother of Amor be present at my beginnings!') captures important programmatic moments from the *Georgics*, both from the preface of Book 2 (45–6 'not here shall I detain you with fictitious song'), and from that of Book 1 (to Octavian) *adnue coeptis* ('give the nod to our beginnings').

The short proem to the *Metamorphoses* (1.1–4) continues an engagement with Callimachus, Virgil, and the entire epic tradition. Reading as most now do *illa* at 1.2 ('you gods also changed those [beginnings]'; see Kenney 1976), the proem connects back to Cupid's actions at the start of the *Amores*, as well as to the fact, only ascertained by the reader with the parenthesis of the second line, that Ovid's elegiac meter has now been changed back to the hexameters he had claimed to be embarking on back then. The final line comments economically on the whole tradition going back through Virgil to Callimachus himself. The gods are asked to lead (*deducite*) the continuous song (*perpetuum . . . carmen*) right down to Ovid's own times. The verb, going through Apollo's Callimachean warning that the Virgilian Tityrus sing a fine-spun song (*Ecl.* 6.3 *deductum dicere carmen*), balances the fact that Ovid has finally come, as Virgil did at the start of *Aeneid* 7, to embrace that which Callimachus had eschewed: the continuous song (*Aet.* 1, fr. 1.4 Pf. ἓν ἄεισμα διηνεκές, 'one continuous song'). It is, of course, a different matter whether we believe the denial of the *Aetia*-like episodicity with which the *Metamorphoses* has always been charged, regardless what 'thematic architecture Ovid's ingenuity might devise or the percipience of modern critics might detect' (Kenney 1973: 116–17). Knox (1986: 9–26) shows convincingly that this basis in Callimachus and Virgil is justified and built upon. If the sixth *Eclogue* is Virgil's *carmen deductum*, so is Ovid's *Met.* 1, which Knox shows may even be seen as a large-scale elaboration of the poetic genealogies of the eclogue, and of other Augustan poets, from the cosmogonical beginnings shared by Silenus' song and Ovid's opening narrative to the stories of Io (doublet to Virgil's Pasiphae in *Ecl.* 6, and treated in the epyllion by Licinius Calvus) and Narcissus.

Stylistic Intertextuality

The best treatment is Kenney (2002), which supplements an earlier treatment of the style of the *Metamorphoses*, to which I confine myself in this Virgilian context. Kenney gets to the heart of the matter that Ovid 'has in effect been criticized for not being Virgil' (2002: 56). The criticisms have to do with being 'underenjambed', 'over-dactylic', with the poet producing 'often only elegiac couplets in disguise'. It may well be that Ovid's stylistic facility was directed in a certain way through more than twenty years of perfecting the self-contained couplet, but difference from Virgil need not imply a lack of ability, but rather point to a more positive desire to forge something radically distinct. Kenney demonstrates with ample examples that Ovidian diction is not notably distinct from that of his predecessor, for instance in the use of 'poetic' or 'epic' words, compounds, and the like. It is in the marshaling of diction that the differences establish themselves, and here Ovid's mode 'is infinitely more straightforward, because that straightforwardness was what the mode in which he was writing called for' (2002: 59).

This gets us to the heart of the Ovidian style, what Bömer (1959) calls the *debasement* of Virgil, and of Ovid's 'profaning' his predecessor, a concept Kenney accepts with the word 'vulgarization' 'in the strict French sense' (2002: 60). By creating a more straightforward style Ovid thus created out of the stuff of Virgil a poetic *koine*, available to lesser poets, and therefore more influential than the style of Virgil to the degree it is imitable. It is a paradox that commentators such as Servius may have seen Virgilian style as ideally normative while it was Ovid who in fact created such normativity.

Mischievous intertextuality

The application of this stylistic process involves more than vulgarization, and rather is profaning in a stronger sense, not now just stylistically, but in the larger engagement with text and meaning. As Tarrant puts it (1997: 61): 'Ovid's appropriations of Virgilian language usually contain an element of mischief'. This becomes particularly potent when ideology is at stake. So at *Ars* 1.453 *hoc opus, hic labor est, primo sine munere iungi* ('this is the task, this the toil, to have sex without having to give her something first') he mischievously quotes and reapplies the Sibyl from *Aen.* 6.128.9 'getting back to the upper air, this is the task, this the toil' (*hoc opus hic labor est*). Or at *Tr.* 2.529–36 Ovid invokes the erotic parts of the *Aeneid* in pleading to Augustus for his own playful verse: Virgil found favor, and yet 'the blessed author of your *Aeneid* brought arms and a man (*arma uirumque*) into Tyrian beds'.

Subversion or Collaboration?

Which brings us to the real heart of the matter: how was Ovid to engage Virgil's great epic poem (what follows modifies and builds on Thomas 2001: 78–83). At times, as with the previous examples, so too when Ovid is directly confronting Virgil's text, the combination of vulgarization and mischief seems to subvert. The phrasing of *Met*. 13.624–5, for instance, is particularly pointed: *sacra, et sacra altera, patrem / fert umeris, uenerabile onus, Cythereius heros* ('holy objects, and a second holiness, his father, the heroic son of Venus carries on his shoulders, a venerable load'). The casual style, the shoulder-carrying cliché already mocked and doubted by Virgil's Dido (*Aen*. 4. 597–9; cf. 2.708, 721), and the fact that *fert umeris* at *Met*. 12.516, with *onus* in the next line, refers to the logs with which the Centaurs are hammering Caeneus into the ground, while Anchises is figured here through the abstracts, *sacra* and *onus*, all of this connotes a certain disrespect at such a solemn moment. The text will become problematic in other ways, a point to which I will return. Similarly, when at *Met*. 13.628–9 Aeneas is said to have left the land of the Thracians 'which was running with the blood of Polydorus' (629 *Polydoreo manantem sanguine terram*), the reading of *Aen*. 3.13–68 recalls Aeneas' triple desecration of the mound under which the murdered Polydorus has been buried. Ovid gives no indication that the Virgilian version ended with proper funeral rites for Polydorus, so partially mitigating Aeneas' actions (*Aen*. 3.62–8). Ovid may therefore be seen as weighting and even subverting the Virgilian text, even though the seeds of subversion are already present in the original.

I will select just a few examples where a problematic aspect of a Virgilian passage is activated in the later text, where the subversion is more a matter of collaboration. In each case there is a hermeneutics in the alluding text amounting to affirmation of the problematic aspect. In some cases recent critics have preferred to stabilize the Virgilian source text and see simply subversion, correction, or destruction in the alluding text, but such a procedure requires a monolithic under-reading of the model that is false to the subversive potential already in Virgil. Where Ovid is apparently 'anti-Virgilian' he may be only targeting the Augustan version. The other, more oppositional Virgil supplies him with the tools. Ovid is frequently brief to the extreme in his references to the *Aeneid*, almost as if that poem is so well known a single word or two, particularly when it sets off an ideological controversy or contrast, lends a powerful intertextual effect to the new setting.

Ovid's engagement with the *Aeneid* in the *Metamorphoses* is a complex and large topic. What seems clear is the fact that, as in the *Heroides* so in his epic, Ovid draws attention to troubled or ambiguous aspects of Virgil's poem. Some scholars have taken the brevity with which Ovid treats the Virgilian aspects of Aeneas' story as evidence that he was not engaging with its conflicts and ideologies—so Galinsky, for whom Ovid is 'merely telling the story *aliter*' and 'restricted himself to presenting an outline of the *Aeneid*, choosing, at various length, one or two of the main episodes of a given book of the *Aeneid* and not entangling himself in the rest' (1975: 219, 225). I would argue rather that the very starkness and brevity of much of Ovid's '*Aeneid*' allows the poet to engage with ideologies in a particularly intense way.

I would argue thus on the grounds that it is virtually impossible to imagine a poet's writing about Aeneas within a generation of the *Aeneid*'s publication without having some degree of engagement with that poem, and without the reader constantly reflecting on the relationship between the two. After all, the *Aeneid* was by now presumably a school text and a classic.

Casali (1995b) and Knox (1995) have recently contributed excellent treatments of Ovid's allusions in *Her.* 7 to Aeneas' separation from Creusa at *Aen.* 2.711, where the hero's injunction has seemed to some to be lacking in conjugal charity (*et longe seruet uestigia coniunx*, 'and let my wife follow our steps from a distance'). Ovid's Dido, as Knox notes, is unambiguous in her charge against Aeneas: *si quaeras ubi sit formosi mater Iuli / occidit a duro sola relicta uiro* ('in case you should enquire into the whereabouts of pretty Iulus' mother, she's dead, left alone, and deserted by her hard-hearted spouse'). That puts the matter unequivocally; it does so, I would argue, and as Knox observes (1995: 221), as an activation of a reading already possible in the model.

Of course, the narrating voice of *Her.* 7 belongs to Dido, who also ends her letter by giving the text of the inscription to be placed on the tomb. The act of killing will be suicide; the cause of death and the weapon will both belong to Aeneas (7.195–6). Again, the text will still be hers, but it will be inscribed for the world to see. And so it is, as we discover at *Fast.* 3.549, when the actual inscription, with precisely the same wording, is now set on her marble tomb, in a post-Dido Carthage: *PRAEBVIT AENEAS ET CAVSAM MORTIS ET ENSEM / IPSA SUA DIDO CONCIDIT VSA MANV* 'Aeneas supplied both the cause of death and the sword / she did herself fall dead by her own hand.'

The fates of Creusa and Dido will come back into play at *Met.* 14.443–4, where Ovid, resuming his '*Aeneid*', responds to the beginning of *Aen.* 7 and its lines on the death and funeral of the nurse Caieta, who provides the aetiology for the place on the coast of southern Latium. She too gets an inscription, also on a marble tomb, which takes us in the direction of Dido, again with Aeneas as subject: he 'rescued me from Greek fire and cremated me with the fire he owed' (*me . . . / ereptam Argolico quo debuit igne cremauit*). In this reading *igne* goes with *ereptam* as well as with *cremauit*, referring to two fires, a nice trope. But if we take *quo debuit* with *ereptam*, we get something more sinister: 'rescued from the Greek fire from which it was an obligation I be rescued' (for the impersonal use cf. *TLL* s.v. *debeo* 102.43–59). Whom did Aeneas *fail* to rescue from Troy? With that question we may turn to the major Virgilian presence in Ovid.

Ovid's '*Aeneid*' (*Met.* 13.623–14.608)

Ovid's '*Aeneid*' opens with the fall of Troy and with Aeneas carrying his father (13.625, *uenerabile onus*) on his shoulders. So far quite traditional, if stylistically a little strange, though not so what follows, perhaps (626–8):

> de tantis opibus praedam pius eligit illam
> Ascaniumque suum profugaque per aequora classe
> fertur ab Antandro.

From all the wealth there the pious one chose that booty (i.e. Anchises) and his own Ascanius, and is borne from Antandros across the seas in exile fleet.

Galinsky comments (1975: 219): 'Ovid's desire to tell the story *aliter* is reflected by his allusion to a tradition, different from that used by Vergil, according to which the Greeks granted Aeneas an honourable departure from Troy with whatever possessions he cared to choose, and he chose his father.' A connected variant of that tradition, appearing in Lycophron (*Alex.* 1263–64), has Aeneas abandoning his wife, children, and father when he is permitted to leave Troy. And not unconnected to that tradition is the one we have already touched on, which has Aeneas betraying Troy (Casali 1995b: 61). Virgil may even have alluded to that tradition, reflected in Aeneas' compromising position on Dido's temple 'mixed in with the Greek leaders' (Serv. on *Aen.* 1.487). So when Ovid has Aeneas selecting his father as *praeda*, and leaving Troy with him and Ascanius, but with no mention of Creusa, and with the question of why Aeneas is granted safe conduct left hanging over the situation but otherwise unaddressed, it may well be that the ambiguities of the Virgilian text are being activated and intensified. In Ovid's reference to Anchises and Ascanius (*praedam . . . Ascaniumque suum*), we may detect an echo of Aeneas' reference at *Aen.* 2.729 *pariter comitique onerique timentem* ('fearing equally for my companion and my burden')—no word of Creusa. As Casali well notes (1995b: 62), with reference to the discussion of this account even in antiquity (Serv. on *Aen.* 1.711, 743, 746), Ovid seems to be indicating that even in Virgil the details are open to differing interpretations, particularly since the account of Creusa's loss is there entrusted to the voice of Aeneas, not the narrator, and it is 'a somewhat confused narrative'. Finally, the reference to *praeda* conspires to conjure up the plundering of a fallen city. And so Ovid's intertextuality has a collaborative effect: he brings out what was already there in Virgil.

It is significant that neither Dido nor Turnus, whose words are so central a feature of the *Aeneid* and of the conflicting sympathies evoked by that poem, utters a single word in Ovid's *Metamorphoses* (just as the important Lavinia utters not a word in the *Aeneid*). That is not accidental, nor is it just a result of the brevity of their appearance, though it may help explain that brevity. The fact is that the narrator of the *Metamorphoses* speaks for the two, and he does so in such a way that he participates fully in the point of view of the two characters, whose point of view is quietly but strongly represented throughout. First, the story of Dido (*Met.* 14. 78–81):

> excipit Aenean illic animoque domoque
> non bene discidium Phrygii latura mariti
> Sidonis, inque pyra sacri sub imagine facta
> incubuit ferro deceptaque decipit omnes.

> Then the Sidonian queen took in Aeneas to her heart and her home, she who would not handle well the divorce of her Phrygian husband, and on a pyre built under the pretext of sacrifice she fell on a sword and, herself deceived, deceived everyone.

Bömer (1986) notes the allusion to Juno's sarcastic words at *Aen.* 4.103 *Phrygio seruire marito* ('slave to a Phrygian husband'), but he limits any authorial ambivalence to the Ovidian site by claiming that *decepta* is strictly the focalization of Dido: it is one thing to have Juno be ironic in this matter (as in the Virgilian instance), quite another to allow a narrator to be so (as in Ovid). Casali has dealt with this in the most recent, and the best, treatment available of Ovid's '*Aeneid*' (1995b: 66–71). We also are told that *mariti* in Ovid means 'partner', not 'husband', on the basis of *Aen.* 4.35: *[Didonem] nulli flexere mariti*. But there the word clearly means 'candidate to be husband' not 'partner': 'no potential husbands swayed her'. At *Her.* 7.69 the Ovidian Dido refers to her status as a spouse of Aeneas (*coniugis . . . deceptae*, 'deceived spouse'), as had the Virgilian Dido at *Aen.* 4.172: *coniugium uocat* ('she calls it a marriage'). Indeed, whereas the Virgilian narrator had reserved *coniunx* for the shade of Sychaeus (as noted by Knox 1995: 214), at *Met.* 14.81 the Ovidian narrator seems to be siding with both Didos, for *decepta* in line 81 confirms Dido's view of her desertion from *Her.* 7, thereby unambiguously assigning responsibility to Aeneas, and affirming Dido's sense of her treatment at *Aen.* 4.330: *non equidem omnino capta ac deserta uiderer* ('I wouldn't seem completely taken in and abandoned').

The end of the *Aeneid*, and specifically the clash of Aeneas and Turnus, is generally deflected in *Met.* 14.445–580. The Callimachean Ovid narrates the epic action with the utmost brevity, and expatiates on two insets, the mission of Venulus to Diomedes (457–526) and the story of the magical Phrygian ships (530–65)—each with its metamorphosis. The remaining narrative, encompassing the second half of the *Aeneid*, from the departure from Circe's island to the death of Turnus, amounts to 23 lines (447–58, 527–31, 568–73), but two details in those lines are of note.

A central issue of the *Aeneid*, and of Turnus' culpability, centers on how we view his relationship with Lavinia. Amata favors the match (*Aen.* 7.56–57), the narrator identifies Turnus as the prime suitor (7.54–56), and even the prophecy of Faunus, which finds that Lavinia is to marry an outsider, concedes that marriage arrangements are under way (7.97 *thalamis neu crede paratis*, 'don't trust in the wedding that has been prepared'). Amata will cling to the slight ambiguity that allows her to point to the Argive ancestry of Turnus (7.367–72). The Ovidian narrator in fact affirms the point of view of Amata and Turnus with emphatically straightforward words: (14.450–51) *bellum cum gente feroci / suscipitur, pactaque furit pro coniuge Turnus* ('war is taken up with a fierce race, and Turnus rages on behalf of his betrothed bride'). Since the very wording resonates with the argument of Turnus at *Aen.* 9.138 (*coniuge praerepta*, 'wife stolen away') and Juno at *Aen.* 10.79 (*gremiis abducere pactas*, 'kidnapping betrothed women from their mother's lap'), the Ovidian version may then be seen as giving narratorial authority to Turnus' viewpoint, even if that viewpoint, in the words of one critic, is an 'attempt to pervert the course of history' (Hardie 1994: 100). Bömer (1986: 160) provides a way out by first quoting *TLL* 4.343, 49 ff. (which does not cite the Ovidian example), where *coniunx* = *sponsa* or *amica* ('fiancée' or 'companion'), and then presenting his own lemma: *Non quae est, sed quae esse cupit* ('not in reality, but wishing to be').

But, of course, the easiest way out would be to see all of this as constituting the focalization or point of view of the character, who does not speak but whose thoughts are presented by the narrator: Dido (thinks she) is deceived (*decepta*), suffering (what she sees as) the divorce of her Phrygian husband (*discidium Phrygii latura mariti*), and Turnus rages on behalf of (the person he thinks is) his betrothed spouse (*pactaque . . . coniuge*). There is obviously a level on which such a reading works, but to the extent that the focalization of these characters is in no way 'deviant' (Fowler 1990), but is rather the sole point of view of this narrative, there is also formed a strong bond and even identity between narrator and focalizer. The Ovidian '*Aeneid*', built at crucial moments on the character speech of the oppositional figures of the Virgilian *Aeneid*, brings to the narrative foreground the case of those oppositional figures.

This phenomenon finds its climax at *Met.* 14.573–80: the death of Turnus (*Turnusque cadit*) is followed by the fall of Ardea (*cadit Ardea*), which leads to the aetiology of the heron (*ardea*; cf. Casali 1995b: 72–5), born from the ruins of the city after Turnus had been killed by the 'sword of the foreigner' (*barbarus ensis*; cf. Casali 1995b: 74–5). The implications are so unpleasant that some have attempted to emend away the unsettling epithet 'foreign' (*barbarus*; cf. Bömer 1986: ad loc.). At *Aen.* 7.468–9 Turnus is presented precisely as the defender of Italy against the outsider: *iubet arma parari, / tutari Italiam, detrudere finibus hostem* ('he orders arms to be readied, orders them to protect Italy and drive the enemy from their territory'). And Juno sarcastically echoes him at *Aen.* 10. 74–8: it is shameful that Turnus is attacking the new Troy and standing on 'his own soil' (*patria . . . terra*); what of it that the Trojans put their yoke on the fields of others (*arua aliena*)? That Turnus and Juno see things that way is not surprising, although it should also be said that their position is a defensible one in the context of the *Aeneid*'s action. But even the strongly Virgilian voice of the exordium at *Aen.* 7.38–39 refers to the Trojans as *aduena . . . exercitus* ('foreign army'). And at *Met.* 14.573–80 the Ovidian narrator again affirms this position of Virgil, the Virgilian Turnus and Juno, subverting Aeneas, but not the *Aeneid*, which contains the seeds of its own subversion. Ovid's *barbarus ensis* has also been referred to the Sibyl's scornful prediction at Tibullus 2.5.48 *iam tibi praedico, barbare Turne, necem* ('already I predict your death, barbarous Turnus'), which captures the same moment in the story (Barnes 1995: 265 n. 73). If so, it seems reasonable to suggest that Ovid is correcting Tibullus' (or his Sibyl's) strongly Augustan reading of the end of the *Aeneid*, as the authoritative narrative voice engages and refutes Tibullus' character.

Virgil Outside Ovid's '*Aeneid*'

Of course, Virgil's presence is hardly confined to those passages of the *Metamorphoses* or *Fasti* that treat the same subject matter of the *Aeneid*. Zingerle (1871: 48–121) is still a useful compendium, even if it does little more than juxtapose parallel texts from within Ovid's '*Aeneid*' and from *Her.* 7 (49–55), and from elsewhere throughout the corpus of both poets (56–111). Zingerle also gathers together numerous instances of parallel phrasing, the same verse endings, and the like. While the Virgilian intertext is for the most part handled briefly, if pungently, within the matching narrative in *Met.* 13–14, the more lengthy interstices may also display the presence of the earlier poet. So, for instance, after Ovid's Aeneas emerges from the Underworld, where Anchises' great instruction is reduced to ten words of Latin (14.118–19 'he taught the laws of those places, and dangers to be undertaken in new wars'—no parade of Romans and no Augustus, we note), the Trojans land at Caieta, north of Cumae (154–7). This landfall is an addition, as is the episode and narration of Macareus (*Neritius Macareus*), a character from the *Odyssey*, absent from Virgil's poem. Macareus will eventually tell the story of Picus' transformation into a woodpecker, but he has an initial function. There is no mention in Virgil after *Aeneid* 3 of Achaemenides, the Greek left behind when Odysseus fled from the Cyclops. Just in case we were wondering what happened to him, Ovid inserts him into his '*Aeneid*' having Macareus recognize Achaemenides at 14.161, then elicits from him an account of all that happened in the land of the Cyclops from the time of Odysseus' departure till the arrival of Aeneas. This includes a speech of the Cyclops. Achaemenides then asks Macareus of his fate, and is in return told the story of Circe (past whose land the Trojans sail in *Aen.* 7.10–24), culminating in the transformation of Picus at the hands of the jealous witch. Thus, Ovid gives us two significant Homeric stories, of the Cyclops and of Circe, each told retrospectively by a Greek witness.

Perhaps a more fundamental aspect of Ovid's use and reuse of Virgil is in passages that thematically have little to do with the texts to which they allude, at least on first impression. So at *Met.* 3.262–72, Juno vents her rage in annoyance that Jupiter has impregnated Semele (with the future Dionysus) in ways that inevitably recall Virgil's Juno angry that she cannot destroy Aeneas and his ships at *Aen.* 1.37–49 (*Aen.* 1.46–7 *ast ego, quae diuum incedo regina Iouisque / et soror et coniunx* ~ *Met.* 3.265–70 *si sum regina Iouisque / et soror et coniunx*). More pointed is the allusion of Actaeon: in deferring the hunt to the next morning (*Met.* 3.149–50 *altera lucem / dum croceis inuecta rotis Aurora reducet*) this borrows from Virgil's Turnus, who does similarly with the contest for Lavinia (12.76–7 *cum primum crastina caelo / puniceis inuecta rotis Aurora rubebit*); the morrow will be fatal for each. Also pointed is the catalogue at *Met.* 13.258 *Alcandrumque Haliumque Noemonaque Prytanimque* in Ulysses' speech, of the Lycians he mowed down on the night-raid, replicating precisely the same line at *Aen.* 9.767 (a context distinct from the Homeric one), but restoring it to its Iliadic context (Ἀλκανδρόνθ᾿ Ἅλιόν τε Νοήμονά τε Πρύτανίν τε), and so a 'correction' of Virgil, as Hardie notes (1994: ad loc.).

Ideology is in the offing at *Met.* 10.106–42, where the story is told of Cyparissus, who was so upset when he killed a handsome, docile stag that he was turned into a cypress tree, on his own request. That this stag is clearly a new version of the one shot by Ascanius at *Aen.* 7.479–504 gives rise to questions about the relative remorse of the two young men. Similarly, at *Met.* 2.358–63, when the Heliades beg their mother Clymene to stop lacerating their bodies (now metamorphosing into tree parts; cf. 362 *nostrum laceratur in arbore corpus*), Aeneas' tree/Polydorus violating (*Aen.* 3.24–48; cf. 41 *quid miserum, Aenea, laceras?*) inevitably comes into play.

Situational intertextuality

On a larger scale, there are instances of a sustained presence of Virgil through-out longer sequences of the *Metamorphoses*. I mention just two, the first more overt, the second mostly atmospheric. The beginnings of consecutive books open alternately with the wedding of Orpheus and Eurydice, the loss of the latter, and the failed attempt to get her back (*Met.* 10.1–85), and with the death of Orpheus, and eventual reunion with Eurydice in the Underworld (11.1–61). These two passages between them are a close reworking of *G.* 4.457–527, Proteus' song of Orpheus and Eurydice. Ovid inverts by having the story told by the primary narrator, and framing the actual songs of Orpheus that take up most of Book 10: Ganymede, Hyacinthus, the Cerastae and Propoetides, Pygmalion, Myrrha, Venus and Adonis (503–739, with Orpheus' quoting Venus' inset song of Atalanta and Hippomenes at 560–707). Ovid's stylistic register is utterly different from that of Virgil's elevated epyllion, simpler and 'profaning' in the sense we have already discussed. At the same time there is mischief at work, with humor deflecting the pathos: when summoned Eurydice is limping from the snakebite; Ovid 'corrects' Virgil in claiming Eurydice made no complaint against Orpheus; and in having him weep for seven days, where Virgil had him weeping seven months; and Orpheus eventually takes up homosexuality, emulating the Thracian people (10.83–5). The tearing apart of Orpheus, which took fewer than three lines in Virgil (*G.* 4.520–2), is spread over 50 in Ovid (*Met.* 11.1–51), again with amusing tropes: the stones the Ciconian women throw drop out of the air, charmed by Orpheus' lyre; that is, until it is drowned out by the Berecynthian flutes and the horns, drums, breast-beating, and howling of the Maenads, who, like Virgil's plague at *G.* 3.517–19, cause agriculture to stop in mid-plowing—in this case because the farmers leave their work in terror.

Again, at a beginning, the beginning of *Met.* 5, Ovid tells the story of Perseus' fight with Phineus (1–235), uncle of Andromeda and betrothed to her, at least in his mind, before she was chained to the rock from which Perseus rescued her. Situa-tionally, we are back in the *Odyssey* with suitors in a dining hall. But the Aeneas–Turnus–Lavinia setup is also clear. Although there is little in the way of specific, dictional intertextuality, there is a sense in which this is a new version of some key parts of the *Aeneid*, but the brutality seems to have been ratcheted up, and there is some clear intertextuality, including Phineus' open allusion at 5.10, *en adsum praerep-tae coniugis ultor* ('look, here I am, avenger of the theft of my bride'), pointing straight at Turnus' wording at *Aen.* 9.138, *coniuge praerepta*, and so tagging Phineus as a new Turnus. Perseus also faces a group of 1000 enemies (157–8), and in this as well as some of the excesses of the narrative there may indeed be a sense of play with the traditions of Iliadic epic, as represented by *Aen.* 7–12 in particular. When Phineus throws the first spear, Cepheus the father-in-law figure withdraws from the fray aver-ring that the action is against his will (43–5), as Latinus had done at *Aen.* 12.285–6 when Tolumnius threw his spear to break the truce. We then meet Athis, an attractive young man, dressed in a Tyrian cloak. Perseus uses a firebrand to smash Athis' face to broken bones (56–8), and we think momentarily of Pallas covered at his funeral with the cloak stiff with purple and gold that Dido had made, after Aeneas had violently killed him. Of course, we also think of the self-emasculating Attis of Cat. 63. But he immediately turns into Euryalus when his friend and declared lover Lycabus (with 61 *ueri non dissimulator amoris*, 'didn't conceal his real love', archly questioning the deflective *Aen.* 5.296 *Nisus (insignis) amore pio pueri*, 'known for pious love of the boy') rushes in only to be killed by Perseus, with a weapon (67, *penetrabile telum*) identical to the one with which Turnus killed Pallas at *Aen.* 10.481 (*penetrabile telum*). Two other characters are immediately killed after first slipping on the blood that now covers the floor (74–8; cf. *tellus madefacta tepebat*), in a gratuitous set of lines were it not for the blood on the ground in both Nisus and Euryalus passages (*Aen.* 5.328–9 *madefecerat*, Nisus slips; 9.333–4 *atro tepefacta cruore / terra torique madent*), with the dictional similarities and changes confirming the intertext.

The remainder of the narrative consists of a vague back-and-forth *aristeia* (catalogue of heroes' killings), very much in the style of those of *Aen.* 9–12, with anecdotes about the killed figure accompanying the description. We are almost in the arena of pastiche in these grotesquely amusing lines (5.74–176), as in the catalogue of those turned to stone by the Gorgon's head (181–209). To take but one example (99–106) we have the death of Emathion, whose justice and intervention reminds of the just and intervening Galaesus, killed at *Aen.* 7.535–9, while the manner of his death, at the altar, looks to the death of Priam at *Aen.* 2.550–8, with the dénouement, his still-talking head keeping up its execrations from the altar onto which it fell (5.104–6), looking to the singing head of Orpheus going down the Hebrus to the Thracian shore (*G.* 4.523–7). The end of the episode has Phineus suppliant like Turnus at the end of the *Aeneid*, and here we find a very different pair of protagonists, all set within the similarity of a fight for the wife (219, *pro coniuge mouimus arma*; 229, *coniunx* is the last word of Perseus; *Aen.* 12.937 Turnus: *tua est Lauinia coniunx*). Unlike Turnus, Phineus begs openly and cravenly for his life, and, unlike the Virgilian Aeneas, Perseus unhesitatingly dispatches his enemy, turning him to stone and taunting him as he does so. How we take this version back to a reading of the end of the *Aeneid* is up to us, but we are unquestionably in the presence of some new version of a parallel moment in human conflict.

Here as everywhere, recognition of the presence of Virgil in Ovid serves to create for the reader an embroidery of Virgilian intertextuality, throughout the *Metamorphoses* in particular, though not exclusively so. We feel we have been down this way before, then realize we have not, but again detect the basis for the faint echoes of other stories, as well as the rewriting of other stories, in the stories we are encountering. So when we do arrive at Ovid's '*Aeneid*' we will not be surprised at what we find, as not just here but in many ways throughout the epic Ovid has repainted the Virgilian canvas, whose palimpsest keeps emerging with varying effects on the mind of the reader. The separation and difference, so often filtered through similarity that invites comparison, is one of the marks of Ovid's genius in successfully competing with the great model history and chance imposed on him.

FURTHER READING

Casali (1995b, 2004–5) is without peer on the topic in question; he captures the relationship between these two poets better than any other scholar. In addition to the works cited in the preceding chapter, useful information can be found in Lamacchia (1960) and Döpp (1969), sound resources and good starting-points for this further study. Knox (1995), Baldo (1995), Smith (1997), Tarrant (1997), and Boyd (2002b) are prerequisites for inquiry into overarching Virgilian intertextuality in Ovid. For more focused investigations of the presence of Virgil in Ovid, Bews (1984) and Miller (2004b) are useful. Ziolkowski and Putnam (2007) is an invaluable collection of materials for study of the reception of Virgil and Ovid's role in it.

PART IV

Critical and
Scholarly Approaches

CHAPTER TWENTY-TWO

Editing Ovid: Immortal Works and Material Texts

Mark Possanza

Immune to Time and the Elements

Any serious inquiry into the meaning and interpretation of a text requires an understanding of its sources, and the rationale for the evaluation of those sources when they offer conflicting evidence, and for the correction of them when their evidence is deficient. Responsible readers will therefore want to familiarize themselves with the history of the text and the critical method that guides the judgment in making decisions about the authentic form and wording of the text. Whether the text under consideration is Anthony Burgess' *A Clockwork Orange* or Ovid's *Heroides*, the question of how accurately the text in the reader's hands represents what the author wrote is a crucial one. In making claims about an author's meaning, critics and interpreters take on the responsibility of making themselves aware of how the text has been transmitted and what kinds of editorial intervention are justified by the circumstances of transmission and the material condition of the documents that transmit the text. The premise behind these observations (and it seems a safe one) is that as objects of criticism and interpretation the author's words are of primary importance and that mistakes, interpolations, and other alterations made during the process of transmission by scribes, secretaries, compositors, and other agents of the transmission are not authorial and therefore, when detected, are to be excluded from the text. The immortal work may outlast the wrack and havoc of the ages but it is undeniably embodied in a material text, an artifact exposed to the thousand natural shocks the text is heir to, and the most harmful shock, apart from physical destruction, is the debasement of the text, both deliberate and accidental, as it passes through the various stages of reproduction by hand or machine. At the end of the *Metamorphoses* our poet, a frequent and reliable prognosticator of his own undying fame, proudly foretells that the work he has now completed will not be obliterated by time or the elements. It appears in the event that these were the least of his worries. The greatest damage has been done by inattentive, errant, or meddlesome human hands attached to inattentive, errant, or meddlesome minds. The poet probably was never seriously worried by the possibility of a successful assault by such puny forces on his immortal opus. Although the threat posed by these seemingly minor hazards of textual transmission do not inspire grandiloquent declarations of imperishability, they are nonetheless real and harmful.

One of the best sources of information about the editing of Ovid's works will be found in the prefaces of critical editions of the poems, the one place, by the way, where the editor's personality is not entirely submerged in the dense code of the *apparatus criticus*, in choice of reading, and in matters of punctuation, orthography, and paragraphing. Here the editor identifies the primary manuscripts, analyzes and reconstructs the history of the transmission, and explains the principles on which the text is founded. Many readers, however, when they take up a critical edition of one of Ovid's works, will either skim or skip the preface. The choice between Ovid's Latin and the editor's will seem an obvious one; the arcana of manuscripts, extant or hypothetical, the symbolic representation of the relationships of progenitors and progeny in a family tree known as the *stemma codicum*, the long Latinized muster role of predecessors in the trade, some famous, some notorious, some long forgotten—all of this seems a boorish intrusion on the elegant world of Ovid's immortal creations, and brings with it an unbearable delay of the pleasure that awaits the reader in the pages of the poet's versatile, irrepressible wit. After all, the reader may think, Ovid's works have been in print for over five hundred years, and a long series of diligent and competent editors and textual critics has by now succeeded in establishing what Ovid wrote to the extent that the manuscript evidence allows; whatever textual problems remain are probably insoluble, and can safely be left to the lucubration of those who have an aptitude for nothing else. These views, however, are based in part on our habituation to the technology of print and print culture, which induce us to believe that the textual artifact itself authorizes its correctness; if it is printed, then it must be correct, or, with a little more reflection, it must be correct because someone approved it before it was printed. And they are due in part to the mistaken notion that the editorial process is extraneous to the work, as if editing is a preliminary process that ends when page one of the text begins. In fact, once a text crosses the threshold from the private into the public sphere, editorial involvement becomes a factor in its making that cannot be discounted or ignored and is present on every page of the text. Editing is a creative activity that puts the art of the book at the service of the art of the author. In the case of texts edited from multiple divergent manuscript copies, editorial involvement is all the more conspicuous because the text of the critical edition is in the last analysis a hypothetical reconstruction, one very large conjecture about the wording and form of the text (Tanselle 1983). The familiarity of the printed format does nothing to diminish the hypothetical nature of the reconstruction. In a moment of supreme authorial pique Ovid asserted that Augustus had no authority over his poetic genius (*Tr.* 3.7.47–48). In the absence of the poet himself, that authority is wielded by his editors.

The familiar neatness and authority of the printed page, the space in which we encounter Ovid's poetry, mask the complexities of the historical process by which it has been transmitted from his own times down to ours. When in our discussions and interpretations of Ovid's poetry we use the rather loose expressions 'what Ovid wrote', 'what Ovid is saying', 'what Ovid means', we are not referring to the text of any single extant authoritative document, the production of which was supervised by the author, but rather to a hypothetical text constructed out of the evidence of multiple divergent copies, which are of varying degrees of reliability, and were produced at many centuries' remove from the author himself. In addition to the staggering amount of textual variation that arose during the manuscript phase of transmission, there is also the variation that has been and continues to be generated by scholars in the form of conjectures, transpositions of verses, deletions of verses and, in some cases, of entire poems judged to be spurious (Lachmann 1876; Tarrant 2000; McKeown 2002), the positing of lacunae where the sense is thought to be deficient, and the division of poems (Heyworth 1995).

Since the appearance of the printed page suggests, and the reader expects, order and certainty in the wording of the text, a brief consideration of disorder and uncertainty in the text will serve as a reminder of the complex variation that is found in the manuscripts and with which editors and readers must come to terms. Readers of the *Metamorphoses* will not advance very far before encountering a significant variant in the transmission. The lines of the proem are quoted here as they were regularly printed before Anderson 1993 and Tarrant 2004.

> In noua fert animus mutatas dicere formas
> corpora; di, coeptis (nam uos mutastis et illas)
> adspirate meis primaque ab origine mundi
> ad mea perpetuum deducite tempra carmen.

> My spirit moves me to tell of shapes changed into strange
> bodies; oh gods (for it was you that changed them),
> inspire what I have begun and from the first beginning of the world
> lead my continuous song down to my own times. (Hill 1985)

Already in the second line there is a poorly attested variant reading *illa*, for the unanimously transmitted *illas*, which requires an editorial decision. These two readings were, until quite recently, the subject of much discussion and controversy. In fact, the choice of reading here might well be described as the most momentous editorial decision in the whole poem. The demonstrative *illas*, referring to *formas* in the first line, is the reading of all the manuscripts and of nearly all printed editions from the two *editiones principes* of 1471 down to Anderson's 1993 Teubner. Although *illas* was the word that confronted readers of the *Met.* through more than five centuries of the print tradition, no one was able to provide a satisfactory explanation of the sense. Defenders of the transmitted text resorted to the following interpretations: 'for you have changed these [forms] also', that is, in addition to transforming yourselves; or, if it is assumed that *et* is displaced and modifies *mutastis*, 'for you have also caused these [transformations]'. In either case the additive force of *et* is by no means clear: the gods' ability to transform themselves or to cause transformation is not being presented by the poet as a reason additional to some other reason for invoking them. The gods might well be invoked, in a poem about metamorphosis, for their power to transform bodies, not for their power *also* to transform them, nor for their power to transform bodies and their own *also*, as if the poet had made a distinction in the first line between bodies human and divine. Translators betray their anxieties about *et* when they treat it as if it were the intensive *ipsi*, emphasizing the appropriateness of the gods as source of inspiration because they are 'the very ones' who cause transformation. Despite the unanimous support of the manuscripts for *illas*, the writing has been judged inelegant, especially since it occurs in the programmatic statement of the poem's theme, and unworthy of the poet. And our understanding of the nature and quality of Ovid's verbal artistry is as valid a criterion for making textual decisions as are the rules of syntax and meter.

A solution to the interpretive problem posed by *illas* comes in the form of the poorly attested reading *illa*, which is recorded as a variant in one manuscript and as a correction in another; it was also conjectured by Lejay. This motley assembly of support may not impress adherents of manuscript authority, but *illa* has been vigorously and persuasively defended (Kenney 1976; Tarrant 1982: 351; Kovacks 1987) and has been shown to yield a sense that is both apposite to the programmatic statement of theme and consistent with our expectations of Ovidian sophistication. With *illa* in the text, referring to *coeptis* earlier in the line, the meaning is 'for you have changed this [my undertaking] as well'; not only are the gods responsible for causing the metamorphosis of bodies, they are also responsible for a poetic metamorphosis, the transformation of the poet from elegist to epic bard; a new, voluminous *corpus* is now in progress, which will be larger than any other of Ovid's works. The poet asks the gods for their support in his undertaking because they are doubly involved in it, causing the transformations that are the subject of the poem and transforming the maker of the poem himself. It is now clear that, in accordance with the traditional structure of prayers, the gods are invoked in virtue of their capacity to exercise their power in the sphere of activity to which the prayer is directed, that is, transformation, but with a peculiar twist, namely that the poet himself bears witness to the efficacy of that power through his own experience of transformation into an epic poet. And it is something of a textual-critical triumph that Anderson, in the 1993 reprint of his Teubner edition, and Tarrant, in his *Oxford Classical Text* of 2004, both promoted *illa* to the text of line 2.

This particular problem of choosing between a unanimously attested manuscript reading (*illas*) and a poorly attested variant (*illa*) illustrates an essential critical principle, and a corollary to that principle. The principle is that the author's meaning, admittedly a subjective reconstruction, takes precedence over the authority of the documents. The reading *illas* was maintained in the text on the basis of what might be called the default defense; it was supported by all the manuscripts and it satisfied the requirements of syntax and meter. The corollary is that in analyzing the sense of the author's words every word counts. As is illustrated by the variant pair *illas* / *illa* the interpretation of *et* was problematic when *illas* was adopted in the text and the sense of the *nam*-clause in relation to its context unclear. However, when *illa* is read, the difficulties surrounding the interpretation of *et illas* and the *nam*-clause are removed. Moreover, the great improvement in sense achieved by adopting the variant *illa* shows what a difference a single word can make for our understanding of the poet's thought, for our overall conception of his habits of style and expression, and ultimately for our appraisal of his genius. Although it may seem that the impact of editorial decisions is localized to individual words, phrases, and lines, their cumulative effect exerts a defining influence on our conception of what Ovid can do with words, and that conception in turn informs the criticism of the text.

Carmina et errores: Ovid in Manuscript

The *Opera Omnia* of Publius Ovidius Naso first appeared in print in 1471. In the centuries before that transformative event Ovid's works were transmitted by a continuous series of manuscript copies, first in the form of papyrus rolls, and then, from the fourth century AD on, in the form of the codex book with which modern readers are familiar. The extant manuscript copies of Ovid's poems, known collectively as the 'direct tradition', though they are not all of equal importance as witnesses to the text, are ultimately derived from texts produced by the author himself and therefore are, along with quotations, excerpts, and paraphrases found in other sources, that is, the indirect tradition, the only physical evidence we have for establishing 'what Ovid wrote'. With the exception of a small fragment dated to the second half of the fifth

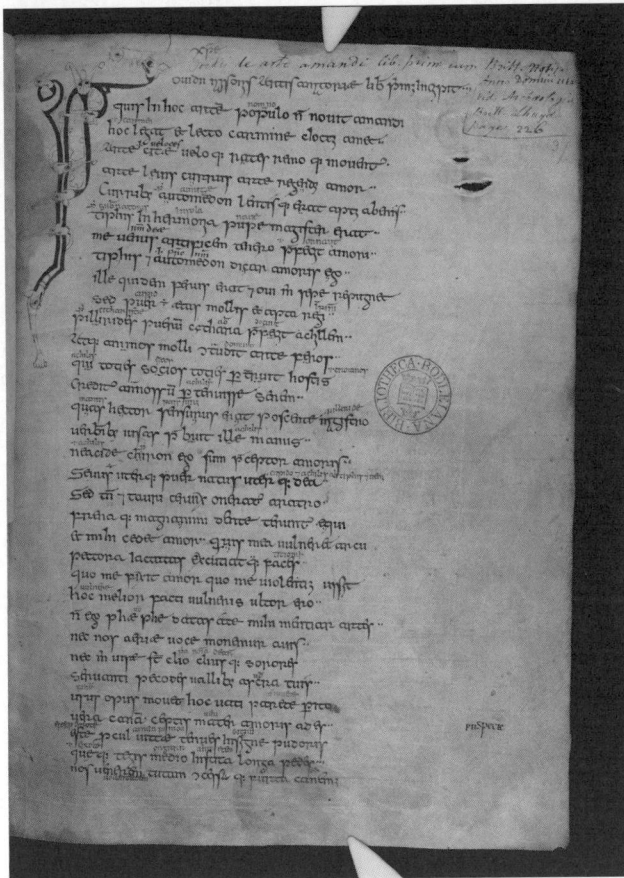

Figure 2: The opening of Book 1 of Ovid's *Ars Amatoria* in the ninth-century manuscript known as 'St. Dunstan's Classbook', with Latin and Old Welsh Glosses (The Bodleian Library, University of Oxford, MS. Auct. F. 4. 32, fol. 37r).

century AD, which contains fifteen lines or traces of lines of *Pont.* 4.9 and nine lines
of 4.12 (Korn 1868: viii–ix; Richmond 1990: v–vi), the extant manuscripts are not
earlier than the ninth century AD. As a result, there can be no substantive discussion
of the editing of Ovid's poetry in the earliest phase of manuscript transmission. Our
ignorance of the nature and quality of the manuscript sources available to those who
sought to safeguard and guarantee the correctness of Ovid's texts in antiquity means
that we are also ignorant of the degree of textual variation that then existed and of
the methods employed to deal with it. That some form of editorial activity took place
is obvious.

Although we do not possess manuscripts of Ovid's poems from late antiquity, with
the exception of the *Epistulae ex Ponto* fragment, or from the beginning of the Middle
Ages, we can glimpse from the indirect tradition what is happening to the text, and
what we see is not encouraging. Seneca's (ca. 4 BC–AD 65) quotation of *Met.* 6.58
reveals that the genuine reading *pauiunt* has been replaced in the manuscripts by a

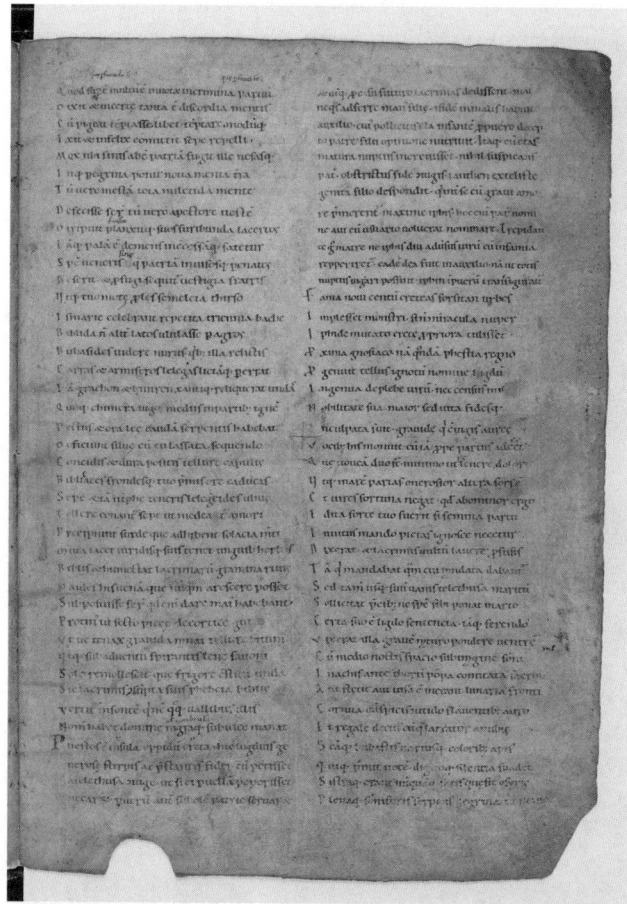

Figure 3:   A leaf from a twelfth-century manuscript in Copenhagen, containing *Met.* 9.629–
695 (Royal Library, Copenhagen, NKS 56, folio, f. 3 recto).

more common synonym *feriunt* (*Epist.* 90.20). And although the reading *pauiunt* is not actually transmitted by any manuscript of Seneca's *Epistulae*, and was restored by conjecture to Seneca's quotation on the evidence of the variant *pariunt* in the ninth century Bambergensis, there can be no doubt that it is correct. Apthonius, the fourth-century author of a metrical treatise, quotes *Her.* 1.2 with the reading *attinet* instead of the *attamen* or *sed tamen* found in the manuscripts. As Housman persuasively argues, *attinet* is far superior in sense to what is transmitted by the direct tradition (Housman 1922; Knox 1995: ad loc.). The poorly attested 'busy bee' (*apis sedula*) at *Met.* 13.928 receives strong support from the grammarian Priscian, dated between the fifth and sixth centuries AD, against the *semine* of all the primary witnesses, which does not yield a satisfactory sense. In one instance, an inscription, *CIL* 6.2.9632, preserves the true reading *cura* at *Tr.* 1.11.12 (*omnis ab hac cura cura leuata mea est*), where all the manuscripts have the interpolation *mens* (*mens leuata mea est*), which must have arisen as an attempt to fill a gap in the line created by the omission of the repeated *cura* (Housman 1937: lx; Luck 1967: 13; 1977). This kind of trivialization, repeated over centuries of transmission, eats away at the very fabric of the poet's genius.

Occupying a unique position between the direct and indirect traditions are the translations of the *Heroides* and the *Metamorphoses* by the Byzantine monk Maximus Planudes (ca. 1255–ca. 1305). Although Ovid's Latin has been transformed into Greek prose, Planudes' conscientiously literal method of translation makes it possible to detect behind the Greek correct readings preserved in his Latin source text which have disappeared from the extant manuscripts (Fisher 1990: 65–98; Palmer 1898: xlvi–liii). To cite one example, at *Met.* 12.256, after the Lapith Pelates has struck the Centaur Amycus with the leg of a table, Amycus is described in the manuscripts as *cumque atro mixtos spumantem sanguine dentes,* which could mean only 'and foaming with respect to his teeth mixed with black blood', an expression peculiar in sense and grammatical construction. In Planudes' translation, however, we find Amycus '*spitting* out his teeth mixed with black blood'. Planudes' Greek indicates that the Latin text he was using had *sputantem*, clearly the correct reading, and not *spumantem*. (Heinsius 1661, without knowledge of Planudes' translation, conjectured and printed *sputantem*, supporting it with parallels cited from Latin poets.) In addition, Planudes comes to the rescue on more than one occasion with the correct spellings of Greek proper names that have been mauled in the direct tradition. Although nothing can be known for certain about the date or provenance of the Latin manuscript, or possibly manuscripts, of the *Metamorphoses* used by Planudes, the fact that it contained readings found nowhere else in the tradition provides yet another indication that true readings may turn up in any witness to the text and that the mongrel is at times preferable to the purebred.

From this rapid survey of the nature of the evidence upon which the texts of Ovid's poems are based, two observation emerge. First, variation abounds; it is the inevitable consequence of the process of transmission. Second, textual variation must be investigated, organized, reported, and evaluated if readers are to understand the historical foundations upon which the edited text is based and also the limitations on what can be achieved in reconstructing what Ovid wrote. (There are two excellent surveys of the transmission, not written in editorial Latin, by Tarrant (1983a) and Richmond (2002), who also gives a brief account of the transition from manuscript to print.)

Corrected and Emended: Ovid in Print

An account of how Ovid's poems have been edited could with some justification begin toward the end of the 1830s, if by 'editing' is meant the application of a set of established procedures designed to produce a text that is based on a critical review of the evidence provided by manuscripts that have been judged to be of independent authority for the constitution of the text. When this method of editing, called 'recension', came into use among classical scholars in the 1820s and 1830s, it shifted the focus of editorial activity from unsystematic attempts to improve or correct, through the sporadic collation of manuscripts that were readily available, a printed text that had established itself as the vulgate, and directed it to the systematic investigation of the manuscripts themselves in order to determine on the basis of their testimony what the transmitted words are. To begin, however, with the modern method of recension is to ignore most of the story and to exclude the person who is generally recognized to be Ovid's greatest editor, Nicolaus Heinsius. If Heinsius did not employ the fully developed method of recension used by editors of the nineteenth century and after, he surpassed his methodologically correct successors in his firsthand knowledge of manuscripts of all of Ovid's works and in his knowledge of Latin poetic diction. The accumulation of material and advances in method do not automatically lead to improved understanding, and modern, of course, does not necessarily mean better. Writing in 1897, Housman could lament that although substantial progress had been made in providing Ovid's works, the amatory poems excepted, with a 'decent *apparatus criticus*', the texts themselves were still in need of an editor. That pessimistic view was the product of Housman's severe appraisal of the work done by Ovid's nineteenth-century editors when set against the achievements of the seventeenth and eighteenth centuries. After taking stock of the lamentable state of critical editions, Housman concluded, 'But Nicolaus Heinsius is dead and buried; and Ovid, in spite of all this new material, is perhaps in a worse condition than he was two hundred years ago' (Housman 1897: 102). It is one thing to know what the testimony of the manuscripts is, it is another to judge the false from the true. The history of editing Ovid's poems is not, at least in Housman's judgment, the story of a steady progress to the reconstruction of 'what Ovid wrote'.

In order to understand the monumental task that has faced Ovid's editors since the invention of printing in the fifteenth century, it is necessary for the reader to have an idea of the imposing bulk of the Ovidian corpus, which is then multiplied by the great number of manuscripts in which the individual works are transmitted. The corpus of Ovid's poetry contains about 34,000 lines, and the manuscripts number in the many hundreds, over four hundred for the *Metamorphoses*, and three hundred for the amatory poems. (A catalogue of *Metamorphoses* manuscripts, an essential editorial tool, wasn't published until Munari 1957; see also Munk-Olsen 1985: 111–181.) Not all of them are of equal value for establishing the text, but a precise determination of the value of each depends ultimately on personal inspection. The difficulties of organizing and assessing this mass of evidence is further complicated by the fact that in the Middle Ages, especially from the twelfth century on, Ovid was a popular author; his poems were much read, studied, and copied. In such an environment industrious readers promoted the migration of readings found in one manuscript into another in the form of marginal or interlinear variants; this is the process known as 'contamination'. When readings are shared in this way, one manuscript effectively becomes two. As a result, the critical review of the manuscripts cannot be confined to those that are judged to be the oldest and the most important; editors must consult later manuscripts as well because they may contain readings that appear genuine and are not found in older witnesses. For Ovid's works in general, the stemmatic organization of manuscripts in a genealogical tree provides an historical outline of the transmission, not a prescription for the selection of variants or for the elimination of witnesses that are younger than the primary manuscripts. (Stemmatic representations of the manuscript traditions of individual works are given in Richmond 2002: 459–483, and Tarrant 1983a.) In short, true readings may turn up in unexpected places and editors must be alert to signs of authenticity in whatever surroundings they may appear.

The most visible and impressive sign of the collaborative nature of the task of editing Ovid is the generations of effort on the part of many scholars to recover the genuine text of the poet's works from this overwhelming mass of often complex and problematic textual evidence. As a result of that collaborative effort Ovid's readers can now acquaint themselves, in the ease and comfort of a modern critical edition, that indispensable instrument of historical scholarship, with descriptions of the primary manuscripts upon which the text is based, and also with the history of the transmission.

The three-volume Ovid published in the Bipontine series of classical texts (Societas Bipontina 1783) contains a useful index of editions covering the period from the two *editiones principes* of 1471 to the year 1779 (it was later updated to 1808 in the Delphin edition of 1812). The index is divided, appropriately enough for Ovid, into four ages (*aetates*). However, for our purposes those four can be reduced to three, without unfairness to those who are excluded. And after the necessary adjustments to the years that punctuate these ages are made, the index provides a convenient framework of chronological stages for studying the progress of Ovid's text in print. Each age is defined by the dominance of a particular edition whose text became the common or vulgate text within each period until it was replaced by another text judged to be superior.

The first age is the age of *incunabula* (1471–1515), those early printed editions that have more in common with the manuscripts of Ovid's poetry than with what we normally think of as an edition. The printing of Gutenberg's 42-line Bible was completed by 1455. The advent of pagan letters in print was not long delayed. In 1465 Cicero's *De Officiis* and *Paradoxa Stoicorum* were printed at Mainz by Johann Fust and Peter Schoeffer, the same men who, in partnership with Gutenberg, had produced the 42-line Bible (Füssel 2005). Six years later in 1471 the complete corpus of Ovid's poetry, along with some spurious additions (Richmond 1981), appeared in two separate and independent editions; one was printed at Rome by Konrad Sweynheym and Arnold Pannartz, and edited by Johannes Andreas (Giovanni Andrea Bussi, 1417–1475), a veritable assembly line of editorial productivity, who writes in his preface that he edited Ovid's works in the summer of 1471 to amuse himself while he was also engaged in editing all of Cicero's speeches (Kenney 1974: 12–17 = 1995: 15–22; Miglio 1978: 69); the other edition was printed at Bologna by Balthasar Azoguidus and edited by Francisus Puteolanus (Francesco Dal Pozzo, d. 1490) whose text of the *Metamorphoses* was to form the basis of subsequent editions in this period (Steiner 1951, 1952). (On the contract between Azoguidus and Puteolanus see Richardson 1999: 31–2.) In overall appearance and page format these books looked very much like the manuscript copies they were designed to replace, impressive folio volumes whose spacious pages are occupied by a single column of text in roman type surrounded by wide margins; and, just as in manuscripts, there was no title page, no pagination, no lineation, and no running titles (Richardson 1999: 122–157). In addition to the benefits of the technological improvements in production, readers now enjoyed the great convenience of having all of Ovid's works gathered together in one or two volumes, rather than divided up among several different manuscripts. Andreas in his preface calls attention to this aspect of his Ovid ('the poet complete in two volumes'), regarding it no doubt as a selling point. This convenience was also going to be of great significance for scholars because the Ovidian corpus now became an accessible, well-defined, and uniform object of study, which would make possible the growth of a community of scholarly discourse, not always well mannered, based on the vulgate text of the editions and directed to the same goal of improving Ovid's text.

A new phase had begun in the transmission of Ovid's works, and the immediate impact of the new technology of print was to make them more accessible to readers through the production of multiple, more or less uniform copies available in a convenient format, and to stabilize the text through the medium of type, which, as contemporaries recognized, made it possible to reproduce the same text with little or no variation in the product, unlike the process of manuscript production which exposed the text during each successive copying to the introduction of errors. In addition to the technology itself, another factor contributing to the stabilization of the text was the printing house practice of hiring a reader and corrector to check the accuracy of what had been set in type, an operation not always successfully carried out (Grafton 1998). Once the text was printed, the field of type on the page provided an effective means of protecting the words form alteration through the intrusion of words written in the margin or between the lines, or through erasure and overwriting. The type established a clear and fixed boundary between what was printed text and what was handwritten text generated by a reader. And if the printed text was somehow effaced, damaged, or lost, there were other copies that could make good the loss.

In referring to Andreas and Puteolanus as 'editors' it must be understood that at this early stage the term means primarily one who prepares printer's copy for the press. In this case, since both men were preparing copy for the first printed texts of Ovid, they used a readily available manuscript of recent date and written in a script that was easy to read for the benefit of the compositors who were setting the text in type. The text of the manuscript would have been of poor quality in the sense that it contained interpolations and corrections in order to remove difficulties, and was in all likelihood of mixed character, containing readings drawn from several manuscript sources in addition to the exemplar from which it was originally copied. To make the weave of this textual fabric even more intricate, Ovid's first editors would have consulted other manuscripts at their disposal in search of readings that would improve, so they believed, the quality of the text they were preparing for the press. As a result of these editorial practices, which were a continuation of the habits inherited from manuscript culture (McKitterick 2003), readers were left in the dark about the sources of the text and how they had been used in constructing it. The immediate goal was to print and sell readable texts of Ovid's poems, not to cumber and even confound the act of reading with the changing forms of his words as they occurred in the manuscripts (Monfasani 1988; Pellegrini 2001: 186–190).

If Ovid's earliest editors were not as energetic in investigating the manuscripts that were available to them or as scrupulous in documenting their sources and what they found in those sources as we would have liked, they did accomplish something of enormous consequence: they produced a common text of all of Ovid's poetry which fostered the growth of a community of learned and ambitious readers who saw the opportunity to improve Ovid's text and enhance their own reputations by displaying their erudition in collections of textual discussions bearing titles like *Annotationes*, *Observationes*, or *Castigationes*. In these early works of textual scholarship Italian humanists deployed their skills as Latinists and as students of Roman culture to recover either by the investigation of available manuscripts or by conjecture 'the true and genuine reading' (*uera et genuina lectio*). As Grafton writes (1983: 14), 'Above all, the very existence of standardized texts ensured that the same critical problems would attract the attention of humanists all over Italy at the same time.' Although the genre of minute and pedantic textual discussions, collected and published in book form, has continued to the present day, the opportunities it affords for preferment, emolument, and reputation are much diminished.

In the second period (1515–1658) the dominant text was that of the second Aldine edition (3 vols. 1515–1516) edited by Andreas Naugerius (Andrea Navagero 1483–1529), humanist scholar, poet, and diplomat. What distinguishes the second Aldine edition from its predecessors is that its text is based on a broader consideration of the manuscript evidence and a more judicious selection of readings. Moreover, Naugerius had a keen appreciation of the variation found in the manuscripts and of the need to present it to readers in an organized way, as evidenced by the volume of notes and textual discussions, *Annotationes*, that accompanied the two volumes of text. In a brief but fascinating preface, which gives a glimpse into the editor's workshop, Naugerius describes his approach to the text. He informs the reader that he has introduced improvements in the text by consulting manuscripts; since in the editor's judgment they are improvements and were found in manuscripts, he does not feel the need to identify them. In the separate volume of *Annotationes* he indicates those places where the text has been altered without manuscript authority and records variants that he feels have a good chance of being right, so that readers can make up their own minds about them. So, for example, in his note on 1.580 Naugerius explains why he prefers Regius' conjecture *Apidanus* to *Eridanus*, which is the reading found in all the manuscripts and in Planudes' translation. Regius' conjecture here and at 7.228, where it does have the support of Planudes' translation, drew some very sharp criticisms from Hercules Ciofanus (1583). *Omnia mutantur* ('everything changes'), says Pythagoras, but apparently not attitudes toward conjectural restorations of the text. When Naugerius deleted an interpolated verse after 8.317 and 9.196 (or 197), he explains that the two verses in question are not found in 'old copies' (*veteribus/antiquis exemplaribus*) and that they are unmetrical. With regard to variants, he is primarily interested in recording readings that may be correct; in some cases he judges all the variants to be correct, as at 2.326 where the readings *factum*, *saxum*, and *fatum* are all recognized as right (*omnia recte*). And finally, he clearly saw the value of Planudes' translation for the textual criticism of the *Metamorphoses*.

Naugerius' editorial procedure serves one basic purpose: to let the reader know that the text of Ovid's poems in his edition is based on what is transmitted in the manuscripts he consulted, except in those places where he has admitted conjectures, and at the same time to inform the reader of what the editor judges to be significant variant readings. Naugerius provided an example that others would follow with less energy and acumen, and his edition became the starting-point for those who were more interested in writing commentaries on Ovid's poems than improving the text. Reprinted, modified, supplemented, and updated in various ways, Naugerius' Aldine edition continued to provide the textual foundation for editions of Ovid for nearly a century and a half (Luck 2002, 2005).

Nicolaus Heinsius, *Verus Sospitator Ovidi*

A new age (1658–1837) dawns in the textual history of Ovid's poems with the work of a scholar who, after three hundred and forty-five years, remains the central figure in any account of the editing of Ovid. No modern editor will fail to mention his name in the preface as the *sospitator Ovidi*; no *apparatus criticus* will fail to cite his numerous contributions to the improvement of the text. Nicolaus Heinsius (1620–1681), scholar, diplomat, and accomplished neo-Latin poet, published a three-volume edition of the works (I, 1658; II, 1659; III 1661; the engraved title page of the first volume bears the year of the last, 1661), together with three volumes of textual notes (undated). This is the first edition of all of Ovid's works to offer the reader texts of the poems that are based on an extensive firsthand knowledge of the manuscript sources and to supplement the printed texts with a full textual commentary in which manuscript variants are recorded and discussed, and alterations of the vulgate text, with which his readers were familiar, are noted. And, it should be observed, that familiarity acted as a break on editorial intervention that might be deemed excessive if a favorite passage was corrupted by the introduction of some newfangled reading. Some indication of the magnitude of Heinsius' achievement is given by the following statistics. Reeve (1976a: 76) has tallied the manuscripts collated by Heinsius between 1636 and 1661; the total is a staggering 286. That figure increases to 458 if individual works are counted separately as the equivalent of a manuscript. Again, J. C. Jahn, a conscientious and industrious editor, based his own edition (1828–1832: 2 vols. only) on Heinsius' text and notes, as they were reprinted in Burman 1727, and wrote in his preface that the criticism of Ovid's poetry depended on the materials assembled by Heinsius. Since Heinsius' brilliance and fertility as an emendator of Ovid have received an eloquent and expert appraisal from Kenney (1974: 57–63 = 1995: 74–82), let it be remarked here that there are two other impressive characteristics of Heinsius as an editor of Ovid. First, there is his steady and confident command of such a vast amount of manuscript and print materials. Some modern editors have been overwhelmed by the sheer volume of evidence that must be reviewed in the course of editing just one of Ovid's works, and have faltered in the attempt to construct a neat and precise presentation of the evidence in the critical apparatus. Heinsius not only achieved an unrivalled knowledge of the manuscript evidence, he was also able to use that knowledge to improve the text significantly. Second, he intuitively employed a method of criticism, 'enlightened eclecticism', to use Tarrant's (1983a: 277) phrase (or less elegantly, he had a good nose for the right reading, regardless of the pedigree of its source), which has stood the test of time as the most productive way to edit Ovid's poems. Our knowledge of what the manuscripts contain and the history of transmission can take us only so far; they cannot help us choose when the choice is between *illas* and *illa*. It is in this area that Heinsius' 'method' continues to be a fruitful example for Ovid's editors. Here it is also worth mentioning that as an editor and textual critic Heinsius is a congenial figure. Those who are not familiar with his work may be surprised to discover that not all textual critics employ the pillory and ducking stool as methods of persuasion (Tarrant 1999).

Heinsius' text, with some changes, and his notes, along with those of other commentators, were reprinted in Burman's monumental edition (1727). A century of textual antiquarianism and textual stagnation followed. Readings were gathered and repeated from printed sources or were culled from the occasional manuscript; the mass of learned exegesis swelled on the page. Many an edition proudly advertised its text as a reprint of the Burman vulgate, *ex recensione Burmanniana* or *Heinsio-Burmanniana*. Heinsius' insistence in his prefaces (1652, 1661) that the improvement of Ovid's text depended on the discovery of better manuscripts and his own commitment to rooting out manuscripts from their dusty dens in the libraries of Europe went unheeded. That situation began to change when the spirit of Heinsius was revived and his example reinvigorated Ovidian textual scholarship in the modern period.

The Modern Critical Corpus

The modern period in the editing of Ovid's poetry began one hundred and seventy years ago with Rudolph Merkel's (1811–1885) edition of *Tristia* and *Ibis* (Berlin 1837). Despite its shortcomings in the establishment of the text (still no significant improvement over Heinsius' edition) and in the organization of the *apparatus criti-cus*, Merkel's edition marks a turning point in the approach to the task of editing Ovid. In a *praefatio* devoted largely to critical method and to Heinsius' work on Ovid, Merkel forcefully maintained that the text had to be based on the evidence of manuscripts judged to be of independent authority; there could be no shirking of the duty to locate, describe, and collate manuscripts (activities that were now facili-tated by the establishment of manuscript collections in public libraries, the publica-tion of library catalogues, and the growth of paleography as a discipline). In making his case for a text based on a systematic assessment of the manuscript evidence, Merkel was inspired not only by the work of Heinsius but also by the critical approach out-lined by the young Karl Lachmann (1816) in his edition of Propertius; uninterpolated manuscripts, Lachmann stressed, are the foundation of the text, not printed editions or late-humanist manuscripts littered with interpolations and elegant improvements. After the century of textual stagnation that followed Burman's edition (1727) Merkel's preface was a wake-up call to scholars who had been satisfied to read or reprint Ovid's poetry without a clearly informed understanding of what the manu-script sources of the text were and by what criteria those sources were employed in establishing the text. Merkel also edited the *Fasti* (1841) along the same line as the *Tristia* and *Ibis* and went on to produce an edition of all of Ovid's poetry in three volumes (1850–1852). The texts in these volumes were not accompanied by an *apparatus criticus* and instead were prefaced by summaries of variant readings and explanations of editorial interventions; in this respect they were a throwback to the editorial practice of an earlier age, though his edition of the *Metamorphoses* stands out for the critical treatment of the evidence and the overall quality of the text.

If Merkel pointed in the general direction of the path to be followed by Ovid's editors, Lachmann gave them their compass bearings. In the preface to his landmark edition of Lucretius (1850) Lachmann gave memorable expression to the method of recension with which his name has long been associated, the stemmatic method based on the determination of the genealogical relationships of manuscripts in order to recover the text of their latest common, no longer extant, ancestor, whenever the conditions of transmission permit such a reconstruction (Timpanaro 2005). But even more impressive, and more valuable, than the reconstruction of a lost ancestor was the demonstration that the text of a work transmitted by manuscript could be estab-lished on strictly historical principles and that the systematic review of the testimony of the independent witnesses to the text provided the only secure foundation for recovering the author's words. An additional benefit was the realization that the great congeries of variant readings that had accumulated over the centuries since the first printed editions from a variety of sources, seldom properly identified, could now be weeded, pruned, and effectively organized as historical knowledge about the transmis-sion within the framework of an *apparatus criticus*.

The impact of Lachmann's *Lucretius* was immediate and profound. Once it was understood that texts could be significantly improved through methodical recension, the hunt was on for better manuscripts; much industry and learning were now expended on collating their readings and delineating their family histories. In the case of Ovid's works it wasn't long before editions of the poems began to appear which have the familiar look of the modern critical edition: a preface in which the manuscripts employed by the editor are identified, dated, and described, and then organized into a history of the transmission; and a text accompanied by a critical apparatus in which the transmitted variants are recorded, along with scholars' conjectures. Among the more ambitious projects of Ovidian textual scholarship published toward the end of the nineteenth century are Korn's *Epistulae ex Ponto* (1868), Ellis' *Ibis* (1881), and Owen's *Tristia* (1889), the last two with extensive prolegomena, Sedlmayer's *Heroides* (1886), preceded by the publication of a *Prolegomena critica* (1878), and Palmer's *Heroides* (1898), which includes Planudes' Greek translation. In this period there also appeared editions of the complete works; noteworthy among them, Riese's *Ovidii Opera* (1871–4), and the *opera omnia* printed in J. P. Postgate's *Corpus Poetarum Latinorum* (1894), a work dedicated to the *manes* of Richard Bentley. At the end of the nineteenth century there was still much work to be done, especially in investigating the manuscripts of the amatory poems and in identifying the numerous manuscripts collated by Heinsius for his editions. Even so, something of permanent value had been achieved; Ovid's editors had replaced a succession of printed vulgate texts that had come to be regarded as authoritative at various stages of the print tradition, often through mere reprinting, with a text based on the systematic investigation of the manuscripts and their interrelationships, the results of which were reported in a critical edition. Not all scholars were satisfied with the texts thus produced, but at least now they held in their hands the evidence which might allow them to improve what they thought wrong-headed on the part of the editor or corrupt in the manuscripts.

The systematic investigation of the manuscripts and the determination of their interrelationships in the process of transmission put the text of Ovid's works on a sounder historical footing than it had hitherto been. Yet at the same time the methods of recension had the unfortunate consequence of inducing editors to elevate a particular manuscript or group of manuscripts to a position of privileged authority because its readings were judged superior in most cases to what was found in the other manuscripts. In an ironic turn of events, the late and interpolated manuscripts that served as printer's copy for Andreas and Puteolanus were now replaced by something potentially more harmful, a *codex optimus* whose preeminence was defended by the application of method. The outcome of such an attitude is visible in the formulas devised by Magnus (1914: xxv–xxvi) for the selection of variants presented by manuscripts of the *Metamorphoses*. Nothing could be farther from the 'enlightened eclecticism' of Heinsius or more incompatible with the realities of the transmission than this mechanical approach. Magnus' great compendium of manuscript evidence and textual scholarship on the poem (Helm 1915; Rand 1916), and Slater's extensive *apparatus crtiticus* 1927 (without a text), two monuments of Ovidian scholarship, are representative of the paradox that underlies much twentieth-century editing of Ovid's poetry: the tremendous amount of energy and labor devoted by scholars to the investigation and collation of manuscripts, even to the point where editors are overwhelmed by the data they have collected, does not necessarily result in texts that are superior in quality to what was achieved by their unmethodical predecessors (Reeve 1974; Hunt 1975). There have been, of course, exceptions to the general conservatism that has prevailed in the twentieth-century editing of Ovid. Kenney's (1961) edition of the amatory poetry successfully revived the spirit of Heinsius when it was languishing under the general enthusiasm to reproduce faithfully the contents of Ovid's manuscripts and to ignore Ovid himself; so too the Teubner *Fasti* (Alton et al. 1997) and, in a different format, George Goold's revision of the Loeb Ovid 1977–1989, which has the distinction, among recent editions, of being the complete corpus prepared by a single hand. And most recently, the high quality of Tarrant's Oxford text of the *Metamorphoses* (2004), based on a truly eclectic approach to the manuscript evidence, augurs well for textual scholarship on Ovid in the twenty-first century (Possanza 2005; Galasso 2006; Ramírez de Verger 2006; Heyworth 2007c). It seems that the example of Heinsius' imperishable achievement is destined not only to act as a standard by which editorial work on Ovid will be judged but also to inspire his true successors with a sense of the high importance of their calling to recover Ovid's words.

FURTHER READING

Readers should collate a manuscript page of one of Ovid's poems against the text of a modern edition, without peeking at the *apparatus criticus*, in order to experience firsthand the complex differences between the manuscript and the printed page as well as the discouraging tedium of the task; facsimiles of pages will be found in Owen (1889), Palmer (1898), Magnus (1914), Slater (1927), and Alton et al. (1997). As a follow-up to that activity readers will gain a better appreciation of the work involved in transforming the raw data of the manuscripts into the familiar text and *apparatus criticus* of a critical edition by studying a page of printed text in relation to the evidence recorded in the *apparatus* and the editorial decisions that are there recorded. Much can be learned from the well-constructed *apparatus* of an exemplary edition: Kenney (1961), Alton et al. (1997), Tarrant (2004). Heinsius' three-volume textual commentary (1661), in its original form or in Fischer's 1758 reprint, is the best place to enter the centuries-long discourse of scholars about 'what Ovid wrote'. Tarrant (1995a) provides an excellent introduction to the procedures involved in editing Latin texts. Tanselle (1983) administers a strong antidote to the empirical bravado of the classical textual critic. The following will give the reader stimulating introductions to the great variety of editorial and critical problems: amatory poems, Goold (1965); *Heroides*, Lachmann (1876), Courtney (1965, 1997–8), and Kenney (1999); *Metamorphoses*, any of Tarrant's articles cited in the bibliography (his promised volume of *observationes* is eagerly awaited); *Fasti*, Alton et al. (1972, 1997: xvi–xxi); *Tristia*, Knox (1997), *Tristia* and *Epistulae ex Ponto*, Housman (1916); *Ibis*, Housman (1918). Reynolds and Wilson (1991) provide a general survey of the transmission of Latin literature (see also Rouse 1992), an introduction to the aims and methods of textual criticism, and a reader's guide to the *apparatus criticus*. West (1973) supplies the aspiring editor with an efficient and informative how-to guide.

CHAPTER TWENTY-THREE

Commenting on Ovid

Peter E. Knox

Introduction

In its most basic aspects the approach to teaching classical texts in the original language has not changed much since antiquity: a teacher with a small group of students parses individual words and phrases, with the aid of commentaries compiled from notes accumulated by his predecessors (Reynolds and Wilson: 9–15). A great deal can be learned about the reception of classical literature from the marginal notes of its readers and the exegetical commentaries of its teachers. Scholars are beginning to make great progress in tapping into the resources to be found in the abundant medieval manuscripts of Ovid, and there are narratives of reception to be found also in the modern commentaries. But explication of the text begins with its first readings in antiquity.

Antiquity

The origins of the modern commentary as a continuous exegesis of a literary text can be traced back to the activity of Greek scholars of the Hellenistic period attempting to elucidate the classic works of their literary past. The commentaries (*hypomnemata*) first produced by scholars like Aristarchus (ca. 215–144 BCE), working in Alexandria on classic authors such as Homer, Hesiod, Aristophanes, and the tragedians, were independent works that circulated separately from the texts they were intended to explain. These commentaries are lost, and the information contained in them is known to us only from the marginal notes (*scholia*) compiled by Byzantine scholars, or transmitted by lexicographers, and encyclopedists (Reynolds and Wilson 1991: 9–15; Pfeiffer 1968: 212–18). Papyrus discoveries have revealed something of the original format of these commentaries, as well as the ways in which even in antiquity marginal comments might take on a more deliberate and formal function than casual notes by students (Cameron 2004: 164–83). The range of topics covered in the notes could be extensive, and individual textual citations (*lemmata*) might elicit explication of problems lexicographical, grammatical, mythological, stylistic, rhetorical, or antiquarian. Nor did ancient commentators refrain from including aesthetic judgments or other literary observations in their notes. As Roman literary scholarship developed, beginning in the second century BCE, the methods of Greek philology were adapted to a Latin context, including the production of commentaries on standard literary works, primarily aimed at the uses of the schools. We also hear of some commentaries produced for non-standard texts that were particularly difficult to interpret, such as one by Lucius Crassicius Pansa on the *Zmyrna* of Helvius Cinna (Kaster 1995: 200–1). But most of the commentaries produced in Latin antiquity had schooling as their primary function.

In a famous passage St Jerome gives us an idea of the circulation of commentaries in the fourth century (*Apol.* 1.16):

> When you were a boy, I think you read the commentaries of Asper on Virgil and Sallust, Vulcatius on the speeches of Cicero, Victorinus on his dialogues; my own teacher Donatus on Terence's comedies, and Virgil; and others on other works: Plautus, Lucretius, Flaccus, Persius and Lucan.

As has often been noted, the most conspicuous name missing from this list is Ovid, for whom no trace of an ancient commentary survives. The scholia found in some medieval manuscripts of the *Ibis* (La Penna 1959) are for the most part of no value, although they do preserve isolated pieces of genuine ancient scholarship. They seem to be the product of a more or less random accumulation of notes identifying mythological allusions, resulting from the activity of ancient and early medieval readers, rather than any focused scholarly activity (Cameron 2004: 180–3).

The only evidence for such scholarly activity on Ovid in antiquity is the collection of prose summaries of the *Metamorphoses* falsely transmitted under the name of Lactantius Placidus. This work, of uncertain date, was compiled as a mythographic companion to the *Metamorphoses* on the model of the similar prose summaries, known as the *Diegeseis*, that Greek scholars composed as a guide to the *Aetia* of Callimachus (Cameron 2004: 52–6). A sample taken from the second book illustrates the limited scope and purpose of the pseudo-Lactantian *Narrationes*. In summarizing the transformation of the sisters of Phaethon into poplars (*Met.* 2.329–66), the Narrator, as this commentator is now known, offers only the bare bones of the story:

> sorores Phaethontis Phaethusa, Lampetie, Phoebe casum fratris dum deflent, deorum misericordia in arbores populos mutatae sunt. lacrimae earum, ut Hesiodus et Euripides indicant, in electrum conversae sunt.

> While Phaethusa, Lampetie, and Phoebe, the sisters of Phaethon, lament their brother's fate, they are changed into poplar trees out of the pity of the gods. As Hesiod and Euripides point out, their tears were changed to amber.

The summary derives some information from sources other than Ovid's text, including the name of one of the sisters, Phoebe, not given by Ovid. This type of aid was intended for the reader who wanted a handy reference to the stories told by Ovid, but it offers none of the information found, for example, in the large-scale commentary of Servius on Virgil. And so, when Ovid acquired an extensive readership in the Middle Ages, the interpretative slate inherited from antiquity was largely blank.

Middle Ages

Ovid continued to be read during the period between the collapse of Roman rule in the West and the Carolingian revival, as scattered testimonia attest, but there is no evidence to suggest that his works were studied in any systematic way or used for pedagogical purposes. Only Virgil among the pagan classics was an accepted component of the scholastic canon of the ninth century; other classic poets of antiquity were only gradually introduced into the canon, and among these Ovid was among the latest to gain entry (Glauche 1970: 12; Munk Olson 1991: 23–55). When medieval readers turned to Ovid in greater numbers, in the twelfth century and after, there was thus no pre-existing framework on which to base interpretation. Scholarly attention has tended to focus on the major allegorizing commentaries of the late Middle Ages, especially the *Ovide Moralisé* of the fourteenth century, but it and its congeners are the products of a longer process of gloss, paraphrase, and commentary that is to be traced in the margins of manuscripts used by students in the medieval

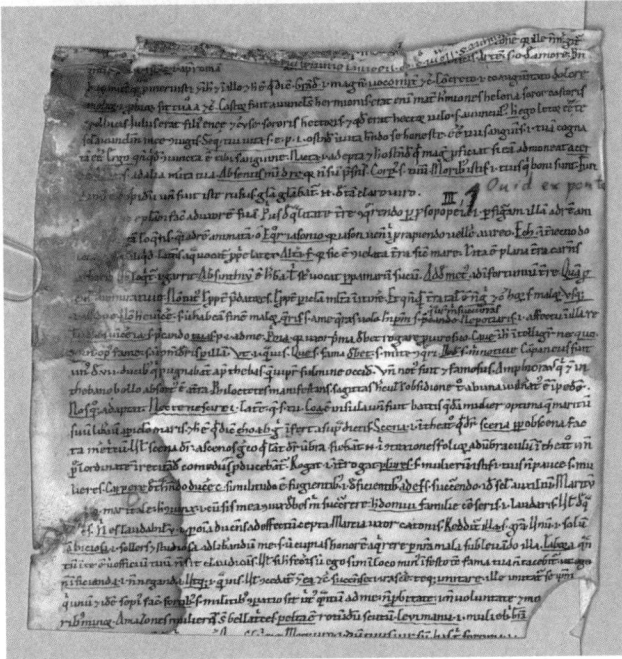

Figure 4: A leaf from a twelfth-century commentary on Ovid's *Epistulae ex Ponto*, with the beginning of Book 3 (Bayerische Staatsbibliothek München, Clm 29208(17)).

schoolroom. The study of literary texts served to instruct students in proper Latin usage, the basic elements of style and expression, correct prosody, and, when appropriately mediated, moral instruction, all tools that might be put to use in study of the Bible and patristic texts. The existence of an annotated text of the *Ars amatoria* from the ninth century, the so-called 'St Dunstan's Classbook', with interlinear glosses in Welsh and Latin, is evidence of the incipient interest in Ovid's Latinity that led incrementally to the more widespread availability of texts in the high Middle Ages (Hexter 1986: 26–41).

Throughout this period the *Metamorphoses* remained the most widely read work of Ovid's, but readers, both in and out of the classroom, devoted themselves to other works as well. From the twelfth century, the period famously dubbed an 'Ovidian age' (*aetas Ovidiana*) by the great medievalist Ludwig Traube (1911: 113), thirty-four surviving manuscripts attest to the popularity of the *Metamorphoses*, and a further eighteen manuscripts of the *Fasti* are evidence of its readership, but next in order are the *Epistulae ex Ponto*, preserved in thirteen manuscripts, more than double the number of the *Heroides* (Munk Olsen 1991: 37). Some sense of the interpretative value attributed by medieval commentators to classical texts can be gleaned from the introductions to their works prefixed to editions, whether accompanied by commentary or not (Quain 1945; Ghisalberti 1946). These *accessus*, as they are called, follow a consistent pattern in dealing with items such as the author's life, the title of the work, the author's intention, the subject of the work, its utility, and which branch of philosophy it should be classified under (*vita auctoris, titulus operis, intentio scribentis, materia operis, utilitas, cui parti philosophiae supponatur*). From one *accessus* to the *Epistulae ex Ponto* we can see how commentators interpreted the text for a Christian readership (Huygens 1970: 34–5):

In hoc libro sicut in ceteris ista inquiri solent: intentio, materia, utilitas, cui parti philosophiae subponatur. Intentio sua est unumquemque persuadere ut vero amico suo in necessitate subveniat, materia sua amici sui sunt, ad quos scribit, mittens singulis singulas epistolas, vel ipsa verba, quibus precatur. Utilitas est maxima, si possit misericordiam consequi apud Octavianum Cesarem intercessione amicorum suorum quibus mittit ipsas epistolas. Ethicae, id est morali scientiae, subponitur, quia in unaquaque epistola agit de moribus.

In this book, as in the others, the following topics are usually investigated: its intention, its subject, its utility, and the branch of philosophy under which it is classified. Ovid's intention is to persuade everyone to come to the aid of a true friend in his time of need; his subject matter is the friends to whom he writes, sending them each separate epistles, or the words with which he makes his entreaty. Its utility is very great, if he can obtain Octavianus Caesar's mercy by the intercession of his friends to whom he sends these epistles. The work is classified under Ethics, that is moral science, because in each letter he deals with morals.

As the surviving *accessus* and accompanying commentaries show (Hexter 1986: 83–136), students were presented with the *Epistulae ex Ponto* as a suitable text not only because it provided a reliable guide to Latinity but also because it supplied appropriate models for dealing with human behavior, the problems of friendship, and issues of character. The interpretative move to approach Ovid's poetry by directing it to the ethical concerns of a medieval Christian audience is even more evident in the great allegorizing commentaries on the *Metamorphoses* of the later Middle Ages.

The earliest of these works is the *Allegoriae super Ovidii Metamorphosin* by Arnulf of Orléans (ca. 1175), the influence of which extended through the end of the Middle Ages and into the Renaissance in the allegorical tradition that continued even alongside the humanistic revolution. Arnulf was well versed in the Ovidian corpus, and in addition to his commentary on the *Metamorphoses*, he produced commentaries on the *Fasti* (Rieker 2005) and notes on *Ars amatoria*, *Remedia amoris*, and *Epistulae ex Ponto* (Ghisalberti 1932: 161–76). The focus of his interest is clear from the *accessus* prefaced to the *Metamorphoses*, also known as Arnulf's *Vita Ovidii* (Ghisalberti 1932: 181):

> Intencio est de mutacione dicere, ut non intelligamus de mutacione que fit extrinsecus tantum in rebus corporeis bonis vel malis sed etiam de mutacione que fit intrinsecus ut in anima, ut reducat nos ab errore ad cognitionem veri creatoris.

> His intention is to tell about change, so that we may not understand only the external change that takes place in corporeal matter both good and bad but also about change that takes place internally, for example in the soul, to lead us from error to knowledge of the true creator.

Arnulf's commentary was influential throughout the period. Drawing on sources such as Fulgentius, the Vatican Mythographers, and the so-called Lactantian *Narrationes*, the *Allegoriae* offers interpretations of Ovid's stories as a 'poetic instruction in an ancient story over time wrapped in a veil of fantasy, the story of nature taught to man with poetic personification, and finally a school of morality for the present and the future' (Ghisalberti 1932: 201).

It is the moral category that most actively engages the hermeneutic ingenuity of Arnulf, in recasting Ovid's morally ambivalent or neutral narratives into a Christian context. So, in his reading, the story of Orpheus in Book 10 becomes an allegory about resisting the ephemeral allurements of this world (*bona huius seculi transitoria et falsa*) and striving for the higher spiritual world, represented by the mountain on which Orpheus sings (*in montem ascendens i. ad virtutes ad quas est ascensus sicut ad vicia descensus*). His abhorrence of women and turn to homosexuality is represented as a rejection of feminine frailty and a turn to manly virtue, for, as Arnulf pointedly reminds the reader, 'women are indeed more prone to sin and vice than men' (McKinley 2001: 66–8).

Following closely upon the commentary of Arnulf, the English schoolmaster John of Garland produced (ca. 1234) a compact poem in 520 lines summarizing the allegories of the *Metamorphoses*. His *Integumenta Ovidii* (Ghisalberti 1933a) often accompanies Arnulf's *Allegoriae* in manuscripts and forms an important component in the intellectual heritage that shaped subsequent developments in Ovidian commentaries of the later Middle Ages. Here is how John of Garland in turn summarizes the tale of Orpheus and Eurydice (407–8):

Pratum delicie, coniunx caro, vipera virus,
Vir ratio, Stix est terra, loquela lira.

The meadow is delights; his wife, flesh; the snake, poison;
The man, reason; the Styx, earth; the lyre, speech.

With such condensed summaries at the ready—the *Integumenta* was probably intended as an aid to memory—the moralizing allegories of the *Metamorphoses* rendered the text safe reading for generations of students and other Christian readers.

In the early years of the fourteenth century, the anonymous French verse *Ovide Moralisé* (de Boer 1915–38) gained a wide audience, as it opened the *Metamorphoses* to multiple readings within the vernacular tradition, with its exuberant re-imaginings of the poem's morality (Demats 1973; Engels 1945). Thus, the tale of Myrrha's incestuous love for her father (10.3478–3795) is at first a condemnation of the sinful nature of the girl's passion, but it concludes by making of her a trope for virginal purity (McKinley 2001: 91; Dimmick 2002: 279–80). The very nearly contemporary work of Giovanni del Virgilio (ca. 1323), a poet in his own right who lectured on Ovid in Bologna, constituted another stream by which the allegorizing tradition reached the expanding public for Ovid's works. His *Allegoriae* offer a paraphrase of the *Metamorphoses* in prose and verse (Ghisalberti 1933b), in which the reconfiguration of Ovid's complex psychological treatment of passion is morphed into parables of virtue. Thus Apollo, in his attempted rape of Daphne, is transformed into an emblem of chastity in pursuit of modesty (1.9):

Nona transmutatio est de Dapne conversa in laurum. Allegoria est hec. Per Phebum intelligo pudicam personam et castam, per Dapnem ipsam pudicitiam quam insequitur casta persona. Per Dapnem converti in arborem intelligo quod pudicitia radicatur in corde illius qui insequitur eam. Per laurum signatur virginitas eo quod semper est virens et redolens.

The ninth metamorphosis concerns Daphne changed to laurel. This is the allegory. I understand Phoebus to be the modest and chaste person; Daphne the very modesty that the chaste person pursues. I take Daphne's transformation into a tree to mean that modesty is rooted in the heart of the one who pursues it. By the laurel virginity is signified, because it is always fresh and fragrant.

Giovanni's standing ensured his allegories a wide audience and their influence is particularly noteworthy in the earliest translations of the *Metamorphoses* into the vernacular (Guthmüller 1975).

The last great work of medieval exegesis is the *Ovidius moralizatus* of Pierre Bersuire (1362), which originally constituted Book 15 of his *Reductorium morale* (Ghisalberti 1933c). It was frequently copied separately and was subsequently attributed to Thomas Walleys, an English Dominican, and the earliest printed editions follow this misattribution. Like its antecedents, the *Ovidius moralizatus* does not reproduce the text of the *Metamorphoses*; it summarizes each story, for which interpretations are then offered. Bersuire takes his definition of the poet's task from Rabanus Maurus (Orgel 1979b):

dicit quod officium poetae est: quae gesta sunt in alias species obliquis figurationibus cum decore aliquo conuertere. Quapropter ibidem dicitur lucanum non fuisse poetam: quia scilicet visus est historias potius quam poetica confecisse.

He says that it is the poet's task to convert events into other forms by indirect figurings with some charm. Accordingly in the same place it is said that Lucan was not a poet, apparently because he was viewed as having composed histories rather than poetry.

True to this view of the poet's mission, Bersuire reinforces a reading based on 'indirect figurings' that convert menacingly attractive pagan deities into more comfortable Christian virtues, as in his interpretation of Bacchus:

Per bacchum qui inebriat: intelligitur vera fides quae feruore deuotionis inebriat seruos Christi. Per semelen intelligitur populus iudaicus: per nymphas intelligo populum gentilem et paganum. Dico igitur quod a principio Iuppiter id est deus pater: semelen id est synagogam: baccho id est feruore fidei impregnauit.

By Bacchus who intoxicates is meant the true faith that intoxicates the servants of Christ with the fervor of devotion; by Semele is meant the Jewish people; the nymphs I interpret as gentiles and pagans. And so I say that Jupiter (i.e. God the Father) impregnated Semele (i.e. the Synagogue) with Bacchus (i.e. the fervor of faith).

The allegorical commentary tradition that culminated in the *Ovidius moralizatus* did not come to an end with the advent of humanism, but from the fifteenth century a new approach to commentary on Ovid was introduced by scholars who in some sense saw it as their role to supply the exegetical apparatus that Ovid had never acquired from the philologists of antiquity.

The Renaissance

The humanists of the mid-fifteenth century practiced the art of the commentary intensively, recording their observations on the ancient texts 'line by line and often word by word' (Grafton 1991: 48). In their practice they saw themselves as continuing the tradition to be observed in the ancient commentaries on canonical texts, Donatus on Terence, Porphyrio on Horace, and especially Servius on Virgil (Kenney 1971a). Many of the humanists' commentaries originated in lectures, some of which are known to us from students' notes, but it became increasingly common for their authors to revise and publish them (Grafton 1991: 48–9). The fact that there were no ancient commentaries on any of Ovid's works combined with another tendency of early humanist scholarship to focus attention on some unexpected works. For the humanist commentary, in the days before the revolution in philological method attributable to Angelo Poliziano, offered a platform from which to showcase the commentator's knowledge on a broad array of topics: rhetoric, mythology, grammar, or history.

One of the first humanists to have his commentaries printed was Domizio Calderini, who, before his untimely death in 1478 at the age of thirty-two, produced commentaries on Martial, Juvenal, and Ovid's *Ibis* (Perosa 1973; Dunston 1968). Like others of his generation, Calderini was attracted to more obscure works that offered ample scope for a pyrotechnic display of erudition in elucidating allusions to minor mythological characters and, not least attractive, the opportunity for polemical engagement with contemporary rivals. Hence, in part perhaps, his attraction to the *Ibis*, 'a work full of anger and obscurity' (Grafton and Jardine 1986: 83). There were similar attractions in the recently rediscovered *Epistula Sapphus*, now usually included in editions of the *Heroides* as the fifteenth poem in that collection. Calderini's commentary was published in a miscellaneous volume produced by Arnold Pannartz in the summer of 1475 (Campanelli 2001: 34–8). The *Commentarioli in Sappho Ouidii*, set out as notes with lemmata but no text, illustrate many of the emerging characteristics that distinguish the humanists' approach from medieval allegorizing.

The question of the authorship of the *Epistula Sapphus* was being hotly disputed at the time, because it was not transmitted with the rest of the *Heroides*, and some alleged that it was actually a translation of a lost poem by Sappho. Calderini addresses this problem in his preface:

> haec autem epistola ab Ouidio composita affectus qui mitiores sunt copiosius exprimit quam ulla alia: nam eam locupletauit poeta ex poematis Sapphus: quae mollissima sunt . . . tantum autem ab est ut hanc epistolam putem a Sappho scriptam ut etiam statuam inferi oportere epistolis Ouidii et statim locandam post Didonem. nam eo ordine poeta scripsit siquidem eius uersibus credimus: paulo ante a nobis recitatis.

> This epistle by Ovid expresses the milder sentiments more abundantly than any other, for the poet has enriched it with selections from the poems of Sappho, which are extremely delicate . . . Moreover, not only do I not believe that this epistle was written by Sappho, I even assert that it ought to be inserted into Ovid's epistles and placed immediately after Dido. For the poet wrote them in that order, if indeed we trust his own verses, which I have cited a little earlier.

Calderini refers to the passage in *Am.* 2.18 where Ovid lists several of the *Heroides*, including a reference to an epistle by Sappho. The appeal to textual evidence is characteristic of the development of humanist philology, and Calderini was on the cusp of this shift, including among his sources a large number of other Latin and Greek authors whom he used to elucidate problems in the text. The application of comparative evidence from other texts was also a hallmark of the new style of commentary.

An instance is found in his explanation of the 'lover's leap' by the temple of Apollo on the island of Leucas in the note on *Her.* 15.165:

> Phoebus. Ad templum acciacum quod in sinu Ambracio est: petra prerupta esse ferebatur. Unde qui se demitterent in mare amoris flamma leuarentur. Id egit prima Sapho ut ex Menandri testimonio Strabo affirmat.

> *Phoebus.* It was said that there was a steep cliff by the Actian on the gulf of Ambracia, from which people might gain release from the fire of love by throwing themselves down

into the sea. Sappho was the first to do this, as Strabo affirms on the testimony of Menander.

Calderini refers to a passage in Strabo's *Geography* (10.2.9), where this bit of local lore is reported. It is often the case, however, that Calderini treats the text merely as a peg for display of specious learning (Grafton and Jardine 1986: 83–94), as in his note on the *ES* 183, where the lyre is mentioned:

> Liram. Primus fecit mercurius ut ante diximus quam tradit orpheo ex testudine ut eratosthenes scribit auctore hygino [*Astr.* 2.7]. Ea relata est in coelum mortuo Orpheo fauore appollinis: quem plurimum apud inferos laudauerat et uoluntate iouis. qui id concessit caliopae filiae matri Orphei.

> As I said previously, Mercury was the first to make one from tortoise shell, which he gave to Orpheus, as Eratosthenes writes, on the report of Hyginus. It was transported to heaven on Orpheus' death by the favor of Apollo, whom he had praised greatly in the Underworld, and by the will of Jupiter, who had granted this to Calliope, Orpheus' mother.

The information hardly assists in interpretation, but in applying a more systematic investigation of sources to explain obscurities in the text, rather than resorting to allegory or invention, Calderini anticipates many of the developments of humanist philology associated with his younger contemporary, Angelo Poliziano, whom he met once in Florence. It is tempting to reflect on how their relationship might have affected the development of classical scholarship, had Calderini not fallen victim to the plague.

Poliziano's initially positive assessment of Calderini was soon altered in the course of his own research, for it was Poliziano, not Calderini, who set the tone for subsequent philological commentary on the classics. Although Poliziano produced commentaries on the *Epistula Sapphus* (Lazzeri 1971) and the *Fasti* (Lo Monaco 1991), his influence was felt largely through the *Miscellanea* (1489), a monographic collection of notes on unrelated interpretative problems. In one chapter (75) he famously dissected Calderini's method, criticizing his frequently reprinted commentary on the *Ibis*. In Calderini's text, line 569 is printed as: *utque loquax in equo est elisus guttur Agenor* ('and as the talkative Agenor was strangled in the horse'). In the accompanying note, Calderini explains, 'as the result of a fall from a horse Agenor's hand became stuck in his mouth and he perished.' Poliziano recognized this as nonsense; indeed, it was entirely a fantasy concocted by Calderini, which Poliziano remedied by emending *Agenor* to *acerno* and rendering the line, 'and as the talkative one was strangled in the maple-wood horse'. By referring to Homer and Tryphiodorus for the story of Anticlus, whom Odysseus strangled inside the wooden horse, Poliziano applied a far higher standard of fidelity to sources and honesty in presentation than had characterized the philology of the mid-fifteenth century (Grafton 1991: 52–4). It would be centuries before Poliziano's methods would be applied consistently by commentators on Ovid's works, but the ramifications of these developments are evident in the bifurcation of the commentary tradition that developed in the sixteenth century.

Early Printed Commentaries

Perhaps the most enduring product of Renaissance scholarship on Ovid was the edition of the *Metamorphoses* published in Venice in 1493 containing the commentary of Raphael Regius (Raffaele Regio). It became in many respects the standard commentary on the poem for the sixteenth century and was reprinted more than sixty times in France and Italy alone during that century; in 1513 Regius could boast that more 50,000 copies were in circulation (Guthmüller 1975: 131). Regius was in many respects the prototypical humanist. He came from Bergamo, and taught in Padua

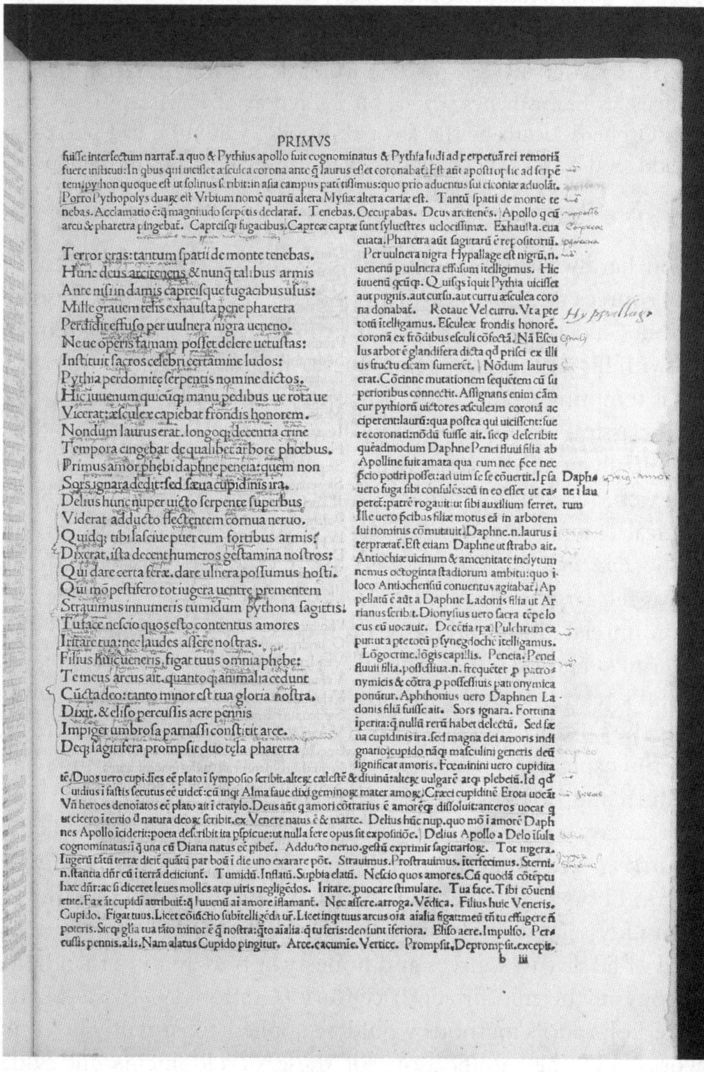

PRIMVS

fuisse interfectum narratur.a quo & Pythius apollo fuit cognominatus & Pythia ludi ad perpetuã rei memoriã fuere instituti:In qbus qui uicisset æsculea corona ante q̃ laurus esset coronabatur.Est aũt apostrophe ad serpẽtem.python quoque est ut solinus scribit:in asia campus patẽtissimus:quo prio aduentus sui ciconiæ aduolãt. Porro Pythopolys duarum est Vrbium nomẽ quarũ altera Mysiæ altera cariæ est. Tantũ spatii de monte tenebas. Acclamatio ẽ:q̃ magnitudo serpẽtis declaratur. Tenebas. Occupabas. Deus arcitenẽs. Apollo q cũ arcu & pharetra pingebatur. Capreisq; fugacibus. Capreæ capræ sunt syluestres uelocissimæ. Exhausta.euacuata.Pharetra aũt sagittarũ ẽ repositoriũ.

Terror eras: tantum spatii de monte tenebas.
Hunc deus arcitenens & nunq̃ talibus armis
Ante nisi in damis capreisque fugacibus usus:
Mille grauem telis exhausta pene pharetra
Perdidit effuso per uulnera nigra ueneno.
Ne ue operis famam posset delere uetustas:
Instituit sacros celebri certamine ludos:
Pythia perdomitę serpentis nomine dictos.
Hic iuuenum quicũq; manu pedibus ue rota ue
Vicerat; æsculeæ capiebat frondis honorem.
Nondum laurus erat. longoq; decentia crine
Tempora cingebat de qualibet arbore phœbus.
Primus amor phębi daphne peneia: quem non
Sors ignara dedit: sed sæua cupidinis ira.
Delius hunc nuper uicto serpente superbus
Viderat adducto flectentem cornua neruo.
Quidq; tibi lasciue puer cum fortibus armis?
Dixerat. ista decent humeros gestamina nostros:
Qui dare certa feræ. dare ulnera possumus hosti.
Qui mõ pestifero tot iugera uentre prementem
Strauimus innumeris tumidum pythona sagittis.
Tu face nescio quos esto contentus amores
Irritare tua: nec laudes assere nostras.
Filius huic ueneris, figat tuus omnia phœbe:
Te meus arcus ait. quantoq; animalia cedunt
Cũcta deo: tanto minor est tua gloria nostra.
Dixit. & eliso percussis aere pennis
Impiger umbrosa parnassi constitit arce.
Deq; sagitifera prompsit duo tela pharetra

Per uulnera nigra Hypallage est nigrũ.n. uenenũ p uulnera effusum itelligimus. Hic iuuenũ qcũq;. Quisq̃s iquit Pythia uicisset aut pugnis.aut cursu.aut curru æsculea corona donabatur. Rotaue Vel curru. Vt a pte totũ itelligamus. Esculeæ frondis honorẽ. coronã ex frõdibus esculi cõfectã. Nã Esculus arbor ẽ glandifera dicta qd prisci ex illius fructu escam sumerẽt. Nõdum laurus erat. Cõcinne mutationem sequẽtem cũ superioribus connectit. Assignans enim cãm cur pythiorũ uictores æsculeam coronã acciperent: laurũ: qua postea qui uicissent: fuere coronati: nõdũ fuisse ait. sicq; describit: queãdmodum Daphne Penei fluuii filia ab Apolline fuit amata qua cum nec pce nec pcio potiri posset: ad uim se se cõuertit. Ipsa uero fuga sibi consulẽs: cũ in eo esset ut caperetur: patrẽ rogauit: ut sibi auxilium ferret. Ille uero pcibus filiæ motus eã in arborem sui nominis cõmutauit. Daphne.n.laurus iterpraetatur. Est etiam Daphne ut strabo ait. Antiochiæ uicinum & amœnitate inclytum nemus octoginta stadiorum ambitu: quo i loco Antiochensiũ conuentus agitabatur. Appellatũ ẽ aũt a Daphne Ladonis filia ut Arrianus scribit. Dionysius uero sacra tẽpe locus eũ uocauit. Decẽtia tpa. Pulchrum caput: ut a pte totũ p synegdochẽ itelligamus. Lõgo crine. lõgis capillis. Peneia. Penei fluuii filia. possessiua.n. frequẽter p patronymicis & cõtra p possessiuis patronymica ponũtur. Aphthonius uero Daphnen Ladonis filiã fuisse ait. Sors ignara. Fortuna iperita: q̃ nullũ rerũ habet delectũ. Sed sæua cupidinis ira. sed magna dei amoris indignatio. cupido nãq; masculini generis deũ significat amoris. Fœminini uero cupiditatẽ. Duos uero cupidines eẽ plato i symposio scribit. alterum cæleste & diuinũ: alterum uulgarẽ atq; plebeiũ. Id qd Ouidius i fastis secutus eẽ uidetur: cũ inqt Alma faue dixi geminorum mater amorum. Græci cupidinẽ Erota uocãt. Vñ heroes denoiatos eẽ plato ait i cratylo. Deus aũt q amori cõtrarius ẽ amorẽq; dissoluit: anteros uocat q ut cicero i tertio d natura deorum scribit. ex Venere natus ẽ & marte. Delius hũc nup. quo mõ i amorẽ Daphnes Apollo iciderit: poeta describit ita pspicue: ut nulla fere opus sit expositiõe. Delius Apollo a Delo isula cognominatus: i q̃ una cũ Diana natus eẽ pibetur. Adducto neruo. gestũ exprimit sagittariorum. Tot iugera. Iugerũ tãtũ terræ dicitur quãtũ par boũ i die uno exarare põt. Strauimus. Prostrauimus. iterfecimus. Sterni.n. stantia dñr cũ i terrã deiciunt. Tumidũ. Inflatũ. Supbia elatũ. Nescio quos amores. Cũ quodã cõtẽptu hæc dñr: ac si diceret leues molles atq; uiris negligẽdos. Iritare. puocare stimulare. Tua face. Tibi cõueniente. Fax ãt cupidĩ attribuit: q̃ iuuenũ ai amore iflamant. Nec assere. arroga. Vẽdica. Filius huic Veneris. Cupido. Figat tuus. Licet cõiũctio subitelligẽda ur. Licet inqt tuus arcus oia aialia figat: meũ tñ tu effugere ñ poteris. Sicq; glia tua tãto minor ẽ q̃ nostra: q̃to aialia. q̃ tu feris: deo sunt iferiora. Eliso aere. Impulso. Percussis pennis. alis. Nam alatus Cupido pingitur. Arce. cacumĩe. Vertice. Prompsit. Deprompsit. excepit.

Daphne i laurum

b iii

Figure 5: A page from Regius' commentary on the *Metamorphoses*, containing his notes on *Met.* 1.440–68 (Herzog August Bibliothek Wolfenbüttel).

and Venice. In addition to the commentary on the *Metamorphoses*, he also produced a commentary on the *Rhetorica ad Herennium*, Quintilian and Persius (Malta 1997). His commentary reflects the humanistic ideal of learning, so for him the *Metamorphoses* is not simply a repository of fable, but 'the basis of a sound liberal education' (Moss 1982: 29). As he puts it in his preface:

> et in primis adolescentibus laudatarum artium studio destinatis sit praelegendum. Non solum enim ueteres historiae quae propter antiquitatem fabularum loco habentur: ex uetustissimis auctoribus collectae eleganter ab Ouidio describuntur: sed ita et geographiae et astrologiae et musicae et artis oratoriae. et moralis naturalisque philosophiae ratio exprimitur: ut cui Ouidii metamorphosis bene percepta sit: facillimum ad omnes disciplinas aditum habiturus . . . esse uideatur.

> And in particular it should be read to young people bound for the study of the accomplished arts. For not only are the old stories (considered fantastic on account of their antiquity), which Ovid has gathered from the earliest sources, elegantly recounted by him; but in like manner he expresses the basis for geography, astrology, music, rhetoric, and philosophy, both moral and natural. As a result anyone who has well understood Ovid's *Metamorphoses* seems likely to have quite easy access to all disciplines.

The moral element remains an important factor in Regius' readings, but stripped now for the most part of its allegorical overlay. So the story of Daphne teaches a lesson, but it is not an overtly Christian message:

> Quid Daphnes in laurum semper uirentem transfiguratione aliud nobis significari putandum est: quam Virginibus pudoris sui sollicitam gerentibus curam immortalem gloriam esse praeparatam?

> What else should we think is signified by the transformation of Daphne into an ever-green laurel than that undying fame awaits maidens who take considered care for their modesty?

Regius also acknowledges the imperatives of inculcating moral virtues and cultivating an elevated Latin style, but his notes address the concerns of a secular society (Moss 1982: 28–31). The commentator's chief task, as Regius sees it, is 'to provide a corrected text and to explain matters that appear to be too difficult in such a way that they can easily be grasped' (*emendate legere: et quae difficiliora videantur: ita exponere: ut facile percipi possint*). His notes accordingly address a wide range of practical difficulties encountered by readers, explaining proper names, glossing unusual words or phrases, explicating allusions, by drawing on a wide range of classical authorities: in his preface he lists 46 Greek poets as sources for the *Metamorphoses*. Regius was not as accomplished a scholar as Poliziano, but his predecessor's influence is evident in his more focused application of philological methods to the explication of the text (Guthmüller 1975: 125–31).

Subsequent commentators on the *Metamorphoses* in the sixteenth century saw their task rather as supplementing, correcting, or refining the work of Regius. The first edition of the observations on the *Metamorphoses* of Jacobus Micyllus (Jacob Moltzer; Classen 1859), which appeared in Basel in 1543, was presented as notes worked into the commentary of Regius. Ercole Ciofani, a native of Ovid's home town, Sulmo, and a passionate advocate of his ancient countryman (Lettere 1981), compiled notes related to Regius' commentary, but focusing almost exclusively on textual matters (Ciofanus 1583). This exemplified a trend in critical work on Ovid, in which the divide between textual criticism and critical exegesis opened wider. In Ovidian scholarship the true heir of the humanist tradition exemplified by Poliziano and Regius was the great Dutch critic Nicolaus Heinsius (Blok 1949), whose edition of Ovid's works in the mid-seventeenth century (Amsterdam 1652) marks a watershed in Ovidian studies. Heinsius' notes, which accompany a reprint of his father's text of Ovid, are a mine of information for the literary critic, bringing together a wealth of information on Ovidian imitations and allusions, for example, but their primary focus is the constitution of the text, not literary exegesis. For that aspect of the *Metamorphoses*, and of Ovid's other works, the student and reader applied to other authorities.

Alongside the commentary of Regius a strain of allegorical interpretation continued to flourish into the sixteenth century and beyond. As early as 1516, the allegorizing notes, or *tropologicae enarrationes*, of Petrus Lavinius, a Dominican friar from Lyons, were incorporated into editions together with Regius' commentary (Moss 1982: 31–6). Among the most influential of the new allegorical commentaries was the *Fabularum Ovidii interpretatio* by Georgius Sabinus, rector of the university of Königsberg, which first appeared in 1554 (Moss 1982: 48–53). The interpretations emphasize rather the compatibility of Ovid with Christian morals, although in many respects the influence of Regius' commentary can be detected. Thus, Sabinus' interpretation of Daphne more closely borrows from Regius than Bersuire: *Ipsius vero Daphnes in arborem semper virentem mutatio docet immortalem gloriam esse paratam virginibus pudicitiam conseruantibus* ('Indeed, Daphne's change into an ever-green tree teaches that undying glory awaits maidens who preserve their modesty'). And allegorical interpretations found in the notes of commentators continued to inform allegorical modes of writing by poets in the Renaissance (Allen 1970; Murrin 1980; Quint 1983).

Exegesis in the Nineteenth Century and After

The intensification of standards of philological scholarship that characterized classical scholarship of the nineteenth century had paradoxical effects on the commentary tradition on Ovid. In part because of the prevailing preferences for Virgil and Horace, who could be read in ways more congenial to contemporary ideologies of political and cultural authority, Ovid's works attracted relatively little scholarly attention, and more importantly did not attract the greater lights. Although there were notable exceptions, for the most part Ovid's amatory works, exile poetry, and the *Fasti* did not participate in the explosion of commentaries on Latin poets in the latter part of that century. Some of the best exegesis of Ovid is to be found in the commentaries produced for schools during this period, for although Ovid had never been thought suitable for the curriculum in antiquity, in the late-nineteenth-century and early-twentieth-century schoolroom he was prized for the accessibility of his Latin and the liveliness of his manner. And so, while a copious commentary on the *Heroides* was begun by Arthur Palmer (1898) and completed by his colleague Louis Purser, in many respects it can be compared unfavorably with the more modest school edition of an appropriately demure selection of epistles by Shuckburgh (1879) for the classic series of school editions published by Macmillan between the once ubiquitous red covers. While scholars on the Continent were primarily interested in textual criticism, the major contribution to the Ovidian commentary tradition during this period was an attempt to provide a comprehensive guide to the *Metamorphoses*. The project was initiated by Moriz Haupt, a disciple of Karl Lachmann, with the publication of a commentary on the first seven books of the poem (1853). The project was eventually completed by a student of his, Otto Korn, and subsequently revised and reprinted several times (Haupt et al. 1966), but the notes rarely rise beyond the level of para-phrase and gloss. On Daphne, for example, Haupt has only this to say: 'The nymph Daphne flees from Apollo's love and is changed into a laurel tree.'

The encyclopedic tendencies of the Continental tradition of commentary that crested late in the twentieth century left their mark on Ovid with the massive commentary on *Metamorphoses* by Bömer, produced in seven volumes over seven-teen years (1969–86). In his introductory remarks Bömer betrays his intuition that a commentary should in fact address other needs, and his own work would be more aptly called 'Remarks on Ovid's *Metamorphoses*' (Bömer 1969: 5). The result is to fragmentize interpretation of the poem, by focusing on the individual word or phrase, with almost resolute avoidance of literary exegesis (Kenney 1972). Where earlier generations of commentators saw it as part of their business to explain the significance of Ovid's tales, from either a religious or moralizing point of view, this is a task that Bömer implicitly defers to others. Daphne is for him neither a literary motif to be explained nor a moral to be pointed, and while he notes that it is no accident that this is the first mythological metamorphosis in the poem (1969: 145), for an explanation the reader is merely referred to Fränkel (1945: 78), while Bömer meanwhile limits his notes to, for example, parallels for *amor* used concretely for 'beloved'.

Current Trends and Future Prospects

The traditional format of the commentary continues to serve as the primary vehicle for making Ovid accessible to readers as new approaches to his works develop in what has emerged as a new *aetas Ovidiana* in recent decades. In tandem with the produc-tion of new critical editions, new commentaries have begun to appear at an accelerat-ing rate. The range of approaches reflects the history of the commentary itself, as well as trends in interpreting Ovid. Once among the most commonly read of Ovid's works, the *Heroides* endured a long period of critical neglect, only to re-emerge as the focus of intense critical activity late in the twentieth century. The profusion of articles and monographs has been accompanied by numerous commentaries on individual poems and selections of poems, a flood that continues unabated. The *Amores* seldom formed part of any curriculum in twentieth-century Latin classrooms, but they are now the focus of one of the most ambitious individual projects on any Latin text. McKeown's four-volume commentary (1987, 1989, 1998, the fourth and final volume has yet to appear) includes also a volume of prolegomena and a critical edition of the poems, while attempting in its copious notes to address Ovid's language, style, and literary interpretation.

In the current proliferation of commentaries on Ovid, it is still the *Metamorphoses* which best illustrates the link with past commentary traditions and the connection with contemporary critical trends. Two recent commentaries illustrate a turn away from the exclusive focus on the individual word or phrase toward a more comprehensive approach that embraces both philological explication and literary exegesis. The Pléiade edition of the *Metamorphoses* (Paduano et al. 2000) contains a text and translation, accompanied by over 800 pages of commentary by Luigi Galasso, that deserve to be more widely known among anglophone readers. Galasso's commentary offers broad surveys on major sections of the poem, offering a guide to reading that shows him as an heir to the tradition of commentary inaugurated by Regius. The new commentary under the general supervision of Alessandro Barchiesi likewise makes gestures to the tradition of variorum commentaries, with portions of the poem allocated to a diverse group of scholars. The appearance of the first volumes (Barchiesi 2005; Barchiesi and Rosati 2007) is further testimony to the vitality of the commentary tradition in continually refashioning our readings of Ovid.

FURTHER READING

The only usable editions of the *Narrationes* are to be found in Magnus (1914) and Slater (1927). Many medieval commentaries on Ovid remain unpublished and can only be inspected in special collections. Coulson's contribution on Ovid in Kristeller et al. (1960–) is eagerly awaited; information about manuscripts containing medieval commentaries on Ovid can be gleaned from Coulson and Roy (2000). Translations of some medieval material can be found in Elliott (1980) and Minnis and Scott (1988). Much Renaissance scholarship also remains unpublished, but as libraries move to digitize their manuscript and rare-book collections this material will become more accessible. The commentary on the *Metamorphoses* by Raffaele Regio, for example, is available online at http://diglib.hat.de/inkunabeln/11-3-poet-2f-1/start.htm, as well as in a facsimile edition (Orgel 1976). Moss (1998) offers sample translations from the most influential Latin commentaries of the sixteenth and seventeenth centuries. Friis-Jensen et al. (1997) is a very helpful resource for the medieval and early Renaissance periods, as is the splendid catalogue to the collection of early printed editions in the Bodleian (Coates et al. 2005). In recent years the role of the commentary as a work of criticism and thus as a vehicle for the reception of classical literature is increasingly the focus of scholarly discussion; starting points for listening in would include the essays collected in Most (1999) and Gibson and Kraus (2002).

CHAPTER TWENTY-FOUR

Ovidian Intertextuality

Sergio Casali

Introduction

The first word that Ovid published, the first word of the first elegy of the first book of the *Amores*, is a 'quotation': <u>*arma*</u> *graui numero* ('<u>weapons</u> with solemn rhythm'). Ovid begins his elegiac collection by creating in the reader the false expectation of an epic poem (as it is well known, the first word of a Latin work could be also used as its title), and in order to do that he 'quotes' the first word of the *Aeneid*. Further-more, as McKeown notes (1989: 12), 'not only is the distribution of consonants in Ovid's first line closely comparable to that in Vergil's, but also the sequence of vowels in the first hemistich corresponds almost exactly (Verg.: *a, a, i, u, e, a, o*—Ov.: *a, a, a, i, u, e, o*; i.e. only an *a* has been displaced). The correspondence of vowels seems too precise to be coincidental.' Ovid begins his poetic career with the most intertex-tual move one could imagine, and the rest of his work will be fully consistent with this beginning. Attention to Ovid's intertextual strategies (quotations, sources, models) has always played a fundamental role in the study of his poetry; but it is true that a turning point, a tangible intensification of the interest in this aspect of the Ovidian corpus, emerged in the middle of the 1970s, to coincide with the rise of a theoretical interest in the very concept of intertextuality in classical literature. It is not by chance that from then on Ovid has been (together with Virgil) the undisputed protagonist of the most important attempts at verifying the various theories of inter-textuality. It is clearly impossible to review in a systematic way all intertextual studies on Ovid, which would require a review of nearly the whole of the Ovidian bibliog-raphy. So, I will limit myself to some key works, indicating also some critical genealo-gies which have played a significant role in stimulating subsequent research.

Mars' and Ariadne's Memories

We can start from the book which has had the greatest influence on recent intertextual studies in Latin. In Conte's chapter entitled 'History and System in the Memory of

Poets', the first two examples of intertextuality discussed are from Ovid (1985: 35–9 = 1986a: 60–3), and for their suggestiveness they have had a success even independent from the theoretical context in which they are located (where Conte suggests an assimilation of poetic memory to a rhetorical function). In the *Metamorphoses*, in the context of the apotheosis of Romulus, Mars reminds Jupiter that once upon a time, in an earlier council of the gods, he had promised to receive Romulus in the sky (*Met.* 15.812–15):

> tu mihi concilio quondam praesente deorum
> (nam memoro memorique animo pia verba notaui)
> 'unus erit, quem tu tolles in caerula caeli'
> dixisti . . .

> Once upon a time, in a council of the gods, you told me (I still remember your pious words: I keep them fixed in my memory): 'There will be one of the yours which you will raise into the blue regions of the sky.'

And in the *Fasti* (2.483–9), Mars speaks in the same way, with the same quotation of Jupiter's words (487). Now, the words of Jupiter's that Mars recalls reproduce exactly a line of the *Annals* of Ennius (fr. 54 Sk.), where in fact Jupiter made that promise to Mars.

A similar instance occurs elsewhere in the *Fasti*, when Ariadne is desperate because Bacchus, the god who had saved her and married her when Theseus had abandoned her on a desert island, has now brought with him from a voyage the daughter of an Indian king to be his lover. Ovid's Ariadne is once again bemoaning her misfortunes on a beach, exactly as when Theseus abandoned her (*Fast.* 3.471–5):

> En iterum, fluctus, similis audite querellas.
>   en iterum lacrimas accipe, harena, meas.
> Dicebam, memini, 'periure et perfide Theseu!';
>   Ille abiit, eadem crimina Bacchus habet.
> Nunc quoque 'Nulla uiro', clamabo, 'femina credat'.

> There, oh waves, yet again hear my laments, similar to my ancient ones! There, oh beach, yet again receive my tears! I used to say, I remember, 'deceitful and perjured Theseus!' He left, and now Bacchus does the same wrong to me. Now again I'll cry: 'Let no woman trust a man!'

In this case, the words Ariadne 'remembers' are the words she had pronounced in the key text for the story of Ariadne in Latin poetry, Catullus' Poem 64 (132–5, 143–4):

> Sicine me patriis auectam, *perfide*, ab aris,
> *perfide*, deserto liquistis in litore, *Theseu?*
> Sicine discedens neglecto numine diuum
> immemor, a, deuota domus *periuria* portas?
> . . . nunc iam *nulla uiro* iuranti *femina credat*,
> nulla uiri speret sermones esse fidelis.

Is this the way, then, *treacherous, treacherous Theuses*, you carried me off from the altars of my fathers for abandoning me on a lonely shore? Is this the way you leave, without fearing the power of the gods—feckless!—to carry home accursed *false oaths?* . . . Now *let no woman believe* any more *a man* who makes an oath, let no woman expect that the words of a man are trustworthy'.

In his discussion of these examples, Conte is interested in making a distinction between allusion as *metaphor* and allusion as *simile*: the first case represents standard allusions, where one poetical phrase alludes to a preceding phrase of another author, and by doing so it assumes for itself the sense, or part of the sense, of the phrase to which it refers ('integrative allusion'); to the second case belong the Ovidian examples, where the memory of the character is, so to speak, tautological, and does not effect any addition in meaning ('reflexive allusion'). Ovid's strategy here is simply to call attention to the very literariness of his discourse, to his operation in a wholly inter-textual world, where the stories already narrated by others can be taken up and continued without a break. The character 'remembers' what is remembered by the poet and the reader; from Ennius or Catullus we can pass to Ovid without any problem.

Conte's discussion of these two examples will recur many times in other treatments of Ovid's literary self-consciousness. For example, Hinds (1987b: 17) recalls the example of Ariadne as 'an especially clear instance of self-referential elaboration of allusion', pointing out that the use of the word *memini* in that passage as a reference to the literary tradition can be seen as an especially elaborated instance of the so-called 'Alexandrian footnote' (Ross 1975: 78), namely the use of words and phrases referring to 'relating' and 'narrating' (e.g. *dicitur, ferunt, fama est*) as techniques for pointing out a poetic allusion. Subsequently, Miller (1993) performed a systematic study of Ovid's use of *memini* and similar phrases for referring to the re-use of a preceding text.

Literary Existence and the Self-consciousness of Poetry

The attention that Conte attracted to these Ovidian examples functioned as a power-ful stimulus to the development of the study of Ovid's 'intertextual imagination', especially in Italy. In 1974 Conte's analysis clearly emphasized the 'artificiality' of Ovid's poetry, its character as metapoetry. Five years later, in the second issue of a new journal edited by Conte himself, Rosati published an article entitled 'Literary existence: Ovid and the self-consciousness of poetry', which can be seen as a real manifesto for the 'formalist' and self-reflexive approach to Ovid's poetry. Rosati's opening words already point the way to an important trend in Ovidian studies (1979: 101): 'To investigate the poetics of Ovid, the last of those who seemed to realize the happy season of poetry at Rome and at the same time the self-conscious heir to Latin "classicism", means to investigate the degree of self-consciousness acquired by that poetry in its most mature expression. Already in his great predecessors Ovid saw how poetry had retreated into itself, had interrogated itself about its own identity (and not only in the frequent discussions of poetics in neoteric and Augustan poetry), also because the need for an answer had become more pressing. Having by now acquired a firm certainty about a role of its own, poetry will not limit itself to protesting its necessity, it will peremptorily claim other rights.'

Rosati takes Book 2 of the *Tristia* as a point of departure. In that poem one can see the very essence of Ovid's poetry: 'art is not the reflex of reality, the sphere of the one is not connected to that of the other by a necessary relationship of identity and mimesis'. Rosati constructs an Ovidian poetics of the autonomy of poetry on the basis of a review of Ovid's programmatic declarations in the course of his production. Intertextuality is an essential element in such a poetics. In this respect, the close of the *Metamorphoses* (15.871–9) is a key example for Rosati (1979: 119–21): 'Vergil too had predicted the immortality of the *Aeneid*, basing it on the immortal destiny of Rome (*Aen.* 9.446–9); and Horace, with greater autonomy, had declared his trust in his own poetic *monumentum* by connecting this eternity, as an outcome parallel to, but independent from, the *Capitolium* (*Carm.* 3.30.1–9). In contrast, Ovid does not take the eternity of Rome as a guarantee of his own immortality; for line 877 [*quaque patet domitis Romana potentia terris*, 'where Roman power extends in conquered lands'] indicates a geographical, not a temporal, extension, to indicate the immense space of the known world. Rather he invokes the 'prophecies of the poets' [879, *uatum praesagia*]: it is they that are the guarantors that assure the eternity of his work, if they have any truth (and *sunt quiddam oracula uatum*: *Pont.* 2.1.55). Paradoxically, the poet's trust in his eternal glory is not based any more on an external element, on a datum of reality, but on the firm self-consciousness of poetry itself, which in that way defines the parameters of its own destiny: as if to say, poetry is immortal, because poetry says so. The only certainty, the only benchmark in relationship to which it is possible to measure the duration of things is not Rome any more, but the eternity of poetry: a significant proof of the degree of autonomy that it has achieved and that it does not hesitate to claim. It is in this way, above all, that one can appreciate the meaning of Ovid's explicit reference to Horace's *sphragis*: if it is true, as Ovid affirms, that the glory of the poets finds the guarantee of its eternity in the *praesagia uatum*, what better way for the poet himself to affirm the proud certainty of his own immortality than to found it, through the gesture of the allusion, on the *praesagia* of a *uates* already consecrated to this glory? The reference to Horace, to that *praesagium*, the truth of which the years were already demonstrating, guaranteed an immortal fame to the person who affirmed such fame in the internal logic of the poetry itself. The measure of the duration of Ovid's work is here the work of Horace, a firmer certainty than that Rome to which the poet cannot get out of paying the ritual homage, though in a shrewdly restrictive way.'

The article closes with a discussion of the concept of intertextuality and the term itself (Rosati 1979: 135–6): 'Conscious of its unyielding otherness from the real, [literature] withdraws into its most authentic dimension: it evades common reality to live in a sort of recreated world, namely the literary Text. Then, those who live in the space of fiction, those who exist in the literary universe are no longer *mendacium*: they acquire an identity of their own, a reality of their own in the realm of appearance. Jupiter and Mars, Ariadne, Byblis, Ulysses, and the other "inhabitants" of literary myth are conscious of an identity and of a past of their own, for which they feel responsible; they are aware of a literary existence of their own that they have already lived in countless other texts. In Ovid's text, where they become aware of this, they come out to declare this awareness of their own, to acknowledge their literary nature. Literature awakens to its nature as an intersection of relations, as a combination of texts: in *intertextuality* it singles out its true dimension. The *sign reifies itself, it becomes the referent*: literature refers only to itself. And then, having definitely escaped the tutelage of the real . . ., this poetry will necessarily be nothing but reflected poetry, poetry which looks at itself in the mirror, and narcissistically alludes to itself.'

With his reference to Jupiter and Ariadne Rosati obviously alludes to Conte's treatment mentioned above; by referring to Byblis and Ulysses he hints at two other articles published in that period: Ranucci (1976), which shows how Byblis in *Met.* 9 self-consciously refers to a different version of her own story, and Labate (1980). In his short note Labate gives another suggestive example of Ovid's attitude toward the stories he narrates and the memory of his characters. In the course of his quarrel with Ulysses for Achilles' weapons in *Met.* 13, Ajax emphasizes that Achilles' shining weapons are not apt for someone like Ulysses, who is accustomed to fighting in night ambushes: the brightness of the helmet could reveal him to the enemy (*Met.* 13.105–6), and the weight of the armor could slow him down (13.115–6). Ajax is surely reminding Ulysses of the context of Homer's *Doloneia* in the tenth book of the *Iliad*, but not so much in the version that Ulysses has really 'lived' (in *Il.* 10), as in the remake which Virgil has made of it in *Aen.* 9: it is there that Euryalus, Ulysses' unlucky literary heir, is revealed to the enemies by the brightness of Messapus' helmet, which he has seized in the course of the night slaughter (*Aen.* 9.373–4), and is slowed down in his escape by the weight of the weapons he has stolen (9.384–5).

Speaking Volumes: The *Heroides* and Intertextual Irony

Alessandro Barchiesi, who had already made an important contribution to the study of intertextuality in Virgil (Barchiesi 1984), is the scholar who has most systematically developed these approaches to Ovid's intertextuality with a series of articles published from the middle of the 1980s (now collected in Barchiesi 2001a). The first of these articles has as its subtitle 'Continuities of the Stories, Continuations of the Texts' (Barchiesi 1986), and, in the familiar form of a collection of short exegetical essays, it offers a number of observations, which lead eventually to a concluding section entitled 'Ovid's Intertextual Imagination'. With this, attention begins to focus on a work of Ovid which was until then rather undervalued, notwithstanding the important monograph of Jacobson (1974), and which was destined to become the main testing ground for analyzing Ovid's intertextual dynamics: the *Heroides*.

There is a sort of 'little *Herois*' also in *Rem.* 263–88, where Circe vainly tries to detain Ulysses. In order to do that, she reminds him, among other things, of the fact that 'a new Troy is not rising again here, (i.e. in Latium, *non hic noua Troia resurgit*), nobody is calling again allies to arms (*Rem.* 281–2). In this case, it is not Circe's literary competence that is being called into question; rather, it is her incompetence:

the sorceress does not know that the things she is presenting to Ulysses as impossible are destined to happen soon after. As the reader of the *Aeneid* knows, a new Trojan War really is on the verge of being fought in Latium, and it is precisely there where a new Troy is fated to rise again: as the disguised Venus says to Aeneas in *Aen.* 1.205–6: *tendimus in Latium . . . / . . . illic fas regna resurgere Troiae* ('we are moving toward Latium . . . there it is granted that the kingdom of Troy rise again') (Barchiesi 1986: 82–93). In this case we find again the same passion for chronological intersections of the stories (Ulysses sails along the coasts of Italy just before the arrival of Aeneas), and we also find a sharing of literary competence between author and reader behind the heroine's back: it happens that she inadvertently anticipates with extreme precision the (intertextual) future in the exact moment when her situation of ignorance is most acute.

This Ovidian technique—ironic prefiguring realized through intertextual anticipation, when a character who lives in a precise moment of the model-text 'unintentionally' foretells his/her own future or others' by using words destined to appear in the continuation of the model-text—finds prominent application in the *Heroides*. The whole of Ovid's work is profoundly intertextual, but certain works and certain parts find their very *raison d'être* in intertextuality. The *Heroides* are elegiac letters that are imagined as written by literary heroines in a precise moment of the 'high level' (usually epic or tragic) text in which they have already lived the most important of their literary lives. They know their past, and they reinterpret it elegiacally (transcoding their story from one genre to another, elegy); but they do not know their future, and readers will amuse themselves in recognizing the unintentional quotation, behind the heroine's back, as has been recently lamented by scholars who have tried to confer new power to the Ovidian heroines (Spentzou 2003).

A very important stimulus to intertextual study of the *Heroides* was provided by Kennedy's oft-cited article (1984) on the epistle of Penelope. Kennedy proposes to take seriously the epistolary status of the first series of the *Heroides* (1–15), and so he asks exactly when and why Penelope writes her letter to Ulysses (*Her.* 1). Asking these questions means to ask when and why Penelope writes within the narrative world of the *Odyssey*, which is the 'objective' reality against which we read *Her.* 1. As for the reason why Penelope writes, we know what the woman says in *Her.* 1.59–62: Penelope asks questions about her husband of every stranger who arrives at Ithaca, and gives them a letter to hand to Ulysses, if ever they should meet him. Clearly, then, someone has arrived at Ithaca now also. And when does Penelope write her letter? We know from lines 37–8 that the letter is clearly dated to the day when Telemachus came back to Ithaca from Sparta and related some news to Penelope about his father. But from the *Odyssey* we also know that the meeting between Telemachus and Penelope takes place the morning before the day on which the suitors are killed. When Penelope writes her letter, therefore, Odysseus, disguised as a Cretan beggar, is already on Ithaca, and very likely it is to him that Penelope is going to give the letter addressed to her husband: 'once we realize it, much of what Penelope says takes on considerable irony: her appeal to Ulysses not to write back, but to come in person (2), her complaints about how slowly time passes for her (7 f.), about how she does not know where he is (57 f.), and above all the closing couplet of the poem, in which she laments "I, who was a girl when you left, though you should come home *immediately* (*protinus ut uenias*, 116), will seem to have become an old woman". Penelope will not have to wait very long to find out her husband's reaction to the physical changes the intervening twenty years have wrought in her' (Kennedy 1984: 417). Kennedy also points out the importance, until now undervalued, of foreshadowing in the poetics of the *Heroides* (1984: 420).

It is precisely with a quotation from Kennedy that Barchiesi begins his article on 'Narrativity and Convention in the *Heroides*' (1987), in which he combines Kennedy's interest in the 'cut' of the model-texts in which the epistles are written with analysis of the crucial importance of the genre of Roman elegy for the poetics of the *Heroides* (cf. Spoth 1992). The essential feature of elegy is the 'constant effect of an individual voice, which attracts toward itself every theme', reinterpreting it monologically. In the same way, the writers of the *Heroides* reinterpret texts which belonged to other genres in the light of the elegiac code (on the concept cf. Conte 1989) and of their monological subjectivity (Barchiesi 1987: 68): 'the contribution of elegy is different, in terms of its quality, from the influences of other genres, because it is not only a matter of materials and narrative techniques, and not even of a unifying theme, love, but above all of a unifying perspective. Elegy teaches the heroines how one can "reduce" every external reality by attracting it toward the *persona* of the lover; and how one can nourish a poetical discourse through the resistance, the unyieldingness of a personal point of view toward the "external" world, while partiality of the point of view and pragmatic direction (the intention of the *Werbung*, the elegiac courtship) back each other up.'

Ironic prefiguring is systematically treated in Barchiesi (1993). A particularly compelling example is found at the beginning of *Her.* 4, where Phaedra begins her seductive letter to Hippolytus with an exhortation to read her epistle without any fear: *Perlege, quodcumque est. Quid epistula lecta nocebit?* (*Her.* 4.3 'Read it all, for what it is worth: what harm can come from reading a letter?') But Ovid's readers know that, on the contrary, letters can be very harmful: it will be the false letter which Phaedra herself, in Euripides' *Hippolytus* (one of the main model-texts of *Her.* 4), will leave on her corpse after her suicide, in which she falsely accuses her stepson of having attempted to seduce her, in order to provoke the anger of Theseus and Hippolytus' own death (Barchiesi 1993: 337).

The studies of Barchiesi have inspired much new criticism of the *Heroides*, both in Italy and in the English-speaking world. Deianira's epistle (9), for instance, has been studied in the light of his work on ironic prefiguring. Deianira insists that Hercules—the hero who has not been destroyed by his many labors and the hatred of his stepmother Juno—has been shamefully conquered by a woman, who has subjected him to her erotic power (namely, Iole, his new concubine, and before her the queen Omphale). Deianira inadvertently anticipates in elegiac-metaphorical terms (the shame of the *servitium amoris*) the laments which Hercules himself will pronounce in the model-text Sophocles' *Trachiniae* when he, the great hero never conquered by any enemy, will be destroyed, in fact, by a woman—Deianira herself, who has poisoned him to death with the gift of the deadly robe of Nessus the centaur (Casali 1995c).

Furthermore, it has been noticed that even when Ovid's model-text has not been preserved, it is possible to verify how the epistles play upon an ironically 'elegiac' prefiguring of the future events that the heroines will meet. Williams (1992) has analyzed the structure of Euripides' lost *Aeolus* and has described the dramatic irony that pervades the letter of Canace (*Her.* 11). Canace writes to her brother Macareus, for whom she has conceived an incestuous love, immediately before committing suicide, as she has been commanded to do by her father Aeolus after his discovery that they have had a baby. Nevertheless, the reader who knows Euripides' *Aeolus* knows that in the very moment when Canace is lamenting her father's unshakeable cruelty and the inexorability of her fate, Macareus is begging Aeolus to spare her life. And the reader also knows that Macareus' attempt is successful: Aeolus annuls the death sentence and Macareus rushes to bring the news to his sister. But it is too late: Canace is dead and Macareus kills himself in turn. The awareness of this tragic irony provides new resonance to the whole epistle.

More recently, again taking her bearings from Kennedy's seminal article (1984) to focus attention on the precise circumstances of the epistolary moment, Fulkerson (2003) suggests that the real addressee of Hypermestra's epistle (*Her.* 14) is not the 'official' one, namely Lynceus, but instead her father Danaus, who keeps her imprisoned. In fact, it is very likely that he will succeed in intercepting and reading the letter. So it is to him, more than to Lynceus, that Hypermestra writes, a strategy that for once will be successful, since, as every reader knows, the heroine is destined to survive and found a royal line at Argos.

Intertextuality and Word Plays: Looking for Ovidian Subtlety

In 1987 Stephen Hinds, author of an important monograph (1987a), to be discussed below, as well as a valuable theoretical reflection on intertextuality (1998), published a general article on Ovid (1987b), which has also played a significant role in the intensification of the scholarly interest in this author. In this article Hinds proposes to counteract three commonplaces about Ovid: (1) that he is a superficial and overly explicit poet, (2) that he is excessively literary, and (3) that he is a passive panegyrist. In arguing against these generalizations, Hinds writes what we can call a veritable manifesto in support of the tendency to take Ovid's lack of seriousness very seriously, especially in the field of intertextuality. The kind of intensified subtlety of analysis that Hinds proposes for Ovid's intertextuality is exemplified in *Am.* 1.5, where, as previous critics have noticed, Ovid describes Corinna's entrance into the bedroom in a way possibly reminiscent of the entrance of Lesbia into the house of Catullus 68. Hinds goes further and sees in Ovid's diction a precise intertextual reference to Catullus: *ecce, Corinna uenit tunica uelata recincta, / candida diuidua colla tegente coma* . . . (*Am.* 1.5.9–10, 'Lo! Corinna comes, draped in an ungirt tunic, with her divided hair covering her fair neck . . .') alludes to Catullus 68.70–1: *quo mea se molli candida diua pede / intulit* . . . ('there with gentle foot my fair goddess made an entry . . .'). As Hinds puts it (1987b: 8), 'The reference to the Catullan goddess is offered for an instant only, as the pentameter opens—only to be withdrawn, as the syntax of the line completes itself. Corinna is not, after all, a *candida diva*: the epiphany fades. The adjective qualifies her *colla*, not herself; and *div-* emerges as the first syllable of *dividua*, qualifying *coma*.' This pushes the envelope in Ovidian subtlety, while also imposing demands upon the competence of the reader, but it is a significant example of a tendency which is surely new in Ovidian criticism. All the more so if we recall another paragraph of Hinds about this passage of *Am.* 1.5, in which the analysis becomes very subtle indeed (10): 'A few bold believers in wordplay may wish to go further, and faster, here. Corinna, a divided *diva* (the allusion in *dividua* alludes to its own processes), aptly inhabits this highly patterned world of borderlines—and of midpoints (lines 1, 2, 26). She is like Catullus' *candida diva* in poem 68, poised on the threshold of definition (line 10); she is like *Semi*ramis, "half" in name (line 11); and she is like Lais, whose etymologically marked name (line 12) makes her half of Catullus' *Lau*damia, half of his Protesi*laus*.'

Another aspect of Ovid's intertextuality considered by Hinds is 'the allusion which is so constructed as to draw attention to its status of allusion' (1987b: 7). We are reminded here, of course, of Conte's example of Mars and Ariadne (and see below the play on *cinnama/Cinna* in Knox 1986). Another is noted by Hinds in *Am.* 2.6, the elegy on the parrot which is clearly inspired by Catullus' poem on Lesbia's *passer* (3). In the opening line of the elegy, 'the conspicuousness of Ovid's allusion to Catullus amounts to an extreme case of self-reference: *psittacus, Eois imitatrix ales ab Indis, / occidit . . .* (*Am.* 2.6.1–2), "The parrot, winged imitator from the Eastern land, is dead . . ." . . . Corinna's engaging *psittacus* is modeled on Lesbia's famous *passer*, or "sparrow": and it is called an *imitatrix ales* by Ovid not just because, as a parrot, its role in nature is to mimic: but because its role in the Latin erotic tradition is to "imitate" that particular bird celebrated by Catullus' (1987b: 7). A similar approach to Corinna's parrot was adopted simultaneously by Boyd (1987).

Hinds proposes other examples of this technique in *Her.* 14.109–100, where Hypermestra closes her digression on the story of Io by saying,

ultima quid referam, quorum mihi cana senectus
    auctor? Dant anni, quod querar, ecce, mei.

Why should I recall far-off things, which are narrated to me by white-haired old men?
Lo, my very years give me reasons to complain.

This is a typical 'Alexandrian footnote' by which Ovid, with a metaliterary gesture, attracts the reader's attention to the 'source' of his own digression. Now, we could ask ourselves whether these 'white-haired old men' (*cana senectus*) who tell the story of Io to Hypermestra allude to some particular source. The most famous treatment of the myth in Latin poetry was certainly the epyllion *Io* by Calvus. By defining the old age which has narrated Io's story as *cana*, Ovid perhaps alludes, through the Roman etymological technique of calling things by their opposites (*a contrariis*), to the word designating old age that is precisely the opposite of *cana*, as far as hair is concerned, namely *calua*. This interpretation may be assisted if indeed the Romans used to contrast the two words in a way that is almost standard: Hinds recalls an anecdote in Macrobius (*Saturnalia* 2.5.7), where Augustus, to reproach his daughter Julia who used to tear away her precociously white hair, asked her 'whether, some years later, she would prefer to be white-haired or bald' (*cana . . . an calua*).

Intertextuality, Genre, Callimacheanism

In 1986 Peter Knox published a book on the *Metamorphoses* which was destined to be very influential. Knox locates himself in the tradition of the Alexandrianism of the so-called 'Harvard school', whose main sources of inspiration are Wendell Clausen (e.g. 1964) and David Ross (1969, 1975), a school that has given a vigorous impulse to the study of intertextuality, including more theoretical approaches (see above; Thomas 1982, 1986). Knox's monograph is centered above all on the genre of the poem, its historical-literary background, and its diction and style—fields in which Knox argues for the fundamental importance of the traditions of elegy and the Alexandrian/neoteric epyllion rather than of traditional epic poetry. But inevitably intertextuality also plays a crucial role in his discussion.

Virgil's sixth *Eclogue*, with the song of Silenus, which starts from a cosmogony to continue on with a catalogue of love myths, is seen as a crucial precedent for the poetic program of the *Metamorphoses* (Knox 1986: 10–14), with comparisons made to the song of Orpheus in Apollonius (1.486–511) and Clymene in Virgil's *Georgis* (4.345 ff.). With its elegiac texture, and echoes from *Am.* 1.1, the story of Apollo and Daphne sets the foundations for the general tone of the narratives of the poem; it is a programmatic declaration 'that the themes which interested him [i.e. Ovid] as an elegist will dominate the narrative to follow' (Knox 1986: 17). An intertextual relationship with the probable model in the Apollo of Euphorion's *Hyacinthus* (fr. 48 P.) is singled out by Knox in Ovid's adaptation of the Propertian and Gallan topos (cf. Ross 1975: 66–9) of the *medicina amoris* and incurable love. In telling the story of Atalanta and Hippomene as an insertion within the tale of Venus and Adonis, Ovid's Orpheus uses it as a kind of Alexandrian self-comment in order to allude to an important literary model of the container-story, namely the *other* version of the myth of Atalanta, the one which involves Milanion. But for Knox the real protagonist of intertextuality in the *Metamorphoses* is Callimachus (Knox 1986: 67–9): he is probably the source of the foundation myth of Cyrene in *Met.* 15, and the entire episode of Pythagoras in *Met.* 15 reveals the influence of the Pythagorean dream of Ennius at the beginning of his *Annals*, a dream that already alludes in a fully Alexandrian way to the dream of Callimachus at the beginning of the *Aitia* (70–2). Further, Ovid's panegyrics of Julius Caesar and Augustus are connected by Knox with the panegyrics of the Ptolemies in the *Aitia* (75–6). A section that has given rise to many discussions is his treatment of the intertextuality of the prologue of the *Metamorphoses* with the prologue of the *Aitia*. Ovid's request to the gods in 1.4 that they inspire him to compose a *perpetuum . . . carmen* has usually been seen as motivated by Ovid's wish to write a 'unified continuous poem', of the type that Callimachus (fr. 1.3) says he was criticized for not having written. But, anticipating the conclusions of Cameron (1995: 303–38), Knox points out that the response to the Telchines in the *Aetia* does not establish oppositions among literary genres, of epic against elegy. Neither the 'unified continuous poem' of Callimachus nor the *perpetuum . . . carmen* of Ovid refers to epic (Knox 1986: 10): 'Callimachus is careful not to distinguish between the epic and elegiac forms . . . The only poets named in the Prologue are elegists, Mimnermus and Philetas (fr. 1.9–12) . . . And Callimachus' most celebrated target [elsewhere in his poetry] was not an epic, but the elegiac *Lyde* of Antimachus. In the polemical setting of the *Aetia* Prologue διηνεκές is a neutral term.' Rather, it is the case that *deducite . . . carmen* in *Met.* 1.4 aligns the poem with the *deductum carmen* of Virg. *Ecl.* 6.5, poetry that is 'subtle' in the Alexandrian and neoteric manner. Ovid's self-consciousness in alluding to his neoteric models is further emphasized through the suggestion that Ovid, in introducing the story of Myrrha in *Met.* 10, which will be modeled on Cinna's *Zmyrna*, plays on the name of his source when he gives a catalogue of aromatic plants: 10.307–9 *sit diues amomo, / <u>cinna</u>maque costumque suum sudataque ligno / tura ferat floresque alios Panchaia tellus* . . . ('Let the land of Panchaia be rich in amomum, let it produce <u>cinna</u>mon, and its costus, and the incenses exuded from wood, and the other flowers . . .').

Shortly after Knox's volume, another book was published, which similarly focuses on issues of genre and intertextuality, albeit from quite a different perspective. Hinds (1987a) proposes a close reading of the two passages in which Ovid narrates the Rape of Proserpine (*Fast.* 4.417–620 and *Met.* 5.341–661). His study aims at a re-examination of the question of the differences in literary genre between the two narratives, with a reconsideration of the classic treatment of Heinze (1919). But the bulk of the book is dedicated to a detailed study of the literary models of Ovid's stories, with a special attention to the programmatic and metaphorical points present in Ovid's poetic texture. Hinds analyzes the complex web of Ovidian references to Hellenistic poets, such as Aratus and Callimachus, and above all discusses the influence of the *Homeric Hymn to Demeter* on both narratives of the Rape of Proserpina, counteracting the common opinion that there is no direct influence of Homer on Ovid's tales.

The influence of Knox and Hinds is clear in two monographs published in the 1990s, which offer deep intertextual readings of passages from the *Metamorphoses*. Keith (1992) is devoted to an analysis of the stories contained in *Met.* 2.531–835. In her first chapter Keith carefully examines the relationship between the story of the crow and the rook in Ovid and in the *Hecale* of Callimachus. Myers (1994) is especially interested in the issues of genre already discussed by Knox (1986) and Hinds (1987): her aim is to show that the *Metamorphoses* 'should be read simultaneously as a cosmogonic epic in the tradition of the lofty "scientific" or cosmological epics of Hesiod and Lucretius and as learned Alexandrian poetry in the tradition of Callimachus' *Aetia*' (Myers 1994: ix). Ample space is devoted to the demonstration of how etymologies, conversations, and narrative situations in the *Metamorphoses* are profoundly indebted to the *Aitia* of Callimachus, an approach which had previously been adopted to the *Fasti* by Miller (1991).

A different way of looking at the intertextual relationship with Callimachus is proposed by Sharrock (1994a), who performs an extremely close reading of the digression on Daedalus and Icarus, and of the epiphany of Apollo in *Ars* 2 (21–98,

493–508), showing how the two Ovidian narratives are studded with self-reflexive references to Callimachean poetics. In particular, in examining the epiphany of Apollo, who unexpectedly appears in order to suggest to the poet-teacher of love the Delphic precept 'know yourself', Sharrock (1994a: 197–290) shows how the epiphany of the god simultaneously reworks different epiphanies of Apollo in the *Aitia*, and how the divine instructions have metapoetic relevance for Ovid's poetic enterprise (cf. Miller 1983).

Intertextuality and Augustanism: Ovid and the *Aeneid*

As we have seen in our brief survey, the study of Ovid's intertextuality often leads to renewed consideration of the theme of Ovid's literary playfulness. But sometimes intertextuality can help to illuminate more 'political' aspects of Ovid's work. This is especially the case in Ovid's intertextual relationship with the quintessential Augustan poem, Virgil's *Aeneid*, a relationship that, as we have seen, was fundamental for Ovid from the very beginning of his career. Virgil is a constant presence in the whole of Ovid's work, but there are Ovidian texts that find their very meaning almost entirely in their relationship with the *Aeneid*. Two examples are *Her.* 7, the letter of Dido to Aeneas, and the so-called 'little *Aeneid*' of the *Metamorphoses* (13.623–14.608), in which Ovid re-tells Virgil's story. The political value of these texts lies in the fact that in them Ovid acts as an *interpreter* of the *Aeneid*, and acting as an interpreter of the Augustan text par excellence means taking up a definite position regarding Augustan discourse as a whole. Ovid does not always have an evident 'political' purpose in his exegetical approach to the *Aeneid*. Sometimes, rather than reacting to Virgil's text in itself, he seems instead to pick up on a certain pedantic attitude of the interpreters of Virgil of his own age. For example, at the end of Book 6 of the *Aeneid*, Aeneas arrives at Caieta (900–1): *Tum se ad Caietae recto fert limite portum. / ancora de prora iacitur; stant litore puppes* ('Then he moves straight toward the harbor of Caieta. The anchor is dropped from the prow, the sterns rest on the shore'). But the following book begins with the aetiological explanation of the name of Caieta: the site takes its name from Aeneas' nurse, Caieta, who dies there (*Aen.* 7.1–4). In the commentary of Servius we find a note which points out Virgil's 'inconsistency' in 6.900 and tries to explain it: *AD CAIETAE PORTVM a persona poetae prolepsis: nam Caieta nondum dicebatur* ('toward the harbor of Caieta: it is an anticipation from the person of the poet: for it was not yet called Caieta'). It is a pedantic observation typical of the ancient exegesis of Virgil, and not only of the fourth and fifth centuries AD, but also of the period immediately following the death of Virgil by, for example, Hyginus, a contemporary and friend of Ovid. Now, in the 'Aeneid' of the *Metamorphoses*, Ovid describes the arrival of Aeneas at Caieta with these words (14.156–7): *Troius Aeneas . . . / litora adit nondum nutricis habentia nomen* ('Trojan Aeneas arrives at the shore which had not yet the name of his nurse'). As Hinds notes (1998: 109 n. 14), in part of an important treatment of Ovid's 'Aeneid', 'Servius' pedantic note on *Aen.* 6.900 is exactly anticipated by Ovid's mock-pedantry.' To be sure, in this case we may also notice a slightly aggressive, irreverent approach toward the text of the *Aeneid*, but probably the first target of Ovid's irony, rather than the *Aeneid* itself, is a certain way of reading the *Aeneid*.

But other Ovidian choices have clear political implications. The seventh epistle of the *Heroides* has been seen as the first example of a 'negative' reading of the *Aeneid* by Knox (1995: 19–25). In his reading of *Aen*. 4, Ovid appears as the prototype of the 'pessimistic', or 'non-Augustan', reader of the *Aeneid*. To give Dido an exclusive point of view and an isolated voice, with no reply from Aeneas, amounts to a dramatic radicalization of the narrative strategy of Virgil, who in *Aen*. 4 had conceded to Dido the possibility of freely expressing her antagonism toward Aeneas' divine mission. Ovid, by giving voice *only* to Dido, emphasizes the 'dangers' that a multivocal epic such as the *Aeneid* involves for the encomiastic and propagandistic intent that apparently characterizes it. Furthermore, it is precisely the most seriously antagonistic aspects of Virgil's Dido that Ovid makes explicit and heightens. So, for example, Virgil's Dido expressed in an oblique and ambiguous way her doubts about the credibility of the narrative which Aeneas has told her about his escape from Troy (*Aen*. 4.596–9); Ovid's Dido picks up this cue and expands it in an extremely harsh way (*Her*. 7.77–80). When she accuses Aeneas of not having done enough to save his wife Creusa during the last night of Troy, or even of having taken the opportunity to get rid of her, Ovid's Dido only makes explicit and exaggerates a suspicion destined to occur quite often to Virgil's interpreters (Knox 1995: 21–2): 'Commentators ancient and modern have been worried by the possible implications of Aeneas' last words to his wife as he flees Troy with his family, reported indirectly by Virgil, *longe seruet uestigia coniunx* (2.711). How Aeneas lost Creusa and how the reader is to judge him are questions enjoined by the ambiguities in Virgil's portrayal of this scene in the *Aeneid*. Ovid's answer, through the voice of Dido, is unambiguous (81–4)'. Aeneas has lied about everything, and Dido is not his first victim (*Her*. 7.83–4): 'if you ask where is the mother of beautiful Iulus, she is dead, abandoned alone by her cruel husband' (*occidit a duro sola relicta uiro*). A similarly 'negative' interpretation of the multivocality of the *Aeneid* has been proposed when in the '*Aeneid*' of *Met*. 13–14 Ovid chooses to abridge the plot of Virgil's poem using in first person, as the epic narrator, words and expressions that in the *Aeneid* Virgil had attributed to the 'partial' speeches of antagonist characters, enemies of Aeneas and of his mission (see Casali 1995b and Thomas 2001: 78–84).

FURTHER READING

The word 'intertextuality' was introduced into the theoretical lexicon by Kristeva (1969: 146), even if in a rather different sense, with reference to a more general interconnection of cultural codes and discourses. For a history and a discussion of the concept of intertextuality in classical studies see Farrell (1991: 3–25) and Edmunds (1995, 2001); theoretical reflections are to be found in Conte and Barchiesi (1989), Fowler (1997), Barchiesi (1997c), and Hinds (1998). An important study that touches on intertextuality through repetition is Wills (1996). Another book that combines a systematic analysis of the Ovidian intertextuality in the *Amores* with an attempt at a theoretical classification is Boyd (1987). Rosati (1983) develops his ideas on self-reflexivity in Ovid's poetics, while a more recent study (Rosati 1999) investigates the imagery of 'weaving' as a self-reflexive metaphor in the *Metamorphoses*. The importance of the stories of Narcissus and Pygmalion for a theoretical approach to Ovidian self-reflexivity is highlighted, from different points of view, by Sharrock (1991; Pygmalion as a figure of the elegiac poet who first creates the woman and then falls in love with his own creation) and by Hardie (2002c: 143–227). Hardie (2002c: 150–65) also offers elegant new perspectives for the study of Ovid's intertextuality: see, for example, the theme of the echo and the reflexion in Lucretius and in the episode of Narcissus in the *Metamorphoses*, and the reading of Perseus' battle in the palace of Cepheus (*Met.* 4–5) in its relationship with Aeneas looking at the pictures in the temple of Juno at Carthage in *Aen.* 1 (178–86). Special attention to intertextuality characterizes the commentaries on single *Heroides* published in the 1990s: Barchiesi (1992), Casali (1995a), Knox (1995), Rosati (1996a), Kenney (1996), Bessone (1997), and Reeson (2001). On intertextuality and 'Augustan discourse', see Barchiesi (1993, 1997a). On Ovid and Virgil, see the essays collected in *Vergilius* 48 (2002) and especially Boyd (2002b). On the political value of Virgilian intertextuality in the *Fasti*, see Brugnoli and Stok (1992). On Ovid as an interpreter of Virgil, the article by Lamacchia (1960) is seminal; regarding the story of Cyparissus as a commentary on the killing of Silvia's stag in *Aen.* 7, Connors (1992–3: 4–12); on the etymologies: O'Hara (1996); on the Theban history in *Met.* 3–4 as developing a 'negative' reading of the *Aeneid*, see Hardie (1990). On *Her.* 7 and the *Aeneid*, see Desmond (1993), Miller (2004a), and Casali (2004–5). On the 'little *Aeneid*' in *Met.* 13–14, see Stitz (1962), Döpp (1969), Baldo (1995), Tissol (1997: 177–91), and Papaioannou (2005).

CHAPTER TWENTY-FIVE

Sexuality and Gender

Alison Keith

Introduction

Ovid characterizes himself in his poetic autobiography as particularly susceptible to amatory passion, no matter how slight the cause: 'my heart was ever soft, no strong-hold against Cupid's darts—a heart moved by the <u>slightest</u> <u>impulse</u>' (*molle Cupidineis nec inexpugnabile telis / cor mihi, quodque <u>levis causa</u> moveret, erat, Tr.* 4.10.65–6). Despite his susceptibility, however, he asserts that no scandal was ever laid at his door (*Tr.* 4.10.67–8; cf. *Tr.* 2.89–90, 349–356, 541–2). This claim may seem disingenu-ous when we recall the scandal of Ovid's relegation to Tomis, the result of 'two crimes—a poem and a mistake' (*duo crimina, carmen et error, Tr.* 2.207). While there is no consensus concerning the poet's mistake, Ovid says that the poem was his three-book *Art of Love* (*Ars amatoria*), which Augustus banished from the public libraries of Rome (*Tr.* 2.8) when he relegated Ovid to Tomis on the charge of teach-ing obscene adultery (*arguor obsceni doctor adulterii, Tr.* 2.212). Ovid denies that there was any crime in the poem (*nullum legisses crimen in Arte mea, Tr.* 2.240) and characterizes the poetry that disgraced him rather as his 'delight' (*delicias, Tr.* 2.78). The word suggests 'an activity that affords enjoyment' (*OLD* s.v. *delicia* 1), particu-larly of a sensual nature. I shall argue in this chapter that Ovidian verse is pervasively sensual even when its subject is not explicitly sexual, as it assuredly often is. In what follows I consider sexuality and gender in the Ovidian corpus in connection with poetry and the body (both female and male), the female body and landscape, the circulation of women, and poetics and gender.

The Matrix of Poetry

The autobiographical passage quoted at the opening of this chapter, in which Ovid admits to an amatory cast of character, implies that his erotic interest was directed to women, since he follows this statement with a series of couplets describing his three marriages (*Tr.* 4.10.69–74). But the passage also lends itself to interpretation as a register of his literary enthusiasms, for it follows Ovid's description of his admission into the ranks of contemporary Roman poets including Propertius, Horace, Virgil, and Tibullus (4.10.39–64) and recalls, in phrasing, descriptions of poetic projects from the very outset of his career. In the first poem of his *Amores*, for example, Ovid represents the poet-lover resisting in vain Cupid's transformation of every second hexameter into a pentameter and the concomitant transformation of his meter from the epic hexameter into the elegiac couplet. Amongst various complaints he makes in response to the god's intervention, the poet-lover observes that he lacks suitable material—'a youth or maiden with her long hair dressed'—for the frivolous measures of elegiac verse (*nec mihi materia est numeris leuioribus apta, / aut puer aut longas compta puella comas, Am.* 1.1.19–20). Ovid thus defines the subject of elegiac poetry as a youth or—the implication is by preference—a maiden with an elaborate coiffure. Certainly the *Amores* features a succession of attractive girls rather than desirable youths. If in the second poem of the collection, moreover, the poet-lover is a captive on display in Cupid's triumphal procession ('look, I admit, I'm your new <u>prize</u>, Cupid', *en ego, confiteor, tua sum noua <u>praeda</u>, Cupido, Am.* 1.2.19), already by the opening of the next poem he has been snared by an unnamed maiden ('I pray for justice: let the girl who has recently made me her <u>prize</u> either love or give me a reason why I should always love', *iusta precor: quae me nuper <u>praedata</u> puella est, / aut amet aut faciat, cur ego semper amem,* 1.3.1–2), whom he entreats to supply him with the material that will bring literary fame: 'offer yourself to me as fertile <u>subject</u> for song; poems worthy of their <u>source</u> will come' (*te mihi <u>materiem</u> felicem in carmina praebe: / prouenient <u>causa</u> carmina digna sua,* 1.3.19–20). In *Tr.* 4.10.65–74 Ovid rehearses the opening movement of the *Amores*, from the shafts of Love in *Am.* 1.1 to the inspiration of a *puella* in *Am.* 1.3, as he recalls his susceptibility to Cupid's darts (4.10.65) and erotic dalliance (4.10.66–8). The *leuis causa* too, which was ever sufficient to arouse his amatory interest (*Tr.* 4.10.66), suggestively evokes both the material suited to elegy's light measures (*numeris leuioribus, Am.* 1.1.19) and the poetry worthy of its source (*causa sua, Am.*1.3.20) that he promises.

Materia

Throughout his career, Ovid seems to have viewed women, both contemporary and mythological, as a particularly congenial subject for his verse. Early in the *Amores*, the poet-lover reminds his new beloved of the celebrity achieved by the heroines of Greek mythology and implies that she too can hope to achieve such fame through the circulation of his elegiac poetry (1.3.21–6):

> carmine nomen habent exterrita cornibus Io
> et quam fluminea lusit adulter aue
> quaeque super pontum simulato uecta iuuenco
> uirginea tenuit cornua uara manu.
> nos quoque per totum pariter cantabimur orbem
> iunctaque semper erunt nomina nostra tuis.

Through poetry they have a name—Io terrified by her horns and the maiden [i.e. Leda] with whom the adulterous Jove sported in the form of a river bird, and she [i.e. Europa] who was conveyed over the sea on the back of a fictitious bull, holding the bending horns with her maidenly hand. We too will be equally celebrated through the whole world, and our name will always be joined with yours.

The promise to make his girlfriend famous in his verse is disingenuous, however, since the poet-lover has not yet named her. Indeed, the withheld name invites her interpretation as poetic construct rather than historical person and the poet's movement from contemporary girlfriend to mythological heroines—Io, Leda, and Europa (two of the three also unnamed)—further facilitates such an interpretation. Even when the girlfriend's name enters the collection two poems later, moreover, the poet-lover introduces her in conjunction with two other legendary women (1.5.9–12): 'Look, Corinna comes, clad in an unbelted tunic, her hair parted over her shining neck, just as beautiful Semiramis is said to have gone into her bedchamber or Lais, beloved by many men.'

The company Corinna keeps throughout the *Amores* is particularly instructive. Ovid clearly invokes the mythological heroines of *Am.* 1.3—Io, Leda, and Europa—for their amatory entanglements, all three the victims of Jupiter's lust. In *Am.* 1.5 too, he seems to have selected the quasi-historical figures of Semiramis and Lais because of their reputations for sexual voracity: Semiramis, the legendary founder of Babylon, was reputed to have had a consuming passion for young lovers, whom she put to death when she tired of them (as she had killed her husband Ninus), while the courtesan Lais, though perhaps historical, bequeathed her name to the courtesans of New Comedy and enjoyed wide posthumous circulation as a stock character in the genre. Even the name of the poet-lover's mistress, Corinna, may be significant in this regard, for Ovid has drawn it from that of a Greek poetess famous for her gynocentric verse, and he thereby bypasses 'the Augustan elegiac procedure of choosing feminised cult names of Apollo for this purpose (Lycoris, Cynthia, Delia) in favour of a return to Catullan practice (Lesbia, from Sappho of Lesbos)' (Hinds 1987b: 6).

The leisurely description of Corinna's figure in *Am.* 1.5 is one of the fullest and most carnal accounts of a mistress' naked body on offer in Latin elegy (1.5.17–22):

> ut stetit ante oculos posito uelamine nostros,
> in toto nusquam corpore menda fuit:
> quos umeros, quales uidi tetigique lacertos!
> forma papillarum quam fuit apta premi!
> quam castigato planus sub pectore uenter!
> quantum et quale latus! quam iuuenale femur!

As she stood before my eyes with her clothing laid aside, nowhere in her whole body was there a blemish. What shoulders, what arms did I see—and touch! How suited for caress the form of her breasts! How smooth her stomach beneath the faultless bosom! How great and how fair her flank! How youthful the thigh!

Stephen Hinds (1987b: 11) has drawn attention to the perfection of Corinna's anatomy, seeing in her form 'the attributes of an idealised mistress; but also, more pointedly than in most elegiac idealisations, the attributes of a goddess, with the stress on her height and faultless physique'. In this respect, he suggests, she anticipates the personified Elegy who explicitly enters the collection as a goddess. Yet Corinna's body also displays a tactile perfection realizable only in a work of art such as a marble statue, an ivory carving, or a finely crafted book of poetry. It is therefore tempting to interpret Corinna's bodily perfection as exemplary not only of the idealized elegiac mistress but also of the aesthetic perfection of the poetry collection in which she is celebrated. Ovid thus represents the subject of his first collection of erotic elegy, Corinna, like her legendary and mythological avatars, as the embodiment of both carnal pleasure and erotic verse.

Occasionally, however, Ovidian elegy assumes the outline of the carnal male body. In the opening poem of the *Amores*, for example, the movement of the elegiac couplet is figured in terms of the tumescence and detumescence of the male member: 'when a new page has <u>risen</u> well with the first verse, the following line <u>shrinks my forces</u> . . . my <u>work rises</u> in six measures, <u>falls back</u> in five' (*cum bene <u>surrexit</u> uersu noua pagina primo, / <u>attenuat neruos</u> proximus ille meos . . . sex mihi <u>surgat opus</u> numeris, in quinque <u>residat</u>*, 1.1.17–18, 27). A sexual double entendre underlies the description of the rhythm of the elegiac couplet in 1.1.17–18 (Kennedy 1993: 57–63), while the pun in 1.1.27 on *opus*, both 'sex' and 'penis' in colloquial Latin (Adams 1982: 157), is facilitated by its proximity to the verbs *surgat* and *residat* (cf. *Am.* 2.15.25, 3.7.75). Ovid employs the same pun at *Am.* 2.10.35–6, where he prays to die in Venus' 'service' (*at mihi contingat <u>Veneris</u> languescere<u> motu</u>, / cum moriar, medium soluar et inter <u>opus</u>*). In this poem full of sexual bravado, the poet-lover lays claim to sexual stamina ('I shall stay the course . . . my body lacks weight [*pondere*], not potency [*neruis*]', 2.10.23–4) and boasts that he often devotes his nights to passion ('I've often spent the course of the night in <u>carnal play</u>, and in the morning I was still <u>serviceable</u> and <u>full</u> of <u>vigor</u>', *saepe ego <u>lasciue</u> consumpsi tempora noctis, / <u>utilis et forti corpore</u> mane fui*, 2.10.27–8).

At other points in the collection too, Ovid maps the anatomy of the elegiac text on to the physique of the elegiac poet-lover (Keith 1999a). In a paraclausithyron in the first book of the *Amores*, the poet-lover asks his beloved's door-keeper to admit him (1.6.3–6), slyly observing that the narrowest opening will suffice since 'long-time love has reduced my body for such service and given me suitable limbs with the loss of weight' (*longus amor tales corpus tenuauit in usus / aptaque subducto pondere membra dedit*). Through an inherent ambiguity in the term *amor*, the long love that has made the lover's body slender may also be interpreted as the poet's lengthy period in the service of Amor, the deity who presides over the refined verse of the *Amores* (1.1.3–4; 2.1.3–4, 38; 2.18.3–4, 15–16; 3.15).

Ovid's lengthy account of the poet-lover's impotence in *Am.* 3.7, often decried as in bad taste, also repays examination in this context, for the poem plays an important role in articulating the final book's program of disengagement from elegy (Keith 1999a). Despite the blandishments of a compliant elegiac *puella*, the poet-lover proves impotent here (*Am.* 3.7.13–14): 'nevertheless, my body, as if touched with chill hemlock, was sluggish, and failed my intent' (*tacta tamen ueluti gelida mea membra cicuta / segnia propositum destituere meum*). The lover's impotence evokes the characteristic aporia of the elegiac lover, but here, paradoxically, it has the further function of metaphorically documenting the poet's flagging interest in elegiac verse for the chill that afflicts the lover's loins (3.7.13) corresponds in literary terms to a frigidity that is antithetical to the exquisite refinement of elegiac style. Here Ovid shapes the speaker's *corpus*, formerly well endowed for erotic encounters (cf. *Am.* 2.10.28, 3.7.23–6), to the task of disengagement from elegiac composition, inasmuch as it is now figured as 'an idle slab . . . mere spectacle and useless weight' (*truncus iners . . . species et inutile pondus*, 3.7.15). The adjective *iners* in this context signals a break with elegiac writing practices for *ars* is a criterion of the utmost importance in defining the stylistic refinement of elegy. In 3.7, Ovid presses to its limits the metaphor that figures the elegiac text as the sexually dynamic or dysfunctional body of the elegiac speaker.

Maria Wyke (1989) has shown that Ovid characterizes the personified genre of Elegy herself in similarly carnal terms. *Elegia* enters the collection in *Am.* 3.1, like Corinna in *Am.* 1.5, with her hair scented and her beauty displayed to sensual effect in a transparent shift (3.1.7–10): 'Elegy appeared, her scented hair bound up and, I think, one of her feet was longer than the other. Her figure was beautiful, her dress almost transparent, her face that of a lover, and the <u>defect</u> in her feet was <u>the source of her beauty</u>' (*uenit odoratos Elegia nexa capillos, / et, puto, pes illi longior alter erat. / forma decens, uestis tenuissima, uultus amantis, / et pedibus <u>uitium causa decoris</u> erat*). The playful references to Elegy's uneven gait allude to the characteristic alternation of hexameter and pentameter lines in her meter, the elegiac couplet. The poet's celebration of the sensual charm of Elegy's unsteady gait is consistent with his observation elsewhere that 'beauty rarely lacks a blemish' (*Ars* 3.261) and the elder Seneca's report that the historical Ovid 'occasionally used to say that a face was the more beautiful for some mole' (*Contr.* 2.2.12). If the unevenness of Elegy's gait only enhances her appeal, the frivolity of her character also adds to the charm of her verse. In *Am.* 3.1 Elegy boasts that she has endowed the genre with her own playful nature ('I am <u>frivolous</u> and so is Cupid, my concern; I am no more overbearing than my <u>subject</u>', *sum <u>leuis</u>, et mecum leuis est, mea cura, Cupido: / non sum <u>materia</u> fortior ipsa mea*, 3.1.41–2). She also claims full credit for the guiles of her protégée Corinna, whom she claims to have instructed in the elegiac arts, in diction that recalls Corinna's entry into the collection two books earlier (3.1.49–52): 'under my tutelage, Corinna learned to deceive her guards and undermine the faith of a closed threshold, to glide from her bed concealed in her unbelted shift and move her feet without stumbling in the night' (*per me decepto didicit custode Corinna / liminis astricti sollicitare fidem / delabique toro tunica uelata soluta / atque impercussos nocte mouere pedes*). The association of poetry with the frivolous erotic escapades of sexually active women persists throughout Ovid's career.

Thus at the outset of the *Ars amatoria*, as at the opening of the *Amores*, Ovid describes his new writing project as the search for a woman to whom to say 'you alone please me' (*elige cui dicas 'tu mihi sola places'*, 1.42) and he characterizes his readership as men in search of the '*material* for an enduring love' who must learn where to find girls (*tu quoque, materiam longo qui quaeris amori, / ante frequens quo sit disce puella loco*, 1.49–50). Molly Myerowitz (1985) has demonstrated that the poetic project of *Ars* 1–2 is the male application of erotic knowledge to the domestication and manipulation of his female raw material, *materia*. If the male lover controls *ars* and thereby represents culture, the female beloved, as raw material, is analogous to nature (cf. Leach 1964). Ovid develops women's symbolic relationship to nature in a variety of ways. In the first book of the poem, for example, he includes a catalogue of mythological heroines who yield to excessive and illicit passion, briefly detailing the incestuous love of Byblis for her brother and Myrrha for her father, expatiating at greater length on Pasiphaë's perverse passion for the bull, and concluding with learned references to her daughter Phaedra's quasi-incestuous infatuation with her stepson Hippolytus, Nisus' daughter Scylla's criminal love for the enemy commander besieging her city, and Clytemnestra's adulterous passion for Aegisthus (1.283–340). Here Ovid represents female passion as excessive, uncontrolled, and, accordingly, properly subject to male rule. We may compare the lessons of the *Heroides*, fictional letters written *in extremis* by the heroines of classical mythology to the lovers who have abandoned them.

Another catalogue of mythological heroines in the *Ars* (2.353–72) illustrates how the male lover's absence makes the susceptible woman's heart grow fonder (2.351–2): 'grant a respite: a rested field gives a better return, and the dry earth absorbs the heavens' rains' (*da requiem: requietus ager bene credita reddit, / terraque caelestes arida sorbet aquas*). Ovid here likens the mistress to a fallow field and the lover to a husbandman who farms his land for the best return, elaborating an observation he makes at the end of the first book of the *Ars* (755–8): 'I was about to conclude, but girls have different dispositions; catch a thousand hearts in as many ways. Nor does the same land bear all things: vines are suited to some, olives to others, while in still others wheat grows green'. Leach has shown that the application of farming imagery to the erotic contests of the *Ars*, through the repeated association of 'women and their love to field, crops and harvest' (Leach 1964: 146), constitutes a parody of Virgil's *Georgics*, but we may note in addition that the metaphor linking women and land respects traditional territorial assignments of gender in classical thought. The metaphor that associates earth with the female body reflects a general propensity in Greek and Latin literature to characterize the earth as a generative female body and, conversely, the generative female body as a fertile field to be ploughed; thus Ovid remarks (2.668) 'one field will bear crops already, another must be planted' (*iste feret segetes, iste serendus ager*). The metaphor is especially pervasive in the second book of the *Ars* where the poet-lover offers instruction to men on the care and cultivation of a mistress, but it recurs as well in the third book (3.101–2, 107): 'I begin with cultivation: wine comes out well from cultivated grapes and from cultivated soil the crops stand tall . . . maidens of old did not cultivate their bodies thus' (*ordior a cultu: cultis bene Liber ab uuis / prouenit, et culto stat seges alta solo. / . . . / corpora . . . ueteres non sic coluere puellae*).

Terra

I have argued elsewhere (Keith 2000: 36–64) that classical poets repeatedly feminize and sexualize the landscapes in which they set male action, and Ovid participates in this tradition not only in the *Ars* but also, especially, in the *Metamorphoses*. In the first book of the poem, for example, the floodwaters Jupiter sends to destroy the human race (sparing only Deucalion and Pyrrha) fertilize the earth, which regenerates the animal kingdom (1.416–37). Ovid represents Mother Earth metaphorically engaged in the process of child-bearing (1.416–17, 434–5) and he explicitly likens this metaphorical child-bearing to the gestation of the child in the mother's womb ('nourished in the vivifying round as if in a <u>mother's</u> belly', *uiuaci nutrita solo ceu matris in aluo*, 1.420). Earlier in the episode, Ovid draws on the metaphor of Mother Earth in his report of Themis' oracle instructing Deucalion and Pyrrha how to regenerate the human race, by 'toss[ing] the bones of their great <u>mother</u> behind them' (*ossaque post tergum magnae iactate <u>parentis</u>*, 1.383). Deucalion only succeeds in overcoming Pyrrha's refusal to desecrate their mother's bones by decoding the oracle's metaphorical underpinnings (1.393–4): '<u>our</u> <u>great</u> <u>mother</u> <u>is</u> <u>the</u> <u>earth</u>; stones, I think, are called bones in the <u>earth's</u> body; we are instructed to toss these behind our backs' (*<u>magna parens terra est</u>; lapides in corpore <u>terrae</u> / ossa reor dici; iacere hos post terga iubemur*). The metaphor recurs in the second book of the *Metamorphoses*, during Phaethon's disastrous ride in the chariot of the Sun just before Mother Earth pleads with Jupiter to prevent him from destroying the world. Commenting on the reduction of 'the waters of the ocean and contraction of water sources' as a result of the fiery heat, the poet-narrator explains: 'they'd hidden themselves in the vitals of their shady <u>mother</u>' (*inter aquas pelagi contractosque undique fontes / qui se condiderant in opacae uiscera <u>matris</u>*, 2.273–4). More commonly in the poem, however, nymphs and mythological heroines are absorbed into the body of Mother Earth, their physical features subsumed into hers. Thus, for example, after Narcissus spurns Echo's advances, the nymph retreats to lonely grottoes where she wastes away for love until she is reduced to pure voice and her bones take on the shape of stones (*uox tantum atque ossa supersunt: / uox manet; ossa ferunt lapidis traxisse figuram*, 3.398–9).

The generative female body is also a sexual body, however, and so the metaphor that describes the earth as a reproductive body can be extended through the application of erotic vocabulary to describe the landscape as a sensual body. Adams (1982: 82–3) charts the development in classical literature of the 'metaphor of the field, garden, meadow, etc. applied to the female pudenda'. Ovid fleshes out the metaphor of the erotic landscape in a succession of erotic narratives in the *Metamorphoses*, including the salacious tale of the oversexed water nymph Salmacis and her spring's insalubrious effect on bathers in Book 4. Introduced as a feature of the natural landscape (Nugent 1990), Salmacis is a clear Lycian spring (*lymphae*, 4.298), home to an indigenous nymph (*nympha*, 4.302) of the same name. Ovid exploits a figural parallel between woman and landscape to describe Salmacis throughout the episode in diction applicable to both spring and nymph (4.302–304, 309–316):

nympha colit, sed nec uenatibus apta nec arcus
flectere quae soleat nec quae contendere cursu,
solaque Naiadum celeri non nota Dianae . . .
nec sua cum duris uenatibus otia miscet,
sed modo fonte suo formosos perluit artus,
saepe Cytoriaco deducit pectine crines
et quid se deceat spectatas consulit undas;
nunc perlucenti circumdata corpus amictu
mollibus aut foliis aut mollibus incubat herbis;
saepe legit flores. et tum quoque forte legebat,
cum puerum uidit uisumque optauit habere.

A nymph dwells in the spring, but one neither fit for the hunt nor accustomed to bend the bow nor to strive in a race; alone among the Naiads she was unknown to swift Diana . . . Nor does she intersperse her leisure with the hardy hunt, but now she washes her beautiful limbs in her spring, often she combs her hair with a box-wood comb and checks her waters to see what becomes her; now she veils her body in a translucent mantle and lies on soft foliage and grasses; often she plucks flowers, and then too she chanced to be plucking flowers, when she saw the youth Hermaphroditus and desired to pluck him.

The interplay between spring and nymph is particularly well developed in the overlap between the attributes lacking to both. Just as the spring Salmacis lacks the Ovidian pool's customary accessories of reeds, sedge, and rushes with sharp points (4.298–9), so the nymph Salmacis foregoes the nymphs' customary activities of hunting and foot-racing (4.302–3). Since rushes with sharp points characteristically supply the material for hunter's arrows with their own sharp points in the poem (e.g. 1.468–71), their omission from the landscape in which the spring is set coheres with the nymph's lack of hunting paraphernalia. Moreover, Salmacis' lack of an *arcus* (4.302, 'hunting bow'), may be related to her spring's lack of an *arcus* (natural 'arch'), such as defines the setting in which Diana bathes earlier in the poem (3.160). The nymph's transparent clothing (4.313) reflects the lucidity of her waters (4.297–8; cf. 4.300). Even Salmacis' use of the clear waters of her spring as a mirror in which to check her appearance (4.311) is paralleled by the description of her eyes blazing like the reflected image of the sun (4.347–9), as though her person itself exhibited the catoptric properties of a mirror.

Salmacis devotes herself to the pleasures of the flesh, rejecting the chaste pursuits of the goddess Diana in favor of the kind of sensual delights on display in Ovid's *Amores*, such as bathing, hair-dressing, admiring her reflection, wearing transparent clothing, and lolling about on soft cushions. The final detail of Salmacis' pleasure in plucking flowers, however, ultimately differentiates her from the 'over-painted nymphs' of Ovid's contemporary Rome, for it draws on the conventional epic association of the well-watered meadow with the rape of nymphs and other nubile maidens in classical literature (e.g. Nausikaa in *Odyssey* 6 and Persephone in the *Homeric Hymn to Demeter*). The epic topography of rape sets a maiden on the verge of marriage in a flowering landscape that figures her erotic appeal in the fountain ringed with grassy banks—in just such terms, indeed, as Salmacis and her spring are described (4.300–1): 'the spring's water was absolutely clear: nevertheless, the edges of the pool were girt with living sod and ever verdant grasses' (*perspicuus liquor est. stagni tamen ultima uiuo / caespite cinguntur semperque uirentibus herbis*). The nubile maiden discovered in a *locus amoenus* landscape is conventionally plucked, like the metaphorical flower she is, by a divine rapist (i.e. she is deflowered). Earlier in the *Metamorphoses*, for example, Jupiter ravishes Io (1.588–600) and Callisto (2.409–31) in similar settings, while in the following book Dis will rape Proserpina as she picks flowers in a meadow beside Lake Henna in Sicily (5.385–95).

Ovid rings a number of changes on the traditional epic *mise en scène*, however, for in this case the nymph is no shrinking violet but a full-blown nymphomaniac, who no sooner sees the youth than she desires him and promptly proceeds to act on her desire by propositioning him in a speech loosely modeled on Odysseus' delicate flattery of Nausikaa in *Odyssey* 6, though far more sexually aggressive (4.320–8). When the youth rejects her amorous advances, Salmacis feigns retreat but lingers to watch him dally in her spring (4.340–7, 350–4):

> at ille,
> ut puer et uacuis ut inobseruatus in herbis,
> huc it et hinc illuc et in adludentibus undis
> summa pedum taloque tenus uestigia tingit;
> nec mora, temperie blandarum captus aquarum
> mollia de tenero uelamina corpore ponit.
> tum uero placuit, nudaeque cupidine formae
> Salmacis exarsit . . .
> uixque moram patitur, uix iam sua gaudia differt,
> iam cupit amplecti, iam se male continet amens.
> ille cauis uelox applauso corpore palmis
> desilit in latices alternaque bracchia ducens
> in liquidis translucet aquis.

But the youth, as though unobserved and in empty grasses, strolls here and there and dips in the playful waters first the tips of his toes and then his ankles; without delay, captivated by the warmth of the caressing waters, he strips the soft clothes from his tender body. Then truly he pleased Salmacis and she blazed with desire for his naked form . . . Scarcely can she endure a delay, scarcely can she postpone her joys, desiring now to embrace him, now scarcely containing herself in her passion. Then slapping his body with cupped palms, he jumps right into the pool, gleaming as his arms move through the translucent waters.

Hermaphroditus' dive into Salmacis' spring invites interpretation as an exploratory dive into adult sexuality; we may compare Dis' assault on Cyane's pool in the following book, after she reproaches him for his rape of Proserpina (5.421–3, 'Dis urged on his team and hurling his royal scepter with his strong arm, buried it in the depths of the spring').

Unlike Dis' determined (and ultimately successful) sexual assault, however, Hermaphroditus' youthful experimentation ends in disaster when the nymph engulfs him rather than surrender her pool to him (4.356–63):

'uicimus et meus est!' exclamat Nais et omni
ueste procul iacta mediis immittitur undis
pugnantemque tenet luctantiaque oscula carpit
subiectatque manus inuitaque pectora tangit
et nunc hac iuueni, nunc circumfunditur illac;
denique nitentem contra elabique uolentem
implicat, ut serpens, quam regia sustinet ales
sublimemque rapit . . .
utue solent hederae longos intexere truncos,
utque sub aequoribus deprensum polypus hostem . . .

'I've won, he's mine!' cried the nymph and throwing off her clothes she immerses herself
in the midst of her waters and holds him as he fights, snatching struggling kisses and
insinuating her hands to touch his unwilling breast, surrounding the youth now on this
side, now on that; finally, as he struggles against her trying to escape, she embraces him
like a serpent caught and carried aloft by an eagle . . . or as ivy is wont to entwine tall
tree trunks or as an octopus catches and holds its prey under water . . .

Clinging to the boy, Salmacis prays to the gods that she and Hermaphroditus be
forever joined together (4.369–72) and her prayer is granted (4.373–5): 'mingled
together, their two bodies are united and one face joins them'. The nymph's embrace
and prayer prove transformative to both parties (4.378–9): 'they are not two but
have a double form, such as could be called neither woman nor youth, but seems
neither and both'. The peculiar being who results from their union—at once bi- and
non-gendered, possessing the attributes of both male and female and therefore of
neither male nor female—may trouble our understanding of the sexed body but in
no way disrupts the traditional territorial assignments of gender. For Ovid names the
hermaphrodite who emerges from the spring 'Hermaphroditus' (4.383), a name
withheld until the end of the tale but already implicit at its outset in the description
of a 'youth born of Mercury [Gk. Hermes] and the Cytheran goddess [Gk. Aphro-
dite]' (4.288). Thus, the sexual union of Salmacis and Hermaphroditus not only
emasculates the latter, but erases the former's subjectivity altogether, leaving her
merely an inert toponym: 'the cause lies hidden, but the violent effect of the spring
is very well known' (4.287; cf. 15.319). The ill-fated coupling of the pair conforms
in no way to the ideal of sexual union recommended by Ovid in his precepts on the
subject at the end of *Ars* 2 (725–8): 'but neither leave your mistress behind, spreading your sails the wider, nor let her outstrip your course. Hasten together to the
goal: then is pleasure [*uoluptas*] full, when woman and man lie equally spent'. If the
Ovidian *praeceptor* commends mutual pleasure as most satisfying for both sexes, the
outcome of the coupling of Salmacis and Hermaphroditus constitutes an object lesson
in the dangers of disregarding his advice.

Homosocial Desire and the Circulation of Female Sexuality

While the subject of Ovidian verse is often sexuality, and specifically female sexuality
at that, Ovid's readership clearly embraced both men and women. The epigram that

prefaces the *Amores*, spoken in the voice of the collection itself, advertises the sensual pleasure (*uoluptas*, 3) on offer in the books now lightened from five to three, but names no dedicatee. Individual poems vary in their addressees from the tutelary gods of elegiac poetry (Cupido/Amor, Elegy, Venus), through the mistress and her slaves, both female and male, to, very occasionally, one of the poet-lover's friends (Atticus, 1.9; Graecinus, 2.10; Macer, 2.18) or rivals (2.19, 3.4). The mistress is the addressee of the majority of the *Amores*, but the inclusion of poems to and about her in a collection that circulated publicly underwrites the poet-lover's bitter renunciation of his love (and love poetry) at the end of the collection (*Am.* 3.12.5–8):

> quae modo dicta mea est, quam coepi solus amare,
>   cum multis uereor ne sit habenda mihi.
> fallimur, an nostris innotuit illa libellis?
>   sic erit: ingenio prostitit illa meo.
> et merito: quid enim formae praeconia feci?
>   uendibilis culpa facta puella mea est.

> She who just now was called my own, whom I alone began to love, I fear I must share with many. Am I mistaken, or did she become known in my little books? So it is—she prostituted herself through my talent. And I deserve it! For what did I do but auction her beauty? My mistress was put up for sale through my fault.

Ovid here both accuses his mistress of prostitution and accepts a measure of responsibility for her circulation among men. Moreover his placement of the poem so close to the end of the *Amores* as a whole invites interpretation in metaliterary terms, as a meditation on the circulation of 'Corinna' among the Roman reading public. He thus literalizes the trope that figures the publication of poetry about an elegiac mistress as the mistress' sexual circulation among men (Fear 2000b).

Within the *Amores*, Ovid models both male and female responses to the circulation of his elegiac poetry. In *Am.* 2.17, for example, he claims that many women want to be celebrated in his amatory verse (2.17.28) and asserts that he even 'knows a woman who puts it about that she's Corinna; what wouldn't she give for it to be so?' (2.17.29–30). The passage provides some illumination concerning the gendered reception of Ovid's poetry and suggests not only that the poet enjoyed a considerable female readership but also that (at least some members of) this readership identified with the position of the textual mistress. In the following poem, by contrast, Ovid describes the reception of his *Heroides* among contemporary poets (2.18.27–8): 'How quickly has my friend Sabinus returned from around the world and himself brought back letters from different places!' Sabinus is represented as responding to Ovid's textual women (Penelope, Phyllis, Oenone, Canace, Medea, Phaedra, and Dido are specifically identified, 2.18.21–6) with the composition of answering epistles from their absent lovers (Ovid mentions Ulysses, Hippolytus, Aeneas, Demophoon, and Jason, 2.18.29–33). To be sure, 2.18 is addressed to an epic poet, Ovid's friend and elder contemporary Macer, whom Ovid urges to write elegy like himself and for whom Sabinus furnishes an exemplary model. Nonetheless, it is perhaps equally illuminating that Ovid characterizes Sabinus' response as one of (literary) identification with the male lovers interpellated by the *Heroides*.

By contrast with the *Amores*, which anticipates a readership of both sexes, Ovid identifies the reader of *Ars* 1–2 as specifically male ('If anyone doesn't know the art of loving, let him read this and, instructed [*doctus*] by perusal of my verse, let him love', *Ars* 1.1–2) and the reader of *Ars* 3 as specifically female (*puellae*, 3.57). The poet explicitly warns respectable women away from the work altogether, not only in the material addressed to men (1.31–4, 2.599–600; cf. *Tr.* 2.247–52) but also in that addressed to women (3.57–8): 'while Venus inspires my talent, seek precepts here girls [*puellae*], whom chastity, the laws, and your own rights allow'. In *Ars* 3, moreover, Ovid mentions his authorship of 'a brief little book . . . of cosmetic aids' (*medicamina formae . . . libellus*, 3.205–6), *Medicamina faciei femineae* as it is called in the manuscripts, which is also addressed to girls and takes the form of a didactic treatise on women's facial cosmetics (*discite quae faciem commendet cura, puellae, / et quo sit uobis forma tuenda modo*, *Med.* 1–2). Many scholars have thought, however, that male readers lurk in the background of *Ars* 3 and the *Medicamina* as unnamed addressees, for they are the 'prime beneficiaries in any case of much of Ovid's instruction' (Gibson 2003: 36). They are also the addressees of Ovid's renunciation of love in the *Remedia amoris* (41–3): 'come to my teachings, deceived youths, whom your own love has utterly betrayed. Learn to be healthy from him through whom you learned to love'.

Analysis of the gendered reception of Ovid's early erotic poetry lays bare the social bonds between elite Roman men that structure not only the reading community at large but also the poet's writing community (exemplified by the poet's friends Sabinus and Macer in *Am.* 2.18). The ostensible projects of *Ars* 1–2 and *Remedia*, along with the implicit projects of *Ars* 3 and *Medicamina faciei femineae*, well illustrate the homosocial dynamics of this reading and writing culture: the volumes serve an elite male community of sexual interest through the expression of friendship, mentorship, class privilege, and even sexual rivalry in their cultivation of the female. This finding is perhaps surprising, given the centrality of female subject matter in Ovid's early poetry, but it is readily apparent in his later writings: the *Fasti* was originally dedicated to Augustus (*Tr.* 2.549–51) but reworked in exile for Germanicus (*Fast.* 1.3–26), while the *Tristia* and *Epistulae ex Ponto* contain individual poems addressed to a wide variety of the poet's elite male acquaintance (including the Princeps himself in *Tr.* 2) in an effort to secure his return to Rome. In these later works Ovid appeals explicitly to homosocial solidarity in making his case for recall from Tomis. Attention to the gendered dynamics of speaker and audience in the *Metamorphoses* invites similar conclusions.

The Poetics of Gender

In the first book of the *Metamorphoses*, in an episode that has been the focus of considerable narratological discussion (Konstan 1991, Wheeler 1999), the god Mercury disguises himself as a shepherd and engages Argus in varied conversation, before beginning to tell him the story of Pan's attempted rape of the nymph Syrinx and the resulting invention of the pan-pipes (1.682–714). Ovid sketches the episode in programmatically pastoral form. The many-eyed Argus, Mercury's interlocuter, is guarding the cow Io (on Juno's orders) and so Ovid depicts him in pastoral guise as a cowherd whose interest is appropriately piqued by the shepherd's pipe which Mercury ostentatiously plays as he traverses the countryside dressed as a goatherd. The story Argus asks Mercury for, moreover, not only explains the origin of the shepherd's pipe and is self-consciously set in Arcadia, the home of pastoral at least since Virgil's *Tenth Bucolic*, but is delivered in the quintessentially pastoral landscape of shaded pasturage. In this tale, then, Ovid deploys vocabulary marked as appropriate to the generic context of pastoral. It is also highly gendered, with male shepherds guarding a female cow and female goats, recounting or listening to a tale about a (male) god trying to rape a (female) naiad. The larger context of Mercury's narrative is similarly gendered, for Jupiter has sent him to secure the release of Io, whom the father of gods and men has already raped and who will eventually bear him a son, Epaphus.

The gendered context of Mercury's tale emerges particularly clearly by contrast with another storytelling sequence later in the poem. Book 4 opens with the tales of the daughters of Minyas, which Ovid shapes in such a way as to offer reflection on stereotypically feminine narrative subjects, themes and settings. At the conclusion of *Met.* 3, the Theban women, warned by the ghastly demise of Pentheus, assiduously worship the new god Bacchus (3.732–3; cf. 4.9–30). Only the daughters of Minyas deny both his descent from Jove and his divinity (4.1–4; cf. 4.272–3). Determined to spurn his rites, the Minyads and their maidservants remain within doors to spin and weave, thus celebrating the rites of Minerva instead of Bacchus (4.31–5). Wool-working constituted women's work par excellence in antiquity, and in Rome a woman's worth had long been defined by her performance of this household duty, as we can see, for example in the story of Lucretia, recounted by Ovid in the *Fasti* (2.741–60). Women's wool-working enjoyed particular esteem in Augustan Rome, where the Princeps boasted that his wife, daughter, and granddaughters wove his clothing (Suet. *Aug.* 64.2, 73). The praise accorded Roman women for spinning and weaving within the domestic sphere stands in sharp contrast to the denunciation of women involved in Bacchic rites by contemporary Roman authors such as Livy (39.8–18) and Virgil (*Aen.*7.385–405). The Minyads implicitly assert their exemplary feminine virtue by drawing a contrast between the Theban women's misguided worship of the false god Bacchus and their own service in the rites of the 'better' goddess, Minerva (*Met.* 4.37–8). Yet despite the sisters' disavowal of Bacchus (the embodiment of unruly feminine emotionalism) and their concomitant endorsement of Minerva (the embodiment of disciplined feminine domesticity), their familial pursuit of the quintessentially virtuous feminine activity of weaving is embedded within the larger community's participation in the quintessentially vicious feminine activity of maenadism. Ovid thus multiply overdetermines the gendered context in which the Minyads tell their tales (Rosati 1999).

When one of the sisters proposes that they tell stories to enliven their work (*Met.* 4.37–41), her suggestion is enthusiastically taken up and she narrates the doomed love of Pyramus and Thisbe (4.55–166). Love stories are a kind of narrative generally assumed to be of particular interest to women in antiquity (despite the fact that almost all our evidence concerning both these narratives and women's predilection for them is derived from male-authored texts), and it is telling that the second Minyad also takes for her subject a tale of love, the 'amours of the Sun' (*Solis referemus amores*, 4.170). The third sister, Alcithoë, also contributes another erotic narrative, that of Salmacis and Hermaphroditus (4.288–388), which we considered above in connection with Ovid's feminization of landscape. Female characters take the lead in all three of the sisters' narratives: the virginal Thisbe in the first Minyad's tale, the vindictive Venus and Clytie in the second sister's sequence, and the seductive water-nymph Salmacis in Alcithoë's narrative. The sisters thus implicitly reject *uirtus*, the traditional focus of classical epic, as a subject of interest either to themselves or to their female audience.

The Minyads' radical gynocentrism emerges particularly forcefully by comparison with the androcentric themes and setting of the tales narrated by the leaders of the Greek army at Troy during a lull in the Trojan War (12.159–62). The Greek chieftains celebrate a feast at which the conversation turns to the subject of virility (*uirtus . . . loquendi / materia est*, 12.159–160). Their talk centers on their exploits in battle, the very stuff of epic verse (12.160–162): 'they mention their enemy's battle and their own, and it pleases them often to recall in turn the dangers encountered and endured' (*pugnam referunt hostisque suamque, / inque uices adita atque exhausta pericula saepe / commemorare iuuat*). In their exclusive focus on virile masculinity and the exploits of war, particularly in the battle of Centaurs and Lapiths that Nestor narrates at great length (12.210–535), the Greek heroes show an androcentrism that is as sweeping as the Minyad's gynocentrism. For the battle of Centaurs and Lapiths (12.210–537), which belongs to the stock of pre-Homeric epic, functions in the *Metamorphoses* as a narrative doublet of the Trojan War, which it displaces from the center to the margins of Book 12 (64–145, 580–628) and overshadows in length. Like the Trojan War (12.5), the battle of Lapiths and Centaurs begins with bride-theft, when the centaur Eurytus snatches Hippodamia from her new husband Pirithous at their wedding feast (12.219–23) and the other centaurs ravish her bridal attendants (12.224–6). The centaurs' rampage thematically parallels Paris' rape of Helen, just as the centaurs' abuse of the generous hospitality of their hosts, Pirithous and the Lapiths, echoes Paris' disregard for the courtesy owed to his hospitable host, Menelaus. The tale Nestor tells, however, like Ovid's own Trojan War narrative of Book 12, focuses relentlessly on the warriors' exploits on the battlefield and their attainment of glory in the fray. Hercules' son Tlepolemus points the moral of battle narrative, when he upbraids Nestor for eschewing mention of his father (12.539–41): 'I'm surprised you've forgotten the exploits that earned Hercules praise, old man. Certainly my father often used to tell me that he had vanquished the cloud-born Centaurs'. In their celebration of martial valor and the father–son relationship, Ovid's heroes self-consciously celebrate the generational transmission of exemplary standards of manliness from father to son that animate classical culture more generally.

Conclusion

This survey of sexuality and gender has, inevitably, failed to do justice to the richness and complexity of these themes in Ovidian poetry. For instance, Ovid's interest in the psychopathology of love—on display throughout the *Heroides* as well as in many of the episodes in the *Metamorphoses*—receives scant attention in these pages, while his recurrent descriptions of sexual violence and particularly rape, the focus of a considerable body of modern scholarship (Curran 1984; Richlin 1992b; Salzman-Mitchell 2005), has gone undiscussed altogether. Nor has this study considered instances of myths of homosexuality and transsexuality in Ovid's poetry. I hope, however, that by analyzing the carnal quality of Ovidian verse and the thematization of sexuality and gender throughout Ovidian poetry, I have brought to light some of the sensual pleasures to be gained from attentive reading of his work.

FURTHER READING

Feminist criticism has spurred interest in gender and sexuality in Latin literature and Roman culture generally, and in Ovidian poetry in particular. Hallett and Skinner (1997) and Ancona and Greene (2005) offer good points of entry to cultural specifics, while the collection of papers in *Helios* 17.2 (1990) is devoted primarily to Ovidian poetry. On the erotics of Ovidian elegy, on which a great deal of exemplary work has been done, see Wyke (1989, 2002), Sharrock (1991, 1994a, 2002a), Desmond (1993), Keith (1994/5, 1997), Farrell (1998), Fear (2000b), and Rimell (2006). On gender and sexuality in the *Metamorphoses*, see Nagle (1988a, 1988b), Nugent (1990), Richlin (1992b), Keith (2000), and Salzman-Mitchell (2005), with full bibliography. Less work has been devoted to gender and sexuality in the *Fasti*, but see Fantham (1983) and Newlands (1995). The exile poetry has more recently been brought into the discussion, with stimulating studies by O'Gorman (1997) and Rosenmeyer (1997).

CHAPTER TWENTY-SIX

Ovid's Generic Transformations

Joseph Farrell

Introduction

Reflecting on Ovid's ludic approach to genre is an activity that begins with Ovid himself. His basic stance is straightforward enough: from the beginning to the end of his career, he insists that he is an elegist. And from many points of view, it is hard to argue with him. Ovid's surviving works consist of about ten distinct titles; nine of these are in elegiacs. If we count lines, the elegiac bias is still clear, if less dramatic: of Ovid's thirty-four thousand surviving lines of verse, about twenty-two thousand (65%) are elegiac couplets. The rest comprise the hexameters of a single poem, the *Metamorphoses*. We know that Ovid also composed an *Aratea*, which was probably, like Aratus' *Phaenomena*, in hexameters, and a *Medea*, which will have used the iambic trimeters and lyric meters of tragedy; but these poems were probably not much more than a thousand lines apiece, so that Ovid's elegiac works will still have been the dominant portion of his *oeuvre*. In view of these facts, it makes sense to regard Ovid primarily as an elegiac poet who experimented only two or three times with other genres.

Generic Complications

On closer reflection, of course, the situation rapidly becomes more complex. In fact, for most of the past two thousand years Ovid's most popular and influential poem has been the 'epic'—i.e. hexameter—*Metamorphoses*. Ovid himself seems to have regarded this poem as his masterpiece. Although he went on after releasing it to produce as many elegies as he had done before, the *Metamorphoses* is such an imposing accomplishment that it almost outweighs Ovid's entire elegiac production. This impression is only strengthened when we examine what Ovid says elsewhere about his generic decisions. As he approached the midpoint of his career, he decided to assemble a definitive edition of his *Amores*, which had previously circulated in five probably separate books (*Am.* pref.; *Tr.* 4.10.61–2; McKeown 1987: 76). It seems likely that it was at this point that he composed *Am.* 1.1 (Farrell 2004: 42–6), the poem that introduces the collection. This poem begins with the poet recalling an attempt to compose epic verse, only to have Cupid appear and steal a foot from the second line, leaving his verses in the form of elegiac couplets. Result: Ovid became an elegiac rather than an epic poet, his subject matter conforming to the meter that he used (*Am.* 1.1.27–30).

If this unusual account of Ovid's poetic initiation suggests that he was forced into elegy against his will, there are many other passages in which he boasts of his position in the canon of Roman elegiac poets, following Gallus, Tibullus, and Propertius (*Ars* 3.333–4, 339–40; *Rem.* 763–6; *Tr.* 4.10.51–4, 5.17–20; see Tarrant 2002b: 15–17). Furthermore, although we haven't enough of Gallus' poetry to be sure, it is clear that Tibullus by implication (e.g. 2.6) and Propertius quite openly (1.7, 1.9, 2.1, 2.10, 2.34, 3.3, etc.) position their poetry as elegiac in contrast to epic and other more 'serious' genres. So from this point of view, we can explain Ovid's call away from epic to the 'diminished' form of epic that is elegy in very conventional elegiac terms. But none of Ovid's predecessors actually introduced his collected works by announcing that he was writing elegy *instead of* epic, or indeed by making an issue of elegy as a genre one way or the other; and none went on later in his career actually to compose a hugely ambitious poem extending to some twelve-thousand lines of epic verse. So while Ovid is definitely to be seen as the fourth and last of Rome's great elegists, he differs from all his predecessors in having strayed so far outside the boundaries of the genre, and also in having spent so much effort within his elegiac compositions testing those boundaries. In fact, with the conceits of the stolen foot and the revised generic program in *Am.* 1.1, Ovid presents elegy as a kind of epic manqué, and thus invites the reader to consider his entire career from an epic perspective. From this point of view, all of the elegiac works prior to the *Metamorphoses* could be regarded as fulfilling the poet's obligation to the god of love before he could finally turn to the epic masterpiece that he had wanted to write in the first place. And by the same token, those elegiac works that follow the *Metamorphoses*—the (deliberately?) truncated *Fasti* and the (supposedly) uninspired and prosaic exile poetry—can be seen as reverting to the lesser form in a way that reflects the diminishment of the poet's talent, a perspective that would reflect a major theme especially of the *Tristia* and the *Epistulae ex Ponto* (Williams 1994: 50–99).

Whatever Ovid meant by these gestures, they had an important influence on his reception. And this is not surprising. It was a very common feature of ancient scholarship to draw inferences, sometimes very specific and far-reaching ones, about all aspects of a poet's life and work from the poetry itself. Modern critics do the same thing, and the procedure is to some extent inevitable. But study of the ancient biographical tradition shows that what appears to be independent evidence about a poet's life, which critics offer up to explain this or that feature of the same poet's work, is often not independent evidence at all, but merely inference drawn from themes in the work (Lefkowitz 1981). A classic example is the statement found in the ancient biographies of Virgil (e.g. *vita Donatiana* 19) that the poet lost property in the land confiscations of the late 40s BC, but regained this property through the good offices of Asinius Pollio, Alfenus Varus, and Cornelius Gallus. In fact, we have no independent evidence that this is true; and the possibility is very strong that the story was invented to explain why Virgil *mentions* the confiscations, why *characters* in Virgil do lose their land and then regain it through the activities of a patron, and why Virgil honors Pollio (4.11–14, 3.84–91; on 8.6–13 see Farrell 1991), Varus (6.9–12, 9.26–9), and Gallus (6.64–73, 10) in several eclogues. So it is possible that Virgil himself had some such experience, but it is equally possible that he did not, and that the story is mere inference drawn from themes in the *Eclogues*.

In a scholarly climate like this, where any aspect of a poet's work might be taken as evidence about his life and work, it mattered a lot what the author himself actually said about his life and work. If we look at the critical reception of Ovid, we find that Quintilian (*Inst.* 10.1.93) faithfully reports the very same view of Roman elegy that Ovid gives us, naming Gallus, Tibullus, Propertius, and Ovid as the four canonical poets of the genre. Quintilian himself considers Tibullus the best of the lot, but acknowledges that others prefer Propertius. Gallus he regards as too dour (*durior*), and Ovid as too silly (*lasciuior*). Of course, Quintilian writes with orators primarily in mind, which limits his perspective, and it is easy to assume that Ovid's 'silliness' in Quintilian's view is a moral deficiency only. But while it probably is that, it may also be that Quintilian objects to a quality that we might regard as the *jouissance* that is characteristic of Ovidian poetry in all its aspects, including that of genre.

For instance, if we ask just what poetry Quintilian has in mind when he talks about Ovid the elegist, the answer is not so clear. Of all Ovid's elegiac works, only the three books of *Amores* are really comparable to the work of the other canonical elegists. Neither Gallus, Tibullus, nor Propertius wrote anything like the erotodidactic works (i.e. *Ars amatoria*, *Remedia amoris*, and *Medicamina faciei femineae*). Late in his career Propertius did write two poems (4.3, 4.11) that may have inspired Ovid to compose the *Heroides*. (It is not impossible that the lines of influence flow in the opposite direction: literature on the question is cited by Knox 1995: 18 n. 44, who is himself skeptical.) Several others clearly anticipate the aetiological themes of the *Fasti* (4.2, 4, 6, 9, 10; see Miller 1982). But these late departures do not outweigh the three books of more conventional elegies that precede them. By contrast, in the context of Ovid's career, the relatively conventional *Amores* appears as a kind of prelude to the prolonged adventure in generic experiment that would dominate the poet's efforts until the end of his life (Harrison 2002; Farrell 2003: 396–403; 2004).

It is in the end a moot point whether Quintilian even considered anything but the *Amores* when he assessed Ovid as an elegist. Either way—whether the erotodidactica, the epistolary works, and the *Fasti* contributed to Quintilian's judgment that Ovid was too silly, or whether he considered these poems totally beside the point— the conclusion we must reach is that he found the majority, and perhaps all, of Ovid's elegiac corpus generically embarrassing. This inference is supported by Quintilian's other remarks about Ovid. For instance, in his discussion of epic poets (*Inst.* 10.1.85–92) he uses the same language that he will again use in describing Ovid's elegies (10.1.88): 'Ovid is quite silly (*lasciuus*) in heroic verse as well, too much in love with his own wit, though some parts are praiseworthy'. Elsewhere we find the same language of disapproval (4.1.77): 'But there is that childishly boring affectation of the schools by which a transition itself produces some sort of epigram and looks for applause on that account as if for a magic trick—the kind of silliness (*lasciuia*) that is habitual in Ovid's *Metamorphoses*'. Quintilian does go on to recognize that such stratagems are forced on Ovid by the need to impose some unity on a sprawling mass of material. Nevertheless, the dominant impression is that Quintilian simply didn't approve of Ovid, and that his disapproval was rooted in characteristics that most readers consider fundamentally, and wonderfully, Ovidian.

The one Ovidian work of which Quintilian does seem to approve is one that is lost. In his notes on the canon of tragic poets, Quintilian states that 'Ovid's *Medea* seems to me to show how outstanding the man might have been if he had chosen to control his talent rather than indulge it' (10.1.98). This verdict is very much in line with Quintilian's complaints elsewhere about Ovid's frivolity. It is also interesting that the Ovidian work of which Quintilian most approves is a tragedy—that is, a poem written in a genre which is, formally at any rate, utterly unambiguous. Having shown that he could do things by the book, as it were, Ovid (in Quintilian's view) wasted his talent by constantly transgressing the laws of literary decorum, including those of genre.

Later ages have, on the whole, been kinder to Ovid, and much more appreciative. The renaissance of the twelfth century has famously been named an 'Ovidian age' (Traube 1911: 115). It was also a period of rampant generic experimentation. The fifteenth and sixteenth centuries as well saw the rise of new genres, particularly the novel. Scholars of early European literature (Kamuf 1982; Kauffman 1986; DeJean 1989; Brownlee 1990) argue convincingly that this most characteristically modern of genres owed a lot to Ovid's generically hybrid *Heroides*—a work that Ovid himself cites as generically innovative (*Ars* 3.346), but that no ancient critic ever mentions. Indeed, until fairly recently these poems were actively disparaged by classicists and even by admirers of Ovid's other works (Wilkinson 1955: 97, 105–6; Jacobson 1974; Kenney 1996: 1). The charges against them were many, but prominent among these was the belief that in choosing the epistolary form Ovid had committed a generic impropriety—for instance, by imposing epistolary form on what were 'really' dramatic monologues (Wilkinson 1955: 86). In retrospect, it is remarkable just how thoroughly a critical mentality dominated by the generic fallacy—the mistaken idea that the success of each and every work ought to be judged in terms of how well it conforms to the requirements of one and only one genre—blinded scholars to the dynamism of these poems, a quality that is clearly demonstrated by their influence on later literature.

Generic Impurities

It was a particular feature of nineteenth-century criticism to insist on generic purity. If we bear this in mind, then it becomes clear that in its time, the foundational modern study of Ovidian genre was a major step forward. Early in the last century, Richard Heinze published a lengthy stylistic assessment of Ovidian narrative in the genre of elegy (1919). He drew his illustrations mainly from the two lengthy narratives of the abduction of Persephone that occur in the elegiac couplets of the *Fasti* and in the heroic hexameters of the *Metamorphoses*. By comparing the two versions, Heinze was able to argue that the elegiac narrative emphasizes the softer emotions—pity, sentimentality, and so forth—while its hexametric counterpart is charged with more powerful sensations, such as anger, terror, and awe. In this way, Heinze parted ways with those who read Ovid's poetry as a hopeless muddle of generic impropriety.

Not long after Heinze's seminal work, Wilhelm Kroll published another essay that would set in motion a rethinking of Heinze's entire frame of reference (1924). The subject of the essay, which is not devoted specifically to Ovid, is the 'crossing of genres,' although it is usually rendered in English by the more promiscuous phrase 'mixing of genres'. Kroll's argument is simple enough: the crossing of genres is not a fault, but a principle of Hellenistic and Roman poetic composition. This simple insight found many adherents among classicists, with the result that both Heinze's idea, that Ovid and other writers generally obeyed specific laws of generic decorum, and Kroll's, that the deliberate violation of these laws was part of the poet's artistry, gave way by the 1970s to a widespread indifference and even hostility to generic criticism altogether (Little 1970).

And as the 1980s wore on, two rather different studies appeared, and the critical atmosphere changed decisively. The first of these (Knox 1986) argued that the *Metamorphoses*, despite its epic metrical form, was an elegiac poem through and through. Knox based his argument on a careful analysis of Ovid's diction and prosody. By such means he was able to prove that there is a substantial continuity between Ovid's elegiac poetry and the apparently epic *Metamorphoses*. The second study (Hinds 1987a) revisited Heinze's material, the Persephone narratives of both the *Metamorphoses* and the *Fasti*. Hinds argued that, in contrast to Heinze's view of definitively contrasting epic and elegiac narratives, what Ovid gives us is a pair of mutually dependent retellings that thematize their own status as representing a particular generic tradition. On this account, much of what Heinze had to say about the epic and elegiac qualities of the *Metamorphoses* and the *Fasti*, respectively, holds true. At the same time, however, the 'epic' *Metamorphoses* narrative does, in keeping with Knox's reading of the poem's generic affiliations, conform to important elegiac protocols; and, what is more, the 'elegiac' *Fasti* narrative exhibits some unmistakably, even ostentatiously, epic elements. Both poems, then, send mixed generic signals. Furthermore, they do so in a notably self-aware, perhaps even a characteristically arch, way. By way of introducing the Persephone narrative of the *Fasti*, Ovid notes that 'you will recognize most of it, but will have to be told a few things' (*plura recognsces, pauca docendus eris*, 4.418). This line has long been read not just as a comment on traditional and innovative elements in Ovid's version of the myth but as a cross-reference to the version that he tells in the *Metamorphoses* (Merkel 1841: cclvi). The knowledgeable reader will find both similarities and differences between the two renditions, not least in respect of their play with conventional generic expectations.

Now, some of the evidence that Hinds and Knox present—or, at least, the kind of evidence they present, evidence that proves neither the *Metamorphoses* nor the *Fasti* to have a stable epic or elegiac character—had been adduced previously to show that, by this period in Latin literary history, 'genre need no longer count for much' (Ross 1975: 37). This is in some sense almost true; but what Knox and especially Hinds showed was that the violation of these rules, and Ovid's ways of violating them, are of real importance. This aspect appeared very clearly in Hind's subsequent essays on '*Arma* in Ovid's *Fasti*' (Hinds 1992a, 1992b). The first of these essays emphasized not only that the *Fasti* mixes paradigmatically epic and elegiac themes and motifs, but that the narrator's anxiety about doing so is itself a major theme of the poem. To begin Book 2, for instance, the narrator remarks that (2.1–10):

> Ianus habet finem. cum carmine crescit et annus:
>   alter ut hic mensis, sic liber alter eat.
> nunc primum uelis, elegi, maioribus itis:
>   exiguum, memini, nuper eratis opus.
> ipse ego uos habui faciles in amore ministros,
>   cum lusit numeris prima iuuenta suis.
> idem sacra cano signataque tempora fastis:
>   ecquis ad haec illinc crederet esse uiam?
> haec mea militia est; ferimus quae possumus arma,
>   dextraque non omni munere nostra uacat.

So much for Janus. The year grows, and so does my poem: here are another month and another book. Now, elegies, be willing to travel under greater sails: I remember that you were once a frail genre. I myself had you as my ready agents in matters of love, when my early youth frolicked in the appropriate meters. I, the same man, now sing the sacred rights and the times that are marked in the calendar: who would have thought that you could get here from there? But this is my soldiery; I carry the weapons that I can, and my right arm is not available for every duty.

Of course, it is easy to take this as a conventional, and not very meaningful, throat-clearing gesture before the poet gets down to the real business at hand. But after he does so, he returns to these proemial thoughts and amplifies them with worry (2.119–26):

> nunc mihi mille sonos quoque est memoratus Achilles
>   uellem, Maeonide, pectus inesse tuum,
> dum canimus sacras alterno carmine Nonas.
>   maximus hic *Fastis* accumulatur honor.
> deficit ingenium, maioraque uiribus urgent:
>   haec mihi praecipuo est ore canenda dies.
> quid uolui demens elegis imponere tantum
>   ponderis? heroi res erat ista pedis.

Now, Homer, singing the sacred Nones in couplets, might I wish I had in me your thousand voices and the heart that told of Achilles. Here the pile of honor grows greatest upon my *Calendar*. My powers fail me; the task is beyond my strength: to sing this day I must be in exceptional voice! Why did I want to put such a burden on my elegies? Madman! This was a theme for epic verse.

The same anxiety that the conventions of the elegiac genre will not support his chosen theme occurs elsewhere in the *Fasti* (e.g. 3.1–10, 4.1–18). In all cases, Ovid regards generic conventions as a matter both of what is appropriate to a particular meter and of what he as a poet is even able to do. But despite these anxious protests, Ovid produces a poem that is, and that has in recent years increasingly been appreciated as, a masterpiece of generic transformation in its successful incorporation of epic, didactic, historical, antiquarian, astronomical, and other elements into what is— metrically, but in other ways as well—an elegiac framework.

Beyond Epic vs. Elegy

The *Metamorphoses* and *Fasti* are Ovid's most ambitious works, and passages such as the twin Persephone narratives suggest that they are bound together in ways that challenge one's usual assumptions about literary unity. For this reason, any account of Ovidian genre that focuses on these works will inevitably foreground the mutually defining relationship between epic and elegy. Other passages, like the beginning of the *Amores*, will strengthen the impression that this dichotomy is what Ovid's generic program is primarily about. Important as it is, though, it is hardly the entire story.

Previously, I noted Quintilian's approval of Ovid's lost tragedy *Medea*, suggesting that the formal clarity of the tragic genre may have been one of the qualities that appealed to Quintilian because it set the *Medea* apart from Ovid's other works. But this quality may have been only apparent; because even if the *Medea* itself was indeed a very straightforward specimen of the tragic genre, in the works that do survive, Ovid does all he can to complicate the picture.

Once again the process begins in the *Amores*. In poem 3.1 Ovid tells of a dream in which he is visited by a pair of equally beautiful goddesses. To tell them apart, Ovid looks at their feet: one wears an elaborate kind of boot called a buskin, while the other has feet of unequal size. The imagery here takes advantage of the fact that in Latin, as in English, 'feet' are units of measurement in poetic meter; so Tragedy has tragic feet, encased in the elaborate and impressive costume that is characteristic of her genre, while Elegy is provocatively barefoot, her beauty undiminished by her defining physical flaw. The dream represents Ovid's choice between two career paths. Just as in *Am.* 1.1 he had tried to write epic, but (under compulsion) gave it up in favor of elegy, here again he remains faithful to elegy, this time by choice, having already proven himself as a tragedian.

As in the case of epic, leaving tragedy behind in favor of elegy virtually announces Ovid's continuing fascination with tragedy. Tragedy rather than epic supplies several of the ladies who 'write' the *Heroides* (most visibly in the cases of Phaedra, Medea, and Deianira, but the letter of Canace too probably alludes to a lost tragic intertext, Euripides' *Aeolus*) and many episodes of the epico-elegiac *Metamorphoses* and *Fasti* are implicated with tragic, and especially Euripidean, intertexts. It is characteristic, for instance, that the Theban cycle as it is told in the *Metamorphoses*—a lengthy episode that has convincingly been read as an essay in cyclic epic, and even as an anti-*Aeneid* (Hardie 1990)—rehearses the demise of Pentheus in a way that depends heavily on Euripides' *Bacchae*. This is only one of many episodes that is so indebted. But not only Greek tragedy is involved: in the *Fasti*, Ovid tells the story of Claudia Quinta, a great beauty whose virtue was doubted, but vindicated when the Magna Mater allowed her to tow into port the ship that was bearing the goddess to Rome. The story would strain credulity, Ovid reports, did not the stage vouch for its veracity (4.326); and here he must refer to a lost *fabula togata* on the theme. Claudia is not only a tragic heroine but also, in view of her great beauty, an excellent emblem of Ovid's elegiac interests; and on this telling, the fact that Claudia maintains the personal virtue that her beauty seems to belie, aligns her with Ovid's elegiac stance in the exile period, a period during which parts of the *Fasti* were either composed or revised (Farrell 2004–2005: 48–52). In the exile poetry itself, tragedy turns up in some surprising places. In *Pont.* 3.2, Ovid relates a story told him by an old Gete or Sarmatian (he isn't clear which) about something that took place long ago in Scythia. The tale proves to be Euripides' *Iphigeneia at Tauris*. This unexpected intrusion transforms Ovid's place of relegation into an authentically 'tragic' landscape, and makes his exile poetry, therefore, more authentically tragic than Euripides himself. But in fact, this isn't the first time that Ovid makes this move. (Nothing in the exile poetry seems to happen for the first time.) In *Tr.* 3.9, the story of how Medea murdered her brother Absyrtus is adduced to explain the name of Tomi, Ovid's place of relegation (from the Greek *tomein*, 'to cut'). This episode has complex, and in one respect less obvious, antecedents. The most complete telling of this story that survives is found in the epic *Argonautica* of Apollonius Rhodius (4.338–506); but it was also the subject of at least one Roman tragedy (frr. 165, 170 Ribbeck), and so probably of an earlier Greek one as well; and the entire manner of the story, which explains a present-day institution (in this case, the name of Tomi) with respect to its origin in the heroic past, looks directly to Callimachus' masterpiece of elegiac narrative, the *Aetia* (not to mention the aetiological motif in Ovid's own poetry, especially the *Metamorphoses* and *Fasti:* see Myers 1994 and Miller 1982, respectively).

Episodes of the Medea story lend themselves to such treatment: the literary tradition is so rich with partial versions in almost every important genre. In Ovid's hands this is all the more true. His tragic *Medea*, as I have been suggesting, however decorous it was per se, tends to obtrude itself into generic contexts where it doesn't belong. To catalogue fully more than the most important appearances, such as the letters to Jason, from Medea and from Hypsipyle, in the *Heroides* (12 and 6, respectively), and the Medea episode in the *Metamorphoses* (7.1–426), would occupy the remainder of this chapter.

Through such factors as his career-long association with Medea, Ovid had a distinctive influence on later Latin poets, especially in epic and tragedy, who are increasingly seen as Ovid's successors in respect of generic inventiveness (Hinds 1993). In this regard, even where the interpretation of Ovid's own poetry is concerned and in spite of the much more generous appreciation of Ovid's generic artistry that has characterized recent criticism, the prevailing theoretical paradigm has not actually changed for years—indeed, in certain key respects, from the time of Quintilian, or even that of Ovid himself. This paradigm involves a conservative and fairly strict identification between specific verse-forms and specific themes. Not only ancient critics but poets as well endorse this conception of genre. The clearest and perhaps most influential statement is that of Horace in the *Ars poetica* (73–85):

> res gestae regumque ducumque et tristia bella
> quo scribi possent numero, monstrauit Homerus.
> uersibus impariter iunctis querimonia primum,
> post etiam inclusa est uoti sententia compos;
> quis tamen exiguos elegos emiserit auctor,
> grammatici certant et adhuc sub iudice lis est.
> Archilochum proprio rabies armauit iambo;
> hunc socci cepere pedem grandesque coturni,
> alternis aptum sermonibus et popularis
> uincentem strepitus et natum rebus agendis.
> Musa dedit fidibus diuos puerosque deorum
> et pugilem uictorem et equom certamine primum
> et iuuenum curas et libera uina referre.

Homer has shown the meter in which one can write about the dire warfare of kings and generals. Lamentation first, then too effective counsel was couched in couplets of unequal verses; but scholars debate, and it is still unclear who first composed delicate elegies. Anger armed Archilochus with suitable iambic verse; the comic sock and the great tragic boots received this foot, because it was suitable for speeches and prevailed over vulgar shouting and was born for getting things done. The Muse assigned lyric poetry to sing the gods and their children, along with the victorious boxer or horse-racer, and the lovesickness of young men in their cups.

As we have seen, Ovid in a number of passages presents a perspective on genre that resembles Horace's in essential respects.

It is well known, however, that poets, despite the ideals that they profess, constantly test the boundaries of genre. Ovid, once again as we have seen, actually trumpets his 'anxiety' about doing so, which is to say, he calls attention to the fact that he does so. Under these circumstances, it may be that the best critical paradigm available would posit the existence of a small number of well-defined, highly prescriptive genres, but would view poetry as taking place to a greater or lesser extent across the frontiers that separate these genres one from another. That is to say that Kroll's ideas about the crossing of genres may define the correct set of generic expectations, or at least the most useful one, for readers to bring to Ovid's poetry (Barchiesi 2001b).

One may ask, though, how hard to press the genetic metaphor in Kroll's 'crossing'. If, let us say, Ovid crosses the genres of epic and elegy, or elegy and tragedy, in a given poem, are we to view the offspring of this crossing simply as a poem or as the first representative of a new genre, descended from each of the parent genres, but different from both? Each of these possibilities seems real. One could cite examples of ancient poems that are themselves generic hybrids, but that were incapable of producing offspring of their own. In some cases, the poems in question did not establish a new genre in antiquity, but succeeded in doing so later on. Much of Ovid's poetry could be so described.

The *Heroides* are a case in point. Ovid boasts of having invented this genre (*Ars* 3.346)—whatever we want to call it. As we have seen, it has clear generic, or genetic, relationships with epic, tragedy, and other genres as well; but it is safe to say that the actual parents are elegy and epistolography. On Ovid's testimony, his example inspired his friend Sabinus to compose replies to the original *Heroides* (*Am.* 2.18.27–34; see Rosati 1996b), and Ovid himself (probably) went on to compose more poems along the lines of the original *Heroides* as well as three pairs of letters, which for the sake of argument we may consider representatives of the same genre as the earlier, single letters. But if we consider the later influence of these poems in antiquity, it would be difficult to maintain that Ovid succeeded in establishing a new genre so much as in opening a space for a generic tour de force that could not be repeated many times. If one traces the specific influence of the *Heroides* on classical Latin poetry, one does find such one-off performances as Byblis' letter to Caunus in *Met.* 9; but more commonly the generically innovative *Heroides* inspire generically more conservative productions, such as the influence that Medea's letter had on Seneca's tragic *Medea* and on Valerius' epic *Argonautica* (Hinds 1993). It would be centuries before the *Heroides* could be said to have inspired a new genre, the heroic epistle as practiced especially by women writers of the Middle Ages (Eloise et al.), and centuries more before this genre would give birth to longer narrative forms that eventually contributed to the formation of the modern novel. It is perhaps a moot point whether these post-antique developments are mere historical accidents having nothing to do with Ovid's own generic ambitions. It is the case, however, that the generic heterogeneity of such works as the *Heroides*, the *Ars amatoria*, the *Metamorphoses*, and the exile poetry all in their different ways gave an important impetus to the development of new genres, not in antiquity but long afterward. What do we make of this fact? Was Ovid that far ahead of his time?

This is not the place to mount such an argument, but let me close by suggesting that Ovid may well have harbored ambitions that his contemporaries and immediate followers simply could not comprehend. His influence on later Latin poetry was great, as critics are beginning to appreciate (e.g. Hardie 2002b). Ovid himself, like other ancient poets and critics, spoke about genre in highly conservative and conventional terms; but he, alone among classical Latin poets, practiced generic composition in a way that seems to call not just for a particular set of assumptions about the way in which he bent strict generic categories to his own purposes, but to require a new set of assumptions and a new set of genres. The need appears most clearly perhaps in the exile poetry, where the elegiac meter of the *Amores* and the erotodidactic poetry, the epistolary form of the *Heroides*, the aetiological narratives of the *Fasti*, and the kaleidoscopic mythical sensibility of the *Metamorphoses* all combine to produce something that is generically new, but which its author disingenuously denies is really poetry at all. By the usual rules of the game, we must consider these poems some species of elegy; this is possible, and Ovid encourages us to do so. But the influence of these poems would be very diverse, so much so that, unlike what we have seen in the case of the *Heroides*, their energy even in antiquity could not be channeled back into more apparently stable genres like epic and tragedy, but gave impetus to less easily classifiable works, or to genres unclassifiable by strictly formal terms (literature of exile, metamorphic literature, heroinism).

In sum, Ovid was a master of the generic gamesmanship that informs so much of Latin poetry. So complete was his mastery that he appears, with the benefit of two millennia's worth of hindsight, to have called into being a new world of genres, or at least to have taken the steps that made this world possible for others to create. His reward, ironically, was to be misunderstood and disparaged by ancient critics. But his influence on future artists more than compensates for the failure of early readers, and perhaps critical appreciation of his achievement is beginning to catch up, as well.

FURTHER READING

Heinze (1919) remains well worth reading for those who have German, but his approach is adopted by Otis (1970), attacked by Little (1970), and summarized more sympathetically and then modified by Hinds (1987a, 1992a, 1992b). All of these works concern primarily the mutually defining relationship between the 'epic' *Metamorphoses* and the 'elegiac' *Fasti*. Individual works have also been studied as variations on the elegiac 'norm', including the *Amores* (Boyd 1997), the *Heroides* (Spoth 1992, in German), the *Ars amatoria* and *Remedia amoris* (Conte 1994), the exile poetry (Williams 1994), and even the *Metamorphoses* (Knox 1986). On Ovid's career as a whole considered from the perspective of elegy, see Harrison (2001) and Farrell (2003 and 2004). On the sources of Ovid's attitude toward traditional genres, see Farrell (2004–5), and for an attempt to assess this attitude in terms that go beyond the ancient categories, see Farrell (1992).

CHAPTER TWENTY-SEVEN

Theorizing Ovid

Efrossini Spentzou

Introduction

For someone born into a comfortable equestrian family, who matured at a time of settled conformity when the political struggles that gave birth to the Augustan regime had passed into memory, Ovid and his poetic corpus are discomforting. His time was of disciplined memories, meticulously constructed narratives, and great rewards for allegiance to, and integration with, a social and political system that was, above all, imperial. And yet, Ovid, often called the *enfant terrible* of Augustan literature, last but not least of the 'Golden Latin' poets, appears at times carelessly directionless, unthinkingly unconciliatory (even vitriolic), and merrily eclectic, an anarchic approach that covered his poetic forms and his ideas. His apprenticeship with love elegy was long: five (of which three survive) books of *Amores*, 21 fictive love letters to lovers (*Heroides*), a manual on the art of love (*Ars amatoria*), and one with cures of love (*Remedia amoris*). Yet any threads of unity running through this amatory corpus are pulled apart by a galaxy of moods and personae, as the poet appears as a distressed, clueless slave of love, a careful, manipulative breaker of hearts, an expert teacher of men of the stratagems to use against women, the confidant of women in their manipulations of men, and even an epic or tragic heroine (occasionally hero) pining for an absent lover. In quick succession, he switches character, sometimes in the course of the same book of poems or even in a single poem.

At long last, the poet turns to serious business (*Metamorphoses*), a continuous epic poem from the beginning of time to the poet's own days (*Met.* 1.3–4), leaving juvenile narrative and other twists behind. Yet, even here there is not very much to remind us of the trusted Aeneadic model, nor of Livy's patient and patriotic account *ab urbe condita*. The poem jerks from the divine misdemeanors of Jupiter and Apollo (Book 1), to infatuated, sometimes incestuous, lovers (Tereus, Myrrha, Byblis), and to unlikely epic heroes who jump up trees to avoid harm (Nestor). And when the panegyric element comes, at the very end, it is punctured by a reminder that all cities rise and fall (*Met.* 15.418–30). If not incredibly convoluted, the transitions from episode to episode are coerced, pedantic, or so flippant that they ridicule the very notion of continuity and progress that the poem promised in the very beginning. These episodes are fragments that paradoxically claim to belong to a whole that defies understanding.

It seems to me that Ovid's protean propensity for transgression, instability, and experimentation has eased the way for critical theorists and exponents of contemporary theoretical approaches to engage with Ovid, and this in itself helps explain the renaissance in Ovidian studies from the early Seventies onwards. An eclectic pick-and-mix of primary material lures the reader toward experiment with multiple critical tools, and a continual stretching of boundaries and roles in the text invites metaphors from distant intellectual fields. Ovid's corpus dares us to find unity (the goal of traditional criticism) in its fierce aberrance, and readers have responded by deploying the weight of a theoretical corpus in the hope that the self-conscious, self-probing drives behind such theories will harness the (literal as well as metaphorical) beasts and force open the Ovidian labyrinth.

Ovid Against the Canon

One of the earliest tricks of theoretically informed scholarship on Ovid was to pitch the *oeuvre* against the classical canon, discussing and exposing prejudices in its formation. The ideology of the canon is a rich field offering insight into questions as complex and culturally important as centers vs. periphery, hegemony vs. subordination, homogeneity vs. diversity, masculinity vs. femininity. An interest, perhaps no more than a natural curiosity, in why Ovid was not in fashion for the first part of the twentieth century and did not become a 'hot topic' until its final decades, swiftly morphed into work on these polarities and Ovid's position within them; Ovidian scholarship of the last forty or fifty years kicked off in the heavy shadow of structuralist polarities. Ovid was awarded a place in the margins, and meaning was generated by his displacement from the establishment, ancient as well as modern. Feminist scholars were particularly fascinated by exposing the political undercurrents of this situatedness (see the special *Helios*, 1990). The Ovidian message was reconstituted in an environment of resistance, held together by a thorough-going anti-Augustanism, that reflected a whole spectrum of political dissidence in a poet refusing to assimilate.

Seminal to this movement was Judith Hallet's (1973) treatment of the entirety of love elegy and its slaves-to-the-*puella* men as an elaborate construction of a counter-culture in conflict with mainstream, male-dominated Augustan culture as promoted by the Princeps, through literature, legislation, architecture, and so on. Further layers of sophistication were added through intertextuality. Stimulated by the newly appreciated self-consciousness of Hellenistic poetry (see e.g. Bing 1988), intertextuality added nuances to more straightforward political readings, giving political edge to word choices, word plays, and intertextual allusions (see e.g. Hardie 1991 and Barchiesi 1997a). Formalism took off, aided by cross-disciplinary practices, such as narratology, and was in itself a sophisticated response to the subversive political messages of Ovidian work (see e.g. Hinds 1987a). In luring his readers toward the intricacies of form and structure, Ovid seemed to succeed in diverting them from political realities; Augustan programs and reforms were curiously sidelined in texts that seemed deliberately to manage attention away from them without, in fact, talking much about them. Yet, other interdisciplinary exercises saw a more pro-Augustan line. Focusing on aetiology allowed Myers (1994) to explore the particularly Italian roots of *Met.* 14 and 15, and trace in Ovid's quirky epic poem of change a discourse on cosmology that bestows a *grauitas* not that dissimilar to Hesiod. Tissol (1997) followed apace, diluting Ovidian subversion and radicalism with a detailed study of Ovid's scientific debts. Hardie's (1997) treatment of the poem's philosophical and other learning concentrated on Ovid's assimilation of the doctrines of Pythagorean philosophy.

In spite of Kennedy's (1992) thoughtful study of the numerous oversimplifications that lurk behind the Augustan/anti-Augustan opposition, an irresistible urge to pin down Ovid's political identity continued to be reflected in a number of diametrically opposed but equally intelligent studies. Perhaps because of its explicit association with politics and history, the *Fasti* has generated some of the most political essays, such as Herbert-Brown (1994) and Newlands (1995), who respectively read the poem as panegyric and subversion. A reappraisal of the terms of study was inevitable. A fresh look at Ovidian politics, consciously avoiding a narrow fascination with the figure of the Emperor and his portrayal, was offered by Habinek (1998), who draws our attention to much broader issues of ideology and the generation of power relations. The exiled Ovid becomes, for Habinek, the colonizing agent whose narrative on the distant tribes of the Danube ultimately propagates the difference between Roman and non-Roman in a perhaps unwitting, but still affective, colonial discourse. Eluding the impasses of a focus on the Emperor, Habinek adopts a Foucauldian interest in the place of Ovidian literature within the discourses that sustained Roman power. The shame of the dishonored Ovid in exile is, for Habinek, the most eloquent explanation of a psychology that sustained the politics of empire. In a retrospective appreciation of his project, Habinek explains how colonial psychology runs through the whole of Ovid's poetry (2002: 59):

> The exile poetry, like the earlier love poetry, presents a story of unrequited love, of a desire for integration foiled by the requirements of honour. In the *Amores* and *Ars amatoria*, the expressed longing for equal love, shared pleasure, simultaneous orgasm, is continually undermined by the conviction that if one is not in charge, one is under control. Thus the figure of the poet on display in the triumph is not just a figure relating the recourses of empire to empire's central authority; it is also an expression of a state of mind that cannot conceive of equality. One is either conqueror or conquered, *triumphator* or *praeda*.

Habinek's determination to expose lurking mechanisms of power behind the literary topoi of Ovidian verse created some unlikely critical alliances. Feminist classicists, who had been quick to embrace Ovid (on this see also Habinek's account in 2002: 61), had been discomforted by the formalist/narratological studies. These formalist studies with their emphasis on generic and programmatic elements in the Ovidian corpus were attacked by Cahoon (1990 and 1996) among others. She felt that the emphasis on the formal contained the risk of a concomitant neglect or demotion of other ethical, emotional, and broadly psychological concerns in the Ovidian *oeuvre*. In her article on the 'fallibilities, gaps, and silences' of Calliope's song in *Met.* 5, Cahoon associates the formalist trends in Ovidian studies with the politics of the academy in the mid-1990s (1996: 46–7):

> Just as treatments of Dido, Camilla, and Creusa are still rare in Vergilian studies . . . so too a more subtle silencing is apparent with regards to the *Metamorphoses* (not to mention the *Heroides*). The scholarly emphasis on Ovid's relations with the poems (and fragments!) of Callimachus, rather than on the connections among characters . . . reflects academic male bonding and Oedipal anxieties. I propose here that a reading attentive to the dynamics of power, psychology, and gender as they are enmeshed in Ovidian narratives . . . will be more timely and of wider appeal than more scrupulously pure narratological approaches . . .

Cahoon's empowering reading of sidelined Ovidian characters recuperates the interest in Ovid as a counter-cultural author of special significance for feminists seeking to appropriate the works of male authors (for more on this see the special issue of *Helios* 1990).

Gendered Readings

A tide of gendered readings of Ovid was to gather throughout the 1990s and beyond. Such studies also mark a gradual, but significant, turn in Ovidian scholarship. Gender relations are only part of wider power relations, and, in this sense, gender came to be a hermeneutic tool for broader deliberations on power. Much as in Habinek's readings of imperial ideology, by seeing literary figures as metaphorical bearers of extensive critiques of the social and political structures, gender studies shifted critical attention from the search for explicit alliances with and oppositions from the powers-that-be to a more nuanced exploration of the ideologies of Roman politics. As the personal came to be increasingly recognized as doubling as the political, attention shifted firmly and consciously to the individual. Within the broader context of gendered approaches to Roman love elegy, studies of Ovid's amatory elegiac poetry have been instrumental in power-conscious readings that celebrate the ways in which Ovidian elegy troubles and experiments with the nature of Roman manhood.

Amongst the most explicit examples, Gamel (1989 and 1998) systematically worked to expose essentializations in gender stereotypes in Roman culture and to read the male individual as an unpredictable unit, transgressing the social imperatives and fashioning of a dominant regime. The concept of performativity, gender as performance, in Gamel (1998) allows masculinity to be seen as a (temporary and changeable) construct. Lindheim (1998), working on dress and identity in the case of Vertumnus of Prop 4.2 and *Met.* 14, further builds on this sense of uncertainty surrounding selfhood in Ovid: by centering Vertumnus' identity on a dress code and his choice of wardrobe, Lindheim (1998: 36) allows, or rather suggests, that the reader might entertain the 'troubling possibility that gendered identity is no more than a tenacious, but ultimately ephemeral, belief in roles that acquire comprehensible meaning in social context'.

Identity is seen as constructed and communicated (performed) and hence being created within a network of communication rather than through an authoritarian and empowered discourse. In this way, identity becomes much more malleable and uncertain, elusive and subversive. Concentrating on communication turned Ovidian scholars toward issues of agency, voice, and, concomitantly, silence. Critics of gender have showcased the elaborate games played with voice in the elegies and *Metamorphoses*. In an article self-consciously called a 'footnote', De Luce (1993) shows us the catastrophic consequences of a woman's silence in the case of raped Philomela in *Met.* 6. Her powers of invention and communication are sharpened by the knife of her brother-in-law and tormentor, Tereus, who cut her tongue to steal her voice. Wild with pain and humiliation, young Philomela finds a way to weave her plight on a tapestry and send it to her sister, Procne. The two finally meet and weave their own terrible plot of revenge and destruction, enabled by conspiracy, silence, and miscommunication: a meal for Tereus, with the cooked limbs of Procne and Tereus' son as the main delicacy. Even when silence does not bite as hard, critics have argued that it can still have a deeply unsettling potential. Corinna's abortion poems are a favorite case study. As Gamel (1989: 183) puts it: 'Both as a phenomenon and as a discursive topic, abortion is difficult, messy, and dangerous. It raises fundamental questions about sexuality, a woman's control over her own body, the relations between the genders, and the powers of the state.' Gamel refers here to the confusing impact that abortion has in male understanding in a patriarchal society. Abortion is a female experience somehow beyond bounds, and a female decision that flaunts male knowledge and control. Almost ten years later, James (1997) took a broader look at the debate; extending the focus to slave rape in what she terms Ovid's *ancilla* passages (*Am.* 1. 7–8 and *Ars* 1.351–98), she investigates the complex layers of interpretation of speech acts performed by hearers, readers, and ultimately the speakers themselves. Her perambulations ultimately lead James to the many (female) silences that punctuate the attempted conversations of the poet-lover in the course of these passages. Far from an entrapping device, these often enforced silences create space, in James' opinion, for alternative interpretative possibilities. 'Although the male narrative gives us no female speech . . . these female silences can encourage us to withdraw from the male perspectives and desires being represented and elucidated, and to look at this language from the point of view of the women involved—to ask, in other words, what Corinna and Cypassis might say if they could speak freely' (73). Looking at the consequences of exile on the exiled persona's voice, Spentzou (2005) also homes in on silence. While his exiled heroines in the *Heroides* discover their voices in writing, Ovid in *Tristia* discovers or returns to writing having lost his physical presence at Rome and accustomed speech. And yet, silence is ultimately deployed by the Ovidian persona, a mode painfully but gradually acquired by the exiled poet to protect himself and his friends and to unsettle Augustus' prescriptive norms, drawing attention to things 'not said' and/or 'non-sayable'.

Narratology and Ovid

Pursuing the contours of voice and silence is obviously not the exclusive prerogative of feminist critics. Narratologists and feminists alike are drawn to the twists of expression in Ovid's long epic poem; discontinuity of voice appears a major riddle able to recruit disparate interpretative and theoretical tools in the pursuit of what seems to be a frustratingly elusive target. An ongoing interest in narrative technique led Tarrant (1995b), for example, to explore the gaps and silences in Cephalus' long narrative of unhappy love for Procris before highlighting allusions, absences, and hidden messages between the (often unuttered) lines in a search for untold stories in the *Metamorphoses* (Tarrant 2005). The list of narratological approaches to the *Metamorphoses* is long. Nagle (1983) on the incest mirror narratives of Byblis and Myrrha, on love triangles in the *Metamorphoses* (1988a), and on a range of erotic pursuits throughout the *Metamorphoses* (1988b) and Janan (1988) on *Met.* 10 have been model studies of the seductively alluring narratives at work in the stories of love and other encounters in the *Metamorphoses*. Blending critical developments in narratology, and especially storytelling, with sophisticated intertextual searches, Keith (1992) in her structuralist approach to *Met.* 2 unravels the meandering reflected, complementary, repetitive, conflicting, embedding, and embedded thematic structures through close readings of the narrators' interconnected stories.

In 2000, Wheeler reckoned an attempt on the complex narrativity of the *Metamorphoses* was due; his intention was to take on these labyrinths in the hope of discovering a fresh, convincing answer to the perennial puzzle of this fragmented *carmen perpetuum*. Wheeler chases thematic emphases and disparities through to their Ovidian denouement. He searches for beginnings in Book 1, only to find that the book of origins is punctuated by repetitive openings (the primordial order emerging out of Chaos, Deucalion and Pyrrha after the Flood, the new world after Phaethon's unwitting destruction of it while struggling, and failing, to restrain the chariot of Sun), all of which undermine meaning through their very own repetition. One certainty emerges from Book 1: that of impending chaos. Wheeler attempts to discern some pillars of continuity in the architecture of the *Metamorphoses*; divine pursuits and the twin stories of Jupiter and Juno offer thematic continuity but in the first cluster of stories emphasize a gradual weakening of parental control, and in the second cluster retell a progressively souring family drama. A complex constellation of narrative agents and devices often creates a seductive illusion of continuity, but ultimately unpredictability emerges as one of the main narrative drives throughout the *Metamorphoses*. Whatever closure might have been machinated in the last book of the *Metamorphoses* with the prophecy of Helenus on Troy's reincarnation as a powerful city and the deification of a descendant of Aeneas (15.444–9) is undercut by the anti-closural, cyclical forces of Pythagorean philosophy, within which Helenus' prophecy is accommodated. The poem concludes with a *sphragis* that does not confirm anything; the only reassuring information concerns Ovid's own undying fame in the centuries to come—but what of Rome and its power to govern the world?

Silences, gaps, and narrative seduction in the recounting of erotic pursuits all point to the unsettling illusions that Ovid is performing on and with his audience throughout this long, meandering text. Inquiries into the narrative demonstrate that meaning in the *Metamorphoses* is constantly reformulated, withheld, and suspended, in fact metamorphosed in and together with the ever-changing world that it purports to capture. As a result, trust in straightforward statements is systematically corroded. Indeed, the reader is wrong-footed and thus made suspicious from the first line of the poem: *In noua fert animas mutates dicere formas / corpora.* (1.1–2). What starts as a seemingly straightforward statement in the first half of the line ('my mind moves me to new forms') gets hijacked by the second half of the sentence, where *noua* ('new') finally meets its corresponding *corpora* ('bodies') and the overall meaning becomes: 'my mind moves me to tell you of forms changed into new bodies'. What seemed a simple, self-contained unit, in the course of one line becomes part of a bigger whole; meaning starts one way and in the process shifts to accommodate the needs of the new structure (see also Wheeler 1999, 8–10). The first four lines encapsulate the *Metamorphoses*: Ovid promises a continuous poem of the history of the world from the early years to his age, an authoritative history from the poet's pen, but the Ovidian narrator all but disappears, allowing a mêlée of other narrators to claim center stage and deliver their histories. As the reader moves deeper into the world of the *Metamorphoses*, these stories are found to have parallel versions, often antithetical. Multiple embedded narrations complicate yet further. Is the authoritative authorial persona behind or against his surrogate narrators? And can we trust the message of a story, once we have become aware of the multiple and contrasting narrations: how can we avoid the nagging thought that another narrator is soon going to present a very, or partially, different tale?

In his study of the multiple audiences of the *Metamorphoses*, Wheeler (1999) sees the uncertainty transmitted in the first line of the epic as permeating through the course of the first book. The subject-matter of Book 1 is the beginning of the world and the reader is treated with a confident quasi-philosophical account of an intelligent demiurge separating the disparate elements, assigning forms and appropriate positions to all things (1.21–86). Yet only too soon this image of harmony, symmetry, and divine, rational causality built starts unraveling in messy, unpredictable ways. The rational demiurge becomes the passionate father of gods who cannot tolerate the wickedness of men and strikes vengefully at Lycaon (1.163–243), eventually flooding the earth, so beautifully made, as a punishment for the sins of its inhabitants. Deucalion and Pyrrha, sole survivors of the Deluge, remake humanity, but from stones (1.348–415). And then, a little later, yet another story of passion jeopardizes the ingeniously crafted Creation: Phaethon, son of the god Sun and Clymene, demands Sun's chariot as a proof of his patrilineage (1.750–2.48). The favor is granted, albeit reluctantly, by his indulgent father, and Phaethon, mastered by his chariot (his tool, his inheritance, and his destroyer), sets the earth afire, triggering another destruction (2.103–327). What started as a universe beautifully arranged by a robust rationalism becomes one hostage to human and divine passions and indulgences. As Wheeler puts it, 'Ovid induces the reader to accept a perfectly coherent and normative view of the world in the opening episode and then proceeds to question it' (1999: 32). The reader reaches the end of Book 1 filled with confusion, but aware that things are not what they seem at first sight. Within all order there is disorder.

But what are readers to do with the burden of this knowledge? Are they meant to live in perpetual disbelief, resisting any engaged reading, from an instinct for self-defense? Wheeler explores the division between internal audiences (the listeners of the stories) and external readers (anyone with the whole fifteen books in written form in their hands) but does not attempt to resolve the dilemma of credulity or skepticism as reading strategies. This dichotomy is explored in the river Achelous' narration of his love for Perimele (8.590–610). As in so many of the *Metamorphoses'* stories, this involves an angry father (Perimele's father), a distraught maiden (Perimele herself), a chivalrous suitor (Achelous), and a *deus ex machina* (Neptune), who saves the girl, thrown into the sea by her father, by turning her into an island. The story elicits two strikingly opposed reactions: Pirithous' god-defying disbelief and Lelex's god-fearing engagement (8.611–9). Ovid does not assist our choice between the two readings, nor is there a model reading anywhere else: stories of belief as well as disbelief, credulity, and cynicism abound. On the one hand, the perverse continuity of the epic, such as it is, is punctuated by (mostly) unpleasant twists that expose the precariousness of any secure understanding and, on the other, the epic abounds in amoral characters who do not believe what they should believe: prime among them is Lycaon, who refuses to believe in Jupiter's divinity, before he tricks him with a deceitful meal in Book 1.

Readers and Illusions: The Imaginary and the Real

Yet, in spite of the multiplicity of possible readings of any situation, Ovid's stories stress that, aside from moral considerations, choosing the wrong reading is disastrous. Narcissus meets his death unable to read properly his own figure on the water, and Cephalus mistakes the rustle of a leaf in the woods for a lurking beast, shoots his javelin, and wounds fatally his beloved (7.835–862). Death lurks behind false readings. By the end of the *Metamorphoses*, Ovid has presented a particularly austere and uncompromising version of response-theory: the author does not determine meanings and the reader has the responsibility and must face the consequences of deciding on the meaning of the text. Earlier critical debates surrounding the closure of the *Metamorphoses*, and especially the politics of Book 15, asked the wrong question: the issue is not whether Ovid or his poetry is Augustan, but how the reader responds to the text. Not even Augustus himself can escape his responsibilities as a reader: in *Tristia* 2 Ovid, exiled at far-flung Constanza on the Danube, accuses his emperor of not reading his verse properly; and how could he, being such a busy man with so much on his plate (207–40). Flattery lies on the surface, but another reading lurks below. Augustus was mentioned as a member of the audience in a sudden, direct apostrophe in *Met.* 1. 204–5: *nec tibi grata minus pietas, Augustem, tuorum est, quam fuit illa Iovi* ('nor was the piety of your people less gratifying to you, Augustus, than it was to Jupiter'). Ovid allows the possibility in the *Tristia* that Augustus had not fulfilled his political and religious duty to read properly.

Intrigued by the authorial and reader-response illusions spun by Ovid, Hardie (2002c) studies illusion throughout the Ovidian *oeuvre*, and in so doing exposes a gaping hole in the middle of the Ovidian universe: Ovid's illusions seem to center on an unexpected absence. Things are not what they seem because things (and people) are absent. But in their absence they are dominant in someone's life; there are present absences or absent presences depending on where one puts the emphasis. Hardie's first example is Ovidian love poetry, a set of poems based on the phantasm of a woman, unnamed until *Am.* 1.4, with many poetic faces but yet stubbornly elusive and silent, who ultimately rejects the lover-poet. Corinna's absence fuels the poet's attraction as well as imagination. Later, Hardie (2002c: 55–9) observes how, in *Am.* 2.15–6, the surroundings of Sulmo serve only as a reminder of the absent *puella* spoiling the loveliness of the landscape. Presence accentuates absence but absence fuels desire and thus ushers the *puella*'s return as a ghostly (absent) presence, marred and enhanced by absence.

This suspended game of erotic conquest is repeated in the first erotic story of the *Metamorphoses*. Apollo desires the nymph Daphne; when she resists and flees (attempting absence), he chases her until she is changed into a tree (1.451–552). Trapped inside the tree's bark, Daphne achieves ultimate absence but will always be present, a rooted presence that claims absence; always visible and available, and yet hermetically aloof. As Hardie puts it (2002c: 46):

> The god of oracular certainty . . . spectacularly falls short not merely of foreknowledge of his own failure but also of the knowledge he seeks of the object of desire. At her first sighting . . . Daphne is subjected to a fetishistic scopophilia, that fragments her person into a blazon of body parts . . . and fantasises about what remains hidden to view. . . . [However] metamorphosis ensures that these secrets will always remain hidden, both from Apollo and from the reader, under the bark that grows round her soft body.

Hardie discovers other such absent presences. He notices the frustrating inability to touch suffered by Hero and Leander, the doomed lovers of *Her.* 18 and 19 separated by Hellespont, and by Pyramus and Thisbe (*Met.* 4.56–166), whose adjoining wall condemns them to corporeal separation. 'Lack' and 'the Other' are key concepts in Hardie's explanation of these numerous absent-presences and they point to a Lacanian reading of the self that he sees emerging through them. Pyramus and Thisbe's love lends itself readily to such an approach. Living in neighboring houses, their mutual love grew together with them, but the fathers ensured that they had no prospect of marriage. Their despair is mitigated by the discovery that their families' houses were divided (or connected!) by a wall which had a narrow chink. The two youths' love flourished as they held secret trysts, grateful for the chink that allowed them to exchange sweet words of love and blow kisses from lips that could never meet. Building on Fowler (2000), Hardie (2002c: 155–5) reads the story as a triumph of love built on lack (of touch) and a desire that can never be consummated.

This is unmistakably Lacanian. The reading of the story through Lacanian lenses refers to two fundamental distinctions/orders within which the individual develops and struggles to achieve self-awareness and a robust sense of subjectivity. In Lacanian thought, all people start in the 'Imaginary order' experiencing life as full, unfettered presence (of themselves next to their mother). Nourished in certainty and plenitude, the Imaginary encompasses all our primary fantasies, the confident images of ourselves that we project to the world. The 'Symbolic order', in contrast, is the world of rules and codes that each individual will encounter as they engage with society. Language operates in the heart of the Symbolic: it empowers people as it enables them to socialize, and yet at the same time it steals some of their individuality as each person agrees to abide by the codes and rules to be able to engage in a comprehensive way with others. The thrust of Lacan's work suggests that, despite misgivings and a sense of loss (of independence and self-adequacy), the individual will as a matter of course adjust to the rules of the Symbolic in order to gain self-awareness, subjectivity, and a place in society. Indeed, for Hardie (and Fowler), Pyramus and Thisbe are an example of the triumph of language over presence, and, more widely, the Symbolic over the Imaginary (Hardie 2002c: 145): 'The chink . . . is a filter that allows their love to be conducted through words, but does not allow Pyramus and Thisbe to enjoy the full presence of each other'.

And yet, Lacan suggests, even though ultimately incurable, regret over the loss of self-adequacy and independence works incessantly and vehemently within the socialized individual, fueling a continuous desire for an Other, in the illusory hope that in this encounter the original full presence and immediate enjoyment will at long last be re-enacted. Desire founded on this perennially nagging absence and lack explains, for Hardie, the near monotonous repetition of episodes, a peculiar kind of monotony that he discovers underneath the marvelous variety of places, people, narrators, colors, and attitudes in the Ovidian narrative (2002c: 66–7):

> Far from finding this an embarrassment, Ovid embraces this monotony, notably this . . . repetition within the first book of the story of Apollo and Daphne in the story of Pan and Syrinx, told by Mercury to Argus . . . [and also] in Book 10, in the doublets of the stories of two dying boyfriends of Apollo, Cyparissus . . . and Hyacinthus.

The self ultimately exists only as a failed self; the only social reality that Ovid recognizes is (Roman) subject-as-lack, which fuels desire for the always elusive Other in a vain quest for a meaning unblemished by the memory of separation and loss. As Hardie puts it: 'desire is the moving force of all signifying processes and is perpetually propelled forward as the desire for something else' (67).

Hardie is not alone in finding inspiration in Lacan. Psychoanalytical reflections on selfhood and subjectivity have proved popular in recent years. Miller (2004a) also offers a Lacanian analysis of Augustan elegy (including Ovid). For Miller, the Emperor and the surrounding political structures and Augustan laws and resurrected customs were intended to provide fixity in society and represent a complex and increasingly dominant Symbolic order. In the gradual move from the virtual anarchy of the civil wars of the first century BC toward the stability of the Principate, the Romans' sense of themselves (the Imaginary order) developed in ever-increasing tension with the Symbolic. Some of the most crippling moments of this tension hint at, even though they could never reflect, aspects of the 'Real order' (Lacan's third dimension) that lurks beneath the constructed and communicable systems of the Symbolic, defining the latter's limitations and the possibility/threat of otherness within its unifying forces and despite its unifying attempts.

Miller is fascinated with this sharp, brief conflict between individual and the Symbolic which runs through the genre of Latin love elegy, starting with Catullus' shock as the structures of the Symbolic change beyond recognition, developing with Tibullus condemned to live in a perennial never-land traumatically split between his Imaginary and a never attained Symbolic, and continuing to rage in Propertius' straining of the structures of the Symbolic to breaking point. But, for Miller, the Symbolic has spread and settled too much by the time we reach Ovid and oppositional tactics are inevitably changed. Instead of setting out to wreak havoc on its patterns, Ovid engages in a subtle and clever interaction with all those fixtures of the prevalent order that he wishes to attack. The best example of this, for Miller, is *Am.* 1.4, a poem of seeming jealousy of the *vir*, the girl's unsuspecting husband. Miller follows the contours of the poem and analyzes the juxtaposed images of the lover and the husband, only to find them sustained by repeated inversions. Ovid would give anything to be in the husband's place, yet the *puella*'s marital love for the husband is bound by the marital law; but she does not need Law to love the poet, her affections for the excluded *amator* are bestowed freely, uncoerced by the Law and thus legitimate. In Miller's words: 'The *amator* . . . is making a claim to legitimacy based precisely on the fact that he has no proprietary claims to Corinna's love. . . . This inversion aligns law, violence, and the *vir* on one side of the equation and places transgression, legitimacy, and the *amator* on the other' (2004a: 175). Ultimately, the erotic site of elegy, by means of its transgressive nature, 'gives the law forbidding transgression its reality' (183). Elegy legitimates Law through its transgressions. 'Thus the *amator* and the *vir*, Amor and Augustus, law and its infraction, are revealed by the *Amores* to be two sides of the same coin' (183); they are revealed to be inversions, and thus shown to be arbitrary, like the rest of Augustus' Symbolic order that Ovid takes so much pleasure in transgressing, mocking, and exposing, but from which he cannot escape.

The desiring subject is also the subject-matter of Rimell's study (2006) of Ovidian lovers. But for Rimell, desire in Ovid is not only an incessant game driven by (Lacanian) lack and an overwhelming sense of an absence at the center of self but is triggered by the conflicting energies and irreconcilable tendencies of the Ovidian selves. If the story of Narcissus in *Met.* 3 is emblematic of an irresistible urge of subjects throughout the Ovidian *oeuvre* to reach out and consume the 'other' that promises an ever-evanescent fulfillment, Rimell turns to another symbol, Medusa, whose story is narrated by Perseus in Book 5, to complement the understanding of desire in Ovid's work. By means of her frightening power to petrify people who dare look at her, Medusa draws attention to the self-realizing potential of the gaze and its workings in the Ovidian stories, elegiac and epic alike. Thanks to Medusa, attention is drawn to another stage in Lacanian psychoanalysis, the mirror stage of identity formation; gazing into the Medusa mirror, subjects become privy to the enemy within, and all those uncharted energies within themselves, that are part of their being, but an alien, frustrating, intimidating part of themselves. Guided by her interest in the Medusa-like mirror imaging, Rimell observes numerous offspring of the

monster scattered in the *Metamorphoses* staring at their opponents (or even randomly), and being victimized as a result (the hundred-eyes Argus that traps Io with
his watchful eye in Book 1, the snake that fascinates and then kills Cadmus' men
prior to the founding of Thebes in Book 3, the hunter Actaeon staring at Diana, and
Pentheus, the King of Thebes, staring at the Maenads, both also in Book 3).

Her insistence in the Medusa motif of looking at oneself through a mirror reveals
Rimell's interest in the relational subject, which, in itself, furthers the Lacanian
subject-as-Lack that motivated Hardie's 2002 study. Discussing texts as different as
the three books of the *Ars amatoria* and Orpheus' love story, song, and death in
Met. 10 and 11, Rimell explores the anxieties and unpredictabilities behind relationships. A relational self is not fixed by hierarchical polarities or an overpowering drive
for sameness. In Rimell's reading, narcissistic reflection is always accompanied by
constant refraction brought about by the multiple Medusa offspring that take over.
As Rimell says (2006: 38): 'In Ovidian poetry, the consistent intertwining of (echoes
of) Narcissus' and Medusa's myths ensures that subjects' relationships with the
mirror, and with their own reflected, projected selves, are in different ways always
fraught and risky'.

In the Medusa mirror, subjects become objects, victors become victims, interiors
become exteriors, once again exposing the arbitrariness of the Symbolic order that
is built on the fixity of such polarities (compare here Miller's readings of the Symbolic
hegemony, above). In the Medusa mirror the subject is terrified and fascinated by
the 'terrible' enemies that are no longer certainly outside but may be lodged within
one's own psyche, family, and city. The Ovidian stories are replete with encounters
with engaging and terrifying creatures: the lover and the husband of *Am.* 1.4 whose
image is refracted in the 'otherness' of a centaur's face, Scylla (*Met.* 8), Byblis (*Met.*
9), and Myrrha (*Met.* 10) (all innocent daughters of 'good families' taken to extremes
by the force of inappropriate passion for father's enemy, brother, and father, respectively), Phaethon (*Met.* 2), Icarus (*Met.* 8) (lured and ultimately destroyed by their
instinct to stretch beyond all rules), and so on and so forth.

Focusing on the moment eyes meet eyes in the mirror, Rimell turns our gaze upon
the corporeality of the selves, and the distances that the bodies have to cover to touch
each other. For her, the space between selves-as-bodies is of paramount importance:
it is the space where hierarchies may collapse, dangerous but irresistible experiments
take place, forbidden or uncontrollable ideas burst into life. Keeping distance is an
intensely political gesture leading to an intensely political type of community. The
contemporary philosopher, Jean-Luc Nancy, has worked extensively for what he calls
'inoperable communities' (the communities that do not sink in consensus) by allowing the distance between the bodies (the space between two sets of eyes) to exist, in
continuous interaction with each other. Discussing this community, Nancy asks
questions that might interest Augustus and Ovid (2005: 154–5):

> What is a community? It is not a macroorganism, or a big family (which is to assume
> that we know what an organism or a family is . . .). The *common*, having in-common or
> being in-common, excludes interior unity, subsistence, and presence in and for itself.
> Being with, being together and even being 'united' are precisely not a matter of being

'one'. Within *unitary* community [*communauté une*] there is nothing but death, and not the sort of death found in the cemetery, which is a place of spacing or distinctness, but the death found in the ashes of crematorium ovens or in the accumulations of charnel-houses.

Looking at each other through the Medusa mirror, the selves in Ovid's multifaceted stories keep stumbling over their selves' darker components. Thinkers of modernity have given this encounter the name of the sublime, another name for Lacan's Real. Eagleton (2005) discusses both concepts, which pertain to the distance between, and within, the selves. Eagleton posits the Real as 'the unfathomable wedge of otherness at the heart of identity which makes us what we are, yet which—because it involves desire—also prevents us from being truly identical to ourselves' (43). Similarly, 'the sublime is a glimpse of infinity which dissolves our identity and shakes us to our roots, but in an agreeable kind of way' (44).

Ovid's engagement with the sublime, his interaction with political orders, his profound elusiveness mean that he is a poet who will continue to fascinate, delight, and puzzle. The Ovidian corpus is both Narcissus' pond and Medusa's mirror in both of which the concerns of the modern are refracted and reflected and it is in its complexity, its familiarity, and unfamiliarity that critics will continue to find inspiration and also incomprehension that will lead them to search through the modern critical tradition. There is a wildness in Ovid that defies or seems to defy attempts to bring the work to order and understanding, a wildness that is political but also engages with the very stuff of human experience. In Ovid's literary world, the characters and readers are in an 'inoperable' community, keeping distances from themselves and from each other, seeking continuous identifications in the hope of achieving presence, continuously refashioning themselves in what is both resistance and subjection to the Symbolic. But next to Narcissus there is Medusa. And as Rimell puts it (2006: 209), 'Medusa makes the wildest illusions real, rock solid'. Ovid exists in the wildest illusions and leads us to an abyss where radical loss and incomprehension go hand-in-hand with radical discovery and understanding.

FURTHER READING

In addition to the works cited in the text, readers may profit from a few items on basic concepts of Lacanian psychoanalysis, for example Lacan (1981: esp. 53–64) and his papers, 'The mirror stage as formative of the function of the I' and 'Aggresivity and Psychoanalysis' in Lacan (1977: 1–7, 8–29). The Lacanian concepts are notoriously difficult to pin down to explicit references; however, the following can act as introductory pointers to further research, especially on the ways in which Lacanian psychoanalysis and especially the tripartite division of the Imaginary, the Symbolic, and the Real can serve as subtle tools for socio-political and literary criticism: Žižek (1992: 3–47), Stavrakakis (1999), and Janan (1994: 1–37).

PART V

Literary Receptions

CHAPTER TWENTY-EIGHT

Ovidian Strategies in Early Imperial Literature

Charles McNelis

Introduction

The twelfth and thirteenth centuries are often referred to as the *aetas Ovidiana* (Traube 1911: 113), but to judge from recent studies of the influence of Ovid's poetry on subsequent Latin literature, the first century AD could also be designated as such. Virgil's influence on the literature of this period is certainly not to be denied, but authors as different as Seneca (Tarrant 1978: 261–3), Lucan (Tarrant 2002a; Wheeler 2002), Martial (Szelest 1999; Williams C. 2002; Janka 2006; Hinds 2007), and Statius (Dewar 2002: 394–401; Keith 2002a) also made significant use of Ovid's poetry. This focus on Ovid's prominent role in Roman literary history owes much to scholarship dating from the 1980s and later that has changed the ways in which both his own poetry and its importance for subsequent Latin literature are read (Hardie 2002b: 34–35 discusses some fundamental critical changes). For instance, it is no coincidence that intense interest in Ovid's narrative techniques has followed in the wake of theoretical work on narratology that dates from the 1970s. And some of the recent scholarship on his *Heroides* partially depends upon an interest in artistic representations of women, a pursuit that has been energized by feminist criticism. Not surprisingly, as our readings of Ovid have changed, it has become possible or even necessary to re-evaluate his importance for later imperial writers. And this process of re-evaluation will continue: Ovid's brilliant deployment of, for example, myth, genre, psychology, and rhetoric makes his poems some of the richest ancient art that we possess. As new critical approaches to such topics emerge, our perceptions of Ovid and his influence will change.

That Ovid's prolific writings respond to a range of approaches is not a peculiarity of modern criticism, however, and in this essay I will focus on instances in which Martial, Seneca, and Statius adapt Ovidian dynamics to their own literary interests. First I will consider Martial's reworking of the *Ars amatoria* as a means of representing a Roman world whose mores and identity defy definition and even legislation.

In doing so, Martial turns the *Ars* into a culturally authoritative poem that invests his own seemingly trifling epigrams with significance. Next, I will turn to the deification of Claudius in Seneca's *Apocolocyntosis* to suggest that the satire treats Ovid's *Metamorphoses* as a definitive text for the imperial period. In particular, Seneca's work suggests that the *Metamorphoses* is foundational for the imperial arrangement of time, history, and apotheosis. Another way in which Ovid's epic shaped imperial literature was in its treatment of myth, and the influence of Ovidian myth upon Statius' *Achilleid* will be the subject of the final section. My interest is not merely to treat Ovid as a source for myth but to explain ways in which allusions to the *Metamorphoses* and its treatment of Achilles underpin Statius' depiction of the cross-dressing warrior and his frustrated mother. In his reworking of an Ovidian depiction of Achilles, Statius sets the *Metamorphoses* against Virgilian epic norms and even reifies a literary-historical divide between the world views of the two epics. These three authors used Ovidian poetry as a powerfully rich model for the conception and production of diverse literary strategies in imperial Rome.

Martial's *Ars Amatoria*

The subjective love elegy that was written by poets like Ovid, Propertius, and Tibullus died out in the imperial period, perhaps because it was dangerous in the established political system (Sullivan 1991: 105). Nonetheless, later imperial poets certainly reworked features of amatory elegy to their own ends. Statius' *Silvae* 1.2, for example, is a hexametric poem about the marriage of Stella and Violentilla, and thus on the surface appears to be as distant as can be from the adulterous relationships of elegiac poetry. Yet Statius consistently incorporates elegiac themes and ideas in his poem (Hardie 1983: 112–5; Nauta 2002: 300; Newlands 2002b: 93). Personified Elegy, for example, attends the celebration of the marriage (1.2.7), and Philetas, Callimachus, Propertius, Ovid, and Tibullus are summoned to sing at the wedding (1.2.251–5). Statius' enumeration of his poetic predecessors recalls the lists of canonical poets—many of whom are elegists—that are familiar from Propertius (2.34) and Ovid himself (*Am.* 1.15), and by continuing such a practice, Statius updates the canon to include Ovid.

While such features highlight the fact that Stella himself was an elegiac poet, Statius' practice also indicates that Roman elegy had been transformed, not forgotten. Indeed, in terms of technical aspects of elegiac composition, Martial has been seen as ably operating within an Ovidian tradition (Kenney 2002: 38), and there are numerous examples of his echoing of Ovidian phrases (Zingerle 1877; Siedschlag 1972; Janka 2006: 280–1 discusses scholarship on Ovid and Martial; Hinds 2007: 114–29 is a full discussion of Martial's generic strategies). In addition, Martial's interest in Ovidian elegy encompasses important themes that his predecessor had worked with: both attempt to bridge the distance between poet and emperor through their writings (Pitcher 1998: 61), and Ovid's poems thus assume a role in the subsequent development of imperial encomium (see e.g. Dewar 1996: 417).

Panegyric, however, is not the only literary strategy that appears in imperial poetry. While both Martial and Ovid deal with the loftiest possible themes of empire and its rulers, their poems are also full of depictions of individuals engaged in less than noble activities. And the two poets often situate these activities in prominent public locations. For example, in 11.47, Martial discusses a man named Lattara who avoids localities in Rome that might lead him to a sexual encounter:

> Omnia femineis quare dilecta cateruis
> balnea deuitat Lattara? Ne futuat.
> Cur nec Pompeia lentus spatiatur in umbra
> nec petit Inachidos limina? Ne futuat.
> Cur Lacedaemonio luteum ceromate corpus
> perfundit gelida Virgine? Ne futuat.
> cum sic feminei generis contagia uitet,
> cur lingit cunnum Lattara? Ne futuat.

> Why does Lattara avoid the baths favored by throngs of women? So as not to fuck. Why doesn't he leisurely stroll in the shade of Pompey's portico, nor seek the doorstep of Inachus' daughter? So as not to fuck. Why does he soak his body, dirty with the Spartan wrestling-mud, in the cold water of the aqueduct of the Virgin? So as not to fuck. Since he avoids the pollution of women in this way, why does Lattara lick a cunt? So as not to fuck.

Martial's diction in the third verse is obviously indebted to the scene in the *Ars amatoria* in which Ovid mentions Pompey's portico as a useful place to find women (*Ars* 1.67 *tu modo Pompeia lentus spatiare sub umbra*). And in the next verse, Martial mentions the temple of Isis, another site that comes from Ovid's list of pick-up spots in Rome (*Ars* 1.77 *nec fuge linigerae Memphitica templa iuuencae*). Martial's topography thus evokes the *Ars*, but as the negative purpose clauses that end each pentameter suggest, the allusions create a deeper literary dynamic: the fact that Lattara avoids places that could lead to sexual encounters of the type which form the subject and goal of Ovid's poem suggests that he 'knows' the *Ars* well and shuns its advice. For the first six verses of the epigram, Lattara seemingly exhibits a stronger moral code than that at work in Ovid's poem.

However, in the final couplet Martial reveals that Lattara's avoidance of these sites does not stem from his upright morality. To the contrary, Martial mockingly questions his character's behavior by revealing that Lattara practices cunnilingus in order to avoid penile intercourse. This kind of oral sex was met with widespread opprobrium in antiquity since it was seen both to befoul one's mouth (Krenkel 1981; Williams 1999: 197–203) and to be unmanly since a man served a woman without using his penis (Williams 1999: 202). Though the model of ancient sexuality that is predicated upon the penetration of an inferior person by a socially superior adult male has been usefully challenged (cf. Dover 1978: 100–9; Davidson 2001), Martial's epigram seems to operate within such a model since it is precisely Lattara's failure to penetrate that is targeted for abuse. In addition, penetration as a form of power had already been raised earlier in the book when Martial offered that cunnilingus was performed by impotent men (11.25). Lattara's activity thus threatens Roman sexual mores in a different and potentially more troubling way than does sex of the type suggested in the *Ars*: sexual mores have been challenged and relativized, and we are left wondering whether the avoidance of an Ovidian kind of sexuality is actually all that bad when compared to behavior that may involve losing one's masculinity.

Such concerns about sexual mores, however, are accommodated to Martial's own epigrammatic ends. Most obviously, the fact that this humorous twist is postponed until the final line is characteristic of Martial's style. This ending serves another epigrammatic purpose in that it undercuts a prominent dynamic of Ovid's poem: whereas the initial verses of 11.47 set up the *Ars* as a disreputable poem that advises about illicit relationships that Lattara seemingly seeks to avoid, Martial upsets this view in the final couplet when he takes away some of the scandal of the *Ars* and seems to highlight instead the salacious nature of his own epigrams (cf. 1.4.8; 3.86). In addition, Martial's narrator does not take on a didactic voice, but rather the narrator has the position, familiar from other epigrams, of a simple chronicler of actual Roman life (Fowler 1995b: 35 discusses epigram and its portrayal of 'real' life). In 11.47, then, Martial imputes a specific literary-historical knowledge to Lattara to rework the *Ars* and its morality to his own epigrammatic program (Hinds 2007: 121–9).

Martial elsewhere uses the *Ars* to investigate the sexual mores of women. For example, in 7.30, Martial lampoons a promiscuous woman named Caelia who has sex with all sorts of foreigners but not with any Romans:

> das Parthis, das Germanis, das, Caelia, Dacis,
> 　　nec Cilicum spernis Cappadocumque toros;
> et tibi de Pharia Memphiticus urbe fututor
> 　　nauigat, a rubris et niger Indus aquis;
> nec recutitorum fugis inguina Iudaeorum,
> 　　nec te Sarmatico transit Alanus equo.
> qua ratione facis, cum sis Romana puella,
> 　　quod Romana tibi mentula nulla placet?

> You provide sexual favors to Parthians, Germans, and Dacians, Caelia. Nor do you reject the beds of Cilicians and Cappadocians. The Egyptian fucker sails from his Pharian city to you, as does the black Indian from the Red Sea. You do not avoid the loins of circumcised Jews, nor does the Alan, with his Sarmatian horse, pass by you. Since you are a Roman girl, what is the reason that no Roman penis pleases you?

Martial's account of these foreigners owes something to the *Ars amatoria*. His designation of an Aethiopian as *niger Indus*, for example, evokes Ovid's similar description (*Ars* 1.53), and the adjective *Memphiticus* also seems to have Ovidian pedigree since the adjective appears for the first time at *Ars* 1.77 (Galán Vioque 2002: 217). Moreover, the epigram ends by stating that no Alan passes by the woman with his horse. This may be a double entendre that plays upon the idea of the *mulier equitans*, a sexual position addressed at *Ars* 3.777–8, a scene which had a clear influence on Martial elsewhere (Hinds 1998: 130–5; Galán Vioque 2002 argues against the double entendre).

In addition to the verbal echoes of Ovid found in this epigram, Martial's overall strategy is Ovidian in that he links sexuality to the new global geography of Rome's imperial world. In the *Ars amatoria*, for example, Ovid mentions that Augustus recreated the sea battle at Salamis between the Athenians and Persians (*Ars* 1.171–2), though he omits that the occasion for the fictive battle was the dedication of the temple of Mars Ultor in 2 BC. Elsewhere, however, Ovid suggests that this temple fulfilled the vow that Octavian had made at Philippi in his fight for imperial control (*Fast.* 5.569–78), and when Ovid adds that young men and women from the whole world were in Rome for the spectacle (*Ars* 1.173–4), it is clear that the mock sea battle symbolizes the coming together of east and west that occurred after Augustus' victory. Yet in the *Ars* this global conquest serves as an opportunity for young lovers to find mates. Even when Ovid segues to the desired conquest of the Parthians by Gaius and to the imagined triumph that will take place (*Ars* 1.177–218), he concludes by suggesting that the ceremony will offer possibilities for the young lover. Roman conquest and the growth of its empire thus aids the cause of Ovid's students, who, if they follow the poet's advice, will become a type of conqueror without needing to 'go abroad.' Indeed, in an earlier expression that echoes his later comment about the opportunities afforded by imperial Rome, Ovid himself had stated that the city had whatever is available in the world and thus there was no reason for a man to look for foreign women (*Ars* 1.55). Through its natural abundance and now through world conquest, Rome has it all.

In 7.30, Martial's depiction of empire includes the Parthians and many other peoples who had come under Roman sway—some quite recently. Domitian had celebrated a triumph over the Dacians in AD 89, a few years before the publication of the seventh book of epigrams (Galán Vioque 2002: 6–7). The mention of the Jews need not refer to the destruction of Jerusalem (and the Temple) by Titus in AD 70, but given that the arch of Titus, constructed after his death in AD 81, emphasizes this particular conquest, such a reference presumably had special resonance in the Flavian period. Cappadocia had been annexed by Tiberius, but Vespasian turned it into a prominent military establishment that stretched all the way to the Euphrates (Levick 1999: 166–9). He also built a fortress at Satala to check the approach of the Alani (Levick 1999: 168–9). And Egypt, Germany, and Cilicia had been under Roman control for some time. So, with the exception of the Aethiopians, Martial follows Ovid's lead by situating Caelia's sexual activity within the recently expanded or strengthened boundaries of the Empire.

Yet in crucial ways, Martial diverges from the *Ars*. For instance, far from being defeated and paraded in a military triumph, Martial's foreigners are now the conquerors. Moreover, Caelia's attraction to these men tweaks the Ovidian idea that Rome possesses whatever is available in the world (*Ars* 1.56 *haec habet . . . quicquid in orbe fuit*): the world is indeed available at Rome, and Caelia has taken advantage of it to the exclusion of Rome itself. Ironically, this incorporation of the world into Rome stems in part from military strength and expansion, yet such a view of masculinity is undercut when a Roman woman spurns an essential attribute of Roman masculinity—the penis. And it is in this fictive display of sexual anxiety about whether or not Roman men are good enough that Martial moves furthest from the correlation of sex and power that generally pervades the *Ars* (See Bowditch 2005, however, for the weakened correlation of force and sex in some of Ovid's 'mythological digressions').

In this epigram as well, Martial reworks Ovidian themes to fit his epigrammatic program. Caelia, for example, is a recurring name for a promiscuous woman in his poetry, and it thus situates this poem in a broader context of epigrammatic fictions about sexuality and imperial Rome. The quadrisyllabic word *Iudaeorum* at the end of the fifth verse creates a spondaic hexameter, and though Martial rarely employs this kind of verse, spondaic lines do appear in his poems with greater frequency than in any poet since Catullus (Galán Vioque 2002: 215). In addition, the repetition of *das* with the meaning of 'to be sexually available' may look to a Greek epigram of Rufinus (*AP* 5.103), who is the first extant writer to use *parexein* in such a way (Galán Vioque 2002: 215). And the tricolon in the opening verse serves another generic purpose since it establishes the norm that is undercut at the last possible moment (Siedschlag 1972: 56–8). This representation of Caelia's sexual practice, then, reworks themes of Ovidian elegy to the form and style of Martial's epigrammatic practice.

Perhaps Martial builds upon Ovidian precedent most of all when he addresses the relationship between imperial law and individual sexuality. Although the connection between Ovid's poem and its Augustan context is complex and disputed, the poem clearly counters the general spirit of Augustus' attempts at moral reform (Gibson 2003: 25–33), and there were numerous aspects of the *Ars* that could be offensive (e.g. Barchiesi 2001a: 91–2). Most notoriously, Ovid's poem works against the Augustan reform of marriage that took place in 18–17 BC when the *lex Iulia de adulteriis* was passed.

The Augustan context of Ovid's poem matters since Domitian reintroduced moral reforms to Rome and modeled himself upon Augustus in order to do so (Jones 1992: 99; Sablayrolles 1994: 125–7). For instance, Domitian condemned those of the senatorial and equestrian classes who had sex with free-born males and thus violated the *Lex Scantina* (Suet. *Dom.* 8.3); he also passed a law forbidding castration (Suet. *Dom.* 7.1). Most significantly, however, Domitian renewed the *lex Iulia de adulteriis* (Pliny *Pan.* 42.1), the very law that Augustus had passed as a cornerstone to his moral reforms. Such reforms are praised by Martial (e.g. 5.75, 6.2, 6.4, 6.22), though he also uses these laws to humorous effect. In the two verses that comprise 6.91, for instance, Martial seemingly applauds the laws yet simultaneously points to their inefficacy in controlling sexual morality:

> Sancta ducis summi prohibet censura vetatque
>   moechari. Gaude, Zoile: non futuis.

> The sacred censorship of the highest leader forbids and bans adultery. Be happy, Zoilus: you do not fuck.

The opening hexameter is full of lofty language that seemingly approves of the law against adultery: the phrase *sancta censura* combines the Roman political office charged with regulating morality with an epithet of the imperial household (Grewing 1997: 490–1), and the words *ducis summi* likewise draw upon long-standing—though unofficial—imperial titles (Syme 1939: 311–12). But the concluding pentameter creates a clear contrast with this tone by bookending the verse with the sexually charged and obscene words *moechari* and *futuis*. Moreover, the epigram's humor stems from the fact that, as is revealed elsewhere (3.82.33; cf. 11.30), the only reason that Zoilus will not violate the law is that he performs oral sex on men. Considering the stigmatization of fellatio (Williams 1999: 197–8), Martial has once again relativized sexual attitudes by creating a situation in which adherence to official morality seems trivial in comparison to the violation of conventional Roman attitudes about sex. So too in 6.45 Martial overturns the idea that, according to the *lex Iulia*, sex within marriage is virtuous when he suggests that in her marriage to Lygdus, a certain woman named Laetoria was better off as an adulteress (*moecha*) than as a wife (*uxor*). Martial here indicates that even seemingly straightforward moral definitions and codes are slippery. Like 11.47—a poem published after Domitian's assassination but so soon thereafter that it allows one to look past chronological demarcations—and other poems in the collections (Garthwaite 1990), then, Martial's poems illustrate an ever-changing and relative morality that defies imperial codification. Social positions, gender roles, and Roman sexual mores are all in flux in Martial's poetic world.

In light of the numerous laudatory poems about Domitian throughout the first nine books of his epigrams, it seems unnecessary to privilege these humorous poems and suggest that Martial is subversive of Domitian's rule. Indeed, Martial does not employ Ovid's didactic stance, thereby distancing himself from such behavior rather than teaching it. And early in his poetry collection (1.4.8), Martial defends his coverage of scandalous themes by stating that it is his poetry that is naughty, not his life. Yet this apologia is indebted to Ovid's own statement at *Tr.* 2.354—a verse in which he defends the *Ars* from criticism of cultural subversion—that his life is modest but his poetry playful, and Martial's evocation of Ovid's complex treatment of poetry and emperors suggests that any view of Martial's relationship to imperial power that is predicated simply upon adulatory poems of Domitian (or even Titus) is also reductive. Rather, the conflicting representations of moral legislation and violations of it coexist in the poetic world that Martial creates. Like Ovid's before him, Martial's Rome contains a full spectrum of life, with his poems taking as their subjects, for example, all sorts of social relations, sexual behavior, mundane objects, and imperial majesty. In Ovidian fashion, Martial's epigrams allow grand national narratives to coexist with individual pursuits of love and sex, and in this way Martial's tiny, seemingly facile (e.g. 4.49, 11.1.14) epigrams lay claim to a verisimilitude and a universality that lofty genres cannot. Epigram thus becomes a valued form in the imperial world since it truly examines what it means to be Roman (e.g. 8.3.20–1, 10.4.7–12).

Martial's transformation of themes and ideas found in the *Ars* reveals that some Augustan elegy flourished and even became 'canonical' in the Empire. Indeed, Martial regularly adopts Ovidian claims for poetic success. or instance, Ovid's idea that his poetry will be read throughout the world (see, e.g., *Ars* 2.740 *cantetur toto nomen in orbe meum*) is regularly picked up by Martial (1.1.2–3 *toto notus in orbe Martialis / argutis epigrammaton libellis*; cf. 3.95.7, 5.13.3, 5.60.4–5, 6.82.4–6, 7.17.10, 11.3; Williams C. 2002). In contrast to the Roman males who have become unattractive to Caelia and subordinate to foreigners, Martial's diminutive epigrams have spread to and conquered the corners of the world. In employing these kinds of Ovidian expressions of poetic power, Martial guarantees both that part of his predecessor's elegiac agenda has indeed been successful and that his own small-scale and seemingly trifling poetry will follow suit.

The Authority of the *Metamorphoses*

In contrast to Ovid's elegiac works and their manifest interest in Roman politics and authority, the extent to which the *Metamorphoses* addresses such themes has been debated. The epic has been viewed as concerned 'primarily with the aesthetics of the neo-Callimachean project' and thereby contrasts with 'the broadly explicit engage-ment with politics' that is found in Virgil and Lucan (Dewar 2002: 393). Others argue that the poem's deep interest in the construction of authority has political ramifications (e.g. Feeney 1991: 218–24), and, moreover, that the separation of politics and aesthetics in Latin poetry is not always distinct (Fowler 1995a).

At least in Seneca's *Apocolocyntosis*, however, Ovid's *Metamorphoses* was read as a politically oriented poem. Early in the satire's treatment of Claudius' deification, Seneca hopes that Nero will live longer than Nestor did (*Apoc.* 4.14 *uincunt et Nestoris annos*). Such a claim is typical of imperial encomium, but the idea here seems to have an Ovidian heritage since both authors express hope for the Emperor's long life by using an adjectival form of Nestor's name (cf. *Met.* 15.838 *Pylios . . . annos*; Scott 1930: 66–8). In addition, the deliberations that take place among the gods in Seneca's scene are patently modeled upon the Roman Senate, and this link between the gods and Roman politics recalls, among other scenes, Ovid's correlation of the councils that take place on Olympus with those of the Palatine (e.g. *Met.* 1.176; Eden 1984: 99). An explicit connection between Seneca and Ovid is made when the deceased emperor, Claudius, seeks to enter the ranks of the gods. Diespiter advocates on behalf of Claudius by shrewdly connecting him to the now-deified Augustus, and the god then proposes that Claudius be recognized as divine from that day forward. In his final attempt to lend a degree of authority and solemnity to his proposal, Die-spiter suggests that the deification of Claudius be appended to Ovid's *Metamorphoses* (*Apoc.* 9.5–6).

Despite the closural strategies—including a sphragis—at work at the end of the *Metamorphoses* (e.g. Barchiesi 1997b: 181–97), Seneca's Diespiter reopens the epic. And he is able to do so because of the way Ovid employs time in his epic: the poem claims that it will move from the creation of the world down to the present day, which, in its contemporary context, means the deification of Julius Caesar and the anticipated apotheosis of Augustus. Diespiter's point that Claudius' deification be added to the end of the *Metamorphoses* suggests that the phrase *ad mea . . . tempora* (*Met.* 1.4) takes on a new meaning for post-Augustans. That is, the linearity of Ovid's epic continues for those living in the imperial system, and Diespiter envisions that the teleological thrust that drives the *Metamorphoses* now continues to Claudius' own day. In short, then, for a satirist living in the post-Augustan imperial world, Ovid's epic served as a model of time-keeping and historical arrangement. Indeed, the mention of the *Metamorphoses* is a substitution for Rome's official *fasti* (Eden 1984: 114), an appropriate move since Ovid's own *Fasti* had explored notions of time and its imperial framework (e.g. Newlands 1995).

In the particular case of the satirical *Apocolocyntosis*, however, the prominent status accorded to the *Metamorphoses* stems from humor as well as an interest in time and apotheosis. After all, the appearance of the Italian god Diespiter is likely poking fun at Claudius' antiquarian interests (Eden 1984: 112). Moreover, in his response to Hercules' speech, Augustus, seemingly annoyed by the fact that Claudius has been compared to him, comically describes how many people his successor has killed and assails his physical maladies (*Apoc.* 10.3–4). Finally, even the legal language that runs through the scene seemingly serves a humorous end by magnifying the mock seriousness of the debate (Eden 1984: 114). In such a context, it seems that Claudius' absurd apotheosis assumes a humorous reading of those that take place in the *Metamorphoses*. After all, the motion to add Claudius' apotheosis to the end of Ovid's epic creates a continuity between Seneca's satire and the *Metamorphoses*; indeed, the *Apocolocyntosis* is itself the link, the metamorphic account that supplements the epic about change. So the satire situates itself as a successor to the epic, and in this way constructs its apotheosis as another incredulous account that builds upon those of the *Metamorphoses*.

A satire, of course, should read its predecessors in such a way, so it is doubtful that Seneca reveals much if anything about Ovid's poem and its view of Augustan Rome. But the *Apocolocyntosis* does impute political significance to the *Metamorphoses* and uses it to formulate an epic view that offers an alternative to that found in the *Aeneid*. Virgil, for instance, refers to the apotheosis of a Caesar in Jupiter's weighty speech that purports to establish a sense of the inevitability of Roman order (*Aen.* 1.288). Ovid's apotheoses, in contrast, appear at the end of an epic that consciously and continually challenges credulity and order, thereby allowing for the possibility of satirical treatments that employ similar tones. In this respect, then, the *Metamorphoses* allows for a powerfully different and influential vision of epic.

In terms of diction and even tone, other Latin writers of the first century AD also treat Ovid's epic as an alternative to Virgil's. Quintilian famously remarked that Ovid was too playful even in epic (*Inst.* 10.1.88). Elsewhere he criticizes Ovid both for puerile and affected transitions in the *Metamorphoses* (*Inst.* 4.1.77) and for creating a spondaic ending to a verse by having the word *Appenninus* occupy the final two feet (*Inst.* 9.4.65; Tarrant (2000: 435) expunges the verse from the poem, however). Among the few other statements that Quintilian makes about Ovid's poetry, the teacher of rhetoric tellingly approves of two phrases that come from the start of *Met.* 13 (*Inst.* 1.5.43, 5.10.41), a book which begins with the highly rhetorical argument between Ajax and Ulysses (Hopkinson 2000: 16–22 discusses the rhetorical nature of the scene). Quintilian's ubiquitous approval of Virgil forms a stark contrast to his few negative or merely lukewarm assessments of Ovidian phrases.

Such a bifurcation of the epic tradition into Virgilian and Ovidian camps is somewhat crude since each post-Virgilian epic confronts the *Aeneid* from a different angle and thus generates its own literary history. Quint, for example, argues that Lucan is central to Western epic since his poem defines itself against the *Aeneid*'s victorious strand by adopting defiant tones (Quint 1993: 8). But by changing the points of comparison between the *Aeneid* and subsequent epic, any sort of literary-historical dichotomy may be broken down (Dewar 2002: 393). Nonetheless, imperial writers do employ such polarizing literary-historical schemes, and the start of Statius' unfinished *Achilleid* puts the Ovidian–Virgilian tension to brilliant use.

The Ovidian Alternative

The stately four-word hexameter (*Ach.* 1.1 *Magnanimum Aeaciden formidatamque Tonanti*) that begins the *Achilleid* suggests that the poem will proceed in a heroically lofty register. However, Statius' use of the verb *deducere* in the proem (*Ach.* 1.7) also brings to mind the appearance of the word in the programmatic opening of Ovid's *Metamorphoses* (Koster 1979: 191–6), an epic that is not exclusively focused on heroic themes. The *Achilleid*'s opening thus points in different literary directions. And as the poem moves past its introductory material and relates Thetis' reaction to Paris' theft of Helen, Statius takes the heroic path and recalls Homeric (Juhnke 1972: 165), and, most forcefully, Virgilian epic. For example, once Paris is on his way across the Aegean and headed back to Troy with Helen, Thetis senses that trouble has started for her son Achilles and springs into action. First she heads to Neptune and asks him to create a storm. The influence of Virgil's Juno, particularly as she appears at the start of the *Aeneid*, is manifest in the scene (Mulder 1955: 122–4). Thetis, for example, replicates the words of the Virgilian Juno when she asks that Neptune sink the fleet (*Aen.* 1.69; *Ach.* 1.72 *obrue puppes*); like Virgil's Juno (*Aen.* 10.91), Thetis characterizes Paris' theft of Helen as a *furtum* (*Ach.* 1.66), and she similarly laments that she had had an opportunity to destroy the fleet earlier (*Aen.* 1.37–49; *Ach.* 1.43); and her mention of Bellona bringing a daughter-in-law to Priam brings to mind Juno's comment in the *Aeneid* that the same war goddess would serve as the *pronuba*, or the marriage-escort, for Aeneas and Lavinia (*Aen.* 7.319–22; *Ach.* 1.33).

Statius' interest in Virgilian goddesses is not limited to Juno. Thetis' scene with Neptune also borrows from the scene in *Aen.* 5 when Venus confronts the sea-god and questions him about the welfare of her mortal son (*Aen.* 5.816–26; Heslin 2005: 107–8). Verbal similarities reinforce the thematic parallels: in both scenes, Neptune's water chariot is accompanied by sea creatures (*Aen.* 5.822; *Ach.* 1.55) and Tritons (*Aen.* 5.824; *Ach.* 1.55), and he then tries to reassure the goddesses through his words. Thetis also recalls the Venus of the *Aeneid* in that both appeal to Jupiter in the opening book of the epic, though in the case of the *Achilleid* it is not Jupiter himself but his brother acting as a 'second Jupiter' (*Ach.* 1.48–9 *secundi . . . Iovis*; Hinds 1998: 96). The similarities between the two goddesses may also be suggested when Thetis, exasperated by the theft of Helen and Venus' role in it, exclaims that 'this is the way Venus behaves' (*Ach.* 1.70 *hi Veneris mores*). Strictly speaking, the words refer to the Judgment of Paris and its fallout, but they could also refer to Thetis' actions. That is, Thetis self-referentially calls attention to the fact that she herself is behaving the way that Venus did at the start of the *Aeneid* by asking a dominant male god to help her endangered mortal son.

The overall tone of Thetis' opening request establishes the scene's Virgilian heritage. Neptune, however, foils Thetis' hopes and she is thus forced to seek other means of trying to save her child. And in pursuing other options, Thetis leaves behind the Virgilian model and adopts an Ovidian strategy when she comes up with the plan of hiding her son, dressed as a young girl, with Lycomedes, king of the island of Scyros. In order to convince Achilles, she informs him that it would be acceptable for him to disguise himself as a girl because Hercules, Bacchus, and Jupiter had all done so (*Ach.* 1.260–3). These mythological exempla are Ovidian. Hercules' service to Omphale had been mentioned in Propertius (4.9.47–8), but had been developed more extensively by Ovid in the *Fasti* (2.305–58) and *Her.* 9, where Hercules is treated as a *seruus amoris* (Casali 1995c: 505). In this sense Thetis' example is apt since, later in the *Achilleid*, Achilles nearly adopts that elegiac role when he comes close to refusing to join the expedition to Troy in order to stay with Deidamia (*Ach.* 1.888–90). So too the tale of Hercules and Omphale in the *Fasti* is relevant because it is an aetion about religious ritual and deceptive clothing, a topic that anticipates Achilles' participation in Bacchic ritual on Scyros. In addition, Thetis' comment that Jupiter had dressed as a woman recalls the scene in the *Metamorphoses* where he fools Callisto by dressing as a devotee of Diana and then rapes her (2.425). Again, this example well fits Achilles' situation since he will don female garb and then force Deidamia to have sex with him. For her third example, Thetis mentions Bacchus' golden clothes. Although gold is conventionally associated with Bacchus (e.g. Seneca *Oed.* 424), the description of him wearing a golden robe echoes Ovid's description of his clothes (*Met.* 3.556 *pictis intextum uestibus aurum*). This example may also pertain to Achilles' impending disguise since Dionysus was involved in the one known ancient ritual that entailed cross-dressing (Heslin 2005: 209–11). Thetis' well-chosen examples all seem Ovidian.

The final example that Thetis offers, however, is perhaps the most Ovidian. She suggests that Achilles think of Caeneus, who had spent time as both male and female (*Ach.* 1.264). This story of gender-bending is briefly alluded to by Virgil (*Aen.* 6.448) and has a hoary tradition (Hesiod, fr. 87 M-W), but the most extensive surviving account stems from *Met.* 12, where it is related by Nestor in the midst of the Trojan War (Keith (2000: 82–6). Caeneus had been a young girl who, after being raped by Neptune and granted a wish by him in recompense, desires to never be harmed in such a way again, and thus she wants to be and is turned into a man (*Met.* 12.202). Ovid goes out of his way to indicate that this story matters particularly for Achilles (Musgrove 1998: 228). For example, Nestor expresses surprise that Achilles had not heard of Caeneus earlier since he hailed from the same part of Greece as Achilles (*Met.* 12.191). Nestor even adds that Peleus would have tried to marry Caenis except his marriage to Thetis had already been arranged (*Met.* 12.193–4). And Achilles'

keen interest in the story of this transgendered warrior is singled out after Nestor
mentions that the transformed Caeneus could not be penetrated by any spear or
sword (*Met.* 12.168), a detail that prompts Achilles to encourage Nestor to tell the
whole of this story (*Met.* 12.176).

This marked attention given to Achilles' interest in Caeneus' story varies a technique from an earlier scene of the *Metamorphoses* in which Theseus listens to Achelous
relate the story of Baucis and Philemon. Ovid reveals that Theseus was particularly
pleased to hear the story (*Met.* 8.726), and this pleasure stems from the fact that the
story of Baucis and Philemon is modeled upon Callimachus' *Hecale*, a poem in which
the Greek hero figures prominently (Kenney 1986: xxviii). Theseus, then, takes a
metadiegetic delight in hearing a story about himself that is hardly part of the standard
heroic repertoire (Rosati 2002: 287). Achilles' interest in the story of Caeneus'
invulnerability, though not as explicit as Theseus' pleasure, certainly invites consideration of his relation to Nestor's account.

Achilles' conspicuous curiosity about Caeneus seems to be explained by the
context. After a day of fighting at Troy, the Greeks discuss Achilles' most recent
martial exploits (*Met.* 12.162–3). In particular, his fight with Cycnus is the focus of
the soldiers' conversation, and this encounter, which Ovid had just related, is yet
another story about a warrior whose body was impervious to wounds. Indeed, it is
this very similarity to Caeneus that prompts Nestor to tell the story about this seemingly indestructible warrior and his major role in battle between the Lapiths and
Centaurs. Eventually, however, the beasts pile whole forests upon Caeneus and thus
seem to kill him, though Nestor believes that Caeneus was metamorphosed into a
bird and thereby escaped death (*Met.* 12.524–35). Both stories of the seemingly
invulnerable Caeneus and Cycnus thus concern their loss of life in an epic battle.

Given that the myth of Achilles' heel was in all likelihood in circulation well before
Ovid (Burgess 1995: 222), it seems hardly coincidental that these two stories of
invulnerable warriors matter to Achilles. That is, while Ovid does not explicitly
mention Thetis' attempt to make her son invulnerable, the emphatic relevance for
Achilles of these two stories of invulnerable warriors prompts one to think of Thetis'
failed attempt to save her son, and readers see that those who had been made impermeable do not escape death in battle. Ovid thus uses the Caeneus myth to hint
at the near-invulnerability and impending death of the paradigmatic epic hero
(Musgrove 1998: 229–30). In using Caeneus in this way, Ovid deflects any emphasis
away from the glory Achilles achieves through his death and burial (e.g. *Od.* 24.36–
94), and instead he handles the hero's death in three quick verses (*Met.* 12.604–6).
As with Theseus and the story of Baucis and Philemon, Ovid reconfigures heroic
subject-matter by narrating a story that serves as an analog to—yet deflects attention
away from—a familiar story about a prominent Greek hero. And the reworking of
mythic content runs even deeper since Ovid recounts a quintessential heroic tale—the
battle between Lapiths and Centaurs—while focusing on the marvelous and even
unbelievable story of Caeneus. Epic narrators and narratives are thus challenged in
Ovid's handling of Achilles and Caeneus (Musgrove 1998: 223).

From the perspective of the *Achilleid*, one surprising point is that in the *Metamorphoses* Achilles had made it all the way to Troy without hearing about this story. After

all, in Statius' epic, Thetis offers the story as a parallel well before he heads to war. In fact, her brief mention of Caeneus suggests that she expects that Achilles is already familiar with the story. Statius is not ignorant of, diverging from, or even correcting the chronological details in Ovid. Rather, he calls attention to the literary-historical background of his epic. By the Flavian period, Achilles had 'heard' the story of Caeneus in Ovid's epic, and thus Statius' Thetis can assume that her child is familiar with the story.

Yet Thetis' assumption of Achilles' familiarity with Ovid's account poses a serious problem: when Achilles heard the Ovidian story of the transgendered warrior, he listened with great interest because of Caeneus' near invincibility. Thetis' appeal to the Ovidian Caeneus is thus tendentious, for she wants her son to think about the part of the myth concerned with gender-bending, not the part about invulnerability and warfare. The tension between the competing lessons of the Caeneus myth is heightened by the fact that Statius' Thetis had already mentioned that she tried to make Achilles invulnerable by dipping him in the river Styx (*Ach.* 1.133–4). This is the initial extant reference to the famous story of Achilles' heel (or, better, ankle), but whatever the original source for the myth may have been, Thetis' failure to make her son invulnerable makes Caeneus an exceedingly appropriate example. After all, both are lost in warfare (at best, Caeneus was turned into a bird). So too Cycnus' death indicates that invulnerability is no guarantee of immortality. Thetis attempts to use myth to save her child, but her selective reading only calls attention to his doomed mortality. And from this perspective, her first three examples of Jupiter, Hercules, and Bacchus suddenly become worrisome for Achilles; in fact, since all are (or become) immortal, the models point to differences between her mortal son and the gods.

Thetis' use of Ovidian myth thus adds to her rhetoric of failure that prominently appears, for example, in the epic's opening scene that is so indebted to Virgil (Heslin 2005: 106–45). In this respect, the works of Statius' predecessors are treated similarly as flawed models for the *Achilleid*. Nonetheless, a significant point of difference between her Ovidian strategy and the Virgilian attempt to gain aid from the Olympians is that she perseveres with the Ovidian model. She seemingly recognizes that a Virgilian world that consists of dominant male Olympians is not for her. In contrast, for her attempt to subvert fate and to bypass Olympian authority, she turns to the *Metamorphoses*. And Thetis' 'reading' makes sense. After all, Ovid's Isis, for example, advises Telethusa to disguise as a boy her daughter Iphis, and the Egyptian goddess then transforms the child from a female to a male (*Met.* 9.705–97). The dilemma of Iphis and Telethusa is not precisely analogous to that of Achilles and Thetis, but the point is clear that gender transformation and a different divine system is part of the world of the *Metamorphoses*. Indeed, the Caeneus episode exemplifies this very idea when a Centaur taunts the warrior by addressing him as Caenis, the feminine form of his name (*Met.* 12.470–6). These kinds of gendered insults form a stock part of the epic tradition (e.g. *Aen.* 9.617, *Il.* 7.96), but in the *Metamorphoses* the ridicule is authentic. Thus, it is to this kind of epic that Thetis mistakenly but understandably turns, since, like other ancients, she found in Ovid's poetry a model for the way she wanted the world to work.

FURTHER READING

The influence of Ovid's poetry on ancient literature requires further study; Galinsky (1989) usefully addresses some parameters of the topic. Individual studies are scattered throughout various journals and monographs from the past century or so, but synthetic analyses or inter-pretations are still needed for topics ranging from diction and style to larger methodological questions. A special issue of *Arethusa* (Frederick et al. 2002) entitled 'The reception of Ovid in antiquity' that deals with Seneca, Lucan, Martial, Statius, and late antique poets serves as an excellent start for some more recent critical concerns as well as bibliography. Ovid's importance for Seneca has been studied better than it has for many authors, for example Tarrant (1978) and Jakobi (1988), though recent studies on the various works of Statius have started to show the fundamental importance of Ovid for Flavian literature, for example Newlands (2002b), Keith (2002a), and Heslin (2005). Hinds (2007) is fundamental for Ovid and Martial. Later imperial writers such as Juvenal and Apuleius have been relatively neglected.

CHAPTER TWENTY-NINE

The Medieval Ovid

John M. Fyler

Introduction

We seem to have entered a new Ovidian age, of critical interpretation and creative adaptation both, which well situates us to think about the medieval *aetas Ovidiana*. Although Ovid as a major Roman poet was never entirely neglected, his work was not awarded the hallowed status of Virgil's *Aeneid*: the surviving manuscripts begin much later, and there are no early Ovidian commentators to match Servius and Macrobius on Virgil. Beginning in the twelfth century, though, and coinciding with the sea-change in Western culture described by R.W. Southern among others, Ovid became the central classical influence on literature and, later, the visual arts. His new importance is signaled by a flurry of allegorizing commentaries, the most notable being the anonymous Vulgate commentary and those of Arnulf of Orléans, John of Garland, Giovanni del Virgilio, and Pierre Bersuire. Many of these commentaries begin with an *accessus*, or introduction, giving a biographical account of the poet and classifying his works by title, subject matter, intention, utility, and philosophical genre. Ovid's life, capping the irreverence of his poetry with his mysterious involvement in scandal and his consequent exile, offers a rich source for the biographer's speculation; and Ovid's own cryptic clues in the *Tristia* and *Epistulae ex Ponto* provoke much conjecture, usually implausible. His life also offers an affecting paradigm for self-characterization in such diverse later writers as Spenser and Nabokov; indeed, 'Boccaccio saw Ovid and Dante both enacting a tripartite career—poets of love, transformation, and exile' (Lyne 2002: 290).

For most medieval poets, however, love and transformation are the focus of concern. The elegiac poems—the *Amores* (often called *Sine titulo*, 'Without a Title', in medieval commentaries) and above all the *Ars amatoria* and *Remedia amoris*— proclaim Ovid to be the supreme authority on the psychology of the lover's mind and the irrationality of the lover-poet's voice, coruscatingly witty, untrustworthy, and almost inevitably self-deluding. Reversing the usually accepted chronology, one commentary claims that the *Amores* follows the *Ars*, so that Ovid the *magister amoris* can put his 'precepts into practice in his own case'; the work evidently lacks a title because the all-too-notorious *Ars* 'had made adulteresses of almost all the married women and maidens' in Rome (Minnis and Scott 1988: 28). The twenty-one letters of the *Heroides* (fifteen from seduced or abandoned legendary women, six from pairs of lovers to each other) provide a less volatile moral meaning, praising chastity and marriage, and encouraging us to 'reject and shun foolish love and adhere to lawful love' (Minnis and Scott 1988: 23). These letters give Ovid the opportunity to ventriloquize women's voices as well as men's, and to display the lover's irrationality and partiality in action—often as a sympathetically portrayed feminine alternative to an epic, heroic, and implicitly masculine perspective. Such complications abound in twelfth-century romance, where women's voices and the new importance of love in the chivalric ideal manifest Ovid's influence. Indeed, a shorthand way of describing the first *roman antique*, the romance of *Eneas*, might be as Ovid superimposed on Virgil—not so much where one might expect it, in the story of Dido, as in the courtship and interior monologues invented for Lavinia.

Narrative complexity is even more notable in the *Metamorphoses*, where the voicing of a story can be at two or three removes, when a speaker repeats another's account of yet someone else's narrative. This poem, epic and mock-epic both, provides a nearly inexhaustible storehouse of myths and legendary narratives. The thirteenth-century Spanish king Alfonso the Wise called it the 'Bible of the pagans'; and for many writers and painters it serves as an essential reference dictionary of classical mythology. Precisely because it feels like a pagan Bible, especially in Book 1, where the Creation narrative is at times strikingly close to the opening of Genesis, the *Metamorphoses* attracts allegorizing interpretations of its meaning. Both this poem and the poems concerned with love have a central place in the medieval schoolroom, with commentaries that gloss unfamiliar words, explain mythical allusions, and comment on details of grammar and rhetoric (Hexter 1986; Demats 1973; Ghisalberti 1946). Scholarly attention to minutiae can foster an obliviousness to poetic nuance. For the author of the *Ovide Moralisé* (Chapter 23), the stories are all that matter, as the springboard for translation and allegorical interpretation: voicing and narrative tone are irrelevant.

Since there are several excellent discussions of the multifaceted medieval Ovid, including those in recent Companion volumes (Dimmick 2002; Hexter 2002), I will focus here on Ovid mainly as he influences three major later medieval writers: Dante, Jean de Meun, and Chaucer. The two sides of Ovid's work, love and transformation, appear in all three, with different emphases and in different combinations. For these poets too, the story is often paramount. But these thirteenth- and fourteenth-century poets also display a pervasive Ovidianism—an attentiveness not only to the literal surface of Ovid's poetry but to his characteristic wit and ironic tone, to his manner as well as his matter.

Dante's Ovid

At a notable moment in *Inf.* 25, Dante enjoins silence on Lucan, who described the malign transformative effects of snake venom on Cato's soldiers, and on Ovid, who described the metamorphoses of Cadmus and Arethusa: 'for if he, poetizing, converts the one into a serpent and the other into a fountain, I envy him not; for two natures front to front he never so transmuted that both forms were prompt to exchange their substance' (25.98–102). Dante had already listed Ovid among the great ancient poets in Limbo, third after Homer and Horace (presumably fourth when we add Virgil, who names and greets them) and ahead of Lucan; they all honor Dante by making him the sixth of their company (*Inf.* 4). But in the course of the poem he poignantly shows that being deferential to the ancient poets, above all Virgil, also requires the Christian poet to move beyond them, changing high tragedy to Christian comedy, correcting ancient errors of fact and interpretation such as the origin of the name Manto (*Inf.* 20) and the eternal fate of Ripheus (*Par.* 20). *Inf.* 25 implies that Ovid's fiction of metamorphosis pales beside the hellish actuality that God created and Dante witnesses, but also that Dante's own fictive imagination of metamorphosis is superior. Much the same thing occurs at the opening of canto 30, where the summarized stories of Athamas and Ino (*Met.* 3) and Hecuba (*Met.* 13), both treated as history, pale next to the punishment of the falsifiers that Dante is about to recount. In the *Purgatorio* he uses a number of stories from the *Metamorphoses* as historical examples for the various sins to be expiated: Niobe and Arachne for Pride, Aglauros for Envy, Procne for Wrath, Midas for Avarice, and the Centaurs for Gluttony. He compares himself to the dying Pyramus recalled to consciousness by Thisbe's name, when he hears Beatrice's as he is about to pass through the purgative flame. Above all, as has been shown in detail, Dante uses Ovidian exemplars—especially Phaethon, Icarus, Jason, Glaucus, and Marsyas—as warning models for his own presumption. They serve as witnesses of his awareness of the dangers they represent and for his own transcendence of them as Christian poet and visionary (Brownlee 1993: 115–18; also see his and others' essays in Jacoff and Schnapp 1991 and esp. Bynum 2001: 184–7).

By inventing a metamorphosis of his own in *Inf.* 25, Dante joins other medieval writers who pay homage to Ovid by copying his example. One anonymous poet invents a story of a priest of Jupiter changed into a libidinous rooster, added in Ovidian hexameters to the margin of a medieval manuscript of the *Metamorphoses* (Anderson 1975). Boccaccio invents a metamorphosis in reverse in the *Caccia di Diana*, when hunted animals are turned into men. Froissart inserts pseudo-Ovidian metamorphoses into his poetry but also, startlingly, uses Ovid's myths as a resonant subtext in the *Chroniques* for his supposedly historical account of Gaston Fébus, count of Foix and Béarn, who rules over a realm of magic and second sight, whose court resembles that of his namesake the Sun god, and whose death reprises Diana's punishments of Callisto and Actaeon (Fyler 1998). Chaucer invents his own story of Alceste metamorphosed into the daisy, in the *Legend of Good Women*, though he almost always deletes such transformations when he retells Ovid's stories, in part at least to avoid evoking the supernatural.

Of all the myths, the most important one for these later writers is Ovid's own favorite. In the *Metamorphoses* and the elegiac poetry both, when Ovid retells the myth of the Golden Age, he performs a complex dance between nostalgia for an innocent past and professed delight in Roman modernity. The figuratively golden has become the gold that can purchase all things, including love; and innocent rustic-ity has turned into sophisticated artifice. In the modern world that Ovid celebrates, only the naturally beautiful woman and the wealthy man can be simple and straight-forward as lovers; everyone else needs to master the amatory art, and the arts of rhetoric and sophistry.

Ovid in the *Roman de la Rose*

For Ovid's medieval heirs the myth of the Golden Age is just as central, by itself and as it is conflated with its Biblical analogue in Genesis. As Dante approaches Paradise, atop the mountain of Purgatory, he is told that 'They who in olden times sang of the Age of Gold and its happy state perhaps in Parnassus dreamed of this place' (*Purg.* 28.139–41). And in his lyric 'The Former Age', Chaucer assigns blame for the loss of primitive innocence equally to 'Jupiter the lecherous' and to the tyrant Nimrod, who built the Tower of Babel. The myth is central in Jean de Meun's *Roman de la Rose*, where it dominates four extended speeches, by Reason, Friend, the Old Woman, and Genius. Throughout it is given a characteristically Ovidian inflection, being used as a key to the history of desire. Just as in Book 1 of the *Metamorphoses* desire origi-nates after the purging flood, in the simultaneously ridiculous and terrifying divine rapists Apollo and Jupiter, so in Jean de Meun, the birth of Venus from the scattered seed of her father Saturn marks the shift from the fulfilled mutual love, common property, and idyllic life of the Golden Age to a fallen world of alienating categories and insatiable desire, especially in its guise as unrequited love.

As in Ovid's *Ars amatoria*, each of the appearances of the Golden Age in Jean de Meun is subjected to irony, though also as in Ovid, with a simultaneous nostalgia for an irretrievable age of innocence. Reason's allegorical account of how Jupiter castrated his father Saturn is followed by Friend's partially suspect vision of the Golden Age as a time of free love and communal property, now replaced by hierar-chies, including the hierarchy of marriage; these hierarchies undo the equality that love requires, so that in the modern world 'true love cannot last' (Horgan 1994: 130). The Vieille, the Old Woman who copies Ovid's character Dipsas (*Am.* 1.8), offers her own version of the way of the world, in which the state of nature, which 'has made all women for all men and all men for all women, every woman common to every man and every man to every woman' (Horgan 1994: 214), has been sup-planted by marriage and law. These constraints must be outwitted by the art that can satisfy universal, natural desire, an art that for women requires bribery and gifts, since they have only a perishable commodity to sell. 'She should not trouble herself to love a poor man, for a poor man is good for nothing: were he Ovid or Homer, he would still be worth less than a couple of drinks' (Horgan 1994: 210), one-upping the advice of Dipsas and the *magister amoris* with a joke at Ovid's own expense.

Finally, Genius, the tutelary spirit of generation, offers an exuberant and quintes-sentially Ovidian commentary on the state of the world. Jupiter, after castrating his father Saturn, usurped his kingdom and ended the Golden Age: he is the founder of agriculture, hunting, the seasons of the year, and the onset of the iron age, 'a cause of great rejoicing to the gods in their halls of everlasting grime and gloom, who are jealous of mankind as long as they see them alive' (Horgan 1994: 311). 'No one ever ploughed until Jupiter came' (Horgan 1994: 310), which inevitably has a bawdy double meaning since Genius has just enjoined love's devotees to 'Plough barons, plough for God's sake, and restore your lineage' by 'ploughing vigorously' (Horgan 1994: 304). Love has become sexual labor in the fallen world; and Jupiter, who has commanded that everyone 'put his mind to achieving happiness', since delight 'is the best thing in the world and the chief good in life', has set the example for all to imitate: 'jolly Lord Jupiter, who so prized delight, gratified his body as much as he liked' (Horgan 1994: 309–10), a sentiment taken almost directly from Phaedra's self-justification for incest (*Her.* 4.133). Procreation, though a good in itself, has become deeply corrupted in this fallen world of desire.

At the poem's end, Pygmalion's love and mad longing for the statue he has created, which Venus rewards by turning the statue into a woman, is followed by the lover's conquest, in which a woman is turned into a building, the fortress that he can subdue and penetrate. This reduction of woman to object echoes the ironies in Ovid's call for a *quod* or *materia* for love and for love poetry. In Genius' frame of reference, which is that of Nature as well, the *Roman* has a happy ending, the pregnancy that apparently results from this conquest; but as in the *Amores* and *Ars amatoria*, the motives and self-knowledge of the narrator are deeply suspect. This is a world in which rhetoric has become sophistry; plain speech is no longer possible and innocence is never rewarded. Reason's effort to promote plain speech, itself problematic in a corrupted world, cannot succeed in countering the Lover's devotion to courtly language. But the Lover's obsessive decorum, in a joke that comes from the French fabliaux, merely leads at the end of the poem to a hilariously obscene periphrastic account of sexual intercourse.

Medieval commentators often read Ovid as an 'ethical pedagogue' (Ginsberg 1998: 62) even as he could be called the 'master of sensuality and shame' by Heloise (Radice 2003: 94), or be accused by Petrarch (in *De Vita Solitaria*) of having a 'lascivious and lubricious and altogether womanish mind' (Martellotti 1955: 532). Petrarch adds that Ovid unsurprisingly considered 'feminine company' to be the height of felicity; so too the deeply Ovidian Chaucer is described by Gavin Douglas as 'al womanis frend'. Whatever accuracy there might be in such descriptions seems to run athwart the charge of Ovidian misogyny, as in Christine de Pizan's complaint against Jean de Meun in the early-fifteenth-century *Querelle de la Rose*. In Jean's defense, Pierre Col argues that the *Roman* is much less dangerous to women than the *Ars amatoria*: since it is written in French, women can read about the possible ruses of their would-be seducers, whereas Ovid writes in Latin, 'which women do not understand' (Hicks 1977: 105). Chaucer's character Pandarus, in *Troilus and Criseyde*, epitomizes such paradoxes, as someone who according to his niece loves the company of women but as the expert practitioner of the *ars amatoria* can also manipulate and deceive her into a love affair.

Ovid and Chaucer

Chaucer in fact offers an especially full territory for exploring the medieval Ovid. His affinity with the Roman poet has been argued for at least since John Dryden, and is already implied by the compliment of the fourteenth-century French poet Eustache Deschamps, who addresses Chaucer as *Ovides grans en ta poëtrie* ('a great Ovid in your poetry', Brewer 1978: 40). Chaucer consults Ovid's Latin text directly and also makes use of some translations and commentaries—almost certainly the *Ovide Moralisé* and perhaps an Italian version of the *Heroides*. Moreover, the medieval writers by whom he is most influenced—including Guillaume de Lorris and Jean de Meun, Dante, Machaut, Petrarch, Boccaccio, and Froissart—are themselves steeped in the Ovidian tradition. Like these other late medieval poets, Chaucer learned most of his classical mythology and much of his love psychology from Ovid. In the *House of Fame* he places Ovid on a pillar of copper as 'Venus clerk', 'That hath ysowen wonder wide / The grete god of Loves name' (1487–9). His allusions to classical myth, which are scattered throughout his work, give evidence of a detailed knowledge. If Chaucer's references are not so learned as Boccaccio's, they are nonetheless sometimes arcane enough to drive all but the best informed modern reader to footnotes or a classical dictionary. Chaucer adopts as well Ovid's characteristically unreliable narrator and ironic temperament (Fyler 1979; Cooper 2005; Simpson 2006).

Chaucer names 'Ovyde' at a number of points in his poetry, three times in the *Legend of Good Women* by his cognomen 'Naso'. Ovid appears second in the list of great classical epic poets at the end of *Troilus and Criseyde* (5.1792), between Virgil and Homer; and the Merchant invokes 'noble Ovyde' ironically, citing his definitive account of lovers' trickery: Pyramus and Thisbe (2125). The Man of Law names him in connection with the *Heroides*, 'his Episteles, that been ful olde' (55), and there are many other references in Chaucer to the 'epistels' of Ovid. The Wife of Bath cites 'Ovides Art' as a chapter in Jankyn's 'book of wikked wyves' (680, 685); 'the remedyes of Ovyde' are mentioned in the *Book of the Duchess* (568), and alluded to in the *General Prologue* portrait of the Wife, the expert in 'the remedies of love' and love's 'art' (475–6). The Man of Law also mentions '*Methamorphosios*' (93), in his somewhat garbled reference to the poetic contest between the Muses and the Pierides.

The extent of Chaucer's direct knowledge of the *Amores* is open to question, since his quotations from the work or allusions to it are arguably second-hand. Even so, Criseyde's mention of the rapidly flowing Symois (*Troilus* 4.1548) may recall *Am.* 1.15.10; several details in the first aubade in *Troilus*, Book 3 (1450–60), seem to come directly from *Am.* 1.13; and the Wife of Bath's lineage, through the Vieille in the *Roman de la Rose*, may be traced back to Dipsas, in *Am.* 1.8. (The aubade and the female expert in love's art, however, both make frequent appearances in the rich Ovidian tradition.) There is at least a possibility that Corinna, Ovid's putative mistress in the *Amores*, is the 'Corynne' of *Anelida and Arcite* (21).

The letters in the *Heroides* are the Ovidian works that Chaucer cites most frequently by name, in large part because the *Legend of Good Women* relies so directly on 'the epistel of Ovyde / Of trewe wyves and of here labour' (G 305–6) for its narratives of women martyrs to Love's religion; the recurring situation of Ovid's work, an abandoned heroine writing to her lover, also lies behind Anelida's epistolary complaint (*Anel.* 204–350). Many of these stories are also cited in two catalogues of Ovidian narrative, one of male 'untrouthe' to women (*House of Fame* 388–426), the other the Man of Law's summary of Chaucer's *Legend* itself (60–76), with its stories of lovers 'Mo than Ovide made of mencioun / in his Episteles, that been ful olde' (54–5). In particular, the narrator's offer, at the end of *Troilus and Criseyde*, to write 'Penopoleës trouthe and good Alceste' (5.1778) probably has *Her.* 1 in mind; Penelope also appears in the Man of Law's summary, along with Alceste and Hypermnestra, as an exemplar of virtuous 'wifhod' (76). Chaucer translates passages from *Her.* 2, 'the letter of Phillis', in the *Legend of Good Women* (2494); the Man of Law identifies her by her 'tree' (65), a detail not mentioned in Ovid, whose Phyllis contemplates an imminent suicide by hanging as one of three possibilities; the same detail appears in the *Book of the Duchess* and the *House of Fame*, as in other later medieval poems and commentaries. Briseis (*Her.* 3) appears as 'Breseyda' in a list of abandoned heroines in the *House of Fame* (398), and as the sufferer of amorous 'wo' in the Man of Law's catalogue. Chaucer may be alluding to Ovid's witticism on the interchangeability of Briseis and Chryseis (*Rem.* 469–76) when Pandarus quotes 'Zanzis' on driving out old love with new (*Troilus* 4.414–15); and Criseyde's fears of what might happen if she tries 'To stele awey by nyght' (*Troilus* 5.702) are notably close in phrasing to Briseis' (*Her.* 3.17–20). Phaedra (*Her.* 4) is linked with her sister Ariadne (*Her.* 10) in the *House of Fame* and in the *Legend of Ariadne*, which derives closely from *Her.* 10 and its medieval glosses, and perhaps as well from Filippo Ceffi's Italian translation; Ariadne is also named by the Man of Law, along with 'The bareyne yle stondynge in the see' (68). The letter of Oenone (*Her.* 5), who was abandoned by Paris (as noted in the *House of Fame*), is evidently making the rounds in Troy, although Troilus has not read it (*Troilus* 1.652–65); Pandarus translates and expands on lines 151–2 (his explanation perhaps indebted to medieval glosses or to Ceffi's translation). The letter may reappear as an ironic backdrop to Criseyde's oath (*Troilus* 4.1551–54); she orders the Simois to return to its source if she fails to return to Troy, echoing an oath on the Xanthus that Paris had memorably failed to keep (*Her.* 5.29–30).

Hypsipyle's story (*Her.* 6) is told at length in the *Legend of Good Women*, where we are directed to her 'letter', 'th'origynal, that telleth al the cas' (1558, 1564); and the *Legend* gives details from Ovid's 'Epistels' that are 'nat rehersed of Guido [delle Colonne]' (1464–65), Chaucer's primary source. Hypsipyle is also mentioned by the Man of Law and in the *House of Fame*, where, as in the *Legend*, she is linked with Medea as one of two women betrayed by Jason (400–1). The Man of Law, referring to *Her.* 9 and 8, mistakenly names 'The pleinte of Dianire and of Hermyon' (66) as part of the *Legend of Good Women*. He names 'Canacee' (*Her.* 11), 'That loved hir owene brother synfully' (79), as the sort of 'wikke ensample' that Chaucer does not recount; but she does in fact appear, 'espied by thy chere', in the *Prologue* to the *Legend* (F265); and her namesake, the Tartar heroine of the *Squire's Tale*, begins an unfinished narrative that seems, as it breaks off abruptly, to threaten an incestuous relationship between Canacee and her brother (668–9). The story of Medea (*Her.* 12) is told in conjunction with Hypsipyle's in the *Legend*; at its end Chaucer quotes from and expands on *Her* 12.11–12 and 19, perhaps with the aid of a manuscript gloss or of Ceffi's translation, and refers us to the original: 'Wel can Ovyde hire letter in vers endyte, / Which were as now to long for me to wryte' (1678–9). Medea and her 'crueltee' are also cited by the Man of Law (72); she is named in the *Book of the Duchess* as the one 'That slough hir children for Jasoun' (727). The Man of Law puts Laodamia (*Her*. 13), incorrectly, in his list of the heroines in Chaucer's *Legend*, though she is mentioned in the work's *Prologue* (F263): she is also named along with Penelope and Portia in Dorigen's lament, but her name here comes from St Jerome's catalogue of women martyrs to chastity (*Franklin's Tale* 1443–47). The story of Hypermnestra, who joins Penelope and Alceste in the Man of Law's trio of exemplary wives (75–6), becomes the final story in the *Legend of Good Women*: Chaucer augments Ovid's account with details he could have found in glosses to *Her*. 14. Chaucer never mentions or makes use of *Her*. 15 (Sappho to Phaon) or 20–21 (the exchange between Acontius and Cydippe); implied references to 16–17 (Paris and Helen) and 18–19 (Leander and Hero) appear in the Man of Law's catalogue (69–70), where their stories are incorrectly cited as being part of the *Legend of Good Women*. There are some general points of comparison between Helen's letter and Criseyde's soliloquy in Book 2 of *Troilus* (2.703 ff.)

The letter of Dido to Aeneas (*Her*. 7) has the most extensive reverberations in Chaucer's poetry. Her story is told at length in the *House of Fame* (239–382, 427–44), which specifically mentions her epistle, 'What that she wrot or that she dyde' (380), and in the *Legend of Dido*. The Man of Law mentions, 'The swerd of Dido for the false Enee' (64), and her suicide for love is also noted along with Phyllis' in the *Book of the Duchess* (731–4). She appears in the list of Venus' devotees (*Parliament of Fowls* 289) and Love's martyrs (*Legend* F263). In the *House of Fame* the narrator refers us to 'Virgile in Eneydos / Or the Epistle of Ovyde' for her story (378–9); in the *Legend of Dido* he invokes 'Virgil Mantoan': 'In thyn Eneyde and Naso wol I take / The tenor, and the grete effectes make' (928–9). This version of the story has a distinctly Ovidian cast, and concludes by translating the opening lines of *Her*. 7 (which are also adapted in *Anel*. 346–50). Chaucer expands the compact zeugma of *atque idem venti vela fidemque ferent?* (and shall the same winds carry off your sails and your honesty?) (*Her*. 7.8) to 'For thilke wynd that blew youre ship awey, / The same wynd hath blowe awey youre fey', and ends with the injunction: 'But who wol al this letter have in mynde, / Rede Ovyde, and in hym he shal it fynde' (1364–67). The differences in detail and emphasis between Virgil and Ovid make Dido's story the *locus classicus* for the uncertainty and unreliability of historical sources. Chaucer so uses the story in the *House of Fame*, which is in this respect a rehearsal for his later, mature consideration of historiography in *Troilus and Criseyde*. Ovid's presentation of Dido's perspective effectively complicates the already complex claims on our sympathies in the *Aeneid*, just as the chaste 'historical' Dido counters Virgil's fiction for a number of later readers, both classical and medieval.

The *Ars amatoria* is the wellspring for a rich medieval tradition; and many of Chaucer's points of contact with it may come primarily through intermediaries, notably the *Roman de la Rose*. Pandarus as *magister amoris* offers a lesson to Troilus on how to write love letters (*Troilus* 2.1023–43; cf. *Ars* 1.467–86) and warns: 'As gret a craft is kepe wel as wynne' (*Tr.* 3.1634), echoing the opening of Book 2 of the *Ars*. The *Summoner's Tale* (2001–03) copies the *Ars* (2.376–8) on the cruelty of a wrathful woman, but Chaucer probably found this phrasing in the *Roman de la Rose*. On the other hand, he also takes some quite distinctive and precise phrasings directly from the *Ars*, suggesting his close acquaintance with the work, and especially with its opening: for example, 'Eacides Chiron' (*House of Fame* 1206, from *Ars* 1.17) and Phoebus shining 'Upon the brest of Hercules lyoun' (*Troilus* 4.32, from *Ars* 1.68 *Herculei terga leonis*), substituting 'brest' for Ovid's 'back'. (This zodiacal detail is original to Chaucer's version of the story; it does not appear in Boccaccio's *Filostrato*.) The *Ars*, 'Ovides Art', is characterized as part of the misogynist tradition in the *Wife of Bath's Prologue* (680).

Chaucer quotes the *Remedia amoris* at second-hand twice in the *Tale of Melibee*. The first notes 'the sentence of Ovide, in his book that cleped is the Remedie of Love' (975) about letting a mother's grief at the death of her child run its course (*Rem.* 127–30). The second, which shows that Chaucer is translating from his French source without reference to Ovid, misunderstands the French *vivre*, which translates Ovid's *uipera*, as a translation of the Latin word *viverra*, 'wesele' (compare *Rem.* 421–2 with *Mel.* 1324). Chaucer appears to make a detailed allusion to the *Remedia*, however, at *Troilus* 4.414–15, where Pandarus quotes Ovid's injunction to let a new love drive out the old. At the equivalent place in the *Filostrato* Boccaccio cites the idea as a common proverb; Chaucer's more elaborate invention of its source in the authority 'Zanzis', that is Zeuxis, gives it a more elevated status as a maxim. In the *Remedia* Ovid attributes this maxim to Agamemnon, who stole Briseis from Achilles to compensate for the loss of Chryseis (462–86). Its anachronistic appearance in *Troilus* is one of several such explosive allusions to Ovid (and Virgil) in the poem.

Chaucer cites 'Ovyde and Titus Lyvius' as the sources for the *Legend of Lucrece*: in fact, his narrative seems to derive entirely from Ovid, and closely follows *Fast.* 2.685–852, as does Gower's retelling in the *Confessio Amantis*, Book 7. It has a number of nearly exact translations of Ovid's phrasing—and perhaps one mistranslation, since *Legend* 1728–29 appears to misunderstand the meaning of *Fast.* 2.751–52: Chaucer has 'the drede doth me so to smerte / That with a swerd it stingeth to myn herte' for *sed enim temerarius ille / est meus, et stricto qualibet ense ruit* ('but my husband is heedless, and with drawn sword he rushes anywhere'). His statement that Lucrece was venerated as 'a seynt' in pagan Rome, 'and ever hir day yhalwed dere / As in hir lawe' (1871–72) is evidently influenced by the appearance of the story in the *Fasti* under February 24, as if in a calendar recording saints' days; at the end of Ovid's narrative, Brutus promises that Lucrece's ghost will be a *numen* for him (2.842). The allusion in the *Parliament of Fowls* (253–6) to Priapus' exposure derives from *Fast.* 1.415–38. The Eagle wants to teach Chaucer star-lore, so that when 'thou redest poetrie, / How goddes gonne stellifye / Bridd, fissh, best, or him or here' (*House of Fame* 1001–3), he will know where they are in the heavens; several of the examples he gives—the Raven, Arion's harp, the Dolphin—are described by Ovid only in the *Fasti*. The stellification of Ariadne's crown, which Chaucer mentions at the end of her *Legend*, is described in *Fast.* 3.513–16, though also at *Met.* 8.176–82.

Chaucer's most frequent Ovidian source is the *Metamorphoses*, both directly and probably by way of the French translation in the *Ovide Moralisé*. He takes extended narratives from the work—notably the stories of Ceyx and Alcyone in the *Book of the Duchess*, of Phoebus and the crow in the *Manciple's Tale*, and of Pyramus and Thisbe in the *Legend of Good Women*. There are a great many more specific allusions as well, along with a number of details from classical mythology that derive from Ovid, either directly or by way of medieval commentaries and poetic texts. (One of the fifteenth-century texts of *Troilus*, H4 [London B.L. MS Harley 2392], contains a number of marginal references to and quotations of specific passages in the *Metamorphoses*.) Ovid's account of the Golden Age and declining world (*Met.* 1.89–150) lies behind Chaucer's lyric 'The Former Age', both directly and through the mediation of Boethius' adaptation of Ovid (*Consolation of Philosophy* 2.m.5). The summary account of the semigods and rustic spirits at *Met.* 1.192–93 is close in phrasing to *Troilus* 4.1541–45 (there is no corresponding passage in the *Filostrato*). In another addition to Boccaccio, Troilus asks Apollo to remember 'when Dane hireselven shette / Under the bark, and laurer wax for drede' (*Troilus* 3.726–27); Daphne is also named in the *Knight's Tale* (2062–64), where she is distinguished as 'Penneus doghter, which that highte Dane' from the 'goddesse Diane'. Argus' many eyes are alluded to in *Troilus* 4.1459 and the *Merchant's Tale* (2111); this common proverbial reference is given particularity in the *Knight's Tale*, which mentions Mercury's appearance to Arcite in a dream, 'Arrayed . . . as he was whan that Argus took his sleep' (1389–90).

The Eagle in the *House of Fame* summarizes the story of Phaethon (*Met.* 2), and Troilus names 'Piros and tho swifte steedes thre, / Which that drawen forth the sonnes char' (3.1703–04), a proper name that created much confusion for the scribes of the poem. The story of Callisto, 'Calistopee', is quickly summarized in the Knight's description of Diana's temple (2056–59). The story of Apollo's revenge on the crow is retold without attribution in the *Manciple's Tale*, though a reference to Ovid may be implied in the Manciple's attribution of the story to 'olde bookes' (106); Chaucer may also be relying on medieval retellings, which include the *Ovide Moralisé*, Machaut, and Gower. Troilus refers to Mercury, Herse, and Aglauros in his prayer reminding all the gods/planets of their loves (3.729–30). He also mentions Jupiter's rape of Europa, in which appears Ovid's widely copied dictum that *maiestas et amor* don't sit well together (*Met.* 2.846–47); Chaucer is one of several medieval poets who quote the dictum but alter its meaning, reading *maiestas* as 'maistrye' or 'sovereignty' rather than 'dignity' (*Franklin's Tale* 764–66). The similar phrasing in the *Knight's Tale* closely echoes *Ars* 3.564: 'Ful sooth is seyd that love ne lordshipe / Wol noght, his thankes, have no felaweshipe' (1625–26).

Actaeon (Book 3) is referred to twice in the *Knight's Tale*, as the victim of Diana's vengeance: 'I saugh how that his houndes have hym caught / And freeten hym, for that they knewe hym naught' (2067–68). Echo appears in the Envoy at the end of the *Clerk's Tale* as the model for archwives' chattering (1189), but in the *Franklin's Tale* as the fatal precedent for Aurelius, who dare not voice his love for Dorigen directly: 'And dye he moste, he seyde, as dide Ekko / For Narcisus, that dorste nat telle hir wo' (951–2) (also see *Book of the Duchess* 735). Book 4, besides providing the source for the *Legend of Thisbe*, contains the most widely influential source for the account of Mars and Venus caught in Vulcan's net, the backdrop for the allegory in the *Complaint of Mars*; Arcite too reminds Mars of his embarrassment (*Knight's Tale* 2389–90), though the story is widely current in medieval poems, notably the *Roman de la Rose*. Chaucer alludes to the madness of Athamas and Ino in Criseyde's oath (*Troilus* 4.1539–40), though with Dante as intermediary (the opening lines of *Inf.* 30). The Man of Law refers to the contest between the Pierides and the Muses in Book 5: '*Methamorphosios* woot what I mene' (93), giving the title in the genitive singular, with *Liber* understood. But the reference 'To Muses that men clepe Pierides' (92) confuses the daughters of Pierus with the Muses themselves, born in Pieria (*Tr.* 5.3.10): *Pieridumque choro* (Simpson 2006: 79 argues that the conflation is deliberate).

The story of Philomela and Procne, from Book 6, is familiar enough that Chaucer must have known it from several sources: in Book 2 of *Troilus* he directly refers (64–70) and alludes (918) to it. In the *Legend of Philomela* he uses Ovid's account directly, with additional details from the French translation by Chrétien de Troyes (included within the *Ovide Moralisé*). (Gower also retells the story in full, in Book 5 of the *Confessio Amantis*.) The *Legend of Medea* makes use of the opening of Book 7 as well as *Her.* 6. The account of Minos and Scylla at the beginning of the *Legend of Ariadne* may owe some of its details to the account in Books 7 and 8. The metamorphosis of Scylla into the bird 'Ciris' (*Met.* 8.151) is recalled at *Troilus* 5.1110, where 'Nysus doughter song with fressh entente' in the early morning: the point of the allusion may be that she, like Troilus, 'stod upon the wal' (*Legend* 1908), or even more, that, as a symbol of betrayal, she comments on Criseyde's failure to return. Chaucer's statement that sacrifices to the Minotaur occurred 'every thridde yeer' (*Legend* 1932) may be due to an understandable misreading of *Met.* 8.171, which speaks of a *tertia sors* 'a third casting of lots' for victims after a further nine years, not nine years altogether—if so, a sign that Chaucer consulted Ovid's version rather closely. Ovid's account of the Calydonian boar hunt is the primary source of *Troilus* 5.1464–84 (for which there is no corresponding passage in Boccaccio); the boar hunt is also mentioned in the *Knight's Tale* (2070–1). The story of Myrrha (*Met.* 10) is cited in *Troilus* 4.1138–9, and MS H4 quotes the Latin original in the margin. The same manuscript notes *Metamorphoses*, Book 5, as the source for the story of Adonis, mentioned at *Troilus* 3.720–1; but the story is widely current, as in the *Roman de la Rose*.

Troilus refers to the reunion of Orpheus and Eurydice in the Elysian fields: his naming of 'the feld of pite' (*Troilus* 4.789) may refer directly to Ovid's *arua piorum* (*Met.* 11.62), quoted in the margin of MS H4. The Wife of Bath refers to 'Ovyde' for the story of Midas and his 'two asses eres' (954), and tells us to read Ovid for 'the remenant of the tale' (981–2): she conspicuously substitutes Midas' wife for his male barber as the irrepressible tattletale. The latter half of Book 11 is taken up by the story of Ceyx and Alcyone, which Chaucer retells at the beginning of the *Book of the Duchess*: he evidently makes use of the versions in the *Ovide Moralisé* and Machaut's *Fonteinne Amoureuse* as well as the original in Ovid. The Cave of Sleep, for which Chaucer adds several details from Statius' *Thebaid*, is also mentioned in the *House of Fame* (69 ff.). The Eagle refers the dreamer to his 'oune bok' (*House of Fame* 712), the unnamed *Metamorphoses*, for the location of the House of Fame; and Ovid's account *(Met.* 12.39–63) provides the source for Chaucer's specific description and broader conception of the House of Fame, including its characteristic mixing of true and false tidings; see *Met.* 12.54–55—*mixtaque cum ueris passim commenta uagantur / milia rumorum confusaque uerba uolutant* ('and everywhere wander thousands of rumors, falsehoods mingled with the truth')—and *House of Fame* 2108–09: 'Thus saugh I fals and soth compouned / Togeder fle for oo tydynge.' Chaucer makes no references to the final three books of the *Metamorphoses*.

There is little evidence in Chaucer's poetry of Ovid's final letters from exile. One passage in the *Squire's Tale* (220–23), on vulgar superstition, is close in phrasing to *Tr.* 4.2.25–26. Chaucer's favorite line, 'For pitee renneth soone in gentil herte' (*Knight's Tale* 1761, etc.), is less close to its Italian analogues, especially when applied to Theseus, than to *Tr.* 3.5.31–32: *quo quisque est maior, magis est placabilis irae, / et faciles motus mens generosa capit* ('The greater someone is, the more easily is he appeased of his wrath; a noble mind grasps good-natured impulses'). And one of the scribal marginalia for *Troilus* 1.712–14—'So ful of sorwe am I, soth for to seyne, / That certainly namore harde grace / May sitte on me, for-why ther is no space'—tells the reader 'Require in Ovidio' (in effect 'cf. Ovid'), presumably *Pont.* 2.7.41–42: *sic ego continuo Fortunae uulneror ictu, / uixque habet in nobis iam noua plaga locum* ('thus I am wounded by the steady stroke of Fortune and now a new blow scarcely has a space in me'). These are at best minimal points of contact—insignificant when compared with Chaucer's continuing and extensive use of Ovid's major works from the beginning of his poetic career to its end.

FURTHER READING

The bibliography on the medieval Ovid is large and continually expanding. The following additional works may be particularly helpful. On the general topic and its implications: Barkan (1986), Bolgar (1954), Edwards (2006), the medieval commentaries edited by Ghisalberti (1932, 1933a, 1933b, and 1933c), Martindale (1988), McKinley (2001), Rand (1925), and the essays in Paxson and Gravlee (1998), and in *Mediaevalia* 1987. For Jean de Meun, Allen (1992) and Minnis (2001); for Dante, Barolini (1984); for Chaucer, Calabrese (1994), Desmond (2006), Hanning (1986), Kiser (1983), Shannon (1929), and Wetherbee (1984).

CHAPTER THIRTY

Ovid in Renaissance English Literature

Heather James

Introduction

It is hard to imagine what the shape of English Renaissance literature might be, if Tudor and Stuart writers and readers had listened to the advice of moral reformers and shunned Ovid. The classical poet's deep learning and eloquence made him vital to the development of English letters, but his sensual and pagan muse posed obvious dangers. If the 'inticing rimes' of 'sweet-lipt Ovid' could 'forc[e] attention' and wonder even from sage and serious readers, how could women and schoolboys (seen as impressionable readers) withstand his seductive appeal (Beaumont 1602: Sig. A3v-4r)? Nonetheless, Ovid's admirers weighed his learning, eloquence, and wit against the wanton, vain, and trifling elements of his verse and came to one conclusion: there had to be a way to retain his gifts to poetry without succumbing to his charms and repeating his moral errors. But how?

Schoolmasters opted for selective reading: Ovid's poetry could be safely mined for its models of eloquence and knowledge of ancient myth and custom. In this view, Ovid's verse was comparable to a garden, replete with rhetorical 'flowers' that one might pluck from context and arrange at will. Schoolboys were trained from early days to read for the beauties of his language: they parsed, memorized, and adapted lines of his verse, leaving questions of interpretation to the schoolmaster, who provided moral lessons from time to time. Their first encounter with Ovid usually came in the form of rhetorical handbooks that collected specimens of eloquence. Such handbooks, or 'florilegia' (gatherings of rhetorical flowers), spared tender students the moral trials of reading Ovid first-hand and, should any intrepid readers venture in on their own, they offered a guide to safe reading. English readers were trained to look for 'excellent and wise Sentences' even in the *Amores* and the *Ars amatoria*, the 'walkes of Venus' that mingled 'delicate flowers' with 'weeds of wantonness' (Peacham 1622: 88).

Renaissance readers put Ovid's eloquence to abundant use. They pored over personal copies of his poems and marked such lines as 'Enuie, the liuing, not the dead, doth bite' (*Am.* 1.15.XX; Jonson 1601: 1.1.81–2), 'We none must blessed call / Before their funerall' (*Met.* 3.136–7; Wither 1620: 80), 'I see the better, I approve it, too: / The worse I follow' (*Met.* 7.20–1; Sandys 1632: 306), and 'a faithful study of the liberal arts humanizes character and permits it not to be cruel' (*Pont.* 2.9.47). They copied choice phrases into commonplace books as records of their reading. They used them in sermons, political discourses, and treatises on topics from marriage and love to moral philosophy. They summoned his wit and wisdom to illustrate their own. Through the art of the commonplace, English readers bound the 'schoolmaster of love' to their rules: they enjoyed the freedom to affirm, discredit, appropriate, or allegorize Ovid at will and suffer no metamorphosis at his hands. Such a method of reading was well suited to fashioning English gentlemen of taste and discernment.

Commonplace wisdom, however, was not up to the task of producing English letters in the form of poems, narrative fiction, and plays. Maxims could *ornament* but not *tell* a tale: the material for characters, plots, and the passions that drive them was to be found in Ovid's poems. Many of the writers who shaped the course of English letters—such as Edmund Spenser, Sir Philip Sidney, Christopher Marlowe, Ben Jonson, John Donne, and John Milton—shut the covers of the rhetorical handbooks and opened Ovid's book. Once the restless and often violent figures of his poetry were released as if from Pandora's box, they could not easily be recalled. Poets of the English Renaissance entered into a long wrestle with the potentially dangerous but alluring errors of Ovid's verse. Is it possible to learn from mistakes, they implicitly ask, or do the lessons of experience inevitably come at too high a price? The figure of Ovid is never far from the scenes in which characters of Renaissance fiction—from Marlowe's Faustus to Milton's Eve—aspire beyond their limits, test precepts and commonplaces that pass for truth, and, quite often, fail as spectacularly as Ovid's Phaethon and Icarus.

Ovid's association with error was complex, comprehending verbal, aesthetic, and political as well as moral activities. His transgressive wordplay, for example, seems to spring from an irrepressible disposition to play with rhetorical and social proprieties. An old anecdote about his life suggests as much. Three of Ovid's closest friends came to him, the story goes, to beg him to let them strike just three lines from the entire body of his verse. Ovid amiably agreed but requested that he be allowed to exempt three lines of his own choosing from the friendly act of censorship. Ovid wrote his cherished lines on one tablet, while his friends inscribed the offending ones on another. When the tablets were compared, the same three lines wondrously appeared on both. The story, which was originally recorded by Seneca the Elder, circulated widely in the Renaissance as testimony that Ovid understood the risks of his poetry and, as one admirer put it, heroically refused to 'suppress . . . the libertie of his verse' (Sandys 1632: unpaginated).

Equally productive were the 'errors' Ovid built into the very form of his verse. No poem experiments more boldly with fluid boundaries than the *Metamorphoses*, which overturns the rules of poetry described in Horace's *Ars poetica*. In lieu of simplicity and uniformity, Ovid produced astonishing generic complexity and thematic variety.

He even made a virtue of the fantastic, creating modern versions of the fabulous sirens and centaurs that Horace urged poets to renounce. While earlier Augustan poets embraced the principle of verisimilitude, Ovid studded his poem with marvels and wonders that appealed to the imagination. He encouraged readers to let their minds wander with the inspired poet, who subordinates nature and convention to ideas and 'rang[es] only in the zodiac of his own wit', as Sidney put it (1966: 24). Ovid's style left Renaissance critics in a quandary. They admired Horace's aesthetic ideals but loved Ovid's creative daring. Although his poem was unorthodox, the wit and skill with which he wove fable into fable were divine.

Ovid constantly toyed with conventions, violated rules, and explored morally ambiguous situations. But there was nothing criminal in his poems until Augustus read some of the irreverent verses of his youth, as the story goes, and exiled him to Tomis on the Black Sea. It made no difference that the charge of licentiousness was likely an official excuse, used to cover up some other offense (Knox 2004). For Ovid and his Renaissance readers, the blame placed on the erotic poetry of his youth changed the significance of his works and career. Before the exile, Ovid possessed the charm and wit to turn any and all materials—even religion, law, and the Emperor's divinity—into subjects for his playful Muse. Afterward, he and his poems were forced to bear the stigma of criminal audacity and moral corruption. The sentence of exile threw into relief the strands of political satire and critique in Ovid's poems and treated them as libel. In Ovid's view, Augustus seized control over interpretation itself, creating a hierarchy of meanings which subordinated all perspectives (including the poet's) to his supremacy. He reduced and determined the meaning of Ovid's poems and, in the process, transformed the poet into a figure from the *Metamorphoses*: Ovid became Actaeon, destroyed by Diana for wandering into her sacred grove. He was also the aspiring Phaethon and Semele, who in different ways came too close to divinity and met the blast of Jove's thunderbolt.

The exile complicated rather than simplified Ovid's reception in Renaissance England. Augustus acted like a prince when he defended the mysteries of state (*arcana imperii*) against the poet's scrutiny and satire. But Ovid, on the other hand, acted as an exemplary citizen and poet when he exposed political abuse. There were risks in praising Ovid's boldness but costs as well in accepting the Emperor's tyrannical judgment against the poet. Is it good to 'be lowly wise' (*Paradise Lost* 8.172) as the angel Raphael counsels Milton's Adam, when he asks about heavenly matters? Or is it the birthright of free citizens to ask questions of established authority, as no less a figure than Milton's God invites Adam to do at the time of his creation? The literature of the English Renaissance records an animated debate about Ovid, who generated questions about authority that were as sensitive in Renaissance England as they were in Ovid's Rome.

Wanton Ovid

The earliest debates about Ovidian verse focused on its sensual appeal and pagan origins. Even positive accounts of his contribution to English education and letters advocated some degree of voluntary censorship. Sir Thomas Elyot placed Ovid second only to Virgil in the school curriculum, asserting that 'righte commendable and noble sentences' were to be found even in his 'mooste wanton bokes', but he also recommended that schoolmasters paraphrase unduly distracting passages (1883: 1.128). Others had harsher words for the poet. Roger Ascham, tutor to Elizabeth I, dismissed Roman comedy and Ovidian elegy out of hand, while Thomas Becon, the Protestant theologian, urged schoolmasters to exclude Ovid from the curriculum and teach eloquence from the psalms. Thomas Brice even penned verse, 'Against filthy writing and such like delighting' (1562), to decry the influx of pagan eroticism into English verse (Huntington Library 18274): 'What meane the rimes that run thus large in euery shop to sell? / With wanton sound, and filthie sense, me thinkes it grees not well, / Tel me is Christ, or Cupid Lord? doth God or Uenus reigne?'

With the sounds of reproach buzzing in their ears, Elizabethans responded to Ovid's myths and eloquence with a combination of fear and excitement. John Lyly used Ovid to flesh out a moral fable of youthful prodigality, while Edmund Spenser found somewhat more positive uses for Ovidian material in his story of Redcrosse's struggle with the passions. Christopher Marlowe by contrast turned the tables on the moralists by repudiating their censure and surrendering his muse to Ovidian sensuality. Ben Jonson, seeking a middle way, satirized the giddy submission of his comic characters to Ovidian sources of inspiration but argued vigorously against the blanket censure of Ovid's fables of the imagination.

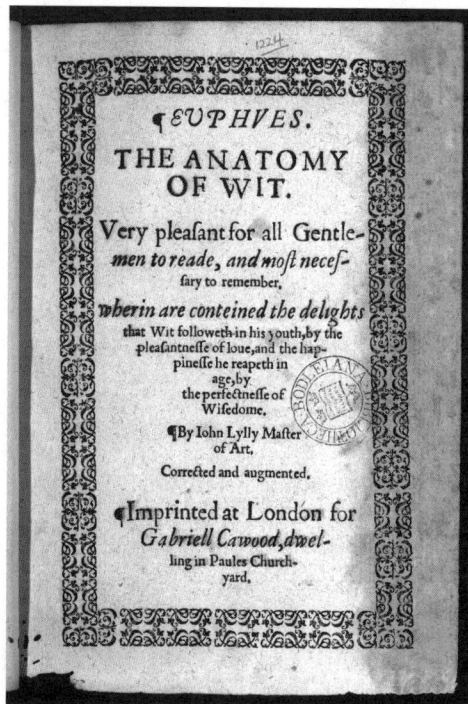

Figure 6: The title page of the 1579 edition of John Lyly's *The Anatomy of Wit* (The Bodleian Library, University of Oxford, Mal. 713 (1)).

Lyly drew on Ovid to ornament his tales of Euphues, a gifted young man with a fatal attachment to rhetoric. Euphues' story begins when he leaves his university home of Athens (i.e., Oxford) to travel to Naples, land of humanist erudition and sensual vice. Having arrived at man's estate, he relishes his newfound ability to make executive decisions (however unwise) about his life and manners: he dazzles the town, ignores the advice of old men, and chooses a bosom friend, Philautus. He shares all aspects of life with his new friend, including the love of his fiancée, Lucilla. Although Euphues never acknowledges his betrayal of Philautus, he is permanently scarred when the beautiful but shallow heroine proves unfaithful to him in his turn. Just as the hero careered out of control when he spurned the advice of his elders, so Lucilla loses her moral bearings when she throws over her father's choice (Philautus) first for Euphues and then for an idle courtier named Curio. Horrified by her failure to distinguish between him and a fop, Euphues glimpses something of the depths of his folly. Recoiling from society, he goes into self-imposed exile at Silexsedra ('seat of flint', impervious to love and pity), where he spends his days in melancholic contemplation and in the writing of moral (and bullying) epistles to friends, who continue to live in the shadow world of social relations.

In the figure and fortunes of Euphues, Lyly makes clever use of Ovid. The hero's life even unfolds along the lines of Ovid's biography, as it circulated in Renaissance texts. Ovid disappointed his father by giving up a career in law for poetry; his infatuation with verse led to his sensational *Amores*, which celebrate Corinna, thought to be the princess Julia, daughter of Augustus. When the inevitable crisis with authority ensued, Ovid went into exile, spending his last years in mental and physical anguish, connected to society only through letters to friends and family and diatribes against enemies. Ovid's life story helped Lyly trace his own ambivalent fascination with the protean qualities of rhetoric. For his tale of youthful indiscretion, he drew on the erotic precepts of Ovid's *Ars amatoria* and the philandering gods of the *Metamorphoses*. When Euphues, betrayed and out of faith in his own judgment, goes into exile, Lyly draws on Ovid's *Tristia*, *Epistulae ex Ponto*, and recantation of love, the *Remedia amoris*. Just as the exiled Ovid laments his former infatuation with rhetoric, so Euphues bids farewell to 'the fine and filed phrases of *Cicero*, the pleasaunt *Eligies* of *Ouid*, the depth and profound knowledge of *Aristotle*. Farewell Rhetoricke, farewell Philosophie, farewell all learning which is not sprenge from the bowels of the holy Bible' (Bond 1902: 1.287). The narrative solution is neat: the fiction ends when the hero and author alike endorse the moralists' censure and banish Ovid.

Yet Lyly's readers see what Euphues cannot: the hero's colossal self-involvement and inability to experience the slightest sympathy or fellow feeling. His encounters with narcissism begin with his bosom friend Philautus, whose name means 'self-love'. Even the faithless Lucilla is his double: both are beautiful, wellborn, and easily inflamed by erotic wit. Although Euphues marvels at her strange 'metamorphosis' after she jilts him, he initiates her transformation into an Ovidian creature through the love games he takes from the *Amores* and *Ars amatoria*. Yet she alone earns a reputation for moral frailty. Euphues repudiates the pagan gods he once cited approvingly: 'Did not *Iupiter* transforme himselfe into the shape of *Amphitrio* to imbrace *Alcmæna*? Into the forme of a Swan to enjoye *Læda*? Into a Bull to beguyle *Iò*? Into a showre of golde to winne *Danae*?' (Bond 1902: 1.236). He converts, while she merely shape-changes into a figure of transgression such as Ovid's Pasiphae or Myrrha, who also assumed control over their love lives and met with disaster. The problem is that Euphues, failing to understand himself, projects his foibles onto others as he scrabbles for the moral high ground (Mount Silexsedra). Ovid's Narcissus was better able to recognize himself in his mirror image. Although Lyly asserts the value of learning from mistakes, his hero seems to reject the lessons of experience instead of learning from them.

In *The Faerie Queene*, Spenser offers a powerful new account of Ovid's role in the construction of literary character. Unlike Lyly, he involves readers in his characters' encounters with the Ovidian imagination, using a technique from classical oratory, in which a speaker hints at what he dares not state openly. According to one rhetorician (Wilson 1553: 105), 'A priuie beginning, or creeping in, otherwise called Insinuation [is useful] when the Iudge is greeued with us, and our cause hated of the hearers.' Spenser slips Ovidian allusions into his *narrative* long before he identifies their role in the moral *allegory*. Such allusions may at first seem irrelevant: they lurk in shadows of ambiguity, then suddenly appear full-blown, like Orgoglio before the hapless Redcrosse in Book I, canto vii. There is no mistaking the Ovidian proportions of Orgoglio, a priapic version of the rebel giants in *Met.* 1, who pile mountain upon mountain in an effort to storm the heavens and overthrow the gods. The question is how Redcrosse, a good man and the patron of holiness, comes to face such an image of his own sexual and spiritual dissidence. How does Spenser prepare for the intrusion of Ovidian sexuality into an allegory of the Christian warrior (Redcrosse), led by truth (Una), who sets out to battle down the dragon (the Antichrist)?

The importance of Ovid to Redcrosse's story is revealed at the midpoint of the book, when the knight, discouraged by the apparent infidelity of Una, sits down to rest by a distinctly Ovidian fountain, dallies with an Ovidian witch (Duessa), and confronts Orgoglio, a grotesque image of his wounded sexual pride. Yet the signs of the wanton Ovidian imagination appear as early as canto i, stanza 6, when Redcrosse and Una are overtaken by a storm at the moment their journey begins (I.i.6; all references from Hamilton 1980):

> The day with cloudes was suddeine ouercast,
> And angry *Ioue* an hideous storme of raine
> Did poure into his Leman's lap . . .

The storm that forces Redcrosse and Una to seek shelter is more pagan than Christian and more sexual than meteorological. Such images often evoke the marriage of heaven and earth, yet this one is hostile: it lashes out at the pair with the wanton destructiveness of Ovid's 'angry' Jove, who harms even those he loves, like Semele, to whom he came as a thunderstorm (Ovid represents himself as Semele to Augustus' angry Jove in his poetry of exile). This image hints that Redcrosse will repeatedly encounter the violent onslaught of his own passions: he will face internal sources of opposition to his mission and mistake them for external threats.

The hint becomes concrete when Redcrosse falls prey to Errour, a monster lurking in the woods in which he and Una seek refuge from the storm. There is at first no visible danger. The pair wanders happily, discussing the natural and moral properties of the various trees. Yet their situation grows confusing as they lose their way and (I.i.10):

> wander too and fro in wayes unknowne,
> Furthest from end then, when they neerest weene,
> That makes them doubt, their wits be not their owne:
> So many pathes, so many turnings seene,
> That which of them to take, in diuerse doubt they been.

Up until this point, the pair seem to share an identical experience of the walk in the woods. Differences between Redcrosse and Una emerge only when they face choices. Arriving at 'a hollow caue, / Amid the thickest woods' of an Ovidian 'labyrinth' (I.i.11), she announces the presence of mortal danger: 'This is the wandring woods, this *Errours den*, / A monster vile, whom God and man does hate' (I.i.13). Una's assertion puts her slightly at odds with Redcrosse: while she urges him to pay attention to the moral threat before them, he sees Errour as a monster from epic romance and a challenge to his heroic virtue.

Unable to juggle the competing demands of moral allegory and martial epic, Redcrosse comes face-to-face with errors that are as much internal as external. He goes, 'full of fire and greedy hardiment,' to 'the darksome hole' (I.i.14):

> And lookèd in: his glistring armor made
> A litle glooming light, much like a shade,
> By which he saw the vgly monster plaine,
> Halfe like a serpent horribly displaide,
> But th'other halfe did womans shape retaine,
> Most lothsom, filthy, foule, and full of vile disdaine.

Redcrosse learns nothing from his visual encounter with Errour: he responds viscerally to her hybrid body, glimpsed in the shadowy light reflected by his armor. His martial presence dwindles even as her grotesque body swells and spills over the bounds of verse and into the next stanza. What does he see? An image of his desires for Una? Of hers for him? Redcrosse successfully battles down the personification of his own potential error. But his distorted perspective, reflected in the grotesque image of the female body, suggests that the threats to his union with Una are not over.

Redcrosse faces his harshest trial at the time and place associated with sexual violence in Ovid's *Metamorphoses*: it is high noon, and the hero seeks shelter from 'the boyling heat' by a fountain in the shades of 'a gloomy glade' (I.vii.4). He is alone and disarmed when Duessa lures him into a love scene by the waters of the fountain, from which Redcrosse drinks, only to find that they chill, melt, and unman him (I.vii.5):

> The cause was this: one day when *Phoebe* fayre
> With all her band was following the chace,
> This Nymph, quite tyr'd with heat of scorching ayre,
> Sat downe to rest in middest of the race:
> The goddesse wroth gan fowly her disgrace,
> and bad the waters, which from her did flow,
> Be such as she her selfe was then in place.
> Thenceforth her waters waxed dull and slow,
> And all that drunke thereof, did faint and feeble grow.

Redcrosse, who strayed from moral allegory into an Ovidian woods and fought with Ovidian forms of error, now drinks directly from an Ovidian fountain or literary source: the story is that of Salmacis and Hermaphroditus, the pleasure-seeking nymph and the underaged object of her desire from *Met.* 4. The Ovidian influences that lead him to sit 'downe to rest in middest of the race' soon unshape him, and the knight finds himself 'Pourd out in loosenesse on the grassy grownd' (I.vii.7). Like a poisoned hero in film noir (e.g. *Dead On Arrival*), he cannot pull himself together to fight this new form of error. He goes through the motions of battle with Orgoglio, the gigantic representation of his own phallic aggression, but his opponent easily defeats him and throws him in a dungeon. Even Arthur, who embodies the chivalric ideals Redcrosse admires, can only pull him from the dungeon. He cannot save him from despair.

Ovid inhabits the morally ambiguous zones of *The Faerie Queene*. He contributes the twists of plot, errors of judgment, and erotic temptations that reveal Redcrosse's heroism and erring humanity. He is vital as well as dangerous to the young knight, devoted to his Christian mission but trained up in classical models of heroism. As the poem's Ovidian subtexts reveal, it is dangerous to follow sensual pleasures and worse to reject them entirely: The demands of the flesh overwhelm Redcrosse, but his despair, which leads him to turn his aggression against his own flesh, endangers his mortal soul. The House of Holiness provides the temporary solace of disembodied contemplation, but Spenser soon returns the hero to his earthly attachments and mission. Only in his last battle does Spenser purge the allegory of Christian identity of its pagan elements. When Redcrosse fights the dragon, falls into the Stream of Life, and emerges as a new man, he steps fully into a Biblical story and casts off the Ovidian coordinates (or contaminants) that gave flesh to the allegory. In Spenser's poem, Ovid provides a potent language through which readers may deliberate the role of sensual pleasure in moral fables.

Christopher Marlowe and Ben Jonson in some ways take opposite positions on the question of how to conjure with Ovid's pagan muse. Marlowe unleashed the libertine Ovid on a delighted readership. He had no patience for Spenser's subtle engagement of readers but mounted an aggressive assault on those who might be hostile to his cause. In *All Ouids Elegies*, he produced the first complete English translation of the *Amores*, without censoring a single poem: ambitious and erudite verses take their place alongside scandalous or trifling poems on sex in the afternoon, adultery, abortion, slave rape, hair loss, the death of a parrot, and impotence. In *Hero and Leander*, he 'blazon[ed] forth the loves of men' and 'powerful gods' (Orgel 1979a; lines 70–1) through his edgily erotic representation of Leander, who represents 'all that men desire' (line 84) and seems too hot for the poem's 'lukewarm' (line 738) heroine to handle. In *Doctor Faustus*, he presented an ambitious man so inspired by pagan loves and learning that he clings to Ovid even as devils gather to drag him to hell. In a doomed attempt to barter with God, Faustus begs for time but, instead of repenting or reciting scripture, he quotes Ovid's wanton plea for more time to linger in his love bed.

Marlowe's Ovid introduced a lyric persona to English Renaissance verse that challenged the going model, derived from the medieval Italian poet Petrarch, who had used Ovid's elegies and *Metamorphoses* to create an influential image of the lyric poet whose desire for one woman, Laura, throws him into restless change. In one poem, Petrarch presents himself a ship buffeted by his own sighs and tears, while in another he imagines his helpless metamorphosis into one Ovidian figure after another. Marlowe, who traced his lyric inspiration back to its pagan roots in Ovid, retained the Petrarchan idea of constantly varying postures of love but removed the stabilizing element of devotion to one woman. The 'ambitious ranging mind' of the Ovidian libertine approves any and all erotic choices his readers could conjure up in their imaginations (Elegy 2.4):

> I cannot rule myself, but where love please
> Am driven like a ship upon rough seas.
> No one face likes me best, all faces move,
> A hundred reasons make me ever love.

This figure fascinated English poets from Donne to Rochester. It turns up in Donne's elegy 'Change' and his sonnets 'The Indifferent' and 'Woman's Constancy', in which the speaker claims he 'can love both faire and browne', rich and poor, town and country, sentimental and steely: 'I can love her, and her, and you and you,' he declares as he builds to his final paradox, 'I can love any, so she be not true' (1, 8–9 in Grierson 1912).

By contrast, Ben Jonson put distance between himself and the libertine Ovid. In the first poem of *The Forrest*, he even imitates and inverts the first erotic elegy of Ovid's *Amores* to explain 'Why I Write Not of Love'. Whereas Ovid claimed that Cupid forced him to write of love, Jonson reverses the case. He was trying his best to bind Cupid in verse, but the god of love utterly refused to cooperate. 'Can Poets hope to fetter mee?' the young god asked (5–12, in Herford and Simpson 1947: 8: 93),

> It is enough, they once did get
> MARS and my *Mother*, in their net:
> I weare not these my wings in vaine.
> With which he fled me: and againe,
> Into my ri'mes could ne're be got
> By any arte. Then wonder not,
> That since, my numbers are so cold,
> When *Loue* is fled, and I grow old.

In this poem, Jonson establishes his difference from the love poets. But he never banishes Ovid from his poetry on moral grounds: to the contrary, he ruefully suggests that Ovid's wanton muse rejected him.

Ovidian eroticism appears as a theme in Jonson's comedies as well. Some of his male protagonists exercise a certain libertine sexuality: the urban wits of *Epicoene*, for example, hold Ovid and attractive boys in high regard. Volpone, however, entirely mistakes his audience when he leaps from his sickbed and reveals to the virtuous Celia that he has one thing on the brain: Ovid. 'My dwarfe shall dance,' he urges (3.212–226; Herford and Simpson 1947: Vol. 5),

> My eunuch sing, my foole make vp the antique.
> Whil'st we, in changed shapes, act OVIDS tales,
> Thou, like EUROPA now, and I like IOVE,
> Then I like MARS, and thou like ERYCINE,
> So, of the rest, till we haue quite run through
> And weary'd all the fables of the gods.
> Then will I haue thee in more moderne formes . . .

This giddy fantasy, stuffed as it is with allusions to sexual metamorphosis, tells us less about Ovid than Volpone, who seems 'weary' of 'the fables of the gods' even before he has finished rehearsing the gamut of sexual scenarios.

Although Jonson can be critical of Ovidian sensuality, he refuses to banish Ovid entirely. In fact, almost every poem of *The Forrest* contains an allusion to Ovid's poetry. Jonson may avoid the *Amores* (Marlowe's terrain) but he embraces the exile poetry, whose ethical and political concerns focus on tyranny and the destructive power of censorship. These themes are also at the heart of his *Poetaster, or the Arraignment*, a play in which Ovid features at the center of a tragic plot, which weighs the poet's erotic mistakes against Augustus' political error of exiling a citizen without trial. For Jonson as for Marlowe, the sentence of exile argued persuasively *for* rather than *against* the liberties Ovid took in his verse. Both poets took a stand and, in different ways, championed Ovid for his refusal to 'suppress . . . the libertie of his verse.'

Heroic Error

A large number of English printed books open with prefaces in which the authors record their wish for the wit, invention, or eloquence of Ovid. This entirely conventional wish speaks to the widespread conviction that England's reputation depended on the ability of modern poets to rival the ancients. Some writers had modest expectations of themselves. Robert Greene, for example, threw in the towel at once, warning readers not to 'looke for any of Ouids wittie inuentions' in his writings, 'but for bare and rude discourses' (1617: unpaginated). Others saw the plain style as a virtue (Huntington Library 18332): why 'pen and paynte [the] prayse' of great men 'With lofty verse heroicall, as was in Ovids days' when one might instead 'tell the troth, and flatter not, but speake as hart doth thinke'? To others, however, skepticism about the heroic idiom suggested a troubling lack of virility in England. How, they asked, might one revive the ancients' masculine virtue without fully surrendering to its rude power? One solution was to project the heroic ethos back in time. The epithets and hyperbole of ancient epic might safely attach to the legendary figures of English history.

In what would seem to be a felicitous choice, some writers concentrated the heroic idiom on England's warrior kings. Shakespeare famously did the honors for Henry V, who led English invasions of France in the Battle of Agincourt, while the Caroline poet Charles Aleyn celebrated the military careers of Edward III and the Black Prince in the Hundred Years War. Although such accounts of the English conquests are largely positive, they tend to be thrilling and disturbing by turns. Warrior kings are unstable figures of heroism, inspiring both patriotic fervor and fear. Aleyn (1631), for example, was clearly worried that Edward III and the Black Prince might look like bloodthirsty tyrants, who satisfied their lust for power on the battlefield. To ward off this danger, he developed a critique of monarchical aggression in his *Battailes of Crescey, and Poictiers* (1631), and ironically focused it on the French king, while lavishly praising Edward III and the Black Prince for their moderation. He carefully presents the French king as insensitive to the suffering of his men, in contrast with the invading Edward III, who is 'a god on earth' (12) because he protects his loving subjects (who were, historically, resentful at being drafted into a foreign war). Edward's son is equally if not more generous: in the battle of Poitiers, he proves that 'Kings are Gods pictures' (117) by showing mercy to his enemies. His act of clemency demonstrates that the English as a race are 'cit'zens of this world', not 'sep'ratists' incapable of 'communion' with Catholic Europe (117): their hearts 'Are *Continents*' and not '*Isles*'.

Aleyn's message of peace and religious toleration is at odds with his heroic genre, which requires violence. This Aleyn delivers to his readers in the high Ovidian style (50):

> Here a hand sever'd, there an eare was cropt;
> Here a chap falne, and there an eye put out;
> Here was an arme lopt off, there a nose dropt;
> Here halfe a man, and there a lesse peece fought.
> Like to dismembred statues they did stand,
> Which had been mangled by times iron hand.

One man leans on his sword as if his dead body were a funereal statue. Another, 'all of whose selfe was as one wound' (50), clings to life because his soul cannot choose an exit from the many wounds. Like Ovid, Aleyn chooses an oddly playful and detached tone to describe heroic bloodshed. Not even the French king is spared: if Philip were 'the subject of old Poetry', he would turn into 'an herb or flowre' and 'by Herbalists [be] enrould, / *Narcissus* like, or Hyacynth of old' (61). Ovid—specifically the tale of Pyramus and Thisbe—comes to Aleyn's mind again when he describes how the green fields of France ran red with blood. Recalling how Pyramus' blood spattered a mulberry and turned its pale berries red, Aleyn writes that if the 'witty feigners of antiquity' such as Ovid had seen this battlefield, 'There had no fruit in all the world beene greene' (114).

As this example suggests, Aleyn turns to Ovid—and to Ovid's ironic narrator—for scenes of violence and death that divide English readers between their insular chauvinism and their hopes for peace with Continental Europe. His Ovidian allusions both enhance and disturb the epic character of the poem, suggesting its division between patriotic fervor and horror at violence as the means of forging a strong nation. The scenes of violence are alternately heroic and grotesque, meaningful and numbing. At the root of the problem is the warrior king, who creates a unified nation by dominating his subjects as well as foreign enemies. Such kings make for ambiguous heroes, because they let the body politic 'bleed / For a distemp'rature [that] lies in the head' (114).

Other verse histories, wise to the problem of the warrior king, gave the heroic Ovid to the rebels. John Weever drew on Ovid to tell the life story of Sir John Oldcastle, the Protestant martyr and rebel, whose boldness eventually led to a 'death! strange death!' which would require 'sweete Ouids wit' to describe (1601: Sig. F1v). When Thomas Gainsford wrote the story of Perkin Warbeck, the commoner who claimed to be Richard IV and fought for the English crown, he used the *Metamorphoses* for scenes of disguise and social-climbing and the *Heroides* for his electric account of the historical women who ambitiously meddled with political history. No one, however, told the story of England's heroic past more successfully than Michael Drayton, who celebrated two legendary rebels: Edmund Mortimer, 'that some-what more than man, / Of the old heroes great and god-like straine' (*England's Heroical Epistles* I.19) and Queen Isabella, the 'bright Queen', who conspired with him to depose Edward II and assume control over the English crown.

In *Mortimeriados* (1596), later reissued as *The Barons Warres* (1603), Drayton divided up Ovid's legacy, giving its questionable aspects to the Queen's chief adviser and the English king. Edward II is the 'lascivious' and 'wanton' king, who lives down to his unheroic epithets by associating with flatterers, alienating his nobles and parliament, and bestowing titles on unworthy men. Ovid's harmful eloquence goes to the crafty Bishop Tarlton, who advises the Queen on mysteries of law and conspires to bring a quasi-legal end to Edward II's rule. Drayton reserves Ovid's heroic eroticism for Mortimer and Isabella. Bypassing opportunities to condemn the rebels, Drayton presents them as the sole figures in this chapter of English history with the vision and desire to re-imagine social convention.

The poem's central books give a riveting account of Isabella's transformation from wronged wife to Ovidian witch: Drayton's Isabella becomes luminous when she assumes the role of England's Medea. Like an Ovidian heroine, motivated by love and the desire to test her own capacity, she plots and oversees Mortimer's escape from prison and travel to France, where she makes him her lover. To concoct a drug for his guards, she gathers herbs—plantan, cold lettuce, poppy, nightshade, cypress,

Figure 7: Image of Phaedra: Robinet Testard, French, about 1500, pigment on parchment. Miniature in Ovid, Épîtres d'Ovide (Letters of Ovid). HM 60 f.17 Phaedra, examining the tip of her pen in an early Renaissance manuscript (Huntington Library ms. HM 60 f. 17). Reproduced by permission of the Trustees of the Huntington Library, San Marino, California.

and mandrake root—and mixes them with the blood of dormice and snakes. Like Ovid, Drayton plays down the menacing elements of his story and expands on the ardent passions of his heroine, who can 'beget life, where was never none, / And put a spirit into the hardest stone' (6.58). In Ovid's story, Medea gathers herbs for a potion to restore youth to an old man (her lover's father). Isabella uses magic to put the guards to sleep and rouse the hero in Mortimer: 'They soundly sleepe, whilst his quicke spirits awake, / Expos'd to perill in the high'st extremes, / Alcydes [i.e. Hercules'] labors as to undertake, / O'er walls, o'er gates, through watches, and through streames' (3.16). Drayton describes Mortimer's heroic escape and travel to France in minute detail. But he does not use the voice of an omniscient narrator. He describes what Isabella sees in her mind's eye: she watches the waters through which he swims grow lovesick for his manly form (in a reminiscence of Marlowe's Leander), while the very breath that passes through his lips makes 'another Milkie Way' and peoples it with 'New creatures' suited to that element (3.21).

Why does Drayton put a positive spin on the night vision through which Isabella conjures the pagan hero within an English nobleman and summons him, through sheer force of will, into her presence? In doing so, he shows acute sensitivity to the potential of Ovidian narratives to produce radically new readings of old texts. Drayton expands on this theme at the poem's end, in an episode devoted to the workings of the lovers' imaginations. The scene takes place in a private chamber designed by Isabella as an earthly paradise, an Eden shaped from pagan materials. For its architectural bones, she chooses pilasters to resemble the constellations as they 'appeare / In their corporeall shapes, with starres inchased, / As by th'old poets they on heaven were placed' (6.31). For the interior design, she presents tapestries of Ovidian metamorphosis: on individual panels she presents images of Apollo and Hyacinthus, Io, Mercury, and Hebe, and Phaethon, blasted from the heavens by Jove. To the series, she adds a new Ovidian scene: Mortimer's heroic escape and welcome in France. For Isabella, Ovid represents a chance to defy convention and reinvent the social world.

When Mortimer and Isabella are at last tracked down and handed over for trial, they are caught in the act of reading Ovid. As they lie 'imparadiz'd' (6.30) in her chamber, the lovers puzzle over the meaning of Phaethon's tale (she laments his fall; he praises his ambition) and Apollo's love for Hyacinthus (she doubts that a god would embrace a boy that way; he demonstrates how it is done). Within the Ovidian cosmos of Isabella's chamber, the pair enjoy a lyric pause in the poem's epic tempo and use it to open up broad questions about the just interpretation of old tales. Ovid's fables had been read and reduced to wise maxims many times over: Io represents ungoverned sexuality, Hyacinthus youthful vanity, and Phaethon the ruinous ambitions of princes. Drayton's lovers reject the moralistic readings of Ovid. Within the protective bounds of their earthly paradise, they raise questions about the way in which texts—Ovid, Genesis, and Drayton's own poem—ought to be read and related to the world. At least some of Drayton's readers will find it hard to rein in their wandering thoughts and fold the story back into a moral parable of the obedience subjects owe monarchs and women owe men. Drayton ends his poem, in fact, not with Isabella's penitence but her curse on her son, Edward III, who broke into her chamber, arrested her lover, and destroyed the world of her desires.

Writing Ovidian Women

Drayton's Isabella, who wrestles with patriarchal traditions in her Ovidian chamber, is not all fiction: many women of the English Renaissance adapted Ovid in painting and tapestry as well as poetry and drama in order to explore their intellectual ambitions, sensual pleasures, and ideological sentiments. When Lady Anne Clifford came into her inheritance, for example, she commissioned a painting, known as the 'Great Picture', that featured her family and her prized books, including Ovid's *Metamorphoses*. Lady Anne Drury painted her own closet, in which scenes of Ovidian metamorphosis represented the ambitions and frustrations of her social and intellectual lives. Ovidian artwork often appeared in great houses. For example, one of the chambers that Francis I designated for the use of Henry VIII was hung with green velvet, embroidered with gold and silver, in which 'euery pane, or pece' contained 'a fable of Ouid in Matamorphoseos embraudered' (Hall 1548: Sig. Ccviiiv). Ovid offered prestige. For women, however, he was also a liability.

To the minds of conservative critics, a woman doomed her virtue when she filled her head with Ovid's tales and erotic precepts. Behavior manuals warned men to keep love poetry away from their wives and daughters. Satirists ridiculed women's desire to read and write love poetry, suggesting such women were wantons and prostitutes. One Jacobean satirist mused about 'this lustie time' (Anton 1616: 52), when:

> women can both sing and sigh in rime,
> Weepe and dissemble both in baudie meetre,
> Laugh in luxurious pamphlets, like a creature
> Whose very breath, some Ouid did create
> With prouocations, and a longing fate.

In this poem, Ovid is synonymous with sexual error in women.

Despite social opposition, many women wrote Ovidian poetry. By appropriating the Ovidian wit, eloquence, and erudition that had long been male prerogatives, women playfully and boldly confronted the supposed error of stepping from one's social place. Christabella Rogers wrote a poem in defiance of Cupid, pitting the 'weapons' of her verse couplets against the love god, whom she hoped to vanquish on the battlefield of moral philosophy (*A Song made by Miss Christabella Rogers,* Folger L.b.707, ca. 1660). Anne Wharton adapted one of his heroic epistles and, even more venturously, wrote a tragedy about Ovid and Julia in *Loves Martyr, or Wit above Crowns*. Isabella Whitney published a poem, 'To Her Unconstant Lover', in which she cited multiple precedents from Ovid's *Heroides* to illustrate her continued fidelity in the face of her lover's faithlessness and, more to the point, to put her poetic credentials on display. A century later, Aphra Behn (the first Englishwoman to make her living by her pen) made a bold foray into Ovid's rude parts in 'The Disappointment', which wittily rewrites a poem about impotence (*Am.* 3.7) as the story of a nymph's embarrassing encounter with sexual failure in an aggressive lover. Disappointment comes when the nymph at last yields to the youth's overtures and reaches for his erection, only to discover—to her horror—there is 'nothing' between his legs (a lack typically imputed to women).

Lady Mary Wroth, the niece of Sir Philip Sidney, wrote of love in her Petrarchan sonnets, *Pamphilia to Amphilanthus*. These sonnets present love as a baffling experience, like finding one's way in a maze, in which grave missteps are possible at every turn (Roberts 1983: 127–8):

> In this strang labourinth how shall I turne?
> Wayes are on all sids, while the way I miss:
> If to the right hand, ther, in love I burne,
> Lett mee goe forward, therin danger is;
>
> If to the left, suspition hinders bliss;
> Lett mee turne back, shame cries I ought returne
> Nor fainte though crosses with my fortunes kiss,
> Stand still is harder, allthough sure to mourne;

Thus let me take the right, or left-hand way,
Goe forward, or stand still, or back retire;
I must thes doubts indure without allay
Or help, butt traveile finde for my best hire;

Yett that which most my troubled sence doth move,
    Is to leave all, and take the thread of love.

In this poem, Wroth explores what it means for a woman to wander in a labyrinth of erotic, moral, and poetic concerns. The hardest choice of all, she writes, is to leave her doubts and dilemmas behind and simply 'take the thread of love'. The last line supplies an important clue to understanding the poem as a version of Daedalus' labyrinth or, better, a critique of its conventional significance in male-authored love poetry. The mythical labyrinth, of course, was designed to conceal the evidence of a woman's monstrous desire: the Minotaur, the half-man, half-beast born of Pasiphaë's passion for a bull. Many male poets before Wroth used the image to describe the emotional and social dangers of love: for them, the moral task before them is that of Theseus, who entered the labyrinth, killed the Minotaur, and retraced his steps (with the help of Ariadne's thread). Wroth, however, cannot or at least does not pretend the Minotaur is an allegorical beast over which she must exert dominance, for it is instead a version of herself as an adulterous lover and a love poet and, as such, a double 'monster'.

In writing her poem, Wroth engages a genre of complaint, in which male poets give voice to the regrets of a fallen woman, such as the much storied and stigmatized Rosamund Clifford, whom Henry II made his mistress and installed at Woodstock, a labyrinthine stronghold designed to keep her in and intruders out. Samuel Daniel told her story as the sinner's tale: his Rosamund recognizes her monstrous error when she gains sexual experience in the king's bed, and confesses herself to be a 'Minotaure of shame' (478, in Sprague 1930: 54). Drayton also told her story: his heroine possesses greater moral agency than Daniel's but similarly sees sexual experience as a sin that transforms her, like one of Ovid's heroines, into a beast. In her poem, Wroth reflects upon the dangers she faces as a love poet, whose verses reveal the passions she is expected to conceal and, if she is unlucky, will leave her open to the charge that she is little more than a 'monster', who should stop writing and 'leave idle bookes alone', as Edward Denny, Baron of Waltham, an enemy of hers, once suggested (Roberts 1983: 32–3).

Some women wrote of love but not eros. Amelia Lanyer wove Ovidian allusions into her *Salve Deus Rex Judaeorum* (1611), which explores the relationship of women to Christ's passion. These allusions underscore Lanyer's ambitions as a poet and commentator on spiritual matters. Katherine Philips, who praised female friendship and virtue in a world dominated by men, also founded her reputation on the eloquence and philosophy of the classics but not their wantonness. She inspired one woman, calling herself 'Philo-philippa', to assert the superiority of the 'matchless Orinda' to men (1–10, in Saintsbury 1968: 496–7):

Let the male Poets their male Phoebus choose,
Thee I invoke, Orinda, for my muse;
He could but force a branch, Daphne her tree
Most freely offers to her sex and thee,
And says to verse, so unconstrain'd as yours,
Her laurel freely comes, your fame secures:
And men no longer shall with ravish'd bays
Crown their forc'd Poems by as forc'd a praise.
Thou glory of our sex, envy of men,
Who are both pleas'd and vex'd with thy bright pen.

Philo-philippa offers a remarkable reading of Ovid's story of Apollo and Daphne as a tale of masculine force rather than poetic merit. In her view, the female poet has the light touch and poetic tact it takes to win Daphne's consent.

Grief was one of the strongest passions that women put into verse. Hester Pulter, who struggled for years with the death of her twenty-year-old daughter, used Ovid to express the state of her 'afflicted sad forsaken soule' (35; Stevenson and Davison 2001: 192). In a haunting poem marking the anniversary of her loss, Pulter observes that the seasons change, the years pass, and Philomela (the nightingale) sings her grief anew, but the moment of her daughter's death remains forever fresh and fixed in her memory (53–8; Stevenson and Davidson 2001: 193):

But what a heart had I, when I did stand
Holding her forehead with my Trembling hand
My Heart to Heaven with her bright Spirit flyes
Whilst shee (ah mee) closed up her lovely eyes
Her soule being seated in her place of birth
I turn'd a Niobe as shee turn'd earth.

To describe her own transformation by grief, Pulter draws on Ovid's Niobe, who boasted of her generativity only to lose all her children to the angry gods. Niobe famously turned into a weeping statue as she held the last and youngest child in her arms. In this poem, the figure of Niobe evokes an extraordinary complexity of feeling that Pulter faces as a devout Christian and grieving mother. Whereas her faith is supposed to give her a heart of flesh (*Ezekiel* 36: 26), her grief gives her one of stone.

Milton's Ovidian Errors

By the late seventeenth century, Ovid had undergone considerable transformation from the licentious and wanton pagan decried by Tudor moralists. For many poets and readers, he came to represent dreams of social mobility and agency. He also spoke to those whose efforts to change their worlds had failed. During the civil war, poets on both sides meditated their spiritual kinship with the exiled Ovid. After the restoration of Stuart rule to England, this version of Ovid belonged to the losers, including John Milton. While he was writing *Paradise Lost*, Milton was in political exile, bound to silence on polemical topics. He had both time and reason to reflect on the long, varied tradition of moralizing Ovid's poetry, with its bold insistence on error over orthodoxy. Milton used Ovidian forms of error to explore the broad terrain between transgression and innovation in his account of the Fall, and he concentrated them in the figure of Eve.

Eve derives no immediate benefits from her association with Ovid. The story she tells of her first experience of consciousness, in fact, casts her as a female Narcissus, evidently prone to error and cut off from the divine truths. As she tells the story, she was drawn to a pool, looked into the waters, saw her own entrancing image, and came fatally close to repeating the errors of Narcissus. Like him, she would have 'pined with vain desire' (Fowler 1971: 466), she tells Adam, had a voice not warned her to leave the pool and go 'where no shadow stays / Thy coming' (470–1). She recalls that she hesitated, when brought to Adam, preferring her own 'winning soft' and 'amiably mild' image (479) to his, but she accepted his claim on her, concluding that 'beauty is excelled by manly grace / And wisdom, which alone is truly fair' (490–1). As she reflects on her first experience, Eve interprets it as a lesson in her necessary subordination to Adam and a rebuke for overvaluing her gifts of beauty. She thus applies one of the standard morals associated with Narcissus' tale to herself.

There is more to Eve's story, however, than a parable of vanity focused on Eve as the first woman. The critique of vanity and spiritual sterility more clearly relates to the Ovidian subtext than to Eve's tale. Unlike Narcissus, Eve did not pore over her various beauties in the pool: she did not fall for starry eyes, ivory skin, divine locks, and sweet blushes but for the responsiveness of its 'answering looks / Of sympathy and love' (464–5). God's first lesson to Eve might be said to emphasize the pleasures of amity and reciprocity rather than reproach. The voice in fact tells her that Adam is hers to 'enjoy / Inseparably thine', and that she will regain her image many times over through him: 'to him shalt [thou] bear / Multitudes like thyself, and thence be called / Mother of human race' (572–5). Eve hears a strict warning in the voice that pulls her from her image, but she might have taken it as a lavish promise of fulfilled desires.

Eve's lesson relates to a less familiar reading of the Narcissus story: the young man who fell in love with himself was sometimes interpreted as a parable of friendship. According to the classical theory of friendship, nothing brings men together as securely as similitude and conformity. 'Similitude is a most firme band, to knit and fasten minds together,' one Renaissance commentator wrote, before citing the example of Narcissus (Hayward 1604: 25): 'This did the poets also signifie, when they fained Narcissus to be in loue with his image. For what is more like vnto vs then our owne image? and whosoeuer loueth another man, what else doth he loue but his owne image in him?' Placed in context of friendship, Eve's lesson in narcissism suggests she is Adam's spiritual equal, not his shadowy subordinate. It even affirms the questions Eve asks in Book 9, when she tries to reason her way through the vexing problem of inequality. It brings her closer, in short, to the radical and iconoclastic ideas that Milton held about marriage: for him, the true basis of marriage was congruence of mind. Anything less was an argument for divorce.

Milton's adaptation of Ovid's story offers a lesson to the reader as well as Eve. It can be dangerous to submit to the obvious moral of a given lesson and declare oneself 'cleared of doubt' (*Paradise Lost* 8.179, in Fowler 1971), 'freed from intricacies' and 'perplexing thoughts' (8.182, 183) when one is in fact not satisfied. Errors of interpretation, moreover, play a crucial role in the development of understanding. In the case of Eve's ambiguous relationship to Ovid's Narcissus, the poem's confirmation of Eve as Adam's companion and a spiritual equal in marriage matters more, not less, if she is first suspected of ties to pagan error, idolatry, and vanity. The more radical reading of the Ovidian text in effect upstages and overturns the conservative reading. This play of meaning suggests, in turn, that Milton's readers, like his Eve, must learn to avoid being 'fixed' to one spot. The understanding must be open to change, even revolution.

FURTHER READING

Barkan's classic study (1986) of Ovidianism in the Renaissance makes for an excellent introduction to the subject; see too Doran 1964. Milton's reception of classical literature, and Ovid in particular, has been the object of several important studies: Martindale (1986), DuRocher (1985), and Martz (1986) are good places to start. On the role of Ovid in cultural politics, see James H. (2003, 2006). Lyne's study of early English translations of Ovid (2001) is essential background for other contemporary receptions.

CHAPTER THIRTY-ONE

Ovid and Shakespeare

Gordon Braden

It is possible that Shakespeare's copy—or one of Shakespeare's copies—of the *Metamorphoses* now resides in the Bodleian: a pocket-sized Aldine text from 1502, with schoolroom annotations, an inscription dated 1682 tracing the ownership back to Shakespeare, and the signature 'W^m Sh^e' (or 'Sh^r' or 'Sh^{re}') on the title page. If authentic, it would make a pair with the British Library copy of John Florio's translation of Montaigne that is signed 'Willm Shakspere' on the flyleaf. The history of Shakespeare forgeries is of course an impressive one, and for neither volume is the case for authenticity very strong (Schoenbaum 1981: 100–4); but if they are forgeries, they are thoughtful ones. We know from other evidence that Shakespeare had a special intimacy with both authors; even if these are not the copies he owned, such copies existed. We have reason as well to think that Shakespeare found something peculiarly dramatic about the idea of a book of Ovid. There are not many books on the prop lists for his plays (Barkan 1986: 243); in three of those few cases, the text between the covers is identifiably Ovidian. In *The Taming of the Shrew* Lucentio disguises his courtship of Bianca as a language lesson, and the Latin couplet that he reads aloud from his book is from the *Heroides* (1.33–4); between the two of them it gets recited three times, and travels some interesting territory (3.1.28–43; see James 2004: 68–71). In a different key, the action of *Titus Andronicus* focuses at one point on another book, desperately important to the mutilated and voiceless Lavinia; 'what booke is that shee tosseth so?' asks her father, to be told by his grandson, 'tis Ovids Metamorphosis, / My Mother gave it me' (4.1.41–43). When they read there the story of Philomela, they know what has happened—and indeed where her assailants got the idea of going the Thracian savagery one better. A decade or so later, in *Cymbeline*, Shakespeare returns to the same conceit, with as always a difference. The predatory Iachimo comes upon his prospective victim sleeping, and inspects the book at her bedside: 'She hath bin reading late, / The Tale of *Tereus*, heere the leaffe's turn'd downe / Where *Philomele* gave up' (2.2.44–6). But no rape follows; the scripted outrage is an omen for what does not happen in the play, for tragedy imagined and avoided. For a moment it is as though Shakespeare's larger journey from the early tragedies to the late romances pivots on this one myth.

These are only three of the most overt signs of Shakespeare's recourse to Ovid's works; evidence is seeded throughout his plays and poems (Fripp 1930: 98–128; Baldwin 1944: II, 417–55; Gillespie 2004: 390–403). In an early attempt at systematic coverage, Robert Kilburn Root concluded that more than four-fifths of Shakespeare's numerous mythological references have their specific provenance in Ovid (Root 1903: 3); that result still stands, and does not cover all things Ovidian. It is tempting to think of Shakespeare as following in the footsteps of his French soul mate: 'The first taste or feeling I had of bookes, was of the pleasure I tooke in reading the fables of *Ovids* Metamorphosies; for, being but seven or eight yeares old, I would steale and sequester my selfe from all other delights, only to reade them' (Montaigne 1965: I, 187). Shakespeare did not have Montaigne's strange experience of possessing Latin as a mother tongue; but if he was indeed a student at the King's New School in Stratford, he would probably have been introduced to Ovid in the original when he was eleven or twelve (for an account of what the lesson would have been like, see Taylor 2000: 1). That seems to have been early enough; Ovid's Latin leaves distinct traces in his work. Some, like Lucentio's lesson, are by way of quotation in the original; the first work of Shakespeare's ever published, *Venus and Adonis* (1593)— Ovidian in its subject-matter—carries a couplet from the *Amores* (1.15.35–36) on its title page. Lavinia's father quotes the *Metamorphoses* (1.150) as he embarks on his revenge (*Titus Andronicus* 4.3.4), and the last words of the young Earl of Rutland (*3 Henry VI* 1.3.48) are a line from the *Heroides* (2.66). At times Ovid's Latin gets under the skin of Shakespeare's English; the description of chaos as *rudis indigestaque moles* (*Met.* 1.7) was particularly infectious: 'foule indigested lumpe'; 'an indigested and deformed lumpe'; 'that indigest / Which he hath left so shapelesse, and so rude'; 'monsters, and things indigest' (*2 Henry VI* 5.1.155, *3 Henry VI* 5.6.51, *King John* 5.7.26–27, *Sonnets* 114.5; on Shakespeare and 'Ovidian decreation', see Velz 1999). The bit in *A Midsummer Night's Dream* about Pyramus and Thisbe meeting 'at *Ninnies* toumbe' (3.1.91 etc.) looks as if it were struck directly off the Latin genitive—*ad busta Nini* (*Met.* 4.88)—and could be a schoolboy joke surviving from the Stratford classroom (Rudd 2000: 116). Shakespeare also knew and used Ovidian works which it would have been inconvenient to access except by reading them in the original. The prime source for *The Rape of Lucrece* (1594), the follow-up to *Venus and Adonis*, is the *Fasti* (2.721–852), for which the first English version was published in 1640. When, sometime before 1597, Juliet warily tells Romeo, 'at lovers perjuries / They say *Jove* laughes' (*Romeo and Juliet* 2.1.134–35), she is quoting from the *Ars amatoria* (1.633), the first English translation of which—by fellow dramatist Thomas Heywood—was not printed until sometime after 1600.

It is on the other hand almost impossible for Shakespeare not to have known the first English version of the *Amores*, by another fellow dramatist, Christopher Marlowe. *All Ovid's Elegies*, published posthumously in the late 1590s but circulating in manuscript before that, had a major impact on the late-Elizabethan literary scene, and its phrasing surfaces numerous places in the works of others. Shakespeare's Portia finds herself quoting it verbatim—'the moone sleepes with Endimion' (*The Merchant of*

Venice 5.1.109 = *All Ovid's Elegies* 1.13.43)—and claims have been made for the extensive presence of Marlowe's translation in the Dark Lady sonnets (Stapleton 1996: 133–53). Stronger and more extensive evidence establishes the long-running relevance of Arthur Golding's translation of the *Metamorphoses*. Its first installment appeared in print in 1565, when Shakespeare was a year old; it became available in complete form in 1567, and was reprinted steadily over the course of his life. Golding's fourteener couplets and eccentric diction can strike later ears as 'clownish' (Fripp 1930: 98) and pose a challenge to our powers of historical sympathy (1.115–20, translating *Met.* 1.101–5):

> The fertile earth as yet was free, untoucht of spade or plough,
> And yet it yeelded of it selfe of every things inough.
> And men themselves contented well with plaine and simple foode,
> That on the earth by natures gift without their travell stoode,
> Did live by Raspis, heppes and hawes, by cornelles, plummes and cherries,
> By sloes and apples, nuttes and peares, and lothsome bramble berries.

Yet the translation was broadly influential in Elizabethan literature and seems to have had for contemporaries a *grauitas* of which history has deprived it; new instances keep coming to light:

> Happie were he could finish foorth his Fate
>   In some unhaunted Desert most obscure
> From all socyetie, from love and hate
>   of worldlie folkes, there might he sleepe secure
> Then wake againe and geve God ever prayse
>   Content with hippes and hawes and bramble berrie

So the Earl of Essex, at a desperate moment in his tumultuous life (Doughtie 1979). The traces of Golding's Ovid in Shakespeare are numerous, varied, and widespread. (There is no comprehensive catalogue, but see Braden 1978: 3–7 and the numerous publications of A. B. Taylor.) The odd word can stick like a burr. 'Roping' in the uncommon sense of 'hanging like a rope,' used twice in *Henry V* and nowhere else in Shakespeare—'Let us not hang like roping Isyckles' (3.5.23), 'The gumme downe roping from their pale-dead eyes' (4.2.48)—can be found in Golding in apposite contexts: '*Isycles* hung roping down' (1.136), 'His crusshed brayne came roping out as creame is woont too doo' (12.478). Shakespeare's fascination with carbuncles can be tracked to Golding's mistranslation of *pyropo* (*Met.* 2.2; Taylor 1985). A wisecrack in *Troilus and Cressida* about 'the fidler *Apollo*' (3.3.293–94) is anticipated in Golding when the god's lyre and plectrum become a 'viall' and a 'bowe' (11.186–88, translating *Met.* 11.167–68; Taylor 1991: 496). In translating Ovid's Pythagorean sermon, Golding quietly shifts one of the processes of endless change from rarefaction—*resolutaque tellus / in liquidas rarescit aquas* (15.245–6)—to something more sensuous: 'The earth resolving leysurely dooth melt too water sheere' (15.270). It is Golding's verb that time and again in Shakespeare mediates these two elements: Coriolanus, coming to tears—'I melt, and am not / Of stronger earth than others'

(*Coriolanus* 5.3.28–9)—or Antony, scorning 'Our dungie earth' and calling in love's name for an end to the old order of things: 'Let Rome in Tyber melt' (*Antony and Cleopatra* 1.1.35–8; Taylor 1994/95: 195–9, with other examples).

Golding's influence on Shakespeare has figured in debates about what Ben Jonson called his 'small Latine', but it is clear now that interest in the translation did not foreclose recourse to the original. Golding avoids just the part of *rudis indigestaque moles* that most fascinated Shakespeare: 'a huge rude heape' (*Met.* 1.7). The intertextual layering can be quite complex, nowhere more so than when Ovid's own name comes up (*As You Like It* 3.3.5–8):

TOUCHSTONE   I am heere with thee, and thy Goats, as the most capricious Poet honest *Ovid* was among the Gothes.
JACQUES (*aside*)   Knowledge ill inhabited, worse than Jove in a thatch'd house.

The mythic reference is to the story of Baucis and Philemon, specifically to Golding's information that 'The roofe therof was thatched all with straw and fennish reede' (8.806); the Latin has a slightly different representation of the material involved: *stipulis et canna tecta palustri* (8.630). The conspicuous Englishness of 'thatch'd' (replicated at *Much Ado about Nothing* 2.1.88–9) poises against the knowing Latinism of 'capricious', which in its root sense means 'goat-like'. Golding's diction represents a strong nativist stand in the sixteenth-century controversy as to how the vernacular should grow, a thoroughgoing Englishing of foreign material (Lyne 1996). Shakespeare seems to have been steadily attracted to the result, but as usual worked both sides of the street to deliberate effect, by which local goats and exotic caprice pun on one another.

Touchstone's joke also has to do with goatishness in the sexual sense; calling Ovid 'honest' while alluding to his banishment invokes through pretended denial his reputation as the poet of erotic license. It seems fair to say that this was his prevailing reputation in Shakespeare's vicinity. For Golding, a committed Puritan whose main interest as a translator was in John Calvin, Ovid is still *Ovide moralisé*, and his stories are 'pitthye, apt and pleyne / Instructions which import the prayse of vertues, and the shame / Of vices, with the due rewardes of eyther of the same' (64–6 in Golding's 'Epistle to the Earl of Leicester'). Two introductory poems give detailed guidance on how to read them this way. Nothing is said of Ovid's exile; the uncanny parallels between the Promethean creation of man and Genesis even suggest that Ovid 'perchaunce' had read the Bible ('Epistle' 445ff.). In the 1590s, though, *All Ovid's Elegies* became a public scandal; there could be no illusions about its manifest content, and available copies were burned by episcopal edict in 1599. In a similar key is a popular series of neo-Ovidian narratives, beginning with *Scylla's Metamorphosis* by Thomas Lodge (1589), of steadily increasing lubricity; John Marston's *The Metamorphosis of Pygmalion's Image* (1598) comes right to the edge of pornography, and its own author calls it 'nasty stuffe' (Marston 1599: E4ʳ). Shakespeare's *Venus and Adonis*, if not as nasty, is in this line. Two other playwrights personated Ovid himself. George Chapman's poem *Ovid's Banquet of Sense* (1595) is an extravagantly mannered narrative of Ovid's attempted and possibly successful seduction of the Emperor's daughter Julia. In Ben Jonson's *Poetaster* (1601) an affair between Ovid and Julia is a going thing, and leads to the poet's banishment from court; his creed is one of unabashed sensuality: 'Beautie, compos'd of bloud, and flesh, moves more, / And is more plausible to bloud, and flesh, / Then spirituall beautie can be to the spirit' (4.10.39–41). The play is among other things a *pièce à clef* about the London literary scene; Marlowe is the readiest candidate for Ovid, but tradition keeps finding something of Shakespeare in him (e.g. Bate 1993: 170).

Ovid and his works court other sorts of disreputability. He is named and quoted several times in Reginald Scot's *Discovery of Witchcraft* (1584), a book which there is reason to think that Shakespeare had read (Gillespie 2004: 445–8). Passages from Ovid are cited on various topics, including poisons and love charms, though the main reason for his presence is Medea's incantation in the *Metamorphoses* (7.192–219). This speech is one of the prime pieces of black magic in classical literature, and is frequently cited in Renaissance discussions of witchcraft; Scot adverts to it no fewer than five times, and takes note of Medea's other appearances in Ovid (Carroll 1985: 237–8, 284; Bate 1993: 252–54; Fox 2007). Scot is not witchhunting; his book is in fact a bracing polemic against belief in the dark arts, and Ovid himself is not so much a target as is the gullibility of such readers as Jean Bodin: 'least some poets fables might be thought lies (whereby the witchmongers arguments should quaile) he mainteineth for true the most part of *Ovids Metamorphôsis*, and the greatest absurdities and impossibilities in all that booke' (Scot 1584: 92). Twice Scot quotes approvingly from the medieval *Canon Episcopi*, which aligns such credulousness with heresy: 'Whosoever beléeveth, that anie creature can be made or changed into better or woorsse, or transformed into anie other shape, or into anie other similitude, by anie other than by God himselfe the creator of all things, without all doubt is an infidell, and woorsse than a pagan' (97; see also 66).

Scot's attitude is an angry version of the one voiced more gently by Theseus in *A Midsummer Night's Dream* (5.1.2–6; for the case that Scot's perspective is indeed that of Shakespeare's play, see Strier 2000: 176–80):

> I never may beleeve
> These antique fables, nor these Fairy toyes.
> Lovers, and mad men have such seething braines,
> Such shaping phantasies, that apprehend
> More, then coole reason ever comprehends.

This in the play that more than almost any other of Shakespeare's is about magic; it is by widespread consent his most Ovidian—'the most magical tribute that Ovid was ever paid' (Rudd 2000: 125). The audience is not in the best position to endorse Theseus' rationality; two acts earlier it witnessed a literal (if not total) human-to-animal transformation—the only one in a Shakespearean play—when Bottom the weaver acquired the head of an ass and was passionately loved in that guise by the fairy queen Titania (her name an Ovidian epithet: *Met.* 3.173 *et aliubi*). The specific metamorphosis traces back to Apuleius, though the story is also told by Scot; *contaminatio* from stories in Ovid's poem can, however, be detected: Midas most obviously (much is made of Bottom's 'faire large eares'; 4.1.4), but also Actaeon (Barkan 1986: 262–63) and Hermaphroditus (Taylor 2004: 58–60). The episode is wildly comic but carries a sense of unreckoned powers being turned loose: 'O monstrous! O strange! We are haunted' (3.1.99). Modern productions usually make clear that Titania's desire ends in bestial copulation, and many discussions stress the sense of lines being crossed into 'the dark sphere of sex where there is no more beauty and ugliness; there is only infatuation and liberation' (Kott 1974: 228).

Bottom's entry into this world interrupts the rehearsal of a play based on another story from the *Metamorphoses*, that of Pyramus and Thisbe. In the last act, after the transformation has been undone, Bottom and his fellows finally stage it, and the theatrical potential of Ovidian material shows a different side. The production includes another bestial metamorphosis, when the joiner Snug dresses as a lion for his part in the lovers' tragedy, though he is so afraid of scaring his courtly audience that he stops to make painfully clear that it is only a clever theatrical device (5.1.221–4):

> know that I, as *Snug* the Joyner am
> A Lyon fell, nor else no Lyons damme.
> For, if I should, as Lyon, come in strife,
> Into this place, 'twere pitty on my life.

He need not of course have bothered; the whole show is fabulously and famously inept. Some of the joke is at the expense of Golding, whose phrasing is scattered about (Muir 1977: 68–77; Forey 1998—though see also Taylor 1989). The budding playwright has chosen Golding's meter for some of the dialogue, and shows off its pitfalls splendidly (5.1.325–30):

> These lilly lippes,
> This cherry nose,
> These yellow cowslippe cheekes
> Are gon, are gon:
> Lovers make mone:
> His eyes were greene, as leekes.

The players never actually get to the Ovidian metamorphosis, involving mulberries; Theseus, as master of ceremonies, is merciful to all concerned: 'No Epilogue, I pray you' (5.1.349).

In a manner of speaking that metamorphosis has already occurred, animating the main plot. We hear earlier of 'a little westerne flower; / Before, milke white; now purple, with loves wound' (2.1.166–7); this is the flower that makes Titania fall in love with Bottom and governs the shifting devotions of Demetrius and Lysander (the women, defying stereotype, never change their love objects) and steers the busy story of the play's four ordinary lovers. The flower is the pansy: 'maidens call it, Love in idlenesse' (168). The myth of its change, narrated by Titania's husband Oberon, is a previously unattested Ovidian aetiology, 'one of the great examples of Ovid reborn in Renaissance garb' (Barkan 1986: 257). Cupid's attempt to shoot his arrow at 'a faire Vestall, throned by the west' (158) is thwarted by 'the chast beames of the watry

Moone' (162), and the diverted shaft lands on the flower and gives its juice the power to make anyone fall madly in love with 'the next live creature that it sees' (172). The fair vestal is, by barely muted implication, Queen Elizabeth; the compliment to her unassailable virginity is standard, but in context gives off some strange vibrations: 'Shakespeare seems to be saying: Cupid won't be gainsaid, so if you want a chaste Queen walking imperially on 'In maiden meditation, fancy-free', her subjects will have to bear mad doting in their love-lives' (Bate 1993: 140; for a more aggressively political reading, see Montrose 1983: 81–5). In having the flower's metamorphosis do what it does to the love lives of his Athenians, Shakespeare inverts the usual Ovidian pattern to make the transformation cause rather than effect: 'instead of a memorial via the oozing blood of the dead lovers, he offers a cause for the passionate blood of the living lovers' (Barkan 1986: 257). The principle behind the resulting whirligig is formulated in a pregnant way by Golding: 'The fancie of thy faultie mind infects thy feeble sight' (4.244; Brown 1999: 64). This line comes in the story of Apollo and Leucothoë, the one that follows that of Pyramus and Thisbe, and gives things a spin not evident in the Latin: *uitiumque in lumina mentis / transit* (4.200–1), that is, the sun god's love-sickness sometimes darkens his beams. Golding sees in the juxtaposition *lumen/mens* a contrast between faculties of perception, and in so doing gives Shakespeare the draft for Helena's incisive if unavailing formulation near the beginning of the play of why lovers seem so out of touch with reality: 'Love lookes not with the eyes, but with the minde: / And therefore is wingd *Cupid* painted blinde' (1.1.234–5). It is a motto not only for the rest of *A Midsummer Night's Dream* ('The lunatick, the lover, and the Poet / Are of imagination all compact', 5.1.7–8), but for much of the rest of Shakespeare's terrain as well: 'Incapable of more, repleat with you, / My most true minde thus makes mine eye untrue' (*Sonnets* 113.13–14).

No other single work has quite the density of Ovidian reference that we find in *A Midsummer Night's Dream*, but there are places where the well seems to reach deeper. Outdoing Bottom's transformation toward the far end of Shakespeare's career is his other onstage metamorphosis, Hermione's return to life in *The Winter's Tale*. Killed sixteen years earlier by the brutal and arbitrary jealousy of her husband Leontes, she reappears as a statue, attributed to the only Renaissance artist named anywhere in Shakespeare: 'a Peece many yeares in doing, and now newly perform'd, by that rare Italian Master, Julio Romano' (5.2.94–6). The repentant Leontes is overwhelmed by the lifelike quality of the statue ('I am asham'd: Do's not the Stone rebuke me, / For being more Stone then it?'; 5.3.37–8), but even more so by the event that the lady Paulina then directs (99–105):

> (*To Hermione*) 'Tis time: descend: be Stone no more: approach:
> Strike all that looke upon with mervaile: Come:
> Ile fill your Grave up: stirre: nay, come away:
> Bequeath to Death your numnesse: (for from him,
> Deare Life redeemes you) (*to Leontes*) you perceive she stirres:
>   (*Hermione slowly descends*)
> Start not: her Actions shall be holy, as
> You heare my Spell is lawfull: doe not shun her.

To which Leontes, touching her: 'Oh, she's warme: / If this be Magick, let it be an Art / Lawfull as Eating' (109–11). This ending is a bold and bizarre move on Shakespeare's part—there is nothing like it in his source, Robert Greene's *Pandosto*, where the wife remains dead—and potentially disastrous in the theater if everything does not go just right; it has proved itself to be one of the most uncannily moving moments in any of his plays. The magic is Ovidian, an enactment of the myth of Pygmalion—though once the air clears we realize that there is no magic, at least of the supernatural sort. Leontes notes right off that the statue renders Hermione as if she had been alive all the intervening time—'*Hermione* was not so much wrinckled, nothing / So aged as this seemes' (28–9)—and we have to assume that she has merely been in hiding; the magic is all in Paulina's scriptwriting and production design. Yet in context the myth has an emotional reality to it that goes beyond theatrical cleverness: 'Shakespeare partly tricks us into imagining that his heroine has actually stood still for sixteen years; and, preposterous as such an image may be, it amounts to the truth, for what is a person deprived of love, family, and society but a block of stone?' The myth also bears a promise that such emotional death can be outlived: 'The husband treats the wife lovelessly, and she becomes a stony lady. With penance, the passage of time, and the fulfillment of the mystic oracle, that hardness can melt in a newly purified love' (Barkan 1986: 284).

The intimation that Ovid's epic theme works at that sort of depth throughout Shakespeare's *oeuvre*, even when magic is not pretended, has driven a good deal of critical analysis. The comedies, especially those involving women disguised as men— doing in play what Ovid's Iphis does for real (*Met.* 9.666–797)—have been notably responsive to such attention (as in Carroll 1985). Some bold claims have arisen along the way: 'when [Shakespeare] takes his inspiration from Ovidian metamorphosis . . . he is touching upon the very heart of his own imagination' (Barkan 1986: 273). This is to renew in a sophisticated mode the much quoted assertion of one of Shakespeare's own contemporaries that 'the sweete wittie soule of *Ovid* lives in mellifluous & honytongued *Shakespeare*' (Meres 1598: OO1ᵛ). The premiere discussion along these lines is that of Jonathan Bate, a thoroughgoing study of Shakespeare's entire corpus on the conviction that 'by reading Shakespeare's reading of Ovid we may come to a remarkably full . . . picture of the sort of artist that Shakespeare was' (Bate 1993: vii). That sort is a somewhat contrary humanist (6):

> his sceptical, dynamic temperament would have had a certain resistance to the humanist implication that 'the essential nature of human beings' does not change; what Ovid taught him was that everything changes . . . and this accorded with his desire as a dramatist to examine human beings at key moments of change in their lives, such as when they fall in love or make a renunciation or, most drastically, decide to kill themselves. Ovid's philosophy of instability modified the 'essentialist' premises of humanism even as his exemplary force sustained it.

This credible perspective gives Bate the confidence to detect connections to Ovid in numerous areas where they have gone unremarked. The effect is sometimes startling, as in the links he makes between Othello's last speech and the fate of Myrrha in the

Metamorphoses (10.499–502: her tears become the 'medicinable gum' of 'the *Arabian* trees' (*Othello* 5.2.359–60)) and the letter in the *Heroides* that leads up to Phyllis' suicide. The latter involves one striking verbal parallel (what have I done, she asks, but love not wisely? (*Her.* 2.27)) and a more general coincidence of occasion and purpose: 'She composes her own epitaph, he his own funeral oration. They create their own myths: the confidence of their rhetorical performances serves to cover up their self-delusions and raise them to exemplary status' (Bate 1993: 190). Across the whole of the Shakespearean corpus Bate sees the lineaments of a systematic recourse to Ovid's account of the Four Ages; it is in part this schema that gives *The Tempest* its special sense of elegiac fulfillment: 'Shakespeare was too much of a sceptic to suppose that he could deliver up the Golden World, but for a moment, through Prospero's theatrical arts, which are of course also his own, he provides some consolation by conjuring the Silver Age back to life. The drama itself becomes a harvest home' (263).

Bate is careful to call many of the connections that he makes 'affinities', rather than, say, allusions (190):

> Allusion and affinity may, but do not necessarily, coexist: an allusion may signal a more far-reaching correspondence, but it may be merely incidental or ornamental; and affinity may be made apparent on the surface of the text, but it may operate at the level of the imagination. . . . Paradoxically, the most profound affinities may be the least demonstrable precisely because they go deeper than the explicit local parallel.

He admits: 'The problem with affinities is that if you're looking for them they're easy to find, but if you're not they cease to exist' (190). With Shakespeare and Ovid, they turn out to be indeed, with the right expertise, impressively easy to find. It is hard to know where to draw the line, or whether there is a line to be drawn. Ovid's big idea can certainly become too big to mean anything in particular: 'The risk of an analysis of "metamorphosis" in Shakespeare is that one may be tempted to discuss changes that are not really matters of morphosis. Since all traditional drama is about change through action . . . the net catches everything in the action, making metamorphosis mean too much and (*ergo*) too little' (Velz 2000: 190). Bate's book has been the object of a particular critique by Charles Martindale. He finds its purportedly historicist methodology 'open to challenge' (Martindale 2000: 199), is unpersuaded by some of the individual readings, and thinks that Bate, 'like most scholars today' (211), overstates Shakespeare's classical learning. In general, Bate 'tends to foreground sameness (partly from a "humanist" belief in the continuity of human nature and concerns)', whereas 'what we need now is an alternative analysis that *rigorously* foregrounds difference' (210). Martindale gestures toward a 'very different' picture from Bate's: 'Bate sees Shakespeare as consistently sceptical and "Ovidian" (as Ovid is now seen), imitating Ovid in a consistent manner. . . . My story was, and remains, that the relationship between Shakespeare and his sources is always more discontinuous and opportunistic than that' (211). Yet Martindale's astringency still leaves the *Metamorphoses* with a very big role in Shakespeare's career (212):

My view is that his sense of it deepened and changed as he grew—though maybe that is another way of saying that three of his late plays, *Cymbeline*, *A Winter's Tale*, and *The Tempest*, construct what is, from my perspective, a peculiarly rich 'Ovid.' Many of the earlier plays are lavishly decked out with Ovidian mythological references in Meres' sweet witty style. In the great tragedies Ovid goes underground, though traces may remain. In general in the three romances there is less superficial Ovidianism, but the plays can be read inter alia as profound meditations on the character of Ovid's greatest poem.

This sketch (answering to the fuller account in Martindale and Martindale 1990: 45–90) is fairly close to the one offered a century earlier by Root (whom Martindale cites), and is not as inconsistent with the picture that Bate paints as the language of academic controversy might make it sound.

Inhibiting any serious attempt to decenter Ovid within the Shakespearean cosmos is the uniquely resonant placement of 'Shakespeare's most sustained Ovidian borrowing' (Bate 1993: 249). At the beginning of the last act of *The Tempest* Prospero enters *'in his Magicke robes'* and readies himself for the last phase of his great plan for regaining his dukedom from his enemies and securing his daughter's place as the future queen of Naples; when alone on stage, he *'drawes a circle with his staffe'* and speaks (5.1.33–40):

> Ye Elves of hils, brooks, standing lakes & groves,
> And ye, that on the sands with printlesse foote
> Doe chase the ebbing-*Neptune*, and doe flie him
> When he comes backe: you demy-Puppets, that
> By Moone-shine doe the greene sowre Ringlets make.
> Whereof the Ewe not bites: and you, whose pastime
> Is to make midnight-Mushrumps, that rejoyce
> To heare the solemne Curfewe . . .

Playful miniature agents from the natural world, only faintly mischievous, much like the lower-ranking fairies in *A Midsummer Night's Dream*—but their power can be incongruously great and fearsome (40–50):

>   by whose ayde
> (Weake Masters though ye be) I have bedymn'd
> The Noone-tide Sun, call'd forth the mutenous windes,
> And twixt the greene Sea, and the azur'd vault
> Set roaring warre: To the dread ratling Thunder
> Have I given fire, and rifted *Joves* stowt Oke
> With his owne Bolt: The strong bass'd promontorie
> Have I made shake, and by the spurs pluckt up
> The Pyne, and Cedar. Graves at my command
> Have wak'd their sleepers, op'd, and let 'em forth
> By my so potent Art.

Building to one of the darkest of arts, the speech becomes a boast and a threat—though at just that point, it takes the turn that defines Prospero's character and the course of the play (50–7):

> But this rough Magicke
> I heere abjure: and when I have requir'd
> Some heavenly Musicke (which even now I do)
> To worke mine end upon their Sences, that
> This Ayrie-charme is for, I'le breake my staffe,
> Bury it certaine fadomes in the earth,
> And deeper then did ever Plummet sound
> Ile drowne my booke.

The long-planned perfection of Prospero's power is also, and by intention, the moment at which he will divest himself of it. He has stated his wish, against a good deal of human and theatrical convention, not to take revenge on his enemies once they are in his power: 'with my nobler reason, gainst my furie / Doe I take part: the rarer Action is / In vertue, then in vengeance' (26–8). Exercising that virtue is simultaneous with a renunciation of his supernatural authority and a return to mortal weakness; afterward, 'Every third thought shall be my grave' (314).

The opening line and middle section of Prospero's soliloquy are taken, at points with great specificity, from the incantation of Medea's that so interested Scot and others (*Met.* 7.197–209; Golding 7.265–77):

> montesque amnesque lacusque,
> dique omnes nemorum dique omnes noctis, adeste!
> quorum ope, cum uolui, ripis mirantibus amnes
> in fontes rediere suos, concussaque sisto,
> stantia concutio cantu freta, nubila pello
> nubilaque induco, uentos abigoque uocoque,
> uipereas rumpo uerbis et carmine fauces,
> uiuaque saxa sua conuulsaque robora terra
> et siluas moueo iubeoque tremescere montes
> et mugire solum manesque exire sepulcris.
> te quoque, Luna, traho, quamuis Temesaea labores
> aera tuos minuant; currus quoque carmine nostro
> pallet aui, pallet nostris Aurora uenenis.

> ye Elves of Hilles, of Brookes, of Woods alone,
> Of standing Lakes, and of the Night approche ye everychone.
> Through helpe of whom (the crooked bankes much wondring at the thing)
> I have compelled streames to run cleane backward to their spring.
> By charmes I make the calme Seas rough, and make the rough Seas plaine
> And cover all the Skie with Cloudes, and chase them thence againe.
> By charmes I rayse and lay the windes, and burst the Vipers jaw,
> And from the bowels of the Earth both stones and trees doe drawe.
> Whole woods and Forestes I remove: I make the Mountaines shake,
> And even the Earth it selfe to grone and fearfully to quake.

I call up dead men from their graves: and thee O lightsome Moone
I darken oft, though beaten brasse abate thy perill soone.
Our Sorcerie dimmes the Morning faire, and darkes the Sun at Noone.

Golding's presence is particularly striking. The translation of *di* as 'Elves' fits the un-Ovidian tone for the first part of Prospero's speech, and 'this rough Magicke' seems to owe its famous adjective to its double appearance in a line of Golding. This passage was the first evidence of Shakespeare's indebtedness to Golding to be publicly noticed, brandished by Richard Farmer in 1767 as proof that Shakespeare did not read his classics in the original (Farmer 1966: 54–55). In fact there are places where Golding is not in the loop—he turns Ovid's *robora* into generic 'trees', but Prospero specifically speaks of assaulting '*Joves* stowt Oke' (see further Baldwin 1944: II, 443–51)—and the case is actually one of the most economical demonstrations of Shakespeare's interest in both the Latin and its English intermediary.

Trace evidence indicates that another classical passage on witchcraft was on Shakespeare's mind as well, from John Studley's fourteener translation of the pseudo-Senecan *Hercules oetaeus*, the text in question (452–72 of the Latin) covers territory similar to Medea's speech ('With waltring surges I have shooke the seas amid the calme') while anticipating Prospero's choice of words in particulars where Golding does not: 'Arte', 'roring', 'oape', and 'noonetyde' (Newton 1581: CC5ᵛ). The generic topic is black magic, and part of the point of the speech in Shakespeare is that Prospero's sternly (and successfully) virtuous intentions draw on dangerous resources. Some critics argue as much by way of the implied allusion to Medea (e.g. Carroll 1985: 235–43; Bate 1993: 249–55); Charles and Michelle Martindale disparage that route—'In this instance it should be plain that the use Shakespeare is making of Ovid is imitative, not allusive'—but they affirm that 'educated members of the audience would recognize the presence of Ovid' (Martindale and Martindale 1990: 23), and in so doing gesture toward another path to the same end: Medea is to Prospero as Medea's author is to Prospero's author.

The tradition of seeing in Prospero an unusually direct Shakespearean self-portrait is almost two centuries old; it continues to annoy scholars, but not all scholars, and shows no signs of going away. Recent discussions have pressed it anew in connection with the Ovidian text behind Prospero's speech of renunciation; that speech comes to look like a final and not entirely happy reckoning of a lifetime's commerce with Ovid, and the book that Prospero promises to drown when he gets the last good out of it becomes figuratively and perhaps (in a sufficiently savvy production) literally the *Metamorphoses*, making its last appearance as a Shakespearean prop (Barkan 1986: 288; Brown 1999: 84; Lyne 2000: 161). The homage is sincere, but many of the things about 'honest Ovid' that might give unease also seem to be in play. The everyday genre of witchcraft that is Ovid's subject in the *Amores* and the *Ars amatoria* (the metamorphical connection was second nature to Shakespeare: 'You have Witch-craft in your Lippes, Kate', *Henry V* 5.2.274) is present in *The Tempest* in the love story of Miranda and Ferdinand, itself part of Prospero's great plan; but his nurturing of it comes with a fear that their desire will break its legal bounds. He threatens Ferdinand with a heart-stopping curse on their marriage if that happens (4.1.15–22):

If thou do'st breake her Virgin-knot, before
All sanctimonious ceremonies may
With full and holy right, be ministred,
No sweet aspersion shall the heavens let fall
To make this contract grow; but barraine hate,
Sower-ey'd disdaine, and discord shall bestrew
The union of your bed, with weedes so loathly
That you shall hate it both.

and he stages a wedding masque whose main plot point is the absence of Venus and Cupid, who meant 'to have done / Some wanton charme, upon this Man and Maide' (94–95). As for Prospero's supernatural charms, theirs is a power whose demonic potential could pervert even a good and wise master; Ovid's Medea, in another passage that found favor in the Renaissance, notes that she sees and approves the better path even as she follows the worse (*Met.* 7.20–1 *uideo meliora proboque,* / *deteriora sequor*). But there is also the thing about witchcraft that so outraged Scot: it is a fraud; it does not really exist outside of the confidence game of which it is part. Prospero's most famous speech, interrupting his wedding masque, is about the dispelling of illusion: initially the illusion of theatrical performance, but expanding as he talks to include 'the great Globe it selfe, / Yea, all which it inherit': 'we are such stuffe / As dreames are made on; and our little life / Is rounded with a sleepe: Sir, I am vext, / Beare with my weakenesse, my old braine is troubled' (*The Tempest* 4.1.153–54, 156–59). The twin valedictions to Ovid and the theater are valedictions to unrealities of love and magic which had looked like everything.

FURTHER READING

The main line of recent analysis of Shakespeare's commerce with Ovid is developed in Carroll (1985), Barkan (1986), and especially Bate (1993); the last work is inclusive in its scope and especially rich and innovative in its detail. Taylor (2000) offers newer essays on particular topics, including the relevant skepticism of Martindale and Velz (see also Martindale and Martindale 1990). The continuing work of A. B. Taylor, in numerous brief articles, on Shakespeare's specific use of Arthur Golding's translation of the *Metamorphoses* shows that venerable topic to be still unexhausted (see also Forey 1998). The text of Shakespeare used above is the edition of 1988.

CHAPTER THIRTY-TWO

Ovid in the Twentieth Century

Theodore Ziolkowski

Introduction

Over the centuries 'Ovidian Ages' have alternated in an almost predictable regularity with the vogue of Virgil. Robert Graves observed that 'whenever a golden age of stable government, full churches, and expanding wealth dawns among the Western nations, Virgil always returns to supreme favour' (Graves 1962: 13). Conversely, in times of political and cultural upheaval Ovid, who has been widely recognized as the 'ur-exile' and whose works exemplify change and metamorphosis, has offered comfort to readers and models to writers. In the twentieth century this alternation proceeded in three principal waves.

Early Modern Ovid

The century began under the aegis of Virgil, the nineteenth centenary of whose birth had been celebrated to international acclaim in 1882 (Ziolkowski 1993: 3–6). Yet even before World War I shattered the confidence and splendor of the grand era of imperialism, which paid lip service to Virgilian *pietas* and *amor patriae*, doubts and uncertainties were evident, conveyed by images from Ovid. In 1912 Richard Strauss' opera *Ariadne auf Naxos*, with its libretto by Hugo von Hofmannsthal, and a series of eight paintings by Giorgio de Chirico presented Ovid's tragic heroine (*Met.* 8.172–82) as a symbol of the loneliness, abandonment, and exile that lay in store for a new generation.

Perhaps the earliest advocate of Ovid was Ezra Pound, himself a voluntary exile from the United States (Ziolkowski 2005a: 36–41). From at least *The Spirit of Romance* (1910), where he described Ovid as 'urbane', 'a Roman of the city', and a skeptical poet for a skeptical age (6), down through his early *Cantos*, which frequently cite Ovid, Pound was a tireless promoter of the Roman poet, whose society, he felt, faced the same problems as did the modern world. At the expense of Virgil, whom he considered a second-rate 'Tennysonian', Pound in his letters incessantly urged Ovid upon his friends as a poet second only to Homer.

Ovid provided the thematic motto as well as the hero's name in James Joyce's *Portrait of the Artist as a Young Man* (1916), which opens with the epigraph *et ignotas animum dimittit in artes* ('and he applies his mind to unknown arts', *Met.* 8.188). Before Stephen Dedalus gives himself wholly to art, he is torn between the contrasting values represented by the two terms of his name: the Christian values of St Stephen and the pagan lure of Daedalean artistry. The novel portrays Stephen's attempts to escape the labyrinth of Ireland with its suffocating Catholic culture and, as he finally departs for Paris, his appeal in the last line to Daedalus: 'Old father, old artificer, stand me now and ever in good stead.' (In *Ulysses* Stephen returns to Dublin, a failed Icarus rather than a successful Daedalus.)

Even more than Pound and Joyce, Osip Mandelstam was an outsider in his own culture—a Jew in an anti-Semitic Russia, a non-practicing Jew among the observant, a Russian born in Warsaw and educated largely abroad, and later an exile who spent much of his life abroad. Small wonder that he was drawn to the ur-exile, whose influence is conspicuous in several poems of his first two volumes: *Stone* (1913) and *Tristia* (1922), which takes its very title from Ovid (Terras 1966). Unlike Pound and Joyce, Mandelstam takes Ovidian themes less frequently than Ovid's own life as the basis for poetic treatment. In one of his most famous poems (*Stone*, no. 80), written following his first visit to the Crimea, he imagines Ovid in exile just across the Black Sea at Tomis, 'Here, amid the quiet fading of nature / Far from the Forum and the Capitol'. Another poem (*Tristia*, no. 104), composed during a subsequent stay in the Crimea, plays explicitly on the famous lines from Ovid's elegy of leave-taking from Rome (*Tr.* 1.3): *Cum subit illius tristissima noctis imago, / Quae mihi supremum tempus in urbe fuit* ('When I am overcome by the gloomy image of that night which was my last hour in Rome').

For intensely personal reasons, then, Pound, Joyce, and Mandelstam—all of whom knew their Ovid in the original from their studies—identified with Ovid as the ur-exile, the victim of a ruthless imperial government not unlike many European states of the early twentieth century. Other high modernists, in whose lives exile constituted a less compelling factor, were attracted more by the theme of transformation that underlies Ovid's *Metamorphoses*.

T. S. Eliot, who later became a conspicuous Virgilian, was drawn in his early poetry to Ovid, whom he had studied at prep school and then at Harvard. Among the several dozen works in seven different languages that Eliot cites as sources to *The Waste Land* (1922) Ovid plays a central role. First, the tale of Tiresias, whom Eliot himself in his notes calls 'the most important personage in the poem, uniting all the rest', begins almost precisely in the middle of the text. (Eliot cites the full Ovidian text, *Met.* 3.320–38, in his notes.) As the witness of the tryst between the typist and the clerk, it is his legendary bisexuality that enables Tiresias to appreciate both the male and the female aspects of the encounter: 'I Tiresias, though blind, throbbing between two lives, / Old Man with wrinkled female breasts'. His function is not just that of an aged voyeur. The entire poem is controlled by his unifying consciousness that assimilates the various figures of the poem, tying together its often seemingly disparate parts and establishing connections between isolated cultural and historical events.

Tiresias' transformation from man to woman and back again reflects on an individual level the more general interest in metamorphosis that permeates Eliot's earliest poems. In 'The Death of Saint Narcissus' (1915) Narcissus, whom Eliot conflates with St Sebastian, imagines in his death throes that he was once a tree, a fish, a young girl. In *The Waste Land* Eliot uses various images taken from the *Metamorphoses*, the most striking of which is the tale of Philomela, who 'by the barbarous king / So rudely forced' is changed into a nightingale and 'Filled all the desert with inviolable voice'.

During that same *annus mirabilis Ovidianus* of 1922, Rainer Maria Rilke, in an unparalleled creative surge of only three weeks, turned out his fifty-five *Sonnets to Orpheus* (1923). Rilke had read selections from works by Ovid, including the *Fasti*, as a schoolboy in Prague. But his cycle of poems addressed to Orpheus was inspired directly by a Latin–French edition of the *Metamorphoses* which his lover Merline had presented to him at Christmas two years earlier. Since the poems are *to* Orpheus, only about a dozen deal explicitly with the figure of the poet. One sonnet (2:13) interprets Orpheus' feelings following the failed rescue of Eurydice from the Underworld; another (1:26) alludes to the poet's dismemberment but concludes with the powerful assertion that all poets are the heir of Orpheus, the ur-poet.

> Nur weil dich reißend zuletzt die Feindschaft verteilte,
> sind wir die Hörenden jetzt und ein Mund der Natur.

> Only because hostility ultimately tore and scattered you
> are we now the hearing ones and a mouth of nature.

Otherwise the poems revolve almost entirely around the middle stage of Orpheus' life—as the poet with the power to transform nature through his song and to capture the essential permanence of being in its most varied transformations.

While Eliot and Rilke explicitly draw on Ovidian images for the theme of metamorphosis in their works, other writers who also knew their Ovid at first-hand tended to find more contemporary analogies for transformation. Franz Kafka, who received a sound training in Latin and read widely in Ovid's works, used an Ovidian theme as the basis of his most famous story, *The Metamorphosis* (*Die Verwandlung*, written 1912). Hermann Hesse, whose letters as a schoolboy frequently cited the *Metamorphoses* as one of his favorite subjects and who translated sections into German hexameters (Ziolkowski 2006: 83), produced in his modern fairy tale *Pictor's Metamorphoses* (*Pictors Verwandlungen*, written 1922) his own version of Ovid's tale of Hermaphroditus, in which the youth is merged with the body of the girl who loves him (*Met.* 4.285–388). Meanwhile, in England both David Garnett (in *Lady into Fox*, 1922) and his friend Virginia Woolf (in *Orlando: A Biography*, 1928) explicitly used Ovidian images in their modern tales of metamorphosis (Ziolkowski 2005a: 87–97; Brown 1999: 201–15).

This lively literary rehabilitation of Ovid, which was begun by European and American poets in the years surrounding World War I and paralleled by a group of writers who, aware of Ovid's model, found in metamorphosis a useful vehicle for their various fictions, came to an abrupt end in the 1930s. Only a few scholars—notably Émile Ripert in his charming *Ovide: Poète de l'amour, des dieux et de l'exil*

(1921) and E. K. Rand, *Ovid and His Influence* (1925)—had turned their attention to the poet, who was still widely regarded as a graceful but lightweight and even licentious figure unworthy of serious study. A few artists, attracted by the theme of metamorphosis, were inspired from time to time by Ovid's work. Picasso issued a folio containing a cycle of thirty vivid etchings based on the *Metamorphoses* (Lausanne, 1931). Other artists were attracted by specific episodes, for example Salvador Dalí's striking *Métamorphose de Narcisse* (1937) and André Masson's *Pygmalion* (1939) (Reinhardt 2001: 48–69).

Generally, however, the rise of fascism in Europe and a renewed national consciousness in the United States called for different literary and historical models—models heralded by the bimillennial of Virgil's birth in 1930, which was celebrated all over the world—most elaborately in Italy, but also in France and Germany as well as in North and South America (Ziolkowski 1993: 17–26). After Virgil had been heralded in 1930 as the poet of empire, the bimillennial of Augustus' birth in 1937 provided an occasion, especially in Fascist Italy and Nazi Germany, for politico-cultural and militaristic propaganda, which seemed to be foreshadowed by Virgil's praise of Augustus, who stormed across Asia imposing Roman rule on 'willing' peoples (*G.* 4.560–62 *Caesar dum magnus ad altum / fulminat Euphraten bello victorque volentis / per populos dat iura*, 'while mighty Caesar thunders to the deep Euphrates and, victorious, gives laws to the consenting peoples'). In this atmosphere there was little room for a poet who represented a pure poetry untouched by politics, who spoke for the rights of the individual rather than the nation, and who proclaimed a world of change and metamorphosis. After his brief flourishing of barely two decades Ovid once again made way for Virgil.

Ovid after the War

Even following World War II Ovid's life and works attracted little attention, despite Hermann Fränkel's attempt at a rehabilitation in his *Ovid: A Poet between Two Worlds* (1945) and despite such musical tributes as Richard Strauss' *Metamorphoses* (1946), a 'study for twenty-three solo strings', and Benjamin Britten's *Six Metamorphoses after Ovid* (1951). But in 1957/58 the situation changed. In preparation for the bimillennial of Ovid's birth L. P. Wilkinson published his pathbreaking introduction *Ovid Recalled* (1955), and the occasion was greeted with international conferences in Italy and with lectures and major publications, both scholarly and popular, in Germany, France, and England (Ziolkowski 2005a: 149–55). This renewed interest was almost immediately reflected in the literature of the period. Writers were attracted by the poet's life, but for two distinctly different reasons: the life of the writer in exile and the critiques of the writer in Rome.

At least since the ninth century poets have identified with Ovid on the basis of his paradigmatic exile (Smolak 1980). This identification, no longer intellectual but actual, intensified in the nineteenth century, as exile became the frequent destiny of such poets as Alexander Pushkin (e.g. his elegy *To Ovid*), Francisco-Manoel Nascimento (cf. Lamartine's ode 'La Gloire'), or Paul Verlaine, who in his melancholy

'Pensée du soir' (in *Amours*, 1888) portrayed Ovid wandering through the horror of the Scythian countryside, much as he had been depicted in Delacroix's painting *Ovide chez les Scythes* (1959).

This identification was readily available to the writers who were driven into exile by the totalitarian regimes of the 1930s—initially such German writers as Hermann Broch, Bertolt Brecht, and Lion Feuchtwanger (Ziolkowski 2005a: 101–03). But the identification was also evident in other countries. John Mansfield witnessed the first wave of political refugees fleeing to England, and his poetic 'Letter from Pontus' (1936)—allegedly written by the elderly Ovid—reflects the resignation that afflicted many of them.

Because he died in the Roman province of Moesia Inferior or Scythia Minor (present-day Dobrudja) Ovid has long occupied a special place in the folklore, culture, and literature of Romania, where he is venerated as the country's tutelary genius, the symbol of its cultural continuity since antiquity, and its first national poet (Mitescu 1972). Accordingly, the bimillennial of Ovid's birth in 1957–1958 provided the occasion in Romania for enthusiastic celebrations that continued for several months. Ovid's life suggested itself immediately to exiled Romanian writers seeking literary analogies for their own destinies.

Vintila Horia's novel *God Was Born in Exile* (*Dieu est né en exil*, 1960) is purportedly a secret journal covering Ovid's eight years at Tomis (present-day Constanta) and based both on extensive historical research as well as Horia's personal experience (Christensen 1995). The Rome from which this Ovid has been exiled is described in terms that evoke modern totalitarian states with their secret police and informers, their conspiracies and assassinations, their atmosphere of terror, and their imperialistic policies. Some of the episodes are based on incidents mentioned in Ovid's epistles from exile. And the book teems with quotations and allusions that demonstrate Horia's familiarity with Ovid's works, with Romanian archaeology, and with Suetonius and other classical sources. But most of the plot is invented and culminates in Ovid's expedition up the Danube to the sacred mountain Kogaionon, where he meets a priest of the Dacian god Zamolxis (Zalmoxis). A Greek physician tells him about the birth of a miraculous child-savior which he witnessed in Bethlehem. Ultimately, left behind by his friends when they flee to the freedom of the Scythian steppes to escape the hostile new centurion from Rome, Ovid dies, hallucinating and alone in Tomis. Early Western reviewers were put off by Horia's suggestion that Ovid was a proto-Christian; but that critique fails to take into account the author's national and ethnic allegiance and the exile's love of Romania and its history. The novel belongs to a tradition of Romanian Ovidianism going back at least three centuries.

Elegien aus dem Nachlaß des Ovid (1963; 'Elegies from Ovid's unpublished works') by the Austrian Marxist Ernst Fischer suggest hidden doubts underlying the author's hitherto stalwart Stalinism, despite an afterword that makes explicit their Marxist basis. He interprets Roman history as a class struggle between aristocrats and plebeians in a Rome corrupted by gold from Egypt, the riches of the Orient, and a slave economy. The *pax Augusta* simply gilded the decadence of a society in which a ruthless dictator so successfully depoliticized Rome that it was difficult to attract young people to the service of the state. The poems, written in vigorous and graceful elegiac

distichs, are divided into three sections. 'Rome' amounts to a hard-hitting social critique along the lines adumbrated in the afterword. 'The Scythian Woman' comprises
love elegies to the woman who has made his exile happy. And 'The Dream' presents
Ovid's/Fischer's visions for the future—a new Golden Age that will come when the
present has disintegrated: a situation symbolized by the rubble from an overthrown
bust of Augustus.

Unlike Horia's novel and Fischer's elegies, Eckart von Naso's *Liebe war sein
Schicksal* (1958; 'Love was his destiny') devotes only a few pages to the period of
exile. The novel, which embeds Ovid's life in a well-informed political and cultural
context, is unified by the theme of love. The chapters, alternating between a modern
narrator and various first-person voices from Ovid's past, tell the extensively fictionalized story of the poet's life in four parts: his early marriage, his love affairs with a
Jewish hetaera and a Roman actress, his encounter with Augustus' daughter Julia,
and the events leading to his exile.

The social criticism underlying Naso's novel is intensified in the brilliant *Nazo
poeta* (1969; 'Naso the poet') by the Polish writer Jacek Bocheński. The capricious
narrator of the novel, styling himself the 'conférencier', portrays Ovid's pre-exilic life
in three stylistically distinct sections: his early life and erotic poems, the scandals at
Augustus' court and the *Metamorphoses*, and an 'Investigation', in which the narrator
surveys the possible scenarios leading to Ovid's exile.

A late example of the conventional biographical novel is still evident in Volker
Ebersbach's novel *Der Verbannte von Tomi* (1984; 'The exile of Tomis'), which
reflects the social situation in the German Democratic Republic in which the author
was educated and lived. This Ovid has been exiled because he became aware of the
sexual infidelities of Augustus' granddaughter and was betrayed by an envious oppor-
tunist. The plot revolves around intrigues at Tomis surrounding the family of the
opportunistic city prefect, who disagrees with Ovid's politics and is contemptuous of
him as a poet. In the confusion of events involving the local Getae the prefect loses
his wife, daughter, and son, and then perishes in a shipwreck as he tries to sail back
to Rome. Ovid, in contrast, makes his peaces with Tomis and establishes friendly
relations with the town's Greek inhabitants. Even when he learns of Augustus' death
he makes no effort to return to Rome.

The drama *Staschek, oder Das Leben des Ovid* (1972; 'Staschek, or The life of Ovid')
by the East German Horst Lange adopts a Brechtian approach. His Staschek is a
proletarian from 'east of the Elbe', who has deserted the cooperative farm where he
worked and, in the twelve scenes of the play, wanders through time and space to
discover that political reality has always and everywhere been the same. He witnesses
Cicero's murder, is beaten by Roman soldiers, and then accompanies Horace to
Rome, where the sycophantic poet writes odes in praise of Maecenas and Octavian.
Leaving Horace for Ovid, who openly ridicules the new matrimonial laws of the
regime and makes fun of Maecenas, he follows the poet to Elba, where Ovid flees to
escape Maecenas' demand that he write a propagandistic ode for the Secular Games.
When Ovid is sent into exile, Staschek tries to make his way to Tomis; but he arrives,
instead, at the frontier town of Bordeaux in AD 485 just as the Visigoths invade the
town. To escape this 'ancient problem' Staschek crosses the nearby river and finds

himself again in an East Germany that has not changed at all. But he has in his pockets the manuscripts of Ovid's works, which he decides might someday be useful. Lange's powerful satire on the role of the poet in history concludes bitterly that the only ones who enjoy success are those who sell out ideologically.

It was not only the Romanians who turned to Ovid after World War II as an analogy for their own experience of exile. But writers in English have tended to view him in a more subjective manner, focusing on his response to the situation of exile. David Malouf is the son of Lebanese refugees who immigrated to Australia. His remarkable poetic novella *An Imaginary Life* (1978), which revolves around personal metamorphosis, only hints at the political reasons for the poet's exile. While he knows much less than Horia about ancient Dacia and its culture—his image of Tomis shows a settlement of mud huts even more primitive than Ovid depicted it—he was drawn to Ovid because the poet lived in 'an age, the dawn of the Christian era, in which mysterious forces were felt to be at work and thinking had not yet settled into a rational mode' (154). Unlike Horia, he is concerned not with the religious atmosphere of the period but with its psychic mood. Set in an era of pre-rational thought in a primitive community still dominated by matriarchy and shamanic magic, his work focuses on the complex relationship between Ovid and a forest child that he encounters in the course of a deer hunt with the villagers and then adopts. When the village becomes unsafe for the boy, whom the villagers suspect of being a lycanthrope, Ovid flees with him across the Ister (Danube) and north into the wilderness. In the visionary conclusion Ovid believes that he has now passed beyond dreams and poetry into 'the last reality' (141), 'the Child's world' (143), a place without time and a space without dimensions. With the boy as psychagogue, Ovid achieves the sense of plenitude and joy foreshadowing the 'new era' that will arrive at some point in the future when 'the millennium of the old gods . . . shudders to its end' (19).

Other Commonwealth poets—C. H. Sisson ('Ovid in Pontus', from *In the Trojan Ditch*, 1974), Seamus Heaney ('Exposure', from *North*, 1975), and Derek Mahon ('Ovid in Tomis', from *The Hunt by Night*, 1983) have similarly transcended narrow political readings of Ovid in exile to see in him an existential model for contemporary humankind. Similarly, in Derek Walcott's poem 'The Hotel Normandie Pool' (*The Fortunate Traveler*, 1981) the poet, sitting at a table beside the hotel pool in Trinidad, is reminiscing about 'the disfiguring exile of divorce'. He notices a 'petty businessman' in sandals, robe, and sunglasses standing 'with Roman graveness' at the edge of the pool. Recalling his own ancestors as 'slave and Roman', he thinks of similarities between the totalitarian state of Augustan Rome and the dictatorships of Caribbean islands. At this point the postfigured Ovid speaks, saying that in his exile he first missed his language and his daughter, but goes on to suggest that he sought out his exile in order to find freedom to write and to escape the political tyranny of Rome. After consoling the poet against detractors who criticize him for his adherence to traditional forms, he wanders back into the hotel and leaves the poet understanding that nature alone endures, superseding all petty human concerns, whether personal, political, or literary.

Ovid was a central influence on the works of Italo Calvino, who invoked the Roman poet in his posthumously published Charles Eliot Norton lectures, *Six Memos for the Next Millennium* (1988), to illustrate the quality of lightness (*leggerezza*) required to offset the heaviness of being. In his earlier introduction to an edition of the *Metamorphoses* (1979) Calvino had stressed another quality he esteemed: the rapidity of the poem. These qualities are both evident in his early postmodern classic *Invisible Cities* (*Le città invisibili*; 1972), where two of the cities bear unmistakable allusions to figures from the *Metamorphoses*: the colored threads linking the houses of Hersilia remind us of Ariadne's thread; and the city of Bauci contains clear allusions to the Ovidian tale of Philemon and Baucis (*Met.* 8.618–724).

The Late Twentieth Century

The second Ovidian wave, which began in the late 1950s, began to ebb in the 1970s as the enthusiasm for the bimillennial commemorations of Virgil's death in 1981– 1982 occupied scholars, and as politicized writers of the late 1960s and 1970s found in Horace's irony and Juvenal's *saeva indignatio* more appropriate vehicles for their political emotions. By the late 1980s, however, a conspicuous revival of scholarly interest was signaled by such collective efforts as *Ovid Renewed: Ovidian Influences on Literature and Art from the Middle Ages to the Twentieth Century* (1988), *Ovidian Transformations: Essays on the Metamorphoses and Its Reception* (1999), and the two-volume Festschrift for the German classicist Michael von Albrecht under the title *Ovid: Werk und Wirkung* (1999). When writers of the 1990s and the new millennium returned to Ovid in this third wave of interest, it was under wholly new auspices. While Ovid's life had not lost its appeal, it was reduced essentially to an analogy for contemporary writers preoccupied with themselves. In addition, the rise of feminism made itself felt—a tendency announced in 1985 by the Women's Classical Caucus of the American Philological Association, which adopted the topic 'Reappropriating the Text: The Case of Ovid' for its annual panel.

While Ovid does not appear in Julia Kristeva's *The Old Man and the Wolves* (*Le vieil homme et les loups*; 1991), his exile prefigures the life of the contemporary thinker in intellectual exile. Her allegorical tale is located in a country named Santa Barbara—a locale, we are told, that might be in New England, the Carpathians, or Greece, but which sounds much like the author's homeland of Bulgaria. The country has been invaded by wolves that have killed thousands of inhabitants—clearly a metaphor for the Soviets who invaded Bulgaria and a philosophical image for a civilization gone 'barbarian' (Santa Barbara). A French journalist, daughter of the former French ambassador, comes to investigate the situation. On her arrival she discovers other mysteries: notably, who killed the Old Man by unplugging his life-support system in the hospital? Ultimately she returns to Paris, leaving the various questions unresolved.

What makes this novel relevant is the Old Man of the title, a former classics master known simply as 'le Vieil Homme'. It is thanks to him that many classical allusions enter the work, which opens with a motto from Ovid (the first two lines of the *Metamorphoses*). The characters frequently quote Ovid, and the theme of metamorphosis—notably the transformation of modern men into wolves—governs the entire work. By the end of the book Stephanie has come to believe that the Old Man has been reincarnated in her—'A metamorphosis that would perhaps have amused the persistent reader of Ovid.'

The Balkan setting is appropriate because the Old Man is also Ovid in exile. 'In which century are we? In the first, in exile on the shores of the Black Sea, dreaming of metamorphoses of human beings who are engaged in a new era . . . or in the present, in Santa Barbara?' (172). His death has introduced her to the realm of myth. The Old Man had dreamed of a world without wolves. He finally died, or was eliminated, because he realized that the wolves have invaded even those closest to him. Although he never appears, Ovid is the dominant presence in this philosophical novel on the power of evil to corrupt: as the author of the *Metamorphoses*, a poem that symbolizes the transformations reshaping the modern world, and as the exiled author, whose destiny prefigures that of the mysterious Old Man, who might even be Ovid reincarnate.

The exiled Ovid makes yet another appearance in Luca Desiato's novel *Sulle Rive del Mar Nero* (1992; 'On the shores of the Black Sea'), which portrays a few months in the life of the elderly and widowed Italian writer Saverio, who is attended by an elderly housekeeper and his grandniece. Now, three months before his eightieth birthday he recalls the bronze monument to Ovid that he saw in Sulmona years earlier and begins to write a novel about Ovid. Drawing parallels between Ovid's exile and his own spiritual isolation, he comes to the conclusion that the human condition is perhaps nothing other than 'a point of grief in the circularity of lives' (153). The third-person account of his daily routine alternates with chapters from his first-person account of Ovid, and the parallels emerge more and more vividly. At the end, as he prepares for his eightieth-birthday celebrations, he sees an apparition in the bathroom mirror: Publius Ovidius. For a short time, he tells the Roman poet, they were companions. Now, he says, he is liberating himself from his model. When Ovid shakes his head, Saverio tries to explain. But Ovid makes him understand that 'life, love, art itself are exile. Not from a preceding blissful existence, but from itself. Exile and life itself are a failure to recognize oneself' (202). Saverio finally understands that the Latin poet has 'infected' him with an awareness of the absurdity of human existence—the constant struggle to reconcile happiness with despair, life with death.

Marin Mincu's *Il diario di Ovidio* (1997; 'Ovid's diary') is a consistently fascinating modern metamorphosis of Ovid. Not really a diary-novel, it is a collection of aphoristic reflections on life, death, religion, morality, metamorphosis, and reincarnation, allegedly penned by the dying Ovid in the last days of his exile. But the work introduces several surprising twists. We are told that Ovid was not forced into exile; instead, he arranged for his own voluntary relegation from Rome because he was disillusioned by life in the capital, where he had witnessed too many incestuous relationships within the imperial family. He also had become disenchanted with his own writing, which now strikes him as aesthetically perfect but ethically insignificant. At Tomis he finds not a primitive outpost but a thriving seaport, a pleasant climate, and a cosmopolitan Getic culture produced from a union of Greek Apollonian and Getic Orphic strains. The reports of hardships in *Tristia* and *Epistulae ex Ponto* are fictions to dissuade acquaintances from visiting him and interrupting the serenity of his last days in this *paradiso terrestre* (49). Like Horia's Ovid, he learns about the monotheistic religion of Zalmoxis with its belief in reincarnation and initially includes that figure as the wise man in Book 15 of the *Metamorphoses*, only later replacing it with Pythagoras. By the end Ovid feels such a desire for spiritual liberation that he offers himself as a sacrifice to the god Zalmoxis and, in the ancient ritual, is tossed into the air and impaled on three spears. The factor linking Mincu's novel with that by Horia, two Romanians living away from their homeland, apart from their familiarity with local history and archaeology and their evident national pride, is the conspicuous interest in questions of comparative religion and Ovid's ties to Zalmoxis—a tradition that goes back to the late sixteenth century in Romania.

In the hands of the various Romanian, English, German, French, and Italian writers the exiled Ovid has undergone a series of metamorphoses that imaginatively transform the poet's life and works into metaphors of modernity. Waldtraut Lewin's *Die Frauen von Kolchis* (1996; 'The women of Colchis') is a feminist fantasy concerning a mild-mannered Roman weaver and his wife, a former prostitute, who go to Colchis to take up land provided by Augustus. Pamphilus is abducted by a tribe of Scythian warrior-maidens—to teach them the art of weaving and to make them pregnant without the aid of their own men, with whom they are in constant conflict. Through Pamphilus' mediation the Scythian women and the Romans come to an agreement whereby the Romans sell their iron weapons to the Scythians in return for gold that the Scythians do not value. Ovid—called 'Publius' or 'the Poet'—enters the story as their neighbor, a clown-like figure of ridicule whom the Romans regard as a nuisance and impractical idealist. When Pamphilus is kidnapped by the Scythians, the poet persuades the wife, Tabea, to accompany him on a 'propaganda tour' of the neighboring farms and villages and to generate enthusiasm for a civilian guard to protect the Roman settlers against the (actually entirely peaceful) Scythians. Lewin's feminist re-visioning of the topic satirizes the principal male figures, who are reduced to the roles of stud (Pamphilus) and naive fool (Ovid).

The feminist impulse is also striking in the lively anthology *Ovid Metamorphosed* (2000), which brings together nineteen writers whose stories are based not only on the *Metamorphoses* but also on the *Ars amatoria*, the *Heroides*, and Ovid's life. Several of the stories amount to feminist updatings of the myths: Michèle Roberts reinscribes Hypsipyle's epistle (from *Heroides*) to a Jason who has just sped off in a blue MG; Joyce Carol Oates relocates the brutal tragedy of Actaeon's offending male gaze to Cape Breton Island in 1923; Patricia Duncker sets Pluto's kingdom into a sleazy contemporary underworld of pornography and violence. The feminist re-visioning of Ovid has also been identified and analyzed in poems based on Ovidian themes by such Commonwealth writers as Margaret Atwood, Jo Shapcott, Jenny Joseph, and Eavan Boland (Merten 2004: 243–326). A further feminist adaptation of Ovid's life and works is offered in Jane Alison's novel *The Love-Artist* (2001), which invents a love affair between the poet and the mysterious Colchian healer Xenia, who becomes the model for Ovid's lost drama *Medea*.

Apart from such postmodern and feminist inventions, rather conventional narratives have continued to appear in various forms: the mystery story (Ron Burns'

'Murderer, Farewell' (from *Classical Whodunnits*, ed. Mike Ashley, 1997), the political thriller (David Wishart's *Ovid*, 1995), or the fashionable comedy (Mavis Cheek's *Aunt Margaret's Lover*, 1994). None of these, however, represents a significant contribution either to Ovidian fiction or to postmodern innovations.

Postmodern Ovid

The most recent shift of emphasis is evident, finally, in *Opium für Ovid: Ein Kopfkissenbuch von 22 Frauen* ('Opium for Ovid: A Pillow Book of 22 Women') by the Japanese writer Yoko Tawada (2000), which continues the feminist impulse using the *Metamorphoses* rather than Ovid's life. Tawada had earlier indicated her affection for Ovid in the three lectures that she delivered as incumbent of the prestigious *Poetik Dozentur* at the University of Tübingen and published under the title *Verwandlungen* (1998; 'Metamorphoses'). Her work, in imitation of the eleventh-century Japanese classic *Pillow Book*, is not so much a collection of stories as a cycle of twenty-two scenes without a plot and connected by overlapping characters. These dreamy scenes, in which almost no men appear, offer portraits of the inner and outer lives of women as they go about their affairs in contemporary Hamburg. While the plots have little to do with Ovid's tales, each of the women is named from a figure from the *Metamorphoses* and characterized by a trait based on her mythic model. There are also explicit allusions to Ovid. The 'opium' of Tawada's title is art, which she cultivates in an effort to avoid the influence of Ovid, whose images tend to creep into her writing like a drug.

The shift of interest from the poet to his poem was evident already in the internationally most successful of late-twentieth-century Ovidian fictions. In Christoph Ransmayr's *Die letzte Welt* (1988; 'The Last World') Ovid occupies the spiritual center but never appears in person. Indeed, the image of the poet that emerges has little connection with the known facts of his life. Ransmayr is concerned neither with the reasons for Ovid's relegation nor with his life during his exile. His interest is focused entirely on the problematic relationship between fiction and reality and on the poet's visionary powers. According to the fiction, the *Metamorphoses* were known in Rome only from recitations before the poet's exile. Cotta, a young admirer of his, hearing that a manuscript of the work survived in Tomis after the poet's death, goes there in search of it. What he encounters is an amazing twilight world hovering between the reality of Rome and the mysteries of the Black Sea, where the ages seem to interpenetrate each other. The town is situated in a timeless realm resembling a backward Balkan country of the early twentieth century—with newspapers and firearms, with dilapidated buses, Christian missionaries, and itinerant film projectionists. Cotta never finds Ovid, but in the course of ten months he meets many residents who knew the poet: the crazy Greek émigré Pythagoras, Ovid's servant; the shop owner Fama, Cotta's source for local gossip; the rope maker Lycaon; the deaf-mute Arachne, who has woven into her tapestries stories told to her by Ovid; the discreet local prostitute Echo; and others.

From various hints Cotta concludes that Ovid must have written poetic episodes featuring all these inhabitants. But the relationship between life and art remains mysterious. It is Cotta's final insight that Ovid 'liberated the world from people and their systems by telling *every* tale to its ultimate end' (287)—that is, by following every human history to its redeeming transformation back into some nature object. Once he had cleared the earth by his metamorphoses of all human beings, Ovid simply entered his own narrative as a stone, a bird, or a bit of moss.

Another typically postmodern adaptation of Ovid is evident in *Het volgende verhaal* (1991; 'The Following Story') by the Dutch writer Cees Nooteboom, which purports to be the deathbed account of his life by Herman Mussert, a fifty-ish classicist from Amsterdam. The story consists essentially of two dreams that Mussert has on the last night of his life. First he recalls a trip to Lisbon that he undertook with his former mistress. Then he imagines a Charon-like voyage from Lisbon to the Amazon in the company of five other men who happen to die at the same moment as he. Each tells his own story, and at the end Mussert prepares to tell his tale, *het volgende verhaal* (which is of course the story we have just read). Ovid enters the narrative as Mussert's favorite poet. Mussert is translating the *Metamorphoses*, and at the time of his death has reached Book 12, the burial of Achilles. Ovid's work is frequently mentioned in the course of his account, and especially his notion of metamorphosis is given an almost postmodern twist: the individual 'I' changes and does not remain constant over the course of a lifetime. The self is only a bundle of ever-changing functions that we choose to label 'I.'

That same year saw the publication of another remarkable Ovidian work, Lawrence Norfolk's *Lemprière's Dictionary* (1991). This brilliant, often fantastic fiction—part historical novel, part detective story—is based on the life of John Lemprière, the author of the well-known *Classical Dictionary* (1788), which has remained a standard handbook of mythology. The adventure story features a mysterious secret society that guides the hero's life and manages to convince him that he possesses mystical powers by staging events—including his father's murder by a pack of hounds—to correspond to incidents from the *Metamorphoses* (here: Actaeon and Diana). At a wild drinking party he witnesses the transformation of a brothel madam into Circe and her patrons into swine. In a warehouse peopled with statues he witnesses a scene out of *Met. 3* (Jason and the dragon's teeth). In his obsession Lemprière begins to see all reality in terms of metamorphoses based on Ovid until, finally, he is healed, marries his beloved, and returns with her to the island of Jersey.

A similarly postmodern, albeit less elaborate, metamorphosis is evident in the lovely *Sogni di sogni* (1992; 'Dreams of Dreams') by Antonio Tabucchi, twenty fictional dreams of figures from history and myth. The 'Dream of Publius Ovidius Naso' represents the wish-dream of the exiled poet, who imagines that he is transformed into a man-sized butterfly with handsome colored wings and brought back to Rome in triumph. Ovid tries to tell the crowds in Rome that he is their poet, but he is unable to speak and emits nothing but a shrill whistle. When the Emperor asks to hear a new poem, Ovid, unable in his insect-form to recite, tries to communicate his verses by gestures. Caesar, annoyed, orders his guards to cut off Ovid's wings, and

Ovid sways out of the palace on his insect legs to encounter a mob now eager to tear him apart. The poet's dancing descent to meet his fate is Tabucchi's acknowledgment of the Ovidian conviction that his poetry will survive—and the postmodern belief that the writer vanishes behind his own work.

The poets have also made impressive contributions. Michael Hofmann's and James Lasdun's anthology *After Ovid: New Metamorphoses* (1994) brings together forty-two different English-language poets dealing with some sixty episodes of the *Metamorphoses* in a variety of meters and forms. The project arose from the editors' perception in the mid-nineties that 'Ovid is once again enjoying a boom'—an appeal they attribute to his mischievous cleverness, his use of shock, and his affinity with contemporary reality. Most of the treatments amount to retellings of familiar tales in a fairly straightforward manner, but others, while staying close to the storylines, rework them in a conspicuously modern idiom, giving them in some cases a modern psychiatric or feminist twist. Christopher Martin's *Ovid in English* (1998) brings together a rich selection of translations by writers from Chaucer, Gower, and Golding down to the present and encompasses not just the *Metamorphoses* but the entirety of Ovid's *oeuvre*. Possibly the most enduring poetic monument to Ovid from the 1990s will be Ted Hughes's dazzling *Tales from Ovid* (1997), which contains twenty-four tales related in a variety of poetic forms and reflecting Hughes's obsession with human passion, including its extreme form of the supernatural.

Inevitably such a resonant boom made its vibrations felt on the stage in the form of Mary Zimmerman's *Metamorphoses* (1998), which brought ten of the tales to life for thousands of theater-goers. The principal scenes, presented without transition, are organized in an alternating rhythm contrasting the themes of destructive passion and the redeeming power of love: Midas is followed by the tale of Ceyx and Alcyone; Orpheus and Eurydice give way to Narcissus. Zimmerman's treatment of Orpheus and Eurydice is characteristic of her postmodern re-visioning. The moment when Orpheus looks back and Eurydice slips back into the Underworld is enacted three times: as a story of love, as a story of time's one-directional movement, and finally as the story of an artist and the loss that comes from sudden self-consciousness. The Phaethon scene is given a humorous twist by casting it as a session between Phaethon, a spoiled brat, and his therapist.

Conclusion

The three progressively strengthening waves of twentieth-century Ovidianism, mirroring the sociopolitical mood of the times in Europe and the United States, enabled the ancient poet to emerge from his role as a precursor of modern alienation and metamorphosis in the 1920s and as a prefiguration of personally experienced political exile in the postwar decades, to become a more generally popular symbol of individual freedom and psychic transformation for a postmodern era—a popularity that will no doubt endure until Ovid is displaced yet again by Virgil in a renewed dedication to nation and society.

FURTHER READING

In addition to works mentioned above, readers wishing to explore further the reception of Ovid from the Middle Ages to the present should consult Rand (1925), Munari (1960), Picon and Zimmermann (1994), Anderson (1995), and Albrecht (2003). Stroh (1969) contains a collection of statements on Ovid from classical antiquity to the early twentieth century, along with a useful bibliography. For purposes of contrasting Ovid's reception with other Roman poets, see Ziolkowski on Horace (2005b), Juvenal (2006), and Catullus (2006/2007).

CHAPTER THIRTY-THREE

Translating Ovid

Christopher Martin

Introduction

The first indignity Ovid had to confront upon disembarking in Tomis was the barbarian language waiting there to swallow him up. Obliged to 'talk Sarmatian' with tribes who lacked even elementary knowledge of Latin, he felt increasingly hard pressed (or so the exile poetry has us believe) to maintain fluency in the father tongue of which he'd become the supreme—though now disgraced—*uates*. At best, he reports, the locals accented their more pervasive contempt with a kind of freak-show awe for the alien guest's plight. Under such demoralizing circumstances, news that an English settler in America would be turning the *Metamorphoses* into his own native idiom over sixteen centuries later may have come as sorry consolation. For an imperial citizen who regarded latter-day Romania as *ultima terra*, the faraway geographic and temporal prospect of tidewater Virginia harbored little attraction. Our modern practice of translation would have struck him as more remote and barbaric still. Translation (always from the Greek into Latin) served in his day as little more than a rhetorical exercise that presumed a bilingual reader's familiarity with the original text. As ravenous as Ovid was for enduring fame, his most unbridled ambitions remained co-terminus with the language of empire (*Met.* 15.877–8 *quaque patet domitis Romana potentia terris / ore legar populi*), and the poet's notorious disdain for editorial encroachments upon his work could only heighten his allergy to the profanations inherent in such extramural tributes. How could even the most elegant couplets into which a foreign enthusiast refashioned his lines seem any more palatable than the Getic jabber at which he now blankly stared? The promise of survival in translation withers before *Tr.* 3.13's exasperated sigh, *quid tibi cum Ponto*? What have I to do with any of these people? What does Pontus, or Virginia, or the discourse of some future empire have to do with me?

An author known chiefly in translation is an author perpetually relegated. Like an exile, the translated writer fears both ostracism within the strange setting, and an absorption that carries even greater risks of self-loss. *Dediscere*, literally 'to un-learn', is a word Ovid uses more than once to describe the cost of yielding to his hosts' outlandish dialects. Translation likewise threatens to displace the text for which it substitutes, until the original ultimately goes 'unlearned' by its new readership. For all our self-congratulatory celebration of Ovid's present-day ascendancy, we're left with a nagging awareness that the poet back in favor among English-speaking readers remains something of a chimera, bred of these many reconstructions and embodying a spirit that may not have animated his own actual *corpus*. Writing at the end of the seventeenth century, John Dryden, Ovid's most formidable English translator, recognized how 'something must be lost in all Transfusion, that is, in all Translations', even as he advocated the practice's essential preservative character: 'but the Sense will remain, which would otherwise be lost, or at least be maim'd, when it is scarce intelligible' (Preface to the *Fables*). Peter Green, one of our chief contemporary Ovidians, likewise affirms that 'all translation, after all (despite post-structural efforts to boost its status), remains in the last resort a *pis aller*' (1994: xxxii), and pointedly differentiates the assumptions of earlier translators from a more recent split between 'the sense of responsibility to one's original, and, in a different sense, to the reader, who today, nine times out of ten, knows nothing whatsoever of the original language, and is far more interested in getting an accurate impression of the poet's own texture and rhythms than in applauding the irrelevant ingenuity of a translator with a gift for clever pastiche' (Green 1989: 232–33). Yet modern assaults on Dryden's essentialist faith that 'the Spirit of an Author may be transfus'd, and yet not lost . . . For thought, if it be translated truly, cannot be lost in another Language' (Preface Concerning Ovid's *Epistles*) have somewhat paradoxically coincided with an unheralded proliferation of English Ovids. Having come to terms with the very mediation that at once distances us from the Latin poet and keeps him in view, we now spend a fair deal of scholarly energy organizing and evaluating the long sequence of translations by which Ovid has become a familiar literary presence.

Shifting English Conceptions

Ovid's progress in English is easily abstracted. Freely appropriated and rendered into Middle English by several of our most prominent fourteenth-century poets, his work emerged as the object of formal translation only in the early modern period. The release of Arthur Golding's complete *Metamorphosis* (so titled) in 1567 moved the practice into high gear, initiating a vogue that extended to George Sandys' recasting of the poem in the late 1620s, and on to the Englishing of the complete canon by 1640. A subsequent generation, largely under Dryden's impetus, took up the torch anew from roughly 1680 to 1700, their efforts culminating in the great afterburn of Samuel Garth's composite *Metamorphoses* in 1717. Barely glimmering amid the undeniably funny but largely reductive parodies of the 1700s, and the even deadlier academic commandeerings of the following century, Ovidian translation experienced a somewhat abrupt renewal in the 1950s, an awakening whose unprecedented momentum shows no sign of abating. I have elsewhere illustrated this history in more extended detail (Martin 1998), but the practitioners' various ambitions and motivations, more idiosyncratic and less given to continuous narrative development, prove more difficult to chart. Largely for this reason, evidence of the ways in which Ovid's translators have construed their office in the self-reflexive commentary accompanying their publications invites our scrutiny and repays our attention.

The curious dividedness of Ovid's reception, set forth in the preceding chapters of this unit, has predictably influenced the translations' tenor over the years. The ambiguity with which his translators have routinely approached their task is on display most conspicuously throughout Dryden's own extensive dealings with the poet. Although Dryden professedly ranked Virgil, Lucretius, and even Chaucer more highly, Ovid exerted a disproportionately vast and complex claim on his imagination. In the preface to his 1700 *Fables, Ancient and Modern,* Dryden confesses how he initially came to the *Metamorphoses* as a sort of epic afterthought. After translating the opening book of the *Iliad* for his miscellany, he recounts,

> I proceeded to the Translation of the Twelfth Book of *Ovid's Metamorphoses,* because it contains, among other Things, the Causes, the Beginning, and Ending, of the *Trojan* war. Here I ought in reason to have stopp'd; but the Speeches of *Ajax* and *Ulysses* lying next in my way, I could not balk 'em. When I had compass'd them, I was so taken with the former part of the Fifteenth Book . . . that I enjoin'd my self the pleasing Task of rendring it into *English.* And now I found, by the Number of my Verses, that they began to swell into a little Volume; which gave me an Occasion of looking backward on some Beauties of my Author, in his former books.

The best seductions are usually the most gradual, Ovid knew, and Dryden's admission wonderfully betrays the frank allure of his reputedly undisciplined and 'luxuriant' original. Moreover, where the chore of casting Virgil's work in English verse had conjured for Dryden an image of the translator as 'poor drudge' who labors to match the glories of Latin to 'a language so much inferior', diminished by 'Old *Teuton* Monosyllables', his work on Ovid—the poet he ultimately declared 'more according to my Genius'—inspired a buoyant affection for 'the best of all my Endeavours in this kind'.

Dryden anticipates this powerful affinity from his earliest published turns at Ovid's poetry. In his editorial preface to the third edition of *Ovid's Epistles translated by several hands* (1683), Dryden elaborates his most explicit ideas on the practice of translation. In addition to a mastery of both the languages involved, the translator must possess an innate character or 'Genius' suited to the endeavor, defined chiefly as a capacity to discern the original author's individuating 'turn of Thoughts, and of Expression', along with the temper to remain faithful to these essential features at all costs. In Ovid's case, this latter demand especially taxed the willingness of those translators 'who dare not cover him', merely 'to blush at the nakedness of their Father', rather than to attempt any correction. 'The sense of an author, generally speaking, is to be Sacred and Inviolable,' Dryden declares: 'If the Fancy of *Ovid* be luxuriant, 'tis his Character to be so, and if I retrench it, he is no longer *Ovid*.' He goes on to protest against the inadequacy of both 'Metaphrase, or turning an Author

Word by Word, and Line by Line, from one Language into another', for its tortuous challenges if not its outright impossibility, and 'Imitation', which 'assumes the liberty not only to vary from the words and sense, but to forsake them both . . . and taking only some general hints from the Original, to run division on the Ground-work'. Dryden ultimately prefers what he terms a 'Paraphrase', which allows greater latitude to expression so long as it does not 'vitiate the sense', which alone remains critical for him in the proper conveyance of Ovid's works.

Dryden speaks from the vantage of a methodological sophistication that underwrites a larger, more self-consciously nationalist endeavor to refine and perfect English letters. His culture had graduated, he believed, to a moment where foreign classics might amplify and enrich the language through translations worthy of their revered status. But on a humbler level, as a basic component of humanist pedagogy, translation starts out chiefly as an undergraduate—indeed, a schoolboy—affair, where curricular function takes precedence over stylistic affect. Two early modern instances exemplify how virtually all corners of the Ovidian canon might be impressed into this

Figure 8:   A woodcut on the title page of Wynken de Worde's 1513 edition of *The flores of Ovide de arte amandi with theyr englysshe afore them*. By permission of the British Library G.9671.

brand of rudimentary service. The first published translation of Ovid into English, Wynken de Worde's 1513 textbook *The flores of Ovide de arte amandi with theyr englysshe afore them*, culled sententious excerpts from the *Ars amatoria* for students' grammatical (if not exactly ethical) edification. The volume's rough frontispiece image, in some respects more striking than its elementary trots of Ovid's lines, depicts a schoolmaster who gazes down upon a trio of young boys presumably engaged in parsing the art of love; the bundle of switches he holds in his lap inflects the picture uncomfortably, reminding us of the grimmer associations that translation likely carried for its early audience. And if *eros* can't stimulate youthful interest, then surely insult can: almost one hundred and fifty years later, on the far side of the first great phase of Ovidian English translation, vituperation replaces foreplay as the paradigm in John Jones' 1658 version of Ovid's invective poem *Ibis*. Identifying himself as 'Teacher of a private School in the City of Hereford', Jones advertises his book as 'Both pleasant and profitable for each sort, Sex, and Age, and very useful for Grammar Schools', however bizarre the pedagogical application of Ovid's densely allusive curses may now strike us. And this time out, it's the instructor's dreary plight that's contrastingly highlighted in the prologue. A man professedly 'almost worne out in Body and Spirits, by that inexpressible labor of Teaching Schoole', Jones nonetheless professes dedication 'to that Sisyphon-toil of the Education of Youth'. In hopes that young scholars might 'find help for composing of a theme' in the text, Jones delivers his translation 'not Periphrastically . . . but punctually (as near as sense and verse could bear it) to render my Poet in English word for word'.

The instructional model struck in these early primers endures in such later offerings as William Massey's 1757 *Fasti*, published with an eye to grammar school circulation, and 'indifferent whether they may call it translation, or paraphrase'. Facing-page prose versions of Ovid's work that proliferated in the nineteenth century follow suit, culminating in the twentieth-century's *Loeb Classical Library* series, durable either as pedagogical aids for the novice or reinforcement for the more capable. Academic credentials bolster the endeavors even of those who inaugurate the last century's renaissance of Ovidian translations. Mary Innes, for example, is introduced on the opening leaf of her 1955 Penguin Classics *Metamorphoses* as having 'spent over twenty years proving to schoolgirls that the classical languages can and should be enjoyed' (1). Undergraduate contexts also purportedly ground the previous year's version by A. E. Watts, who had initially aimed 'at a rendering that should elucidate for the student everything in the Latin, including even the grammar' (1980: ix). By this late turn, however, these more modest foundational goals had become something of a liability, and no longer pardoned whatever limitations the translator's talents might reveal: Watts' labors unhappily met with the opprobrium of Robert Lowell, who attacked the translation as 'freakishly stiff and floppy, a Minotaur, uneasy in both natures' (1987: 152), and Horace Gregory likely has Innes and Watts in mind when he faults recent versions of the poem as part of 'the conspiracy to keep Ovid in a nineteenth-century classroom' (1958: xxvii).

Outside the academy, of course, translation gradually came to serve the grander cultural purpose of broadening the foreign text's exposure to a more eclectic readership. This aspiration is first articulated, suitably, by William Caxton, one of English humanism's premier brokers, who stands as both the nation's earliest printer and its first 'professional' translator. Caxton's design to put the entire work before an English-speaking audience—anticipating the reformers' revolutionary outlook toward scripture by several decades—attested to a new conviction that Ovid's poem merited a broader domain in and of itself. Ironically, his prose translation of the complete *Metamorphoses*, which likely never saw print, remains a curious, Janus-like anomaly that offers the last instance of what we might think of as a 'medieval' Ovid even as it betrays the more novel tendencies that shape its execution. Caxton's beautifully ornate, partially illuminated manuscript employs a French redaction of the moralized Latin version as its source. Yet alongside this casual pre-modern indifference to a densely mediated original, the translator displays a freshly meticulous attention to comprehensiveness, detail, and fidelity absent from Chaucer's and Gower's earlier, less deliberated English borrowings from the poet. The 'Prohemye' announces his 'purpose to translate this sayd book of methamorphose in to Angylysshe tonge aftir the lytyl connyng that god hath departed to me to thend that yt myght be the better & souner understanden. And that it might cause ensiewe more fruyt vnto the lovyng & preysyng of allmighty god that of nothyng all created and made al thyngs good.' The 'ryght subtil style' that so distinguishes Ovid will, for Caxton, implicitly remain intact, his translation (divinely inspired, after a modest fashion) furthering rather than compromising the author's comprehensibility. Poised on the threshold between two distinct eras, the work provides a fascinating and still largely unappreciated portrait of cultural transition.

Golding's and Sandys' Legacies

As Raphael Lyne has pointed out, the *Metamorphoses* will always serve as a primary barometer for Ovid's reception in any given period since 'this capacious work actually contains the various strands of Ovid's importance in one brilliantly but tenuously organized whole' (2001: 1). The notion also applies to the prefatory commentary included with the milestone English translations of the poem that signpost the practice's maturation from period to period. Over the course of the century following Caxton's, English translation participated in a nationalist fervor nourished by the country's growing prestige on the European political and cultural stage, effectively folding respected foreign works into the native literary canon. Not surprisingly, Ovid inspired one of the most celebrated achievements in this vein, Arthur Golding's remarkable 1567 Englishing of the complete *Metamorphoses*. In many respects, the attitude Caxton had expressed in his unpublished 'Prohemye' survives in his Elizabethan successor, though the blend of modesty and exuberance evident in Golding's prefatory comments—cast in the fourteener couplets he uses to render the entire work—takes a quantum leap beyond the earlier version's staid prose. Golding has made Ovid 'so well acquainted with our toong', he proclaims (177–84),

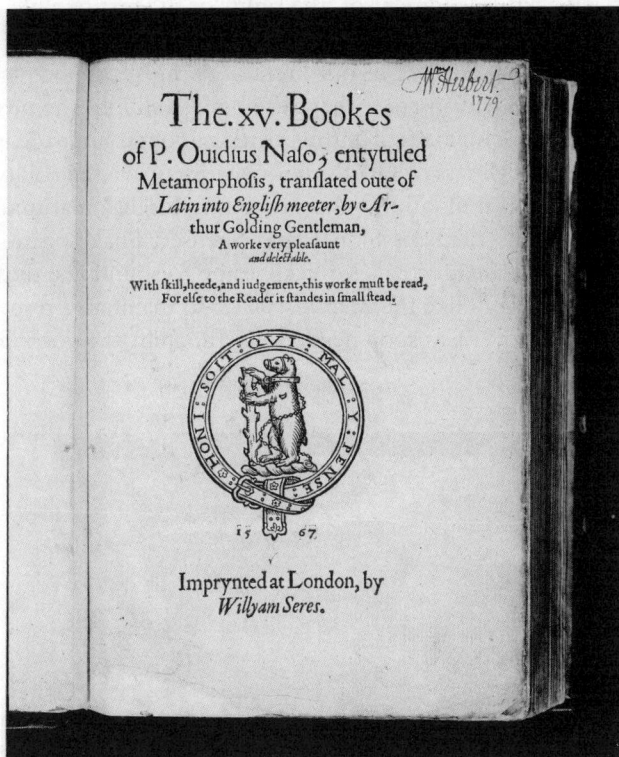

Figure 9: Title page of Golding translation, *The XV Bookes of P. Ouidius Naso*, 1567. Reproduced by permission of the Trustees of the Huntington Library, San Marino, California.

As that he may in English verse as in his owne bee soong.
Wherein although for pleasant style, I cannot make account,
To match myne author, who in that all other dooth surmount:
Yit (gentil Reader) doo I trust my travail in this cace
May purchace favour in thy sight my doings to embrace:
Considring what a sea of goodes and Jewelles thou shalt fynd,
Nor more delyghtfull to the ear than fruteful to the mynd.

Here again, Ovid's natural superiority of 'pleasant style' mitigates rather than exacerbates the text's intimidating challenges: professedly unable to rise to his poet's sublime heights, Golding affably determines to follow his own genius, well suited to the expansiveness of the Latin original. Though not the first to bring humanist preoccupation with the unmediated text to bear in his handling of Ovid—an anonymous 1560 translation of the Narcissus myth had secured this distinction—he put Ovid's poem in its entirety before the vernacular audience, generally stripped of the earlier tradition's moralizing tendencies. In Lyne's view, Golding's 'preservation of an Ovidian ambivalence, and contribution of his own, are significant decisions', and the translator's implicit acknowledgment of 'the rights of the text to a life of its own is in itself a change' (Lyne 2001: 32 and 53). The publication's profound influence over virtually all of the authors at work in our literature's most prolific period cannot be overstated, sparking an Ovidian craze that developed well into the next century.

In Golding we find the unchecked enthusiasm of a poetic language inventing itself, fueled by the narrative richness of Ovid's uniquely discursive sensibility. Invigorating as readers would find this translation, modern literary English matured quickly under the sponsorship of such talents as Sidney and Spenser, Shakespeare and Marlowe, Donne and Jonson, and the fourteener quickly came to sound like the quaint accents of an earlier day. For a work like the *Metamorphoses* to maintain a respectable English cadence, a serious makeover was soon needed. Fortunately, the poem found just such

Figure 10: A plate from the translation of the *Metamorphoses* by George Sandys (1632), accompanying the opening of Book 8, showing Icarus' fall among a composite of other scenes from this book. Courtesy of the Warden and Fellows of All Souls College, Oxford.

a renovated voice in the gifted George Sandys, whose crisp heroic couplets high-lighted the wit and philosophical tilt—traits then at their highest courtly premium—of Ovid's myths. Almost as importantly, in its final 1632 form his publication takes the shape of a scholarly reference edition as much as a glorified 'artistic' presentation of the poem: there the translator appends a running commentary to each of the fifteen books, intending 'to collect out of sundrie Authors the Philosophicall sense of these fables', and supplies illustrations of each book's 'many Figures'. This pictorial feature, as Sandys expresses it in his prefatory address to the reader, itself amplifies the transla-tion visually: 'as the rarest peeces in Poets are the descriptions of Pictures', he explains, 'so the Painter expresseth the Poet with equall Felicitie'. The illustrations also afford the dignified regalia that a work like the *Metamorphoses* richly deserves, 'that so excel-lent a Poem might with the like Solemnity be entertained by us, as it hath beene among other Nations: rendered in so many languages, illustrated by Comments, and imbelished with Figures: withall, that I may not prove less gratefull to my Author, by whose Muse I may modestly hope to be rescued from Oblivion'.

The ambition that resonates within the final clause boldly discloses Sandys' aware-ness of what's at stake in his enterprise: far more than a mere purveyor of another's labors, the translator steps forward as an artistic voice in his own right, eligible to share, however distantly, in the distinction of his source. Sandys also betrays a growing sense of mission behind the translator's enterprise in the emphasis he places upon his own pains: 'To the Translation I have given what perfection my Pen could bestow; by polishing, altering, or restoring, the harsh, improper, or mistaken with a nicer exactnesse than perhaps is required in so long a Labor.' This sense of pride and dedication is firmly entrenched by decade's end, when John Sherburne announces the degree of 'strictnesse' and 'care' he devotes to his author's meaning in his 1639 version of the *Heroides*, which strives for 'sweetnesse too, as much as could conve-niently be attained, having throughout observed a verse for verse traduction'. His express sensitivity to the ill fit between the poems' elegiac form and the 'English *Decasyllable*' that he employs further suggests anxieties over formal as well as substan-tive fidelity. That same year, Zachary Catlin expounds in his *De Tristibus: or Mourn-efull Elegies* even more thoroughly on 'the paines of the Translatour', which 'as they are liable to much exception, so are they not uncapable of some Apologie'. However self-promotional, Catlin's vision of his work's audience comprehensively stakes out translation's broad cultural claim: 'from the mere *English* Reader, loe here *Ovid* is turn'd his owne Countryman: to the raw Scholler, loe here *Ovid* speaking by an Interpreter; To them that can survive without bladders, this translation will not only bring delight, but if they please with the matter to observe the propriety of both the tongues, it may *Miscere utile dulci*, bring them in delight and profit both'. He likewise identifies the discriminating eye that the translator must bring to his task: 'If any wish my veine had been more lofty, he must know it was the part of me a Translator, not to soare beyond mine Authors straine, who was not here a stately *Maro*, or a Tragicall *Sophocles*, but a quick-spirited and nimble-witted *Naso*.' The enhanced sense of duty to the source establishes the legacy that Dryden and his successors to our own day inherit as they reformulate Ovid's lines for an increasingly demanding vernacular readership.

Expanding Perimeters

From the start of the early modern period, then, translation presumed to democratize Ovid for a growing audience whose capabilities did not extend to ancient languages. The pitch to a progressively more abstracted 'general reader' comes to sound quaint by the time of John Jump's rambling preface to his *Epistles of Ovidius Naso* (1857), which inquires, 'Why should the Cantab and the Oxonian monopolize a delightful feast? Why not you, O general reader, be admitted to a table so invitingly served?' Even the pedestrian fare he set out included 'elucidations' designed to edify 'the class of readers' unfamiliar with matters classical. Lonely in his trade, Jump more interestingly directs his work 'to gain the good will of my fair countrywomen', an appeal with its own extended history. Presumed literate in only the mother tongue, women had become conventional targets of Ovid's translators, particularly those presenting the *Heroides*. Wye Saltonstall's dedication of his 1636 version 'To the Vertuous Ladies and Gentlewomen of England' draws this notion out at rather libidinous length:

> since this booke of *Ovids*, which most Gentlemen could reade before in Latine, is for your sakes come forth in English, it doth at first addresse it selfe as a Suitor, to woo your acceptance, that it may kisse your hands, and afterward have the lines thereof in reading sweetened by the oder of your breath, while the dead letters formed into words by your divided lips, may receive new life by your passionate expression, and the words married in that Ruby colour Temple, may thus happily united, multiply your contentment.

Isaac Tinckler's prefatory tribute to Gower's *Fasti* several years later exerts greater restraint in its claim that, with his friend's translation, 'Now Ovid hath his wish, that he may be / In English read upon a Ladies knee'.

In the lap of such condescension, however, women would soon try their own fortunes at turning Ovid's verse. Aphra Behn's contribution to the 1680 volume *All Ovid's Epistles* belies the modest disclaimer she advances in a manner that provokes Dryden's editorial praise, despite his reservations about freely rendered 'imitations': 'I was desir'd to say that the Author who is of the *Fair Sex*, understood not *Latine*. But if she does not, I am afraid she has given us occasion to be asham'd who do.' The counterpoint provided by her reworking of Oenone's epistle to Paris, set against the wooden, more literal version of John Cooper also included in the text, manages to confirm Dryden's point splendidly. For instance, Cooper awkwardly presents Oenone's early indictment of Paris, besotted by his newly discovered royal status:

> Tho' now a Prince, not yet so great you was,
> When a fam'd Nymph, I stoop'd to your Imbrace:
> A Slave you was (forgive what I have said)
> Slave as you was, I took you to my Bed.

Behn expands these lines to convey the ambiguous affection that the outraged Oenone still harbors for her former consort:

Wou'd Heav'n, when first I saw thee, thou hadst been
This Great, this Cruel Celebrated Thing,
That without Hope I might have gaz'd and bow'd,
And mix'd my Adoration with the Crowd:
Unwounded then I had escap'd those Eyes,
Those lovely Authors of my Miseries.

Behn's example pioneered the way into Ovidian territory for subsequent women poets like Anne Killigrew, Anna Laetitia Barbauld, and the manumitted slave Phillis Wheatley—whose skillful handling of the Niobe episode from *Met.* 6 offsets her former master's understated account of how she had displayed 'great Inclination to learn the Latin tongue, and has made some Progress in it'. By 1842, fifteen years before Jump assayed to extend the ladies his helping hand, Emma Garland had already become the first woman to publish a translation of an entire Ovidian work, her *Ovid's Epistles, in English Verse*. Noting the double challenge faced by a writer 'if that Author be a lady, and happen to be a Latinist', and recognizing the squeamishness that her own century might likely feel toward Ovid's 'luscious' verse, Garland nonetheless shared Dryden's sense that any temptation to bowdlerize the text would violate her project. She therefore aimed 'to give the most pure and delicate English that strict fidelity to her Author would allow, to every idea and line contained in his Love Letters'. Her genuine passion and affection for the verse, moreover, shielded her from the more stuffy, domine-like character unfortunately depressing so many Victorian attempts at Ovidian translation. Garland's self-effacing and sadly obscure publication stands worthily even against more formidable competition than her century offered. Whether she could have anticipated a time when the gender boundaries she knew would finally be loosened, her accomplishment forms an important bridge between the pioneering work of writers like Behn and the responses of contemporary female Ovidians like Florence Verducci and Betty Rose Nagle, now active in the discipline.

From the humble to the grandiose, translation's chemistry has always involved an odd blend of deference and vanity, often evident in the variety of metaphors that translators have adduced to characterize their task. In the first English go at the complete *Heroides*, George Turbervile modestly retired to the kitchen: 'If it be so that thou mislike any thing,' he tells his readers, 'impute the blame to the cooke. For doutlesse the Cates of themselues in their kinde, are passyng curious, but for want of cunning in dressing the same, maye appere nothing delectable to the eie, nor toothsome to the taste.' Sixty years on, Robert Hatton's translation of the spurious *Nux* as 'Ovid's Walnut-tree transplanted' offers an apology by means of an elaborate but apt comparison of the translator to the gardener:

This our tree, standing in open and unfenced ground, I haue made bold to seise vpon and remoue hither: By which transplanting of a stocke so growne and conveyed so farre, it is no maruell if it now droope in our cold English soyle; especially by reason of the unskillfulnesse of the gardner, Who being but a fresh apprentice to the translating trade, may iustly feare that this Latine plant will be thought more rudely battered by his rough English penne, then euer it was by the staues of Rustick Passengers.

Saltonstall, in his second outing with an Ovidian work, more lyrically hopes that the English of his *Tristia* 'can but like the Eccho, send backe the soft Musicke of his lines'. The tributes prefacing Gower's 1640 *Fasti* comprise a virtual anthology of figures for the translator's office. 'C. M.', for instance, calls up a sartorial analogy to proclaim how Ovid, 'Cloth'd in the Britain garb and modest fashion / Looseth no virtue of the Latine nation', where Isaac Tinckler reverses the comparison, inquiring, 'Was his old Romane gown thread-bare and old. / Whom thou hast rob'd in cloth of English gold?' More ghostly analogies also obtain. Tinckler himself goes on to suggest, 'Thy soul was in his breast, or his in thine. / He's metempsychos'd', a notion Villiers Harrington amplifies in his tribute, 'Divine Translatour! tell me; Didst thou call / For *Ovids* ghost, that he might tell thee all / His well-spun lines could mean? or hast thou got / His very soul into thy breast?' The verses of one 'Ed. Bosworth' in praise of Jones' *Ibis* demonstrate the lurid excess to which the prospect of translation can excite a reader's imagination:

> No flyings out, your Muse though free, is bound
> To word for word, to render, not confound
> The Genuine sense so justly, that we might
> Say *Ovid's* self did dictate, you did write.
> No rack here shewn to make a word confess
> Then what it signifies or more or less:
> No virgin Muse here forc'd, no violence,
> Or rape committed upon word or sense;
> Each word so fitly married, as if ment
> To shew you woo'd well first, and had consent.

Whatever Jones' self-perception of his vocation's thankless tedium, his friends found in his extracurricular activities a genuine source of release for their own frustrated creativity.

If self-abnegation and ambition vie in the personal analogies that translators and their supporters call up, evaluations are often less demurring when directed at others in the field. Since multiple translations of a single work implicitly beg comparison, practitioners have typically trained severely critical eyes upon their competition. While some of Ovid's translators have regarded their rivals with honest graciousness— Thomas Peend, unfortunately at work on a version of the *Metamorphoses* at the same time as Golding, defers to his contemporary's clearly superior accomplishment— others have been severe in their judgments. Dryden, for example, denigrated Sandys and his entire literary milieu as mere 'versifiers' who only 'evaporated' Ovid's poetry, since 'They neither knew good Verse, nor lov'd it; they were Scholars 'tis true, but they were Pedants. And for a just Reward of their Pedantick pains, all their Translations want to be Translated, into *English*.' Though Dryden later softened this stance, Samuel Garth would resuscitate the charges against Sandys' 'verbal' rendering in his editorial preface to the 1717 composite *Metamorphoses*, suggesting that if the earlier translator had made the necessary improvements in the poem (a practice, curiously, that Dryden himself would not have allowed), 'perhaps other translations of the

Metamorphoses had not been attempted'. In an even more aggressive spirit, John Sherburne promotes his own 1639 version of the *Heroides* by claiming that he undertook the work 'in the humble, and modest hope, of rectifying the wrongs our Author hath sustained through the attempts of a too-too busie pen', presumably that of Saltonstall, who had released his version of the epistolary poems three years earlier. At a bit more of a remove, Massey compares his new rendering of the *Fasti* with a sneer at Gower's *Festivalls* of a century before: 'The language and versification of that performance is such that I could reap little or no help from it; and I flatter myself, that a comparison, made between his version and mine, would be no disadvantage to me.' A similar attitude survives in Melville's claim (1990) that he translated the love poetry to provide an alternative to Green's well-known Penguin edition, 'widely available and in my view wholly unsatisfactory.' Fastidiously, Melville likewise grants Golding's *Metamorphoses* only 'a clumsy charm', takes issue with Dryden's efforts to 'improve' upon the source (something he attributes this to 'the arrogance of his age'), and has little time for recent American versions of the poet 'whose main value is as a warning of the difficulty of the task'. Green himself cautions against that 'greatest pitfall, to be avoided at all costs, . . . the self-indulgent literary pastiche, dated almost before it is written' (1982b: 80), and offers a balanced critique of Guy Lee's 'free' rendering of the *Amores* which 'jettisons a whole mass of fustian, and is sharply alive to jokes and nuances', though at the cost of boiling 'all the formal richness out of the poems' (Green 1989: 228). Whatever one makes of such dismissals or endorsements, the passions animating the debate illustrate the investment in establishing a responsible representation of Ovid's achievement that has always enlivened the field, now perhaps more than ever before.

Contemporary Revisions

Regardless of his deepening sympathy for Ovid's poetic, Dryden never attempted to translate an entire Ovidian text. This perhaps stems not so much from a lack of application or interest as from the sense of democratic diversity he perceived within Ovid's literary manner, more acclimated to the committee approach remarked in the *Epistles* volume. There, he advertises, readers may find the poet translated 'by divers hands, that you may at least have that variety in the *English*'. The notion that Ovid is better served by various talents finds its apogee in Garth's remarkably seamless patchwork of the entire *Metamorphoses*, which gathers Dryden's translations along with the work of some of the day's leading poets. Joseph Addison, who also contributes to the volume, likewise observes how 'There is so great a variety on the arguments of the Metamorphoses, that he who would treat 'em rightly, ought to be a master of all styles, and every different way of writing.' The resuscitation of the miscellany approach so prevalent in Dryden's day in the radical 1994 anthology *After Ovid* attests to the endurance of his early impression. The editors Michael Hofmann and James Lasdun, who remark on the way a renewed appreciation of Ovid coincides with refurbished interest in 'the notion of poetic translation', aim to present 'an Ovid remade, made new', by inviting established poets 'to translate, reinterpret, reflect on, or completely re-imagine the narratives' (1994: xi–xiii). The resulting collection, offering a variety of inventive approaches that showcases the contributors' distinctive techniques as much as it throws new light (however glimmering or oblique) upon the poem's familiar myths, reconfirms how freshly Ovid's narratives continue to inspire English writers. The late Ted Hughes, whose gripping version of the creation story opens the work, would expand his contribution in one of his very last publications, 1997's *Tales from Ovid*. Hughes presents Ovid in a way that seems to mirror and justify his own selective manner:

> His attitude to his material is like that of the many later poets who have adapted what he presents. He, too, is an adaptor. He takes up only those tales which catch his fancy, and engages with each one no further than it liberates his own creative zest. Of those he does take up . . . he gives attention to only a proportion, sketching the others more briefly in ornamental digressions or cramming them as clusters of foreshortened portraits into some eddy of his unfurling drift. (1997: viii)

Hughes' powerful lines seem almost to reverse the analogy of the original poet animating his translator. Preferring immediacy over a reverential distance from his source, he aims to possess his original, as a way of further realizing his 'own creative zest'.

If Hughes' *Tales from Ovid* continues the work of *After Ovid*, it also can be seen to depart from that miscellany, in so far as the poet's implicit attempt to reconvene the poem's narratives in a unified sensibility manifests certain reservations about the anthology format. Other modern translators have been vocal in their opposition to eclectic approaches to Ovid and the liberties they encourage. Whatever splendid byproducts such efforts may yield, some feel, they cannot be said to represent 'an author's thoughts', which constitutes the principal burden of a translator's project: as Dryden elegantly puts it, ''tis not always that a man will be contented to have a Present made him, when he expects the payment of a Debt.' Rolfe Humphries, for instance, recounts his initial temptation to render the *Metamorphoses* in a variety of meters and stanzaic forms, 'one story in eight-beat couplets, another in Spenserian or Byronic stanzas, and so on', a virtuoso impulse he resisted since the poem is 'all of a piece, as much as *The Canterbury Tales*, and there was fun enough in the original, variety and richness enough, for all the metrical sameness, so that to perform feats of generosity would have been an intolerable license on the part of the translator, a chopping up of the texture, an intolerable insult' (1955: ix). The broader ambitions of numerous contemporary Ovidians to translate not just entire works, but works across the canon—Green's *Amores, Ars amatoria, Remedia amoris, Tristia,* and *Epistulae ex Ponto*; Melville's *Metamorphoses, Amores,* and *Tristia*; David Slavitt's exile poems and *Metamorphoses,* to name but a few— also implicitly lend these various parts of the poet's *oeuvre* a more individuated stamp for their English audience, even though the fact that no one translator has yet taken on all the poet's work still suggests the unique challenges that Ovid continues to pose.

The sheer quantity of available translations has freed up and even encouraged English readers to formulate preferences for particular episodes or poems across the many versions. It has likewise proved liberating for the translators themselves. Slavitt, for example, clearly takes solace in the vast resources at our disposal: aware that we can (and hopefully will) compare his versions to the 'faithful, literal translations [that] are available for those who wish to consult them', he can without apprehension take as his goal 'a text that is lively and readable in English' (1990: vi). If a reader enjoys the poetry, the distance from the original can be as provocatively stimulating as engagement with the standard itself. Whether we agree that 'all translation is crazy' (1990: viii), we can readily concur with his notion that 'A translation is, after all, an account of a reading' (1994: xii), an idea resonating well with Hughes' observations. Slavitt's moving version of the exile poems more than justifies his relaxed outlook. At the same time, Green's excellent *Erotic Poems*, well-laden with a superlative commentary, confirms that greater literalism need not undercut the energy or readability of Ovid's text, something also evident in Charles Martin's most recent *Metamorphoses*, likely to become the edition of choice for the next generation of English readers seeking ready access to the poem. The diversity that Dryden and his peers had favored within the miscellany publications has moved outward in the marketplace, and the fruitful competition steers us closer to the ever-more comprehensive vision of the poet so coveted by those modern audiences for whom Ovid's own language has fallen silent.

Barbarus hic ego sum, Ovid had proclaimed in *Tr.* 5.10: around here, *I'm* the barbarian. However much his proleptic statement stirs our regret, it remains no less true now than it was when he composed the line almost two thousand years ago. Sensing the importance of his companionship for our own enjoyment and self-understanding, we have compensated by sponsoring a vigorous and regular industry of translation, keeping the works alive artificially now that we have allowed the language in which they were written to fade out of earshot. Yet the master poet of change and adaptation knew what it meant to make due, and confesses by *Pont.* 4.13 that he had begun even to compose in Getic, however reluctantly. Although he resigns himself to be merely a 'poet among the natives', Ovid wrote with an eye to posterity, training his long-range vision on a future audience as assiduously as he did on the ideals, foibles, and failures of his own moment. The best translators, in response, have always been those most capable of intuiting how the original author foresaw his artistic fortunes in later, fantastic, and alien circumstances. From the casual appropriations of Chaucer to the most meticulous demands of contemporary scholarship, from humanist reinventions of the seventeenth century to the free-form exploits of recent poets, Ovid has known many such translators in English. All have essayed to distill what Dryden regarded as an essential core, even if their impressions often clash with one another. The 'divers hands' have passed the poet down in a continuum that forms a traceable history unto itself, pointing out what Ovid has always had to do, literally or periphrastically, with us.

FURTHER READING

For a survey of English translations of Ovid since the Middle Ages—including many of the items mentioned in this chapter—see my anthology (1998). Critical studies of the tradition have, for obvious reasons, tended to focus on the work of sixteenth- and seventeenth-century translators. See especially Pearcy (1984), Lyne (2001), and Oakley-Brown (2006). For a more general discussion of early modern translation practice, see Morini (2006). While Ovidianism of the eighteenth and nineteenth centuries still awaits broader treatment, Theodore Ziolkowski offers a fine discussion of twentieth-century European and American reception; see Chapter 32 and the readings suggested there. For the best general review of Ovid's legacy, see the collection of essays edited by Charles Martindale (1988).

Bibliography

Acosta-Hughes, B. 2002. *Polyeideia: The* Iambi *of Callimachus and the Archaic Iambic Tradition.* Berkeley.

Acosta-Hughes, B. 2003. Aesthetics and recall: Callimachus Frs. 226–9 Pf. reconsidered. *CQ* 53. 478–89.

Acosta-Hughes, B. and Stephens, S. A. 2002. Rereading Callimachus' *Aetia*, fr. 1. *CPh* 97: 238–55.

Acosta-Hughes, B. and Stephens, S. A. 2009. *Callimachus in Context.* Forthcoming.

Adams, J. N. 1982. *The Latin Sexual Vocabulary.* Baltimore.

Adams, J. N. and Mayer, R. (eds). 1999. *Aspects of the Language of Latin Poetry.* London.

Ahern, C. F. 1990. Ovid as *vates* in the proem to the *Ars Amatoria*. *CPh* 85: 44–8.

Ahl, F. M. 1984. The art of safe criticism in Greece and Rome. *AJP* 105: 174–208.

Ahl, F. M. 1985. *Metaformations. Soundplay and Wordplay in Ovid and Other Classical Poets.* Ithaca.

Albrecht, M. von. 1983. Ovide imitateur de Tibulle. *LEC* 51: 117–24.

Albrecht, M. von. 2000. Ovids *Amores* und sein Gesamtwerk. *WS* 113: 167–80.

Albrecht, M. von. 2003. *Ovid: Eine Einführung.* Stuttgart.

Albrecht, M. von and Zinn, E. (eds). 1968. *Ovid.* Darmstadt.

Aleyn, C. 1631. *Battailes of Crescey, and Poictiers.* Cambridge.

Alföldi, G. 1985. *The Social History of Rome.* London.

Allen, A. W. 1950. Sincerity and the Roman elegists. *CPh* 45: 145–60.

Allen, D. C. 1970. *Mysteriously Meant: The Rediscovery of Pagan Symbolism and Allegorical Interpretation in the Renaissance.* Baltimore.

Allen, G. 2002. Ovid and art. In Hardie 2002a: 180–99.

Allen, P. L. 1992. *The Art of Love: Amatory Fiction from Ovid to the Romance of the Rose.* Philadelphia.

Altman, J. G. 1983. *Epistolarity: Approaches to a Form.* Columbus, Ohio.

Alton, E. H., Wormell, D. E. W., and Courtney, E. 1972. Problems in Ovid's *Fasti*. *CQ* 23: 144–51.

Alton, E. H., Wormell, D. E. W., and Courtney, E. (eds). 1997. *P. Ovidi Nasonis Fastorum Libri Sex.* 4th edn. Stuttgart and Leipzig.

Ancona, R. and Greene, E. (eds). 2005. *Gendered Dynamics in Latin Love Poetry*. Baltimore.

Anderson, W. S. 1975. A new pseudo-Ovidian passage. *CSCA* 8: 7–16.

Anderson, W. S. (ed.). 1993. *P. Ovidii Nasonis Metamorphoses*. Leipzig.

Anderson, W. S. (ed.). 1995. *Ovid: The Classical Heritage*. New York.

Anderson, W. S. 1997. *Ovid's Metamorphoses: Books 1–5*. Norman.

André, J. (ed.). 1968. *Ovide: Tristes*. Paris.

André, J. (ed.). 1977. *Ovide: Pontiques*. Paris.

Anton, R. 1616. *The Philosophers Satyrs*. London.

Armstrong, R. 2005. *Ovid and his Love Poetry*. London.

Arrathoon, L. A. (ed.). 1986. *Chaucer and the Craft of Fiction*. Rochester, Mich.

Asper, M. 1997. *Onomata Allotria: Zur Genese, Struktur und Funktion poetologischer Metaphern bei Kallimachos*. Stuttgart.

Asquith, H. 2005. From genealogy to *Catalogue*: the Hellenistic adaptation of the Hesiodic catalogue form. In Hunter 2005a: 266–86.

Atherton, C. 1998. *Form and Content in Didactic Poetry*. Bari.

Austin, R. G. 1971. *P. Vergili Maronis Aeneidos Liber I*. Oxford.

Bakker, J. T. H. 1946. *Publi Ovidii Nasonis Tristium Liber V*. Groningen.

Baldo, G. 1995. *Dall'Eneide alle Metamorfosi. Il codice epico di Ovidio*. Padua.

Baldwin, B. 1990. Philaenis, the *doyenne* of ancient sexology. *CL* 6: 1–7.

Baldwin, T. W. 1944. *William Shakspere's Small Latine and Lesse Greeke*. Urbana.

Barbu, N., Dobroiu, E., and Nasta, M. (eds). 1976. *Ovidianum. Acta Conventus Omnium Gentium Ovidianis Studiis Fovendis*. Bucarest.

Barchiesi, A. 1984. *La traccia del modello*. Pisa.

Barchiesi, A. 1986. Problemi d'interpretazione in Ovidio. Continuità delle storie, continuazione dei testi. *MD* 16: 77–107 (= Barchiesi 2001a: 9–28).

Barchiesi, A. 1987. Narratività e convenzione nelle *Heroides*. *MD* 19: 63–90 (= Barchiesi 2001a: 29–48).

Barchiesi, A. 1988. Ovid the censor. *American Journal of Ancient History* 13: 96–105.

Barchiesi, A. 1991. Discordant muses. *PCPhS* 37: 1–21.

Barchiesi, A. 1992. *P. Ovidii Nasonis Epistulae Heroidum 1–3*. Florence.

Barchiesi, A. 1993. Future reflexive: two modes of allusion and Ovid's *Heroides*. *HSCP* 95: 333–65 (= Barchiesi 2001a: 105–27).

Barchiesi, A. 1997a. *The Poet and the Prince: Ovid and Augustan Discourse*. Berkeley.

Barchiesi, A. 1997b. Endgames: Ovid's *Metamorphoses* 15 and *Fasti* 6. In Roberts et al. 1997: 181–208.

Barchiesi, A. 1997c. Otto punti su una mappa dei naufragi. *MD* 39: 209–26 (= Barchiesi 2001a: 141–54).

Barchiesi, A. 2001a. *Speaking Volumes: Narrative and Intertext in Ovid and Other Latin Poets*. London.

Barchiesi, A. 2001b. The crossing. In Harrison 2001: 142–63.

Barchiesi, A. 2002. Narrative technique and narratology in the *Metamorphoses*. In Hardie 2002a: 180–99.

Barchiesi, A. 2005. *Ovidio Metamorfosi Volume I (Libri I–II)*. Milan.

Barchiesi, A. 2006. Women on top: Livia and Andromache. In Gibson et al. 2006: 96–120.

Barchiesi, A. and Rosati, G. 2007. *Ovidio, Metamorfosi. Volume II (Libri III–V)*. Milan.

Barkan, L. 1986. *The Gods Made Flesh: Metamorphosis and the Pursuit of Paganism*. New Haven.

Barnes, W. R. 1995. Virgil: the literary impact. In Horsfall 1995: 257–92.

Barolini, T. 1984. *Dante's Poets: Textuality and Truth in the* Comedy. Princeton.

Barsby, J. A. (ed.). 1973. *Ovid's* Amores: *Book One*. Oxford.

Bastianini, G. 1996. Tipologie dei rotoli e problemi di ricostruzione. *Atti del V seminario internazionale di papirologia*: 21–42.

Bastianini, G. and Casanova, A. 2006. *Callimaco cent' anni di papiri*. Florence.

Bastianini, G., Gallazzi, G., and Austin, C. 2001. *Posidippo di Pella Epigrammi (P. Mil. Vogl. VIII 309)*. Milan.

Bate, J. 1993. *Shakespeare and Ovid*. Oxford.

Bauman, R. A. 1992. *Women and Politics in Ancient Rome*. London.

Beard, M. 1987. A complex of times: no more sheep on Romulus' birthday. *PCPhS* 33: 1–15.

Beard, M., North, J., and Price, S. 1998. *Religions of Rome: Volume I: A History*. Cambridge.

Beaumont, F. 1602. *Salmacis and Hermaphroditus*. London.

Berman, K. E. 1972. Some Propertian imitations in Ovid's *Amores*. *CPh* 67: 170–7.

Berman, K. E. 1975. Ovid, Propertius and the elegiac genre. Some imitations in the *Amores*. *RSC* 23: 14–22.

Bernsdorff, H. 2007. *P. Oxy.* 4711 and the Poetry of Parthenius. *JHS* 127: 1–18.

Bertini, F. (ed.). 2001. *Giornate filologiche 'Francesco Della Corte'*. Genoa.

Bessone, F. 1997. *P. Ovidii Nasonis: Heroidum Epistula XII: Medea Iasoni*. Florence.

Bews, J. P. 1984. The Metamorphosis of Virgil in the *Tristia* of Ovid. *BICS* 31: 51–60.

Bidart, F. 1997. *Desire: Poems*. New York.

Bing, P. 1988. *The Well-Read Muse: Present and Past in Callimachus and the Hellenistic Poets*. Göttingen.

Binns, J. W. (ed.). 1973. *Ovid*. London.

Blänsdorf, J. 1995. *Fragmenta Poetarum Latinorum*. Stuttgart and Leipzig.

Blok, F. F. 1949. *Nicolaas Heinsius in dienst van Christina van Zweden*. Delft.

Bolgar, R. R. 1954. *The Classical Heritage and Its Beneficiaries*. Cambridge.

Bolgar, R. R. (ed.). 1971. *Classical Influences on European Culture A.D. 500–1500*. Cambridge.

Bömer, F. 1959. Ovid und die Sprache Vergils. *Gymnasium* 66: 268–88.

Bömer, F. 1969. *P. Ovidius Naso: Metamorphosen. Kommentar. Buch I–III*. Heidelberg.

Bömer, F. 1986. *P. Ovidius Naso: Metamorphosen. Kommentar. Buch XIV–XV*. Heidelberg.

Bond, R. W. (ed.). 1902. *The Works of John Lyly*. Oxford.

Bonner, S. F. 1949. *Roman Declamation*. Liverpool.

Booth, J. 1991. *Ovid*, Amores II. Warminster.

Boucher, J.-P. 1965. *Études sur Properce: problèmes d'inspiration et d'art*. Paris.

Bowditch, P. L. 2005. Hermeneutic uncertainty and the feminine in Ovid's *Ars Amatoria*: the Procris and Cephalus digression. In Ancona and Greene 2005: 271–95.

Bowersock, G. W. 1965. *Augustus and the Greek World*. Oxford.

Boyd, B. W. 1987. The death of Corinna's parrot reconsidered: poetry and Ovid's *Amores*. *CJ* 82: 199–207 (= Knox 2006: 205–16).

Boyd, B. W. 1997. *Ovid's Literary Loves: Influence and Innovation in the* Amores. Ann Arbor.

Boyd, B. W. (ed.). 2002a. *Brill's Companion to Ovid*. Leiden.

Boyd, B. W. 2002b. 'When Ovid reads Vergil . . .': a response and some observations. *Vergilius* 48: 123–30.

Boyd, B. W. 2006. Two rivers and the reader in Ovid, *Metamorphoses* 8. *TAPA* 136: 171–206.

Boyle, A. J. (ed.). 1995. *Roman Literature and Ideology: Ramus Essays for J. P. Sullivan*. Bendigo.

Boyle, A. J. 2003. *Ovid and the Monuments: A Poet's Rome*. Bendigo.

Braden, G. 1978. *The Classics and English Renaissance Poetry: Three Case Studies*. New Haven.

Brandt, P. (ed.). 1902. *P. Ovidi Nasonis de Arte Amatoria libri tres*. Leipzig.

Brandt, P. (ed.). 1911. *P. Ovidi Nasonis Amorum Libri Tres*. Leipzig.

Bretzigheimer, G. 2001. *Ovids* Amores. *Poetik in der Erotik*. Tübingen.

Brewer, D. (ed.). 1978. *Chaucer: The Critical Heritage. Volume I, 1385–1837*. London.

Brown, S. A. 1999. *The Metamorphosis of Ovid from Chaucer to Ted Hughes*. London.

Brownlee, K. 1993. Dante and the classical poets. In Jacoff 1993: 141–60.

Brownlee, M. S. 1990. *The Severed Word: Ovid's 'Heroides' and the Novela Sentimental*. Princeton.

Brugnoli, G. and Stok, F. 1992. *Ovidius παρῳδήσας*. Pisa.

Brunelle, C. 1997. *Gender and Genre in Ovid's Remedia Amoris*. Diss. University of North Carolina at Chapel Hill.

Brunelle, C. 2000–1. Form vs. function in Ovid's *Remedia Amoris*. *CJ* 96: 123–40.

Brunelle, C. 2002. Pleasure, failure, and danger: reading Circe in the *Remedia*. *Helios* 29: 55–68.

Brunt, P. A. 1988. *The Fall of the Roman Republic and Related Essays*. Oxford.

Buchan, M. 1995. *Ovidius Imperamator*: beginnings and endings of love poems and empire in the *Amores*. *Arethusa* 28: 53–85.

Buck, A. and Herding, O. (eds). 1975. *Der Kommentar in der Renaissance*. Boppard.

Burgess, J. S. 1995. Achilles' heel: the death of Achilles in ancient myth. *CA* 14: 217–43.

Burman, P. 1727. *P. Ovidii Nasonis Opera Omnia*. 4 vols. Amsterdam.

Butrica, J. L. 1997. Editing Propertius. *CQ* 47: 176–208.

Bynum, C. 2001. *Metamorphosis and Identity*. New York.

Cahoon, L. 1988. The bed as battlefield: erotic conquest and military metaphor in Ovid's *Amores*. *TAPA* 118: 293–307.

Cahoon, L. 1990. Let the Muse sing on: poetry, criticism, feminism, and the case of Ovid. *Helios* 17: 197–211.

Cahoon, L. 1996. Calliope's song: shifting narrators in Ovid, *Metamorphoses* 5. *Helios* 23: 43–66.

Cairns, F. 2006. *Sextus Propertius. The Augustan Elegist*. Cambridge.

Calabrese, M. A. 1994. *Chaucer's Ovidian Arts of Love*. Gainesville.

Cameron, A. 1968. The first edition of Ovid's *Amores*. *CQ* 18: 320–33.

Cameron, A. 1995. *Callimachus and his Critics*. Princeton.

Cameron, A. 2004. *Greek Mythography in the Roman World*. New York.

Cameron, Averil. (ed.). 1989. *History as Text*. London.

Campanelli, M. 2001. *Polemiche e filologia ai primordi della stampa. Le* Observationes *di Domizio Calderini*. Rome.

Canali, G. 1961. Angelo Sabino. *Dizionario Biografico degli Italiani* 3: 234–5.

Carroll, W. C. 1985. *The Metamorphoses of Shakespearean Comedy*. Princeton.

Casali, S. 1995a. *Heroidum Epistula IX: Deianira Herculi*. Florence.

Casali, S. 1995b. Altre voci nell'*Eneide* di Ovidio. *MD* 35: 59–76 (= Knox 2006: 144–65).

Casali, S. 1995c. Tragic Irony in Ovid, *Heroides* 9 and 11. *CQ* 45: 505–11.

Casali, S. 2004–05. Further voices in Ovid *Heroides* 7. *Hermathena* 177–8: 141–58.

Casali, S. 2006. The art of making oneself hated: rethinking (anti-)Augustanism in Ovid's *Ars Amatoria*. In Gibson et al. 2006: 216–34.

Cavallo, G., Fedeli, P., and Giardina, A. (eds) 1989. *Lo spazio letterario di Roma antica, Vol. I: La produzione del testo*. Rome.

Cheney, P. and de Armas, F. A. (eds). 2002. *European Literary Careers: The Author from Antiquity to the Renaissance*. Toronto.

Christensen, P. G. 1995. Vintila Horia's treatment of Ovid's religious conversion in *Dieu est né en exil*. *Journal of the American Romanian Academy of Arts and Sciences* 20: 171–85.

Chwalek, B. 1996. *Die Verwandlung des Exils in die elegische Welt: Studien zu den* Tristia *und* Ex Ponto *Ovids*. Frankfurt.

Ciofanus, H. 1583. *In Omnia P. Ovidii Nasonis Opera Observationes*. 2nd edn. Antwerp.

Citroni, M. 1989. Marziale e la letteratura per i Saturnali. *ICS* 14: 201–26.

Citroni, M. 1995. *Poesia e lettori in Roma antica*. Rome and Bari.

Citroni, M. 2006. The concept of the classical and the canons of model authors in Roman literature. In Porter 2006: 204–34.

Citroni Marchetti, S. 2000. *Amicizia e potere nelle lettere di Cicerone e nelle elegie Ovidiane dall'esilio*. Florence.

Claassen, J. M. 1987. Error and the imperial household: an angry god and the exiled Ovid's fate. *AClas* 34: 31–47.

Claassen, J. M. 1988. Ovid's poems from exile: the creation of a myth and the triumph of poetry. *A&A* 34.2: 158–69.

Claassen, J. M. 1989a. Carmen and poetics. In Deroux 1989: 252–66.

Claassen, J. M. 1989b. Meter and emotion in Ovid's exilic poetry. *CW* 82: 351–65.

Claassen, J. M. 1990a. Ovid's wavering identity: personification and depersonalization in the exilic poems. *Latomus* 49: 102–16.

Claassen, J. M. 1990b. Ovid's poetic Pontus. *PLLS* 6: 29–45.

Claassen, J. M. 1996. Exile, death and immortality: voices from the grave. *Latomus* 55: 577–90.

Claassen, J. M. 1998. Ovid's exilic vocabulary. *Akroterion* 43: 67–98.

Claassen, J. M. 1999a. *Displaced Persons: The Literature of Exile from Cicero to Boethius*. London.

Claassen, J. M. 1999b. The vocabulary of exile in Ovid's *Tristia* and *Epistulae ex Ponto*. *Glotta* 75: 134–71.

Claassen, J. M. 1999c. *Exsul ludens*: Ovid's exilic word games. *CB* 75: 23–35.

Claassen, J. M. 2001. The singular myth: Ovid's use of myth in the exilic poetry. *Hermathena* 170: 11–64.

Claassen, J. M. 2003. 'Living in a place called exile': the universals of the alienation caused by isolation. *Literator* 24: 85–111.

Claassen, J. M. 2004. *Mutatis mutandis*: the poetry and poetics of isolation in Ovid and Breytenbach. *Scholia* 13: 71–107.

Claassen, J. M. 2007. Literary *anamnesis*: Boethius remembers Ovid. *Helios* 34: 1–35.

Classen, J. 1859. *Jacob Micyllus, Rector zu Frankfurt und Professor zu Heidelberg von 1524 bis 1558, als Schulmann, Dichter und Gelehrter*. Frankfurt.

Clausen, W. 1964. An interpretation of the *Aeneid*. *HSCP* 68: 139–47.

Clausen, W. 1994. *A Commentary on Virgil: Eclogues*. Oxford.

Clay, D. 1998. The theory of the literary persona in antiquity. *MD* 40: 9–40.

Coates, A., Jensen, K., Dondi, C. et al. 2005. *A Catalogue of Books Printed in the Fifteenth Century Now in the Bodleian Library*. Oxford.

Coffey, M. 1976. *Roman Satire*. London and New York.

Coletti, M. L. 1981. Rassegna bibliografico—critica degli studi sulle opere amatorie di Ovidio dal 1958–78. *ANRW* 31.4: 2385–2435.

Commager, S. 1974. *A Prolegomenon to Propertius*. Cincinnati.

Condos, T. 1997. *Star Myths of the Greeks and Romans: A Sourcebook*. Ann Arbor.

Connors, C. 1992–3. Seeing cypresses in Virgil. *CJ* 88: 1–17.

Conte, G. B. 1985. *Memoria dei poeti e sistema letterario*. 2nd edn. (1st edn 1974). Turin.

Conte, G. B. 1986a. *The Rhetoric of Imitation: Genre and Poetic Memory in Virgil and other Latin Poets*. Ithaca.

Conte, G. B. 1986b. L'amore senza elegia: I *Remedia amoris* e la logica di un genere. In Lazzarini 1986: 9–53.

Conte, G. B. 1989. Love without elegy: the *Remedia amoris* and the logic of a genre. *Poetics Today* 10: 441–69.

Conte, G. B. 1994. *Genres and Readers: Lucretius, Love Elegy, Pliny's Encyclopedia*. Baltimore.

Conte, G. B. and Barchiesi, A. 1989. Imitazione e arte allusiva. Modi e funzioni dell'intertestualità. In Cavallo et al. 1989: 81–114.

Cooper, H. 2005. The classical background. In Ellis 2005: 255–71.

Copley, F. 1947. *Seruitium amoris* in the Roman elegists. *TAPA* 78: 285–300.

Coulson, F. T. and Roy, B. 2000. *Incipitarium Ovidianum. A Finding Guide for Texts in Latin Related to the Study of Ovid in the Middle Ages and Renaissance*. Turnhout.

Courtney, E. 1965. Ovidian and non-Ovidian *Heroides*. *BICS* 12: 63–66.

Courtney, E. 1980. *A Commentary on the Satires of Juvenal*. London.

Courtney, E. 1993. *The Fragmentary Latin Poets*. Oxford.

Courtney, E. 1997–1998. Echtheitskritik: Ovidian and non-Ovidian *Heroides* again. *CJ* 93: 157–166.

Crabbe, A. 1981. Structure and content in Ovid's *Metamorphoses*. *ANRW* II.31.4: 2274–2327.

Cucchiarelli, A. 1997. *La nave e l'esilio (allegorie dell'ultimo Ovidio)*. *MD* 38: 215–24.

Curran, L. C. 1984. Rape and rape victims in the *Metamorphoses*. In Peradotto and Sullivan 1984: 263–86.

D'Alessio, G. 1996. *Callimaco*. Milan.

Dalzell, A. 1996. *The Criticism of Didactic Poetry: Essays on Lucretius, Virgil and Ovid*. Toronto.

Dante Alighieri. 1970–75. *Commedia*, ed. C. Singleton. Princeton.

Davidson, J. 2001. Dover, Foucault and Greek homosexuality: penetration and the truth of sex. *Past and Present* 170: 3–51.

Davis, J. T. 1977. *Dramatic Pairings in the Elegies of Propertius & Ovid*. Bern.

Davis, P. J. 1995. *Praeceptor amoris*: Ovid's *Ars Amatoria* and the Augustan idea of Rome. *Ramus* 24: 181–95.

Davis, P. J. 1999. Ovid's *Amores*: a political reading. *CPh* 94: 431–49.

Davis, P. J. 2006. *Ovid and Augustus: A Political Reading of Ovid's Erotic Poems*. London.

Davisson, M. H. T. 1996. The search for an 'alter orbis' in Ovid's *Remedia Amoris*. *Phoenix* 50: 240–61.

De Boer, C. 1915–38. *Ovide moralisé. Poème du commencement du 14ième siècle. Publié d'après tous les manuscrits connus*. Amsterdam.

De Caro, A. 2003. Si qua fides: *gli* Amores *di Ovidio e la persuasione elegiaca*. Palermo.

Dee, J. H. 2006. *Repertorium Ovidii Metamorphoseon Hexametricum*. Heidelberg.

DeForest, M. 1993. *Woman's Power, Man's Game: Essays on Classical Antiquity in Honor of Joy K. King*. Wauconda, Ill.

Degrassi, A. 1963. *Inscriptiones Italiae* 13.2. Rome.

DeJean, J. 1989. *Fictions of Sappho, 1546–1937*. Chicago.

De Jonge, T. H. J. 1951. *Publii Ovidii Nasonis Tristium liber IV commentario exegetico instructus*. Groningen.

Della Corte, F. 1973. *I Tristia*. Genoa.

De Luce, J. 1993. 'O for a thousand tongues to sing': a footnote on metamorphosis, silence, and power. In DeForest 1993: 305–21.

Demats, P. 1973. *Fabula: trois études de mythographie antique et médiévale.* Geneva.

Depew, M. and Obbink, D. (eds). 2000. *Matrices of Genre: Authors, Canons, and Society.* Cambridge, Mass.

Deroux, C. (ed.). 1980. *Studies in Latin Literature and Roman History II.* Brussels.

Deroux, C. (ed.). 1989. *Studies in Latin Literature and Roman History V.* Brussels.

Deroux, C. (ed.). 1997. *Studies in Latin Literature and Roman History VIII.* Brussels.

Deroux, C. (ed.). 2006. *Studies in Latin Literature and Roman History XIII.* Brussels.

Desmond, M. 1993. When Dido reads Vergil: gender and intertextuality in Ovid's *Heroides* 7. *Helios* 20: 56–68.

Desmond, M. 2006. *Ovid's Art and the Wife of Bath: The Ethics of Erotic Violence.* Ithaca.

Dewar, M. 1996. *Claudian: Panegyricus de Sexto Consulatu Honorii Augusti.* Oxford.

Dewar, M. 2002. *Siquid habent veri vatum praesagia:* Ovid in the 1st–5th centuries A.D. In Boyd 2002a: 383–412.

Diggle, J. and Goodyear, F. R. D. (eds). 1972. *The Classical Papers of A. E. Housman.* Cambridge.

Dilke, O. A. W. (ed.). 1954. *Statius: Achilleid.* Cambridge.

Dillon, J. 1994. A Platonist *Ars Amatoria. CQ* 44: 387–92.

Dimmick, J. 2002. Ovid in the Middle Ages: authority and poetry. In Hardie 2002a: 264–87.

Dimundo, R. 2003. *Ovidio. Lezioni d' amore.* Bari.

Döpp, S. 1969. *Virgilischer Einfluss im Werk Ovids.* Munich.

Doran, M. 1964. Some Renaissance 'Ovids'. In Slote 1964: 44–62.

Dörrie, H. (ed.). 1971. *P. Ovidii Nasonis Epistulae Heroidum.* Berlin and New York.

Doughtie, E. 1979. The Earl of Essex and occasions for contemplative verse. *English Literary Renaissance* 9: 355–63.

Dover, K. 1978. *Greek Homosexuality.* London.

Dover, K. J. 1971. *Theocritus. Select Poems.* London.

Downing, E. 1990. Anti-Pygmalion: the *praeceptor* in *Ars Amatoria,* Book 3. *Helios* 17: 237–49.

Duckworth, G. E. 1969. *Vergil and Classical Hexameter Poetry. A Study in Metrical Variety.* Ann Arbor.

Due, O. S. 1974. *Changing Forms. Studies in the Metamorphoses of Ovid.* Copenhagen.

Dunston, J. 1968. Studies in Domizio Calderini. *IMU* 11: 71–150.

Du Quesnay, I. M. Le M. 1973. The *Amores.* In Binns 1973: 1–48.

Durling, R. M. 1958. Ovid as *praeceptor amoris. CJ* 53: 157–67.

DuRocher, R. J. 1985. *Milton and Ovid.* Ithaca.

Dyck, A. R. 1996. *A Commentary on Cicero, De Officiis.* Ann Arbor.

Dyson, J. T. 2001. *King of the Wood: The Sacrificial Victor in Virgil's Aeneid.* Norman.

Eagleton, T. 2005. *Holy Terror.* Oxford.

Eco, U. 1994. *Six Walks in the Fictional Woods.* Cambridge, Mass.

Eden, P. 1984. *Seneca:* Apocolocyntosis. Cambridge.

Eder, W. 2005. Augustus and the power of tradition. In Galinsky 2005: 13–32.

Edmunds, L. 1995. Intertextuality today. *Lexis* 13: 3–22.

Edmunds, L. 2001. *Intertextuality and the Reading of Roman Poetry.* Baltimore.

Edwards, R. R. 2006. *The Flight from Desire: Augustine and Ovid to Chaucer.* New York.

Elliott, A. G. 1980. Accessus ad auctores: twelfth-century introductions to Ovid. *Allegorica* 5: 6–48.

Ellis, R. 1881. *P. Ovidii Nasonis Ibis.* Oxford.

Ellis, S. (ed.). 2005. *Chaucer: An Oxford Guide.* Oxford.

Elyot, Sir Thomas. 1883. *The Boke of the Gouernour*, ed. H. H. S. Croft. 2 Vols. London.

Engels, J. 1945. *Études sur l'Ovide moralisé*. Groningen.

Evans, H. B. 1983. *Publica Carmina: Ovid's Books from Exile*. Lincoln.

Fairweather, J. 1987. Ovid's autobiographical poem, *Tristia* 4.10. *CQ* 37: 181–96.

Fantham, E. 1983. Sexual comedy in Ovid's *Fasti*: sources and motivation. *HSCP* 87: 185–216.

Fantham, E. 1997. Images of the city: Propertius' new-old Rome. In Habinek and Schiesaro 1997: 122–35.

Fantham, E. 1998. *Ovid: Fasti Book IV*. Cambridge.

Fantham, E. 2004a. *Ovid's* Metamorphoses. New York.

Fantham, E. 2004b. *The Word of Cicero's* De Oratore. Oxford.

Fantuzzi, M. and Hunter, R. 2004. *Tradition and Innovation in Hellenistic Poetry*. Cambridge.

Farmer, R. 1966. *An Essay on the Learning of Shakespeare*. New York.

Farrell, J. 1991. *Virgil's Georgics and the Traditions of Ancient Epic*. Oxford.

Farrell, J. 1992. Diaologue of genres in Ovid's 'Lovesong of Polyphemus' (*Metamorphoses* 13.719–897). *AJP* 113: 235–268.

Farrell, J. 1997. Towards a rhetoric of (Roman?) epic. In Dominick 1997: 131–46.

Farrell, J. 1998. Reading and writing the *Heroides*. *HSCP* 94: 307–38.

Farrell, J. 2002. Greek lives and Roman careers in the classical *uita* tradition. In Cheney and de Armas 2002: 24–46.

Farrell, J. 2003. Classical genre in theory and practice. *New Literary History* 34: 383–408.

Farrell, J. 2004. Ovid's Virgilian career. *MD* 52: 41–55.

Farrell, J. 2004–2005. Precincts of Venus: towards a prehistory of Ovidian genre. *Hermathena* 177–178: 27–69.

Fear, T. (ed.). 2000a. *Fallax Opus: Approaches to Reading Roman Elegy* (= *Arethusa* 33.2).

Fear, T. 2000b. The poet as pimp: elegiac seduction in the time of Augustus. In Fear 2000a: 217–40.

Feeney, D. C. 1991. *The Gods in Epic*. Oxford.

Feeney, D. C. 1992. *Si licet et fas est*: Ovid's *Fasti* and the problem of free speech under the Principate. In Powell 1992: 1–25 (= Knox 2006: 464–88).

Feeney, D. C. 1998. *Literature and Religion at Rome*. Cambridge.

Feeney, D. C. 1999. *Mea tempora*: patterning of time in the *Metamorphoses*. In Hardie et al. 1999: 13–30.

Feeney, D. C. 2004. Introduction to Raeburn 2004.

Feldherr, A. 2002. Metamorphosis in the *Metamorphoses*. In Hardie 2002a: 163–79.

Ferguson, J. 1960. Catullus and Ovid. *AJP* 81: 337–57.

Fisher, E. A. 1990. *Planudes' Greek Translation of Ovid's Metamorphoses*. New York and London.

Fitzgerald, W. 1995. *Catullan Provocations*. Berkeley.

Fitzgerald, W. 2000. *Slavery and the Roman Literary Imagination*. Cambridge.

Foley, J. M. (ed.). 2005. *A Companion to Ancient Epic*. Oxford.

Forbes Irving, P. M. C. 1990. *Metamorphosis in Greek Myth*. Oxford.

Forbis, E. P. 1997. Voice and voicelessness in Ovid's exile poetry. In Deroux 1997: 245–267.

Forey, M. 1998. 'Bless thee, Bottom, bless thee! Thou art translated!': Ovid, Golding, and *A Midsummer Night's Dream*. *Modern Language Review* 93: 321–29.

Fowler, A. (ed.). 1971. *Milton. Paradise Lost*. London and New York.

Fowler, D. P. 1990. Deviant focalization in Virgil's *Aeneid*. *PCPhS* 36: 42–63.

Fowler, D. P. 1995a. Horace and the aesthetics of politics. In Harrison 1995: 248–66.

Fowler, D. P. 1995b. Martial and the book. *Ramus* 24: 31–58.

Fowler, D. P. 1997. On the shoulders of giants: intertextuality and classical studies. *MD* 39: 13–34.

Fowler, D. P. 2000. Pyramus, Thisbe, King Kong: Ovid and the presence of poetry. In *Roman Constructions: Readings in Postmodern Latin*. Oxford.

Fox, C. 2007. Authorizing the metamorphic witch: Ovid in Reginald Scot's *Discovery of Witchcraft*. In Keith and Rupp 2007: 165–78.

Fox, M. 2004. Stars in the *Fasti*: Ideler (1825) and Ovid's astronomy revisited. *AJP* 125: 91–133.

Fränkel, H. 1945. *Ovid: A Poet Between Two Worlds*. Berkeley.

Fränkel, H. (ed.). 1961. *Apollonii Rhodii Argonautica*. Oxford.

Fraser, P. M. 1972. *Ptolemaic Alexandria*. Oxford.

Frécaut, J.-M. 1972. *L'esprit et l'humour chez Ovide*. Grenoble.

Fredrick, D., Konstan, D., Dugan, J. et al. (eds). 2002. The reception of Ovid in antiquity. *Arethusa* 35.3.

Friis-Jensen, K., Munk Olsen, B., and Smith, O. L. (1997). Bibliography of classical scholarship in the Middle Ages and the early Renaissance (9th to 15th centuries). In Mann and Munk Olsen 1997: 197–251.

Fripp, E. I. 1930. *Shakespeare Studies: Biographical and Literary*. Oxford.

Froesch, H. 1968. *Ovids* Epistulae ex Ponto I–III als Gedichtsammlung. Diss. Bonn.

Fuhrmann, M. 1968. Die Funktion grausiger und ekelhafter Motive in der lateinischen Dichtung. In Jauss 1968: 23–66.

Fulkerson, L. 2002. Writing yourself to death: strategies of (mis)reading in *Heroides* 2. *MD* 48: 145–65.

Fulkerson, L. 2003. Chain mail: Hypermestra and the dual readership of *Heroides* 14. *TAPA* 133: 123–45.

Fulkerson, L. 2004. *Omnia vincit amor*: why the *Remedia* fail. *CQ* 54: 211–23.

Fulkerson, L. 2005. *The Ovidian Heroine as Author: Reading, Writing, and Community in the* Heroides. Cambridge.

Füssel, S. 2005. *Gutenberg and the Impact of Printing*. Aldershot and Burlington.

Fyler, J. M. 1971. *Omnia vincit amor*: incongruity and the limitations of structure in Ovid's elegiac poetry. *CJ* 66: 196–203.

Fyler, J. M. 1979. *Chaucer and Ovid*. New Haven.

Fyler, J. M. 1998. Froissart and Chaucer. In Maddox and Sturm-Maddox 1998: 195–218.

Gaertner, J. F. 2005. *Ovid:* Epistulae ex Ponto, *Book I*. Oxford.

Gaisser, J. H. 1993. *Catullus and His Renaissance Readers*. Oxford.

Galán Vioque, G. 2002. *Martial, Book VII. A Commentary*. Leiden.

Galasso, L. 1995. *P. Ovidii Nasonis, Epistularum ex Ponto liber II*. Florence.

Galasso, L. 2006. L'edizione di Richard Tarrant delle *Metamorfosi* di Ovidio: una discussione. *MD* 57: 105–36.

Galasso, L., Paduano, G., and Perutelli, A. 2000. *Ovidio, Opere II: Le metamorfosi*. Turin.

Gale, M. 2005. Didactic epic. In Harrison 2005: 101–15.

Galinsky, K. 1967. The Cipus episode in Ovid's *Metamorphoses* (15.565–621). *TAPA* 98: 181–191.

Galinsky, K. 1975. *Ovid's* Metamorphoses. *An Introduction to the Basic Aspects*. Berkeley.

Galinsky, K. 1989. Was Ovid a Silver Latin poet? *ICS* 14: 69–89.

Galinsky, K. 1996. *Augustan Culture. An Interpretive Introduction*. Princeton.

Galinsky, K. (ed.). 2005. *The Cambridge Companion to the Age of Augustus.* Cambridge.

Gamel, M.-K. 1989. *Non sine caede*: abortion politics and poetics in Ovid's *Amores. Helios* 16: 183–206.

Gamel, M.-K. 1998. Reading as a man: performance and gender in Roman elegy. *Helios* 25: 79–95.

Ganzenmüller, W. 1911. Aus Ovids Werkstatt. *Philologus* 70: 274–311.

Garthwaite, J. 1990. Martial, Book 6, on Domitian's moral censorship. *Prudentia* 22: 12–22.

Gee, E. 2000. *Ovid, Aratus, and Augustus.* Cambridge.

Geisler, H. J. (ed.). 1969. *P. Ovidius Naso Remedia Amoris, mit Kommentar zu Vers 1–396.* Diss. Freie Universität, Berlin.

Ghisalberti, F. 1932. Arnolfo d'Orléans, un cultore di Ovidio nel sec. XII. *Memorie del Reale Istituto Lombardo di scienze e lettere* 24: 157–234.

Ghisalberti, F. 1933a. *Giovanni di Garlandia: Integumenta Ovidii. Poemetto inedito del secolo XIII.* Milan.

Ghisalberti, F. 1933b. Giovanni del Virgilio, espositore delle *Metamorfosi. Giornale Dantesco* 34: 3–110.

Ghisalberti, F. 1933c. L' 'Ovidius moralizatus' di Pierre Bersuire. *Studi Romanzi* 23: 6–136.

Ghisalberti, F. 1946. Medieval biographies of Ovid. *JWCI* 9: 10–59.

Gibson, R. K. 1998. Didactic poetry as 'popular' form: a study of imperatival expressions in Latin didactic verse and prose. In Atherton 1998: 67–98.

Gibson, R. K. 2003. *Ovid, Ars Amatoria Book 3.* Cambridge.

Gibson, R. K. 2005. Love elegy. In Harrison 2005: 159–73.

Gibson, R. K. 2006. Ovid, Augustus, and the politics of moderation in *Ars Amatoria* 3. In Gibson et al. 2006: 121–42.

Gibson, R. K. 2007. *Excess and Restraint: Propertius, Horace, and Ovid's Ars Amatoria.* London.

Gibson, R. K. and Kraus, C. S. (eds). 2002. *The Classical Commentary. History, Practices, Theory.* Leiden.

Gibson, R. K., Green, S. J., and Sharrock, A. R. (eds). 2006. *The Art of Love: Bimillennial Essays on Ovid's Ars Amatoria and Remedia Amoris.* Oxford.

Gildenhard, I. and Zissos, A. 2000. Inspirational fictions: autobiography and generic reflexivity in Ovid's proems. *G&R* 47: 67–79.

Gill, C. 1987. Two monologues of self-division: Euripides, *Medea* 1021–80 and Seneca *Med.* 893–977. In Whitby et al. 1987: 25–37.

Gillespie, S. 2004. *Shakespeare's Books.* London.

Ginsberg, W. 1998. *Ovidius ethicus?* Ovid and the medieval commentary tradition. In Paxson and Gravlee 1998: 62–71.

Giovannini, A. (ed.). 2000. *La révolution romaine après Ronald Syme. Bilans et perspectives.* Vandoeuvres, Genève.

Glauche, G. 1970. *Schullektüre im Mittelalter. Entstehung und Wandlungen des Lektürekanons bis 1200 nach den Quellen dargestellt.* Munich.

Godman, P. 1995. Ovid's sex-life. *Poetica* 27: 101–8.

Gold, B. K. (ed.). 1982. *Literary and Artistic Patronage in Ancient Rome.* Austin, Tex.

Golding, A. 1966. *Shakespeare's Ovid*, ed. W. H. D. Rouse. New York.

Goold, G. P. 1965. Amatoria critica. *HSCP* 69: 1–107.

Goold, G. P. 1966. *Noctes Propertianae. HSCP* 71: 59–106.

Goold, G. P. (ed.). 1977–1989. *Ovid.* 5 vols. Cambridge, Mass.

Goold, G. P. 1983. The cause of Ovid's exile. *ICS* 8: 94–107.

Goold, G. P. 1992. *Paralipomena Propertiana. HSCP* 94: 287–320.

Gordon, C. J. 1992. *Poetry of Maledictions: A Commentary on the Ibis of Ovid.* Diss. McMaster.

Gow, A. S. F. 1952. *Theocritus.* Cambridge.

Gow, A. S. F. and Page, D. L. 1968. *The Greek Anthology: The Garland of Philip. Vol. II.* Cambridge.

Gow, A. S. F. and Scholfield, A. F. 1953. *Nicander: The Poems and Poetical Fragments.* Cambridge.

Gradel, I. 2002. *Emperor Worship and Roman Religion.* Oxford.

Graf, F. 2002. Myth in Ovid. In Hardie 2002a: 108–21.

Grafton, A. 1983. *Joseph Scaliger: A Study in the History of Classical Scholarship. I: Textual Criticism and Exegesis.* Oxford.

Grafton, A. 1990. *Forgers and Critics: Creativity and Duplicity in Western Scholarship.* Princeton.

Grafton, A. 1991. *Defenders of the Text.* Cambridge, Mass.

Grafton, A. 1998. Correctores corruptores? Notes on the social history of editing. In Most 1998: 54–76.

Grafton, A. and Jardine, L. 1986. *From Humanism to the Humanities: Education and the Liberal Arts in Fifteenth- and Sixteenth-Century Europe.* London.

Graves, R. 1962. The Virgil cult. *The Virginia Quarterly Review* 38: 13–35.

Green, P. 1982a. *Carmen et error*, πρόφασις and αἰτία in the matter of Ovid's exile. *CA* 1: 202–20.

Green, P. 1982b. *The Erotic Poems.* Harmondsworth.

Green, P. 1989. *Classical Bearings: Interpreting Ancient History and Culture.* London.

Green, P. 1994. *Ovid: The Poems of Exile.* Harmondsworth.

Green, S. J. 2004. *Ovid, Fasti I: A Commentary.* Leiden.

Green, S. J. 2006. Lessons in love: fifty years of scholarship on the *Ars Amatoria* and *Remedia Amoris.* In Gibson et al. 2006: 1–22.

Greene, E. 1997. *The Erotics of Domination. Male Desire and the Mistress in Latin Love Poetry.* Baltimore.

Greene, R. 1617. *Alcida, Greenes metamorphosis.* London.

Greetham, D. C. 1995. *Scholarly Editing: A Guide to Research.* New York.

Gregory, H. 1958. *The Metamorphoses.* New York.

Grewing, F. 1997. *Martial, Buch VI: Ein Kommentar.* Göttingen.

Grewing, F. (ed.). 1998. *Toto Notus in Orbe.* Stuttgart.

Grierson, H. (ed.). 1912. *The Poems of John Donne.* Oxford.

Griffin, J. 1985. *Latin Poets and Roman Life.* London.

Gross, N. P. 1996. *Amores* 1.8: whose amatory rhetoric? *CW* 89: 197–206.

Günther, H.-C. 1997. *Quaestiones Propertianae.* Leiden.

Günther, H.-C. (ed.). 2006. *Brill's Companion to Propertius.* Leiden.

Guthmüller, B. 1975. Lateinische und Volkssprachliche Kommentare zu Ovids *Metamorphosen.* In Buck and Herding 1975: 119–39.

Guthrie, W. K. C. 1955. *The Greeks and their Gods.* Boston.

Gutzwiller, K. J. 1998. *Poetic Garlands: Hellenistic Epigrams in Context.* Berkeley.

Habinek, T. 1998. *The Politics of Latin Literature: Writing, Identity, and Empire in Ancient Rome.* Princeton.

Habinek, T. 2002. Ovid and empire. In Hardie 2002a: 46–61.

Habinek, T. and Schiesaro, A. (eds). 1997. *The Roman Cultural Revolution.* Cambridge.

Hall, E. 1548. *The vnion of the two noble and illustre famelies of Lancastre [and] Yorke*. London.

Hall, J. B. (ed.). 1995. *P. Ovidi Nasonis Tristia*. Stuttgart and Leipzig.

Hallett, J. P. 1973. The role of women in Roman elegy: counter-cultural feminism. *Arethusa* 6: 103–24.

Hallett, J. P. and Skinner, M. B. (eds). 1997. *Roman Sexualities*. Princeton.

Halperin, D. M. 1990. *One Hundred Years of Homosexuality*. London and New York.

Hamilton, A. C. (ed.). 1980. *Spenser. The Faerie Queene*. London and New York.

Hanning, R. W. 1986. Chaucer's first Ovid: metamorphosis and poetic tradition in *The Book of the Duchess* and *The House of Fame*. In Arrathoon 1986: 121–63.

Harder, M. A. 1993. Aspects of the structure of Callimachus' *Aetia*. In Harder et al. 1993: 99–110.

Harder, M. A. Forthcoming. *Callimachus* Aetia. *Introduction, Text and Commentary*.

Harder, M. A., Regtuit, R. F., and Wakker, G. C. (eds). 1993. *Callimachus*. Hellenistica Groningana I. Groningen.

Hardie, A. 1983. *Statius and the Silvae*. Liverpool.

Hardie, P. 1990. Ovid's Theban history: the first *anti-Aeneid*? *CQ* 40: 224–35.

Hardie, P. 1991. The Janus episode in Ovid's *Fasti*. *MD* 26: 47–64.

Hardie, P. 1992. Augustan poets and the mutability of Rome. In Powell 1992: 59–82.

Hardie, P. (ed.). 1994. *Virgil Aeneid Book IX*. Cambridge.

Hardie, P. 1997. Questions of authority: the invention of tradition in Ovid's *Metamorphoses* 15. In Habinek and Schiesaro 1997: 182–98.

Hardie, P. (ed.). 2002a. *The Cambridge Companion to Ovid*. Cambridge.

Hardie, P. 2002b. Ovid and early imperial literature. In Hardie 2002a: 34–45.

Hardie, P. 2002c. *Ovid's Poetics of Illusion*. Cambridge.

Hardie, P. 2005. The Hesiodic *Catalogue of Women* and Latin poetry. In Hunter 2005a: 287–98.

Hardie, P. 2006. *Lethaeus Amor*: the art of forgetting. In Gibson et al. 2006: 166–90.

Hardie, P., Barchiesi, A., and Hinds, S. (eds). 1999. *Ovidian Transformations. Essays on Ovid's* Metamorphoses *and its Reception*. Cambridge.

Harries, B. 1990. The spinner and the poet: Arachne in Ovid's *Metamorphoses*. *PCPhS* 36: 64–82.

Harris, W. V. 1989. *Ancient Literacy*. Cambridge, Mass.

Harrison, S. J. (ed.). 1995. *Homage to Horace: A Bimillenary Collection*. Oxford.

Harrison, S. J. (ed.). 2001. *Texts, Ideas, and the Classics: Scholarship, Theory, and Classical Literature*. Oxford.

Harrison, S. J. 2002. Ovid and genre: evolutions of an elegist. In Hardie 2002a: 79–94.

Harrison, S. J. (ed.). 2005. *The Blackwell Companion to Latin Literature*. Oxford.

Haupt, M. 1853. *Die Metamorphosen des P. Ovidius Naso*. Leipzig.

Haupt, M. 1875. *Opuscula: Vol. I*. Leipzig.

Haupt, M., Korn, O., and Ehwald, R. 1966. *P. Ovidius Naso Metamorphosen. Erster Band: Buch I–VII; Zweiter Band: Buch VIII–XV*. Corrected ed. by M. von Albrecht. Zurich.

Häuptli, B. W. 1996. *Publius Ovidius Naso. Ibis, Fragmente, Ovidiana*. Zürich.

Hayward, Sir John. 1604. *A Treatise of Vnion of the Two Realmes of England and Scotland*. London.

Heinsius, N. 1652. *Operum P. Ovidii Nasonis Editio Nova*. 3 vols. Amsterdam.

Heinsius, N. 1661. *Operum P. Ovidii Nasonis Editio Nova*. 6 vols. Amsterdam.

Heinze, R. 1915. *Vergils epische Technik*. Leipzig.

Heinze, R. 1919. Ovid's elegische Erzählung. *Berichte der Sächsischen Akademie zu Leipzig, Philologisch-historisch klasse*, 71.7.

Heinze, R. 1960. *Vom Geist des Römertums,* ed. E. Burck. 3rd edn. Stuttgart.

Heinze, T. 1997. *P. Ovidius Naso:* Der XII Heroidenbrief: Medea an Jason *mit einer Beilage: Die Fragmente der Tragödie* Medea: *Einleitung, Text und Kommentar.* Leiden.

Helm, R. 1915. Review of Magnus 1914. *Göttingische Gelehrte Anzeigen* 177: 505–54.

Helzle, M. 1988. Ovid's poetics of exile. *ICS* 13: 73–83.

Helzle, M. 1989. *Publii Ovidii Nasonis Epistularum ex Ponto liber IV. A commentary on Poems 1 to 7 and 16.* Hildesheim–Zürich–New York.

Helzle, M. 2003. *Ovids Epistulae ex Ponto. Buch I–II Kommentar.* Heidelberg.

Helzle, M. 2005. Sabinus in Ovid's exile poetry. *Scholia* 14: 71–9.

Hemelrijk, E. 1999. *Matrona Docta: Educated Women in the Roman Élite from Cornelia to Julia Domna.* London.

Henderson, A. A. R. (ed.). 1979. *P. Ovidi Nasonis Remedia Amoris.* Edinburgh.

Henderson, J. 2006. In Ovid with bed (*Ars* 2 and 3). In Gibson et al. 2006: 77–95.

Henrich, D. and Iser, W. (eds). 1983. *Funktionen des Fiktiven* (Poetik und Hermeneutik 10). Munich.

Henry, M. M. 1995. *Prisoner of History: Aspasia of Miletus and her Biographical Tradition.* Oxford.

Herbert-Brown, G. 1994. *Ovid and the Fasti. A Historical Study.* Oxford.

Herbert-Brown, G. (ed.). 2002a. *Ovid's* Fasti: *Historical Readings at its Bimillennium.* Oxford.

Herbert-Brown, G. 2002b. Ovid and the Stellar Calendar. In Herbert-Brown 2002a: 101–28.

Herescu, N. I. (ed.). 1958. *Ovidiana. Recherches sur Ovide.* Paris.

Herford, C. H. and Simpson, P. (eds). 1947. *Ben Jonson.* Oxford.

Herrmann, L. 1938. La faute secrète d'Ovide. *RBPH* 17: 695–725.

Heslin, P. 2005. *The Transvestite Achilles: Gender and Genre in Statius'* Achilleid. Cambridge.

Hexter, R. J. 1986. *Ovid and Medieval Schooling.* Munich.

Hexter, R. J. 2002. Ovid in the Middle Ages: exile, mythographer, lover. In Boyd 2002a: 413–42.

Hexter, R. J. 2006. Sex education: Ovidian erotodidactic in the classroom. In Gibson et al. 2006: 298–316.

Heyworth, S. J. 1995. Dividing Poems. In Pecere and Reeve 1995: 117–148.

Heyworth, S. J. 2007a. *Cynthia: A Companion to the Text of Propertius.* Oxford.

Heyworth, S. J. 2007b. Propertius, patronage and politics. *BICS* 50: 93–128.

Heyworth, S. J. 2007c. The OCT *Metamorphoses.* Review of Tarrant 2004. *CR* 57: 104–9.

Hicks, E. (ed.). 1977. *Le Débat sur le Roman de la Rose.* Paris.

Higham, T. F. 1958. Rhetoric in Ovid. In Herescu 1958: 32–48.

Hill, D. E. (ed. and trans.) 1985. *Ovid. Metamorphoses I–IV.* Warminster.

Hinds, S. E. 1985. Booking the return trip: Ovid and *Tristia* 1. *PCPhS* 31: 21–32 (= Knox 2006: 415–40).

Hinds, S. E. 1987a. *The Metamorphosis of Persephone: Ovid and the Self-Conscious Muse.* Cambridge.

Hinds, S. E. 1987b. Generalising about Ovid. *Ramus* 16: 4–31 (= Knox 2006: 15–50).

Hinds, S. E. 1989. Review of Knox 1986. *CPh* 84: 266–71.

Hinds, S. E. 1992a. *Arma* in Ovid's *Fasti*: Part 1: genre and mannerism. *Arethusa* 25: 81–112.

Hinds, S. E. 1992b. *Arma* in Ovid's *Fasti*: Part 2: genre, Romulean Rome and Augustan ideology. *Arethusa* 25: 113–53.

Hinds, S. E. 1993. Medea in Ovid: scenes from the life of an intertextual heroine. *MD* 30: 9–47.

Hinds, S. E. 1998. *Allusion and Intertext. Dynamics of Appropriation in Latin Poets.* Cambridge.

Hinds, S. E. 1999. After exile: time and teleology from *Metamorphosis* to *Ibis.* In Hardie et al. 1999: 48–67.

Hinds, S. E. 2000. Essential epic: genre and gender from Macer to Statius. In Depew and Obbink 2000: 221–44, 302–4.

Hinds, S. E. 2002. Landscape with figures: aesthetics of place in the *Metamorphoses* and its tradition. In Hardie 2002a: 222–49.

Hinds, S. E. 2007. Martial's Ovid/Ovid's Martial. *JRS* 97: 113–54.

Hofmann, M. and Lasdun, J. (eds). 1994. *After Ovid: New Metamorphoses.* London.

Holleman, A. W. J. 1971. Ovid and politics. *Historia* 20: 458–66.

Holleman, A. W. J. 1976. *Femina virtus:* some new thoughts on the conflict between Augustus and Ovid. In Barbu et al. 1976: 341–55.

Hollis, A. S. 1970. *Ovid, Metamorphoses Book VIII.* Oxford.

Hollis, A. S. 1973. The *Ars Amatoria* and *Remedia Amoris.* In Binns 1973: 84–115.

Hollis, A. S. 1977. *Ovid Ars Amatoria Book I.* Oxford.

Hollis, A. S. 2006. Propertius and Hellenistic poetry. In Günther 2006: 97–125.

Hollis, A. S. 2007. *Fragments of Roman Poetry, c. 60 B.C.–A.D. 20.* Oxford.

Holzberg, N. 1997. Playing with his life: Ovid's 'autobiographical' references. *Lampas* 30: 4–19 (= Knox 2006: 51–68).

Holzberg, N. 2002. *Ovid: The Poet and his Work.* Ithaca (= 1998. *Ovid: Dichter und Werk.* Munich).

Holzberg, N. 2006. Staging the reader response: Ovid and his 'contemporary audience' in *Ars* and *Remedia.* In Gibson et al. 2006: 40–53.

Hopkinson, N. 2000. *Ovid: Metamorphoses XIII.* Cambridge.

Horgan, F. (trans.) 1994. *Guillaume de Lorris and Jean de Meun: The Romance of the Rose.* Oxford.

Horsfall, N. 1979. Epic and burlesque in Ovid, *Met.* viii.260 ff. *CJ* 74: 319–22.

Horsfall, N. (ed.). 1995. *A Companion to the Study of Virgil.* Leiden.

Horsfall, N. 2003. *The Culture of the Roman Plebs.* London.

Housman, A. E. 1897. Ovid's *Heroides. CR* 11: 102–6 (= Diggle and Goodyear 1972: 380–7).

Housman, A. E. 1916. Ovidiana. *CQ* 10: 130–50 (= Diggle and Goodyear 1972: 917–39).

Housman, A. E. 1918. Transpositions in the *Ibis* of Ovid. *JPh* 34: 222–38 (= Diggle and Goodyear 1972: 969–81).

Housman, A. E. 1920. The *Ibis* of Ovid. *JPh* 35: 287–318 (= Diggle and Goodyear 1972: 1018–42).

Housman, A. E. 1922. *Attamen* and Ovid, *Her.* 1.2. *CQ* 16. 88–91 (= Diggle and Goodyear 1972: 1052–1055).

Housman, A. E. (ed.). 1937. *M. Manilii Astronomicon Liber Primus.* 2nd edn. Cambridge.

Hubbard, M. 1974. *Propertius.* London.

Hughes, T. 1997. *Tales from Ovid.* New York.

Humphries, R. 1955. *Metamorphoses.* Bloomington.

Hunt, J. D. 1996. *Garden and Grove: The Italian Renaissance Garden in the English Imagination.* Princeton.

Hunt, J. M. 1975. Review of Dörrie 1971. *CPh* 70: 215–24.

Hunter, R. 1989. *Apollonius of Rhodes:* Argonautica, *Book III.* Cambridge.

Hunter, R. 1993. *Jason and the Golden Fleece*. Oxford.

Hunter, R. 1996. *Theocritus and the Archaeology of Greek Poetry*. Cambridge.

Hunter, R. 1999. *Theocritus: A Selection*. Cambridge.

Hunter, R. (ed.). 2005a. *The Hesiodic* Catalogue of Women: *Constructions and Reconstructions*. Cambridge.

Hunter, R. 2005b. The Hesiodic *Catalogue* and Hellenistic poetry. In Hunter 2005a: 239–65.

Hunter, R. 2006a. Sweet nothings. In Bastianini and Casanova 2006: 119–31.

Hunter, R. 2006b. *The Shadow of Callimachus. Studies in the Reception of Hellenistic Poetry at Rome*. Cambridge.

Huskey, S. J. 2002. Ovid and the fall of Troy in *Tristia* 1.3. *Vergilius* 48: 88–104.

Hutchinson, G. O. 1988. *Hellenistic Poetry*. Oxford.

Hutchinson, G. O. 2006. The metamorphosis of metamorphosis: *P.Oxy.* 4711 and Ovid. *ZPE* 155: 71–84.

Huygens, R. B. C. (ed.). 1970. *Accessus ad auctores, Bernard d'Utrecht, Conrad d'Hirsau 'Dialogus super Auctores'*. Leiden.

Huys, M. 1991. *Le poème élégiaque hellénistique P. Brux. Inv. E. 8934 et P. Sorb. Inv. 2254 : édition, commentaire et analyse stylistique*. Brussels.

Innes, M. 1955. *Metamorphoses*. Harmondsworth.

Iser, W. 1983. Akte des Fingierens oder 'Was ist das Fiktive im fiktionalen Text?' In Henrich and Iser 1983: 121–51.

Jacobson, H. 1974. *Ovid's Heroides*. Princeton.

Jacoff, R. (ed.). 1993. *The Cambridge Companion to Dante*. Cambridge.

Jacoff, R. and Schnapp, J. T. (eds). 1991. *The Poetry of Allusion: Virgil and Ovid in Dante's 'Commedia'*. Stanford.

Jacques, J.-M. 2002. *Nicandre: Oeuvres*, ii. *Les thériaques; fragments iologiques antérieurs à Nicandre*. Paris.

Jäger, K. 1967. *Zweigliedrige Gedichte und Gedichtpaare bei Properz und in Ovids* Amores. Tübingen.

Jahn, J. C. (ed.). 1828–1832. *P. Ovidii Nasonis Quae Supersunt Opera Omnia*. 2 vols. Leipzig.

Jakobi, R. 1988. *Der Einfluss Ovids auf den Tragiker Seneca*. Berlin.

James, H. 2003. Ovid and the question of politics in early modern England. *English Literary History* 70: 343–73.

James, H. 2004. Shakespeare's learned heroines in Ovid's schoolroom. In Martindale and Taylor 2004: 66–85.

James, H. 2006. The poet's toys: Christopher Marlowe and the liberties of erotic elegy. *MLQ* 67.1: 103–27.

James, S. L. 1997. Slave-rape and female silence in Ovid's love poetry. *Helios* 24: 60–76.

James, S. L. 2003. *Learned Girls and Male Persuasion: Gender and Reading in Roman Love Elegy*. Berkeley.

Janan, M. 1988. The Book of Good Love? Design versus desire in *Metamorphoses* 10. *Ramus* 17: 110–37.

Janan, M. 1994. *'When the Lamp is Shattered'. Desire and Narrative in Catullus*. Carbondale and Edwardsville.

Janka, M. (ed.). 1997. *Ovid, Ars amatoria Buch 2*. Heidelberg.

Janka, M. 2006. *Paelignus, puto, dixerat poeta* (Mart. 2.41.2): Martial's intertextual dialogue with Ovid's erotodidactic poems. In Gibson et al. 2006: 279–98.

Janko, R. 2005. Sappho revisited. *Times Literary Supplement*, 23 December.

Jauss, H. R. (ed.). 1968. *Die nicht mehr schönen Künste. Grenzphänomene des Ästhetischen.* Munich.

Jenkyns, R. 1992. *The Legacy of Rome. A New Appraisal.* Oxford.

Johnson, P. J. 1997. Ovid and poetic *facundia.* In Deroux 1997: 231–44.

Jolivet, J.-C. 2001. *Allusion et fiction épistolaire dans les* Héroïdes: *Recherches sur l'intertextualité ovidienne.* Paris.

Jones, B. W. 1992. *The Emperor Domitian.* London.

Jonge, P. de, Jonkers, E. J., Mulder, H. M. et al. (eds). 1955. *Ut Pictura Poesis. Studia Latina P. J. Enk Septuagenario Oblata.* Leiden.

Jonson, B. 1601. *Poetaster, or The Arraignment.* London.

Jonson, B. 1925–52. *Ben Jonson,* ed. C. H. Herford and Percy and Evelyn Simpson. Oxford.

Juhnke, H. 1972. *Homerisches in römischer Epik der flavischer Zeit.* Munich.

Kamuf, P. 1982. *Fictions of Feminine Desire: Disclosures of Heloise.* Lincoln.

Kaster, R. A. 1995. *Suetonius:* De Grammaticis et Rhetoribus. Oxford.

Kauffman, L. S. 1986. *Discourses of Desire: Gender, Genre, and Epistolary Fictions.* Ithaca and London.

Keith, A. M. 1992. *The Play of Fictions: Studies in Ovid's* Metamorphoses *Book 2.* Ann Arbor.

Keith, A. M. 1994/5. *Corpus eroticum:* elegiac poetics and elegiac *puellae* in Ovid's *Amores. CW* 81: 27–40.

Keith, A. M. 1997. *Tandem venit amor:* a Roman woman speaks of love. In Hallett and Skinner 1997: 295–310.

Keith, A. M. 1999a. Slender verse: Roman elegy and ancient rhetorical theory. *Mnemosyne* 52: 41–62.

Keith, A. M. 1999b. Versions of epic masculinity in Ovid's *Metamorphoses.* In Hardie et al. 1999: 214–39.

Keith, A. M. 2000. *Engendering Rome.* Cambridge.

Keith, A. M. 2002a. Ovidian personae in Statius' *Thebaid. Arethusa* 35: 381–402.

Keith, A. M. 2002b. Sources and genres in Ovid's *Metamorphoses* 1–5. In Boyd 2002a: 235–69.

Keith, A. M. and Rupp, S. (eds.). 2007. *Metamorphoses: The Changing Face of Ovid in Medieval and Early Modern Europe.* Toronto.

Kennedy, D. F. 1984. The epistolary mode and the first of Ovid's *Heroides. CQ* 34: 413–22 (= Knox 2006: 69–85).

Kennedy, D. F. 1992. 'Augustan' and 'anti-Augustan': reflections on terms of reference. In Powell 1992: 26–58.

Kennedy, D. F. 1993. *The Arts of Love: Five Studies in the Discourse of Roman Love Elegy.* Cambridge.

Kenney, E. J. 1958. *Nequitiae poeta.* In Herescu 1958: 201–9.

Kenney, E. J. 1961. *P. Ovidi Nasonis Amores, Medicamina Faciei Femineae, Ars Amatoria, Remedia Amoris.* 2nd edn. 1994. Oxford.

Kenney, E. J. 1962. The manuscript tradition of Ovid's *Amores, Ars Amatoria,* and *Remedia Amoris. CQ* 12: 1–31.

Kenney, E. J. 1965. The poetry of Ovid's exile. *PCPhS* 191: 37–49.

Kenney, E. J. 1969a. On the *Somnium* attributed to Ovid. *Agon* 3: 1–14.

Kenney, E. J. 1969b. Ovid and the law. *YCS* 21: 241–63.

Kenney, E. J. 1970a. That incomparable poem the '*Ille ego*'. *CR* 20: 290.

Kenney, E. J. 1970b. Love and legalism: Ovid, *Heroides* 20 and 21. *Arion* 9: 388–414.

Kenney, E. J. 1971a. The character of humanist philology. In Bolger 1971: 119–28.

Kenney, E. J. 1971b. Review of Duckworth 1969. *CR* 21: 200–3.

Kenney, E. J. 1972. Materie superatur opus. *CR* 22: 38–42.

Kenney, E. J. 1973. The style of the *Metamorphoses*. In Binns 1973: 116–53.

Kenney, E. J. 1974. *The Classical Text*. Berkeley (= Kenney 1995).

Kenney, E. J. 1976. Ovidius prooemians. *PCPhS* 22: 46–53 (= Knox 2006: 265–73).

Kenney, E. J. 1979. Two disputed passages in the *Heroides*. *CQ* 29: 394–431.

Kenney, E. J. 1982. Books and readers in the Roman world. In Kenney and Clausen 1982: 3–32.

Kenney, E. J. 1986. Introduction to Melville 1986.

Kenney, E. J. 1990. Introduction to Melville 1990.

Kenney, E. J. 1995. *Testo e metodo*. Rome.

Kenney, E. J. 1996. *Ovid: Heroides XVI–XXI*. Cambridge.

Kenney, E. J. 1999. *Vt erat novator*. Anomaly, innovation and genre in Ovid, *Heroides* 16–21. *PBA* 93: 399–414.

Kenney, E. J. 2001a. Textual notes on Ovid, *Metamorphoses* 7–9. *CQ* 51: 545–50.

Kenney, E. J. 2001b. Review of Bretzigheimer 2001. *BMCR* 2001.10.39.

Kenney, E. J. 2001c. 'Est deus in nobis . . .': Medea meets her maker. In Papanghelis and Rengakos 2001: 261–83.

Kenney, E. J. 2002. Ovid's language and style. In Boyd 2002a: 27–89.

Kenney, E. J. 2005. On the number of books in Ovid's *Metamorphoses*: a postscript. *CQ* 55: 650.

Kenney, E. J. and Clausen, W. V. (eds.). 1982. *The Cambridge History of Classical Literature II. Latin Literature*. Cambridge.

Kidd, D. 1997. *Aratus: Phaenomena*. Cambridge.

King, C. 2003. The organization of Roman religious beliefs. *CA* 22: 275–312.

King, R. J. 2006. *Desiring Rome. Male Subjectivity and Reading Ovid's* Fasti. Columbus.

Kirk, G. S. 1970. *Myth: Its Meaning and Functions in Ancient and Other Cultures*. Cambridge.

Kirk, G. S. 1972. Aetiology, ritual, charter. Three equivocal terms in the study of myth. *YCS* 22: 83–102.

Kirk, G. S. 1974. *The Nature of Greek Myths*. London.

Kiser, L. J. 1983. *Telling Classical Tales: Chaucer and the* Legend of Good Women. Ithaca.

Kleve, K. 1983. Naso magister erat—sed quis Nasonis magister? *SO* 58: 89–109.

Klopsch, P. 1967. *Pseudo-Ovidius de Vetula*. Leiden.

Knaack, G. 1880. *Analecta Alexandrina-Romana*. Greifswald.

Knox, P. E. 1983. Cinna, the *Ciris*, and Ovid. *CPh* 78: 309–11.

Knox, P. E. 1985. The Epilogue to the *Aetia*. *GRBS* 26: 59–65.

Knox, P. E. 1986. *Ovid's* Metamorphoses *and the Traditions of Augustan Poetry*. Cambridge.

Knox, P. E. 1993. The Epilogue to the *Aetia*: an epilogue. *ZPE* 96: 175–8.

Knox, P. E. 1995. *Ovid: Heroides. Select Epistles*. Cambridge.

Knox, P. E. 1997. Review of Hall 1995. *BMCR* 97.3.31.

Knox, P. E. 2004. The poet and the second prince: Ovid in the age of Tiberius. *MAAR* 49: 1–20.

Knox, P. E. (ed.). 2006. *Oxford Readings in Ovid*. Oxford.

Konstan, D. 1991. The death of Argus, or what stories do: audience response in ancient fiction and theory. *Helios* 18: 15–30.

Korn, O. (ed.). 1868. *P. Ovidii Nasonis Ex Ponto Libri Quattuor*. Leipzig.

Koster, S. 1979. Liebe und Krieg in der 'Achilleis' des Statius. *WJA* 5: 189–208.

Kott, J. 1974. *Shakespeare Our Contemporary.* New York.

Kovacs, D. 1987. Ovid, *Metamorphoses* 1.2. *CQ* 37: 458–65.

Kraus, W. 1968. Ovidius Naso. In Albrecht and Zinn 1968: 67–166.

Krenkel, W. 1981. Tonguing. *Wissenschaftliche Zeitschrift der Wilhelm-Pieck-Universität* 30: 37–54.

Kristeller, P. O. et al. (eds). 1960– . *Catalogus Translationum et Commentariorum.* Washington, D.C.

Kristeva, J. 1969. *Sèméiôtikè. Recherches pour une sémanalyse.* Paris.

Kroll, W. 1924. *Studien zum Verständnis der römischen Literatur.* Stuttgart.

Küppers, E. 1981. Ovids *Ars Amatoria* und *Remedia Amoris* als Lehrdichtungen. *ANRW* 2.31.4: 2507–51.

Labate, M. 1980. Ulisse, Eurialo e le armi di Achille. Ov. *Met.* XIII 98 sgg. *A&R* 25: 28–32.

Labate, M. 1984. *L'arte di farsi amare: modelli culturali e progetto didascalico nell' elegia ovidiana.* Pisa.

Labate, M. 1987. *Elegia triste ed elegia lieta. Un caso di riconversione letteraria. MD* 19: 91–129.

Labate, M. 1990. Forme della letteratura, immagini del mondo: da Catullo a Ovidio. In Momigliano and Schiavone 1990: 923–65.

Labate, M. 2006. Erotic aetiology: Romulus, Augustus, and the rape of the Sabine women. In Gibson et al. 2006: 193–215.

Lacan, J. 1977. *Ecrits. A Selection* (A. Sheridan trans.). London.

Lacan, J. 1981. The unconscious and repetition. In Miller 1981: 17–64.

Lachmann, C. (ed.). 1816. *Sexti Aurelii Propertii Carmina.* Berlin (repr. 1973 Hildesheim).

Lachmann, C. [1848] 1876. De Ovidii epistulis. In *Kleinere Schriften*, vol. 2, ed. J. Vahlen. Berlin: 56–61.

Lachmann, C. 1850. *T. Lucreti Cari De Rerum Natura Libri Sex.* Berlin.

Lafaye, G. 1904. *Les Métamorphoses d'Ovide et leurs modèles grecs.* Paris.

Lamacchia, R. 1960. Ovidio interprete di Virgilio. *Maia* 12: 310–30.

Landolfi, L. 2000. *Scribentis imago: eroine ovidiane e lamento epistolare.* Bologna.

La Penna, A. 1957. *Ibis.* Florence.

La Penna, A. 1959. *Scholia in P. Ovidii Nasonis Ibin.* Florence.

La Penna, A. 1963. *Orazio e l'ideologia del principato.* Turin.

La Penna, A. 1977. *L'integrazione difficile: un profilo di Properzio.* Turin.

La Penna, A. 1979. L'*usus* contro Apollo e le Muse. Nota a Ovidio, *Ars Am.*, 1, 25–30. *ASNP* 3.9: 985–97.

Lazzarini, C. (ed.). 1986. *Ovidio, Rimedio contro l'amore.* Venice.

Lazzeri, E. (ed.). 1971. *Angelo Poliziano: Commento inedito all'Epistola Ovidiana di Saffo a Faone.* Florence.

Leach, E. W. 1964. Georgic imagery in the *Ars Amatoria. TAPA* 95: 142–54.

Leary, T. J. 1990. On the dating of Ovid's *Ibis. Latomus* 49: 99–101.

Lechi, F. 1988. *Piger ad poenas ad praemia velox:* un modello di sovrano nelle *Epistulae ex Ponto. MD* 20–21: 119–32.

Lechi, F. 1993. Ovidio: *Tristezze.* Milano.

Lee, G. 1958. The authorship of the *Nux.* In Herescu 1958: 457–71.

Lee, G. 1962. *Tenerorum lusor Amorum.* In Sullivan 1962: 149–79.

Lee, G. 1968. *Ovid's* Amores. London.

Lee, G. 2000. *Ovid in Love* (illustrated reprint of Lee 1968). London.

Lefkowitz, M. 1981. *Lives of the Greek Poets.* Baltimore.

Lehmann, P. 1927. *Pseudo-antike Literatur des Mittelalters.* Leipzig.

Lehnus, L. 2006. Prima e dopo αἱ κατὰ λεπτόν. In Bastianini and Casanova 2006: 133–47.

Lelli, E. 2005. *Callimachi Iambi XIV–XVII.* Rome.

Lenz, F. W. (ed.). 1938. *P. Ovidii Nasonis Epistulae ex Ponto.* Turin.

Lenz, F. W. (ed.). 1956. *P. Ovidi Nasonis Halieutica, Fragmenta, Nux. Incerti Consolatio ad Liviam.* Turin.

Lenz, F. W. 1968. Das pseudo-ovidische Gedicht *De Sompnio. MLatJb* 5: 101–14.

Lenz, L. 1997. Tibull in den Tristien. *Gymnasium* 104: 310–17.

Leo, F. 1878. *De Senecae Tragoediis Observationes Criticae.* Berlin.

Lerer, S. (ed.). 2006. *The Yale Companion to Chaucer.* New Haven.

Lettere, V. 1981. Ercole Ciofano. *Dizionario Biografico degli Italiani* 25: 661–3.

Levick, B. 1999. *Tiberius the Politician.* Revised edn. London.

Liebeschuetz, J. H. W. G. 1979. *Continuity and Change in Roman Religion.* Oxford.

Lightfoot, J. L. 1999. *Parthenius of Nicaea.* Oxford.

Lindheim, S. 1998. I am dressed, therefore I am? Vertumnus in Prop. 4.2 and in *Metamorphoses* 14.622–771. *Ramus* 27: 27–38.

Lindheim, S. 2003. *Mail and Female: Epistolary Narrative and Desire in Ovid's* Heroides. Madison.

Lipking, L. 1988. *Abandoned Women and Poetic Tradition.* Chicago.

Little, D. A. 1970. Richard Heinze: Ovid's elegische Erzählung. In Zinn 1970: 64–105.

Little, D. A. 1982. Politics in Augustan poetry. *ANRW* 2.30.1: 254–370.

Littlewood, R. J. 1975. Ovid's Lupercalia (*Fasti* 2.267–452): a study in the artistry of the *Fasti. Latomus* 34: 1060–72.

Littlewood, R. J. 1980. Ovid and the Ides of March (*Fasti* 3.523–710): a further study in the artistry of the *Fasti.* In Deroux 1980: 301–21.

Littlewood, R. J. 2006. *A Commentary on Ovid's* Fasti, *Book 6.* Oxford.

Liveley, G. 2006. Ovid in defeat? On the reception of Ovid's *Ars Amatoria* and *Remedia Amoris.* In Gibson et al. 2006: 318–37.

Livrea, E. 1973. *Apollonii Rhodii Argonauticon Liber IV.* Florence.

Llewellyn, N. 1986. Illustrating Ovid. In Martindale 1988: 151–66.

Lloyd-Jones, H. 2005. *Supplementum Supplementi Hellenistici.* Berlin.

Lloyd-Jones, H. and Parsons, P. J. 1983. *Supplementum Hellenisticum.* Berlin.

Lo Monaco, F. (ed.). 1991. *Angelo Poliziano: Commento inedito ai Fasti di Ovidio.* Florence.

Lowell, R. 1987. Ovid's *Metamorphoses.* In *Collected Prose,* ed. Robert Giroux. New York, 152–62.

Luck, G. 1967. *P Ovidius Naso: Tristia. Band I: Text und Übersetzung.* Heidelberg.

Luck, G. 1977. *P. Ovidius Naso: Tristia. Band II: Kommentar.* Heidelberg.

Luck, G. 1982. Notes on the text of Ovid's *Metamorphoses. AJP* 103: 47–61.

Luck, G. 2002. Ovid, Naugerius and We, or: how to create a text. *Exemplaria Classica* 6: 1–40.

Luck, G. 2005. Naugerius' notes on Ovid's *Metamorphoses. Exemplaria Classica* 9: 155–226.

Lucke, C. (ed.). 1982. *P. Ovidius Naso Remedia Amoris, mit Kommentar zu Vers 397–814.* Bonn.

Luque Moreno, J. 1995. Tibulo a través de Ovidio. *Emerita* 63: 341–51.

Lyne, R. 1996. Golding's Englished *Metamorphoses. Translation & Literature* 5: 183–200.

Lyne, R. 2000. Ovid, Golding, and the 'rough magic' of *The Tempest*. In Taylor 2000: 150–64.

Lyne, R. 2001. *Ovid's Changing Worlds: English* Metamorphoses, *1567–1632*. Oxford.

Lyne, R. 2002. Love and exile after Ovid. In Hardie 2002a: 288–300.

Lyne, R. O. A. M. 1979. *Seruitium amoris. CQ* 29: 117–30.

Lyne, R. O. A. M. 1980. *The Latin Love Poets from Catullus to Horace*. Oxford.

Lyne, R. O. A. M. 1995. *Horace: Behind the Public Poetry*. New Haven.

Lyne, R. O. A. M. 2007. *Collected Papers on Latin Poetry*. Oxford.

Mack, S. 1988. *Ovid*. New Haven.

Maddox, D. and Sturm-Maddox, S. (eds). 1998. *Froissart Across the Genres*. Gainesville.

Mader, G. 1991. Panegyric and Persuasion in Ovid, *Tr.* 2.317–336. *Latomus* 50: 134–49.

Magnus, H. (ed.). 1914. *P. Ovidi Nasonis Metamorphoseon Libri XV. Lactanti Placidi Qui Dicitur Narrationes Fabularum Ovidianarum*. Berlin.

Malta, C. 1997. *Il Commento a Persio dell' umanista Raffaele Regio*. Messina.

Maltby, R. 1999. Tibullus and the language of Latin elegy. In Adams and Mayer 1999: 377–98.

Maltby, R. 2002. *Tibullus: Elegies: Text, Introduction and Commentary*. Cambridge.

Mann, N. and Munk Olsen, B. (eds). 1997. *Medieval and Renaissance Scholarship*. Leiden.

Mariotti, S. 1962. Epigrammata Bobiensia. *RE* Suppl. 9: 37–64.

Marlowe, C. *ca* 1582. Translation of the *Amores* in: R. Gill (ed.). *All Ovids elegies, Lucans first booke, Dido Queene of Carthage, Hero and Leander*, Oxford 1987.

Marston, J. 1599. *The Scourge of Villanie. Corrected*. London.

Martellotti, G. (ed.). 1955. *Francesco Petrarca: Prose*. Milan.

Martin, A. J. M. 2004. *Was ist Exil?* Hildesheim.

Martin, C. 1998. *Ovid in English*. Harmondsworth.

Martindale, C. 1986. *John Milton and the Transformation of Ancient Epic*. London.

Martindale, C. (ed.). 1988. *Ovid Renewed: Ovidian Influence on Literature and Art from the Middle Ages to the Twentieth Century*. Cambridge.

Martindale, C. (ed.). 1997. *The Cambridge Companion to Virgil*. Cambridge.

Martindale, C. 2000. Shakespeare's Ovid, Ovid's Shakespeare: a methodological postscript. In Taylor 2000: 198–215.

Martindale, C. and Martindale, M. 1990. *Shakespeare and the Uses of Antiquity*. London.

Martindale, C. and Taylor, A. B. (eds). 2004. *Shakespeare and the Classics*. Cambridge.

Martini, E. 1933. *Einleitung zu Ovid*. Prague.

Martyn, J. R. C. 1981. Naso—*desultor amoris* (*Amores* 1–3). *ANRW* 31.4: 2436–59.

Martz, L. L. 1986. *Milton, Poet of Exile*. 2nd edn. New Haven.

Massimilla, G. (ed.). 1996. *Aitia: Libri Primo e Secondo*. Pisa.

McGinn, T. A. J. 1998. *Prostitution, Sexuality and the Law in Ancient Rome*. New York.

McKeown, J. C. 1979a. Ovid, *Amores* 3.12. *PLLS* 2: 163–77.

McKeown J. C. 1979b. Augustan elegy and mime. *PCPhS* 25: 71–84.

McKeown, J. C. 1984. *Fabula proposito nulla tegenda meo*. Ovid's *Fasti* and Augustan politics. In Woodman and West 1984: 169–87.

McKeown, J. C. 1987. *Ovid: Amores Vol. I. Text and Prolegomena*. Liverpool.

McKeown, J. C. 1989. *Ovid: Amores Vol. II. A Commentary on Book One*. Leeds.

McKeown, J. C. 1998. *Ovid: Amores Vol. III. A Commentary on Book Two*. Leeds.

McKeown, J. C. 2002. The authenticity of *Amores* 3.5. In Miller et al. 2002: 114–128.

McKie, D. S. 1986. Ovid's *Amores*: the prime sources for the text. *CQ* n.s. 36: 219–38.

McKinley, K. L. 2001. *Reading the Ovidian Heroine: 'Metamorphoses' Commentaries, 1100–1618*. Leiden.

McKitterick, D. 2003. *Print, Manuscript, and the Search for Order 1450–1830*. Cambridge.

McLennan, G. 1972. *Arte allusiva* and Ovidian metrics (imitation of Tib. in *Am.* 3.9). *Hermes* 100: 495–6.

Meckelnborg, C. and Schneider, B. 2002. *Odyssea: Responsio Ulixis ad Penelopen*. Munich.

Melville, A. D. 1986. *Metamorphoses*. Oxford.

Melville, A. D. 1990. *The Love Poems*. Oxford.

Melville, A. D. 1992. *Ovid: Sorrows of an Exile. Tristia*. Oxford.

Meres, F. 1598. *Palladis Tamia: Wit's Treasury*. London.

Merkel, R. 1837. *P. Ovidii Nasonis Tristium Libri Quinque et Ibis*. Berlin.

Merkel, R. 1841. *P. Ovidii Nasonis Fastorum Libri Sex*. Berlin.

Merkel, R. 1850–1852. *P. Ovidius Naso*. 3 vols. 2nd edn. 1875–1884.

Merklin, H. 1968. Arethusa und Laodamia. *Hermes* 96: 461–94.

Merli, E. 2004. On the number of books in Ovid's *Metamorphoses*. *CQ* 54: 304–7.

Merten, K. 2004. *Antike Mythen—Mythos Antike. Posthumanistische Antikerezeption in der englischsprachigen Lyrik der Gegenwart*. Munich.

Michalopoulos, A. N. 2000–2. Ovid's mythological exempla in his advice on amatory correspondence in the *Ars amatoria* and *Remedia amoris*. *Sandalion* 23–25: 39–48.

Michalopoulos, A. N. 2006. *Ovid Heroides 16 and 17: Introduction, Text, and Commentary*. Leeds.

Michels, A. 1967. *The Calendar of the Roman Republic*. Princeton.

Miglio, M. 1978. *Giovanni Andrea Bussi: Prefazioni alle edizioni di Sweynheym e Pannartz prototipografi romani*. Milan.

Millar, F. 1973. Triumvirate and principate. *JRS* 63: 50–67.

Millar, F. 2000. *The First Revolution: Imperator Caesar, 36–28 BC*. In Giovannini 2000: 1–38.

Millar, F. and Segal, E. (eds). 1984. *Caesar Augustus. Seven Aspects*. Oxford.

Miller, J.-A. (ed.). 1981. *The Seminar of Jacques Lacan, Book Eleven: The Four Fundamental Concepts of Psychoanalysis*. New York.

Miller, J. F. 1982. Callimachus and the Augustan aetiological elegy. *ANRW* II 30.1: 371–417.

Miller, J. F. 1983. Callimachus and the *Ars Amatoria*. *CPh* 78: 26–34.

Miller, J. F. 1986. Disclaiming divine inspiration: a programmatic pattern. *WS* 20: 151–64.

Miller, J. F. 1991. *Ovid's Elegiac Festivals: Studies in the* Fasti. Frankfurt and Bern.

Miller, J. F. 1992. The *Fasti* and Hellenistic didactic: Ovid's variant aetiologies. *Arethusa* 25: 11–31.

Miller, J. F. 1993. Ovidian allusion and the vocabulary of memory. *MD* 30: 153–64 (= Knox 2006: 86–99).

Miller, J. F. 1996–97. Lucretian moments in Ovidian elegy. *CJ* 92: 384–98.

Miller, J. F., Damon, C., and Myers, K. S. (eds). 2002. *Vertis in usum. Studies in Honor of Edward Courtney*. Munich.

Miller, P. A. 1994. *Lyric Texts and Lyric Consciousness: The Birth of a Genre from Archaic Greece to Augustan Rome*. London.

Miller, P. A. 2004a. *Subjecting Verses: Latin Love Elegy and the Emergence of the Real*. Princeton.

Miller, P. A. 2004b. The Parodic Sublime: Ovid's Reception of Virgil in *Heroides* 7. *MD* 52: 57–72.

Minnis, A. J. 2001. *Magister Amoris: The* Roman de la Rose *and Vernacular Hermeneutics*. Oxford.

Minnis, A. J. and Scott, A. B. (eds). 1988. *Medieval Literary Theory and Criticism, c.1100– c.1375: The Commentary Tradition*. Oxford.

Mitescu, A. 1972. Ovid's presence in Romanian culture. *Romanian Review* 26: 54–57.

Moles, J. L. 1991. The dramatic coherence of Ovid, *Amores* 1.1 and 1.2. *CQ* 51: 551–4.

Momigliano, A. and Schiavone, A. (eds). 1990. *Storia di Roma*. 2.1. *La repubblica imperiale*. Turin.

Monfasani, J. 1988. The first call for press censorship: Niccoló Perotti, Giovanni Andrea Bussi, Antonio Moreto, and the editing of Pliny's *Natural History*. *Renaissance Quarterly* 41: 1–31.

Montaigne, M. de. 1965. *Montaigne's Essays*. (J. Florio trans.). London.

Montrose, L. A. 1983. 'Shaping fantasies': figurations of gender and power in Elizabethan culture. *Representations* 2: 61–94.

Morgan, K. 1977. *Ovid's Art of Imitation: Propertius in the* Amores. Leiden.

Morini, M. 2006. *Tudor Translation in Theory and Practice*. Aldershot.

Moss, A. 1982. *Ovid in Renaissance France. A Survey of the Latin Editions of Ovid and Commentaries Printed in France before 1600*. London.

Moss, A. 1998. *Latin Commentaries on Ovid from the Renaissance*. Signal Mountain, Tenn.

Most, G. W. (ed.). 1998. *Editing Texts. Texte edieren*. Göttingen.

Most, G. W. (ed.). 1999. *Commentarie—Kommentare*. Göttingen.

Mouritsen, H. 2001. *Plebs and Politics in the Late Roman Republic*. Cambridge.

Muir, K. 1977. *The Sources of Shakespeare's Plays*. London.

Mulder, H. M. 1955. Fata vetant. De imitandi componendique in Achilleide ratione Statiana. In Jonge et al. 1955: 119–28.

Munari, F. 1957. *Catalogue of the Mss of Ovid's Metamorphoses*. London.

Munari, F. 1960. *Ovid im Mittelalter*. Zurich.

Munk Olsen, B. 1985. *L'étude des auteurs classiques latins aux XIe et XIIe siècles*. Vol. 2. Paris.

Munk Olsen, B. 1991. *I Classici nel Canone Scolastico Altomedievale*. Spoleto.

Murgatroyd, P. 1975. *Militia amoris* and the Roman elegists. *Latomus* 34: 59–79.

Murgia, C. E. 1986a. The date of Ovid's *Ars Amatoria* 3. *AJP* 107: 74–94.

Murgia, C. E. 1986b. Influence of Ovid's *Remedia amoris* on *Ars amatoria* 3 and *Amores* 3. *CPh* 81: 203–20.

Murrin, M. 1980. *The Allegorical Epic: Essays in its Rise and Decline*. Chicago.

Musgrove, M. 1998. Nestor's centauromachy and the deceptive voice of poetic memory (Ovid *Met.* 12.182–535). *CPh* 93: 223–31.

Myerowitz, M. 1985. *Ovid's Games of Love*. Detroit.

Myerowitz, M. 1992. The domestication of desire: Ovid's *parva tabella* and the theater of love. In Richlin 1992a: 131–57.

Myers, K. S. 1994. *Ovid's Causes. Cosmogony and Aetiology in the Metamorphoses*. Ann Arbor.

Myers, K. S. 1999. The metamorphosis of a poet: recent work on Ovid. *JRS* 89: 190–204.

Mynors, R. A. B. 1990. *Virgil: Georgics*. Oxford.

Nagle, B. R. 1980. *The Poetics of Exile: Program and Polemic in the* Tristia *and* Epistulae ex Ponto *of Ovid*. Brussels.

Nagle, B. R. 1983. Byblis and Myrrha: two incest narratives in the *Metamorphoses*. *CJ* 78: 301–15.

Nagle, B. R. 1988a. A trio of love-triangles in Ovid's *Metamorphoses*. *Arethusa* 25: 11–31.

Nagle, B. R. 1988b. Erotic pursuit and narrative seduction in Ovid's *Metamorphoses*. *Ramus* 17: 32–51.

Nancy, J.-L. 2005. *Being Singular Plural*. Stanford.

Nauta, R. 2002. *Poetry for Patrons*. Leiden.

Newlands, C. E. 1992. Ovid's narrator in the *Fasti*. *Arethusa* 25: 33–54 (= Knox 2006: 351–69).

Newlands, C. E. 1995. *Playing with Time: Ovid and the Fasti*. Ithaca.

Newlands, C. E. 2002a. *Mandati memores*: political and poetic authority in the *Fasti*. In Hardie 2002a: 200–16.

Newlands, C. E. 2002b. *Statius' Silvae and the Poetics of Empire*. Cambridge.

Newlands, C. E. 2005. Ovid. In Foley 2005: 476–491.

Newton, T. 1581. *Seneca His Tenne Tragedies*. London.

Nicoll, W. S. M. 1977. Ovid *Amores* 1.5. *Mnemosyne* 30: 40–8.

Nims, J. F. 1965. *Ovid's Metamorphoses. The Arthur Golding Translation of 1567*. New York.

Nisbet, R. G. M. 1982. Great and lesser bear (Ovid *Tristia* 4.3). *JRS* 72: 49–56.

Nisbet, R. G. M. and Hubbard, M. 1970. *A Commentary on Horace: Odes, Book I*. Oxford.

Nisbet, R. G. M. and Hubbard, M. 1978. *A Commentary on Horace: Odes, Book II*. Oxford.

Nisbet, R. G. M. and Rudd, N. 2004. *A Commentary on Horace: Odes, Book III*. Oxford.

Nisetich, F. 2001. *The Poems of Callimachus*. Oxford.

Nugent, S. G. 1990. This sex which is not one: de-constructing Ovid's Hermaphrodite. *differences* 2.1: 160–85.

Oakley-Brown, L. 2006. *Ovid and the Cultural Politics of Translation in Early Modern England*. Aldershot.

Obbink, D. 1999. Anoubion, Elegiacs. *POxy* 66: 57–109.

O'Gorman, E. 1997. Love and family: Augustus and Ovidian elegy. *Arethusa* 30: 103–23.

O'Hara, J. J. 1996. Vergil's best reader? Ovidian commentary on Vergilian etymological wordplay. *CJ* 91: 255–276 (= Knox 2006: 100–22).

Oliensis, E. 2004. The power of image-makers: representation and revenge in Ovid's *Metamorphoses* 6 and *Tristia* 4. *CA* 23: 285–321.

O'Neill, K. N. 1999. Ovid and Propertius: reflexive annotation in *Amores* 1.8. *Mnemosyne* 52: 286–307.

Onians, R. B. 1954. *The Origins of European Thought about the Body, the Mind, the Soul, the World, Time, and Fate*. 2nd edn. Cambridge.

Orgel, S. (ed.). 1976. *Metamorphoseos libri moralizati*. New York.

Orgel, S. (ed.). 1979a. *Christopher Marlowe: The Complete Poems and Translations* Harmondsworth.

Orgel, S. (ed.). 1979b. *Pierre Bersuire: Metamorphosis Ovidiana Moraliter . . . Explanata*. New York.

Osborne, R. 2005. Ordering women in Hesiod's *Catalogue*. In Hunter 2005a: 5–24.

Otis, B. 1970. *Ovid as an Epic Poet*. Cambridge.

Otón Sobrino, E. 1999. Tibulo en Ovidio. In Schubert 1999: 153–5.

Ottone, M. D. 2003. *Epic and Elegy in Ovid's Heroides: Paris, Helen, and Homeric Intertext*. Diss. Duke.

Owen, S. G. (ed.). 1889. *P. Ovidi Nasonis Tristium Libri V*. Oxford.

Owen, S. G. (ed.). 1915. *P. Ovidii Nasonis Tristium Libri Quinque, Ibis, Ex Ponto Libri Quattuor, Halieutica, Fragmenta*. Oxford.

Paduano, G., Perutelli, A., and Galasso, L. 2000. *Ovidio: Opere. II. Le metamorfosi*. Turin.

Pailler, J. M. and Sablayrolles, R. (eds). 1994. *Les années Domitien: colloque organisé à l'Université de Toulouse–Le Mirail*. Toulouse.

Palmer, A. 1898. *P. Ovidi Nasonis Heroides*. Oxford.

Papaioannou, S. 2005. *Epic Succession and Dissension: Ovid, Metamorphoses 13.623–14.582 and the Reinvention of the Aeneid*. Berlin and New York.

Papanghelis, T. D. 1987. *Propertius: A Hellenistic Poet on Love and Death.* Cambridge.

Papanghelis, T. D. 1989. About the hour of noon: Ovid, *Amores* 1.5. *Mnemosyne* 42: 54–61.

Papanghelis, T. D. and Rengakos, A. (eds). 2001. *A Companion to Apollonius Rhodius.* Leiden.

Papathomopoulos, M. 1968. *Antoninus Liberalis: Les Métamorphoses.* Paris.

Parker, H. N. 1992. Love's body anatomized: the ancient erotic handbooks and the rhetoric of sexuality. In Richlin 1992a: 90–111.

Parsons, P. J. 1977. Callimachus: Victoria Berenices. *ZPE* 25: 1–50.

Pasco-Pranger, M. 2002. Added days: calendrical poetics and the Julio-Claudian holidays. In Herbert-Brown 2002a: 251–74.

Pasco-Pranger, M. 2006. *Founding the Year: Ovid's* Fasti *and the Poetics of the Roman Calendar.* Leiden.

Paxson, J. and Gravlee, C. (eds). 1998. *Desiring Discourse: The Literature of Love, Ovid through Chaucer.* Selinsgrove.

Peacham, H. 1622. *The Compleat Gentleman.* London.

Pearcy, L. T. 1984. *The Mediated Muse: English Translations of Ovid 1560–1700.* Hamden, Conn.

Pecere, O. and Reeve, M. D. (eds). 1995. *Formative Stages of Classical Traditions: Latin Texts from Antiquity to the Renaissance.* Spoleto.

Pellegrini, P. 2001. Per gli incunaboli di Giovanni Calfurnio, umanista editore. *IMU* 42: 181–281.

Peradotto, J. and Sullivan, J. P. (eds). 1984. *Women in the Ancient World: The Arethusa Papers.* Albany.

Pérez Vega, A. (ed.). 2000. *P. Ovidio Nasón: Cartas desde el Ponto.* Madrid.

Perosa, A. 1973. Calderini, Domizio. *DBI* 16: 597–605.

Petrovic, I. and Petrovic, A. 2003. Stop and smell the statues. Callimachus' Epigram 51Pf. reconsidered (four times). *MD* 51: 179–208.

Pfeiffer, R. (ed.). 1949–53. *Callimachus.* Oxford.

Pfeiffer, R. 1968. *History of Classical Scholarship: From the Beginnings to the End of the Hellenistic Age.* Oxford.

Phillips, C. R. 1992. Roman religion and literary studies of Ovid's *Fasti. Arethusa* 25: 55–80.

Pianezzola, E., Baldo, G., and Cristante, L. 1991. *Ovidio: l' Arte di Amare.* Milan.

Picon, M. and Zimmermann, B. (eds). 1994. *Ovidius redivivus: von Ovid zu Dante.* Stuttgart.

Pinotti, P. (ed.). 1988. *P. Ovidio Nasone, Remedia amoris.* 2nd ed. 1993. Bologna.

Pitcher, R. A. 1998. Martial's debt to Ovid. In Grewing 1998: 59–76.

Porte, D. 1985. *L'étiologie religieuse dans les* Fastes *d'Ovide.* Paris.

Porter, J. I. (ed.). 2006. *Classical Pasts. The Classical Traditions of Greece and Rome.* Princeton.

Possanza, D. M. 2005. Review of Tarrant 2004. *BMCR* 2005.6.27.

Postgate, J. P. 1894. *Corpus Poetarum Latinorum.* 2 vols. 2nd edn. 1905. London.

Pound, E. 1910. *The Spirit of Romance.* London.

Powell, A. (ed.). 1992. *Roman Poetry and Propaganda in the Age of Augustus.* London.

Powell, J. U. 1925. *Collectanea Alexandrina.* Oxford.

Prinz, K. 1914. Untersuchungen zu Ovids *Remedia amoris,* I. *WS* 36: 36–83.

Prinz, K. 1917. Untersuchungen zu Ovids *Remedia amoris,* II. *WS* 39: 91–121 and 259–91.

Pucci, J. 1998. *The Full-Knowing Reader: Allusion and the Power of the Reader in the Western Literary Tradition.* New Haven.

Puelma, M. 1982. Die Aitien des Kallimachos als Vorbild der römischen Amores-Elegie. *MH* 39: 221–246 and 285–304 (= Puelma 1995: 360–407).

Puelma, M. 1995. *Labor et Lima. Kleine Schriften.* Basel.

Pulbrook, R. M. 1985. *P. Ovidi Nasonis Nux elegia.* Maynooth.

Putnam, M. C. J. and Hankins, J. 2004. *Maffeo Vegio: Short Epics.* Cambridge, Mass.

Quain, E. A. 1945. The Mediaeval Accessus ad Auctores. *Traditio* 3: 215–64.

Quinn, K. 1959. *The Catullan Revolution.* Melbourne.

Quinn, K. 1982. The poet and his audience in the Augustan age. *ANRW* 2.30.1: 75–180.

Quint, D. 1983. *Origin and Originality in Renaissance Literature: Versions of the Source.* New Haven.

Quint, D. 1993. *Epic and Empire.* Princeton.

Raaflaub, K. A. and Toher, M. (eds). 1990. *Between Republic and Empire: Interpretations of Augustus and His Principate.* Berkeley.

Radice, B. (trans.). 2003. *The Letters of Abelard and Heloise.* London.

Raeburn, D. 2004. *Ovid Metamorphoses. A New Verse Translation.* London.

Ramírez de Verger, A. 2006. A New Edition of Ovid's *Metamorphoses.* In Deroux 2006: 315–34.

Rand, E. K. 1916. The New Critical Edition of Ovid's *Metamorphoses.* (Review of Magnus 1914). *CPh* 11: 46–60.

Rand, E. K. 1925. *Ovid and his Influence.* Boston.

Ranucci G. 1976. Il primo monologo di Biblide. Ovidio, *Metamorfosi* IX, vv. 474–516. *ASNP* 6: 53–72.

Reeson, J. 2001. *Ovid: Heroides 11, 13 & 14: A Commentary.* Leiden.

Reeve, M. D. 1974. Review of Dörrie 1971. *CR* 24: 57–64.

Reeve, M. D. 1976a. Heinsius's manuscripts of Ovid: a supplement. *RhM* 119: 65–78.

Reeve, M. D. 1976b. The tradition of *Consolatio ad Liviam. RHT* 6: 79–98.

Reeve, M. D. 1977. Review of Due 1974. *CR* 27: 112–13.

Reeve, M. D. 1983. Grattius. In Reynolds 1983: 181–2.

Reinhardt, U. 2001. *Ovids Metamorphosen in der modernen Kunst.* Bamberg.

Reitzenstein, E. 1935. Das neue Kunstwollen in den *Amores* Ovids. *RhM* 84: 62–88.

Renner, T. 1978. A papyrus dictionary of metamorphoses. *HSCP* 82: 277–93.

Reynolds, L. D. ed. 1983. *Texts and Transmission: A Survey of the Latin Classics.* Oxford.

Reynolds, L. D. and Wilson, N. G. 1991. *Scribes and Scholars: A Guide to the Transmission of Greek and Latin Literature.* 3rd edn. Oxford.

Richardson, B. 1999. *Printing, Writers and Readers in Renaissance Italy.* Cambridge.

Richlin, A. (ed.). 1992a. *Pornography and Representation in Greece and Rome.* New York.

Richlin, A. 1992b. Reading Ovid's rapes. In Richlin 1992a: 158–79.

Richmond, J. 1962. *The Halieutica Ascribed to Ovid.* London.

Richmond, J. 1976. The authorship of the *Halieutica* ascribed to Ovid. *Philologus* 120: 92–106.

Richmond, J. 1981. Doubtful works ascribed to Ovid. *ANRW* 2.31.4: 2744–83.

Richmond, J. (ed.). 1990. *P. Ovidii Nasonis Ex Ponto libri quattuor.* Leipzig.

Richmond, J. 2002. Manuscript traditions and the transmission of Ovid's works. In Boyd 2002a: 443–83.

Rieker, J. R. 2005. *Arnulfi Aurelianensis Glosule Ovidii Fastorum.* Florence.

Riese, A. 1871–4. *P. Ovidii Nasonis Opera.* Leipzig.

Rimell, V. 2006. *Ovid's Lovers. Desire, Difference, and the Poetic Imagination.* Cambridge.

Rivero Garcia, L. 2004. A reading of Ovid, *Amores* 2.15. *Hermes* 132: 186–210.

Robathan, D. M. 1968. *The Pseudo-Ovidian De Vetula.* Amsterdam.

Roberts, D., Dunn, F., and Fowler, D. (eds). 1997. *Classical Closure.* Princeton.

Roberts, J. A. (ed.). 1983. *The Poems of Lady Mary Wroth*. Baton Rouge.

Root, R. K. 1903. *Classical Mythology in Shakespeare*. New York.

Rosati, G. 1979. L'esistenza letteraria: Ovidio e l'autocoscienza della poesia. *MD* 2: 101–36.

Rosati, G. 1983. *Narciso e Pigmalione. Illusione e spettacolo nelle Metamorfosi di Ovidio*. Florence.

Rosati, G. 1996a. *P. Ovidii Nasonis Heroidum Epistulae XVIII–XIX*. Florence.

Rosati, G. 1996b. Sabinus, the *Heroides* and the poet-nightingale: some observations on the authenticity of the *Epistula Sapphus*. *CQ* 46: 207–16.

Rosati, G. 1999. Form in motion: weaving the text in the *Metamorphoses*. In Hardie et al. 1999: 240–53 (= Knox 2006: 334–50).

Rosati, G. 2002. Narrative techniques and narrative structures in the *Metamorphoses*. In Boyd 2002a: 271–304.

Rosati, G. 2006. The art of *Remedia Amoris*: unlearning to love? In Gibson et al. 2006: 143–65.

Rosen, R. and Farrell, J. 1986. Acontius, Milanion, and Gallus: Vergil, *Ecl.* 10.52–61. *TAPA* 116: 241–54.

Rosenmeyer, P. A. 1997. Ovid's *Heroides* and *Tristia*: voices from exile. *Ramus* 26: 29–56.

Rosenmeyer, P. A. 2001. *Ancient Epistolary Fictions: The Letter in Greek Literature*. Cambridge.

Ross, D. O. 1969. *Style and Tradition in Catullus*. Cambridge, Mass.

Ross, D. O. 1975. *Backgrounds to Augustan Poetry: Gallus, Elegy and Rome*. Cambridge.

Rouse, R. H. 1992. The transmission of the texts. In Jenkyns 1992: 37–59.

Rudd, N. 1976. *Lines of Enquiry: Studies in Latin Poetry*. Cambridge.

Rudd, N. 2000. Pyramus and Thisbe in Shakespeare and Ovid. In Taylor 2000: 113–25.

Ruepke, J. 2007. *Religion of the Romans*. Cambridge.

Rutherford, I. 2001. *Pindar's Paeans: A Reading of the Fragments with a Survey of the Genre*. Oxford.

Sablayrolles, R. 1994. Domitien, l'Auguste ridicule. In Pailler and Sablayrolles 1994: 113–44.

Saerent, C., De Smet, R., and Melaerts, H. (eds). 1987. *Studia varia Bruxellensia ad orbem Graeco-Latinum pertinentia. Dertig jaar Klassieke Filologie aan de Vrije Universiteit Brussel*. Leuven.

Saintsbury, G. 1968. *Minor Caroline Poets*. Oxford.

Salzman-Mitchell, P. B. 2005. *A Web of Fantasies: Gaze, Image and Gender in Ovid's* Metamorphoses. Columbus.

Sandys, G. 1632. *Ovids Metamorphosis, Englished, Mythologiz'd, and Represented in Figures*. London.

Scaliger, J. J. 1572. *Publii Virgilii Maronis appendix*. Leiden.

Scheid, J. 1992. Myth, cult and reality in Ovid's *Fasti*. *PCPhS* 38: 118–31.

Scheid, J. 2003. *An Introduction to Roman Religion*. Bloomington and Indianapolis.

Schiesaro, A. 2001. Dissimulazioni giambiche nell'*Ibis*. In Bertini 2001: 125–36.

Schiesaro, A. 2002. Ovid and the professional discourses of scholarship, religion, and rhetoric. In Hardie 2002a: 62–75.

Schneider, O. 1856. *Nicandrea: Theriaca et Alexipharmaca*. Leipzig.

Schoenbaum, S. 1981. *William Shakespeare: Records and Images*. London.

Scholte, A. 1933. *Publii Ovidii Nasonis Ex Ponto liber primus commentario exegetico instructus*. Diss. Groningen.

Schoonhoven, H. 1980. *Elegiae in Maecenatem: Prolegomena, Text and Commentary*. Groningen.

Schubert, W. (ed.). 1999. *Ovid: Werk und Wirkung*. Frankfurt.

Scot, R. 1584. *The Discoverie of Witchcraft*. London.

Scott, K. 1930. Emperor worship in Ovid. *TAPA* 61: 43–69.

Scullard, H. H. 1981. *Festivals and Ceremonies of the Roman Republic*. London.

Sedlmayer. H. (ed.). 1886. *P. Ovidi Nasonis Heroides*. Vienna.

Sedlmayer. H. 1878. *Prolegomena critica ad Heroides Ovidianas*. Vienna.

Segal, C. P. 1969. *Landscape in Ovid's Metamorphoses*. Wiesbaden.

Segal, C. P. 1998. Ovid's metamorphic bodies: art, gender, and violence in the *Metamorphoses*. *Arion* 5: 9–41.

Sellar, W. Y. 1892. *The Roman Poets of the Augustan Age: Horace and the Elegiac Poets*. Oxford.

Shakespeare, W. 1988. *The Complete Works: Original-Spelling Edition*. Eds. S. Wells and G. Taylor. Oxford.

Shannon, E. F. 1929. *Chaucer and the Roman Poets*. Cambridge, Mass.

Sharrock, A. R. 1991. Womanufacture. *JRS* 81: 36–49.

Sharrock, A. R. 1994a. *Seduction and Repetition in Ovid's Ars Amatoria II*. Oxford.

Sharrock, A. R. 1994b. Ovid and the politics of reading. *MD* 33: 97–122 (= Knox 2006: 238–61).

Sharrock, A. R. 1995. The drooping rose: elegiac failure in *Amores* 3.7. *Ramus* 24: 152–80.

Sharrock, A. R. 2000. Intratextuality: texts, parts, and (w)holes in theory. In Sharrock and Morales 2000: 1–39.

Sharrock, A. R. 2002a. Gender and sexuality. In Hardie 2002a: 95–107.

Sharrock, A. R. 2002b. Ovid and the discourses of love: the amatory works. In Hardie 2002a 150–62.

Sharrock, A. R. 2003. Review of Volk 2002. *CPh* 98: 306–9.

Sharrock, A. R. 2006. Love in parentheses: digression and narrative hierarchy in Ovid's erotodidactic poems. In Gibson et al. 2006: 23–39.

Sharrock, A. R. and Morales, H. (eds). 2000. *Intratextuality: Greek and Roman Textual Relations*. Oxford.

Shuckburgh, E. S. 1879. *P. Ovidii Nasonis Heroidum epistulae XIII*. London.

Shulman, J. 1980–81. *Te quoque falle tamen*: Ovid's anti-Lucretian didactics. *CJ* 76: 242–53.

Sidney, Sir Philip. 1966. *A Defence of Poetry*. Ed. J. A. Van Dorsten. Oxford.

Siedschlag, E. 1972. Ovidisches bei Martial. *RFIC* 100: 156–61.

Simpson, J. 2006. Chaucer as a European writer. In: Lerer 2006: 55–86.

Skutsch, O. (ed.). 1985. *The Annals of Quintus Ennius*. Oxford.

Slater, D. A. 1927. *Towards a Text of the Metamorphosis of Ovid*. Oxford.

Slavitt, D. 1990. *Ovid's Poetry of Exile*. Baltimore.

Slavitt, D. 1994. *The Metamorphoses of Ovid*. Baltimore.

Slote, B. (ed.). 1964. *Literature and Society*. Lincoln, Neb.

Smith, R. A. 1994. Fantasy, myth, and love letters: text and tale in Ovid's *Heroides*. *Arethusa* 27: 247–73 (= Knox 2006: 217–37).

Smith, R. A. 1997. *Poetic Allusion and Poetic Embrace in Ovid and Virgil*. Ann Arbor.

Smolak, K. 1980. Der verbannte Dichter (Identifizierungen mit Ovid in Mittelalter und Neuzeit). *WS* 14: 158–91.

Societas Bipontina. 1783. *Publii Ovidii Nasonis Opera*. 3 vols. 2nd edn. 1805. Zweibrücken.

Solodow, J. B. 1977. Ovid's *Ars Amatoria*: the lover as cultural ideal. *WS* 11: 106–27.

Solodow, J. B. 1988. *The World of Ovid's Metamorphoses*. Chapel Hill.

Sommariva, G. 1980. La parodia di Lucrezio nell' *Ars* e nei *Remedia* ovidiani. *A&R* 25: 123–48.

Spentzou, E. 2003. *Readers and Writers in Ovid's* Heroides: *Transgressions of Genre and Gender.* Oxford.

Spentzou, E. 2005. Silenced subjects: Ovid and the heroines in exile. In Ancona and Greene 2005: 318–40.

Speyer, W. 1971. *Die literarische Fälschung im heidnischen und christlichen Altertum.* Munich.

Spoth, F. 1992. *Ovids Heroides als Elegien.* Munich.

Sprague, A. C. (ed.). 1930. *Samuel Daniel, Poems and A Defence of Ryme.* Cambridge, Mass.

Staffhorst, U. 1965. *P. Ovidius Naso, Epistulae ex Ponto III 1–3.* Diss. Würzburg.

Stahl, H.-P. 1985. *Propertius: 'Love' and 'War'—Individual and State under Augustus.* Berkeley.

Stapleton, M. L. 1996. *Harmful Eloquence: Ovid's* Amores *from Antiquity to Shakespeare.* Ann Arbor.

Starr, R. J. 1987. The circulation of literary texts in the Roman world. *CQ* 37: 213–23.

Stavrakakis, Y. 1999. *Lacan and the Political.* London.

Steiner, G. 1951. Source-editions of Ovid's *Metamorphoses. TAPA* 82: 219–31.

Steiner, G. 1952. The textual tradition of the Ovidian incunabula. *TAPA* 83: 312–18.

Steudel, M. 1992. *Die Literaturparodie in Ovids Ars Amatoria.* Hildesheim.

Stevenson, J. and Davidson, P. (eds). 2001. *Early Modern Women Poets: An Anthology 1560– 1700.* Oxford.

Stitz, M. 1962. *Ovid und Vergils Aeneis. Interpretation Met. 13.623–14.608.* Diss. Freiburg.

Strier, R. 2000. Shakespeare and the Skeptics. *R&L* 32: 171–96.

Stroh, W. (ed.). 1969. *Ovid im Urteil der Nachwelt: Eine Testimoniensammlung.* Darmstadt.

Stroh, W. 1971. *Die römische Liebeselegie als werbende Dichtung.* Amsterdam.

Sullivan, J. P. (ed.). 1962. *Critical Essays on Roman Literature: Elegy and Lyric.* London.

Sullivan, J. P. 1991. *Martial: The Unexpected Classic.* Cambridge.

Syme, R. 1939. *The Roman Revolution.* Oxford.

Syme, R. 1978. *History in Ovid.* Oxford.

Syme, R. 1986. *The Augustan Aristocracy.* Oxford.

Szelest, H. 1999. Ovid und Martial. In Schubert 1999: 861–4.

Tanselle, G. T. 1983. Classical, biblical, and medieval textual criticism and modern editing. *SB* 36: 21–68.

Tarrant, R. J. 1978. Senecan drama and its antecedents. *HSCP* 82: 213–63.

Tarrant, R. J. 1981. The authenticity of the Letter of Sappho to Phaon (*Heroides* XV). *HSCP* 85: 133–53.

Tarrant, R. J. 1982. Editing Ovid's *Metamorphoses*: problems and possibilities. *CPh* 77: 342–60.

Tarrant, R. J. 1983a. Ovid. In Reynolds 1983: 257–84.

Tarrant, R. J. 1983b. Pseudo-Ovid: *Nux.* In Reynolds 1983: 285–6.

Tarrant, R. J. 1995a. Classical Latin literature. In Greetham 1995: 95–147.

Tarrant, R. J. 1995b. The silence of Cephalus: text and narrative technique in Ovid *Metamorphoses* 7.865 ff. *TAPA* 125: 99–111.

Tarrant, R. J. 1997. Aspects of Virgil's reception in antiquity. In Martindale 1997: 56–72.

Tarrant, R. J. 1999. Nicolaas Heinsius and the rhetoric of textual criticism. In Hardie et al. 1999: 288–300.

Tarrant, R. J. 2000. The soldier in the garden and other intruders in Ovid's *Metamorphoses*. *HSCP* 100: 425–38.

Tarrant, R. J. 2002a. Chaos in Ovid's *Metamorphoses* and its Neronian influence. *Arethusa* 35: 349–60.

Tarrant, R. J. 2002b. Ovid and ancient literary history. In Hardie 2002a: 13–33.

Tarrant, R. J. 2004. *P. Ovidi Nasonis Metamorphoses*. Oxford.

Tarrant, R. J. 2005. Roads not taken: untold stories in Ovid's *Metamorphoses*. *MD* 54: 65–90.

Taylor, A. B. 1985. The non-existent carbuncles: Shakespeare, Golding, and Raphael Regius. *N&Q* 230: 54–55.

Taylor, A. B. 1989. Golding's Ovid, Shakespeare's 'Small Latin', and the real object of mockery in 'Pyramus and Thisbe'. *ShS* 42: 53–64.

Taylor, A. B. 1991. Shakespeare and Golding. *N&Q* 236: 492–99.

Taylor, A. B. 1994/95. Melting earth and leaping bulls: Shakespeare's Ovid and Arthur Golding. *Connotations* 4: 192–206.

Taylor, A. B. (ed.). 2000. *Shakespeare's Ovid*. Cambridge.

Taylor, A. B. 2004. Ovid's myths and the unsmooth course of love in *A Midsummer Night's Dream*. In Martindale and Taylor 2004: 49–65.

Taylor, J. H. 1970. *Amores* 3.9. A farewell to elegy. *Latomus* 29: 474–7.

Terras, V. 1966. Classical motives in the poetry of Osip Mandel'stam. *SEEJ* 10: 251–65.

Thibault, J. C. 1964. *The Mystery of Ovid's Exile*. Berkeley.

Thomas, E. 1964. Variations on a military theme in Ovid's *Amores*. *G&R* 11: 151–64.

Thomas, R. F. 1982. Catullus and the polemics of poetic reference (64.1–18). *AJP* 103: 144–64.

Thomas, R. F. 1986. Vergil's *Georgics* and the art of reference. *HSCPh* 90: 171–98.

Thomas, R. F. 1993. Callimachus back in Rome. In Harder 1993: 197–215.

Thomas, R. F. 2001. *Virgil and the Augustan Reception*. Cambridge.

Timpanaro, S. 2005. *The Genesis of Lachmann's Method*. (G. W. Most trans.). Chicago.

Tissol, G. 1997. *The Face of Nature. Wit, Narrative, and Cosmic Origins in Ovid's Metamorphoses*. Princeton.

Tissol, G. 2002. The house of fame: Roman history and Augustan politics in *Metamorphoses* 11–15. In Boyd 2002a: 305–35.

Toohey, P. 1996. *Epic Lessons: An Introduction to Ancient Didactic Poetry*. London.

Tränkle, H. 1960. *Die Sprachkunst des Properz und die Tradition der lateinischen Dichtersprache*. Wiesbaden.

Trapp, J. B. 1973. Ovid's tomb: the growth of a legend from Eusebius to Laurence Sterne, Chateaubriand and George Richmond. *JWCI* 36: 35–76.

Traube, L. 1911. *Einleitung in die lateinischen Philologie des Mittelalters*. Munich.

Treggiari, S. 2005. Women in the time of Augustus. In Galinsky 2005: 130–50.

Tsantsanoglou, K. 1973. The memoirs of a lady from Samos. *ZPE* 12: 183–95.

Tsitsiou-Chelidoni, C. (2003). *Ovid* Metamorphosen *Buch VIII. Narrative Technik und literarische Kontext*. Frankfurt.

Velz, J. W. 1999. Ovidian creation in Milton and decreation in Shakespeare. In Schubert 1999: 1035–6.

Velz, J. W. 2000. Shakespeare's Ovid in the twentieth century: a critical survey. In Taylor 2000: 181–97.

Verdière, R. 1992. *Le secret du voltiger d'amour ou le mystère de la relegation d'Ovide*. Brussels.

Verducci, F. 1985. *Ovid's Toyshop of the Heart*. Princeton.

Veremans, J. 1987. Tibulle 1.6 et Ovide. In Saerent et al. 1987: 125–33.

Vessey, D. W. T. 1976. Philaenis. *RBPH* 54: 78–83.

Veyne, P. 1988. *Roman Erotic Elegy. Love, Poetry and the West.* Chicago.

Vian, F. 1952. *La guerre des géants: le mythe avant l'époque hellénistique.* Paris.

Vian, F. (ed.). 1974–81. *Apollonios de Rhodes: Argonautiques.* 3 vols. Paris.

Videau-Delibes, A. 1991. *Les* Tristes *d'Ovide et L'élégie romaine.* Paris.

Volk, K. 2002. *The Poetics of Latin Didactic: Lucretius, Vergil, Ovid, Manilius.* Oxford.

Volk, K. 2005. *Ille ego:* (mis)reading Ovid's elegiac persona. *A&A* 51: 83–96.

Volk, K. 2006. *Ars Amatoria Romana*: Ovid on love as a cultural construct. In Gibson et al. 2006: 235–51.

Wallace-Hadrill, A. 1987. Time for Augustus: Ovid, Augustus and the *Fasti.* In Whitby et al. 1987: 221–30.

Wallace-Hadrill, A. 1989. Rome's cultural revolution. *JRS* 79: 157–64.

Wallace-Hadrill, A. 2005. *Mutatas formas*: the Augustan transformation of Roman knowledge. In Galinsky 2005: 55–84.

Watson, L. 1991. *Arae: The Curse Poetry of Antiquity.* Leeds.

Watson, P. 1983. Mythological *exempla* in Ovid's *Ars Amatoria. CPh* 78: 117–26.

Watson, P. 2002. *Praecepta amoris*: Ovid's didactic elegy. In Boyd 2002a: 141–65.

Watts, A. E. 1980. *The Metamorphoses of Ovid.* San Francisco.

Weever, J. 1601. *The Mirror of Martyrs.* London.

Weinstock, S. 1971. *Divus Julius.* Oxford.

West, M. L. 1966. *Hesiod: Theogony.* Oxford.

West, M. L. 1973. *Textual Criticism and Editorial Technique.* Stuttgart.

West, M. L. 1985. *The Hesiodic Catalogue of Women: Its Nature, Structure, and Origins.* Oxford.

West, S. 2000. Lycophron's *Alexandra*: 'Hindsight as foresight makes no sense'. In Depew and Obbink 2000: 153–66.

Wetherbee, W. 1984. *Chaucer and the Poets: An Essay on* Troilus and Criseyde. Ithaca.

Wheeler, A. L. 1910. Erotic teaching in Roman elegy and the Greek sources. Part I. *CPh* 5: 440–50.

Wheeler, A. L. 1911. Erotic teaching in Roman elegy and the Greek sources. Part II. *CPh* 6: 56–77.

Wheeler, A. L. 1925. Topics from the life of Ovid. *AJP* 46: 1–28.

Wheeler, S. M. 1999. *A Discourse of Wonders. Audience and Performance in Ovid's* Metamorphoses. Philadelphia.

Wheeler, S. M. 2000. *Narrative Dynamics in Ovid's* Metamorphoses. Tübingen.

Wheeler, S. M. 2002. Lucan's reception of Ovid. *Arethusa* 35: 361–80.

Whitby, M., Hardie, P., and Whitby, M. (eds). 1987. *Homo Viator: Classical Essays for John Bramble.* Bristol.

White, P. 1993. *Promised Verse. Poets in the Society of Augustan Rome.* Cambridge, Mass.

Wiggers, N. 1977. Reconsideration of Propertius 2.1. *CJ* 72: 334–41.

Wildberger, J. 1998. *Ovids Schule der 'elegischen' Liebe: Erotodidaxe und Psychagogie in der Ars Amatoria.* Frankfurt.

Wilkinson, L. P. 1955. *Ovid Recalled.* Cambridge.

Wilkinson, L. P. 1963. *Golden Latin Artistry.* Cambridge.

Williams, C. 1999. *Roman Homosexuality.* New York.

Williams, C. 2002. Ovid, Martial and poetic immortality: traces of *Amores* 1.15 in the epigrams. *Arethusa* 35: 417–33.

Williams, G. D. 1992. Ovid's Canace: dramatic irony in *Heroides* 11. *CQ* 42: 201–9.

Williams, G. D. 1994. *Banished Voices: Readings in Ovid's Exile Poetry.* Cambridge.

Williams, G. D. 1996. *The Curse of Exile: A Study of Ovid's* Ibis. Cambridge.

Williams, G. D. 1997. Writing in the mother-tongue: Hermione and Helen in *Heroides* 8 (a Tomitan approach). *Ramus* 26: 113–137.

Williams, G. D. 2002. Ovid's exile poetry: *Tristia, Epistulae ex Ponto* and *Ibis*. In Hardie 2002a: 233–48.

Wills, J. 1998. Divided allusion: Virgil and the Coma Berenices. *HSCP* 98: 277–305.

Wills, J. 1996. *Repetition in Latin Poetry: Figures of Allusion*. Oxford.

Wilson, T. 1553. *Art of Rhetorique*. London.

Wiseman, T. P. 1971. *New Men in the Roman Senate. 139 BC–AD 14*. Oxford.

Wiseman, T. P. 1998. *Roman Drama and Roman History*. Exeter.

Wiseman, T. P. 2002. Ovid and the stage. In Herbert-Brown 2002a: 275–99.

Wiseman, T. P. 2008. *Unwritten Rome* Exeter.

Wither, G. 1620. *Exercises Vpon the First Psalme*. London.

Woodman, A. J. and West, D. (eds.). 1984. *Poetry and Politics in the Age of Augustus*. Cambridge.

Woytek, E. 2000. *In medio et mihi Caesar erit*: Vergilimitationen in Zentrum von Ovids *Remedia amoris*. WS 113: 181–213.

Wray, D. 2001. *Catullus and the Poetics of Roman Manhood*. Cambridge.

Wray, D. 2003. What poets do: Tibullus on 'easy' hands. *CPh* 98: 217–50.

Wright, E. F. 1984. *Profanum sunt genus*: the poets of the *Ars Amatoria*. PQ 63: 1–15.

Wyke, M. 1987. Written women: Propertius' *scripta puella*. JRS 77: 47–61.

Wyke, M. 1989. Reading female flesh: *Amores* 3.1. In Cameron 1989: 113–43 (= Knox 2006: 169–204).

Wyke, M. 1995. Taking the woman's part: engendering Roman love elegy. In Boyle 1995: 110–28.

Wyke, M. 2002. *The Roman Mistress*. Oxford.

Yavetz, Z. 1969. *Plebs and Princeps*. 2nd edn. 1988. Oxford.

Zanker, P. 1988. *The Power of Images in the Age of Augustus*. Ann Arbor.

Zetzel, J. 1981. On the opening of Callimachus, *Aetia* II. ZPE 42: 31–3.

Zetzel, J. E. G. (ed.). 1995. *Cicero, De Re Publica: Selections*. Cambridge.

Zetzel, J. E. G. 1996. Poetic baldness and its cure. *MD* 36: 73–100.

Zingerle, A. 1869–71. *Ovidius und sein Verhältnis zu den Vorgängern und gleichzeitigen römischen Dichtern, 1–3*. Innsbruck.

Zingerle, A. 1877. *Martial's Ovid-Studien*. Innsbruck.

Zinn, E. (ed.). 1970. *Ovids Ars amatoria und Remedia amoris: Untersuchungen zum Aufbau*. Stuttgart.

Ziolkowski, J. and Putnam, M. C. J. 2007. *The Virgilian Tradition*. New Haven.

Ziolkowski, T. 1993. *Virgil and the Moderns*. Princeton.

Ziolkowski, T. 2005a. *Ovid and the Moderns*. Ithaca.

Ziolkowski, T. 2005b. Uses and abuses of Horace: his reception since 1935 in Germany and Anglo-America. *IJCT* 12 (2005): 183–215.

Ziolkowski, T. 2006. Two Juvenal delinquents: Robert Lowell and Durs Grünbein. *CML* 26: 12–32.

Ziolkowski, T. 2006/2007. Anglo-American Catullus since the mid-twentieth century. *IJCT* 13: 409–30.

Zissos, A. and Gildenhard, I. 1999. Problems of time in *Metamorphoses* 2. In Hardie et al. 1999: 31–47.

Žižek, S. 1992. *Looking Awry. An introduction to J. Lacan through Popular Culture*. Cambridge, Mass.

Zumwalt, N. 1977. *Fama subuersa*: theme and structure in Ovid *Metamorphoses* 12. *CSCA* 10: 209–222.

Index

Index

Minotaur 438
Minyades 230
Minyas, daughters 367–8
mistresses, immortality reflected in elegiac poetry
  284
moderation 102, 111, 114
Moltzer, Jacob (Jacobus Micyllus) 338
Mons Sacer 132
Montaigne, Michel Eyquem de 442, 443
Montanus 29, 38
Mopsus 161
moral values, Augustan age 200, 202–3
Mortimer, Edmund 434–6
Moschus, *Europa* 223, 227
Mother Earth (*Metamorphoses*) 361
Mukterismos (sarcasm) 34
mulieres 125
Munari 318
Muses 57, 109, 142, 143–4, 165, 246
Musgrove, M. 161
mutability 151–2
Myerowitz, Molly 91, 360
Myers, K. S. 351, 383
Myrrha 149, 360, 392
  and intertextuality 351
  medieval commentaries on 332
  portrayal 230, 233, 256, 421
  psychology 234
  story reflected in Shakespeare's *Othello* 449–50
mythology
  Ars amatoria 94
  in the *Heroides* 78, 80–2, 84
  Ibis 190–3
  in the *Metamorphoses* 45
  as metaphor 173
  Ovid's use 88, 144, 145–6, 269–70, 398
  Propertius' use 269–70

Nagle, Betty Rose 386, 479
Nancy, Jean-Luc 392–3
Narcissus 231, 262–3, 391, 392, 440, 441, 457,
  475
narrative techniques, Tibullus' use 290
narratives, Propertius' use 272–4
narrativity, *Metamorphoses* 159–63, 412
narratology, Ovid's use 272–4, 373–4, 386–8,
  397
Nascimento, Francisco-Manoel 458
Naso, Eckart von 460
Naugerius, Andreas (Andrea Navagero) 321–2
Nausikaa 363
nautical imagery, *Remedia amoris* 116–17
negatives, accentuation in management of love
    affairs (*Remedia amoris*) 112–13
Nemesis (Tibullus' mistress) 258, 280, 281, 282,
  284, 291, 292

neotericus 254
neoterism 22, 24, 25
Neptune 51, 164, 388, 406, 407
Nero (Emperor) 404
Nestor 148, 159–61, 162, 368, 404, 407–8
New Comedy, influence 100
Newlands, C. E. 271, 383
Nicaenetus 233
Nicander of Colophon 101, 105, 115, 225,
  229–32, 242, 243–4
Ninus (Semiramis' husband) 357
Niobe 205
Nisus 173, 306
Nonae Caprotinae festival 122
Nooteboom, Cees 466
Norfolk, Lawrence 466
the novel 373
Numa Pompilius 54–5, 133, 157
Nux 212–13, 479

Oates, Joyce Carol 464
Odysseus 173, 192, 363
Oeneus 222
Oenone 32–3, 79, 87, 417, 478–9
O'Hara, J. J. 295
Oldcastle, John, Sir 434
Omphale, Hercules' service to 407
Ops Augusta, cult 138
oratory *see* rhetoric
Orestes, friendship for Pylades 173
Orgoglio (Spenser, *Faerie Queene*) 428, 430
Orion, daughters 230
Ornithogonia 228–9
Orpheus 305, 306, 331–2, 421, 457
Otis, B. 162
otium 111
Ovid: Werk und Wirkung 462
Ovid
  aetiologies 224–6
  autobiography 177–8
  blurring of boundaries between genres 104
  on book production 21
  calendar 126–30
  Callimachus' influence 236–9
  character 204–6
  commentaries on 327
    Antiquity 327–9
    early printed commentaries 335–8
    humanists 333–5
    Middle Ages 329–33, 411–12
    modern period 338–40
  concerns with the literary public 21–2
  and Corinna 272
  critical appreciation of Catullus 257–63
  critical receptions 372–3, 381–4, 397
    gendered readings 384–5